Journalism in the Civil War Era

(Second Edition)

Kimberly Wilmot Voss
General Editor

Vol. 8

The Mediating American History series
is part of the Peter Lang Media and Communication list.
Every volume is peer reviewed and meets
the highest quality standards for content and production.

PETER LANG
New York • Berlin • Brussels • Lausanne • Oxford

David W. Bulla and Gregory A. Borchard

Journalism in the Civil War Era

(Second Edition)

PETER LANG
New York • Berlin • Brussels • Lausanne • Oxford

Library of Congress Cataloging-in-Publication Data

Names: Bulla, David W., author. | Borchard, Gregory A., author.
Title: Journalism in the Civil War Era / David W. Bulla and Gregory A. Borchard.
Description: Second edition. | New York: Peter Lang, 2023.
Series: Mediating American history; vol. 8
ISSN 2331-0588 (print) | ISSN 2166-6474 (online)
Includes bibliographical references and index.
Identifiers: LCCN 2022029453 (print) | LCCN 2022029454 (ebook)
ISBN 978-1-4331-9793-2 (hardback) | ISBN 978-1-4331-8721-6 (paperback)
ISBN 978-1-4331-8722-3 (ebook pdf) | ISBN 978-1-4331-8723-0 (epub)
Classification: LCC E609. B83 2023 (print) | LCC E609 (ebook) |
DDC 071/.3—dc23
LC record available at https://lccn.loc.gov/2022029453
LC ebook record available at https://lccn.loc.gov/2022029454
DOI 10.3726/b18269

Bibliographic information published by **Die Deutsche Nationalbibliothek**.
Die Deutsche Nationalbibliothek lists this publication in the "Deutsche
Nationalbibliografie"; detailed bibliographic data are available
on the Internet at http://dnb.d-nb.de/.

© 2023 Peter Lang Publishing, Inc., New York
80 Broad Street, 5th floor, New York, NY 10004
www.peterlang.com

Joseph Redding Bulla
(1927-1986)
Industrial Engineer for AT&T
Commander in the U.S. Naval Reserves

David B. Sachsman
(1945-2022)
Director of the Symposium on the 19th Century Press, the Civil War,
and Free Expression
University of Tennessee at Chattanooga

Contents

Illustrations

Foreword
By Harold Holzer

Like many American Presidents before and after the Civil War, Abraham Lincoln never shied away from complaining about alleged press abuse—what he called "gas from newspaper establishments."[1] Once, a White House visitor asked Lincoln if he believed the press was reporting on his Administration fairly and accurately. Here was an irresistible chance for the President to vent. He had only recently been subjected to the latest round of what an admirer called "violent criticism, attacks, and denunciations" from both "radicals" and "conservatives," and Lincoln was no doubt chafing over the opprobrium.[2]

According to one account of this incident (as spun by White House artist-in-residence Francis B. Carpenter), the President considered the question for only a few seconds before he was characteristically "reminded of a little story." It seemed that a pair of immigrants "fresh from the Emerald Isle" was traveling West when, one evening, the men were loudly greeted by "a grand chorus of bullfrogs"—a cacophony they had never heard before. Unable to discover the source of the deafening "B-a-u-m!—B-a-u-m!," one frightened Irishman turned to the other and whispered: "And sure ... it is my opinion it's nothing but a '*noise!*'" As far as Lincoln was concerned, Carpenter insisted, loud criticism was nothing but "noise." Rebukes "rarely ruffled the President."[3]

And yet his Administration—the Union army—and in at least one documented case, Lincoln himself—censored and shut down more newspapers, and arrested and imprisoned editors more often, and in greater numbers, than any other civilian or military authority in the nation's history. In personally acting against the *New York World* and *New York Journal of Commerce* on May 18, 1864, Lincoln deployed unusually harsh language in commanding the army to "take possession by force, of the printing establishments ... prevent any further publication therefrom," and to arrest the offending editors "until they can be brought to trial before a military commission." According to Lincoln's order, the two papers had "wickedly and traitorously" printed a "false and spurious" presidential proclamation "to give aid and comfort to the enemies of the United States, and to the rebels now at war against the government."[4] In truth, the fake proclamation did no such thing; Lincoln and his Secretary of War, Edwin M. Stanton, clearly overreacted, deeply worried that the Administration's true, secret conscription plans had been leaked to the press. Sometimes, gas and noise proved impossible to ignore.

Here is the enduring anomaly that scholars of Lincoln and the Civil War press have explored in earnest for some four score years—a question repeatedly asked, but never fully answered, by biographers, historians, and political scientists. Why did a war that generated more press coverage, wider readership, and greater journalistic opportunity, than any event to date also ignite the most widespread censorship and suppression? Was Lincoln, the savior of the Union, also the enemy of a free press—indeed, guilty of the very tyranny of which many Democratic editors accused him at their peril?

The response is usually straightforward: partisanship transformed the press into enemies of the people. Observers have convincingly demonstrated that the Civil War era press largely covered the war and the White House through the lens of politics, for newspapers of the era were deeply enmeshed in political organizations, Democratic and Republican. Many editors served as politicians, and many politicians as editors. Several members of Lincoln's initial Cabinet had run newspapers, including Simon Cameron and Gideon Welles. Lincoln's crackdowns targeted only Copperhead journalists, and were often applauded by pro-war, anti-slavery Republican editors.

But as this new book shows, the story is far more complicated. Politics was only one of the factors animating wartime newspaper coverage. To those who think the press differed only politically, or by region—North and South—this study will come as a revelation. It explores both small-town and big-city papers, civilian and military publications, and not only the unsurprising difference in coverage in the North and South, but unanticipated differences East and West. It addresses the influence of personal, if sometimes pseudonymous journalism, and probes the power of advertising to encourage positive policy change, or in the case of slave-auction and runaway-slave ads, to perpetuate policy of the inhumane variety.

The book also explores the technological changes that brought news to Americans more rapidly, and more widely, than ever before—inviting closer scrutiny and greater suspicion, just as social media does today—and it weighs the perennial dilemma facing journalists torn between partisan loyalty and editorial integrity. Here, too, are reminders that readers of the day did not consume only war news and political coverage; they were also treated to both hyper-local and international stories, to woodcut illustrations and, eventually, photographs, and to reports on business, culture, and even the weather.

Of course, the focus on these pages inevitably returns to military and political coverage, and how it impacted the rise of Lincoln and the preservation of the Union, even when it meant covering up the most disastrous federal battlefield defeats. Whether or not it answers the lingering questions about the President's tough stance against editors who went beyond criticism and, in his view, flirted with treason, remains open to debate. At the very least, the book helps us understand how a man lionized after his death as a savior and liberator could present himself during his presidency as both a St. Sebastian enduring slings and arrows, and a Torquemada who willingly assumed the role of grand inquisitor. Perhaps it should never be forgotten that Lincoln once revealingly blurted out to Lawrence Gobright of the Associated Press: "I have always found what I say to be true."[5]

On another memorable occasion, resulting in a slightly different version of the Irish "noise" story, Lincoln was—again—asked how he felt about yet one more denunciatory volley by the press. His response did little to solve the mystery of the Janus-like nature of the Civil War President's attitude toward coverage and criticism, or narrow the reputational chasm between his images as tolerant forgiver and the relentless censor.

"That reminds me," Lincoln replied, "of a farmer who lost his way on the Western frontier. Night came on, and the embarrassments of his position were increased by a furious tempest which suddenly burst upon him. To add to his discomfort, his horse had given out, leaving him exposed to all the angers of the pitiless storm.

"The peals of thunder were terrific, the frequent flashes of lightning affording his only guide on the road as he resolutely trudged onward, leading his jaded steed. The earth seemed fairly to tremble beneath him in the war of elements. One bolt threw him suddenly upon his knees.

"Our traveler was not a prayerful man, but finding himself involuntarily brought to an attitude of devotion, he addressed himself to the Throne of Grace in the following prayer for his deliverance:

'O God! Hear my prayer this time, for Thou knows it is not often that I call upon thee. And, O Lord! If it be all the same to thee, give us a little more light and a little less noise.'

"I wish," the President concluded sadly, "there was a stronger disposition manifested on the part of our civilian warriors to unite in suppressing the rebellion, and a little less noise as to how and by whom the chief executive office shall be administered."[6]

Yet despite the presidential complaints and crackdowns, the "noise"—the unrelenting, occasionally unsettling, reports from the era's "civilian warriors"— never abated. At least this book sheds "a little more light" on the story.

Notes

1 Michael Burlingame and John R. Turner Ettlinger, eds., *Inside Lincoln's White House: The Complete Civil War Diary of John Hay* (Carbondale: Southern Illinois University Press, 1997), 188 (entry for April 24, 1864).
2 Francis B. Carpenter, *Six Months at the White House: The Story of a Picture* (New York: Hurd & Houghton, 1866), 154.
3 Ibid, 155.
4 Lincoln to General John Adams Dix, May 18, 1864, in Roy P. Basler, ed., *The Collected Works of Abraham Lincoln*, 8 vols. (New Brunswick, NJ: Rutgers University Press, 1953-55), 7:345-46.
5 L. A. Gobright, *Recollections of Men and Things at Washington During the Third of a Century* (Philadelphia: Claxton, Remsen, & Haffelfinger, 1869), 337, 338. Lincoln made the remark after complaining about unauthorized, premature press reports.
6 Alexander K. McClure, *"Abe" Lincoln's Yarns and Stories: A Complete Collection of the Funny and Witty Anecdotes that Made Lincoln Famous as America's Greatest Story-Teller* (New York: Henry Neil, 1901), 80.

Preface

The Times that Were

"The illusion that the times that were are better than those that are, has probably pervaded all ages." Horace Greeley, *The American Conflict*, Vol. 1 (New York, Chicago, Hartford: O. D. Case, 1866), 21.

This second edition of *Journalism in the Civil War Era* revisits areas explored in the first edition (Peter Lang, 2010) by re-examining the contributions of newspapers and magazines to the American public's understanding of the nation's greatest internal conflict. Both editions document the effect the Civil War had on journalism and the effect journalism had on the Civil War. *Journalism in the Civil War Era* describes the politics that affected the press, the constraints placed upon journalism, and the influence of technology on communications. It profiles the editors and reporters who covered the war and examines typical newspapers of the era, while providing a broad account of journalism in the mid-nineteenth century. The authors, David W. Bulla and Gregory A. Borchard, wrote this book intending it as an important reference for scholars and students, as well as a supplementary text for courses in journalism history, U.S. press history, civil rights law, and nineteenth-century history.

The second edition of *Journalism in the Civil War Era* expands on topics from the first edition by adding perspective on particular issues that are in need of updating since its original publication. This edition does this, first, by broadening the scope of the initial text to look at international coverage of Civil War issues and post-war issues facing the press, and adds chapters centered on abolitionism in the press, naval battles, and the role of classified ads during the era. Further, it expands on analyses of Abraham Lincoln's legacy, with the press's coverage of his assassination as a starting point.

This edition continues to provide a broad account of journalism during the Civil War, reflecting on the political, military, legal, and journalistic issues of the era. Its chapters examine these various facets of the journalism of the period, and the theme of the development of the wartime press emphasizes the professional, political, social, economic, legal, and military factors that affected it. It began as academic conversations between the authors when they were doctoral students at the University of Florida almost twenty years ago. More specifically, the authors began making presentations on their findings in the late 1990s at the University of Tennessee, Chattanooga's Symposium on the 19th Century Press, the Civil War, and Free Expression, and discovered a like-minded interest in exploring underdeveloped areas of press and Civil War-era scholarship. At least in part, Peter Lang published these conversations in 2010's first edition of this book. Since then, the authors have maintained their scholarship on the subject. (You now will see a recently reissued 2015 book by Borchard and Bulla, *Lincoln Mediated: The President and the Press through Nineteenth Century Media*, referenced throughout *Journalism in the Civil War Era*.) Dialogue between the authors will no doubt continue well after publication of this second edition of *Journalism in the Civil War Era*.

Given the durability and popularity of the Civil War as a subject among amateur and professional historians, this book again targets a wide audience. What makes this particular endeavor unique stems from the time in which the authors produced it—one in which the press as we know it has changed in ways more dramatic than those of any other era. Historians have documented how, in the years leading to the Civil War, an explosion of technological innovation contributed to the democratization of the press—comparable in some respects to the era in which we now live. Yet, as traditional members of the press wait to see if newspapers will continue to exist in a context of predominantly digital media, historians (ourselves included) continue to reconstruct the past based on our best sources—in this case, the leading newspapers of the Civil War. This re-issue of *Journalism in the Civil War Era* accordingly comes at a critical time: a period in which historians and citizens alike are reinterpreting the value of the printed word in contributing to social discourse and maintaining the foundation necessary for a functioning representative democracy.

Remarkably, a very real and recent calamity has also befallen the nation in the form of a pandemic, making our current situation in history compounded by changes in the press and acute questions about mortality. According to the August 2021 issue of *Time* magazine, the United States passed a landmark in the fight against COVID-19 when the death toll surpassed 620,000 people—a figure traditionally cited as the number of deaths during the Civil War. "The grim comparison is telling, not only because of the sheer size of the death toll, but also because it carries a bleak secondary meaning," writes Rachel Lance, a Ph.D.in biomedical engineering.

> The Civil War, infamous for having the highest American death toll of any war in history, was the last major American conflict before the greater public understood how diseases spread. It was therefore the last war where the bulk of the deaths—two-thirds, in fact—were not from bullets and bombs, but from viruses, parasites and bacteria. Unfortunately, today's COVID-19 death toll shows that many have approached the virus with a medical attitude hardly updated from 160 years ago.[1]

While a study of the role of the press in covering the recent pandemic certainly merits a different text altogether, recurring contemporary reports of widespread death tolls rivaling those of the Civil War provide context on the press in covering catastrophic events.

Social upheaval accompanying recent events has also revealed the ways in which our contemporary understanding of the past hardly matches the perspectives of previous generations—from those during and immediately after the Civil War through today. Confederate General Robert E. Lee, for example—long considered an icon among those who insist the Civil War was about something other than slavery—has assumed a new role among historians who have reevaluated his legacy vis-à-vis contemporary social justice movements.

Veneration of Lee—along with almost every Confederate (and sometimes non-Confederate) personality from the era—is no longer taken for granted, as identity-conscious activists have increasingly targeted memorials as relics from a past that should be shunned.[2]

Regarding the roles and perspectives of this book's authors, some have stayed the same and others have changed since publication of the first edition. On a personal level, Bulla has roots in a Southern tradition and Borchard in a Northern

Image I.1 "Statues and Sculpture. Robert E. Lee in Statuary Hall." United States Capitol, Washington, DC. Theodor Horydczak, photographer, 1951.[3]

one. Our different backgrounds, we believe, continue to contribute to a nuanced interpretation of the press and of the war's participants. Bulla's scholarship has focused more intensely on the issues of slavery and abolition, as well as international journalism, while Borchard's work has tended toward editing books and articles on the history of journalism in general.

Interpreting historical materials discovered since 2010 relied on the same method used in the first edition: analyzing primary sources such as personal letters, editorial musings, books, newspaper articles, and historical artifacts. We found these materials in a number of locations, including archival searches of libraries, at museums and historical societies, in online searches, and in some cases, through the exhausting but satisfying process of transcribing microfilm. The scope of sources generally ranges from the Penny Press Era (1830s) to Reconstruction (1870s), and the items featured bore directly on the major themes of this book, including the era's cultural, economic, institutional, political, and technological issues.

The picture of the press during the Civil War that readers will discover is one of a group of participants who played a role in reshaping a nation—a nation that had come into existence only a few generations before. The war was a Second Revolution, in both political and professional senses, as technological innovations of the time facilitated faster and more-efficient means of newspaper production. This revolution in the production of news turned the penny press on its head, as the largest daily publications became complex institutions that made fewer demands of actual labor from leading editors and publishers. As a result, well into the twentieth century advertising agents replaced functions formerly reserved for editors.

This book contributes to literature on the subject by including analyses based (in terms of historiography) in cultural and developmental perspectives; that is, our interpretations analyze the roles of both society and technology in shaping events.[4] It features an examination of a typical newspaper—not just the popular urban penny papers, but a small-town newspaper in the Midwest. At the same time, it revisits the contributions of leading editors and publishers, such as Horace Greeley, editor of *The New York Tribune*, who used his newspaper as a way to advance press freedoms under unprecedented circumstances. The book describes journalism as a specialized profession by including an analysis of technology's role in carrying timely information to a national audience. It features the beginnings of visual representations of war via Mathew Brady's photographic exhibitions, and explains the development of journalistic conventions such as the inverted pyramid and the use of graphics (particularly maps). It describes the role of press organizations, including the Associated Press, in diffusing war information and the reaction of readers to major policy issues—including emancipation, taxation, conscription, and suspension of the writ of habeas corpus. In short, *Journalism in the Civil War Era* synthesizes work on individual subjects—both those that have been examined to some extent in secondary literature and those that have not—along with unexplored primary sources to form new interpretations of issues that have often gone missing in other accounts of the press and the war.

Although countless scholars have addressed either the press or politics during the nineteenth century, fewer have played a particularly direct role in shaping our interpretation of the interconnection of the two during the Civil War. For example, one of the leading works on the press during the Civil War, Robert S. Harper's *Lincoln and the Press* (1951), looks at both the pro- and anti-war press; however, written more than half a century ago, it focuses on Lincoln's political relationship with the press, not on the relationship between the press and society.

In some respects, a comparable, more-recent book, *The Civil War and the Press* by David Sachsman, S. Kitrell Rushing, and Debra Reddin van Tuyll (1999), although exceptional in individual contributions, touches on issues explored in this book but lacks a cultural or developmental theme.[5]

Books offering general treatments of journalism during the Civil War have tended, meanwhile, to focus only on the contributions of individual editors. While *Bohemian Brigade* by Louis M. Starr (1954) and *The Greenwood Library of American War Reporting* by Amy Reynolds and Debra Reddin van Tuyll (2005) both provide extraordinary analyses of Civil War reporting, they focus more on issues of press freedoms than on the technological or developmental aspects of journalism. Among sources by writers with a professional journalism background, James Moorhead Perry's *A Bohemian Brigade: The Civil War Correspondents, Mostly Rough, Sometimes Ready* (2000) provides a colorful account of the subject but does not explore the social context examined in our book.[6] Topical studies, while useful for interpreting specific subjects, also rarely fully explore the larger cultural or developmental arcs in which their topics played a role. For example, *Editors Make War*, by Donald E. Reynolds (1971), looks at Confederate editors who pushed the war in the South without wholly contrasting them with their counterparts in the North. *Fanatics and Fire-Eaters* by Lorman A. Ratner and Dwight L. Teeter (2003), another example, examines specific events—six key developments leading up to the war—and how the nation's newspapers covered them, but its timeline ends with the hostilities at Fort Sumter.

While dozens of other compelling books could be added to this list, *Hated Ideas and the American Civil War* (2008) by Hazel Dicken-Garcia and Giovanna Dell'Orto in particular shows how newspapers from a wide spectrum of political perspectives framed the most controversial issues of the war. Examining in detail free-speech issues, their book lays a foundation for additional work on the role and evolution of the First Amendment, as described in Bulla's work on Lincoln's suppression of the press and Borchard's analysis of the president's sometimes-contentious relationship with Horace Greeley of *The New York Tribune*.[7]

Indeed, press historians who read our story critically will note the recurrence of *The New York Tribune* as a primary source. We have also cited scores of newspapers from the era, not the least of them the industry-leading New York *Herald*, but the fact that Greeley's *Tribune* plays a major role deserves explanation.[8] Historians interested primarily in the developmental aspects of the American press might rightfully point to James Gordon Bennett's *Herald* as among the most influential newspapers of era—outselling its competitors and devoting its vast resources to covering the war in an unparalleled manner.[9] However, the

Tribune, for our purposes, described the events of the era in more clearly intellectual terms, illustrating a cultural transformation beyond business sales alone. (It is worth noting that Edwin Emery, an honored media historian, observed that while few nineteenth-century figures come close to Lincoln in being the subject of historical studies, Greeley is among that small number).[10]

While the preceding secondary sources all played roles in interpreting the primary sources of our first edition, scholars have published numerous books on the subject since 2010. The following list is a sample of remarkable titles by year with publishers:

- Patricia G. McNeely, Debra Reddin van Tuyll, and Henry L. Schulte, *Knights of the Quill: Confederate Correspondents and their Civil War Reporting*, Purdue University Press, 2010.
- Gregory A. Borchard, *Abraham Lincoln and Horace Greeley*, Southern Illinois University Press, 2011.
- Ford Risley, *Civil War Journalism*, Praeger, 2012.
- Debra Reddin van Tuyll, *The Confederate Press in the Crucible of the American Civil War*, Peter Lang, 2013.
- Harold Holzer, *Lincoln and the Power of the Press: The War for Public Opinion*, Simon and Schuster, 2014.
- Gregory A. Borchard and David W. Bulla, *Lincoln Mediated: The President and the Press through Nineteenth Century Media*, Transaction, 2015; Routledge, 2020.
- Mary M. Cronin, ed. *An Indispensable Liberty: The Fight for Free Speech in Nineteenth-Century America*, Southern Illinois University Press, 2016.
- David B. Sachsman, ed. *A Press Divided: Newspaper Coverage of the Civil War*, Routledge, 2017.
- Ford Risley, *Dear* Courier: *The Civil War Correspondence of Editor Melvin Dwinell*, University of Tennessee Press, 2018.
- David B. Sachsman, and Gregory A. Borchard. *The Antebellum Press: Setting the Stage for Civil War*, Taylor & Francis, 2019.
- Elizabeth Mitchell, *Lincoln's Lie: A True Civil War Caper through Fake News, Wall Street, and the White House*, Counterpoint, 2020.
- Mary Cronin and Debra Reddin van Tuyll, eds., *The Western Press in the Crucible of the American Civil War*, Peter Lang, 2021.

You will find references to these texts and others woven throughout our narrative. At the same time, an annotated listing of publications near the end of this second edition provides for historiographical purposes sources issued between the first edition and this one.

The resulting story you will read in the following pages details the interaction between society and the press. This account affords readers the opportunity to examine both the achievements and shortcomings of members of the press. It should also encourage readers to explore and analyze the value of press freedom during the war—a time when that freedom came under intense fire. In subscribing to an observation made by Greeley that "the illusion that the times that were are better than those that are, has probably pervaded all ages," the authors also reject an amateurish misconception of history as simply a collection of "names and dates."[11] The story in the pages that follow is, rather, part of an organic body of work that contributes as much to an understanding of the present as it does the past.

Notes

1 Rachel Lance, "As U.S. COVID-19 Deaths Top the Civil War's Toll, We're Repeating Disease History," *Time*, August 14, 2021.

2 Janell Ross, "Richmond's Robert E. Lee Statue Is Gone, Now It's Up to the City to Shape What That Means," *Time*, September 9, 2021.

3 "Statues and Sculpture. Robert E. Lee in Statuary Hall," Library of Congress, accessed October 27, 2021, at <loc.gov/item/2019681623>.

4 William David Sloan, *Perspectives on Mass Communication History* (Hillsdale, NJ: Lawrence Earlbaum, 1991), 5-9; James D. Startt and Sloan, *Historical Methods* (Northport, AL: Vision Press, 2003), 19-40.

5 Robert S. Harper, *Lincoln and the Press* (New York: McGraw-Hill, 1951), 418; David B. Sachsman, S. Kittrell Rushing, and Debra Reddin van Tuyll, eds., *The Civil War and the Press* (New Brunswick, NJ: Transaction Publishers, 2000), 309-24.

6 Louis M. Starr, *Bohemian Brigade* (New York: Alfred A. Knopf, 1954), 367; Amy Reynolds, Reddin van Tuyll, *The Greenwood Library of American War Reporting: The Civil War, North & South*, Vol. 3 (Westport, CT: Greenwood Press, 2005), 530; James Moorhead Perry, *A Bohemian Brigade: The Civil War Correspondents, Mostly Rough, Sometimes Ready* (New York: John Wiley and Sons, 2000), 305.

7 Donald E. Reynolds, *Editors Make War* (Nashville, TN: Vanderbilt University Press, 1970), 310; Lorman A. Ratner and Dwight L. Teeter, *Fanatics and Fire-Eaters: Newspapers and the Coming of the Civil War* (Champaign, IL: University of Illinois Press, 2003), 232; Hazel Dicken-Garcia and Giovanna Dell'Orto, *Hated Ideas and the American Civil War* (Spokane, WA: Marquette Books, 2008), 350.

8   James Parton, *Life of Horace Greeley* (New York: Mason Brothers, 1855), 281; Frederic Hudson, *Journalism in the United States* (New York: Harper Brothers, 1873), 529.

9   Perry, *A Bohemian Brigade*, 49.

10   Edwin Emery, Michael Emery and Nancy Roberts, *The Press and America, An Interpretive History of the Mass Media*, 9th ed. (Boston: Allyn and Bacon, 2000), 105.

11   Horace Greeley, *The American Conflict*, Vol. 1 (New York, Chicago, Hartford, CT: O. D. Case, 1866), 21.

Acknowledgements

Librarians at these locations helped locate or provide documents: Dayton, Ohio, Public Library; Des Moines, Iowa, Public Library; Duke University Special Collections; George A. Smathers Library at the University of Florida; Goshen, Indiana, Public Library; Herman B Wells Library and Lilly Library at Indiana University; Indiana State Library; Jackson Library at the University of North Carolina at Greensboro; Library of Congress; Lied Library at the University of Nevada, Las Vegas; Literary And Philosophical Society, Newcastle (UK); New York Public Library; Parks Library at Iowa State University; Philip Robinson Library, Newcastle (UK) University; Roux Library at Florida Southern College; and the Walter Davis and Louis R. Wilson libraries at University of North Carolina at Chapel Hill.

Staff at these museums and historical societies provided contextual information: The American Antiquarian Society in Worcester, Massachusetts; Center for History in South Bend, Indiana; Chicago Historical Society; Greensboro, North Carolina, Historical Museum; Indiana Historical Society; Iowa Historical Society; Lincoln Museum in Fort Wayne, Indiana; and the Maryland Historical Society.

Personnel at these national parks and battlefields provided historical background: Andersonville (GA) National Historic Site (prison); Antietam;

Appomattox; Chancellorsville; Chattanooga-Chickamauga; Confederate Powder Works Chimney, Augusta (GA); Ford's Theatre; Fredericksburg; Gettysburg; Harpers Ferry; Kennesaw Mountain; Lincoln home in Springfield, Illinois; Manassas; Shiloh; Stones River; and the Tredegar Iron Works in Richmond, Virginia.

Other materials featured include text supplied by Gale's Nineteenth Century U.S. Newspapers archives, the Chronicling America website, the University of North Carolina at Greensboro's "North Carolina Runaway Slaves Advertisements" projects, and the online archives of the Library of Congress, which provided invaluable information in the form of nineteenth-century images and documents that did not require reproduction permission.

Thank you, also, to Eric P. Ries for proofing our manuscript, and thanks to Kashalah Robinson for help with research on runaway slave advertisements. A shout of gratitude, too, to Clark A. Borchard, whose collections of books on the Civil War and whose press entrepreneurship has inspired a lifetime of study.

1

A Typical Newspaper of the Era: The St. Joseph Valley *Register*

"I have endeavored to so conduct myself, the paper, and the business as to advance your political and pecuniary interest. I have never been guided by other motives." Alfred Wheeler to Schuyler Colfax, June 20, 1856.

Organizers had originally promoted the event as a protest of President James K. Polk's veto of a bill that would have invested federal funds into Chicago, a city of rising importance in the West.[1] Instead, it became a meeting of leading Whig and liberal Democratic politicians and editors, unlike any of the era, before or since.

Among the delegates at the July 1847 Chicago Harbor and River Convention, Schuyler Colfax, editor of Indiana's St. Joseph Valley *Register*, headed the list of secretaries in charge of the event. Attendees included Abraham Lincoln, a rising Whig just beginning a term in the U.S. House; Horace Greeley, the popular editor of *The New York Tribune*; David Dudley Field, famed lawyer and reformer; and Edward Bates, the presiding officer, who in 1861 became attorney general in Lincoln's cabinet. The 20,000-plus other conventioneers had met to help promote the constitutional power of Congress to appropriate money for infrastructural improvements throughout the West. Leaders such as Henry Clay, Martin Van Buren, and Lewis Cass read letters and made addresses that led to resolutions, unanimously adopted, that called on Congress to fund construction of canals and railroads.[2]

While Colfax and Greeley had already formed a professional relationship through correspondences on all things in politics and print, the convention marked the first time Lincoln and Greeley first appeared together on the same stage and in print. Greeley's *Tribune* featured the event, and in addition to noting Greeley's roles as both a participant and a reporter, it introduced Lincoln to readers as "a tall specimen of an Illinoisan, just elected to Congress from the only Whig district in the State" who spoke "briefly and happily."[3]

The convention signaled the power of populism during the era and at the same time revealed that voters found Congress to be out of touch with their interests. The failure of all branches of government to address in particular the role slavery would play in the West's newly admitted states led to what historians have since described as the Civil War, or as the Second American Revolution. Editors at the time described it as "The War Between the States," "The Great Rebellion," "The War for Southern Independence," or "John Brown's War."

At the time, two primary types of newspapers existed in the Civil War era. In major cities on the East Coast, penny papers were popular. These papers, among them Greeley's *Tribune*, emphasized local news, along with local, state, and national politics, featuring information that ordinary citizens in the Eastern cities found useful. Publishers circulated tens of thousands of daily copies produced by steam presses, often requiring sophisticated operations with dozens of laborers completing discrete tasks. Among the employees were reporters who during the Civil War covered the events from the front lines. Elsewhere, in another kind of publishing, editors oversaw operations more modest. Most ran four-page weeklies with politics dominating the agenda.[4] These weeklies included a smattering of local news, but also ran fiction and poetry. These newspapers, some of which converted to daily operations, ran war news from the telegraph and clippings from exchange papers. The majority of American papers fit the latter type, and one of them more or less epitomized it: Schuyler Colfax's St. Joseph Valley *Register*. Colfax, a New York native whose family moved to Indiana when he was thirteen, was a prominent politician on the national stage.[5] He was a Republican congressman from Indiana, Speaker of the U.S. House of Representatives, and vice president under Ulysses S. Grant. His South Bend newspaper was relatively small, never having more than a few thousand readers.[6] Like many mid-nineteenth-century journalists, Colfax maintained a partisan journal, and his advanced the cause of the Republican Party in northern Indiana.

Colfax's correspondence with his editor, Alfred Wheeler, who ran the paper's daily operations, show how the two men divided assignments and labor, and how they worked to promote Colfax's political career. Along the way, Colfax became a national political figure and nearly procured the editorship of Greeley's nationally prominent *New York Tribune*. Meanwhile, Wheeler would rise from printer to editor to publisher.

Image 1.1 "Carte d'visite: Schuyler Colfax, 1823–1885." From the Brady National Photographic Art Gallery, Washington, DC. At the age of 19, Colfax became the editor of the *South Bend Free Press*. In 1845, he purchased the newspaper and changed its name to the St. Joseph Valley *Register*. He embarked on a political career that included roles as a U.S. Representative, Speaker of the House, and the 17th Vice President of the United States.[7]

Yet the Hoosier journalist also oversaw the development of an ever-improving newspaper, thanks in part to changes in business practices. One of the most profound transformations in the newspaper business in the middle of the nineteenth century was the rise of distinct roles for the various workers. The days of the single-person operation, with perhaps one or two printer's apprentices, were ending, and Colfax moved to make the *Register* a more sophisticated operation, one that not only served a political interest but also functioned as a small business with modest profits.

One of the features of American journalism in the middle of the nineteenth century was this transition from the political to the pecuniary, but by today's standards, the journalism of Colfax's era seems almost entirely about personal and party politics. Indeed, 80 percent of the newspapers in the United States were still political in nature at the dawn of the Civil War, yet more American newspaper owners found themselves trying to make a living—and in some urban settings, significant profits—from their endeavors. Colfax, like many editors in Indiana and other interior states, straddled the line between the political and commercial.

Building the Flagship

Editors and publishers of the Civil War era provided leadership for 31 million readers, with many of them either having side careers as politicians or, later, entering the world of politics after the war, believing the 888 million copies of papers printed per year positively influenced the public. Although the journals of the North and South may not have been this influential, the publishers operated under this assumption. These newspapers at the same time emphasized the discovery of fact. Reporting as a profession was in its infancy, having begun to emerge in the 1830s and 1840s with the rise of the urban penny papers, but by the Civil War, approximately 500 men and women served as reporters. They used observation as their main tool for gathering facts, but they also talked to officers and their men. Hundreds of soldiers wrote home to their papers to provide their views of various battles. The journalism of mid-century had already produced a desire for undiluted information that could help citizens make decisions about both the trivial and the profane. When the war began, newspapers, mostly those with larger circulations, dispatched reporters to the front lines to collect the news.

Colfax's newspaper followed this model, and although he lived an extraordinary life for an editor, his biography reveals important traits in the evolution of the news industry in general. Born in New York City in 1823, he began his career in journalism at sixteen, working as a printer and writing for newspapers in South Bend. His grandfather, William Colfax, a general in the Revolutionary War, was married to Hester Schuyler, a cousin of another Revolutionary War general, Philip Schuyler. The South Bend politician's father, Schuyler Colfax, Sr., married Hannah Stryker and worked at a Wall Street bank, but contracted tuberculosis and died before his son was born. Hannah Colfax remarried to George W. Matthews of Baltimore and moved to New Carlisle, Indiana. Schuyler Colfax, who had left school in New York when he was only ten years old, worked in his stepfather's store, in the local post office, and on nearby farms. The Matthews family moved to South Bend in 1841, and Schuyler Colfax would call South Bend home until his death in 1885. In 1841, the town had less than 1,000 inhabitants. George Matthews, a Whig, won election as auditor of St. Joseph County, and his stepson served as deputy auditor. Matthews frequently served as either trustee or clerk of South Bend before becoming city treasurer in 1865, by which time he was a Republican. He won one election by a vote of 1,014 to 68. The family was first Presbyterian and then Dutch Reformed.

From 1841 to 1843, Colfax sent dispatches to Horace Greeley at *The New York Tribune*, thus inaugurating a long relationship with one of the journalistic luminaries of American history. Greeley told the boy to send him "what you see and learn about Politics, Business, Crops, etc."[8] Colfax followed the advice by writing about banking, internal improvements, agriculture, politics, and temperance. After covering the Indiana Senate for the pro-Whig *Indiana State Journal* in Indianapolis, Colfax served as editor of the pro-Whig South Bend *Free Press*, focusing on politics. Colfax and Albert W. West purchased in 1845 an interest in the *Free Press*, a newspaper that William Millikan had established in 1836. They discontinued it after nine years, but bought the newspaper building and press. In September of 1845, they commenced publishing, renaming the pro-Whig paper the St. Joseph Valley *Register*. Colfax remained in publishing for three decades, during which he rose with the fortunes of a new political organization, the Republican Party, and ultimately achieved national political prominence. West sold his interest in the paper in 1846, leaving Colfax the sole proprietor.

From the beginning, Colfax emphasized the political nature of the journal: "In Politics, we shall be inflexibly Whig, believing those principles the best and safest and wisest for the administration of our Government."[9] The editor expressed strong disdain for slavery, and Colfax, a descendent of Puritans, was pro-temperance. However, he said the paper would not be as reformist as Greeley's: "With the position of the *Tribune* as regards Fourierism and some of the other Reforming views of that paper we do not concur. This is well known to Mr. Greeley."[10] Other issues he would discuss would include women's rights—he was for them—and Mormonism. The owner said the *Register* would be a journal of record for the news of the day. Indeed, when no Democratic journal existed in the county, the *Register* would cover that party's events, personalities, and policies. Regarding other news items, Colfax indicated the newspaper would cover agriculture and education. Furthermore, it would record the progress of society in the St. Joseph River Valley, although it would have little crime news, as was the case with the penny papers of the East Coast. Colfax felt crime news was too sensational. He wanted a journal on a higher plain, emphasizing business, agriculture, education, and internal improvements, including the building of more railroads. The paper also served a watchdog function, criticizing local government when improvements were not made or they were not made fast enough. Another feature included dispatches from Greeley as he traveled across the growing nation, as well as letters from South Bend residents who had moved to California in search of gold.

A decade later, Colfax won election to the U.S. House of Representatives, and in leaving for Washington, D.C., he handed over the newspaper to Alfred Wheeler, a veteran printer. The study that follows looks at the written exchange between Colfax and Wheeler in the 1850s and 1860s. It shows a hierarchical relationship that was critical to the success of the newspaper, especially since Colfax spent so much time in Washington, D.C., and yet had a significant say in how the paper looked, what information it transmitted to the citizens of South Bend, and the tone of that transmission. Colfax and Wheeler worked as a team to make the *Register* one of the best newspapers in Indiana. Their relationship was professional and cordial, but the congressman had the upper hand even as Wheeler had to make the gate-keeping decisions about what would go into the paper every day.

A portion of their correspondence and other Colfax letters shows the dynamic relationship between publisher and editor as they worked to publish their newspaper. The purpose was twofold, as Wheeler wrote in a June 20, 1856, letter to his employer. "I have endeavored to so conduct myself, the paper, and the business as to advance your political and pecuniary interests. I have never been guided by other motives."[11]

Wheeler saw the *Register* as the flagship of his boss' political fortunes, but he also saw it as a vehicle for making money. Toward that end, he considered a major part of his duties to be financial in nature, selling advertising, running down subscribers to get them to pay their subscriptions ($1.75/year), and keeping account of the paper's transactions. Thus, Colfax's newspaper was exemplary of the Popular Press era in that it not only tried to make a profit by including news, but also remained partisan, connecting politicians with potential voters. Colfax, with no small advantage from his paper's support, built a political career that nearly took him to the top of the U.S. government. Letters to and from other journalists also flesh out the nature of the mid-century press. Some of these are included in this study, such as those to Greeley and Charles Dana of *The New York Tribune* and Henry Jarvis Raymond of *The New York Times*.

Then, after his political career ended in scandal, he remained publicly active as an author, journalist, and lecturer. Colfax's book about a journey he took west with Springfield, Massachusetts, *Republican* editor Samuel Bowles—at the behest of Lincoln just before his assassination—became a popular travelogue. At one point, there was a plan to make him the editor of *The New York Tribune* after Greeley's death in 1872, but that deal fell through when Whitelaw Reid made himself permanent editor.[12] Thus, Colfax in effect remade himself into a literary man. Accordingly, no longer in the political storm, he gave up his newspaper and retired to a quiet life of letters.

The relationship between Colfax and Wheeler described in these letters demonstrates the various functions of their journalistic operation and serves as a case study in skill differentiation in a mid-nineteenth-century newspaper endeavor. Colfax, as owner and occasional editor, had developed a reputation for journalistic excellence and was taking the business risk. He also used the weekly journal to advance his personal—and party—political fortunes. Wheeler was a skilled printer, and his objective was to make the *Register* the leading newspaper in South Bend and serve as Colfax's eyes and ears back home when the legislator was away in Washington or on one of his many journeys around the country.

A weekly published on Thursdays, the *Register* had an initial subscription list of two hundred fifty, and its dimensions were twenty-two by thirty-two inches. The text initially flowed over six columns, though Colfax increased it to a seven-column format in September 1847. In 1848, the first telegraph line connected New York and Chicago, providing a major benefit for newspapers that could tap into it. South Bend was on the line, and Colfax took advantage, including news of the world beyond the St. Joseph Valley. Later, after the laying of the transatlantic cable, Colfax began to include European news in the *Register*.

At first a fur-trading outpost on the St. Joseph River, South Bend grew rapidly in the years Colfax was a journalist. In 1850, its population was 1,652. A decade later, it had climbed to 3,832; by 1870, 7,206; and in 1880, 13,280.[13] The immigrant population of the city nearly tripled, from 17 to 47 percent of the population, with most of the immigrants from Germany, Poland, and Ireland. Change was abundant during Colfax's four decades in South Bend, a town best known for the Studebaker Manufacturing Company, a maker of covered wagons. One of the best ways to see it was that when he started the *Register* in 1845 the telegraph was just coming to St. Joseph County. By his death in 1885, the city already had telephone lines. The journalist, who had married Evelyn Clark in 1844, was worth $1,600 when he bought the *Free Press*. This included his joint ownership of a home with his stepfather, George W. Matthews. Colfax's biographer, Willard H. Smith, believed it was unlikely the editor had to borrow much money to make his portion of the payment on the paper.

Publishing Politics

Colfax, who wrote a weekly column for the *Register* for eighteen years, actively participated in politics on the state and national level. In 1847, he won nomination for the clerk of the Indiana House of Representatives, but he lost in the election. Nonetheless, he stayed in Indianapolis, sending back dispatches to the *Register* and reporting for The Indiana *State Journal*. During his time in Indianapolis, he had the opportunity to be part of an ownership group of two papers, first the

Tippecanoe *Journal* and then the Cincinnati *Gazette*. He declined, preferring to have only one journalistic enterprise. In 1848, the South Bend resident was a delegate to the national Whig convention. In 1850 and 1851, he served as a delegate to Indiana's Constitutional Convention in Indianapolis, where he served on the committees on banking and public institutions. Colfax opposed a law that would make it illegal for freed Blacks to enter Indiana, and even proposed a law that would give Blacks the right to vote. It never gained enough support.

Then, in 1851, when Colfax ran for Congress the first time, James Davis, an attorney, served as editor of the *Register*. Colfax believed that he could not practically run the paper during campaign. This arrangement continued Colfax's tendency to delegate authority at the *Register*, much in the way Baltimore *Sun* publisher Arunah S. Abell and other penny press editors in the East did. During the congressional campaign, against Democratic incumbent Graham N. Fitch, Colfax continued to oppose slavery, although he refused to pledge a repeal of the Fugitive Slave Law. Colfax did say he would not renounce his anti-slavery convictions just to win the election. The South Bend editor did in fact lose—by a mere 200 votes. In 1852, he returned to the Whig national convention, working to have Mexican-American War hero Winfield Scott nominated for president.

In 1854, Colfax decided to run again, and he hired Wheeler to help run the newspaper. Wheeler then took over the everyday operation of the paper in 1855 when Colfax, defeating Norman Eddy on a wave of support from those who opposed the admission of new slave states from the Kansas and Nebraska territories, began seven terms in the U.S. House of Representatives.[14] By this time, Colfax, who thought slavery was morally wrong, was a moderate Republican who opposed its expansion in the territories. Colfax's victory over Eddy was part of a change in Indiana politics, as the Republicans, taking the place of the defunct Whigs, won nine of the eleven Hoosier seats in Congress. After the Whigs' demise, the newspaper supported the Republican Party for the rest of its history.

Colfax's relationship with Wheeler exemplified the emerging division of labor in the era. As publisher, Colfax was the majority owner of the paper for much of the time they worked together. He had Wheeler serve as the editor in charge of day-to-day operations. Colfax, meanwhile, charted the paper's political course and provided feedback on the quality of each edition of the paper. Wheeler's expertise as a printer and editor helped develop the *Register* into a formidable journalistic enterprise. He compensated his editor well, and Wheeler became a partner in the *Register* and held the position until November 1865, selling it to Archibald Beal, former editor of the Mishawaka *Enterprise*. Alfred B. Miller and Elmer Crockett were involved in owning and running the *Register* in the late

1860s and early 1870s, but they left to form the *Tribune*, which began on March 9, 1872. The *Register* Printing Company formed in 1875, the same year the newspaper became a daily. In 1887, it finally closed, and owners sold its equipment to the *Tribune*, which is South Bend's daily newspaper today.

The *Register* was representative of the typical small-town newspaper of midcentury in that it had a limited circulation, but it grew steadily thanks to Colfax's political ascension and consistent upgrading of the paper. Beginning in 1853, the *Register* printed on a Northup Power Press, the first in the state outside of Indianapolis. Wheeler said that the press printed 1,000 sheets per hour.[15] In the 1850s, the *Register* was a weekly and cost $1.50 a year. It had the largest circulation in the northern part of the state, boasting its reach extended into every county in Northern Indiana from the Lake to the Wabash. It was "the largest of all the papers in the State, except those at the Capital," and it "considerably exceeds even those in size."[16] The *Register* also advertised printing services—books, "Job," "Fancy," and card printing.

Colfax exchanged letters with other journalists, usually discussing politics or journalism. Charles A. Dana of *The New York Tribune* sent Colfax a letter on June 28, 1851, asking the South Bend editor to give him a sense of how things were going for the congressional election in Indiana. Dana was writing on behalf of Greeley, who had conducted an early form of straw poll to try to predict and influence national political races. Dana asked Schuyler Colfax his opinions about the 1852 presidential race and the Fugitive Slave Law. Dana also commented that Colfax had written Greeley a letter, but it had been lost "among a stack of papers he left behind him [on a trip to Europe to a world's fair] for removal and destruction."[17]

Wheeler began working at the *Register* as a printer in 1851. A native of New York, he came to South Bend in 1840 after living first in Michigan and then in Bristol, Indiana. The correspondence between Colfax and Wheeler started even before Wheeler became editor of the *Register*. In a letter from Wheeler to Colfax, dated August 23, 1853, the former wrote that he could "tinker up your press so that it will work better than it does now at all events."[18] He discussed the importance of using felt rollers, and how the Toledo *Blade* had a steam-powered press, which he said was more efficient, noting that sheets of paper "come out better and lay better." Wheeler wrote that the *Blade*'s press has a "steady and uniform motion." In the margins, he noted, "Your Seal Press has arrived." In a letter dated August 29, 1853, he told Colfax that the newspaper had fifty new subscribers. Wheeler, who worked to improve the paper's circulation, said he collected $24.16 for the paper.

Explaining that the *Register* was growing, and that he hoped to earn both a raise and a higher position, Wheeler told Colfax in spring 1855 that he could not work for less than nine dollars a week. The owner wrote that he had assumed Wheeler would gain a share of the *Register* eventually. "I should have offered you half the *Register* on easy terms of payment," Colfax noted.[19] The publisher worried that Wheeler would walk. Before Colfax could settle matters with Wheeler, a fire razed the newspaper office in August 1855. Colfax decided to rebuild, but he wanted the *Register* to modernize. He wanted to hire an editor whose politics exactly matched his own, confiding in Wheeler that he had three candidates in mind—but that one opposed the Know Nothings, another one was too radical on abolition, and the third lacked journalistic experience. That is when he decided to make Wheeler his editor. Colfax announced the hiring in November 1855. At the same time, the owner promised to write regularly from Washington. He said he would provide a "faithful portrayal of the political movements at the Capital."[20] Colfax served as both a reporter and an interpreter of national political news.

The owner and editor had an agreement about what should happen to the *Register* in the case of Colfax's death while he served in Congress. In a letter to his close friend Charles M. Heaton Sr., Colfax shared the information in the memorandum of agreement between the congressman and Wheeler. If Colfax were to die, Wheeler would get the "office, fixtures, subscription list, and good will of the St. Joseph Valley *Register*" on the condition that Wheeler would pay Colfax's legal heirs $3,000 in six $500 installments over thirty-three months. Interest for not paying on time would be 10 percent.[21]

Wheeler, who rarely wrote much in the letters about local news and tried to live by Colfax's dictum to avoid crime news, nonetheless sensed interesting stories. The editor mentioned a messy romantic situation in town and told the story of how a South Bend woman had visited relatives in Illinois and sent a letter back to her husband, David Stover, telling him that she was leaving him and that he should seek a divorce. She planned to leave Stover for a Dr. Brainard, who also sent his spouse a letter saying he was leaving her. Wheeler said that the editorials would be slender if Colfax did not send some news to South Bend. He also asked the publisher to purchase type the next time he was in New York. The editor reported that he delayed paying for ink to a man named Thompson, that he had exchanged type with a man in Elkhart, and that he was selecting mail to forward to Colfax. Wheeler reminded Colfax to hurry his correspondence back to South Bend. The editor noted that too often it arrived late and appeared two weeks later than both editor and publisher desired, especially since Colfax's letters from the East were quite popular with *Register* readers.

Another typical activity for Wheeler was collecting newspapers for his boss. These included the LaPorte *Times*, South Bend *Forum*, Bluffton *Banner*, Vincennes *Gazette*, and Indiana State *Sentinel* of Indianapolis. Wheeler was also busy with content, and one way he tried to fill the pages of the paper was to run all of Colfax's House speeches that appeared in *The Globe*, a journal that covered Congress. However, his most important duty may have been just keeping his employees satisfied. "[Andrew] Tipton has thrown out some hints about wishing to quit the business," he wrote Colfax, "but I think he will stay till his year is out."[22] Later, Tipton told Wheeler that he had to return to his home because his father was sick and confined to bed. Eventually, Tipton received his release, and the editor began to search for a replacement. He preferred a boy to learn the trade, but believed his boss would probably want a "regular apprentice" with experience in printing. A year later, Tipton returned at $200 a year after another veteran employee resigned.

Politics was a consistent theme in the letters. Wheeler and Colfax often discussed the fact that political support depended on giving the right people political patronage. In a letter dated December 23, 1855, Wheeler told the congressman that he was putting three columns of advertising on the front page of the next issue, something that frustrated him because he preferred political news. The editor also told Colfax that the LaPorte *Times* of December 5 had no mention of the congressman. Wheeler read many newspapers carefully, but he read The St. Joseph County *Forum*, the pro-Democratic competitor, with acute interest. He consistently told Colfax not to take invective against him in the *Forum* too seriously. Wheeler wrote that the people in Colfax's district put little faith in the words of the Democratic paper's editors, the father-son combination of Ariel E. and William H. Drapier.

Wheeler sent Colfax a letter in the summer of 1856 telling the congressman that the citizens of South Bend eagerly anticipated each of his offerings from Washington. "I am very glad my letters are 'popular' with our readers," Colfax replied, "for they are always written under very disadvantageous circumstances … with people talking to me every minute or so." Politics was central to the exchange between publisher and editor. The "Old Liners," Wheeler wrote, perceived "the necessity of putting forward their strongest man, and I am afraid that [John C.] Walker will be discarded."

Notwithstanding the Sentinel's denial, the Pharos says that [William Z.] Stuart is a candidate for the nomination. I agree with you that Walker would be the weakest candidate. [Norman] Eddy, or Stuart, or [Charles W.] Cathcart would be much stronger. Perhaps also [David A.] Turpie would be, but I don't know anything about him.[23]

Stuart won the Democratic nomination, and during the 1856 congressional race, Wheeler counseled Colfax not to look like he wanted to be re-nominated. In a June 20 letter, Wheeler noted that a rumor was floating around South Bend that Colfax declined the nomination. The *Forum* apparently was spreading the word, reporting on the "puzzle of silence" from Wheeler in not denying that Colfax had turned down the nomination. Wheeler told Colfax to ignore the *Forum* article, hoping that Colfax would not think he had erred in keeping silent and defended that strategy. Wheeler worried the margin was getting closer, but he predicted victory. In summer 1856, he wrote that despite German defections to the Democratic Party, Colfax would win St. Joseph County by 300 votes. As it turned out, Colfax prevailed over Stuart in the general election with a majority of 1,036. However, the news was not as positive across the state. The Republicans lost the governor's race and six of the state's eleven congressional seats.

Wheeler also told Colfax that his readers wanted plenty of news from Kansas, so he "gave them Kansas news."[24] Wheeler lamented that German immigrants gravitated toward the Democrats because of their opposition to prohibition, which was the law in Indiana. A teetotaler, Colfax was a proponent of Indiana's prohibitory law. The editor also reported that voters in South Bend generally found the nomination of John C. Frémont agreeable. In that same June letter, Wheeler touched on business matters. He reported that advertising was crowding reading material in the columns of the *Register*. The editor reported the paper bill was $279.75 going back to the previous fall. Wheeler said he owed the paper vendor $125.75.

On September 10, 1856, Colfax reported on a riot in Lafayette. As usual, he began his letter with "Friend Wheeler" and closed it "Yours truly." Supporters of the Democratic candidate running against Colfax had attacked a wagon that flew the stars and stripes, and in the melee, an Irishman had been shot. A man on horseback named John Zeffel, who tried to rescue his wife on the wagon, was knocked off his horse. The rioters chased the man and used axes to wound him. Colfax assumed the man died. The Irish had sufficient numbers to take over the town, Colfax said, and assaulted a man named Samuel Fisher. They also attacked a physician. Colfax claimed he was also threatened and that one of the rioters struck his horse and said he would do the same to the congressman. The rioters also threatened the life of another man for joining the Republicans after having been a Democrat.[25]

In a September 30, 1856, letter to Wheeler written in Crown Point, Colfax informed his editor about payments by several subscribers. "Political prospects flattering," he wrote, noting Republican gains in Jasper County by the scores and in Lake County by the hundreds, with a projected majority of 600. "Some say more," he added. He told Wheeler he would like to make two speeches per day on the Friday, Saturday, and Monday before the election, speaking in five towns in the district.[26] Two years later, in the next campaign, Colfax discussed canvassing with his opponent, John C. Walker, who wanted to confine the campaigning to thirteen stump speeches and no more. They could not come to terms and campaigned separately. Colfax told Wheeler he was worried about his throat and an old bronchial condition.[27]

Looking East

Abraham Lincoln, the rising star of the West, recognized early the importance of consolidating the support of Republicans in Indiana and Illinois in order to succeed in the 1860 election. In mid-1859, he wrote Colfax, asking him to help "hedge against divisions in the Republican ranks generally, and particularly for the contest of 1860." He wrote, "In a word, in every locality, we should look beyond our noses; and at least say nothing on points where it is probable we should disagree."[28]

Wheeler felt that Abraham Lincoln would win the presidency in 1860, but at great cost. In March of that year, he wrote, "I believe that the man who will probably go into the Convention with a higher vote on the first ballot than either Bates, Seward, Chase or Cameron, stands the best chance of the nomination— and that man is Abe Lincoln." Wheeler believed Lincoln would pull in a heavy vote from Indiana and Illinois. He added that Pennsylvania and Illinois would decide the Republican nominee for president. He also observed that the winner of the Chicago convention would not get a single electoral vote from a slave state. "I do not like the way things are shaping themselves on the Democratic side."[29]

On May 27, 1860, Wheeler reported that South Bend Republicans received news of Lincoln with enthusiasm. He said even some Democrats regarded Lincoln favorably and would vote for him if Douglas lost the nomination. South Bend and St. Joseph County Democrats, Wheeler wrote, were "discouraged, disorganized and demoralized, and thus far do not even show fight," adding that if Douglas did not earn the Democratic nomination, they would let the county go to Lincoln. If Douglas were nominated, conversely, "they will revive." He was confident the Republicans would win in St. Joseph County: "The signs are conspicuous, the feeling is right, the current is setting strongly for us, and I now feel more confident and hopeful than I ever did before." He mentioned that some Democrats had switched parties and attended the recent county Republican convention. Colfax, who had been friendly with Stephen Douglas in 1858, supported Edward Bates for president and arranged to have Indiana's delegates support him. In a June 14, 1860 letter, Wheeler reported that Colfax won re-nomination for Congress by acclamation and without opposition.[30]

After Lincoln won the November election, Joseph Medill's *Chicago Tribune* was one of several groups outside of Indiana to support Colfax for a cabinet position. Medill floated Colfax's name for postmaster general. Colfax received a letter dated January 30, 1861, from Robert Carter, who worked for *The New York Tribune* and the *Cyclopaedia*. Colfax had asked the *Tribune* to support him for postmaster general. Then, a delegation of legislators from Minnesota sent Lincoln a letter February 27, 1861, deeming Colfax "eminently well qualified" for postmaster general. H. G. O. Morrison, the lieutenant governor of Minnesota, signed the letter, which had twenty-six co-signers.[31]

In a letter of January 29, 1861, Wheeler reported that all Republicans in St. Joseph County opposed the Crittenden Compromise, and that they would reject any arrangement in which the federal government would regulate slavery. He said Republicans of the county favored "masterly inactivity." Yet he went on to adopt a pro-Douglas position of popular sovereignty. He was willing to accept slavery "as a local institution" that "can exist only by virtue of State or local laws, and the people of the Territories by legislation can either introduce or prohibit slavery therein." He also believed the Crittenden Compromise would receive a majority vote if a referendum were held in Indiana, although not in Colfax's Second District.

Wheeler told Colfax he was glad to see that the congressman's prospects for postmaster general were "improving, although I do not yet feel sanguine."[32] He feared Indiana would have no representation in the cabinet, although he believed Caleb Smith had the best chance among Hoosiers to serve in the administration. This proved an accurate forecast, as Lincoln, still stinging from Colfax's support of Douglas and then Bates, made Smith postmaster general. Once again, Wheeler noted that Colfax's dispatches reached South Bend too late to make the latest edition of the *Register*. He did mention that the subscription list had "increased quite rapidly" in St. Joseph County, although he did not give a specific figure. "We must certainly try to get new type in the spring," he concluded.[33]

Lukewarm on Lincoln, Colfax aligned increasingly with the Radical Republicans. When Colfax sought to become Speaker of the House in 1863, Lincoln was one of his opponents. Postmaster Montgomery Blair and Colfax were friends, but the Indiana congressman soured on Blair after he discovered the latter opposed him for the speakership. Nonetheless, Colfax was at the White House the night that Lincoln signed the Emancipation Proclamation. He remained a careful observer of the administration and was close to Salmon P. Chase, the secretary of the Treasury.

In a January 1862 missive, Wheeler defended his competence as a journalist after Colfax had complained about the quality of the paper.

> I *do* [Wheeler's emphasis] read the proof of your letters and remarks, but I am quite certain that your experience as proof-reader has made you acquainted with the fact that errors *marked* are not *always corrected* [Wheeler's emphasis]. And you are also aware that in most cases we are in our haste to get to press, obliged to dispense with revising. Some of the errors you speak of I distinctly recollect were made in the proofs, and perhaps all. We are short of at least half a full hand, and for the last few weeks, I have had to work all the time both night and day, and even some on Sundays.[34]

Wheeler indicated he was focused on reading editorials and gathering news. "And generally on Wednesday forenoon I have to read proofs, set up late news, set type, and make up the forms; so that if some errors do get in the paper it is no great wonder."[35] He also had additional work when employees were sick.

Perhaps no issue was more important to Colfax than the post office. He served as the chair of the Committee on Post Offices and Post Roads from 1859 to 1862. His major achievement was re-organizing the overland mail service to California, but in January 1862, he introduced the unpopular House Number 215. This bill would make it illegal to circulate newspapers on postal roads or routes by the railroads (usually done by baggage masters or other agents), express companies, common carrier, or steamboats. The fine for such an offense would be one hundred dollars. If the bill passed, newspapers would face postal charges if sent in such a way, contradicting a long-standing practice that exempted newspapers from postal charges.

Editors across the country worried that Colfax's bill would cause many consumers to choose not to subscribe to out-of-town newspapers, especially *The New York Tribune*, because the cost of mailing them would be passed on to the readers, or they would get to readers so late that they would be irrelevant. The Cincinnati *Enquirer* opposed the bill, warning that it would not support any member of

Congress for re-election who voted for it.[36] The *Enquirer* accused the federal government not of just trying to quell freedom of the press, but the press itself, as the postal privilege was vital to the free flow of public information. The Cincinnati editors wrote that they did not know why Colfax was proposing such a bill at a time when he ought to devote his resources to winning the war.

However, the status quo favored major newspapers from large cities, not the rural and small-town press. Free papers from Chicago, Cincinnati, and New York came into St. Joseph County, and readers often preferred these journals to the *Register* and other small-town papers. From the perspective of the hinterland press, urban papers were becoming a monopoly, and Colfax, a member of the small-town press fraternity, now held a critical office as the chair of the Committee on the Post Office and Post Roads. He suggested he was not protecting country journalism; rather, he was enacting legislation more agreeable to the press than the proposed war revenue tax on newspapers that simmered in the House Ways and Means Committee.

Greeley, the editor of *The New York Tribune* and one of Colfax's long-time friends, claimed the bill would raise little revenue for the federal government. Greeley said the bill "would seriously diminish the number of journals disseminated and read."[37] He encouraged Colfax and his committee to continue the work it had done to improve the postal system, but he urged the Indiana congressman not to pass this bill. James Gordon Bennett's *New York Herald* castigated Colfax's bill for burdening citizens with an additional tax. The public, not newspapers, had the most to lose from the bill, according to the *Herald*.[38] In the end, House 215 never advanced to the Senate with a vote of sixty for and seventy-five against defeating it.

Although there is no evidence that Colfax and Wheeler discussed the Post Office bill, they continued their exchanges even as the former was about to retire from the *Register*. In a letter to Wheeler dated November 25, 1862, Colfax said he would not take a cabinet position even if offered. He also told Wheeler that he nearly was killed on Long Island Sound when a schooner hit his steamer en route from New York from Newport, Rhode Island. Colfax her displayed a dry sense of humor: "But it didn't sink & so I escaped, missing what would have been a happy day for our Dem. Friends."[39]

Henry C. Bowen of New York wrote a letter to Colfax dated February 7, 1863, in which the former mentioned that Colfax's song about John Brown was growing in popularity. Bowen said members of New York's Plymouth Church sang the song at a lecture by Wendell Phillips, and again at a speech by Frederick Douglass. Colfax discontinued his weekly column in the *Register* in 1863, but the letters about journalism and politics continued—much of it dealing with the editorial war between Republicans and Democrats. "We must have success in the field and energy in the Administration if we are to have any hope of saving the Nation," he told Williamson Wright of Logansport in May 1864. "It's fashionable in the papers to abuse Congress, but although Congressmen may be slow in acting, they have done all that the Government has asked of them and more."[40] Meanwhile, Colfax gave Wheeler majority control of the *Register*. As it turned out, the price for Colfax's three-fourths control of the newspaper was $3,750. The congressman trusted his editor so much that by 1865 Colfax required no security from Wheeler in the form of a down payment.

Colfax had powerful friends in journalism, and he exchanged ideas with them. In a letter from Henry J. Raymond dated February 15, 1865, *The New York Times* editor told Colfax that he was tired of political posturing and worried about Major General Nathaniel P. Banks, a political appointee. "Why in heaven's name can't men rise above party feeling?" Colfax asked. "I don't mean party relation but the spirit of partisanship—and save the country first?"[41]

The *Tribune* Calling

As the end of the war neared, Colfax was in position to see the administration up close. Lincoln's letter of March 5, 1865, invited Colfax to the second inaugural ball and asked him to speak with the president. Secretary of War Edwin M. Stanton, in a March 29, 1865, letter indicated that movements by troops under General Ulysses S. Grant would bear significant results by the time Colfax received the letter. This was, of course, an allusion to the war's end. He also exchanged letters with the ambitious Greeley, who said he would not decline any political office until it was offered to him.

Colfax remained a dominant political figure on the national stage after the war. Beginning in 1863, he held the office of Speaker of the House for three terms before becoming vice president under Grant. He also was inching closer to a direct role in *The New York Tribune*, one of the nation's most prestigious newspapers. In a letter from Samuel Sinclair of the *Tribune* dated March 24, 1866, Sinclair informed Colfax that Greeley wanted the Speaker to take charge of the editorial department of the newspaper in July, August, and September of that year. Sinclair said that Greeley would have "his history finished by that time and he badly needs rest and relaxation." Sinclair said that Greeley thought Colfax was more capable of running the *Tribune* editorial department and judging the political situation than anyone else was. "Can you not do better for the party and the country, here during that period than you could anywhere else?" Sinclair asked. It appeared Greeley wanted Colfax to come work for the *Tribune* permanently, and that this was intended to be a sampling of the work environment. Sinclair said the "old proposition is always open whenever you choose to open it."[42]

Colfax, who did not take the 1866 offer, would have a similar proposal from Greeley in 1872, but he did not finalize the agreement. Sinclair and William Orton, the majority owners of the *Tribune*, pressed for an affirmative answer from Colfax, but he asked for a delay. Colfax then learned that their hold on the majority was weak, and he hesitated. Whitelaw Reid, a top reporter during the Civil War, soon secured the majority with outside money and made himself editor. In a February 1, 1869, letter to Samuel Bowles of the Springfield *Republican* in Massachusetts, Colfax wrote about his plans for a revised book about a journey they had shared to the West. Lincoln had commissioned Colfax to take a trip across the country and write about what he saw. Colfax and Bowles embarked, with the former keeping notes for a book. He wrote it when he returned, and Bowles served as publisher. A first volume came out in 1878 and second in 1881. The title *was Across the Continent: A Summer's Journey to the Rocky Mountains, the Mormons, and the Pacific States*. During the excursion, Colfax discussed plural marriage with the Mormons. He listened considerately to the arguments for polygamy before countering that it had not been part of church doctrine at its founding. One report of the debate was characterized as constituting a rare example of free expression in Salt Lake City.[43] Colfax would print a booklet on the open exchange titled "The Mormon Question."

He expressed amazement at what they had seen on the journey and was optimistic the West would open for expansion. He called Colorado, Wyoming, Utah, Nevada, California, Oregon, and Washington "our new West." Colfax called the railroad "the highway of Nations," writing "lightning trains will render travel a pleasure, instead of a fatigue." He predicted that publishing the book "will increase the number of those who will not only add to their enjoyment and knowledge, but also strengthen the patriotic ties which bind together such distant regions as the Atlantic & Pacific States, into one harmonious Republic."[44]

Colfax's political career ended after Massachusetts Congressman Oakes Ames accused him and other congressmen of receiving stock and dividends in the Crédit Mobilier Company at below-market prices in return for their influence. Congress had chartered the Union Pacific Railroad in 1862 with a federal subsidy for a transcontinental railroad, also establishing Crédit Mobilier to construct it and attract private investors. Ames lent money to colleagues—including fifteen House members, six members of the Senate, and Colfax—to purchase shares at half of their market value. Stockholders in the Union Pacific and Crédit Mobilier, who were usually the same people, paid themselves exorbitant profits. On the eve of the 1872 election, *The New York Sun* exposed Ames and his cohorts, revealing they had taken for their personal use more than $23 million intended for a congressionally approved permanent endowment for construction. After the election, the House voted to censure Ames for bribing House members. Democratic Representative James Brooks of New York was also censured for his involvement. James A. Garfield (R-Ohio) recovered from the scandal to win the presidential election of 1880, only to die shortly thereafter by assassination.

Colfax decided the best course of action was to resign the vice presidency and retire from politics, which he did in early 1873. At that time, he was vice president of the Knoblock Furniture Company and the Birdsell Colver Huller Company, both in South Bend. Yet neither post provided him with adequate income. In addition to his writing projects, including poetry in *Harper's Bazaar*, he launched a career as a public speaker. A major part of his oratory work was devoted to temperance. Colfax played a leadership role in the Washingtonian Movement, which supported prohibition. He also spoke to the Odd Fellows, soldiers' reunions, religious groups, colleges, agricultural bodies, and fairs. His most famous engagement came at the unveiling of the Lincoln monument in Springfield, Illinois, in October 1874.

The *Register* grew, but it also reflected South Bend—a small city growing rapidly in terms of population and industry, but surrounded by farming on the flat, post-glacial plain just southeast of Lake Michigan. Much of the newspaper's success was due to the clear, open communication Colfax had with Wheeler, who managed daily tasks in South Bend so that his boss could pursue national political aspirations. Both men benefited from their relationship. Eventually, Colfax turned the entire operation over to Wheeler, including ownership—a reward to Wheeler for making the *Register* a respected journal—while Colfax's political and journalistic achievements nearly landed him editorship of Greeley's *Tribune*.

Editors like Colfax and Greeley helped set the agenda for public opinion and then colored—framed—how the debate would proceed. Although most historians now somewhat downplay Greeley's effect on Lincoln's announcing the Emancipation Proclamation with his "Prayer of Twenty Millions" editorial in *The New York Tribune* in August 1862, Greeley certainly affected public opinion with his nationally circulated newspaper. He and other more radical Republican editors moved Lincoln away from the center on the issue of slavery, and this moved emancipation to the top of the public agenda.

Colfax's career as a journalist had progressed through stages, from reporter for local newspapers, to correspondent for a New York paper, to owner and editor of a local paper, and finally to man of letters. Ownership and editorial responsibilities for the *Register* represented the bulk of that career. He revived a defunct newspaper and turned it into one of Indiana's best. He modernized it with telegraphic news, a powerful industrial press, and coverage of topics important to Hoosiers. Yet he also used the newspaper to further his political career and to espouse temperance and abolition, his favorite causes. Indeed, the success of the *Register* as an oracle of information for South Bend's citizens made it even more of a political organ. The paper not only helped Colfax build his own personal political career, but it helped him build the base of the Republican Party in northern Indiana. Like his friend Horace Greeley in New York with the *Tribune*, and, for that matter, editors elsewhere, Colfax wanted a modern paper, but he also used the *Register* to advance very specific political causes.

Notes

1 Thurlow Weed, *Life of Thurlow Weed Including His Autobiography and a Memoir*, Vol. 1 (Boston and New York: Houghton Mifflin and Company, 1883–84), 148.

2 Ovando James Hollister, *Life of Schuyler Colfax* (New York: Funk and Wagnalls, 1886), 42, 43.

3 New York *Tribune*, July 17, 1847; Harlan Hoyt Horner, *Lincoln and Greeley* (Urbana, IL: University of Illinois Press, 1953), 1, 2.

4 David J. Russo, "The Origins of Local News in the U.S. Country Press, 1840s–1870s," *Journalism Monographs*, 65 (February 1980), 4; Donald L. Shaw, "At the Crossroads: Change and Continuity in the American Press News 1820–1860," *Journalism History*, 8, 2 (Summer 1981): 41.

5 Willard H. Smith, *Schuyler Colfax: The Changing Fortunes of a Political Idol* (Indianapolis, IN: Indiana Historical Society, 1952), 366, 367.

6 Smith, "Schuyler Colfax, Whig Editor, 1845–1855," *Indiana Magazine of History*, 34, 3 (September 1938): 262, 263; Dean R. Esslinger, *Immigrants and the City: Ethnicity and Mobility in a Nineteenth-Century Midwestern Community* (Port Washington, NY: Kennikat Press, 1975), 108.

7 "Carte d'visite: Colfax, Schuyler, 1823-1885," Library of Congress, accessed July 1, 2021, at <loc.gov/item/mss4429700129>.

8 Greeley to Schuyler Colfax, Colfax MSS, Manuscript Division, Indiana State Library, Indianapolis, IN, L36, 1782–1886 (hereafter, Colfax MSS, ISL).

9 St. Joseph Valley (IN) *Register*, September 12, 1845.

10 Ibid, October 3, 1845.

11 Colfax MSS, Letters from Colfax to Alfred Wheeler, 1855–1862, Lilly Library, Indiana University, Bloomington, Indiana (hereafter, Colfax MSS, Lilly).

12 Smith, *Schuyler Colfax*, 366, 367.

13 U.S. Census, 1850, 1860, 1870.

14 Colfax MSS, Northern Indiana Center for History, South Bend, Indiana.

15 Colfax MSS, Lilly, letters to Wheeler, 1855–1862.

16 St. Joseph County (IN) *Register*, July 14, 1853.

17 Colfax MSS, ISL, Folder Three.

18 Colfax MSS, Lilly, letters to Wheeler, 1855–1862.

19 Colfax to Wheeler, Library of Congress, MMC-0199, April 13, 1855.

20 St. Joseph Valley (IN) *Register*, November 22, 1855.

21 Colfax Collection, Northern Indiana Center for History, South Bend, Indiana, Vincent Bendix Reading Room, Box 1, 162–8, November 19, 1855.

22 Colfax MSS, Lilly, letters to Wheeler, 1855–1862.

23 Colfax to Wheeler, Library of Congress, MMC-0199, June 26, 1856.

24 Colfax MSS, Lilly, letters to Wheeler, 1855–1862.

25 Colfax MSS, ISL.

26 Ibid.

27 Colfax Papers, Indiana Historical Society, Indianapolis, IN, M55, Folder Three.

28 Lincoln to Colfax, May 17, 1859, in Ronald C. White, *A. Lincoln: A Biography* (New York: Random House, 2009), 298, 299.

29 Colfax MSS, Lilly, letters to Wheeler, 1855–1862.

30 Ibid.

31 Colfax MSS, IHS, Folder Four.

32 Ibid.

33 Colfax MSS, Lilly, letters to Wheeler, 1861–1864.

34 Ibid.

35 Ibid.

36 Cincinnati *Enquirer*, January 23, 1862.

37 New York *Tribune*, January 20, 1862.

38 New York *Herald*, January 20, 1862.

39 Colfax MSS, ISL, Folder Four.

40 Ibid.

41 Colfax, MSS, IHS, Folder Four.

42 Ibid.

43 Indianapolis (IN) *State Journal*, October 9, 1869.

44 Colfax MSS, IHS, Folder Four.

2

Journalism and Politics: New York and the 1860 Election

"The past is dead. Let the dead past bury it, and let its mourners, if they will, go about the streets." Horace Greeley, from a speech cited in Thurlow Weed, *Life of Thurlow Weed*, Vol. 2, 271.

Traditional accounts of Abraham Lincoln's presidential bid have detailed his rise from life in a humble log cabin to his famous campaign as "The Rail Splitter," a title he earned at the 1860 Republican Convention in Chicago. Less-mythic events—those based in intense and sometimes petty political rivalries—also contributed to his nomination. Before the convention, Lincoln had developed a network of press support in the West. Historians have documented some of these relationships. Jay Monaghan's *The Man who Elected Lincoln* (1956), for instance, explores Lincoln's crucial cultivation of *Chicago Tribune* editors Dr. Charles Henry Ray and Joseph Medill.[1] Interestingly, however, these accounts have largely neglected Lincoln's antebellum relationship with Horace Greeley, editor of *The New York Tribune*, who helped turn the vote of delegates at the convention in a way that not even Lincoln had expected.

The growing political rifts between North and South have been the subject of extensive study, but the press-related issues that contributed to Lincoln's nomination stemmed from rifts on a number of levels. The first, most striking split emerged from the polarized interpretations of the Constitution published in the leading newspapers of the North and South—with editors of the former tending to paint the Union as perpetual and those of the latter seeing it as a compact that ensured the rights of individuals and states to dissent and, if necessary, secede.

Perhaps the most significant tensions that directly affected Lincoln were those associated with the competing interests of Republicans in the North, between the older Eastern establishment and the newer group of politicians and editors in the Midwest.

Leading Republicans in New York included powerbroker Thurlow Weed and his associate William H. Seward, the latter a senator and former governor, whom Weed felt should be the Republican candidate in 1860. Weed presumed that Horace Greeley, who had worked with Weed and Seward on various campaigns, lending editorial support of his *Tribune*, would support Seward, if for no other reason, because he was a New Yorker. Along with Henry Raymond, whose *New York Times* had grown to usurp Greeley's *Tribune* as the doctrinaire standard for Republican interests in the East, New York's Republicans envisioned a different political strategy for the party than did their counterparts in the West. Eastern Republicans saw Chicago as a satellite for industrial interests, and they assumed the role of dictating how to delegate responsibility for initiatives in the West, including the development of infrastructure projects and homestead legislation. The West, under the leadership of the equally staunch Republican *Chicago Tribune*, saw the national debate over the fate of territories as rightfully addressed by their own representatives, constituents, and readers. Combined with internal, interpersonal struggles among the once-formidable firm of Seward, Weed, and Greeley, the Chicago Convention resulted in Lincoln's nomination. The nexus of power, in both politics and the press, no longer rested solely in Manhattan.

An analysis of events before, during, and after May 1860 from the perspectives of Greeley's *Tribune* and Raymond's *Times* provides an account of press influence on Lincoln's nomination. Although scholars have already noted Lincoln's shrewd political instincts and ability to manage Illinois newspapers, extenuating circumstances made his victory possible. Exploration of the correspondences of Weed, Seward, Greeley, and Raymond in the East, and those from Lincoln, Medill, and Lincoln's supporters in the West, reveals how splits within the Republican Party strengthened Lincoln's bid for the presidency. At the same time, while the rift between Republicans in the East cast doubt upon the anticipated selection of Seward, the split between Republicans in the East and the West was not large enough to jeopardize Lincoln's success in the fall.

The Road to Chicago

The roots of Lincoln's career grew from the complex partisan formations of the antebellum era. After the 1833 creation of the Whig Party, Thurlow Weed, a powerful New York lobbyist and editor of The Albany *Evening-Journal*, discovered Greeley and hired him in 1837 to edit the *Jeffersonian*, a campaign paper that promoted William H. Seward for Governor. Greeley produced the newspaper in Weed's Albany office and subsequently cited the affiliation, which continued to engineer campaigns throughout the 1840s, as "the firm of Seward, Weed, and Greeley."[2] The resounding success of Greeley's follow-up newspaper, The *Log Cabin*, which he published in 1840 to promote the campaign of William Henry Harrison, the first Whig president, made Greeley nationally famous. His most enduring contribution to journalism, though, came shortly after his involvement with the 1840 election.[3]

Although Harrison died shortly after assuming office, Greeley launched *The New York Tribune* in 1841 to continue promoting the Whig Party. He edited the *Tribune* for the next thirty years, covering the stories of the day but, more importantly, blending information with interpretation and a sincere, passionate belief in the general benevolence of humanity. First attracting 500 subscribers, by the end of the *Tribune's* second month circulation had reached 11,000. By the end of the decade, it nearly outsold *The New York Herald* as a leading penny press newspaper, averaging nearly 200,000 copies per week.[4] The content was alert, cheerful, and aggressive, and attacks on the newspaper from rivals only increased its sales, with readers drawn to its extensive coverage of issues that directly interested them, including farming reports and market prices, as well as political campaigns and the endeavors of great literary and intellectual figures. Greeley's readers spanned the Northeastern elite to Midwestern farmers who read the *Tribune* from one account "next to the Bible."[5]

Greeley's chief rival was James Gordon Bennett, Sr., a maverick publisher who had launched the *Herald* in 1835. The Scottish immigrant had perfected a business model for the emerging penny press industry with large circulation rates and cheap advertising, popularizing the newspaper by publishing stories of crime and scandal. Bennett generally supported Democratic policy, but was also shrewd enough to put his economic interests above partisan loyalty. Although generally pro-Democrat throughout the 1840s, Bennett supported Republican candidate John C. Frémont in 1856, Simon Cameron for the Republican nomination in 1860, Democrat John Breckinridge in the general election in 1860, Ulysses S. Grant for the Republican nomination in 1864, and Lincoln for reelection that year. Throughout the Civil War, Bennett maintained his edge over rivals by featuring premier reporting, correspondence, and commentary—at times promoting the Union cause with more vigor than the staunchest Republican newspapers of New York.

In an age dominated by sensationalism and the rivalry epitomized by Bennett and Greeley, Henry Raymond, a former *Tribune* contributor, founded the *Times*. Raymond had left the *Tribune* in 1841 for, he said, economic reasons, but in the following decade, in the editorial content he had penned as managing editor of the *Courier and Enquirer*, it became clear that Raymond found Greeley's eccentricities incompatible with his own no-nonsense style. Shunning the scandalous content of the *Herald* and the "isms" of the *Tribune*, Raymond's *Times* became a favorite news source for the business class—gaining the support of Thurlow Weed and William H. Seward, Greeley's associates, and eventually of President Lincoln.

Although Lincoln, upon assuming the presidency, more closely followed the advice of Raymond than that of Greeley, he had begun reading the *Tribune* regularly early in his political career, which had launched at about the same time that Greeley began publishing. Lincoln began using the press as a political tool as early as 1836, when he published a letter in the Sangamon *Journal*, calling on voters to support his bid for reelection to the Illinois state legislature. He was a twenty-seven-year-old candidate who lived in the village of New Salem. "I go for all sharing the privileges of the government who assist in bearing its burdens," he wrote, making known that he favored suffrage rights for all who paid their taxes, "by no means excluding females," a common trait among members of the emergent Whig Party.[6] In the fall election, the voters of Sangamon County sent seven men to the legislature, with Lincoln at the head of the delegation.

Lincoln enjoyed a role of importance as Whig floor leader, and the Sangamon *Journal* began publishing his speeches, the first appearing in January 1837. To his contemporaries, Lincoln served as a model up-and-coming political star among those in the Age of Jackson who offered resistance to the sometimes-dark underside of the populism of the era. In 1846, Lincoln became a member of the U.S. House and gained national exposure for his opposition to the Mexican War. As Lincoln's term neared its end, that unpopular position cost him the support necessary for reelection—his opponents dubbed him "Spotty Lincoln," and as veterans from the war returned to Lincoln's home district in large numbers, they elected the Democratic candidate. Whigs held Lincoln responsible for loss of the seat, which they had for years almost taken for granted. Lincoln used loss of the House seat to pursue his legal career and, in time, would reemerge as a candidate for the Senate as a member of the Republican Party, which later launched him to the presidency.

Meanwhile, Whigs in the East increasingly recognized Chicago as a vital new hub, essential for the kinds of transportation and infrastructural developments prescribed by Henry Clay's nationalist vision, the American System. Western Whigs (and later Republicans, with Lincoln foremost among them) benefitted directly from the strategy and Clay's idea of a vast, interconnected web of markets and business activity. However, while Eastern Whigs often had the luxury of vacillating in their support of Western candidates (with Greeley and Raymond, for example, suggesting the victory of Stephen A. Douglas over Lincoln in the 1858 Senate campaign would benefit the Republicans in the long term), *The Chicago Tribune*, first published in 1847, consistently supported Lincoln in his endeavors.

Raymond, since his debut as Greeley's assistant, had risen in the ranks of New York's Whigs throughout the 1840s as the managing editor of the *Courier and Enquirer*, calling for conditions that promoted free-market capitalism. Having become weary of the sometimes-petty antagonisms between rival editors and the sometimes equally petty content of the penny press, in 1851, he founded *The New York Times* and devoted the newspaper, he wrote, to reporting fact-driven news and delivering commentary "without passion."[7] This style at the time must have struck readers as novel, but it later contributed to the newspaper's fame. Throughout the 1850s, as Greeley and Raymond competed for the lead role of spokespersons for New York's business and labor interests, Raymond eventually gained favor in the eyes of Weed and Seward as a steady voice for Whig (and later Republican) policies.[8]

After Winfield Scott's catastrophic defeat in 1852, the Whig Party collapsed. Members of the old Whig Party came together again in the following years over the admittance of new states in the West, namely Kansas and Nebraska, under a new banner and new party organization, the Republicans. Seward had since become an outspoken Senator, and Weed, as his financial backer, naturally expected Greeley to support a presidential bid for Seward in either 1856 or 1860. However, Weed had not realized how deeply resentful Greeley had become over years of neglect at the hands of his partners, who, Greeley said, had failed to support him in his own political aspirations.[9] In a final moment of frustration, after Greeley had asked Weed to nominate him for New York governor in 1854 and Weed had declined, Greeley had responded by writing a bitter resignation letter addressed to Seward that dissolved his connection to the firm.

These tensions among New York's editors and politicians resembled national antagonisms. In 1854, Congress attempted to resolve a growing crisis over the admission of new states by passing the Kansas-Nebraska Act, which included a provision that abrogated the Missouri Compromise. Popular outrage at the repeal found expression at meetings, at conventions, and in newspapers, leading, in sections of the North, to a new organization dedicated to opposing the expansion of slavery. When Asahel N. Cole, editor of The Genesee Valley *Free Press* in Allegany County, New York, called a convention for those opposed to the legislation, he contacted Greeley about naming the group. Greeley suggested "Republican," and in May 1854, the *Free Press* became the first newspaper to display the name of the party in its masthead.[10] When Joseph Medill, who had become editor of *The Chicago Tribune*, called upon a collation in the Midwest to help nationalize the new party, Greeley encouraged him, writing, "Go ahead, my friend, with your proposed Republican Party, and may God bless you. I hope you will have the best of luck."[11] In 1856, Republicans nominated John C. Frémont as their candidate for president, with a platform of ideas that had been associated with free labor, free soil, and protectionism.

Events in Kansas, which had contributed to the formation of the party, by 1856, had descended into armed confrontation. Indeed, reporters there might have argued the first shots of the Civil War did not take place at Fort Sumter, but rather, with the violence in what was dubbed "Bleeding Kansas." Coverage of the fighting there came from reporters such as James Redpath, a correspondent for Greeley's *Tribune*, who reported on militant abolitionist John Brown.[12] In Kansas, Brown had instigated the Pottawatomie Massacre of proslavery settlers. This made him instantly notorious, but more generally bespoke the growing intensity with which abolitionists were willing to fight. Although Redpath, also an abolitionist, tempered his accounts of the slaughter, the debate over Popular Sovereignty had reached a bloody conclusion for a national audience.

Fighting over what kind of constitution Kansans would adopt, free or slave, played a role in debates around the country—and nowhere more notably than in the Illinois contest for Senate between Lincoln and Stephen Douglas in 1858. The controversy over the fates of lands in the West, more generally, also deepened a rift between Republicans in the East and West. Republicans in the East, including Weed, Seward, Greeley, and Raymond, were thrilled when Douglas, a Democrat, had sided with the Republicans in opposing President James Buchanan over the Lecompton Constitution for Kansas, which essentially guaranteed the rights of slaveholders. When Douglas, who had championed Popular Sovereignty, maintained the people of Kansas had not received the opportunity to vote in a legitimate election, the East saw reason to support him for another term, believing tensions in Kansas could be pinned on Democrats and, in turn, strengthen the chances for a Republican president from the East.

Republicans fully expected *The New York Tribune* to support their candidates; when Greeley was at first silent about Lincoln's Senate bid, publishing nothing on his behalf, Illinois Republicans were shocked. When Greeley praised Douglas, writing in the *Tribune*, "His course has not been merely right, it has been conspicuously, courageously, eminently so," Lincoln's supporters were outraged. Adding to their injuries, Greeley counseled Republicans in the East that they should support Douglas's reelection or face defeat themselves.[13]

When Douglas defeated Lincoln, Republicans in Illinois naturally blamed Greeley. "Damn Greeley, etc.," exclaimed a voter from Paris, Illinois, "they have done Lincoln more harm than all others."[14] Others in the West derided Seward and Weed as "Pharisaical old Whigs," as they had promised to support Lincoln financially and politically but then changed tactics, realizing Lincoln's loss could lead to a Seward presidency.[15]

Lincoln, for his part, did what he could to avoid taking *The New York Tribune*'s support for Douglas personally. "I do not charge that G. [Greeley] was corrupt in this. I do not think he was, or is," he wrote. "It was his judgment that the course he took was the best way of serving the Republican cause."[16] However, he privately confided in Illinois Senator Lyman Trumbull that Greeley had disgusted him by allowing the sacrifice of a fellow Republican. "What does *The New York Tribune* mean by its constant eulogizing and admiring and magnifying Douglas?" Lincoln asked. "[W]e would like to know it soon; it will save us a great deal of labor to surrender at once."[17] On another occasion, Lincoln complained to his law partner William Herndon simply, "Greeley is not treating me right."[18]

Chicago mayor and Lincoln supporter John Wentworth vowed revenge. "Our business is war, war, war on them!" he wrote in a letter to Lincoln. "They cannot war on us, for we have said nothing, have done nothing, have no candidates." Wentworth feared Seward, Weed, and "others of that school" had sold Lincoln's chances because they wanted "as little said about slavery as possible." He advised Lincoln to prepare instead for the Republicans' next major contest, the 1860 presidential race.[19] Indeed, Lincoln did not give up his political aspirations, and instead gave speeches to audiences outside of Illinois while his supporters initiated designs for his nomination. The convention, scheduled to meet in Chicago, was perfectly suited for Lincoln's advantage; however, outside of the Midwest, voters knew little about him.

Events in late 1859 changed his status, opening the opportunity to speak to a national audience, as John Brown re-emerged as a national figure with another sensational attack on the institution of slavery. Brown sought to start a slave insurrection with the takeover of the federal arsenal at Harpers Ferry, Virginia. The failed attempt resulted in his capture, trial, and execution.[20] By the time of his death, correspondents, editors, and readers nationally began reinterpreting the problems of regional differences, states' rights, and property (that is, slaves) with a newfound sense of urgency—even panic.[21] The day after Brown's execution, Greeley's newspaper featured full coverage of the event with news and editorials, suggesting the epitaphs of Brown and his raiders would "remain unwritten until the not distant day when no slave shall clank his chains in the shades of Monticello, or by the graves of Mount Vernon."[22] In the North, Brown achieved the status of a martyr, with Reverend Theodore Parker describing him as "a saint."[23] Such sentiments enraged the South, with the Alabama Montgomery *Mail*, among other newspapers, calling for the execution of Greeley (who had published Parker's letter) as a traitor, demanding his exile to "some uninhabited island" where beasts could prey on him as the least of possible sentences.[24]

Lincoln took the opportunity to speak about Brown's raid and the ensuing firestorm in a speech at New York's Cooper Union in February 1860 that would come to be considered among his most important addresses. He clarified the views he had expressed about slavery in the 1858 debates and affirmed that he did not wish to see it expand into Western territories. Lincoln held that the founders would agree with this position. He then addressed accusations that Republicans were a "sectional" party that only represented the interests of the North and incited slave rebellions, dismissing allegations that the Republicans had backed Brown. "John Brown was no Republican," Lincoln said, "and you have failed to implicate a single Republican in his Harpers Ferry enterprise." The final portion of the speech called on Republicans to put reason above emotion in their actions, and ended with the call for his audience to "have faith that right makes might, and in that faith, let us, to the end, dare to do our duty as we understand it." Politically, the event raised Lincoln's stature among his audience in the East, with even Henry Raymond running the speech in its entirety on the front page of the *Times* the next day.[25]

Splitting Rails

Horace Greeley and Abraham Lincoln had served as Whigs together in the Thirtieth Congress. Greeley's term, as a representative for the Sixth District of New York, was short, only three months, but he used it to advocate homestead legislation and expose Congressional misspending. Since their terms in the House, many Republicans saw Lincoln as espousing their policies more consistently than the *Tribune* had done, as Greeley often vacillated on economic policy and his interpretation of the Constitution. Meanwhile, Lincoln's ascent from obscurity to challenge the Democratic machinery had appealed to voters otherwise disenfranchised. The mythic connotations of rugged individualism and the Western frontier spirit, which Greeley had first promoted in his *Log Cabin* newspaper, were reborn, and in time made a central part of Lincoln's life story. Greeley's promotion of Lincoln's story before, during, and after his presidential campaign included accounts in the *Tribune* of how the successful Illinois lawyer was first reared in poverty to "the very humblest White stratum of society" and earned his own livelihood by "the rudest and least recompensed labor." Lincoln—a true frontiersman, the *Tribune* noted—had cleared primeval forests, split rails, operated a flatboat, and had supported his widowed mother and his younger siblings with a self-education accomplished "by the evening firelight of rude log cabins."[26]

Before the 1860 convention, Republicans nationally were divided, with Eastern Republicans promoting Seward's experience and those in the West celebrating Lincoln's honesty and self-reliance. Thurlow Weed, still a venerable force in national politics, had hatched a scheme in the winter of 1859–60 to furnish, through the New York legislature, charters for city railroads, whose grantees were in turn to supply several hundred thousand dollars for the Republicans, through which Seward would directly benefit in his presidential campaign. Although Greeley had, beginning in 1854, become increasingly independent of Weed and Seward, Weed, at least, proceeded with the assumption that *The New York Tribune* would endorse a Seward presidency. However, the loyalties of *The Chicago Tribune*, also aligned with the Republican Party, were unquestioned: Medill and Ray supported Lincoln unconditionally, describing him, not Seward, as the nation's "model statesman." Lincoln used "no tricks of oratory, nothing for mere stage effect, but inspired by the grandeur of his theme." The Chicago newspaper suggested, "the Republican Party, and, indeed, the whole American people, have reason to be proud of Abraham Lincoln."[27]

Despite their preference, Lincoln's supporters recognized that the choice of the leadership of the party rested entirely on either Seward or Lincoln, and that a choice of anyone else at the upcoming convention would be "fatal."[28] The Democrats called their convention first, and on April 23, 1860, nominated Lincoln's old rival Stephen A. Douglas; however, the results from the Convention were inconclusive, as a group of delegates who had demanded the adoption of a pro-slavery platform marched from the convention hall in protest of the Douglas nomination. Fearing a Douglas ticket would compromise the interests of the South, they called for another convention, causing the Democratic Party to be "deliberately split," Weed later wrote in his *Memoirs*, with "one section subsequently nominating Mr. Douglas, of Illinois, and the other Mr. Breckenridge, of Kentucky."[29]

Weeks later, the Republicans opened their convention with most of the furor on the opening day, May 16, surrounding the presence of Horace Greeley, who had managed to secure for himself the role of delegate from Oregon. Rumors swirled that there had been a break in the New York delegation, which, it was supposed, would put Seward's nomination over the top quickly. Instead, fliers distributed throughout the streets of Chicago stoked the divisions: "Greeley at the Tremont: Weed at the Richmond House." The streets and hotels nevertheless were crowded with enthusiastic friends of Seward, and even his opponents did not appear to believe that he could be defeated.[30]

Lincoln's supporters had organized quietly at first, but in the week before the election, they had resolved to make their candidate not only the next nominee, but also the president. On May 10, 1860, the Illinois Republicans had met in Decatur to consolidate their support and develop a strategy for the upcoming national convention. In one of the most famous campaign stunts in American political history, Richard J. Oglesby, a vigorous young politician from Decatur, had consulted with John Hanks, an elderly first cousin of Lincoln's mother, and located two rails from a fence that Lincoln allegedly had erected in 1830. On the first day of the meeting, Oglesby organized a display of the rails adorned with labels advertising them as split by Lincoln himself. "Honest Abe" could not pass up the opportunity for self-promotion. "It is true I helped build a house for my father," he said. "Whether these are some of the identical rails I cannot say. Quite likely they are."[31]

Lincoln went to Chicago with a new image: not a country bumpkin or small-town lawyer, but, rather, a strong and honest frontiersman. At the end of the first day, his chances still appeared slim, with the first round of voting indicating Seward had indeed taken a lead with delegates. But Seward had not secured the margin necessary for the nomination; the count was Seward 173.5, Lincoln 102, and Simon Cameron of Pennsylvania 50.5. William Butler, among Lincoln's friends to aid during the convention, provided updates indicating that rifts among Eastern Republicans were beginning to show. "No material change in sentiment of public opinion amongst delegates since yesterday," he wrote. "The strife between delegates from New York and Pennsylvania still rage high. Pennsylvania will never go for Seward."[32]

Greeley, meanwhile, lobbied on the convention floor against Seward. He focused on delegates from Pennsylvania and told them the interests of the Eastern establishment would corrupt Seward. When Cameron, a Pennsylvania senator, dropped out after the second ballot and cast his support to Lincoln, the difference narrowed to Seward 184.5 and Lincoln 181. "Your friends are doing all that can be done for you," Butler wrote Lincoln in a follow-up note, which also included the encouraging information that Chicago Mayor John Wentworth had lent his efforts to gaining hometown support.[33] In light of Lincoln's gains in the second round of voting, the role of players at the Chicago convention—from Ogelsby, Butler, and Wentworth to Seward, Weed, and Greeley—has subsequently been the subject of debate and even some controversy. Although historians have focused primarily on the contributions of Lincoln's supporters in Illinois, Greeley played an undoubtable role.

Weed's account of a seemingly innocuous encounter between Greeley and an old friend of Weed's, Julius Wood of Columbus, Ohio, in hindsight contained an exchange of critical importance to the outcome of the final vote. "We shan't nominate Seward," Greeley had said to Wood months before the convention—"we'll take some more conservative man, like Pitt Fessenden or Bates." According to Weed, Wood told Seward "Greeley is cheating you. He will go to Chicago and work against you." Seward responded: "My dear Wood ... your zeal sometimes gets a little the better of your judgment."[34]

The next two votes on the floor of the Chicago convention proved pivotal. With the exposure of Weed's plans for lucrative New York railroad contracts, the delegates of Indiana also turned to Lincoln, whose numbers had risen to 231.5 votes to Seward's 180. And in the final vote, according to Greeley, with Lincoln pulling in the lead, "others were rapidly transferred to him, until he had 354 out of 466 in all, and his nomination was declared."[35]

When Weed learned of Seward's defeat, he reportedly broke down in tears, claiming he had been unaware that Greeley had held deep-seated resentments over his secondary role in New York politics. Weed could see no mistake in his management of Seward's campaign, and he called on Henry Raymond of *The New York Times*, his most reliable supporter in the New York press, to blame Greeley for the misfortune.

Raymond began running accounts in the *Times* of the events in Chicago that cast Greeley in an unflattering light. Announcing what had taken place in 1854, he declared that Greeley was "deliberately wreaking the long-hoarded revenge of a disappointed office-seeker."[36] There was truth to the allegation, as Greeley's letter had complained bitterly that Seward and Weed had tried to "humiliate" him by nominating Henry Raymond for the role of lieutenant governor. "No other name could have been put upon the ticket so bitterly humbling to me," Greeley had written, "as that which was selected."[37]

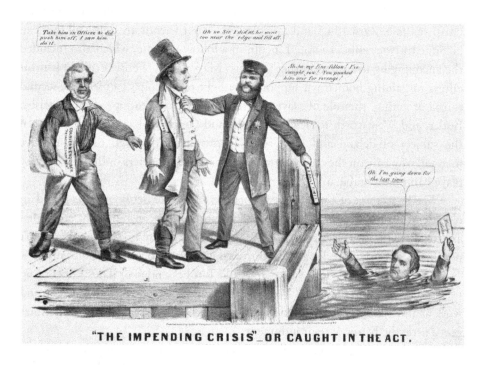

"THE IMPENDING CRISIS"_OR CAUGHT IN THE ACT.

Image 2.1 "'The Impending Crisis'—or Caught in the Act." New York: Currier & Ives, 1860. This print derives its title from the 1857 Hinton Rowan Helper pamphlet "The Impending Crisis," an influential antislavery document. The crisis depicted here centers on New York Senator William H. Seward, whose loss of the Republican presidential nomination to Abraham Lincoln was widely attributed to the machinations of New York *Tribune* editor Horace Greeley. Seward flounders in the water at the end of a pier, crying, "Oh I'm going down for the last time." Henry J. Raymond, an ardent Republican and publisher of *The New York Times*, grabs Greeley by the collar and says to him, "Ah, ha my fine fellow! I've caught you! You pushed him over for revenge." Greeley pleads, "Oh no Sir, I didn't. He went too near the edge and fell off." *Courier & Enquirer* editor James Watson Webb (left) exclaims, "Take him in Officer. He did push him off. I saw him do it." Webb carries a copy of his own newspaper, inscribed with the motto "Principles not men," which may allude to Webb's recent abandonment of the Whig party for the Republicans.[38]

Seward's supporters, who expected to campaign for him through Election Day in November, had already printed thousands of pamphlets and circulars that were ready for distribution as soon as word of the nomination had arrived. Reflecting on Seward's loss, one description of the outcome cast the materials as lying hopelessly idle and in piles "rendered a dead and cumbrous mass of useless material, unfit for any but one purpose."[39] Seward, for his part, met the news about his defeat as well as expected, agreeing to the request of the Republicans to issue a statement of support for Lincoln. However, in efforts to make the Republicans still appear divided, at least a few Democratic newspapers in the North either ignored the speech or downplayed it, making it necessary for Seward to write to Lincoln directly. Seward included a copy of the speech from *The New York Times* as evidence that he had done what was expected. He assured Lincoln that his supporters in New York would support the Illinoisan in November.[40]

Meanwhile, Greeley, who faced accusations of engaging in petty personal politics, gave a speech just a few days after the convention, saying, "The past is dead. Let the dead past bury it, and let its mourners, if they will, go about the streets." Weed responded bitterly: "The 'mourners,' to whom Mr. Greeley alludes ... constitute the rank and file, as well as the intelligence and patriotism of nearly every Republican state in the Union."[41] The *Times*, in response, claimed Seward would have undoubtedly won the nomination had Greeley not exploited the apprehensions of Pennsylvania delegates in particular.

Greeley faced criticism from the *Tribune*'s rivals, as well as from editors ordinarily in line with the Republican's calls for reform. For example, an illustration in *Vanity Fair*, June 2, 1860, titled "Et Tu, Greeley?" compared the turn of events in Chicago to Julius Caesar's assassination in the Roman Senate. The artist depicted Seward as Caesar, dying on the floor, after Greeley (Brutus) stabbed him, with Raymond depicted as Mark Antony and Francis Blair Sr., editor of the *Congressional Record*, as Casca. Lincoln was portrayed as a small Black man, as "Black Republican" was a derogatory term used to associate the party with abolitionism.[42]

War's Eve

With Seward faithfully throwing his support to Lincoln—and despite exposure of the rift with Greeley—Republicans agreed to work together toward to capture the White House in November. In contradistinction, the split among Democrats threatened to undermine the legitimacy of the election. While Lincoln held a popular advantage over rival candidate—including Stephen Douglas, the Northern Democrat; John Breckenridge, the Southern Democrat; and John Bell, the Constitutional Unionist—it was not clear he would receive the constitutionally required electoral vote. Secessionists entertained the possibility the House might have to decide the election, which would give them grounds to question the integrity of the results, and ultimately the Union itself. Positing that an unpopular Republican presidency could result in disaster, Greeley, who by now fully and clearly supported Lincoln for both personal and political reasons, entreated conservatives "by nature or fortune, not by trade," to realize an election decided by the House could upset the balance of power permanently. He called on those who had misgivings about a Republican presidency to vote for Lincoln, realizing that failure to support him would result in a "chronic weakness" in an administration that would have no hold on the country's confidence—"baffled at every step," he said, "and paralyzed by a mortifying consciousness of impotence."[43]

Greeley, in turn, published a report from the Republican Central Campaign Club that held out more optimism. It indicated that Lincoln enjoyed resounding support in the West, and that his popularity would allow him to "sweep the seven or eight Western States like a tornado" and "run like chain lightning from the Allegheny to the Missouri." Moreover, the Democrats had expected Seward's nomination, and the results in Chicago had "disarranged their nicely-adjusted progamme."[44] Greeley had longed for a return to news subjects less intense than secession, slavery, and treason, but Lincoln's ascent to the presidency occurred during conflict and political failures, with Congress having developed no lasting solution for disputes over land in the West, and with President Buchanan failing to stop the violence in Kansas.

New York Tribune readers—indeed, audiences everywhere—understood the election of 1860 as a historic event, and Greeley capitalized on the most controversial issues of the campaign. *Tribune* sales representatives told potential customers that their subscriptions were important, as increased circulation of the newspaper would do much toward "a correct decision" in the presidential election. Readers were encouraged to induce "honest and moderate" working-class Democrats to read the *Tribune* for one year. Wealthy Republicans were an especially attractive demographic: "the cheapest and surest way to influence voters."[45]

The total circulation of the *Tribune's* editions reached almost 300,000, and the newspaper's increased sales brought responsibilities Greeley had not anticipated. With his staff working at maximum levels, the number of advertisements in each issue peaked, and by Election Day, the *Tribune* announced that increased operations made it necessary for clients to submit ads on an early deadline.

Distribution of the *Daily Tribune* reached an unprecedented 72,500 copies daily, with the demand "for correct and trustworthy election returns," Greeley wrote, carrying the sale of his paper to this number.[46] Greeley's personal schedule was booked, too. "Friends who receive no answer to their invitations to speak will understand that I am unable to do more than fulfill existing engagements," he wrote. "My time is absorbed."[47]

In Southern states, supporting a Republican candidate was virtually impossible. The *Tribune* noted the difficulty, and in a response to a reader's question advised Southerners to "not vote at all" if they could not do so with a ballot that included Republican candidates. "But (in many, if not most cases) you can vote for Lincoln—you will if you have but manly courage," he wrote. "If you know any voters of like faith with yourselves, agree beforehand with them on the hour at which you will together go quietly to the polls and offer your votes for Lincoln Electors: if they are refused, or if they are accepted and then destroyed or not returned, your duty is performed."[48] A particularly provocative *Tribune* editorial suggested the Democrats were "playing 'possum" by throwing the election. "Slavery Extension" had been driven "by dire necessity," to playing dead. "It has no other remaining resource," Greeley wrote, "and die it must—unless it can avoid that catastrophe by merely seeming to be dead." He accused journals in the North of supporting the ruse by publishing pro-slavery propaganda, which claimed the Republicans were fighting "a chimera—or, rather, pretending to fight one, in pursuit of sinister ends."[49]

On Election Day, Republican organization was credited for strong returns in New York City in particular. Members of the Wide Awake Club, a militia-like group of Lincoln supporters, made appearances at the polls, ostensibly to minimize fraud. The final returns reflected a fragmented electorate, but "Honest Abe the Rail Splitter," the sixteenth president of the United States, carried an electoral majority, even though he won only 40 percent of the vote. Totals in Illinois and New York reflected the national electoral split. Lincoln won the northern part of his home state and lost to Douglas in the south. He won much of New York, but lost New York City, in part because of Bennett's warning that Republicans would cause laborers to compete with millions of emancipated, former slaves and that Blacks would, in the words of Benjamin Wood of *The New York Daily News*, find New York City in swarms "thicker than blackberries."[50]

Although New York City had voted against Lincoln, in a show of appreciation for Greeley's efforts to promote his campaign, Republicans asked him to speak at New York's Stuyvesant Institute in a rally the night after their 1860 victory. A crowd greeted the *Tribune* editor with applause. Greeley and thousands of revelers were satisfied that the administration would bring, in his words, a renewed appreciation for "all great, just, and true expositions of the law of righteousness and freedom." Greeley expressed pride that the election proved Republican Party was "not a man-worshiping party." He could afford to make the statement, because at the time of his speech, he enjoyed greater popularity in New York than did Lincoln.[51]

"Let Them Go!"

Throughout December, leading Republican politicians and editors in the East and West competed with each other for positions of power. Lincoln, who had initially believed the chatter of secessionists was idle, found himself more closely allied with Henry Raymond's *New York Times* than with any of the other leading newspapers in the East. Raymond, one of the penny press' most conservative members, had written Lincoln one week after the election and called on him to take precautionary measures in his ascent to the presidency. The president should tell Southerners they misunderstood the Republicans, Raymond wrote, and that the new administration would correct the error by assuaging their fears. Yet, the first Republican presidency had indeed spread alarm through Southern states and second-guessing in the North—a condition of the national spirit that was, even Lincoln recognized, "not what either party, or any man devised, or expected."[52]

Lincoln, at the time perhaps erroneously, rebuffed the appeal for appeasement and blamed tensions on a misunderstanding in the South of the Yankee character. Only by the "actual experience" of a Republican administration could the South remove their fears, Lincoln replied to Raymond. "My views upon every prominent political issue are before the country [and] accessible to everyone who desires to know them."

> I have too much faith in the good sense [and] patriotism of the people of the South to apprehend any violent disruption on their part from the mere fear of future aggressions—while I have too much faith in their honor to expect them to submit to such aggression when actually committed. I think with you that they will take counsel of their judgments, instead of their fears.[53]

Lincoln's response evinced a pragmatic approach to politics, built on a trust in fellow Americans, an approach that Raymond understood and echoed in the pages of his newspaper.

In New York, meanwhile, leading Democratic newspapers that had helped sway the vote in urban areas against Lincoln coalesced in recognizing him as the president of the Union. James Gordon Bennett, editor of *The New York Herald*, offered Lincoln his unlikely approval, suggesting that Lincoln reward Greeley for his role in securing the new administration's rise to power. In an interview with *The Chicago Tribune*'s Joseph Medill, Bennett called Lincoln "a man of good and honest intentions" but added that he feared the president would fall victim to the influence of Seward, who would denounce Lincoln for trusting Southern loyalties to the Union. Bennett had little doubt that Lincoln would undertake his duties faithfully, Medill wrote, but Republicans in the West would need to keep watch on Weed, who would have "black mailed any job and contract" and made at least a million dollars with Seward's election.[54] Greeley should expect at least a foreign mission or a cabinet position, Bennett said—and, indeed, Greeley had apparently assumed that his role in the Chicago convention would earn him a role in government.

As Bennett anticipated, letters from Greeley's associates arrived in Lincoln's mail recommending Greeley for office. John W. Forney, a Pennsylvania editor, encouraged Lincoln to find an appointment for Greeley primarily because a wide audience, from the Northeast to the Midwest, read and admired the *Tribune*. Greeley's influence on the masses, Forney wrote, made him an ideal candidate for federal office, as Greeley was "the first journalist in America"—a populist "entitled to the thanks of his party" for his vigor, courage, and integrity.[55] However, Lincoln, who had grown accustomed to the publisher's eccentricities and sometimes-erratic behavior, passed on the opportunity to appoint Greeley to any position. In what Greeley must have taken as another devastating insult, Lincoln instead appointed Seward secretary of state and left the *Tribune* editor to tend to his newspaper.

In response, for the next four years Greeley did his best to remain a loyal Republican, but at the same time hounded Lincoln, apparently out of personal bitterness, by attacking the president's war policy in the *Tribune*. More immediately, Greeley's remedy was to seek the Senate in a campaign supported primarily by the *Tribune*. In 1861, he styled himself as the Republican candidate and almost won the Senate bid, but Weed, in an ironic twist of revenge, managed to secure instead the selection of Ira Harris, a rival Republican.

Lincoln's most loyal supporters in the Illinois press, meanwhile, increasingly saw Greeley's *New York Tribune* as a bastion of duplicity. *The Chicago Tribune*, beginning with Greeley's misbegotten 1861 bid for the Senate and until his final campaign as a presidential candidate in 1872, criticized him as a naked opportunist with only his own interests in mind. Although "Uncle Horace," as he was affectionately known among Midwestern audiences, maintained a loyal following for the literary and informative content of his newspaper, his colleagues regarded him as unreliable and even detrimental to the conservative ideals of union promoted by Lincoln.

By April 1861, the drums of war rumbled throughout the nation, and when it was clear that Lincoln could not stop the threats of secessionists to dissolve the Union without war, Bennett's *Herald* attacked the administration for plunging the nation into "an abyss of ruin." Bennett, reflecting the confusion that had engulfed editors across the nation, retreated from his earlier, even-handed treatment of Lincoln and used the *Herald* to call for the overthrow of the president and the Republican Party. When the war became a fixture of news, Bennett changed course again, establishing his newspaper as the leading source for coverage ensuing battles, and sending more correspondents into the field than did any other newspaper in the nation.

Opinions published in the *Tribune*, whether Greeley's or his editors, vacillated before and after the inauguration, giving readers the impression that the North did not take the threats of secessionists seriously, or at least that the president did not know how to address them. "If South Carolina shall be left to stand alone, we think she must ultimately recede," read one editorial.[56] "But if ever seven or eight States send agents to Washington to say 'We want to get out of the Union,'" read another, "we shall feel constrained by our devotion to Human Liberty to say, 'Let them go!'"[57] Readers in the South understood the statements as an indication that the new administration would violate their rights, and for the next four years, the war, it seemed, proved the judgments of Lincoln and editors in both the East and Midwest wrong. Secession was South Carolina's remedy. Other states followed. War ensued.

Notes

1 Jay Monaghan, *The Man Who Elected Lincoln* (Westport, CT: Greenwood Press, 1956), 334.

2 Frederic Bancroft, *The Life of William H. Seward*, Vol. 1 (Gloucester, Mass: Harper and Brothers, Peter Smith, 1900, 1967), 372; Gregory A. Borchard, *The Firm of Greeley, Weed, and Seward: New York Partisanship and the Press, 1840–1860*, Ph.D. Dissertation (Gainesville: University of Florida, 2003): 151-55; Hudson, *Journalism in the United States*, 529, 549; Henry Luther Stoddard, *Horace Greeley, Printer, Editor, Crusader* (New York: G. P. Putnam's Sons, 1946), 170, 171; Glyndon G.

Van Deusen, *Horace Greeley, Nineteenth-Century Crusader* (New York: Hill and Wang, 1953, 1964), 249-53; Van Deusen, *Thurlow Weed: Wizard of the Lobby* (Boston: Little, Brown and Company, 1947), 97, 201; Van Deusen, *William Henry Seward* (New York: Oxford University Press, 1967), 251; Robert C. Williams, *Horace Greeley: Champion of American Freedom* (New York and London: New York University Press, 2006), 175; Weed, *Life of Thurlow Weed*, Vol. 1, 554.

3 Borchard, *"The New York Tribune* and the 1844 Election: Horace Greeley, Gangs, and the Wise Men of Gotham," *Journalism History*, 33, 1 (Spring 2007): 51-9.

4 Parton, *Life of Horace Greeley*, 281; Hudson, *Journalism in the United States*, 529.

5 Bayard Taylor, *Life and Letters of Bayard Taylor*, Vol. 1 (Boston: Houghton, Mifflin and Company, 1884), 263.

6 Harper, *Lincoln and the Press*, 1.

7 "A Word about Ourselves," New York *Times*, September 18, 1851.

8 Greeley to Weed, August 17, 1847, *Thurlow Weed Papers* [microfilm], New York: University of Rochester; Weed to Hamilton Fish, January 16, 1850, *Weed Papers*.

9 Borchard, "From Pink Lemonade to Salt River: Horace Greeley's Utopia and the Death of the Whig Party," *Journalism History*, 32, 1 (Spring 2006): 22-33.

10 Weed, *Life of Thurlow Weed*, Vol. 2, 241.

11 DeAlva Stanwood Alexander, *A Political History of the State of New York* (New York: Henry Holt and Co., 1906), 205-21; George Henry Payne, *History of Journalism in the United States* (Westport, CT: Greenwood Press Publishers, 1920), 291.

12 John R. McKivigan, *Forgotten Firebrand: James Redpath and the Making of Nineteenth-Century America* (Ithaca and London: Cornell University Press, 2008), 43-60.

13 White, *A. Lincoln: A Biography*, 247.

14 David Herbert Donald, *Lincoln* (London: Jonathan Cape, 1995), 211, 242.

15 David Davis to Abraham Lincoln, November 7, 1858, *Abraham Lincoln Papers at the Library of Congress*, Galesburg, IL: Knox College, accessed July 1, 2021, at <memory.loc.gov/ammem/alhtml/malhome.html>; Norman B. Judd to Lincoln, October 20, 1859, *Lincoln Papers*, accessed July 1, 2021, at <loc.gov/item/mal0198200>.

16 Lincoln to William Kellogg, December 11, 1859, in Don E. Fehrenbacher, *Lincoln: Speeches and Writings, 1859–1865* (New York: Library of America, 1989), 102.

17 Lincoln to Lyman Trumbull, December 28, 1857, *Lincoln Papers*, accessed July 1, 2021, at <loc.gov/item/mal0537000>.

18 Rose Strunsky, *Lincoln* (New York: MacMillan, 1914), 101.

19 John Wentworth to Lincoln, April 19, 1858, *Lincoln Papers*, accessed July 1, 2021, at <loc.gov/item/mal0075200>.

20 "The Harper's Ferry Insurrection," "Further Developments of the 'Irrepressible Conflict,'" "The Legislature of Tennessee on the Harper's Ferry Affair," "The Harper's Ferry Insurrection," "Antecedents of Ossawatomie Brown," "How We

Feel!" *Valley Spirit*, November 9, 1859, *The Valley of the Shadow*, accessed July 1, 2021, at <valley.lib.virginia.edu>.

21 Borchard, "*The New York Tribune* at Harper's Ferry: Horace Greeley on Trial," *American Journalism*, 20, 1 (Winter 2003): 13-31.

22 "John Brown Dead," New York *Tribune*, December 3, 1859.

23 "Letter from Theodore Parker," New York *Tribune*, December 27, 1859.

24 "What is Asked of Republicans," The Montgomery *Mail*, Alabama, quoted in New York *Tribune*, December 31, 1860.

25 Donald and Harold Holzer, eds., *Lincoln in the* Times: *The Life of Abraham Lincoln as Originally Reported in the New York* Times (New York: St. Martin's Press, 2005), 18.

26 "Brady on Rail-Splitting," New York *Tribune*, October 23, 1860.

27 "Mr. Lincoln's Speeches," Chicago *Tribune*, March 2, 1860.

28 "Press and *Tribune* v. Seward," Chicago *Tribune*, April 7, 1860.

29 Weed, *Life of Thurlow Weed*, Vol. 2, 260.

30 Ibid, 269.

31 Charles Carleton Coffin, *Abraham Lincoln* (New York: Harper and Brothers, 1893), 188.

32 William Butler to Lincoln, May 15, 1860, *Lincoln Papers*, accessed July 1, 2021, at <loc.gov/item/mal0266500>.

33 Butler to Lincoln, May 16, 1860, *Lincoln Papers*, accessed July 1, 2021, at <loc.gov/item/mal0267400>.

34 Weed, *Life of Thurlow Weed*, Vol. 2, 269.

35 Greeley, *Recollections of a Busy Life* (New York: Arno, 1868), 390, 391.

36 Bancroft, *The Life of William H. Seward*, Vol. 1, 524-40.

37 Greeley, *Recollections of a Busy Life*, 315-21.

38 "'The Impending Crisis'—Or Caught in the Act," New York: Currier & Ives, 1860. <loc.gov/item/2003674580>.

39 "Political Intelligence," New York *Tribune*, June 3, 1860.

40 William H. Seward to Lincoln, October 8, 1860, *Lincoln Papers*, accessed July 1, 2021, at <loc.gov/item/mal0394600>.

41 Weed, *Life of Thurlow Weed*, Vol. 2, 271.

42 "Et Tu, Greeley?" *Vanity Fair*, June 2, 1860.

43 "The Presidency in Congress," New York *Tribune*, September 27, 1860.

44 "Republican Central Campaign Club," New York *Tribune*, June 1, 1860.

45 "Office of the *Tribune*," *Horace Greeley Papers*, Durham, NC: Duke University.

46 New York *Tribune*, November 8, 1860.

47 "To the Republicans of the Union," New York *Tribune*, October 11, 1860.

48 "The Republicans of the Slave States," New York *Tribune*, October 12, 1860.

49 "Playing Possum," New York *Tribune*, October 1, 1860.

50 New York *Herald* and New York *Daily News*, cited in Edwin G. Burrows and Mike Wallace, *Gotham: A History of New York City to 1898* (Oxford: Oxford University Press, 2000), 865.

51 "The Republican Jubilee," New York *Tribune*, November 9, 1860.

52 Greeley, *Greeley's Estimate of Lincoln* (Hancock, NY: Herald Printery, unpublished, 1868?), 26.

53 Henry J. Raymond to Lincoln, November 14, 1860, *Lincoln Papers*, accessed July 1, 2021, at <loc.gov/item/mal0449700>.

54 Joseph Medill to Lincoln, July 5, 1860, *Lincoln Papers*, accessed July 1, 2021, at <loc.gov/item/mal0342900>.

55 John W. Forney to Lincoln, November 12, 1860, *Lincoln Papers*, accessed July 1, 2021, at <loc.gov/item/mal0444800>.

56 "Are We Going to Fight," New York *Tribune*, November 30, 1860.

57 "The Right of Secession," New York *Tribune*, December 17, 1860.

3

Horace Greeley's New York *Tribune*

"If you can find, any person anywhere professing to have any proposition of Jefferson Davis in writing, for peace, embracing the restoration of the Union and the abandonment of slavery, whatever else it embraces, say to him he may come to me with you." Abraham Lincoln to Horace Greeley, July 9, 1864.

The war began with words: certainly opinionated and sometimes incendiary interpretations of the Constitution. By the end of the actual fighting, Horace Greeley could rightfully take pride in his efforts to publish as many views on a subject as possible. Greeley, a Universalist who opposed slavery and supported labor rights, crusaded against capital punishment, smoking, drinking and adultery; and promoted women's rights, vegetarianism, and trade protection. He earned both admiration and scorn for his open-minded approach to publishing, all the while holding a belief that a divine benevolence would eventually restore the Union. He may have been incorrect in the final analysis, but his newspaper reflected this belief and attracted readers to it because of his sincerity.

Other leading newspapers in New York devoted space to editorials that reflected the personal positions of respective editors, but the *Tribune* thrived on both Greeley's opinions and those of contributing writers. Henry Raymond's *New York Times* mastered a model of news that focused on facts, and James Gordon Bennett's *New York Herald* enjoyed an unrivaled pool of reporters; but, the depth of thought behind the writings published in the *Tribune* demonstrated the complexity of addressing the war's human dimensions—not just the raw names, dates, and places associated with it.

Abraham Lincoln appreciated Greeley's stature among readers, and he understood it, as the two had followed each other's careers since their days as fellow legislators in the Thirtieth Congress. Beginning in the late 1840s, Lincoln sought to distinguish himself as an opponent of the Mexican War and Greeley likewise advocated of homestead legislation. The two held essentially compatible goals—albeit with different means of achieving them, which sometimes created political friction. As the gravity of the Civil War became apparent and touched the lives of all Americans, tensions between Lincoln and Greeley at times became more than either man could bear.

Developments during the war that colored the relationship between Greeley and the Lincoln administration included the *Tribune*'s bellicose tone before the Battle of Bull Run, discussion surrounding the role of abolition in the war, and, finally, Greeley's role in a failed peace effort that President Lincoln had commissioned in the war's final year. Although historians can argue that Greeley erred in his analyses more often than not, he did so no more frequently than did other editors, generals, and elected officials. In fact, the *Tribune* fared just as well as did other papers in this respect—and even better considering the crucial role Greeley played in making abolition a subject the public understood to be a political necessity.

Seven Sleepless Nights

The relationship between Greeley and Lincoln inspired content in the *Tribune* that was politically productive, though at times rooted in antagonisms. Greeley's first comments on the secession crisis, which had reached a critical level with Lincoln's election to the presidency in November 1860, indicated that he thought the president should allow the South to "go in peace." However, by January 1861, beliefs in a peaceable dissolution of the Union clearly were ill founded, and Greeley, of all editors in the North, stood to lose prestige with continued reassurances that the nation could avoid war. After Lincoln's inauguration, the *Tribune* ran a series of "stand firm" editorials, which readers accepted as part of a position Lincoln also advocated—that secession was simply not an option.[1]

On April 12, 1861, with the first shots of the Civil War, Greeley—or at least the *Tribune*'s policy—vacillated again. "Sumter is temporarily lost, but Freedom is saved!" he wrote. "It is hard to lose Sumter, but in losing it we have gained a united people. Long live the Republic."[2] From June 26 to July 4, 1861, the *Tribune* ran a series of columns, "The Nation's War-Cry," calling on Lincoln to send federal troops into Virginia to capture the Confederate capitol in Richmond.[3] Greeley was away from the newspaper at the time the call to arms was written, leaving managing editor Charles A. Dana in charge. Fitz-Henry Warren, the *Tribune*'s Washington correspondent, wrote the material, but Greeley had a burdened conscience after the rout of the Union Army in the first battle of Bull Run—a fight attributed, at least in part, to the *Tribune*'s role in pressuring Lincoln to fight. The outcome of such pressure was a fiasco for the Union known as the "Great Skedaddle" in which thousands of unprepared troops fled the battlefield. Reports published in his own newspaper startled Greeley, who realized the *Tribune* had played a role in pressuring the government to act. "The strange and disastrous retreat of our troops from their well-contested position at Bull's Run to their old quarters at Arlington yesterday formed the topic of much gloomy conversation and somber conjecture," the *Tribune* reported. "It was only when the fighting was done, and the ridiculous panic turned the heads of the men, that they seemed to waver."[4]

Greeley also panicked at the news. In fact, from a number of accounts, he suffered a nervous breakdown. Forced to apologize to his audience for the *Tribune*'s content before Bull Run, he blamed at least part of the content on Dana. Hurriedly defending the *Tribune* to readers shocked by Bull Run, Greeley published a column within days of the fiasco.

> I am charged with what is called 'opposing the administration' because of that selection, and various paragraphs which have from time to time appeared in the *Tribune* are quoted to sustain this inculpation. The simple fact that not one of those paragraphs was either written or in any wise suggested or prompted by me suffices for that charge.[5]

However, Greeley had a difficult time convincing himself that he had played no role in the Union rout. He soon thereafter wrote Lincoln a frantic letter with language that reflected his tormented state, a condition called "brain fever" by his contemporaries. "This is my seventh sleepless night—yours, too, doubtless—yet I think I shall not die, because I have no right to die. I must struggle to live, however bitterly," he wrote Lincoln. "You are not considered a great man, and I am a hopelessly broken one. You are now undergoing a terrible ordeal, and God has thrown the gravest responsibility upon you. Do not fear to meet them."[6]

Lincoln, slow to anger, hid the letter for three years before quietly disclosing its contents in a private conversation. However, he did gripe publicly after Bull Run that the press had treated him poorly. In a speech, he cited a *Tribune* editorial that complained that Union regiments, which had begun burying troops after waving the truce flag, encountered Confederate soldiers who were seizing Blacks who had helped with the burials and sent them back into slavery. "Horace Greeley said in his paper," Lincoln said, "that the government would probably do nothing about it. What *could* I do?"[7]

In measures still considered controversial, Lincoln responded to the press by suspending the writ of habeas corpus, allowing for the prosecution of newspaper content that jeopardized Union war efforts. Greeley and other members of the Fourth Estate, whether intentionally seeking to protect their rights or simply trying to attract readers, had published sensitive military operations, and in doing so had infuriated the president's generals by allowing Confederate leaders to anticipate Union troop movements. On one such occasion, the *Tribune* revealed the battle plans of General William Tecumseh Sherman in North Carolina. The incident cost Sherman troops and his strategy at the time, leading the general to remark, "If I could have caught Mr. Greeley during the war, I would have hung him."[8]

Greeley's Prayer

The opening year of the war went disastrously for the Union, and it was clear Lincoln would need to reconsider his strategy of preserving the Union at all costs. Abolitionists had pressured Lincoln to end slavery almost immediately after he had assumed the presidency, believing that it was the right thing to do, but also that, as the war progressed, it would demoralize the South and contribute to Union victory. While Lincoln approved of the principle of abolition, he did not see his power as president as including the role of ending it, and hoped to postpone action on slavery at least until it had obtained wider public support.

At the beginning of the war, Lincoln disagreed with the abolitionists' strategy. He harbored a deep-seated hatred for slavery his entire life and opposed its spread, but he hoped it would eventually die without necessitating federal action that violated the Constitution. Later in the war, Lincoln felt the need to defend the stance, which he described as "naturally antislavery." In a letter to Kentucky editor A. G. Hodges, he wrote that if slavery was not wrong, nothing was wrong. "I cannot remember when I did not so think and feel," he wrote. "And yet I have never understood that the Presidency conferred upon me an unrestricted right to act officially upon this judgment and feeling. It was in the oath I took, that I would to the best of my ability preserve, protect, and defend the Constitution of the United States."[9]

Lincoln's stance on the issue changed in response to unfolding events—including legislation passed by Congress in July 1862, the Second Confiscation Act, which allowed for the freeing of the slaves of everyone in rebellion against the government. The legislation provided the signal desired by abolitionists, who called on Lincoln to enforce the change and demonstrate an increased intolerance for the institution. However, Lincoln had already drafted what he termed the Preliminary Proclamation, the first version of the Emancipation Proclamation, and read an initial draft of it to secretaries William H. Seward and Gideon Welles in July 1862. Hearing the language of what would become the Emancipation Proclamation rendered both secretaries at first speechless. According to Seward biographer Glyndon Van Deusen, when Lincoln read the draft of the final Proclamation to the Cabinet, the Secretary of State expressed fear that the measure would both represent a sign of desperation and would inspire an insurrection by those in the North who did not support abolition.[10] When Lincoln found Welles apparently too confused to respond, he let the matter drop, but he raised the issue again in a regularly scheduled Cabinet meeting later in July, to a mixed reaction. While Lincoln had wanted the advice of his advisors only on the style of the Proclamation, not its substance, they had a good deal to say about both. Secretary of War Edwin M. Stanton advocated its immediate release, correctly interpreting the Proclamation as a military measure that would both deprive the Confederacy of slave labor and bring additional men into the Union Army. Treasury Secretary Salmon P. Chase also supported it, but Postmaster General Montgomery Blair foresaw defeat in the fall elections. Attorney General Edward Bates, a conservative, opposed equality for Blacks but gave his qualified support.

Lincoln's decision to wait on issuing the Emancipation Proclamation demonstrated his uncanny ability to step mentally away from immediate circumstances and evaluate a situation objectively. He had clearly held sincere convictions about preserving the Union, as previous attempts to press abolition had elicited a similar response from him. In an exchange between Lincoln and Greeley, the most famous example, the *Tribune* had called upon Lincoln to wage war against the South in the name of ending slavery. The editorial, published under the title "The Prayer of Twenty Millions," which referred to the interests of Northern laborers, urged the president to use the Second Confiscation Act to allow Union commanders to free the slaves under Confederate control. On August 20, 1862, Greeley published the prayer, which held that the Union had suffered from the "mistaken" deference of Lincoln to the institution of slavery.[11]

Remarkably, Lincoln chose to reply to Greeley by publishing his letter in the *National Intelligencer*, whose editors were pro-Union but not staunch supporters of the president and decidedly against emancipation. Using the press in this way signaled an open defiance of Greeley by suggesting that mainstream editors would appreciate the measure even more than the radicals and abolitionists who followed the *Tribune*. The substance of his response indicated that he believed, as he had since assuming office, that his first task was to preserve the Union. "The sooner the national authority can be restored," he wrote, "the nearer the Union will be 'the Union as it was.'"

Lincoln's response was striking in a number of ways—that he responded at all, that he did so quickly, and that he chose to do so via a telegraphic transmission to a competing newspaper. "I intend no modification of my oft-expressed personal wish that all men, everywhere, could be free," Lincoln wrote, having already decided privately to issue the Emancipation Proclamation; however, his public response was to preserve the Union, whether that meant keeping or abolishing slavery.

> I would save the Union. I would save it the shortest way under the Constitution. The sooner the national authority can be restored; the nearer the Union will be "the Union as it was." If there be those who would not save the Union, unless they could at the same time *save* slavery, I do not agree with them. If there be those who would not save the Union unless they could at the same time *destroy* slavery, I do not agree with them. My paramount object in this struggle *is* to save the Union, and is *not* either to save or to destroy slavery. If I could save the Union without freeing *any* slave I would do it, and if I could save it by freeing *all* the slaves I would do it; and if I could save it by freeing some and leaving others alone I would also do that. What I do about slavery, and the colored race, I do because I believe it helps to save the Union; and what I forbear, I forbear because I do *not* believe it would help to save the Union. I shall do *less* whenever I shall believe what I am doing hurts the cause, and I shall do *more* whenever I shall believe doing more will help the cause. I shall try to correct errors when shown to be errors; and I shall adopt new views so fast as they shall appear to be true views.[12]

Having waited for the right time to demonstrate his willingness to free the slaves without sacrificing the Union, Lincoln saw the bloody victory of General George B. McClellan's Army of the Potomac over Confederate General Robert E. Lee at the Battle of Antietam (or Sharpsburg) as something more than symbolic gesture. In the September 17, 1862, fight, both sides suffered more than 23,000 casualties combined—the most deadly day of American history. Although Union troops died in greater numbers than Lee's, the battle ended in a tactical draw, perhaps at best a tactical victory, for McClellan, who forced Lee's men to retreat, but then failed to pursue them and deliver a crushing blow. Regardless, Lincoln saw signs that the North could carry on a fight and inflict severe damages to Lee's formidable record of consecutive victories. Within the week, Lincoln's Cabinet met to refine the draft of the edict Lincoln had developed in July, and on September 22, Lincoln issued a preliminary Emancipation Proclamation.

The *Tribune* celebrated what appeared to be the president's conversion to the abolitionist cause with extensive coverage of the event the following day. After the fact, Greeley claimed he had understood that the president was deliberating emancipation before Antietam, but the public recognized Greeley as having helped to advance the cause. The *Tribune* of September 23 pronounced that the Emancipation Proclamation would usher in a new era of freedom, "the beginning of the end of the Rebellion." Readers could celebrate the beginning of the nation's new life effective January 1, 1863, the beginning of the "emancipation of a race."[13] The *Tribune's* reaction did not necessarily reflect sentiment elsewhere in the North, which varied from endorsement of Lincoln's actions to resentment and rejection.

The *New York Times* at first referred to the decree as the most far-reaching document ever issued by the government, maintaining that its wisdom was unquestionable and its necessity indisputable.[15] A month later, the *Times* more calculatingly declared that the loyal states had received it well, the Border States had remained in the Union, and the army was not offended, Southern leaders feared the new policy, and that Europe reacted favorably to it.[16] Writing on behalf of Northern Democrats who resented the president's actions, James Gordon Bennett's *Herald* met the proclamation with skepticism. While the proclamation left slavery untouched in areas where Lincoln could enforce the decree, Bennett observed, the president had no way of enforcing his decree in areas directly affected by it. "Friends of human rights will be at a loss to understand this discrimination," Bennett wrote. "As a war measure it is unnecessary, unwise, illtimed, impracticable, outside the Constitution, and full of mischief."[17]

Elsewhere, the Emancipation Proclamation produced a reaction of indignant hostility, especially in the South. The Richmond (VA) *Whig* described the proclamation as "a dash of the pen to destroy four thousand millions of our property" and as "a bid for the slaves to rise in insurrection."[18] That city's *Examiner* described it as a "startling political crime." Referring to the proclamation in his January 12, 1863, message to the Confederate Congress, President Jefferson Davis declared that the act had rendered the restoration of the union "forever impossible."[19]

Image 3.1 "Horace Greeley statue, *Tribune* Office." As many of the images of Greeley in the Library of Congress' archives have been reproduced in a number of publications, this particular image is remarkable inasmuch as it features both a statue of Horace Greeley and *The New York Tribune* office. The bibliographic information for this image does not include a date for the photograph; however, the *Tribune* office building was destroyed in 1966, and the passersby appear to wear clothes from the early twentieth century.[14]

While Greeley had called for decisive action, he saw the proclamation in less dogmatic terms than did the most strident supporters of either states' rights or abolition. Yes, he understood the Emancipation Proclamation as part of a revolution, but its significance for him was largely indirect and strategic. It represented only a step toward other reforms that would require Reconstruction and additional years of struggle. Regardless, the times were indeed revolutionary, as settlers in the West would attest. In December 1860, twelve years after Greeley had first called on Congress to deliberate homestead legislation, the House passed the Homestead Bill by a decisive vote of 132 "Yeas" to 76 "Nays." The *Tribune* celebrated the victory, congratulating "the industrious poor of the cities and of all the Atlantic hives of population on the opening of a way of escape from their ever recurring embarrassments and sufferings."[20] President Buchanan, who left office soon thereafter, vetoed the bill, but in 1862, Lincoln signed the Homestead Act, granting 160 acres of public land to a settler after a five-year residence with improvements. Although the legislation never measured up to the ideals set by enthusiasts who had hoped to give poor men farms, it did become an important part of westward expansion after the war.

Union Victory and Greeley's Defeat

On Independence Day, July 4, 1863, the commemoration of the eighty-seventh birthday of the nation's founding, newspapers around the country filled their pages with reports of an epic battle in the Pennsylvania countryside. Between the first and third of July, more than 160,000 American soldiers had clashed in the areas surrounding Gettysburg, and coverage of the aftermath established new precedents in the professionalism of journalism—both in regard to the level of reporting and in commentary on the event. While newspapers in the North celebrated the victory of Union General George Gordon Meade over the advancing armies of Confederate General Robert E. Lee, Southern newspapers did not depict Gettysburg as a failure. However, by all accounts, Union forces turned back the Rebel invasion, and the battle marked a turning point. New York's leading newspapers—the *Herald*, *Times*, and *Tribune*—provided similar perspectives on the events at Gettysburg, inasmuch as each was generally hopeful and at the same time sober about the tremendous costs to both the combatants and the citizenry. Greeley's response, perhaps the oddest of them all, was again to publish high-handed calls for the president to act decisively alongside columns that suggested the war was lost.

During the first week of July 1863, the *Herald*, as the nation's leading supplier of war-related news, had featured front-page maps of Gettysburg and illustrations of the battlefield. Editor James Gordon Bennett, ordinarily ambivalent about Lincoln's war objectives, recognized Gettysburg as a "Great Victory Won!" and wrote that the victory in Pennsylvania had "settled the fate of the rebellion," as Union armies dispelled "the clouds and darkness which lately overshadowed us."[21] The *Herald* also highlighted the human toll of the battle, publishing accounts reproduced in papers around the nation of "Gettysburg after the Battle"— describing the ruin that had spilled from the field into the town and destroyed houses and yards. "Little of the enclosure remains save the wicket gateway, from which the gates have been torn," as artillery fire destroyed most of the landmarks of the time, leaving cemetery headstones shattered, "and fences and lawns trampled, turning beautiful fields into a dirty, corpse-filled landscape."[22] Indeed, after the battle, one of the most enduring stories that circulated well after the war was that of efforts to remake the Pennsylvania countryside into a hallowed ground.

Putting aside his usual attempts to promote the *Times* as an objective source for news and news alone, Henry Raymond also described Gettysburg in a mix of glowing and horrific terms. Although the Union victory was a "splendid triumph" and the Army of the Potomac's "greatest victory," it was also in many ways the worst battle of the war. From accounts in the *Times*, Confederate soldiers had retreated from Gettysburg so swiftly that their surgeons left behind the wounded—the writer called the action cowardly and infamous, observing the Southern wounded "complained bitterly of the cruelty of their surgeons in thus forsaking them."[23] The people of Gettysburg, according to the *Times*, were meanwhile spared the worst of the horrors, as General Lee, it alleged, had entered Pennsylvania with the intent of engaging in a "career of general ravagement." The carnage could have been much worse had Lee been allowed the opportunity to "loose reign to the passions of his soldiery," the *Times* suggested, "and we have no doubt that Pennsylvania would have been the scene of atrocities quite as horrible as those of the barbaric generals and military hordes."[24] Although the *Times*, of course, could not and did not always abide by its pronounced objective treatment of news, given the location of the battle and its relative proximity to New York, coverage of Gettysburg contained an extraordinary amount of personal interpretation.

Greeley also described the battle as the "most terrific fight of the war" and announced "the complete, overwhelming, magnificent victory of the Army of the Potomac."[25] But by early 1863 he had already concluded that the war was hopeless, and in his editorials, he began advocating for a restoration of the Union to its state before the outbreak of war. The suggestion constituted yet another one of the editor's baffling vacillations, as he essentially suggested that Lincoln should rescind the Emancipation Proclamation, even though he himself had urgently pressed him to enact it.

While the Union victory at Gettysburg had raised Greeley's spirits for the moment, he had already taken it upon himself to write to William Cornell ("Colorado") Jewett, a Peace Democrat from Maine who had offered to help establish ties between representatives of the North and South in efforts to negotiate peace. Greeley suggested in the correspondence that negotiations could not be between unofficial persons, but should be, rather, "between the government of the United States and the accredited authorities of the Confederates"—and that the Confederates must take the initiative.[26] With the *Tribune* publishing an appeal to representatives from England, France, or even Switzerland to help mediate an end to the war, Lincoln had to develop a strategy for both satisfying Greeley and keeping the latter's defeatist attitude from reaching his considerable, sympathetic audience.

After the brief respite of victory at Gettysburg, Greeley resumed his criticisms of Lincoln's war efforts, for a time indicating the *Tribune* would not endorse Lincoln's re-election. In spring 1864, Greeley had belittled the president as "not one of those rare, great men who mold their age into the similitude of their own high character, massive abilities, and lofty aims."[27] Lincoln—apparently knowing that Greeley would fail, and in so doing learn some restraint—responded by asking him to mediate in a peace mission to Canada in which he would arrange with representatives of the Confederate government a meeting to discuss terms for a cessation of conflict. The meetings, which did indeed prove futile, took place in July 1864. The *Tribune* editor was to meet with Confederate emissaries with Lincoln's orders: "If you can find any person anywhere professing to have any proposition of Jefferson Davis in writing, for peace, embracing the restoration of the Union and the abandonment of slavery, whatever else it embraces, say to him he may come to me with you."[28]

Greeley discovered that the Confederates did not take the negotiations seriously. After weeks of pursuing what he thought were grounds for a lasting peace, without having received any indication that the Confederate representatives were interested, he wrote Jewett again. His July 1864 correspondence gave Jewett the impression that Lincoln had empowered him to negotiate as a representative of the Union. Greeley suggested that "the fearful expensiveness of the war" would result in "bankruptcy and ruin" for both North and South, and he maintained that Lincoln had commissioned him to seek measures to avoid such catastrophic results. Greeley then suggested his own "Plan of Adjustment"—a proposal encompassing a restored Union, the utter abolishment of slavery, complete amnesty for all political offenses, and restoration of citizenship to all. In addition, Greeley proposed a grant of $400 million to the Confederates that would compensate for the losses of slaveholders, plus representation for them in the House. Upon receiving word of the proposals, both Lincoln and the Southern negotiators naturally and thoroughly dismissed them, as Greeley had not even bothered to verify if they had met with the approval of either Lincoln or Davis.[29]

Lincoln responded by writing Greeley two letters on the same day indicating he was "disappointed" that he had not received a response to his previous request to meet with a Confederate representative in the peace effort. "I was not expecting you to send me a letter, but to bring me a man or men."[30] The Southern representatives had taken Greeley's proposal no more seriously. "It must be confessed that Mr. Greeley, in his hysterical, deluded, and Quixotic course in this affair, cuts a shabby and pitiable figure," one wrote. "He also bitterly reproaches Mr. Lincoln for the whole past, and insists upon it that nine tenths of the whole American people, North and South, are sick of slaughter and anxious for peace on almost any terms; that a peace might have been made last month by 'an honest, sincere effort,' but it was now doubtful."[31] On one issue, both Lincoln and the Southern representatives agreed: Greeley had fooled himself into misrepresenting his own government. Greeley, unsurprisingly, narrated the events differently, suggesting that Lincoln had failed the nation by leading it into a "desperate, agonizing war."[32]

Upon collapse of the talks, Greeley exploited his mistakes by publishing the contents of the letters between Lincoln and him. He wrote Lincoln, requesting his permission—rather insisting upon it—to publish the contents in their entirety. Lincoln first responded that he would not object to publication but believed that certain details about the meetings would put in danger certain war objectives, as well as demoralize readers in the North. "With the suppression of a few passages in your letters in regard to which I think you and I would not disagree," Lincoln wrote, "I should be glad of the publication."[33] Greeley persisted and insisted that he would publish all of the material or none at all, to which Lincoln responded days later.

> Herewith is a full copy of the correspondence, and which I have had privately printed, but not made public. The parts of your letters which I wish suppressed are only those which, as I think, give too gloomy an aspect to our cause, and those which present the carrying of elections as a motive of action. I have, as you see, drawn a red pencil over the parts I wish suppressed.[34]

Exasperated—already anticipating Greeley's response—Lincoln turned to Henry Raymond, a stalwart supporter of the administration. "I have proposed to Mr. Greeley that the Niagara correspondence be published, suppressing only the parts of his letter over which the red pencil is drawn in the copy which I herewith send," he wrote.

> He declines giving his consent to the publication of his letters unless these parts be published with the rest. I have concluded that it is better for *me* to submit, for the time, to the consequences of the false position in which I consider he has

placed me, than to subject the *country* to the consequences of publishing these discouraging and injurious parts [emphasis in original].[35]

Lincoln included in the correspondence a copy of the letters, not intending Raymond to publish them. Newspapers throughout the North eventually published the letters, marking what Greeley must have thought as a marginal victory for press freedoms, although he clearly had motives other than the First Amendment in mind. Raymond, upon seeing the letters published on front pages of leading newspapers, reportedly exploded with rage. "Yes, all the newspapers will publish my letter," Lincoln said, replying to the question of why he did not more aggressively suppress the printing of the letters, "and so will Greeley."

> The next day he will take a line and comment upon it, and he will keep it up, in that way, until, at the end of three weeks, I will be convicted out of my own mouth of all the things which he charges against me. No man, whether he be private citizen or President of the United States, can successfully carry on a controversy with a great newspaper, and escape destruction, unless he owns a newspaper equally great, with a circulation in the same neighborhood.[36]

Indeed, the incident marked a formal souring of Lincoln's attitude toward Greeley. For years, since the *Tribune* had first vacillated in its support of the president, alternating it with inconsistent criticisms, Lincoln had tolerated Greeley as a valuable ally despite his eccentricities. However, in an August 19 Cabinet meeting, the president resigned to the fact that Greeley had worn out his usefulness. He was like "an old shoe—good for nothing new, whatever he has been," Lincoln said, "so rotten that nothing can be done with him. He is not truthful; the stitches all tear out."[37]

Historians generally also give Greeley poor marks for his performance; he had become at best a caricature of himself, a victim of the policies he sought to espouse: "The party for which he was so largely responsible had become the entrenched party of the north, determined on vengeance," wrote biographer Jeter Allen Isley. "The wages of battle were hatred, and Greeley saw his hopes of a harmonious society within the nation crumble about his feet."[38]

In fact, Greeley's attempt at peacemaking had been so heavy-handed that Secretary of State William H. Seward had threatened to prosecute him under the Logan Act, which prohibited American citizens from negotiating with foreign representatives. Lincoln dismissed Seward's threats against Greeley and joked that Greeley had actually aided in the successful prosecution of the war. The South, prior to this time, Lincoln said, had engaged successfully in a defensive war, and Greeley's over-earnest advocacy of peace had, "on the principles of antagonism, made the opposition urge on the war."[39]

In a final insult to Greeley's efforts, he again took criticism from his rivals at *The Chicago Tribune*. The Chicago editors published details from Greeley's travels that suggested he had quaked "with terror" in his correspondences with Lincoln. The accounts noted Greeley's own writings at the time had focused on the "bleeding, bankrupt, almost dying" Union that longed for peace and shuddered "at the prospect of fresh conscriptions, of further wholesale devastation, and of new rivers of human blood." Greeley's language indicated, in the estimation of the Chicago paper, that "next to Greeley's fear of the Rebels," Lincoln's contempt for Greeley was "the most salient feature of the correspondence." Lincoln must have arranged the entire mission, the column concluded, simply to let Greeley realize that his vacillating and inconsistent calls for both a prosecution of the war and an end to it were "his own folly."[40]

Greeley's Estimate of Lincoln

In the end, Lincoln proved himself a more reliable friend to Greeley than Greeley was to him. Throughout summer 1864, Greeley persisted in attempting to set up a convention for an alternative presidential candidate, one who would defeat Lincoln in the election. "Mr. Lincoln is already beaten," Greeley wrote. "He cannot be elected. And we must have another ticket to save us from utter overthrow."[41] Had General William T. Sherman not conquered Atlanta late in the summer, Greeley would have most likely gotten his way, as Lincoln's reelection depended on the stunning blow.

As the war came to a brutal close, Raymond's consistent news format trumped in the minds of many readers Greeley's less predictable (and sometimes wrong-headed) sentiments. The *Herald* remained New York's leading newspaper. Although James Gordon Bennett had actively opposed Republican initiatives and supported Democratic candidate George McClellan, he had earned Lincoln's respect through years of intensive reporting and trustworthy editing. In February 1865, Lincoln offered Bennett a ministerial appointment to France, which Bennett declined, writing Lincoln that he appreciated the offer but doubted that, at his age, he could perform the duties required, and preferred to maintain the *Herald*.

As Lincoln was preparing plans for his second administration, making appointment offers to Bennett and others who might serve on his Cabinet, he met with Greeley for a final time. Greeley later reflected on the occasion with one of his most poignant observations of the president. Lincoln's face was "haggard with care, and seemed with thought and trouble," he wrote. "It looked care-plowed, tempest-tossed, and weather-beaten, as if he were some tough old mariner." Judging from his "scathed, rugged countenance," Greeley feared the president would die. "I do not believe he could have lived out his second term had no felon hand been lifted against his priceless life."[42]

Lincoln had managed to either forgive or forget years of the *Tribune's* antagonisms. Sometime after the meeting told George G. Hoskins, New York Republican Assembly Speaker, he valued the support of the *Tribune* for the Union as much as a division of troops. Lincoln had intended to appoint Greeley to the Postmaster General position in his next administration, or so Hoskins reportedly told Greeley.[43] Greeley had long desired the position, and upon hearing the news, his attitude toward the president improved, at least temporarily.

Months later, Greeley by chance encountered Hoskins in New York and took the occasion to inquire about his pending Cabinet appointment. Hoskins, feeling his word was in jeopardy, boarded a train that Friday evening, April 14, 1865, to remind Lincoln about Greeley. On Saturday, Hoskins arrived in Washington with Greeley's blessing to secure the appointment; however, as Hoskins was riding on the train, an assassin fired a bullet into the president's head as Lincoln sat in Ford's Theatre.[44] As Hoskins was arriving in the nation's capital, the president died.

News of the president's death shook the nation, with newspapers devoting an unprecedented—and perhaps unsurpassed—amount of attention to the final moments of Lincoln. "The death of President Lincoln naturally excites universal and profound solicitude as to the immediate future of the country," *The New York Times* reflected. Lincoln's "sudden removal from the stage of events," it continued, "naturally excites anxiety and apprehension in the public mind."[45] Greeley was naturally also devastated, as his eulogies to Lincoln published in the *Tribune* of April 16, 17, and 18 revealed. Among his most compelling words included the sentiment that few graves would subsequently be more visited "or bedewed with the tears of a people's prouder, fonder affection, than that of Abraham Lincoln."[46]

A year later, Greeley again ran for Senate, promoting himself in the winter of 1866–67 by advocating "universal amnesty" for former Confederate leaders. The suggestion hurt him, as Yankees throughout the North generally thought a more appropriate fate for Jefferson Davis and his supporters was death. Greeley also supported the right to vote for African-Americans and quickly lost the support of New York's Democrats. In another among a string of defeats, Greeley lost his bid, and in a typical fashion received some of the harshest criticism of his campaign from the Lincoln loyalists at *The Chicago Tribune*. The Chicago editors campaigned against Greeley's bid, describing him as a man who could not be trusted, and as "an unreliable commander in action; a misanthrope in victory, and a riotous disorganizer in defeat."[47]

During Reconstruction, the *Tribune* promoted universal suffrage and advocated amnesty for all Southerners, including Jefferson Davis; when Greeley signed the bail bond for former Confederate President Jefferson Davis in 1867, it cost the *Tribune* thousands of readers. At about the same time, Greeley published *The American Conflict*, his account of the Civil War, for which *The Chicago Tribune* again blasted him. Although the text contains an admirable amount of primary materials, documenting issues tied to the history of the conflict dating to the nation's founding, the Chicago newspaper was correct to note that Greeley had failed in an obvious respect: He paid scant attention to the primary figure in the war, Lincoln. The newspaper noted that the account consisted primarily of news stories from Greeley's own editorial perspective, "full of the imperfect information which necessarily characterizes a report for a daily paper when it deals with questions which go to make history." The paper further suggested that Greeley had done so because of his exclusion from the Lincoln Cabinet.[48]

By 1868, Greeley had again begun to exhibit traits that had dogged him chronically throughout his life, including an erratic temperament accompanied by the publication of unpredictable opinions. He had attempted to clear his record with the autobiography *Recollections of a Busy Life*, which remarkably contained a number of insightful passages about nineteenth-century life, but it also attempted to minimize his role in the Lincoln administration. Reflecting on the suggestion that he had helped Lincoln obtain the presidency by backing his nomination at the 1860 Republican Convention, "I was somewhat surprised to meet there quite a number who, in conversations with me and others, had unhesitatingly pronounced his [Seward's] nomination unadvisable, and likely to prove disastrous, now on hand to urge it," he wrote. "I did much less than was popularly supposed."[49]

The same year, Greeley also penned a tribute to Lincoln, one of the few public accounts of the political and editorial relationship between the two. Although the 1868 manuscript later titled *Greeley's Estimate of Lincoln* contained sincere ruminations on Lincoln, Greeley did not publish it. Indicative of his state of mental duress, the manuscript's handwriting is virtually illegible, for the most part reduced to scribbles. Greeley apparently intended to deliver the address as a speech, but he most likely never did. Years later, after Greeley had died, the document was published in *The Century*, requiring years of painstaking transcription by American writer and lecturer Joel Benton. The publication included references to letters from readers published in *The Century* that suggested Greeley might have delivered the contents as a speech in both Washington and New York; however, one of the letter writers provided only a vague recollection of having heard it, perhaps in 1870. Among the telling aspects of the document, Greeley's reflections indicated that he had finally come to terms with his exclusion from the Lincoln Cabinet. Although the slight had clearly bothered him during the war, Greeley recognized that Lincoln's decisions were sound. Lincoln was "the one providential leader, the indispensable hero," Greeley wrote, "fitted by his very defects and shortcomings for the burden laid upon him." In Greeley's estimate, Lincoln was "simply a plain, true, earnest, patriotic man, gifted with eminent common sense, which, in its wide range, gave a hand to shrewdness on the on hand, humor on the other, and which allied him intimately, warmly with the masses of mankind."[50]

Greeley's legacy includes his admirable attempts to publish as many angles as possible on any given issue. His efforts led to the perception that he was inconsistent, a trait that worked at times to his advantage, capturing the attention of both his readers and the president. But in other instances, he erred in siding with sentiments that were not at all in step with what Lincoln or the nation either wanted to read or, indeed, needed at the time. When the *Tribune* succeeded in capturing the sentiments of its audience, readers applauded Greeley, as they did when Lincoln issued the Emancipation Proclamation. But when Greeley failed, as he did in attempting to negotiate peace, Lincoln and others made sure he knew it.

Notes

1 "No Compromise!" New York *Tribune*, February 18 to February 28, 1861.

2 New York *Tribune*, April 12, 1861.

3 "The Nation's War Cry," New York *Tribune*, June 26 to July 4, 1861.

4 "The Latest War News," New York *Tribune*, July 23, 1861.

5 "Just Once," New York *Tribune*, July 24, 1861.

6 Greeley to Lincoln, July 29, 1861, *Lincoln Papers*, accessed July 1, 2021, at <loc.gov/item/mal1092100>.

7 "Reply to Chicago Emancipation Memorial," December 13, 1862, in Fehrenbacher, *Lincoln: Speeches and Writings*, 362.

8 William Sherman to John W. Draper, March 15, 1870, in Stanley P. Hirshson, *The White Tecumseh, A Biography of General William T. Sherman* (New York: John Wiley, 1997), 289.

9 Greeley, *Greeley's Estimate of Lincoln*, 26.

10 Van Deusen, *William Henry Seward*, 333.

11 "The Prayer of Twenty Millions," New York *Tribune*, August 20, 1862; Greeley, *The American Conflict*, Vol. 2, 250.

12 "Lincoln's Reply to Greeley," Chicago *Tribune*, August 25, 1862.

13 New York *Tribune*, September 23, 1863.

14 "[Horace] Greeley Statue, *Tribune* Office," Library of Congress, accessed July 1, 2021, at <loc.gov/item/2014699235>.

15 New York *Times*, September 23, 1862.

16 Ibid, October 22, 1862.

17 New York *Herald*, January 3, 1863.

18 Richmond (VA) *Whig*, October 1, 1862.

19 Richmond (VA) *Examiner*, January 7, 1863.

20 "Passage of the Homestead Bill," New York *Tribune*, December 6, 1860.

21 New York *Herald*, July 4, 6, 7, 1863.

22 Ibid, July 9, 1863.

23 New York *Times*, July 3, 6, 1863.

24 "What Pennsylvania Has Escaped," New York *Times*, July 6, 1863.

25 New York *Tribune*, July 4, 6, 8, 1863.

26 Greeley to William Cornell ("Colorado") Jewett, January 2, 1863, in James Parton, *Life of Horace Greeley, Editor of the New York Tribune, From His Birth to the Present Time* (Boston: James R. Osgood and Company, 1872), 469.

27 "Opening the Presidential Campaign," New York *Tribune*, February 23, 1864.

28 Lincoln to Greeley, July 9, 1864, in Fehrenbacher, *Lincoln: Speeches and Writings*, 606.

29 Greeley, *The American Conflict*, Vol. 2, 664.

30 Lincoln to Greeley, July 15, 1864, in Fehrenbacher, *Lincoln: Speeches and Writings*, 608.

31 Francis Nicoll Zabriskie, *Horace Greeley, The Editor* (New York: Funk and Wangalls, 1890), 252-56.

32 Greeley, *Recollections of a Busy Life*, 404.

33 Lincoln to Greeley, August 6, 1864, in Abraham Lincoln, John George Nicolay, John Hay, *Abraham Lincoln: Complete Works*, Vol. 2 (New York: Century, 1894), 559.

34 Lincoln to Greeley, August 9, 1864, in Fehrenbacher, *Lincoln: Speeches and Writings*, 618.

35 Ibid, August 15, 1864, 619.

36 Chauncey DePew, *Reminiscences of Abraham Lincoln* (New York: North American Review, 1888), 436.

37 Howard K. Beale, ed., *The Diary of Gideon Welles* (Boston: Houghton, Mifflin, 1911), 112.

38 Jeter Allen Isley, *Horace Greeley and the Republican Party* (Princeton, NJ: Princeton University Press, 1947), 334.

39 Donald, *Lincoln*, 414.

40 "Greeley vs. Lincoln," Chicago *Tribune*, August 15, 1865.

41 Horner, *Lincoln and Greeley*, 351.

42 "The President's Health," New York *Tribune*, March 17, 1865.

43 William Harlan Hale, *Horace Greeley: Voice of the People* (New York: Harper and Brothers, 1950), 288, 289.

44 Greeley, *Greeley's Estimate of Lincoln*, Compiler's Note; Edward Everett Hale, *James Russell Lowell and His Friends* (Boston and New York: Houghton, Mifflin and Company, 1899), 178, 179; Harper, *Lincoln and the Press*, 347; Harry J. Maihafer, *War of Words: Abraham Lincoln and the Civil War Press* (Washington, DC: Brassey's, 2001), 253.

45 "The Effect of President Lincoln's Death on National Affairs," New York *Times*, April 17, 1865.

46 New York *Tribune*, April 19, 1865.

47 "Mr. Greeley for Senator," Chicago *Tribune*, November 17, 1866.

48 "H. G. and A. L.," Chicago *Tribune*, February 9, 1869.

49 Greeley, *Recollections of a Busy Life*, 390.

50 Greeley, *Greeley's Estimate of Lincoln*, 14, 15; Joel Benton, *Greeley on Lincoln* (New York: The Baker and Taylor Company, 1893), 6; Benton, "Greeley's Estimate of Lincoln," *The Century; A Popular Quarterly*, 42, 3 (July 1891): 371.

4

News Spin: Fredericksburg, Stones River, and Chancellorsville

"We are sure that the country, as much as it will criticize the attack made with only the imperfect information that [Burnside] possessed, will warmly applaud the moral courage and the care for his men which impelled him to retreat rather than renew an engagement, the result of which was hardly doubtful." *Chicago Tribune*, December 19, 1862.

An objective reporter of three critical battles in the second year of the war would have most likely concluded without much deliberation that Confederate armies had prevailed. However, readers of newspapers North and South would have undoubtedly had conflicting reports about exactly who won, how they did it, and why each side was credited with victory. Editors played roles in reporting the same facts in remarkably different ways, setting a precedent for what press practitioners later dubbed "spin." Although the record shows that the battles resulted in Union defeats (one being a draw), editors interpreted the facts differently, for purposes political or economic. Although other battles during the war also illustrated the tendency of the press to both represent and in some cases misrepresent the facts, Fredericksburg, Stones River, and Chancellorsville provide case studies in the way editors delivered news to an audience that sought in earnest the truth.

This study shows that the newspaper accounts were a medley of on-the-scene dispatches from correspondents, official military reports, casualty lists, graphical information (primarily maps), and editorial interpretation that sometimes resulted in opposing accounts of the same event. On the other hand, these three distinct battles shared commonalities as reported in the press, as well as in their role during the war. Fredericksburg was perhaps the low-water mark for the Union's Army of the Potomac. Major General Ambrose E. Burnside had taken over from George McClellan in November 1862 and had heeded President Abraham Lincoln's call to take the war to the enemy. An engineering mishap foiled Burnside's initiative, and the December 13 battle offered Confederates a tragic opportunity for target practice. Burnside had one and half times as many men at his disposal as Confederate Lee, but when the Union Army crossed the Rappahannock River and occupied the town, it met stiff resistance on the western side of the river from the Army of Northern Virginia. Positioned on a hillside west of town known as Marye's Heights, the Confederates clipped the Union right in perhaps the worst carnage the Union would see in the war.

The two other battles set the tone of newspaper coverage: In the first, a few weeks later, in Tennessee, Major General Braxton Bragg led the South to a very narrow tactical victory at Stones River near Murfreesboro, though the North did justly claim a strategic triumph. The bloody battle on the plains of Tennessee resulted in 24,000 casualties—just a few thousand less than at Antietam just three months before, but the highest percentage of casualties of any single Civil War clash. Then, in May 1863, the South would win again, this time defeating yet another leader of the Army of the Potomac, Major General Joseph Hooker, at Chancellorsville, near Fredericksburg. The battle at Chancellorsville resulted in more than 30,000 casualties. While the colossal failures of Union regiments primarily were attributable to the inexperience of the North's leading generals, Lincoln took the brunt of the criticism and found himself forced to reconsider his strategy to preserve the Union.

Three Battles, More than Two Versions Each

New York *Tribune* Editor Horace Greeley, who initially had indicated support for Lincoln's war strategy, reconsidered that stance within months of the war's outbreak. "I do not believe that this war can or ought to be prosecuted through the present year," he wrote, having determined that if the nation were to fall, history would "lay the blame on Abraham Lincoln and his cabinet, with the half-hearted commanders of their forces and the scoundrelly contractors who armed and fed those forces."[1] By early 1862, Greeley's sentiments had soured even more. "If this country is worth saving, it will be saved. If not, let it be damned as it ought," he wrote. "If we are a nation of robbers and thieves, let us accept the fate that we deserve."[2]

Image 4.1 "Virginia. Newspaper Vendor and Cart in Camp." Alexander Gardner, photographer, November 1863. A photograph from the main eastern theater of war while General Meade was in Virginia features several different newspapers made available on the front lines.[3]

Greeley understood the direct role newspapers could and would play in the war and sought to use the *Tribune* as a source of influence both for his target audience (readers in general) as well as—additionally—soldiers themselves. He encouraged correspondents to distribute the *Tribune* directly to troops. "I am authorized by a Republican to spend $500 of his money in increasing the circulation of the *Tribune* in the Army of the Potomac. I want you to make arrangements to that effect directly," he wrote to correspondent Samuel Wilkeson.[4]

> You ought to go down at once to the Rappahannock, see Gen. Hooker and others influential there, show them the treasonable articles from day to day appearing in the *Herald* and *World* (especially the latter), and suggest that the circulation of journals which try to disorganize and disaffect the Army ought to be stopped peremptorily, and that of loyal journals promoted instead.[4]

With the weekly edition of *The New York Tribune* alone reaching circulation levels of more than 200,000 issues, and with more than 100 million words in 2,500 newspapers and magazines written about the war, journalists during the Civil War nevertheless almost never wrote what would become the staple of twentieth-century journalism—neutral, objective, and balanced accounts.

While members of the press sensed an ownership in at least part of the outcome of the war, writers felt the need to provide information within very specific production constraints, not just giving their readers an agenda of items of what to think about; they also provided the interpretation. Editors on the winning side of a battle often overplayed triumphs, while those on the losing side tended to hold back information.

Many battles were stalemates and others resulted only in strategic successes, not overwhelming victory, resulting in published accounts sometimes based on faulty interpretation. Field reporters faced obstacles in transmitting their dispatches back to the newspaper office, including censorship or intimidation from military officers, downed telegraph lines, and dirty tricks from competing reporters. Reporters also had to rely on officers for information. More often than not, it was inaccurate because of the chaos attendant to military action. To maintain their relationships with sources, reporters tended to sanitize the battles—although some of the best were extremely critical, especially as the war reached its second and third years. Even if relatively independent dispatches did find their way into publication, newspapers remained fiercely partisan in the Civil War, and editors spun results.

The New York dailies had the most comprehensive and current coverage of the battles. For example, the *Daily Tribune* had front-page stories on the Fredericksburg campaign from December 8 through 25. This included battle reports, analyses of strategy and tactics, and casualty lists. Horace Greeley's eight-page *Tribune* also carried reports and editorials on its inside pages. The newspaper, too, ran reports from Richmond newspapers for a Southern view. There was so much detail that it was hard to tell if the battle was conclusive or not. Greeley's paper claimed that Fredericksburg saw the most intense fighting of the war to date. Greeley admitted in a headline on December 16 that the Union had not succeeded in the battle: "The Object Sought Unattained." After the fighting of December 13, the *Tribune* correspondent said there had been an official order to renew the battle the next day. However, he was skeptical that this could happen, writing, "When the hard usage nearly the whole of our right has experienced will become fully known to Gen. Burnside, the order will undoubtedly be countermanded."[5] The newspaper would quote a Southern officer who claimed that even an army of 500,000 would not have been able to carry Marye's Heights. "He said our men exhibited the greatest bravery, but he considered the Rebel position impregnable," the *Tribune* correspondent wrote.[6]

Like the *Tribune, The New York Herald* had hyperactive coverage of the battle. James Gordon Bennett's *Herald* promised that its coverage "comprises a full and complete account of all the memorable transactions delineated by eye witnesses of all they portray."[7] For weeks, the *Herald* led each edition with the conflict in Virginia. The lead story usually had ten headlines, such as, "Important from Virginia," "The Great Battle Commenced on the Rappahannock," "Bombardment and Partial Destruction of Fredericksburg," etc., with that particular article including a lead-in written by a *Herald* editor, followed by information from a correspondent and official Union Army reports.[8] However, the *Herald*'s most prominent information came in the form of maps. Most days, this independent-but-conservative newspaper had a new map to show its reader, usually placed above the fold in the center. On some days, those maps covered the entire front page. One map showed the relationship between Fredericksburg and Richmond, another provided a close-up of downtown Fredericksburg, and yet another showed where various Union generals were bivouacked. These woodcut illustrations helped the reader see where the action was occurring. The *Herald* of December 14 described a "tremendous battle" for which the editors were "waiting for the details and results." Bennett's newspaper reported rumors that the strength of Lee's army was 200,000. The *Herald* figured that the number was closer to 150,000. In fact, Lee had less than 80,000 men. The early forecast from even the conservative *Herald* was that while "the battle is reported as exceedingly desperate, we anticipate the most glorious results."[9]

A story from a competitor of the *Herald*, the *Evening Express*, published under the headline "The War" on December 15, described in detail Burnside's battle plan, preparations for the engagement the day before it would begin, and then the events on the day of the battle. However, the *Evening Express* story focused on strategy and troop movements, and it was highly accurate, clearly with a correspondent on the scene. When Union troops reached the outskirts of Fredericksburg, Confederate artillery and snipers began shooting, and the *Express* reporter wrote, "The Rebel Sharpshooters now opened from all sides with fearful effect. The vigor of the fire of the Rebel artillery also steadily increased, and when the [Union] line reached the foot of the second range of hills, a perfect hail of lead fell upon it."[10]

Meanwhile, Henry Raymond's pro-Republican *New York Times* reported that the battle had begun in a heavy fog. In an update on the back page on

December 14, a headline read, "Our Troops Met by a Terrible Fire of Artillery and Musketry."[11] The *Times* correspondent wrote that the Confederates were positioned behind a stone wall and in houses at the base of and on Marye's Heights. The next day, the *Herald* conveyed an ominous tone: "Serious Loss of Union Officers" and "Immense Strength of the Rebel Works."[12] Four days after the battle, the lead *Herald* headlines were "The Disaster" and "Fredericksburg Abandoned by Burnside." Still, Bennett was relatively benevolent to Burnside, holding that he had retreated from Fredericksburg "in time to save his army from the chances of annihilation."[13] The *Herald* mentioned that Confederate snipers fired at Union soldiers who tried to bury the dead the night after the battle. Likewise, the pro-Democratic *Evening Express* was more likely to be critical. Editors James and Erastus Brooks ran an editorial under the headline "Battle, or Slaughter? Which?" The editors reported Union casualties between 10,000 and 20,000, remarking, "Despite all this sacrifice, we seem to be in a worse military position than when on this side of the Rappahannock." The editors also attacked the Union Army's use of "attack by column" on an entrenched force.[14] Furthermore, the Brooks brothers defended Burnside, saying he had received inadequate resources in the attack and that he had simply obeyed his orders from Washington—ones that the *Express* editors believed to be too politically motivated.

The *Tribune* seemed in denial. Greeley's paper displayed a headline on the Monday after the Saturday battle that claimed "No Damage Done Our Forces." Greeley surmised that the Confederates had put all of their available men in the hills surrounding Fredericksburg. He dismissed the rumored 200,000 Confederate States of America (C.S.A.) troops, but estimated Southern strength to be 100,000 to 150,000: "Sheltered by their natural and artificial defenses, they very nearly held their own throughout the obstinate and protracted fight of Saturday, and probably inflicted more loss in killed and wounded than they suffered."[15]

If the *Tribune*'s editorials were defensive about the results of the battle, Greeley still tried to provide readers with a steady stream of facts. A major feature of the *Tribune* reporting was lists of the dead, wounded, and missing. A first extensive list came on December 16. It spanned four columns, with two rows in each column—eight columns of copy. A similar four-column list ran two and four days later, and on December 22 the newspaper printed a list that started on the last column of the front page and continued through two and a quarter columns on the eighth page. In that same edition, the *Tribune* ran four columns of those hospitalized in Washington from wounds received at Fredericksburg. The information on both sets of lists included the first name or initial, last name, and regiment. The *Tribune* typically did not include any specificity about the nature of the wounds. However, some companies provided that information, and it was included in the lists. Eleven days after the battle, a *Tribune* reporter put Union losses at 12,000 after the paper had put those losses at 9,400 only a few days earlier, quoting Southern officers as saying that they had lost only 3,000. Greeley defended Burnside's performance and inveighed against Democratic editors who were pleading with Lincoln to end the savage war. The *Tribune* editor accused Democratic critics of attempting to "destroy every vestige of public trust in those called to administer the Government, including the President who must remain President for the next twenty-seven months."[16]

The New York Times reporter was unsparing in his description of the Union loss. After the Saturday battle, he indicated, Burnside had failed "to accomplish the object sought," and the "the result thus far leaves us with a loss of ten to fifteen thousand men, and absolutely nothing gained."[17] To illustrate that loss in firepower, the *Times* ran a casualty list in small agate type that comprised two and one-half columns on December 18. Each column was divided in half, amounting to five columns of dead and wounded.

J. W. Gray's Cleveland *Plain Dealer* described the news of Burnside's defeat as "incredible," yet "sadly, gloomily, discouragingly true."[18] The Boston *Daily Advertiser* called the loss a "bitter disappointment," but editors Nathan Hale, Charles Hale, and Charles F. Durham preached patience to their readers. They urged the government to let the Army of the Potomac rest and restock for the winter, so that the force would be ready for battlefield success in the spring. "With such a force in such good condition," they wrote, "we hope it may be within the plans of the generals in command to strike somewhere a decisive blow from which the military strength of the rebellion may find it difficult to recover."[19] The *Advertiser* also reported on the death of the Reverend A. B. Fuller, a chaplain for the Massachusetts Sixteenth. A ball from a musket hit Fuller, and "in five minutes, he fell dead."[20] The pro-Republican newspaper included a lengthy biography of the Unitarian minister, whose resume included twice being chaplain of the Massachusetts legislature.

The Philadelphia (PA) *Public Ledger and Daily Transcript* sensed something was wrong at Fredericksburg when the federal government suspended transmission of news on the telegraph. This is always "construed into a defeat or a reverse," the editors wrote, and, anticipating the news, prepared for "the melancholy lists of killed and wounded." The *Public Ledger* offered one of the most accurate descriptions of the suicidal advance of the Union soldiers against the Confederates at Marye's Heights. "Not a single spade was used nor a ditch dug, nor an entrenchment thrown up, but solid columns of men, as brave as ever shouldered a musket, were dashed impetuously at the foe, and almost as quickly were swept out of existence by the concentrated fire of the Rebel artillery and rifles." A moderate, pro-Lincoln journal, the *Public Ledger* praised Burnside for fighting "gallantly and dashingly" and pinned blame for the failure on radical Republicans who had demanded the advance. The Philadelphia editors hoped Burnside would now find a new, more "eligible" way to Richmond.[21]

On the same day that the *Public Ledger* told its readers of the debacle at Fredericksburg, the Cincinnati *Daily Commercial* called the battle "a tremendous loss." Its correspondent termed it "a shocking blunder and disaster," adding, "We did not gain a single position of importance on Saturday, and our loss was severe."[22] On December 20, the Ohio newspaper asked for a congressional investigation into the failure. In particular, the editor wanted to know why Burnside did not find an easier and swifter method of entering Fredericksburg than the pontoons that were used too late.

The pro-Lincoln *Chicago Tribune* initially was optimistic about Burnside's progress. It praised the general's order and quoted it: "Forward the whole line!" The next day, though, a headline in Joseph Medill's newspaper called Fredericksburg a "Desperate Conflict."[23] On December 16, Medill praised the Seventh Michigan Regiment for leading the Army of the Potomac across the Rappahannock. "The Western soldiers point the way to victory," the *Tribune* editor wrote.[24] By December 18, the Chicago newspaper put Union losses at 750 killed, 4,000 wounded, and 500 missing—a total of 5,250—but the next day wrote that the total was much higher (13,000) in an article headlined "Thrilling Details of Bravery and Slaughter." Medill's journal also suggested a congressional committee was on its way to Fredericksburg to investigate the battle. The paper ran a map of Fredericksburg that included the positions of key Union generals and the locations of pontoon crossings, Union batteries, and Confederate entrenchments and sharpshooters. The *Tribune* provided an account of Burnside's retreat to the other side of the Rappahannock. "We are sure that the country, as much as it will criticize the attack made with only the imperfect information that he [Burnside] possessed, will warmly applaud the moral courage and the care for his men which impelled him to retreat rather than renew an engagement, the result of which was hardly doubtful."[25]

Southern newspapers were generally cautious in their initial reporting of the battle on the Rappahannock. The *Missouri Republican*, which relied on government and East Coast journal accounts of the battle, had called Fredericksburg a "terrible slaughter" and written that the Army of the Potomac had made no

Image 4.2 "Campaign in Virginia: A Street in Harper's Ferry during the Passage of the Potomac by the National Troops from Maryland, October 24, 1862." *Frank Leslie's Illustrated Newspaper* (November 15, 1862), 113. This front-page illustration depicted two Zouave fighters for the Union Army riding on mules through the streets of the Virginia town. The date associated with the event, October 24, 1862, took place before Union's costly defeats at Chancellorsville and Fredericksburg.[26]

substantial progress.[27] The St. Louis newspaper also surmised that Burnside had retreated across the Rappahannock because of inclement weather. A pro-Democratic paper, the *Republican* blasted the impatience of the North in forcing Burnside to be too aggressive. Later, George Knapp's paper concluded that the Union Army was "overwhelmed with disaster" and that the C.S.A. had "great advantage" in its position on Marye's Heights.[28]

However, early reports of the engagement in the Atlanta *Intelligencer* suggested on December 14 that only "skirmishing" had taken place—although the newspaper commented that a "considerable portion" of the city had been destroyed. Two days later, it noted that the accounts of the battle were truncated due to a downed telegraph line. Still, the Atlanta newspaper was able to run a dispatch from Robert E. Lee saying that the enemy had been "repulsed at all points thanks to God. As usual, we have to mourn the loss of many brave men."[29] Initial reports of the battle in Southern journals conceded Burnside would probably take the town, with the Richmond *Enquirer* suggesting Lee was "cheerful and confident" and that his commander, Stonewall Jackson, had examined the field, remarking "in the coming fight Jackson's men will be no laggards."[30] The *Weekly Standard* of Raleigh, North Carolina, commended Union corps commander Joseph Hooker's maneuvers in preparation for the battle. Editor William W. Holden also noted that thirty-eight Union regiments were about to see their tours of duty expire, and that none of the soldiers in those regiments had re-enlisted.[31]

The Southerners used sharpshooters in the town to pick off Union engineers once the latter finally began to build temporary bridges across the river. Then, when the town was evacuated, the Rebels took positions on Marye's Heights and assaulted Burnside's men as they tried to advance up the hill. The Lynchburg *Virginian* reported on December 15 that the Union Army had occupied Fredericksburg. "It is said that an entire company of our troops, on picket near the river, were surprised and captured," the *Virginian* correspondent wrote. "Sharp skirmishes ensued in the streets of Fredericksburg and about eight o'clock our forces relinquished the place to the enemy."[32] Charles W. Button's newspaper emphasized the severity of Union Army tactics. Button reported that Union troops set fire to the post office, a church, a bank, and houses. His reporter also noted that only a few hundred people had stayed in the city, and speculated that some had switched loyalties to the Union. The newspaper played the story more prominently the next day, leading the commentary column at the top of the second page with the latest information and interpretation of events. Editor Button began by writing: "Up to this writing we are unable to present a clear and lucid exposition of affairs on the Rappahannock."[33] He noted that the closest telegraph station was several miles from the front. Still, he waxed poetic, writing, "So far as matters are developed, we have reason to believe that the God of Battles has blessed our arms again, though even this reflection is saddened by the thought that our victory has its price." Button reported that Brigadier General Thomas R. R. Cobb of Georgia had died on December 13 and that Major General A. P. Hill was wounded in the fighting.

The Richmond *Enquirer* waxed poetic about Cobb, an attorney who had helped lead Georgia out of the Union: "Virginia, on whose soil he died, mourns with Georgia over the loss of one of her noblest sons."[34] The Lynchburg editor also surmised that the Fredericksburg attack was part of a larger Union strategy that included attacks on Richmond and on Confederate supply lines in North Carolina. Another *Virginian* story that day recounted the suffering of the dispersed civilian population of Fredericksburg: "Their peaceful and happy homes have been wrenched from them by the ruthless hand of the invader, and given over to war's worst devastations," Button observed. He noted that the former citizens of the city had hurried away from the Union Army, leaving behind most of their possessions. "Poor Fredericksburg, bright on the page of a historic past, long the seat of a generous hospitality, a refined cultivation, an elegant sociability—now how changed, with its altars broken, its steeples shattered, its homes desolate, and its people despoiled and scattered!" The editor praised a group of Lynchburg residents who were taking up a collection for the Fredericksburg refugees. One day later, Button wrote that the suffering was worth it—that it would "make our liberties only the more pure and precious when they are won, as they assuredly will be."[35]

The *Virginian* relied on the reporting of the Richmond *Enquirer*'s correspondent in the field. He noted that Burnside commanded in person. He also commented that Stonewall Jackson, along with A. P. Hill, "bore the brunt of the battle, and nobly did they sustain themselves." The reporter supplied a list of casualties, including notable officers and ordinary soldiers. He emphasized the dead and wounded from Virginia regiments, but he also wrote that Hill's division had lost approximately three hundred men. The *Weekly Standard* of North Carolina noted that Confederate losses were heavy, but added that those of the enemy were "far greater than ours."[36] It also noted that the ground was more favorable to the Rebels, and that reports erroneously had Hooker killed, though he was in fact working with a wound from a previous battle.

By December 18, five days after the battle, the *Virginian* was at last calling the outcome: "The Glorious Victory on Heights of Fredericksburg." The Richmond *Enquirer* reporter wrote that Lee was "highly pleased with the result," and the correspondent reported that Union casualties amounted to "many thousands." Editor Button's commentary that day asked what would happen next in the war, writing that Burnside "had measured his skill with that of Gen. Lee, and it proved unequal to the contest." He described Burnside, formerly "the new hope of the North and anointed of Abraham," as having failed miserably, like his predecessors. "The same cup of defeat and disaster which they drank, he has swallowed; and most probably the same fate as theirs awaits him."[37]

Button would be right on this score, as Lincoln would sack Burnside a month later. However, for the moment, the Lynchburg editor only could speculate what the Army of the Potomac would do next. He told his readers that Lee ought to prepare for a second battle at Fredericksburg. He also gleefully noted that the *Washington Republican*, once so enthusiastic about the "On to Richmond" strategy, was now favoring the Army of the Potomac's switching to a winter mode and ceasing active operations. Button reiterated his claim that Fredericksburg had been a great Southern victory, noting the disparity between casualties. Reports suggested the Union suffered 15,000 casualties, and by contrast, the South only had 2,000 dead, wounded, and captured. The *Virginian* reported Burnside, in his report to Washington, claimed losses were no more than 5,000.

Button was now ebullient. "The world never saw a better army than that now marshaled under the greatest soldier of the age, Gen. Robert E. Lee."[38] Holden, in the *Standard*, wrote there is "no doubt that Gen. Lee has been successful. He has repulsed the enemy in heavy forces at several points, and now holds Fredericksburg with no enemy in its vicinity."[39] The Lynchburg newspaper published a description of the battle from *The New York Herald* under the headline "Great Slaughter of Federal Troops." The *Herald* correspondent, however, gave the advantage at Fredericksburg to the Union.

> Where they [the Confederates] fought behind their works, they were not believed to have lost as heavily as we did. Thus, those engaged where the enemy kept behind their fortifications estimate our loss at much more than theirs, while those whom they met in open field insist that their killed and wounded are at least double ours.[40]

Button observed that the Confederates were considerably outnumbered, but the superior numbers of the Yankees gave the Rebels "more numerous ranks to fire into." As it turned out, the C.S.A. soldiers were more skilled with their rifles. "Upon the while, the result at Fredericksburg is in the highest degree encouraging." The Lynchburg newspaper portrayed Southern soldiers as noble and heroic.

By contrast, the Yankees were "savages." Button noted reports of the ransacking of every home in Fredericksburg "from garret to cellar." All household items were destroyed—china, furniture, pianos, windows. Worst of all, the abolitionist soldiers drank all of the town's liquor.[41]

Northern and Southern newspapers ran transcripts of Burnside's testimony before the Senate on December 23. He defended his aggressive approach, which had Lincoln's approval. Burnside testified that at all times his army would be between the enemy and Washington.[42] The Senate committee concluded that no one was to blame for the defeat. *The New York Herald*, which had claimed that the best army in the world had been defeated by an "army of ragamuffins," commented that in effect the federal government was covering up the defeat. "We warn President Lincoln to beware of this disastrous result," Bennett wrote, adding a rhetorical comment in the form of a question: "or he will lead his administration, as Burnside led our army, to a Fredericksburg—victory?"[43] In Raleigh, *Weekly Standard* editor Holden claimed Northern newspapers were calling Fredericksburg the Union's "most disastrous flogging they have had" to that point in the war.[44]

Another type of news published after Fredericksburg was lists of casualties. For example, the *Chronicle & Sentinel* in Augusta, Georgia, ran several columns of that state's casualties. The information came from C.S.A. Army Assistant Adjutant General James M. Goggin's headquarters in Fredericksburg, dividing the list into brigades and then subdividing them into companies, giving each soldier's rank and name, and then whether killed or wounded. For the wounded, there was an attempt to give a brief description of the injury, such as "Col. Robt. McMillan, wounded slightly in right arm."[45] The *Weekly Standard* ran a table of killed and wounded from four North Carolina regiments, as well those in two C.S.A. brigades and seven divisions. The totals for North Carolina's troops were forty killed and 343 wounded. The Raleigh newspaper also ran a list of Tar Heel officers who had arrived at Richmond hospitals.[46] Several weeks later, the *Standard* printed a full list of wounded North Carolinians, along with a regimental breakdown of killed and wounded. The list filled nearly two columns. Meanwhile, the Southern editors eagerly waited for news from Tennessee, as rumors circulated of a great battle brewing southeast of Nashville, and it was believed that another Confederate victory would galvanize the peace contingent in the North.

Calling a Draw

The battle at Stones River took place from December 31, 1862, through January 2, 1863. It was a narrow decision with significant casualties so that either side could claim triumph. Because it was in the western theater, New York newspapers did not cover it with quite the same intensity as they had Fredericksburg. Still, they followed the action and were more willing to term it a decisive victory than did the Southern journals.

The coverage began on January 1, 1863, with *The New York Tribune* writing that Union Major General William S. Rosecrans of Ohio had put his army in motion and attacked the Army of Tennessee under Major General Braxton Bragg of North Carolina. Early news of the battle was favorable for the Union's Army of the Cumberland, which pushed Bragg's army for several miles, and the *Times* claimed that Rosecrans then drove Bragg's army for seven or eight miles. Two days later, the *Tribune* correspondent (whom the paper said was with Rosecrans throughout the conflict) portrayed Stones River as "one of the most ferocious battles of modern times," with 2,500 Union losses and Confederate casualties reportedly "larger." Later *Tribune* coverage indicated "a great struggle in Tennessee" amid "severe fighting," with Union losses at 4,000.[47] Eventually, both the *Tribune* and *Times* declared Stones River a Union victory. The *Times* had Union casualties at 6,500, with "Rebel losses much heavier."[48] The *Herald* continued its practice of including maps with its coverage. Maps of Tennessee from Nashville to Tullahoma were commonplace. The *Herald* termed Stones River a "terrific battle" with "desperate and sanguinary fighting."[49] Gordon's newspaper praised the bravery of the Union troops and hailed Rosecrans for conducting himself "fearlessly amid the carnage."[50]

The Philadelphia (PA) *Public Ledger and Daily Transcript* reported cautiously during the first few days after the battle, noting the fighting had gone back and forth. It called the Union troops "heroic and their [the Confederates'] loss terrible." It was not until January 6, 1863, that the *Public Ledger* declared Union victory. Its editors praised the "preserving and skillful efforts of the courageous leaders of the Union army."[51] Likewise, while the Springfield *Republican* in Massachusetts spoke of a "federal victory"—albeit with a great cost in the loss of many Union officers—it also noted that the contest appeared "to have been one of the most desperate and bloody of the war."[52]

The Louisville (Ky.) *Journal* printed official correspondence, including Rosecrans' dispatch that suggested the enemy was in full retreat.[53] The Boston *Daily Advertiser* quoted the *Journal*'s reports and called Stones River a "Complete

Federal Victory."[54] The Cleveland *Plain Dealer* told its readers that Rosecrans had "gained a splendid victory." Editor Gray's newspaper reported on officers from Cleveland either killed or taken prisoner, commenting: "Nobly have these young soldiers distinguished themselves, and their valor and devotion will live forever in the hearts of their countrymen."[55] Other newspapers, such as M. D. Potter's Cincinnati *Daily Commercial*, took a more cautious tone, reporting that intelligence from the front was favorable. Editor Murat Halstead preferred not to cast the battle as a victory or a defeat. Instead, he let readers judge for themselves from the dispatches of the newspaper's reporter in Murfreesboro. The editor wrote the "probabilities are that it [his correspondent's report] is correct" in calling Rosecrans successful.[56]

The staunchly Republican *Chicago Tribune* called the battle three days of "Terrific Fighting" without a definitive result.[57] The next day, however, the paper called Stones River a complete Union victory, though reiterating the loss in men was heavy. The *Tribune* claimed the win in Tennessee, combined with successes at Vicksburg and in Arkansas, "lit up the horizon and revived the drooping spirits of the loyal people." Still, the Republican paper wrote that a "long and rugged road" remained for the Union to travel "before the great rebellion is completely extinguished."[58] Joseph Medill's journal also reported on the trip of the Chicago Sanitary Commission to the battlefield.

The *Missouri Republican* focused on the performance of Missouri regiments in the battle. The St. Louis newspaper printed a letter from Lieutenant Colonel Bernard Laibold, a brigade commander, who said the state's regiments "behaved with a gallantry and bravery which must swell the heart of every Missourian with pride."[59] In Des Moines, Iowa, the *Daily State Register* spoke of the "Great Battle in Murfreesboro" and relied on telegraphic reports transmitted by East Coast newspapers.

Down South, the Richmond *Examiner* painted a less-clear picture of the Tennessee battle. The editors observed that correspondents in the field provided "favourable but vague accounts" of Confederate progress. The report from Bragg was "positive and satisfactory," with 4,000 Union prisoners accompanied by a "general repulse of the enemy." Yet the published account of Bragg's communiqué suggested the battle was not complete. The Richmond paper was careful not to predict the ultimate outcome of the battle. Still, it hoped Rosecrans would retreat, thus leaving all of Tennessee in the hands of the Confederates. Furthermore, the paper claimed the army fighting before Vicksburg would never touch the soil of the United States again "except as paroled prisoners." The *Examiner* lauded Bragg.

The merit of this brave and able officer has been obscured by his late campaign in Kentucky. That campaign failed, and failed because General Bragg was not a proper person to manage such a movement. But in his proper place, the Confederate service affords no better office than General Bragg.[60]

Bragg, in command of the Army of Mississippi, had been defeated at the Battle of Perryville, Kentucky, October 8, 1862, with a period following in which both the Confederate and Union forces in Kentucky retreated to safe ground.

The Augusta *Chronicle & Sentinel* did not have a reporter at Murfreesboro. It ran the account from the Knoxville *Register* that was rather sketchy. It told of a Confederate retreat under Lieutenant General Joseph Wheeler, an Augusta native, and Brigadier General John A. Wharton, who was wounded in the battle, with relatively few casualties. The *Register* correspondent added that the Army of Tennessee had dug in, winning "fresh laurels."[61] For the Richmond *Examiner*'s editors, Bragg had become the Southern army's best general in the field, based on his performance against Rosecrans at Murfreesboro. Perhaps the *Examiner* wanted Bragg seen as successful because he had C.S.A. President Jefferson Davis' backing at a time when some of his senior officers wanted him replaced by Joseph E. Johnston, who was commander of the entire Western army. Yet it was also true that Bragg took the battle to Rosecrans, attacking first on the morning of December 31. The Richmond newspaper and its readers appreciated an aggressive general, and such a trait in a commanding officer was one of the C.S.A.'s major advantages in the war, especially since the opposite trait was common in Virginia by the now-relieved Union General George C. McClellan.

The Lynchburg *Virginian* published Bragg's official dispatch on December 31. It said that ten hours of "hard fighting" had driven Rosecrans' army "from every position except his extreme left, where he has successfully repulsed us."[62] Bragg claimed that the Confederate Army had taken 4,000 prisoners, including two brigadier generals. The Lynchburg newspaper's assessment of the battle at Murfreesboro was that it was not a complete victory, but that Bragg "struck a stout blow for the liberation of Nashville. We are the assailants. We attacked the enemy in their chosen position."[63]

The Greensborough *Patriot* in North Carolina called Murfreesboro a "victory" for the South. The *Patriot*, which termed the enemy the "Abolitionist army," described Bragg and Major General Leonidas Polk, who had attended the University of North Carolina before going to West Point, as having "displayed great judgment and heroism" at Murfreesboro.[64] Like other Southern journals, the *Patriot* reprinted Bragg's dispatches from the front. It also reprinted what other Southern newspapers were saying about the battle. These included a Chattanooga (TN) *Rebel* report that claimed Union prisoners from the battle came from seventy-eight different Yankee regiments.

The Greensboro (formerly Greensborough) newspaper also printed an optimistic editorial from the Vicksburg *Citizen* proclaiming that Bragg's army would give Rosecrans "a better whipping" in an anticipated rematch: "We will clean them out so thoroughly that their friends at home will never find out what has become of them."[65] In Raleigh, Holden's *Weekly Standard* also pronounced Murfreesboro a Southern triumph. It reported the capture of 4,000 Yankee prisoners, but also described the fighting on January 2 as among the "most desperate and bloody" of the war.[66] Holden hoped that future telegraphic dispatches would indicate that Bragg had routed Rosecrans.

Such news never came. Now some Southern newspapers were being less kind to Bragg, who would retreat despite the fact that his army inflicted more casualties than it suffered. Indeed, Rosecrans would build a fort at Stones River and stockpile material for nearly a half-year to help the Union's war effort in Tennessee. "We fear that our victory in Murfreesboro is about to be barren of results, as so many others of ours have been," observed Nathan S. Morse, the editor of the Augusta *Chronicle & Sentinel*.[67] Holden in Raleigh had a similar lament: "The results of the battle of Murfreesboro, Tenn., are not as gratifying and successful as we had hoped."[68] On the other hand, Rosecrans did not pursue Bragg and failed to offer any kind of attack against the Army of Tennessee. In other words, Rosecrans displayed the kind of passivity that had often driven President Lincoln to despair with McClellan. Still, when word arrived in Washington that Bragg had been expelled from Murfreesboro, Lincoln, Secretary of War Edwin M. Stanton, and General in Chief Henry W. Halleck all hailed Rosecrans.

The Augusta *Chronicle & Sentinel* continued to provide dispatches after the battle had ended. On January 5, the Augusta newspaper reported that all was quiet in Murfreesboro, but noted the enemy was "in strong force" just three miles northwest, and that Nashville had been reinforced.[69] Newspapers also published lists of enemy prisoners captured in battle. These included the rank and name of the enemy soldier, his regiment, and the site of capture. Southern newspapers emphasized captured officers. Other stories dealt with the aftermath of battle. For instance, *The Chicago Tribune* ran stories about aid for the wounded and sick. Joseph Medill's newspaper urged readers to contribute to the U.S. Sanitary Commission, "the proper channel for all parties" to help those injured and ill soldiers at Murfreesboro.[70]

In spring 1863, the focus of the two nations returned to northern Virginia, just southwest of Fredericksburg, at a house at the intersection of the Orange Turnpike and Orange Plank Road. On the border of a thick wood, the Chancellor's House would witness a textbook Southern victory, although one that the Confederate Army's commanding officer believed to be of only marginal significance. The battle represented the anticipated re-match between Lee's Army of Northern Virginia and the Army of the Potomac after the Confederates had notched a victory the previous December at Fredericksburg. It was the major story of the first two weeks of May. Only the arrest by the demoted Burnside and the military trial of former Ohio Congressman Clement L. Vallandigham briefly challenged Chancellorsville for the nation's lead news.

New York's *Tribune* and *Herald* each ran a map on May 5 that showed where Chancellorsville was situated relative to Fredericksburg. By May 7, the *Tribune* still had not determined a winner, though the battle had ended the day before. However, Greeley's newspaper reported that Major General Joseph Hooker's troops had taken 8,000 Confederate prisoners. The *Herald* called the fighting "terrible" and "desperate."[71] One day, later, Greeley expressed "a disagreeable shock" over the battle's outcome, in which Hooker retreated across the Rappahannock.[72] The *Herald* reported that Hooker's "retrograde movement" and a loss of "ten thousand or more" men had created "intense excitement" in New York.[73] The *Herald* editors opined that Major General Daniel E. Sickles of New York should replace Hooker. The *Times* was unwilling to concede and called Hooker's retreat a response to a storm that caused "a great rise" in the Rappahannock.[74] Likewise, the Philadelphia *Public Ledger* saw no defeat in the battle. It ran a headline on May 6 calling the battle a "Great Victory." The editors claimed the news to that point seemed "highly favorable to the Union cause."[75]

The Boston *Daily Advertiser* reported on May 6 that the situation at Chancellorsville was critical for the Union Army. It reported that Stonewall Jackson had routed Union Major General Oliver O. Howard's Eleventh Corps, that Southern soldiers had fought with "Desperate Valor," and that the federal government had employed a "rigid" censorship of the telegraph.[76] That same day, elsewhere in the paper, the *Advertiser* also stated that Jackson had been stymied, and that the Chancellor's house had been burned to the ground. Charles Hale's newspaper ran casualty lists on May 7, highlighting the dead, wounded, and captured from New England. The *Advertiser* described the battle's end as another "bitter disappointment" for the Union. The Army of the Potomac was the best-manned and supplied force the country had ever seen, according to Hale and his co-editors. Hooker, moreover, had an effective plan of battle, but "it has pleased

Providence to send us reverse instead of victory, and to defer to yet again the day when a Union army shall enter the capital of the Rebel confederacy."[77]

The Cincinnati *Daily Commercial* praised Hooker and initially disputed reports in some New York newspapers that he had retreated across the Rappahannock. Later, the *Commercial* admitted defeat was possible and urged its readers not to give into "despondency."[78] Editor Murat Halstead claimed Hooker had retreated in part because of a severe thunderstorm that made it impossible to keep the necessary provisions available to the Union Army, and that a week after the battle, Hooker had re-crossed the river and was on his way to Richmond—proving he had not been defeated. On the other hand, the pro-Democratic *New York Evening Express* termed Chancellorsville a loss because Hooker had failed in his attempt to reach Richmond. James and Erastus Brooks, criticizing Union strategy, wrote, "No keen eyed man of any occupation ever expected Hooker to reach Richmond by the route he has taken."[79]

The *Chicago Tribune* declared "the Situation Hopeful" in a May 7 headline about the battle near Fredericksburg, but the next day, the Republican newspaper reported that Hooker had marched back across the Rappahannock.[80] Hooker had judged the enemy too powerful, and thus the retreat was necessary, according to the *Tribune*, especially since Major General John Sedgwick's VI Corps had separated from the main Union force. The *Tribune* urged its readers not to despair: "The greater the disaster, the more courage we need to meet it—the more wise and resolute must be our councils." It was time for more men, not for turning back, Medill wrote. "Let the Conscript law have its fullest effect, not upon whites alone, but upon Blacks. Let us raise a whole army of Blacks, and throw their muscle, also, against the enemy."[81]

The pro-Democratic *Missouri Republican* reported "Hard Fighting at Chancellorsville" and the "Whole Army in Motion."[82] The St. Louis newspaper criticized the Lincoln administration for censoring the telegraph to prevent news of the battle from reaching the public. Still, George Knapp's journal praised the valor of the troops—in particular Brigadier General George Stoneman of the U.S. Cavalry—while trying to remain neutral on a verdict. Then, on May 10, the *Republican* printed an incredible front-page story (based on a rumor from Philadelphia) claiming a Union force from the peninsula had captured Richmond. In the *Republican* that same day, the editors stated that the story was a "cruel fiction."[83]

Southern journals sounded a different note, with the Lynchburg *Virginian* claiming Lee would have destroyed Hooker's army if a thunderstorm had not stopped the fighting. The newspaper reminded readers to keep the victory in perspective: the Union had a far greater army, and although Hooker had prepared for a victory that would have "annihilated our forces," Lee still won. Since Hooker's army came nowhere near Union goals, the Southern victory was as a major one, as reflected in Lee's praise for his soldiers. "Under the trying vicissitudes of heat and storm you attacked the enemy entrenched in the depths of a tangled wilderness, and again on the hills of Fredericksburg fifteen miles distant," Lee said.

> By your valor, triumphant on so many fields, [you have] forced him once more to seek safety beyond the Rappahannock, while glorious victory redounds to your praise; and you are especially called upon to return grateful thanks to the only giver of victory, for the signal deliverance He has wrought for us.[84]

The Augusta *Chronicle & Sentinel* published an intimate account of the battle with a letter from a Georgia soldier named Henry L. Leon, who wrote that bullets had hit him twice, but he was not severely hurt. Leon said he would only miss a week of duty. He mentioned the loss of three comrades in the Georgia Tenth Regiment. "The Yankees are badly whipped, and thousands of them killed," he added. "The Yankees have left their dead on the field without burying them, and it is a horrible sight to see."[85] Three weeks after the battle, Raleigh's *Weekly Standard* published a list of North Carolina's dead and wounded. It took up two and a half columns, and the end of each regiment listed included a tally of killed, wounded, and missing, with most of the regiments suffering more than one hundred casualties.[86]

"Jackson's Fame Will Endure"

The Southern victory had a major cost: the death of Lieutenant General Thomas J. "Stonewall" Jackson, Lee's top officer, who died May 10 after a wound from friendly fire eight days earlier. Jackson had attempted a night attack after the day battle at Chancellorsville, believing victory was within his grasp if he could push the Union Army once more. Attacking from the west worked, but it did not allow Jackson enough daylight hours to complete his task. He restlessly tried to organize and rally his men just up the road from the Chancellor's House, but darkness made it difficult to tell who was who. Unfortunately, for the general, soldiers from the North Carolina Seventh Regiment under C.S.A. Brigadier General James H. Lane accidentally shot Jackson as he travelled along Orange Turnpike near the intersection with Bullock Road. The Tar Heel soldiers knew Union troops were not far away and mistakenly took Jackson's party for the enemy at about 9:30 p.m. After three. 57-caliber bullets struck Jackson—his left arm shot twice and his right wrist once—he was taken to a field hospital behind the Confederate lines. He survived the wounds, but C.S.A. Surgeon Hunter H. McGuire had to amputate his severely wounded left arm at the field hospital to prevent gangrene. After the surgery on May 3, an ambulance transported him to a cottage on the Chandler farm twenty-seven miles away near Guinea's Station. The Virginia general died a week later of complications from pneumonia.

No other soldier killed in the war spurred such a journalistic outpouring. Prose in the Southern papers was more poetic, but Northern journals also ably captured the significance of the event. Jackson brought comparisons to Napoleon, and his loss was seen as ominous for the Southern cause. The Augusta *Chronicle & Sentinel* suggested the jubilee that rang through the land with news of the Fredericksburg victory had been interrupted by the dirge of a bereaved people. Editor Nathan Morse called Jackson brave, bold, patriotic, successful, and pure. He attempted to put his life in perspective, comparing him favorably to Napoleon: "Coming generations of boys will dwell on the exploits of Jackson in the Shenandoah Valley with an interest and amazement equal to anything which was ever excited by the record of the wonderful campaigns of the great French conqueror."[87] The Lynchburg *Virginian* emphasized Jackson's religious fervor: "He cared nothing for men, but the cause was everything for him. He prayed as well as labored for it, devoutly asking God's blessing upon what he did, with a single view to a great end."[88] The Richmond *Enquirer* praised Jackson by running the official dispatches of the Virginia Military Institute, where the general had served as a professor before the war.

Govan Hill, VMI's acting adjutant, wrote that Jackson "was peculiarly our own" and told the corps of cadets that the general's memory "is very precious to you. You know how faithfully, how conscientiously he discharged every duty."[89] *Weekly Standard* editor W. W. Holden wrote: "The death of no other citizen of the Confederate States would have as deep a grief. The loss which the cause has suffered by his removal from the world cannot be overstated." Holden used themes of patriotism and religious zeal seen in the other Southern papers, claiming Jackson's "fame will endure."[90] Under the general's obituary, Holden ran a short report about the Chancellorsville victory and a list of Tar Heel casualties. Elsewhere on the same page, he published a dispatch on the battle from a correspondent of the Richmond *Examiner*. The Atlanta *Intelligencer* reiterated the melancholy theme, saying that Jackson's death "cast a gloom over this community. ... Peace to his ashes."[91]

A week later, Holden featured a whole column's worth of information about Jackson on the front page of the *Weekly Standard*, including a dispatch from the *Examiner* on the general's body lying in state at the Confederate Capitol in Richmond. The story told of Jackson being placed in an "elegant metallic burial" casket covered by the Confederate flag.[92] Elsewhere, the Raleigh editor ran an article about the details of Jackson's death, although it did not mention that the regimental soldiers who mistakenly shot him at Chancellorsville were from North Carolina. The story also noted that Jackson was further hurt when he fell as the federals fired upon his litter-bearers. Jackson believed the pneumonia that ultimately would kill him was started from the injuries he received when he fell from the litter.

Northern newspapers were equally profuse in their praise of the Virginian. The Cleveland *Plain Dealer* commented that Jackson's loss "will be as severely felt by the Rebels as the loss of a battle—nay, as the loss of an army."[93] *The New York Herald* wrote that Jackson was "the most brilliant Rebel general developed by the war. From his coolness and sagacity, rapid movements and stubbornness in fight, and his invariable good fortune, he resembled Napoleon in his early career more than does any other general of modern times."[94] The *Herald* also ran a profile of Jackson's life. It stretched for an entire column and included high-lights of the battles he had won. *The New York Times* argued that the South had "unquestionably lost by far their greatest military leader," adding, "his death is a tremendous and irreparable loss to the secession cause, as no other Rebel of like character has been developed during the war. He will figure in history as one of the ablest of modern military leaders."[95] The *Tribune* reported that military bands on December 12 played "dirges a greater portion of the afternoon" in memory of Jackson.[96] The general exercised, the *Tribune* noted, "a great personal influence over his men, never wearing a showy uniform, often marching on foot, and going into battle with a musket in his hand, and in the dress of a private, so as to elude the delicate attentions of hostile sharpshooters." Greeley concluded: "There is no man left in the Rebel service whose loss would be so generally or keenly felt."[97] The Philadelphia *Public Ledger* observed that Jackson "gave our generals more trouble than all the others put together."[98] The Cincinnati *Daily Commercial* commented: "His name will forever be prominent, shining with a brilliant but baleful light, in the records of these strange and significant times."[99] *The Chicago Tribune* suggested that history, "when she recounts her final verdict against the infamous rebellion," would rank Jackson among "the most active and determined of its misguided agents."[100]

It is not possible to conclude that Jackson's death changed the tide of the war, as other factors contributed to the North's march toward victory. In spring 1863, the Army of Northern Virginia had proven to be dominant over the Army of the Potomac in the first two years of the war. With the exception of Antietam, the Confederates had seemed to win every major clash in the Eastern theater, and yet, as historian Allan Nevins put it, Robert E. Lee's army was in the long run "permanently weakened" by every encounter, while the Union military continued to gather strength both in human and material resources.[101] The North simply was the stronger nation, and was fated to win if the South could not deliver a dramatic blow. Furthermore, Lee sensed that Chancellorsville was not a decisive victory because he was unable to pursue Joseph Hooker's force. While Southern newspapers thanked Lee for yet another success, he worried about how he would carry on without Jackson. "Our loss was severe," he wrote of Chancellorsville, "and again we had not got an inch of ground."[102] Still, as historian Gary Gallagher observed, the series of Lee triumphs "nurtured among the Confederate citizenry an expectation of continued success. That expectation in turn would sustain hopes for Southern independence during two more years of grinding war."[103]

Victories Revised

Perhaps the North as a whole was less restless with this setback because Hooker had reconstructed his army so well and because Lee suffered. Furthermore, news of the battle—and the defeat—was relatively slow to reach newspaper readers in the North, so the sense of panic was mitigated. Many papers only began reporting on it upon its completion, and the truncation of the telegraph dispatches from the front and from Washington contributed to the relative dearth of information. Regardless, Fredericksburg, Stones River, and Chancellorsville brought insecurity and fear to the North, especially after significant conservative Democratic gains in the House of Representatives and in state legislatures in the 1862 fall elections. Only the split decision at Murfreesboro, coming after the Fredericksburg debacle, provided a little daylight for the Northern journals. Perhaps the Northern newspapers' more intensive reporting and their greater degree of graphic coverage contributed to this overall air of uncertainty—the better the reporting of defeat, the greater the sense of public skepticism.

Conversely, Southern editors were ecstatic. Their new nation might just become recognized internationally, and the gains of Northern Democrats might mean the Copperheads—the opposition group in the Union advocating peace—might actually sway public opinion enough to end the war and cement a two-nation solution to the irrepressible conflict. Still, the Confederate press never explained how Jackson's dramatic flanking action on May 2 at Chancellorsville really did not give Lee any significant advantage in the battle. That march was a textbook maneuver, but it took so long and spread out Jackson's army so much that the former VMI professor was unable to attack early enough in the day to gain decisive victory. Still, Hooker had failed—and failed dramatically—and Chancellorsville was a Southern victory. For the Union, another general had tried to destroy Lee's army, and another had disappointed his president, the Congress, and his nation.

Before Gettysburg and Vicksburg, editors in New York, Cleveland, and Chicago had urged resolve and patience amid the uncertainty the heavy losses had brought to the North in 1862. Editors in Richmond, Raleigh, and Atlanta had meanwhile preached hope and confidence, but the losses of July 4, 1863, shattered their optimism. While newspapers North and South had different tones, the majority in both sections attempted to analyze precisely what had occurred on the battlefield, often with partial or faulty information. Military campaigns took days and sometimes weeks or months, and reporters had to rely on rumor and distant observation, while governments on both sides squelched the telegraph lines.

What correspondents could report with certainty was that a given battle was fought fiercely, contested severely and desperately, the firing was hot, the hospitals were overcrowded, and that innuendo abounded. Reporting from the front was at best sketchy, and quoting sources had not yet become a staple of American journalism. Meanwhile, editors back in the home office struggled to assess what was happening in the field and had to rely on correspondents' judgment. Moreover, newspapers that could not afford reporters at the front repeated accounts from elsewhere, relying on what was published in the New York dailies.

Journalistic practices used during these major battles followed a pattern of placing the news—information—on the front page and interpretation of developments on the second. Newspapers with greater resources covered battles intimately and daily via correspondents in the field, and constantly updated information with telegraphic updates and even special telegraphic editions. Newspapers with fewer resources, meanwhile, had to rely on military dispatches, clippings from other journals, and letters from soldiers to tell the stories of battles. Urban dailies already produced sophisticated information, and, by contrast, small-city dailies and the weeklies operated in a more interpretive mode, emphasizing editorial opinion. Regardless, each paper attempted to make meaning of the fighting—to determine a winner and characterize the results' significance in the overall war. It was a clumsy process that yielded many mistakes (i.e., the *Missouri Republican*'s headline about Richmond's capture), but the press believed it offered readers a valuable public service.

Within a year, the tone of editorial spin took a dramatic turn in another direction, as Confederate victories yielded to setbacks and Union armies for the first time made dramatic gains. Changes to interpretation came with the concurrent results of Gettysburg and Vicksburg. Throughout the North, editors heralded the victory at Gettysburg as a long-awaited triumph—in the words of The Hartford *Daily Courant*, a "glorious day for the Republic" and a sign that the Confederacy had finally been "broken."[104] Other Northern newspapers, less prone to celebrate, saw Gettysburg as a victory, but a costly one. Among them was The Boston *Daily Advertiser*, which questioned whether the Lincoln administration or the Pennsylvania governor had prepared in any way for Lee's invasion.[105] Reports elsewhere, such as in the Philadelphia *Public Ledger*, included inaccurate information, mistakenly claiming that Gettysburg featured 22,000 Union soldiers against 50,000 Confederates. In fact, Lee had 89,000 men, while Meade, who had replaced Hooker on June 28 as commander of the Army of the Potomac, had 122,000 men at his disposal. The *Public Ledger* was correct to suggest that the first week of July 1863 would "hereafter be regarded as one of the most memorable in the history of our country, and considering that the fate of the republic probably rested upon it, one of the most momentous which has ever occurred to any nation."[106]

Descriptions of events outside the North conveyed dramatically different angles, as editors in the South simply may have wanted to believe Lee had not lost. A correspondent for the Savannah (Ga.) *Republican*, for example, claimed the Union had sustained twice as many casualties as the Confederacy, when in fact the Union had suffered just over 23,000, to the C.S.A.'s 28,000-plus. Furthermore, the Savannah reporter wrote, Lee had retreated to Hagerstown, Maryland, in a strategic move because Meade's forces had retired, allowing Lee to reopen communication lines, and "for other reasons not proper to mention, though satisfactory."[107] Editors Nathaniel Tyler and W. B. Allegre of the Richmond *Enquirer* steeped their accounts in even more denial, suggesting that although the South could carry on a defensive war for another forty years, gaining peace through Union surrender at Gettysburg would have been "altogether to our disadvantage." Gettysburg was in fact, they claimed, a "magnificent victory" for Lee, but they also noted its cost. Still, they believed the South was on a new path to peace and independence, and they were "firmer than ever in the belief that peace will come to us only in one way—by the edge of the sword."[108] Now that the Southern soldier had gained an appetite for fighting in the North, he would want more. Cincinnati would be razed, and the four slave states in the Union would return to the Southern fold.

Regardless of the glorious—albeit conflicting—accounts of the events at Gettysburg, it remains a historical curiosity that another military event of equal, if not greater, significance—the surrender of Vicksburg to General Ulysses S. Grant—received less attention in the contemporary press. The geographic distance of Vicksburg from the major publishers of the East no doubt interfered to some degree with its presence on the news page, as assigning reporters to cover the event, let alone transmit it, would have provided logistical and economic challenges. In addition, the surrender of Vicksburg occurred on July 4, concurrent with the outcome of the battle of Gettysburg.

Newspapers did take note, with the Philadelphia *Public Ledger* calling Vicksburg "the second great victory" of the week, noting that the citizens of St. Louis seemed even more gratified by news from Mississippi than from the Eastern campaign. "Grant's victory at Vicksburg is no less important to the cause of the Republic, and decisive against rebellion," the editors wrote, "than the rout of Lee in Pennsylvania."[109] An account from St. Louis of events in Mississippi from the pro-Democratic *Missouri Republican* described it as the most important Union triumph of the war. In its coverage of Gettysburg, *Republican* editor George Knapp had relied on reports from the Baltimore *American*, declaring Gettysburg a victory but also noting that both sides had suffered terrible losses. The twin victories prompted the newspaper to make a political point: Knapp wondered why Grant received praise for his long, gradual war on the Mississippi while Lincoln had taken the Army of the Potomac from McClellan when the general used a similar strategy on the Peninsula in Virginia. "McClellan is to-day in retirement because he conducted war on military principles, just as Grant has done," the editorial noted. "The distance between Grant and Washington City has been his salvation as an officer."[110]

Maybe it was the draft. Maybe it was the inclusion of Black soldiers. Maybe it was the tattered condition of the Confederate Army. Maybe it was the string of unprecedented and far-reaching congressional legislation—including the Homestead Act, the Morrill Act, emancipation, and the transcontinental railroad. Concretely, it would be Lee's decision to undertake a second invasion of the North two months after Chancellorsville with his smaller army. This time, the Virginian, without his greatest aide in Jackson, would witness a reversal of fortune. Now under General George G. Meade, the Army of the Potomac gained victory at Gettysburg, Pennsylvania. Simultaneously, in the West, Major General Ulysses S. Grant captured Vicksburg, Mississippi, after months of grueling battle. Whatever advantage the South had gained from its two victories in northern Virginia and the draw in Middle Tennessee it all but lost in 1863 on the Fourth of July.

Notes

1 Greeley to Wilkeson, January 17, 1862, unpublished letter, courtesy Seth Kaller, Inc., Historic Documents & Legacy Collections.
2 Ibid, February 3, 1862.
3 "Virginia. Newspaper Vendor and Cart in Camp," Library of Congress, accessed November 4, 2021, at <loc.gov/resource/cwpb.01140>.
4 Greeley to Samuel Wilkeson, May 27, 1863, unpublished letter, courtesy Seth Kaller, Inc., Historic Documents & Legacy Collections.
5 New York *Tribune*, December 16, 1862.
6 Ibid, December 19, 1862.
7 New York *Herald*, December 15, 1862.
8 Ibid, December 12, 1862.
9 Ibid, December 14, 1862.
10 New York *Evening Express*, December 15, 1862.
11 New York *Times*, December 14, 1862.
12 New York *Herald*, December 15, 1862.
13 Ibid, December 17, 1862.
14 New York *Evening Express*, December 16, 1862.
15 New York *Tribune*, December 15, 1862.
16 Ibid, December 23, 24, 1862.
17 New York *Times*, December 17, 1862.
18 Cleveland *Plain Dealer*, December 17, 1862.
19 Boston *Daily Advertiser*, December 18, 1862.
20 Ibid, December 16, 1862.
21 Philadelphia (PA) *Public Ledger and Daily Transcript*, December 17, 1862.
22 Cincinnati *Daily Commercial*, December 17 1862.
23 Chicago *Tribune*, December 13, 14, 1862.
24 Ibid, December 16, 1862.
25 Ibid, December 19, 1862.
26 "Campaign in Virginia—A Street in Harper's Ferry during the Passage of the Potomac by the National Troops from Maryland, October 24, 1862," Library of Congress, accessed July 1, 2021, at <loc.gov/item/2002714248>.

27 *Missouri Republican*, December 16, 17, 1862.
28 Ibid, December 21, 1862.
29 Atlanta *Intelligencer*, December 14, 1862.
30 Richmond (VA) *Enquirer*, quoted in the Lynchburg *Virginian*, May 4, 1863.
31 Raleigh (NC) *Weekly Standard*, May 6, 1863.
32 Lynchburg *Virginian*, December 15, 1862.
33 Ibid, December 16, 1862.
34 Richmond *Enquirer*, quoted in the Lynchburg *Virginian*, December 17, 1862.
35 Lynchburg *Virginian*, December 16, 1862.
36 Raleigh (NC) *Weekly Standard*, December 17, 1862.
37 Lynchburg *Virginian*, December 18, 1862.
38 Ibid, December 19, 1862.
39 Raleigh (NC) *Weekly Standard*, May 13, 1863.
40 New York *Herald*, quoted in the Lynchburg *Virginian*, December 22, 1862.
41 Lynchburg *Virginian*, December 19, 20, 1862.
42 Ibid, January 1, 1863.
43 New York *Herald*, quoted in the Lynchburg *Virginian*, January 2, 1863.
44 Raleigh (NC) *Weekly Standard*, December 31, 1862.
45 Augusta (GA) *Chronicle & Sentinel*, January 1, 1863.
46 Raleigh (NC) *Weekly Standard*, December 24, 1862.
47 New York *Tribune*, January 3, 5, 1863.
48 New York *Times*, January 6, 1863.
49 New York *Herald*, January 3, 4, 1863.
50 Ibid, January 4, 1863.
51 Philadelphia (PA) *Public Ledger and Daily Transcript*, January 5, 1863.
52 Springfield (MA) *Republican*, January 3, 1863.
53 Louisville (KY) *Journal*, January 7, 1863.
54 Boston *Daily Advertiser*, January 4, 1863.
55 Cleveland *Plain Dealer*, January 5, 6, 1863.
56 Cincinnati *Daily Commercial*, January 5, 1863.
57 Chicago *Tribune*, January 5, 1863.
58 Ibid, January 8, 1863.
59 *Missouri Republican*, January 16, 1863.
60 Richmond (VA) *Examiner*, January 2, 1863.
61 Augusta (GA) *Chronicle & Sentinel*, January 4, 1863.
62 Lynchburg *Virginian*, January 2, 1863.
63 Ibid, January 4, 1863.
64 Greensborough (NC) *Patriot*, January 8, 15, 22, 1863.
65 Vicksburg *Citizen*, quoted in the Greensborough (NC) *Patriot*, January 22, 1863.
66 Raleigh (NC) *Weekly Standard*, January 7, 1863.
67 Augusta (GA) *Chronicle & Sentinel*, January 6, 1863.

68 Raleigh (NC) *Weekly Standard*, January 7, 1863.

69 Augusta (GA) *Chronicle & Sentinel*, January 5, 1863.

70 Chicago *Tribune*, January 7, 1863.

71 New York *Herald*, May 7, 1863.

72 Ibid, May 8, 1863.

73 Ibid, May 9, 1863.

74 New York *Times*, May 8, 1863.

75 Philadelphia (PA) *Public Ledger and Daily Transcript*, May 11, 1863.

76 Boston *Daily Advertiser*, May 6, 1863.

77 Ibid, May 8, 1863.

78 Cincinnati *Daily Commercial*, May 8, 1863.

79 New York *Evening Express*, May 8, 1863.

80 Chicago *Tribune*, May 7, 1863.

81 Ibid, May 8, 1863.

82 *Missouri Republican*, May 4, 5, 1863.

83 Ibid, May 11, 1863.

84 Lynchburg *Virginian*, May 11, 1863.

85 Augusta (GA) *Chronicle & Sentinel*, May 12, 1863.

86 Raleigh (NC) *Weekly Standard*, May 27, 1863.

87 Augusta (GA) *Chronicle & Sentinel*, May 12, 1863.

88 Lynchburg *Virginian*, May 12, 1863.

89 Richmond (VA) *Enquirer*, May 22, 1863.

90 Raleigh (NC) *Weekly Standard*, May 13, 1863.

91 Atlanta *Intelligencer*, May 12, 1863.

92 Raleigh (NC) *Weekly Standard*, May 20, 1863.

93 Cleveland *Plain Dealer*, May 13, 1863.

94 New York *Herald*, May 14, 1863.

95 New York *Times*, May 14, 1863.

96 New York *Tribune*, May 13, 1863.

97 Ibid, May 14, 1863.

98 Philadelphia (PA) *Public Ledger and Daily Transcript*, May 14, 1863.

99 Cincinnati *Daily Commercial*, May 14, 1863.

100 Chicago *Tribune*, May 7, 1863.

101 Allan Nevins, *The War for the Union, Volume II: War Becomes Revolution* (New York: Charles Scribner's Sons, 1960), 429.

102 Robert E. Lee, quoted in Gary Gallagher, *The Battle of Chancellorsville* (Washington, DC: Eastern National, 1995), 53.

103 Gallagher, *The Battle of Chancellorsville*, 55.

104 Hartford (CT) *Daily Courant*, July 9, 1863.

105 Boston *Daily Advertiser*, July 6, 1863.

106 Philadelphia (PA) *Public Ledger and Daily Transcript*, July 6, 1863.

107   Savannah (GA) *Republican*, July 14, 1863.
108   Richmond (VA) *Enquirer*, July 8, 1863.
109   Philadelphia (PA) *Public Ledger and Daily Transcript*, July 8, 1863.
110   *Missouri Republican*, July 4, 5, 8, 9, 1863.

5

Journalistic Practice and Technological Change

"What Hath God Wrought?" Samuel F. B. Morse's first official transmission, opening the Baltimore-Washington telegraph line, May 24, 1844 (The Book of Numbers, 23:23).

Before the Civil War, American newspapers operated primarily for political purposes. While this remained the case throughout a war fought largely for political reasons, journalism changed rapidly in the mid-nineteenth century, with several technological innovations affecting the press dramatically. Major developments included improvements in the steam press; diffusion of a telegraphic network; inclusion of graphical art and illustrations such as portraits, tables, and maps; and the advent of documentary photojournalism. While the general transformation of news from political purposes to informative ones made it a fixture unlike in any time before, the catastrophic events of the Civil War—a nation divided, hundreds of thousands dead, the institution of slavery hanging in the balance—brought a new emphasis to the purpose of the press.

Technology changed reporting during the war. The telegraph especially affected news by quickly transmitting information over long distances and conveying a unified impression of events, since the telegraph was a single channel. Improvements in the reproduction of woodcuts also played role, pushing the top urban dailies—specifically *Harper's Weekly* and *Frank Leslie's Illustrated Newspaper*—into the early days of the Visual Age. Further, photographic images shaped readers' understanding of the war, as improvements in the ability of the steam press to produce newspapers at greater speeds and at greater volume facilitated the expansion of newspaper audiences.

The Printing Press and Telegraph

Hundreds of years before the Civil War, Johannes Gutenberg had set into motion a revolution in information delivery that is still very much with us today. Changes brought about by the introduction of his fifteenth-century press eventually led to Civil War-era printers being able to produce information quickly and efficiently. This process wrested the power over information from elites and put it into the hands of a democratized electorate. Average people could increasingly understand both economic issues and their rights as defined by a civil law, and in the 1860s, American publishers could produce tens of thousands of papers each day using modern machines that had stemmed more recently from the industrial revolution.

In 1814, Friedrich Koenig of Germany developed a two-cylinder steam press capable of printing on both sides of a sheet of paper by using a movable bed that carried the type back and forth for inking after each impression, producing eleven hundred newspapers per hour. By 1830, David Napier in England fine-tuned Koenig's press so that it could produce more than 3,000 papers per hour. By 1843, Richard M. Hoe of New York had invented a rotary device known as the "lightning press," which American publishers began using in 1846. Hoe used horizontal cylinders for the flat bed of the Koenig press and sunk curved iron beds into the cylinders. At first, the improved Hoe press could produce 12,000 newspapers per hour, and by the Civil War, it cranked out 20,000 per hour. *The New York Herald*, reporting on Fort Sumter, produced 135,000 Sunday issues using the Hoe press. Many newspapers, including *The New York Tribune*, paid tribute to the invention with an engraving of it in their nameplate at the top of the front page.

Another critical innovation was development of the round stereotype by Swiss inventor James Dellagana. Working in London in 1855, Dellagana created curved, solid casting plates that were one-sixth-inch thick. The plates were hollow and easy to handle. The type was impressed on a soft mold, making a type-plate. This made it possible to run type across columns and ushered in larger headlines—a particularly significant innovation, as editors could now run bold, multi-decked headlines announcing the results of battles. It also enhanced the appeal of advertising space by facilitating bigger ads that brought in more revenue. The *Times of London* was the first to use these plates, beginning in 1857.

These improvements in the printing press allowed newspapers to package the news in unique ways. Before, editors simply filled the columns with text. Headlines were relatively small, only a few points bigger than the main body type. Now, papers used both graphics and multi-decked headlines. These headlines could emphasize several aspects of a news story. For example, in its reporting of the battle of Fredericksburg, Virginia, in December 1862, *The Chicago Tribune* ran a headline that featured several decks: "From Fredericksburg. The War in Virginia. Our Forces Recross the River. They Remove their Pontoon Bridges. Special Dispatch to Gov. Morton."[1] Not to be outdone, *The New York Tribune* employed even more headers and subheads: "The Battle of Fredericksburg. A Full and Detailed Description. A Council of the Generals. A Charge of the Rebel Works Decided on. The Organization of the Forces. The Gallantry and Bravery of Our Troops. The Most Intense Fighting of the War. Some of the Rebel Works Carried. Our Troops Obliged to Fall Back. Great Strength of the Rebel Positions. The Object Sought Unattained."[2] Yet those two could not match the Cleveland *Plain Dealer*, which used fifteen decks for its coverage of the battle. Among the fifteen was a line that vastly overstated the strength of the Rebel forces at Fredericksburg: "Rebel Army Estimated at 200,000 Strong."[3] The technology had advanced changes, if not precision, in Civil War journalism.

With the exception of the printing press itself, no single invention in human history has had a more profound effect on mass communication than the electronic telegraph. It produced an age of information, and, in the middle of the nineteenth century, suddenly made speed the key trait of its transmission and reception. Telegraphy had existed for centuries, but not in an electronic form. It consisted first of smoke signals and then later, in France, a complex system of line-of-sight signals invented by Claude Chappe in 1792. His optical telegraphy system, which lasted approximately half a century, relied on a system in which one elevated station flashed signals using pivoting shutters to another over distances that could not exceed the horizon. Chappe's system had its own code, with thousands of symbols. However, it was limited to daytime use and was weather-dependent. The electronic telegraph, transmitted over wires, overcame both of those problems and covered virtually unlimited distances.

Danish physicist Hans Christian Oersted's discovery in 1819 that a wire carrying an electronic current had an effect on a magnetized needle compass sowed the seeds of the modern electronic telegraph. In Great Britain, William F. Cooke and Sir Charles Wheatstone invented an electronic signaling device that had five needles. Railroad operators applied the invention as a way of helping control traffic. However, the needle system proved too inefficient. A telegraph that used an electromagnet replaced it after American Joseph Henry developed, in 1830, a device that could ring a bell on a wire that was more than a mile in length. Then, in 1838, Samuel F. B. Morse and Alfred Vail improved on Henry's invention by developing a telegraphic key that imprinted a code of dots and dashes on a roll of paper. Morse constructed a code that corresponded to the alphabet and the numbers zero to nine.

Journalistically, electronic telegraphy had the greatest impact on reporting news. As mass communication historian Hazel Dicken-Garcia observed, the telegraph was largely responsible for improving access to news during the war.[4] Only fifty years before, a story published by a Charleston, South Carolina, newspaper about an event in New York might be twenty days old when it reached its audience in the Southern port city. Now the telegraph enabled journalists to transmit and receive information instantly over long distances. Thus, newspapers benefited from Morse's innovation, as it had once taken days—even weeks—to spread from one region of the nation to another could appear in print the next day.

In a larger context, the telegraph had a transformative effect on society in general. Communications scholar James Carey described this process in a seminal work on the telegraph, tracing much of our modern understanding of time and space to the development of instant messaging. "The simplest and most important point about the telegraph is that it marked the decisive separation of 'transportation' and 'communication,'" Carey wrote. "Until the telegraph, these words were synonymous. The telegraph ended that identity and allowed symbols to move independently of geography and independently and faster than transport."[5]

Morse's invention delivered up to three times more information per minute than had the old optical telegraph.[6] By the beginning of the Civil War, the electronic device allowed journals to place additional information about the various theatres of war from the previous day. During the war, newspapers that had once carried only a few columns of telegraphic news now had several pages of it. An editor for a daily would stay late into the night to get telegraphic updates. Newspapers would also have telegraphic editions—between-cycle publications that provided up-to-date information of battles in progress. During especially significant events, there might be several telegraphic editions in a single day. All of this made the Civil War newspaper far more informative than its antebellum counterpart had been, although the trend was not as strong in smaller cities and towns across the continent.

On May 24, 1844, Morse made the first official telegraphic transmission using his device by opening the telegraph connection between Baltimore and Washington, D.C.—communicating via dots and dashes the perhaps ominous question "What Hath God Wrought?" from the Bible (Book of Numbers, 23:23). Forty miles away, Morse's associate Alfred Vail received the electric signals and returned the message. As those who witnessed it understood, this demonstration would change the world. The speed at which messengers could travel previously limited both the quality and quantity of content delivered. Therefore, "when Morse tapped out those four words on his electric telegraph," historian Daniel Walker Howe notes, "he was not only decoupling communication from travel and enabling and speeding up commerce, but also fostering globalization and encouraging democratic participation."[7]

The first practical use of Morse's invention was reporting of the Whig National Convention in Baltimore in 1844. Using a line between Washington and Annapolis, Morse transmitted the news that Henry Clay of Kentucky had won the nomination for president. A correspondent in Baltimore had gathered the information and had traveled by train to Annapolis. There, he gave the information to a telegraph operator stationed near the depot, who tapped out Clay's name to the waiting receiver in the nation's capital. When the train from Annapolis arrived in Washington, passengers thought they were bearing fresh news. However, they were merely confirming what Morse already had proclaimed to be the truth. Thus, on that day in May, "Speed with Heed" became the new mantra of American journalism. A communication revolution had occurred, and the telegraph was king. A nation of regional interests suddenly opened upon itself—a phenomenon described by Howe as giving "new urgency to social criticism and to the slavery controversy in particular."[8]

Newspaper editors in New York were among the first to realize the potential of the new invention. Along with a daily newspaper in Philadelphia, they formed the Associated Press wire service to share information over long distances. Before the Associated Press (originally the New York AP), the newspapers had competed for time on the wire, and this was too costly. Furthermore, managing all of the information transmitted was a task beyond the abilities of even the best-managed metropolitan dailies.[9] The AP originally had bureaus in New York, Albany, and Washington, and it established favorable relationships with Western Union and the American Telegraph Company. These newspapers cooperated with each other originally, as they wanted to share news from the war in Mexico. Yet competing editors began to worry that these few urban newspapers would come to dominate the shape of news in the country, and thus began forming their own wire services.[10] By 1860, more than 50,000 miles of telegraph wire stretched across the country, much of it along railroad routes, with a line from New York to San Francisco opening in 1861. Ironically, as editors touted the telegraph as an instrument of unity, advocating westward expansion, in the East the nation had grown increasingly divided over slavery.[11]

Early in the war, William H. Pritchard established the Southern Associated Press in Richmond under after the Union military commandeered the American Telegraph Company and cut Southern access to its lines. However, editors disdained the Southern AP's high prices, unreliability, and generally poor quality. Thus, in February 1863, the Press Association of the Confederate States of America was born. By May of that year, it had forty-four subscribers. Centered in Atlanta, the Press Association had twenty reporters from Virginia to Mississippi who earned twenty-five dollars a week.[12] John S. Thrasher, its superintendent, put a premium on speed, clarity, and conciseness. He also believed that dispatches should be free of opinion and should not reveal military secrets. Thrasher had correspondents in Richmond and Charleston, and with the Confederate Army. One of the problems the Press Association faced was that reporters sometimes were not located at the scene of battle. Accounts of the fighting at Vicksburg in spring and summer 1863 came from a correspondent in Jackson, Mississippi.[13] His dispatches were woefully inaccurate, especially in terms of the Union military campaign's progress in finally capturing the port city.

Because newspapers paid for the telegraph by the word, reporters learned to write concise narratives. For some, this meant the omitting certain rhetorical devices, as well as sacrificing opinion for more emphasis on fact. Some correspondents began using a summary lead, fearing the enemy might cut their dispatches during transmission. The sooner they could transmit the story, the better, so it made sense to put the most important information at the top. Still, the majority of newspapers were not located along telegraph lines, so the postal exchange of newspapers remained an important way to diffuse the news of the day. Thus, stories were printed in the newspapers at the end of the line. Then papers beyond the line clipped those stories and printed them in their publications. This process took advantage of the fact that newspapers could exchange with other journals through the mail at no charge.

Image 5.1 "Rebel Telegraph Operator near Egypt, on the Mississippi Central R.R." *Frank Leslie's Illustrated Newspaper*, March 18, 1865. With the risk of enemy combatants intercepting sensitive information by tapping the wires of telegraphs for messages, the inverted pyramid style of news delivery ensured that the most important information would at least reach the intended receiver before any additional information was lost to an interfering party.[14]

While publishers relinquished almost all of the space reserved for editorials to war coverage, technology enhanced reporting—allowing for increases in quantity, quality, and transmission speed of news. As a result, what has since become an enduring feature of news—the inverted pyramid—became standardized practice. While publishers for particular reasons had used the inverted pyramid before the Civil War, this practice became more and more widely used as standard journalistic protocol, with the rationale stemming from war strategy.

Likewise, with the widespread publication of sensitive information in popular newspapers—much to the dismay of Union generals—Union Secretary of War Edwin Stanton required writers to include bylines as a way for the government and potential prosecutors to determine if the author inadvertently or intentionally disclosed to Southern intelligence news that jeopardized the lives of troops. For example, *The New York Tribune* at one point in the war revealed General William Tecumseh Sherman's plans of attack. Southern commanders adjusted their strategy accordingly and cost the Union lives. Stanton attempted to quell reckless publication with the bylines requirement, but Sherman called for censorship. "If I could have caught Mr. Greeley," the general said after the incident, "I would have hung him."[15]

As the telegraph began to put the country on one mass communication channel—in effect providing an increasingly objective story of what was happening in the war through more fact-based reporting—the temptation to fashion the narrative increased. In particular, the freedom to send uncensored reports from the field faced the obstacle of government interference. The first inkling of this occurred after the First Battle of Bull Run in July 1861, when reporters discovered their officials had censored their dispatches. Early in the battle, their transmissions faced no governmental obstruction. However, when the battle turned to favor the Confederates, Winfield Scott, chief of the Union Army, ordered termination of transmissions. Because of the news blackout, Northern newspapers wrongly reported the battle to be a victory.

The Illustrated Press

The most prolific use of graphics during the Civil War came from two magazines, *Harper's Weekly* and *Frank Leslie's Illustrated Newspaper*. Both of these publications began publishing after the Mexican War, so they became the first American journals to cover warfare with extensive graphical art. James, John, Wesley, and Fletcher Harper had christened Harper and Brothers publishing in 1825, and Fletcher began publishing *Harper's Monthly* in 1850. He originally intended the publication as a vehicle to promote authors such as Dickens and Thackeray, but it was so successful that it became *Harper's Weekly* in 1857.

Harper's primary competitor, Frank Leslie, was born Henry Carter in Suffolk, England. Leslie was an illustrator who had begun his journalistic drawing career with the *Illustrated News*, which P. T. Barnum and H. D. and A. E. Beach had owned. Leslie developed a publishing empire based on graphic journalism, and his strengths as a publisher came from the in-house engraving department and presses he designed for pictorial work, giving him an advantage with both price and quality of illustrations.[17]

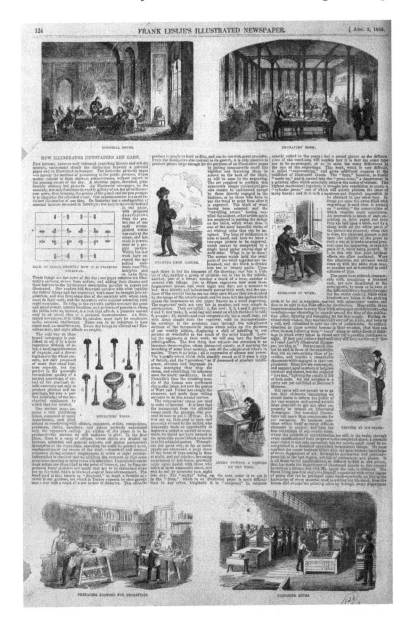

Image 5.2 "How Illustrated Newspapers are Made." *Frank Leslie's Illustrated Newspaper,* 2 (August 2, 1856): 124. The Library of Congress includes the following description of this image: "Ten illustrations showing editorial rooms, engravers' room, artists at work, engraving tools, etc., at offices of *Frank Leslie's Illustrated Newspaper.*"[16]

Both *Harper's* and *Leslie's* used woodcuts that were then impressed upon paper to create the images. These engravings came from illustrations made by sketch artists in the field. Both publications had to be weeklies because the process of creating the images took too long for a daily newspaper. While each covered sixteen pages, *Harper's* sold for six cents an issue and *Leslie's* for ten, with the former having a larger bankroll and thus being able to afford running costly illustrations at a loss, while Leslie had to make ends meet. Speed was increased by using a multiple-block system in which a drawing was divided into four or five segments. A different engraver worked on each block, and the blocks were then locked into a frame. A master engraver cut the lines that crossed the various blocks.

By the eve of the Civil War, *Harper's* circulation had reached 200,000 and *Leslie's* 100,000. The two magazines had sizable pools of sketch artists and reporters who spent much of their time behind enemy lines—drawing the disdain of Confederate officers, who generally saw Northern journalists as spies. Both magazines used large illustrations on their front page, but they also carried woodcuts on the interior pages. Pages eight and nine contained a large pictorial, known a century later as "double-truck" artwork. The first major event directly related to the Civil War that these two covered was John Brown's raid on Harpers Ferry in October 1859. In the first issue that depicted the raid and its immediate aftermath, *Harper's* ran illustrations of Marines storming the engine house, Brown lying wounded in prison, wounded mutineers in prison, Brown and his son awaiting a physical examination, a schoolhouse in the mountains where Brown stored weapons, and drawings of weapons used in the raid.[18] *Leslie's* artwork depicted the interior of the engine house.[19] The next week, *Harper's* featured Brown's trial, showing Brown talking to his attorney, the conspirators at their arraignment, and the courtroom in Charleston.[20] A month later, *Leslie's* ran an engraving of Brown ascending the scaffold just before his execution.[21]

The year that followed Brown's raid entailed, not coincidentally, the most consequential presidential election in U.S. history, with the press playing an unprecedented role in shaping public opinion. An image of Abraham Lincoln—the first of many taken while he was the Republican nominee—became so well known that he credited it in helping his election.[22]

Image 5.3 "Abraham Lincoln, Candidate for U.S. President, Three-quarter Length Portrait, before Delivering his Cooper Union Address in New York City." Mathew B. Brady, photographer, February 27, 1860. Lincoln spoke at the Cooper Union Institute in Manhattan the day of this photograph.[23]

Lincoln's address at Cooper Union clarified the views he had expressed about slavery in the 1858 debates and affirmed that he did not wish to see it expand into Western territories.[24] Before delivering it, Lincoln had taken a stroll on Broadway with a group of Republicans who were hosting his speech. He visited Brady's studio at the corner of Bleecker Street for a portrait. In the photograph, he stood still and beardless next to a table, resting his hand on a small stack of books.[25] The photograph, the "Cooper Union Portrait," became a model for distributed engravings, and the image would be the basis for campaign posters in the 1860 election.

Remarkably, the November 10, 1860, issue of *Harper's Weekly*, a leader in popularizing illustrated materials, published the woodcut version of the photo on its cover, heralding Lincoln's election (the mirrored reversal of the Lincoln image reflects the stenciled version of the photograph when transposed to a woodcut impression). This particular sketch by Winslow Homer for *Harper's* came off the press November 3, even before Lincoln's election.[26]

Homer had adapted Brady's photograph for the illustration, augmenting the original by adding more drapery for symmetry and an inkstand next to the books, suggesting a contemplative Lincoln. The illustration also includes a window with a view of bison grazing on a peaceful prairie in the background, promoting—in the view of *Harper's Weekly* editors—harmony between North and South that would ensue under Lincoln's administration.[27]

Yet, only months later, the war broke, and at the start of it, an engraving in *Harper's* showed citizens watching the bombing of Fort Sumter from a Charleston, South Carolina, rooftop. An engraving in that edition depicted citizens in New York gathered to support the federal government's war effort. Yet another drawing was of Harpers Ferry, with a reprint of a story about Brown's raid. Others showed regiments marching in New York, Jersey City, and New Jersey, as well as the Massachusetts Sixth attempting to resist rioters as it transited through Baltimore. A final engraving showed Union officers at Fort Sumter.[29]

A typical edition of *Harper's Weekly* can be found in its publication on the eve of the battle at Antietam, Lee's first invasion of the North. The September 20, 1862, cover was a single illustration of an officer holding a bearded standard-bearer. A fallen soldier is looking up at the stars and stripes while another marches forward with his musket pointing toward the sky. On page four is an illustration of Major General Don Carlos Buell in Decherd, Tennessee. The accompanying story appears several pages later and notes that Buell had readily employed freed slaves to work his camp, as directed by President Lincoln. Three illustrations on page five depict the defense of Cincinnati from Rebel invasion. The largest illustration in *Harper's* covered the eighth and ninth pages: a scene from Second Bull Run, which had been fought a month earlier. Major General Franz Sigel, a corps commander, appears on horseback in the foreground. Sigel gives an order to another officer, who salutes. While the battle rages in the background, several soldiers in front of Buell relax on the ground. Three other soldiers, each standing, are in conversation. Smoke fills much of background as soldiers march in columns and officers race around on horseback. A dead or wounded horse lies on the ground, and two men are carrying a third man on a litter from the field. The report that accompanied the illustration, filed by a correspondent of *The New York Tribune*, appeared on the previous page. On the next page is a map of Tennessee and Kentucky, showing the Western theater of Union operations. On page twelve are portraits of two fallen generals, Isaac J. Stevens and Phil Kearney. Also on that page is an illustration of the Hygeia Hotel in Old Point Comfort, Virginia. The next page had a portrait of Colonel Fletcher Webster, the son of Daniel Webster, who had been killed in the Second Battle of Bull Run on August

Image 5.4 "Hon. Abraham Lincoln, Born in Kentucky, February 12, 1809." While the outcome of the vote would not be certain for another week or two, *Harper's Weekly* issued this cover, confident in Lincoln's victory.[28]

30, 1862. Two illustrations at the bottom of the page accompanied a piece of fiction. On page sixteen, a Confederate soldier looks across the Ohio River at a father and son. The son says, "Daddy, Old Secesh's [secession] coming across sure." The father replies: "All right, Sonny! But I've been waiting a blessed long time for him."[30] A final illustration shows a volunteer at home with his wife and children.

The magazines often ran panoramic prints of battle. These highly detailed illustrations gave a sense of a battle's scope. They featured action, which made the prints far less static than portraits and maps. One such woodcut from *Harper's* shows a skirmish at Gettysburg. In it, a Union artillery battery fires from a hill at distant Confederate troops. Another landscape shows the Union center as a group of officers watches the battle from a battery on a bluff. A third shows a shell exploding during the battle.[31] Five months later, *Leslie's* featured a woodcut of the dedication of the Gettysburg battlefield, accompanied by a report on the ceremony, including the verbatim text of President Abraham Lincoln's address.[32] Both magazines put a premium on portraits of Union officers. *Harper's* cover for the Gettysburg edition was not George G. Meade, the commander of the Army of the Potomac, but, rather, Ulysses S. Grant, who had achieved the victory at Vicksburg. *Leslie's* ran portraits of generals with features and news stories on battles. Among the generals featured by *Leslie's* were Grant, William T. Sherman, William S. Rosecrans, Phillip H. Sheridan, John M. Schofield, John F. Reynolds, John Sedgwick, George H. Thomas, Benjamin F. Butler, Lewis Wallace, John Pope, John Buford, and Joseph Hooker, as well as admiral David G. Farragut of the U.S. Navy.

Likewise, the magazines emphasized images of President Lincoln. For example, *Leslie's* ran illustrations of Lincoln and General George McClellan reviewing the troops near Washington, D.C., in September 1861 and at Harrison's Landing, Virginia, in July 1862.[33] *Harper's* ran a cartoon of the president standing next to a tree with an ax in hand. The tree has "Slavery" written on it, and a barefoot man cowers in the upper branches, with the caption reading, "Now, if you don't come down, I'll cut the Tree from under you."[34] *Leslie's* also had humorous illustrations, such as one of Lincoln playing badminton with Jefferson Davis using a shuttlecock named Vallandigham, after the former Ohio congressman arrested by Ambrose Burnside in May 1863, whom Lincoln had exiled to the South after a military commission convicted him. The illustration depicted Davis as saying, "No good sending him here." To which Lincoln replied, "He's none of mine, anyhow."[35]

Harper's often ran engravings of non-combat wartime scenes.[36] In May 1863, it ran a front-page illustration of a sentry on picket duty in the swamps of Louisiana. In the same issue, *Harper's* included a woodcut of Black "contrabands" going into the Union lines. Another illustration showed a hospital on a ship on the Mississippi River. *Harper's* also printed a collage of women titled "Our Women and the War."[37] It included nuns, members of the U.S. Sanitary Commission, a woman bowing to a passing soldier, and a wife with an ill husband. Artist Winslow Homer often did drawings for *Harper's*, including a scene in camp for the Thanksgiving 1862 issue.[38] Union soldiers are seen drinking, smoking, and playing cards in front of a tent, with signs for cider, herring, and pies.

Both illustrated journals went beyond the use of maps to help create a visual interpretation of reality. They also published portraits of key political and military leaders, as well as landscape portrayals of the war's various settings—hiring artists to do the original drawings, and then converting the drawings into carvings on wood blocks, which in turn were imprinted on paper. Between 1861 and 1865, these two magazines in particular devoted an increasing amount of space to visuals, but they were not the only publications to do so. A competitor was the *New-York Illustrated News*, which also featured portraits of generals, battles, camp scenes, and civilian life. Later named *Demorest's New York Illustrated News* after merging with a fashion magazine, it published color covers and carried less news than either *Harper's* or *Leslie's*. In September 1862, The *Southern Illustrated News*, first published in Richmond, Virginia, by Ayres and Wade, focused on portraits of key Confederate generals, with its premier issue featuring one of General Stonewall Jackson on the cover.

Yet another journal that carried engravings was a British publication, The *Illustrated London News*. For example, at Bull Run in July 1861, artist Frank Vizetelly showed Union soldiers running during the heat of the battle.[39] Like the other magazines, the *Illustrated London News* often ran engravings of everyday scenes, such as ships trying to break up ice on the East River in New York, a street scene in Richmond, or Southern refugees on the Mississippi seeking a ride down the river.[40] The London magazine published dramatic illustrations also, such as the burning of a Black orphanage during the New York draft riots of July 1863, Jefferson Davis signing documents just two days before the fall of the Confederate government, and Lincoln's body carried past New York's City Hall before a banner on the building that reads "The Nation Mourns."[41]

Image 5.5 "Reading the War News in Broadway, New York." *Illustrated London News* (June 15, 1861), 563. This image depicts reception of the news among Americans for British readers under a column header "The Civil War in America (From our Special Artist and Correspondent.)"[42]

Newspapers did use some illustrated portraits, but were more likely to incorporate maps into their publications. In coverage of major battles, both New York's *Tribune* and *Herald* offered the most comprehensive daily use of graphics. Both newspapers prominently displayed maps on their front pages. The maps covered more than one column and led to changes in layout design. Some of the maps covered nearly the entire front page above the fold. For example, during the Gettysburg campaign of the first week of July 1863, the *Tribune* published a map showing General George G. Meade's headquarters sandwiched between Marsh Creek and Rock Creek south of Cemetery Hill.[43] The various corps of the Army of the Potomac surrounded Meade's headquarters. The map also showed the position of the Confederate lines and artillery. A series of small rectangles represented the buildings of downtown Gettysburg to the north of the battlefield. The next day the *Tribune* ran a map of Vicksburg, Mississippi, where the Union was notching a similarly major victory.[44] This map was much broader in scope. It included the surrounding countryside, showing Yazoo City to the north and Clinton to the east. It also noted the location where William T. Sherman and his troops crossed the Big Black River by pontoon at Bridgeport on their march from Jackson.

The *Herald*'s reporting of these two battles was comprehensive. James Gordon Bennett's newspaper included significant uses of maps not only on the front page but also interior, where battle reporting often went on for pages. On July 1, the *Herald* carried a map of General Robert E. Lee's second invasion of the North.[45] It included Washington to the south and Harrisburg, Pennsylvania, to the north. It emphasized the location of roads, rail lines, and rivers. Two days later, the *Herald* had two maps, one of Gettysburg and the other of Carlisle, Pennsylvania, where the Confederates had destroyed an army barracks and gas works.[46] On the Fourth of July, it ran two maps, one showing the position of Union troops around Gettysburg and the other predicting Lee's likely retreat path back to Virginia.[47] The most detailed map of the battle was published two days later, focusing on Cemetery Hill. Most journals of this era, however, relied exclusively on text to describe what had happened in battle. They relied on the reporting of correspondents in the field or clipped dispatches from the leading urban newspapers of the East Coast. These pieces were based mostly on observation. Reporters did talk to officers and soldiers, but rarely quoted them.

Newspapers outside New York also used illustrations. For example, the Greensboro, North Carolina, *Times* used graphics to emphasize culture. Editors James W. Albright and C. C. Cole subtitled their journal "An Illustrated Southern Family Paper" and printed a logo on the front page depicting three women, each plying an artistic craft. One played a harp, another wrote in a large book, and the third held a brush and palette. However, the editors did not have the ability to produce illustrations as fast as the major New York papers or the pictorial magazines. Thus, their offerings were not tied to news stories, and instead typically used a large woodcut on the front page and a few stock graphics on the inside pages. A noteworthy series of sketches profiling American presidents ran in the *Times*, with one of James Buchanan in 1859, for example, including an eagle underneath the profile.[48]

In 1864, another Greensboro newspaper, the *Daily Southern Citizen*, included a political cartoon on its front page showing W. W. Holden, editor of The *Standard* in Raleigh, reading the "Working Man's Address." Holden had run for governor as an anti-war candidate and hoped to get the laborers' vote, but, as noted in the Greensboro paper, the "returns came pouring in from the western counties showing that the workingmen had rejected their valiant champion." The Greensboro newspaper also printed a four-column box for the 1864 gubernatorial race, listing the candidates across the top with the state's 100 counties down the left side, and totals for each candidate at the bottom of the box. Holden, the editor of The *Standard* in Raleigh, it reported, received no votes in several counties, and the *Daily Southern Citizen* claimed Holden burst into rage after reading results of the polling.[49]

Graphics

Other newspapers that used graphics to complement political news included The Boston *Daily Advertiser*, which ran a graphic for the mayoral election above a box positioned sideways for the aldermen elections.[50] The Cleveland *Plain Dealer* used graphics in its coverage of the 1862 Republican congressional commission, depicting ballots with the names of the candidates and the number of votes they received.[51] In Davenport, Iowa, Edward Russell's *Daily Gazette* ran the state's congressional races of 1862 in tabular form, basing breakdowns on the returns for both the Republican and Democratic candidate in each district county.[52] The *Gazette*'s rival, the *Daily Democrat and News*, ran two tables—one with the overall county-by-county results for secretary of state and state auditor, and the other the same races with votes from soldiers.[53] The Burlington *Hawk-Eye* in Iowa ran names of the officers of the state Republican Party in a table. It gave the district, the officer's name, and the county where they lived.[54] The newspaper also published the names of candidates for the state's top three offices.

Another form of graphics was the use of boxed tables within text. These broke up the text-heavy layouts that usually stretched over seven, eight, or nine columns. For example, the Fayetteville *Observer* in North Carolina used a one-column graphic to summarize casualties and other significant information from the battle of Stones River in Murfreesboro, Tennessee. The *Observer* included the numbers of prisoners taken, artillery and small arms confiscated, Union wagons destroyed, and casualties on both sides—claiming the Union had suffered 14,000 casualties, contrasted to only 4,500 for the Confederacy. At the bottom of the table was a "Balance" of 9,500 in favor of the Confederate military.[55] Charlotte's *Western Democrat* used a similar graphic for Stones River, showing the difference, as well, and concluding the Confederacy had 10,000 fewer casualties.[56] *The Standard* of Raleigh used a similar table to publicize the number of corps in the Army of the Potomac, including the name of each corps commander.[57] The Boston *Daily Advertiser* ran a box with the names of deserters in it, giving the soldier's name, regiment, company, and hometown.[58] The Cincinnati *Daily Commercial* ran a list of "Deceased Soldiers in New Albany Hospitals," which gave the soldier's name, company, and regiment.[59] The *Daily Commercial* would also run casualty graphics of individual regiments when officers mailed such information to the newspaper. For example, the *Daily Commercial* carried information about the Indiana Thirty-sixth Volunteers.[60] The graphic included names of those killed in action and those who died of wounds or from disease, followed by a written report from Colonel William Grose, the regiment's commanding officer. The regiment had fought at Shiloh and Stones River with a loss of 192 dead out of just over 1,000 men.

In North Carolina, the Greensborough *Patriot* published a table showing the 1860 census and ran a box detailing the relative financial health of twenty-one schools in Guilford County.[61] Raleigh's *Daily Progress* used a graphic to list the members of the Confederate and state governments, including a graphic included the number of free citizens and slaves in each state. It also ran market information with a graphically depicted commodity in one column and its price in a second column, with a series of dots between.[62] Its rival, *The Standard*, ran a similar commodity table, though it was harder to read because it did not include the dots between market item and price.[63] Another Greensboro newspaper, *The Watchman and Harbinger*, used a graphic to show how much money could be donated to cover the expenses of sending the paper to soldiers.[64] The *Western Democrat* of Charlotte ran a graphic that divided officers in North Carolina regiments by rank. In July 1863, the *Western Democrat* published information about the state's tax law in graphical form.[65]

Virginia's Richmond *Examiner* was generally a very gray newspaper, but it ran census data as graphics in an attempt to show that the slave states were more prosperous than the free states. One box showed per capita income of each type of state. Individuals in the slave (or mixed) states earned $152 more per year. In the narrative that accompanied the box, the *Examiner* claimed that the "mixed labour States, instead of falling behind, have actually accumulated fifty percent more wealth to proportion to their population than the free labour states."[66] Likewise, in the North, the Boston *Daily Advertiser* used a boxed graphic to show loans, deposits, specie in banks, and circulation of dollars in the city's banks.[67] In Ohio, the Cleveland *Plain Dealer* ran market reports, with commodity names in caps, followed by the price.[68] While the Cincinnati *Daily Commercial* included graphics for imports, exports, and commodities at the city market, *The New York Evening Express* ran a table of stock prices that showed the trend over several weeks, also showing the value of commodities over a two-year period.[69] An Iowa newspaper, the Muscatine *Courier*, ran a large table that gave a long list of census information for Muscatine County.[70] The items included the number of dwellings, families, and those eligible to vote. It also had the number of males and females in the county, as well as foreigners, Blacks, blind, deaf, and insane followed by a long list of commodities, property, and machinery.

Another typical graphical box was that for railroad schedules. In Raleigh, the *Standard* included the distances between towns in the state. The *Western Democrat*'s graphic told whether a train was going east or west, and what time it would leave Charlotte.[71] The table reminded passengers to pay their fare with exact change. *The Hawkeye* in Burlington, Iowa, ran a table for the Burlington and Missouri River Railroad showing when passenger and freight trains were scheduled to leave heading both east and west.[72] The table gave the times trains would go through various Iowa cities. The Boston *Daily Advertiser* provided information about ocean steamers in a boxed format.[73] This graphic covered four columns, giving the name of the steamer, its port of origin, where it was bound, and when it would set sail. Half of the column was devoted to ships leaving England and the other from North American ports. Another box showed the condition of ships in the Navy yard in Brooklyn, New York.[74] The Cleveland *Plain Dealer* used a graphic to show the arrival and departures of boats and trains.[75]

Other kinds of graphics published in newspapers that could afford them include images used to accentuate a range of stories, from business to religion to sports, with many urban newspapers running extensive market quotations. For example, the *Daily Advertiser* provided wholesale commodity prices in Boston on a daily basis. The quotes shared how many goods were sold at what prices.[76] Another staple was a box with imported foreign goods at the port of Boston.[77] This gave the name of the commodity and the total value of the goods coming into the port. The *Daily Advertiser* also had advertisements for stocks within a boxed format. The Baltimore *Sun* reported business failures in a boxed format.[78] The *Daily Times* in Dubuque, Iowa, and the Augusta, Georgia, *Chronicle & Sentinel*, among many papers, ran a calendar at the beginning of each year.[79] The graphical box had the days of the week at the top and the months by day underneath. This was divided in half, with the first six months on the left side and the second six on the right. *The New York Herald* used informational graphics to show the number of railroad and steamboat accidents, as well as crime and fire statistics, in a single year.[80] *The Watchman and Harbinger* in Greensboro, North Carolina, ran names of attendees to a Methodist conference in graphical form.[81] It divided them into ministers and lay people. Like many newspapers, the Charleston *Mercury* in South Carolina ran a list of letters not yet delivered.[82] The Cleveland *Plain Dealer* covered the Ohio State Fair by running a box with types of animal and numbers of each entered in competition. A graphic of horses listed

"Thorough Bread," "Roadsters," "General Purposes," "Draft," Sweepstakes," and "Jacks and Mules."[83] The *Daily Democrat and News* in Davenport had tables listing the number of troops expected for recruitment in each of the city's six wards. The *Democrat* also ran weather information in a table. It included pressure, temperature, and measurable precipitation.[84] Likewise, the Cincinnati *Daily Commercial* published a daily capsule of weather data in a small box in its "Local Matters" column.[85] This three-column graphic included time of observation, barometric pressure, and temperature.

Most graphics appeared in advertising, and many newspapers, including the Atlanta *Intelligencer*, put their advertisements on the front page, something that had been common practice since the mid-eighteenth century. *The Hawk-Eye* of Burlington, Iowa, saved its biggest engraving for a publisher's advertisement. The Hawk-Eye Steam Printing House promoted steam presses "running night and day."[86] The illustration showed the building in which the presses operated. The publishing house printed newspapers, books, and job printing. Another large advertisement in *The Hawk-Eye* was for E. M. Eisfield, a Philadelphia-based clothing company that had a store in Burlington. The Eisfield ad, headlined "Prospects Are Bright for the American Nation," included interpretation of the news. Another Eisfield ad told readers "No Foreign Interference by Europe— Good News from the East."[87] While Great Britain did not interfere in the war by recognizing the Confederacy, at that point the news was not very "good" in the East, as the Army of the Potomac had just lost a battle at Chancellorsville, Virginia. The Boston *Daily Advertiser* extensively used graphics in advertisements. For example, the John Tracey & Co. distillery ad included five cases of wine, and a woodcut of an open safe accompanied the Tremont Safe and Machine Co.[88] The Cleveland *Plain Dealer* carried an advertisement for joining the Mississippi Squadron of the U.S. Navy.[89] The graphic included the various positions available and the pay for each rank. At the bottom, the graphic told where interested individuals could join—St. Louis, Cincinnati, Louisville, Cairo, Chicago, Erie, and Memphis. David D. Porter, the acting rear admiral, signed it.

Other popular uses of graphics included logos on the editorial page. The Dubuque *National-Demokrat*, a German-language newspaper in Iowa, used an eagle on top of an American flag; a series of flags, guns, and a drum; or simply a Union flag.[90] The Fort Madison *Plain Dealer* had an eagle perched on a banner that read "Democracy."[91] The eagle, clutching bunting, echoed President Andrew Jackson's words, "The Union—It Must Be Preserved." The Boston *Daily Advertiser* had a man climbing a flagpole. As he does, he clutches a hammer as he looks above the Stars and Stripes.[92] Sometimes, an editor printed patriotic images with news stories, especially when connected with major events. On the eve of Gettysburg, the Dubuque *Daily Times* carried an eagle with a snake in its clutches.[93] The eagle is perched on a U.S. emblem. A week later, above a story on the battle of Vicksburg, the *Daily Times* published a Union flag blowing in the wind.[94] The Boston *Daily Advertiser* would run the seal of Massachusetts when it printed official acts of the legislature.

A final noteworthy and increasingly popular graphic included images accentuating sports news. For example, the *Daily Advertiser* ran a box score for a game between the Sophomore Club of Brown College and the Base Ball Club of Harvard College. The box score was positioned between a game report and a brief editorial about the sport. The graphic was divided in half. Harvard's nine was on the left side, Brown's on the right. The names of the players were matched with how many runs they scored. Underneath the box, one line told which players had hit homeruns. (By the way, Harvard won, 27–12.) "If we cannot have cricket," the editorial noted, "by all means let us have baseball."[95] The Cleveland *Plain Dealer* used a box for horseracing. Under the headline "The Trotting Race," the newspaper reported on head-to-head races between horses named Country Boy and Excelsior.[96] The *Plain Dealer* told who won each of four races and the winning times.

Photojournalism and the New Literacy

Although photography was in its infancy and not yet mass-produced, it had a significant impact on Civil War journalism. Actual photographs of the Civil War appeared only in exhibitions, but the visual record of the conflict captured the horrors of war in a way never before seen. Consumers were more likely to see works of traveling art, such as Goodwin and Wilder's "Polyorama of the War."[97] The exhibition promised to tell the story of the "First Dread Signal at Sumter down to the Last Grand Battle."[98] The owners said the polyorama would engulf the senses of its viewers with fire and smoke, as well as thunderous sounds. Illustrated magazines began to use photographs by taking the originals and converting them into a wood engraving for use in the mass production of images.

Enterprising photographers opened salons throughout the county where they exhibited their pictures and promoted this innovation. Moreover, soldiers and politicians routinely visited photographers to have their pictures taken, and Lincoln's use of photography gave him a major advantage historically over previous presidents. Mathew Brady was close to Lincoln and received permission to accompany the Union Army to the front. The so-called "Brady wagon" included a dark room where plates where developed in the field. Humidity and dust often plagued the operation.

One of Brady's leading photographers was Alexander Gardner, who covered Antietam. There, a few weeks after the battle, Gardner took a famous photograph of Lincoln meeting with George McClellan and other Union officers. Three other famous Gardner photographs depicted the carnage at the foot of Round Top, the corpse of a sharpshooter, and a field of dead horses around the Troseel House at Gettysburg. Another graphic representation of war was a photograph Gardner took of the skeletal remains of soldiers at Cold Harbor, Virginia.

In this photograph, among the most harrowing from the battlefield—or what once was a battlefield—an African American sits with a stretcher full of skulls and partial corpses as he and other men reinter the dead months after the battles of Gaines' Mill and Cold Harbor.

The photograph exemplifies the limits of photography during the Civil War. Rather than depicting battles as they unfolded, photographers often had to content themselves with scenes of post-battle carnage—shocking, but literally and figuratively lifeless.

The following excerpt from a caption for the picture originally published in Alexander Gardner's *Photographic Sketch Book of the War* describes a "sad scene" in language that would have resonated with contemporary readers.

> It speaks ill of the residents of that part of Virginia, that they allowed even the remains of those they considered enemies, to decay unnoticed where they fell. The soldiers, to whom commonly falls the task of burying the dead, may possibly have been called away before the task was completed. At such times the native dwellers of the neighborhood would usually come forward and provide sepulture for such as had been left uncovered.[100]

On a symbolic level, African Americans, possibly former slaves, perform the grim task of cleaning up the battlefield. Such images of death, in many ways, took center stage in the photographic work coming out of the Civil War. A less famous Gardner photograph showed *The New York Herald*'s headquarters with the Army of the Potomac—which included a horse drawn carriage with the name of the newspaper on the side. The photo shows that the journalists were not stuck in an office, but rather were on the scene at the front. After the war, Gardner published a collection of his best work in the *Photographic Sketch Book of the War*.

Image 5.6 "A Burial Party on the Battle-field of Cold Harbor, April 1, 1865." John Reekie, photographer, in *Gardner's Photographic Sketch Book of the War*, Alexander Gardner, Washington, DC: Philp and Solomons, 1865-66, v. 2, no. 94, 1866.[99]

Timothy H. O'Sullivan's photograph of Alfred Rudolph Waud, an important illustrator, captures a meta-historical moment. O'Sullivan, another Brady affiliates, took some of the era's most famous photos, and Waud—who was born in England in 1828 and immigrated to the United States in 1850—drew illustrations for newspapers and periodicals as a "special correspondent," a title used for contributors such as artists, photographers, and writers.

O'Sullivan presents his subject in a convergence of a popular form of media (illustrations) and an emerging one (photographs).[102] The fact that the photograph itself depicts Waud at the Devil's Den site on the Gettysburg battlefield confers an additional context for the viewer to consider, as on July 2, 1863, Devil's Den— the site of some of the bloodiest fighting of the battle—would have undoubtedly triggered an association with the larger events of the war. Beyond the scope of either the subject or the photographer lies an even larger event—the battle itself. While Waud and O'Sullivan appear to work peacefully, an epic battle—a pivotal moment in the Civil War—takes place at a distance unknown and invisible to

Image 5.7 "Gettysburg, Pa. Alfred R. Waud, Artist of *Harper's Weekly*, Sketching on Battlefield." Timothy H. O'Sullivan, photographer, July 1863. In this photo, Waud prepares a sketch of the battle of Gettysburg for *Harper's Weekly*.[101]

the viewer. (With more than 50,000 casualties, historians generally recognize the three days of conflict at Gettysburg as the costliest battle of the war).[103]

Waud would have sent a drawing such as this to his editors, who would then convert it into a woodcut or a copperplate engraving for print publication. Leading illustrated newspapers during the war used woodcuts that were then impressed upon paper to create images for mass reproduction in the press. A multiple-block system increased speed by having drawings divided into four or five segments. A different engraver worked on each block, and then the blocks were locked into a frame. A master engraver cut the lines that crossed the various blocks.[104]

The process of transcribing the continuous tone image of photography into the line engravings of newspapers posed challenges. Camera speeds at the time were too slow to take photos of active battle, so photojournalists were left to document only the before and after of military action. Moreover, problems with using sketch artists who sometimes were not actually at the scene of battle—and instead relied on what reporters told them about a skirmish—did not outweigh the slowness of the photographic process, and at this point in history, drawings were cheaper than photographers, so publishers of illustrated journals continued to rely on sketched engravings. Precise representations of battles would have to wait for another war.

Image 5.8 "The Progress of the Century: The Lightning Steam Press, the Electric Telegraph, the Locomotive, [and] the Steamboat." New York: Published by Currier & Ives, 1876. This lithograph depicts a number of technological innovations that influenced both the course of the Civil War and development of the press during the nineteenth century. A man using the telegraph in the foreground—as well as the steam press, steamboat, and locomotive in the background—cumulatively represent progress.[105]

Meantime, technology and the war itself had played a major role in developing a nation of readers. By the 1860s, at a time of such great political instability, readers demanded information on the daily events that affected their friends and family members who had gone to battle—events that more often than not detailed horrific struggles of life and death. Newspapers prompted many of those who could not read to take an interest in acquiring the skill. The concurrent expansion of the railroads, at a rate of more than 1,000 new miles each year in the 1850s, allowed publishers to sell newspapers over vast distances, with the weekly edition of *The New York Tribune* in particular circulating widely in the West. With the amount of track jumping from 8,589 miles in 1850 to 30,591 in 1861—and the greatest increase in mileage coming in the states that today make up the Midwest—Greeley's *Tribune* prospered, with circulation climbing to 200,000.[106]

Along with the railroads, the postal service was another major channel for delivering newspapers and magazines. In the 1850s, the post office would typically deliver more than 100 million journals in a single year, with the bulk of those being newspapers.[107] In 1860, of the nation's 3,300 newspapers, 373 were dailies.[108]

The wartime press struggled to maintain standards of precision and reliability, as technology generated vast quantities of information and journalists faced the challenge of separating fact from fiction. The press of the era still served partisan interests, and editors interpreted the events of the day in terms of party doctrine, with almost no editor immune from the call to interpret. However the country's journalists had new ways to spread information and fashion the news—namely through visual representations such as woodcut illustrations, maps, and fact boxes—and they could deliver such information to a large audiences, faster and faster.

Notes

1 Chicago *Tribune*, December 17, 1862.

2 New York *Tribune*, December 16, 1862.

3 Cleveland *Plain Dealer*, December 15, 1862.

4 Dicken-Garcia, *Journalistic Standards in Nineteenth-Century America* (Madison, WI: University of Wisconsin Press, 1989), 55.

5 James Carey, *Communication as Culture* (New York and London: Routledge, 1989), 213.

6 David W. Bulla, "The Popular Press, 1833–1865," in *The Age of Mass Communication*, Sloan, ed. (Northport, AL: Vision Press, 2008), 142.

7 Daniel Walker Howe, "What Hath God Wrought," *American Heritage*, 59, 4 (Winter 2010), accessed July 1, 2021, at <americanheritage.com/what-hath-god-wrought>.

8 Howe, *What Hath God Wrought: The Transformation of America, 1815–1848* (New York: Oxford University Press, 2007), 7.

9 Menaham Blondheim, "The Click: Telegraphic Technology, Journalism, and the Transformations of the New York Associated Press," *American Journalism*, 17, 4 (Fall 2000): 39.

10 William E. Huntzicker, *The Popular Press, 1833–1865* (Westport, CT: Greenwood Press, 1999), 96.

11 Ibid, *The Popular Press*, 94.

12 Brayton Harris, *Blue & Gray in Black & White: Newspapers in the Civil War* (Washington, DC: Brassey's, 1999), 8.

13 Ford Risley, "The Confederate Press Association: Cooperative News Reporting of the War," *Civil War History*, 47, 3 (2001): 222, 230.

14 "Rebel Telegraph Operator near Egypt, on the Mississippi Central R.R.," <loc.gov/resource/cph.3a02101>, accessed July 8, 2021.

15 Borchard, *Abraham Lincoln and Horace Greeley* (Carbondale, IL: Southern Illinois University Press, 2011), 76.

16 "How Illustrated Newspapers are Made," Library of Congress, accessed August 30, 2021, at <loc.gov/item/98510934>.

17 Huntzicker, "Picturing the News: Frank Leslie and the Origins of American Pictorial Journalism," in Sachsman, Kittrell Rushing, and Reddin van Tuyll, eds., *The Civil War and the Press*, 312.

18 *Harper's Weekly*, November 5, 1859.

19 *Frank Leslie's Illustrated Newspaper*, November 5, 1859.

20 *Harper's Weekly*, November 12, 1859.

21 *Frank Leslie's Illustrated Newspaper*, December 17, 1859.

22 Charles Hamilton and Lloyd Ostendorf, *Lincoln in Photographs: An Album of Every Known Pose* (Norman, OK: University of Oklahoma Press, 1963), 35.

23 "Abraham Lincoln, Candidate for U.S. President, Three-quarter Length Portrait, before Delivering his Cooper Union Address in New York City," Library of Congress, accessed July 1, 2021, at <loc.gov/pictures/item/98504529>.

24 Lincoln, "Address at Cooper Institute, New York City," February 27, 1860, in Roy P. Basler, ed., *The Collected Works of Abraham Lincoln*, 9 vols. (New Brunswick, N.J.: Rutgers University Press, 1953-55), 4:60-7; Donald and Holzer, *Lincoln in the Times*, 18; Naomi Rosenblum, *World History of Photography* (New York: Abbeville Press, 1997), 191.

25 Roy Meredith, *Mr. Lincoln's Camera Man, Mathew B. Brady* (Mineola, NY: Dover, 1974), 59.

26 Borchard and Bulla, *Lincoln Mediated: The President and the Press through Nineteenth Century Media* (New York: Routledge, 2020), 32-34.

27 David Tatham, *Winslow Homer and the Pictorial Press* (Syracuse, NY: Syracuse University Press, 2003), 95, 96.

28 "Hon. Abraham Lincoln, February 12, 1809," Library of Congress, accessed July 1, 2021, at <loc.gov/pictures/item/98518286>.

29 *Harper's Weekly*, May 4, 1861.

30 Ibid, September 20, 1862.

31 Ibid, July 25, 1863.

32 *Frank Leslie's Illustrated Newspaper*, December 5, 1863.

33 Ibid, September 24, 1861, August 2, 1862.

34 *Harper's Weekly*, October 11, 1862.

35 *Frank Leslie's Illustrated Newspaper*, June 20, 1863.

36 *Harper's Weekly*, May 9, 1863.

37 Ibid, September 6, 1862.

38 Ibid, November 29, 1862.

39 *Illustrated London News*, August 17, 1861.

40 Ibid, March 29, 1862, July 5, 26, 1862.

41 *Illustrated London News*, August 15, 1863, May 20, 1865, July 22, 1865.

42 "Reading the War News in Broadway, New York," Library of Congress, accessed July 13, 2021, at <loc.gov/resource/cph.3c12561>.

43 New York *Tribune*, July 7, 1863.

44 Ibid, July 8, 1863.

45 New York *Herald*, July 1, 1863.

46 Ibid, July 3, 1863.

47 Ibid, July 4, 1863.

48 Greensboro (NC) *The Times*, August 13, 1859.

49 Greensboro (NC) *Daily Southern Citizen*, August 16, 1864.

50 Boston *Daily Advertiser*, December 9, 1862.

51 Cleveland *Plain Dealer*, September 24, 1862.

52 Davenport (IA) *Daily Gazette*, November 4, 1862.

53 Davenport (IA) *Daily Democrat and News*, December 13, 1862.

54 Burlington (IA) *The Hawk-Eye*, July 7, 1863.

55 Fayetteville (NC) *Observer*, January 19, 1863.

56 Charlotte (NC) *Western Democrat*, January 20, 1863.

57 Raleigh (NC) *The Standard*, May 13, 1863.

58 Boston *Daily Advertiser*, December 17, 1862.

59 Cincinnati *Daily Commercial*, December 13, 1862.

60 Ibid, December 12, 1862.

61 Greensborough (NC) *Patriot*, April 12, 1861, December 25, 1863.

62 Raleigh (NC) *Daily Progress*, November 11, 29, 1862.

63 Raleigh (NC) *The Standard*, March 15, 1865.

64 Greensboro (NC) *The Watchman and Harbinger*, November 6, 1863.

65 Charlotte (NC) *Western Democrat*, January 13, July 7, 1863.

66 Richmond (VA) *Examiner*, January 10, 1863.

67 Boston *Daily Advertiser*, July 2, 1862.

68 Cleveland *Plain Dealer*, December 16, 1862.

69 New York *Evening Express*, May 9, 1863.

70 Muscatine (IA) *The Courier*, July 30, 1863.

71 Charlotte (NC) *Western Democrat*, January 27, 1863.

72 Burlington (IA) *The Hawk-Eye*, December 16, 1863.

73 Boston *Daily Advertiser*, July 2, 1862.

74 Ibid, September 1, 1862.

75 Cleveland *Plain Dealer*, August 16, 1862.

76 Boston *Daily Advertiser*, August 9, 1862.

77 Ibid, August 11, 1862.

78 Baltimore *Sun*, January 2, 1863.

79 Dubuque (IA) *Daily Times*, January 8, 1863.

80 New York *Herald*, January 1, 1863.

81 Greensboro (NC) *The Watchman and Harbinger*, November 27, 1863.

82 Charleston (SC) *Mercury*, January 3, 1863.

83 Cleveland *Plain Dealer*, September 20, 1862.

84 Davenport (IA) *Daily Democrat and News*, December 6, 1862.

85 Cincinnati *Daily Commercial*, May 15, 1863.

86 Burlington (IA) *The Hawk-Eye*, January 1, 1863.

87 Ibid, May 7, 1863.

88 Boston *Daily Advertiser*, May 13, 1863.

89 Cleveland *Plain Dealer*, December 15, 1862.

90 Dubuque (IA) *National-Demokrat*, April 16, 19, 1860.

91 Fort Madison (IA) *Plain Dealer*, January 2, 1863.

92 Boston *Daily Advertiser*, August 13, 1862.

93 Dubuque (IA) *Daily Times*, July 1, 1863.

94 Ibid, July 8, 1863.

95 Boston *Daily Advertiser*, June 30, 1863.

96 Cleveland *Plain Dealer*, September 20, 1862.

97 Fort Wayne (IN) *Dawson's Daily Times & Union*, May 23, 1863.

98 Cleveland *Plain Dealer*, May 12, 1863.

99 "A Burial Party on the Battle-field of Cold Harbor, April 1, 1865," Library of Congress, accessed July 1, 2021, available at <loc.gov/pictures/item/2002713100>.

100 Alexander Gardner, *Gardner's Photographic Sketch Book of the War* (Washington, DC: Philip and Solomons, 1865–66), Vol. 2, no. 94.

101 "Gettysburg, Pa. Alfred R. Waud, Artist of *Harper's Weekly*, Sketching on Battlefield," Library of Congress, accessed July 1, 2021, available at <loc.gov/pictures/item/cwp2003000198/PP>.

102 Meredith, *Mr. Lincoln's Camera Man*, 3.

103 James McPherson, *The Battle Cry of Freedom* (New York: Oxford University Press, 1988), 659-69.

104 Borchard, Lawrence J. Mullen, and Stephen Bates, "From Realism to Reality: The Advent of War Photography," *Journalism & Communication Monographs*, 15, 2 (June 2013): 66-107.

105 "The Progress of the Century—The Lightning Steam Press, the Electric Telegraph, the Locomotive, [and] the Steamboat," Library of Congress, accessed July 1, 2021, at <loc.gov/resource/ppmsca.17563>.

106 McPherson, *Ordeal by Fire: The Civil War and Reconstruction* (Boston, MA: McGraw-Hill, 2001), 19.

107 Richard B. Kielbowicz, *News in the Mail: The Press, Post Office, and Public Information, 1700–1860s* (Westport, CT: Greenwood Press, 1989), 107.

108 McPherson, *Ordeal by Fire*, 19; Harris, *Blue & Gray in Black & White*, 9.

6

A Battle of Content: Party Press vs. Informative Press

"When will they learn who are their best friends and who are their enemies. It seems as if never." Wilmington (NC) *Daily Herald*, October 20, 1859.

According to the historical record, the Civil War began in April 1861, but decades before the outbreak of formal military activities, written records reflected the impending conflict. Many of the most dramatic accounts of fighting included specific commentary on the role slavery would—or would not—have in the nation's future. The words and actions pointed toward what would be an eventual culmination in John Brown's raid on Harpers Ferry in 1859. Literature including David Walker's *Appeal* (1829), Harriett Beecher Stowe's *Uncle Tom's Cabin* (1852), and Hinton Helper's *The Impending Crisis* (1857)—interspersed with Nat Turner's 1831 slave revolt, the murder of abolitionist editor Elijah P. Lovejoy in 1837, and the caning of Charles Sumner in 1856—ratcheted tensions among proponents of regional interests. However, Brown's insurgency in October 1859 brought together preceding issues in political, legal, and journalistic terms like no other event, marking a watershed in the development of the press as an instrument of partisanship and a deliverer of news.

The Frankfort (Ky.) *Commonwealth* provided just a sample of a wide range of reactions from newspapers across the country, but it also summarized the tone of North and South. Denouncing the raid, it appreciated other newspapers in the North for doing the same, noting that nearly everyone condemned the "wicked and insane projects of Brown and his hair-brained associates." Moreover, it noted, politicians, "including the most inveterate Republicans," and common people had joined the editors in the condemnations. Interestingly, the newspaper suggested, it was "not going too far to assert that in case there had been any necessity for their aid, thousands of true men in the North would have promptly taken up arms in behalf of the Southern slaveholder against the brutality and of the slave."[1] The response in Tennessee was less conciliatory, as the *Republican Banner and Nashville Whig* suggested Brown's attempts to liberate slaves was the result of "designing" politicians in the North. Remarkably, it described the raid as "a preface to the history of a civil war in which the same scenes will be re-enacted on a larger scale, and end in the dissolution of our glorious Union."[2] Elsewhere in Tennessee, the Nashville *Union and American* described the Harpers Ferry raid as the "legitimate" result of abolitionism, which encouraged "fanatics to riot and revolution."[3] The response in Charleston, South Carolina, was perhaps the most outraged, with the *Mercury* describing the raid as a provocation, "a concerted movement of abolitionists" and "a prelude to what must and will recur again and again, as the progress of sectional hate and Black Republican success advances to their consummation."[4]

Northern newspapers also generally condemned the attack on the federal armory, although some newspapers showed sympathy for the cause of abolition. *The Chicago Tribune* predicted that Brown's attempt to rally slaves was "but the beginning of like endeavors, which will horrify the country."[5] The Chicago newspaper blamed the attack on the policies of the Democratic Party—in particular, Stephen A. Douglas' concept of popular sovereignty. The *Tribune* claimed the conservative party was "utterly blind" to the "impending crisis," that slaves were becoming more intelligent, and that those Blackmen who had tasted freedom in the North or in Canada now knew the truth about the oppressive nature of slavery.

Meanwhile, Southern journalists initially struggled in their efforts to report the news, as some of their editors reacted with a state of denial. For example, the Richmond (VA) *Whig* commented that the news was "greatly exaggerated, as such occurrences usually are."[6] In the first days after the raid, news trickled into Southern cities and towns with minimal firsthand reporting by Southern newspapers. For instance, the Charleston, South Carolina, *Daily Courier* relied on the Baltimore *Sun* for its reports on the raid. The first coverage in the *Daily Courier* came in its October 19 edition. Information was unreliable in the first days after the initial raid. The Wilmington, North Carolina, *Daily Herald* at first reported 750 slaves had joined the revolt, but later reduced the number to twenty.[7] The Augusta, Georgia, *Chronicle & Sentinel* went further, calling John Brown's raid "reckless, fool-hardy, and insane."[8] The Wilmington, North Carolina, *Daily Herald*, which reported that President James Buchanan had ordered extra men to guard the armories in Washington, held that the "poor deluded negro, of course, is the greatest sufferer" in the wake of the news from Harpers Ferry. "When will they learn," the editorial continued, "who are their best friends and who are their enemies. It seems as if never."[9] Six days after the raid, the *Daily Herald* published a five-column narrative of the "Insurrection at Harper's Ferry" highlighting the actions of the Marines to stop the raid and take Brown and his conspirators into custody. Colonel Robert E. Lee of Virginia led the Marine detachment, which took charge of the prisoners.

As the Southern coverage of the Harpers Ferry raid and the trial and execution of Brown demonstrated, the mid-century press had two primary functions: interpreting news within certain political orientations and informing the public.[10] However, editorials marshaled the facts of a high percentage of published information to fit into various political perspectives. Newspapers of the 1860s that claimed to be independent were not neutral—not when the nation was about to splinter—as they were not yet able to separate themselves from their deeply entrenched political functions. Yes, there was plenty of information in a Civil War newspaper that did not take sides—shipping news, weather reports, train schedules, crop reports, social news, and church news. Still, the majority of editors saw their enterprise in political terms; that is, an editor was a political leader who would help a party develop or secure a power base.

Nonetheless, war makes information an essential commodity, as readers want to know how battles are progressing, who is winning, who is losing, and what is likely to happen next. Readers want to know the names of those killed, wounded, or missing, and how a husband, father, son, uncle, cousin, or neighbor is faring. The newspapers of the Civil War provided that information for the public, and because of the development of the telegraph and railroad lines, as well as improvements in printing, the press could deliver the news faster than ever before. Furthermore, newspapers illustrated the sheer intensity of the war by printing the long list of casualties, eventually bringing the news-consuming public to a tipping point. Information began to overwhelm political interpretation.

Covering East to West

The Baltimore *Sun* set the tone for war coverage by giving Brown's raid as many column inches as did any newspaper in the country and at one point calling the event a "short, sharp, terrible drama, provoked by a handful of enthusiasts, fanatics, and adventurers." Its coverage of Brown's execution was even more concise: "Captain Brown was hung to-day at quarter past 11 o'clock."[11] The *Sun* also had stories about pro-and anti-Brown religious services, about how African Americans responded to the execution, and about Brown's will and the transport of his body to its final resting place. Yet the one sentence about Brown's execution in the *Sun* spoke volumes. A white American had tried to start a revolt of Black slaves in the South.

The *Sun*, a penny paper, recognized the extraordinary nature of the event, and the fact that it bloviated less than did most journals of the era and commented on the seamlessness of Brown's execution demonstrated a new national reality—that Brown's death brought a sense of Southern military pride. Indeed, the *Sun* editors remarked on the efficiency of the military's handling of the hanging. The *Sun* and other Southern newspapers also noted that there was no attempt by abolitionists to spring Brown at the last moment. In effect, these lines point to the fact that the militarization of the South was now in full swing. Brown's raid, trial, and execution hurtled the nation from the irrepressible conflict between slavery and freedom to the impending crisis between North and South.

During the war, the telegraph contributed greatly to this change in the nature and content of journalism. The presence of a large reporting corps in the field made possible the delivery of a wide variety of stories. Because the war took place in the front and back yards of average Americans, the nation's newspapers poured great resources into its coverage, especially in terms of labor. Some five hundred men and women covered the war.[12] By contrast, only a handful had covered the Mexican War.

From the summer 1861 forward, the reporting corps struggled to keep ahead of events in a war of more than 10,000 battles. Just as casualties in the Civil War exceeded those of all previous American wars combined, the first major battle of the war, Bull Run, in Manassas, Virginia, in July 1861, had more casualties than any previous American war. The South won the battle, and the North realized the war was not going to be a short one. Citizens of both sides in the conflict also saw the cost in lives. The lists of dead, wounded, and missing were long, with the Union suffering approximately 3,000 and the Confederates about 2,000 casualties. On that summer day, 36,000 men began fighting. At the end of it, 5,000 were gone. The Baltimore *Sun* published casualty lists from the start. Three days after the July 21 battle, the *Sun* ran a list of the dead and wounded that covered two columns on its editorial pages. Those listed were mainly from New England and the upper Midwest. The information was clear and concise.

Here was a typical report: "Capt. Todd, of Brattleboro, Vt., 23, shot in the throat, ball passed completely through within sixteen inches of the jugular vein—will recover."[13]

The Cleveland *Plain Dealer*'s coverage of First Bull Run was comprehensive. J. W. Gray's pro-Democratic newspaper attacked not Lincoln but Horace Greeley. Gray and his brother, A. N. Gray, believed Greeley had driven the federal government to act before it was ready. The first group of Union volunteers had signed up for three months and their tours of service were about to expire. The Lincoln administration put pressure on the Army to take some action before those men's three months were completed. Greeley had pushed for an attack, and both he and the editors at the *Plain Dealer* argued for the raising of a mighty army. However, after the fight, the Ohio journal also ran a cartoon of Greeley running from the battle toward Washington, noting that an Ohio regiment made the last stand on the field at Manassas before the Union Army raced for Washington. The Cleveland newspaper claimed that the work of the Ohio men "saved us from great losses." The *Plain Dealer* also defused the notion that the Confederate Army was going to follow the victory at Bull Run with an attack on Washington. It ran a *New York Times* story that described the Rebels in poor condition after the battle to maintain the offensive. Nine days after the battle, the *Plain Dealer* ran a profile of George B. McClellan, which included a woodcut drawing of the major general. At the time, McClellan was the commander of the Department of the Ohio. The *Plain Dealer* called him the "Napoleon of America," adding, "McClellan has no political aspirations, thank God! He is all General."[14] Two weeks after the battle, the Cleveland paper began running lists of the killed and wounded. The initial list only included officers. Later, the newspaper would begin carrying the names of both officers and soldiers.

The Baltimore *Sun* reported on the retreat of Major General Irvin McDowell's forces back to the federal capital. The lead story on July 24 called Bull Run "one of the most severe and sanguinary [battles] ever fought on this continent, and it ended in the failure of the Union troops to hold all the positions which they sought to carry, and which they actually did carry, and in their retreat to Centreville." That same day, the Baltimore newspaper ran long casualty lists. Officers' names came at the top of a list, followed by the names and regiments of the soldiers. The next day, the *Sun* called Bull Run a "disastrous defeat" and concluded the Confederate Army under Brigadier General P. G. T. Beauregard was "more numerous and even better commanded, equipped and organized."[15] On July 27, the *Sun* ran an eyewitness account of the battle. The writer commented: "The agony of this overwhelming disgrace can never be expressed in words, or understood by those who only hear the tale repeated. I believe there were men upon that field who turned their faces to the enemy, and marched to certain death, lest they should share the infamy which their fellows had invited and embraced."

The *Sun* also lambasted the political nature of the Union military. Its editors noted that while in Europe military leaders managed campaigns, in the United States politicians have a say in how an operation will go. "When a campaign projected by so mixed an assembly proves unsuccessful, the responsibility involved is generally disclaimed by all parties," the *Sun* wrote. The Baltimore paper also criticized those in the North who looked to Greeley's *Tribune* as the official source for military information—such an approach had pushed for a battle before General-in-Chief Winfield Scott and the Army had devised an effective strategy. In August, the *Sun* ran an article from the Paterson *Register* in New Jersey that suggested the peace wing of the Democratic Party was "growing stronger and stronger" with conservatives questioning what could be "gained by all this bloodshed and devastation."[16] Three days later, the *Sun* reported on grassroots peace movements in Maryland.

The battle at Bull Run led *The New York Tribune*'s front page on Sunday, July 21. Headlines of eight and twelve lines accompanied the two main stories on Saturday's events in northern Virginia. One read, "The Armies Only One Mile Apart." The next day, the newspaper had a headline that read "Great Victory!" The article described the engaged forces as "the most numerous ever opposed in deadly fray on the continent of America." The *Tribune* reported heavy losses on both sides, and that the Confederates had retreated from the field after the Union Army had "silenced" the Rebel batteries. Horace Greeley's paper also claimed that the Union had 50,000 forces at Bull Run, compared to 70,000 for the Confederates. The next day, though, Greeley reported the "strange and disastrous retreat of our troops."[17]

Keeping pace with its chief rival, the *Tribune*, *The New York Herald*'s lead story that day contained nineteen headlines. The *Herald* ran a large map of the area from Washington to Manassas on July 19, also publishing a long list of the officers in charge of the Union Army—from McDowell at the top to the acting brigadier generals in charge of the various regiments. On July 21, the day of the battle, the *Herald* included a map of Manassas Gap Junction, where the Orange & Alexandria met the Manassas Gap Railroad. The Confederate troops amassed at the junction while McDowell's men were to the northeast at Bull Run, the tiny creek near Centreville. All of the war stories came under the heading, "The Rebellion."

The next day, the *Herald* declared Bull Run to be a "Brilliant Union Victory!" and reported that the Confederate Army had been "routed," their batteries captured, and the infantry driven back to Manassas in the greatest battle in the history of the nation—adding that losses on both sides were "immense." The *Herald*'s Bennett claimed Bull Run to be one of the "great military achievements which, in ancient and modern times, have overthrown or marked the beginning of the downfall of empires, kingdoms, and revolutionary enterprises." Like the *Tribune*, the *Herald* reversed itself on July 23, later brandishing Bull Run a "Disaster." The *Herald* claimed the battle was going well for the Union until 20,000 men under Brigadier General Joseph E. Johnston reinforced the Confederates. Bennett described the Union retreat as a "panic" that began with a group of teamsters and eventually included a number of citizen spectators. The newspaper also reported that the army in the field had not followed the attack plan of Winfield Scott, the commander. Bennett also noted that the Lincoln administration had asked McClellan to transit from West Virginia to Washington to take command of the Union Army. A few weeks later, the *Herald* reported the Confederates fought bravely, and they were "abundantly supplied with cannon and all the munitions of war."[18] By contrast, the Union soldiers had poor leadership. With McClellan at the helm, Bennett and his editors expected more. They also did not expect to be disappointed. The *Herald* believed the war would be over by the following May.

Although nowhere near as influential a journal as the *Tribune* or *Herald*, *The New York Times* was a formidable newspaper by the time of the Civil War. On July 23, it called the result a "Disaster to the National Army." Under a headline titled "Disasters of the Battle," a *Times* correspondent wrote that the Confederates had captured a Rhode Island battery. This article included lists of engaged regiments and the dead and wounded. The reporter also claimed Confederate reinforcements had come by railroad and that the Southern soldiers greeted their arrival with cheers.[19] Another New York newspaper, the *Journal of Commerce*, while more concerned with a tariff bill recently passed by Congress, called Bull Run a "serious disaster" after Johnston's Confederates arrived, suggesting the Union troops, "worn by fatigue, seem to have at once become panic stricken."[20]

The Dubuque, Iowa, *Herald* devoted far less column space devoted to the Battle of Bull Run than did its Eastern counterparts. Because it was so far from the field of battle, the Dubuque newspaper did not have the same reporting resources, as did many of the Eastern newspapers. The *Herald* reported that early on it looked like the Union would carry the day, but that later the Northern soldiers panicked. This caused a "disorderly retreat" and "dreadful" loss of life. Editor Dennis A. Mahony wrote that the Confederates had an advantage of some

15,000 soldiers but that next time the Union Army could expect reinforcement, and when the call of "Forward to Richmond" came again, the match would be conducted with "such prudence and judgment, that if a battle ensues, it will be one of success for the Federal Government."[21]

Three days later, the *Herald* ran lists of the dead and wounded. Soon newspapers all over the country began including casualty lists. However, these lists would provide only a partial representation of those who died in the war, as almost certainly the majority of the dead and wounded never were listed. Chaplains were generally responsible for the duty of compiling such lists, but only about half of all regiments for both armies even had chaplains.[22]

Soldiers also had their own newspapers. Union regiments would commandeer a newspaper office once they re-conquered a city. They would learn to set type and operate the press, leading to publication of regimental newspapers. One historian found that as many three hundred regimental papers were published during the war.[23] These newspapers included descriptions of camp life and successes of regiments in battle.

While the country's journalists cut their teeth on the battle at Bull Run and focused on the battles in the East, equally significant action was taking place in the western theater. Chickamauga, fought just south of Chattanooga, Tennessee, was typical of the western action. The second-bloodiest battle of the war, Chickamauga took place September 19 and 20, 1863, and produced a Confederate victory. Like other major western battles—Shiloh, Stones River, and Vicksburg—this clash in northwest Georgia took a high toll. Indeed, Chickamauga had the second highest number of casualties in the war—approximately 34,500 dead, wounded, and missing—with only Gettysburg spilling more blood during the four years of the war.

The Richmond *Examiner*, although reduced to two pages during the war, followed the events in Georgia with interest. Accustomed to Southern battlefield wins that did not add up to ultimate victory, the *Examiner* praised General Braxton Bragg for his careful assessment of the Chickamauga triumph. The *Examiner* also suggested the victory had no meaning without the recapture of Chattanooga. Union Major General Williams Rosecrans had occupied the Tennessee city since September 9, with the battle for its possession in November, resulting in a Northern victory. Yet, if Chattanooga were to be recaptured, then, according to the *Examiner*, the Confederate victory at Chickamauga would be one of the war's most important developments. Describing the ground at Chickamauga as "literally strewn with dead Yankees," the newspaper also reported on the death of Major General John Bell Hood. However, that report proved to be untrue. Hood was wounded, and a surgeon amputated his right leg. Thinking they were penning his obituary, the *Examiner* editors wrote: "As the leader of the brave Texas in the numerous battles in Virginia, his name is intimately connected with brilliant campaigns, and will long live in the memory of a grateful people."[24]

The New York Tribune called Chickamauga a "desperate engagement" and one of the "greatest battles of the war," in which the Confederates tried to put themselves between Rosecrans and Chattanooga. The next day, the *Tribune* claimed that Union losses were "very heavy" and that Rosecrans had an inferior force. By September 23, the *Tribune* called Chickamauga a Union disaster, although it could not gauge the degree of the calamity. The *Tribune* continued to claim Rebel forces were superior, between 70,000 and 96,000 men, and, putting Union losses at 12,000, reported Major General Ambrose E. Burnside would send the Army of the Ohio as reinforcements from Knoxville.[25]

As was the case with most battles in the war, the well-staffed *New York Herald* provided comprehensive coverage of Chickamauga. This included maps of the Chattanooga area. Early coverage in the *Herald* called the battle "desperate" and praised the "Esprit du Corps of the Union Troops." On the first day of the battle, according to the *Herald*, the Confederates attacked Union Major General George Thomas's left wing. Although it was a "savage engagement," the Union held, but later it faced a reinforced Southern force. Bennett's newspaper claimed Bragg's attempt to get in-between Rosecrans and Chattanooga had failed. On September 22, the *Herald* carried a large front-page map of southeast Tennessee, northeast Alabama, and northwest Georgia under the headline "The Battle Field near Chattanooga," and reported that Thomas had "handsomely" repelled the Rebel attack on the Union left.[26]

The New York Times called Chickamauga neither a crushing defeat nor a magnificent victory, although it conceded that it was a tactical Southern triumph. The *Times* called it a "temporary check" on Rosecrans' army. However, the newspaper also recognized that other Union successes that summer tempered the discouraging news from northwest Georgia. These included, of course, the victories at Gettysburg and Vicksburg, but also the win at Port Hudson and the possession of Knoxville and Little Rock. Because of the broader trend of Union success, *Times* editor Henry J. Raymond believed "the days of the rebellion are few and full of trouble to its authors." During the battle near Chattanooga, the *Times* also printed an editorial about the peace movement in North Carolina, saying it was now for peace because "a continuance of the war involves subjugation, and subjugation means ruin."[27]

Typical of many newspapers far from the war front, the Des Moines, Iowa, *Daily State Register* relied on exchange newspapers for its information about Chickamauga. After the first day of the battle, the *Register* reported that the Union Army was doing well and that Major General George H. Thomas had triumphed. However, the dispatch also claimed that Thomas had retreated to Rossville. The next day, a *Register* editorial called Chickamauga "about an even thing thus far" and wrote that the Confederates had concentrated their forces expecting to "wipe out the army of the Cumberland."[28] Newspapers singled out the dead from their cities. For example, the Baltimore *Sun* reported on John Keyser, a city resident shot in the right groin during battle who later died from the wound.[29]

News from Washington

Aside from direct accounts of battle, newspapers also featured legislative news. One of the first actions Congress took was an income tax to help pay for the war. Passed in August 1861, it tax met with relatively mild resistance from Northern editors, in part because Republican journalists favored the war, and they knew it would come at a significant fiscal cost, especially after the failure at Bull Run. *The New York Tribune*, one of those Republican papers, did note that the state of New York would pay $2.6 million of the total $20 million the income tax would raise—but a "very large portion of course falling upon the city."[30]

In a time well before the existence of the Internal Revenue Service, the *Tribune*'s editors believed each state would be in charge of assessing and collecting. *The New York Times* covered congressional deliberations on the income tax, but Henry J. Raymond's newspapers also chronicled disaffection with banks during the war. This included riots at several banks in Milwaukee in June 1861. Four banks and a real estate office faced damages to their buildings, and several employees were hurt. Eventually, after the fire department tried to disperse the rioters by spraying water on them, a German regiment arrested approximately fifty rioters. Those arrested were upset at bank failures because the banks had lost money on Southern state bonds that had become worthless. Other rioters threatened to attack the jail to earn their friends' release. Wisconsin's governor declared martial law in Milwaukee.

Other New York newspapers expressed no support for the tax. The *Herald* claimed Congress passed the income tax bill hastily, and reported that the tax would be 3 percent on all incomes "in excess of $800" and 5 percent on the "incomes of all non-residents."[31] The *Journal of Commerce* was uncomfortable with the fiscal policy of Congress in general. It was aghast at a House Ways and Means Committee report indicating that the war would cost the federal government $1.25 million per day, mainly because it wondered how long the war would last. The *Journal* suggested the country was just beginning to feel "the oppressive bearing" of the war debt upon the country.[32]

The Baltimore *Sun* did not oppose the tax. It ran daily transcripts of congressional sessions and first commented on the income tax on August 6, 1861. The newspaper held that the $20 million raised by the tax would help pay for the war. Arunah A. Abell's newspaper complained that it contained seventy-six sections, making it far too long and expressed apprehension about the tax. The tax was for income in excess of $800 after all other taxes were taken into consideration. In other words, according to the *Sun*, $800 would be deducted from the sum that the federal government taxed an individual.[33]

The New York Herald also covered resolutions passed by the House of Representatives giving President Lincoln indemnity from any unconstitutional actions taken by the administration, including suppression of newspapers. The *Herald*, which was generally critical of Lincoln, supported such indemnity, calling civil war a "singular circumstance."[34] Other Democratic editors also generally blasted the controversial Enrollment Act of 1863, asking how the Lincoln administration could coerce Northerners into fighting a war that he had made about freedom. Republican editors were less critical, although they had ridiculed the Confederacy for having a draft for more than a year before the Union finally resorted to conscription. With Southern newspapers generally supporting Jefferson Davis's use of conscription, the Richmond *Examiner* had claimed it "held our armies together and reinforced them with thousands of free troops."[35] Most Northern newspapers eventually accepted conscription and began printing lists of those drafted, often on the front page. *The New York Times'* lists included a last name, first initial, and township by county.

Another important early political issue was ensuring the allegiance of the Border States—Delaware, Maryland, Kentucky, and Missouri. Lincoln wanted them in the Union but wished to avoid coercing them. This evolved into a two-phase plan. The first stage involved strong-arm tactics that included suspension of civil liberties, such as freedom of the press. Journalists in Maryland and Missouri felt the narrowing of press freedoms most intensely, especially in 1861 and 1862. Then the Lincoln administration employed a more subtle method to keep the Border States from leaving.

Although it did not come from Congress, the greatest federal policy of the war was emancipation. When Lincoln announced the Emancipation Proclamation on September 22, 1862, the Republican press either praised the announcement or asked why it had taken so long to occur. Democratic editors were either skeptical or critical. The *Missouri Republican* supported the freeing of slaves in the South, as their owners had forfeited their rights by unconstitutionally leaving the Union. However, the *Republican* editors worried that slave owners in Missouri might lose their property. "As to loyal men, who do insist that neither the laws of war nor the behests of political classes, and the assumptions of executive power, give a justifiable pretext for interference with property, which under our charter of liberties," noted the pro-Democratic paper in St. Louis, "it is their privilege to hold. They have the right, guaranteed by their allegiance, to be protected in their property."[36] The *Daily Empire* in Dayton, Ohio, went further than the St. Louis paper. William D. Logan, editor of the Democratic journal, wrote that in adopting emancipation, the Lincoln administration had "annihilated every vestige of Constitutional and civil liberty, so long the cherished heritage and boast of the true American citizen."[37]

International news played a prominent role in the Civil War press because of intense interest in what England and France might do. American newspapers followed the press of those two nations and hired reporters to write from Europe. The *Journal of Commerce* in New York kept a close eye on the French. Early in the war, it reported that the French press thought Lincoln would prosecute the war more expeditiously and that he should make emancipation its central cause. There was also concern that the United States might go to war with Cuba in order to gain a place for Black refugees at the end of the domestic conflict. *Journal* editors attacked the quality of the French information about the Civil War, pointing to the "deficiency" of their sources—namely, overreliance on the English press. *Journal* leadership expressed relief that France opted to remain neutral to and recognize only the United States as a legitimate government. Thus, *Journal* editors wrote, the French declined to recognize any kind of equality between the warring states.[38] The *New York Times* reported on movements of British troops to Canada, holding that they were unnecessary, as the United States did not intend to invade its northern neighbor. The *Times* criticized the British press as trumping up alarm over American intent. The real worry for the Union was that the British might recognize the Confederacy.

Non-War News

American newspapers had made city news a fixture of journalism by midcentury, with editors devoting portions of at least one page to crime, municipal government, and accidents. For example, *The Chicago Tribune* published a story about a Black man arraigned in police court for the rape of a 10-year-old mulatto girl—the only witness called in the hearing. The *Tribune* commented that her "testimony was exceedingly ambiguous."[39] Interestingly, the article named both the accused and the accuser; the former was held on $800 bond. Similarly, the Baltimore *Sun* reported on riots that broke out in Detroit after a mulatto man, who happened to be a saloonkeeper named William Faulkner, molested both a white girl and a Black girl. Of course, the avenging mob took out their frustrations on the Black community. According to the *Sun*, "One colored woman made her appearance at the door [of her house] with a little child in arms, and appealed to the mob for mercy."[40]

The Springfield, Massachusetts, *Republican* reported on an abandoned infant girl who had died from strangulation and left no clues as to her parentage.[41] Based on an exchange with *The Chicago Post*, the Baltimore *Sun* reported on the death of an elderly Irish couple in the Illinois city who had died of heat exhaustion in August 1861. The *Post* story concluded with the coroner's jury report, which stated that the couple died from "'an accumulation of ills, old age, poverty, insufficiency of food, excessive heat, want of proper ventilation, and lowness of spirits, caused by homesickness.'"[42] A *Chicago Tribune* story in 1863 told of a 60-year-old man who died in bed, which he shared with his 15-year-old son. The coroner said that man had heart disease, according to the *Tribune*.[43]

Other local stories were more pedestrian, such as an item that appeared in the Springfield *Republican* about two men arrested for failure to obey city dog laws—although the story had a twist, inasmuch as the two were public officials from a nearby town. Moral twists made recurring appearances in the reporting of local news. The Springfield *Republican* had six lines about a preacher who had run off with "beautiful and accomplished" girl. Added at the end of article were these words: "More shame to her."[44] Sometimes the stories were just weird or unusual. For example, the Wilmington, North Carolina, *Daily Herald* wrote about a woman named Eleanor E. Southall who killed a large alligator "with a lightwood knot."[45]

Business news had a prominent place in Civil War newspapers. The Cleveland *Plain Dealer* provided daily market reports. The paper would give the price for a commodity and the level of sales. For example, on a summer day in 1861, the

Plain Dealer announced that butter sales were "very dull and prices nominal."[46] New York's *Journal of Commerce* put a business spin on much of its reporting. As was typical of the era, the newspaper included quantities of information in table formats, including weekly bank statements from the major institutions in New York, the daily stock quotations, the tonnage of commodities on board ships coming into the New York Harbor, and commodities being carried by rail. Similar in weight to the shipping news was information about the railroads. While the business sections included frequent stories about rail accidents, most of the information on transportation came in the form of train schedules. City newspapers included the name of the train station, the name of the train company, the line's destination, the time the train left, and its scheduled arrival time at various cities. Typical of papers in the hinterland, the *Daily State Register* in Iowa boasted about the best routes to major cities. For example, the *Register* touted the Galena & Chicago & Cedar Rapids Railroad as being the fastest line to Chicago. The *Register* claimed the trip to Chicago would take only twenty-four hours. Newspapers also included boxes about when mail trains arrive in various cities in a state or region. Another part of the business section included shipping news. *The New York Herald* gave the names of ships, their destinations, and their arrival dates, also including lists of ships that had cleared customs.

Another important type of news concerned religion—not necessarily weekly notices for services, but rather information about changes in pastors or guest ministers. For example, the Springfield *Republican* reported on the movements of various ministers, including the resignation of a Congregational pastor in New Marlboro, Massachusetts. Another item mentioned a minister who was "uneasy in his Presbyterianism," to whom church officials granted a release from service in the United States. The church allowed him to move to Canada.[47] The Baltimore *Sun* reminded Catholic readers about church services on the Festival of the Annunciation.[48] *The New York Tribune* covered the building of new churches. Of a Presbyterian church under construction on 55th Street near Lexington Avenue, the *Tribune* commented that the new building was of "considerable proportions" and was being built in the area where the draft riots in July 1863 had been centered. The church would hold five hundred congregants, according to the *Tribune*, which also kept a close watch on the migration of men and women to Utah to join the Mormons.[49]

The *Daily State Register* in Des Moines, Iowa, reported that the community was upset by the removal of a Methodist bishop. "He goes, but his work remains, and his home will long be in the hearts of our citizens," the writer commented.[50] The Dubuque *Herald* ran a weekly church directory that included the names of the church and pastor and the time of worship service. In Indiana, the *Daily Sentinel* noted that a group of churches had worked to raise money for the Indianapolis Orphan Society.

Coverage of education was generally limited to local issues involving common (public) schools. The Dubuque *Herald* in Iowa ran a list of the names of students promoted at various primary and secondary schools after exams, and was pleased to note that the results were "highly satisfactory."[51]

Weather did not dominate the news, but newspapers carried short articles about it when extremes occurred. The Wilmington *Daily Herald* ran an item about a thunderstorm in Wake County, North Carolina, that produced hail that accumulated three or four inches on the ground. The storm also "injured the crops seriously."[52] The Baltimore *Sun* reported on thunderstorms in the Midwest that caused vessels to break from their moorings. Streets were flooded, and wharves and railroad tracks damaged. The *Sun* also reported that flooding saved the pressroom of the Sandusky, Ohio, *Register* from fire. The *Sun* story stated that in Chicago the storm "blew the fiercest about three o'clock on Monday morning, accompanied by a fearful display of thunder, lightning and rain."[53]

The Springfield *Republican* termed temperatures above ninety degrees "extreme heat" during summer 1862. On another day, when the temperature reached the upper eighties, the newspaper called the weather "disagreeably hot and sultry."[54] Newspapers often reported on violent weather in other parts of the country. The Baltimore *Sun* told of a "destructive tornado" in Shelbyville, Kentucky, noting that the twister damaged the roofs of the courthouse and two churches.[55] Weather writing was often more poetical. For example, the Wilmington *Daily Herald* personified this 1859 thunderstorm: "Last night we were visited with quite a nice little shower of refreshing rain, and the earth this morning looked grateful as we came out."[56] On the other hand, *The New York Tribune* commented on the relative absence of violent weather in summer 1861: "This general absence of hurricanes and thunder-storm is in strong contrast with our experience of last year."[57] The *Daily Sentinel* in Indianapolis offered a most succinct, though qualified, description of the weather in April 1862: "Yesterday was a windy day, somewhat."[58] That summer, a correspondent for the Springfield *Republican* chronicled a meteor he had witnessed in Massachusetts. "It surpassed the planets in brightness," he wrote, "and intermitted its light at intervals of 10 to 15 seconds, fading and reappearing gradually like a revolving light."[59]

Health stories were also prevalent, especially those that dealt with disease. The Wilmington *Daily Herald* reported that a disease was killing hogs. The *Herald* claimed charcoal would "prove an effective remedy."[60] The Baltimore *Sun* reported on a yellow fever epidemic in Key West, Florida. The article noted that eighteen of fifty-six men in the New York 110th Volunteer Regiment had died of the disease. The news brief also confirmed the death of the Key West district attorney and the "master of the colored school."[61] The *Sun* also reported on attempts to help sick and dying soldiers. For example, the journal reported on a shipment of ice from Providence, Rhode Island, to the U.S. Sanitary Commission in Washington, D.C. Many health stories involved accidents, such as a Baltimore article about a Black woman who burned herself while lighting an oil lamp. The domestic was trying to light the lamp with the stove, but oil accidentally went into the flames, igniting. Her clothes immediately caught fire. Although severely burned, the woman was "out of danger."[62] Some of the health stories involved the unusual. For example, the Wilmington *Herald* ran a story about a Black woman who was experiencing intense pain from a toothache and suddenly died, adding, "This case has excited considerable interest and surprise in the neighborhood."[63]

Agricultural news had a central place in the newspapers of the Civil War. Sometimes newspapers would boast about the ability of farmers to produce a particular crop. A Wisconsin newspaper touted the ability of local farmers to raise tobacco. The editor wrote that Wisconsin ought to grow its own tobacco and "thus retain a large sum of money which are annually sent abroad."[64] The *Daily Sentinel* in Indianapolis reported in spring 1862 that its expert on peaches said the buds on the trees were unscathed by the winter weather. The *Sentinel* also reported "every indication" suggested there would be a "full if not an extraordinary crop" of apples that summer.[65] Like industrial news, agriculture reporting also included accident news. The *Daily State Register* in Iowa reported on a Charles Swetfigger, who was killed when an arm and leg were severed in a reaper accident. The article ended thusly: "He left a family."[66]

Science and industrial news was also common, especially in the larger cities. *The New York Tribune* wrote about advances in science. For example, it carried an 1861 story on a new process for baking bread. The *Tribune* pointed to the advantages of the new method, which was the use of carbonic acid "in a pure state under pressure." These plusses included faster productivity and greater cleanliness in baking the bread.[67] In covering a science and technology fair, the *Tribune* told readers "no family can possibly afford to do without" a washing machine, adding that the machine's wringers and squeezers were the most important exhibits at the fair.[68]

The New York Times ran a story about a dockworker strike a month before the Gettysburg battle, reporting that it was generally successful in getting men not to cross the line and work for the old wage. "A riot is anticipated," the story continued, "and a strong police force is in readiness to quell it."[69]

Newspapers also ran marriage announcements and death notices. *The New York Tribune* had a formula for marriage notes. It would give the last name of both parties, and then where and when the ceremony took place. Also included were the names of the fathers and their professions. The *Tribune's* obituaries included name, age, where death came, some identification (usually profession), and sometimes information about the funeral.

Another area that received attention was sports. Sports covered included horseracing, billiards, hunting, rowing, boxing, baseball, cricket, and chess. The Baltimore *Sun* included a report on the Goodwood Cup, a British horse race that had begun in 1808. The winner was a horse named Starke, owned by an American. The report noted that Starke answered the call of his jockey in the stretch run "in a gallant manner, and after protracted finish landed the American colors first by a head only."[70]

The *Sun* also mentioned that an American ice skater named Jackson Haines was moving to England to try to make a living performing in Europe, and that a race "between fat men" scheduled in Philadelphia required a minimum weight of 250 pounds for participants.[71] The Cleveland *Plain Dealer* boosted a local establishment named Richard's Billiard Rooms, saying its seven tables would give fans of the game a "principal resort during the winter."[72] New York and Boston newspapers covered baseball, and papers in New York and Indiana covered cricket. For example, the Brooklyn *Eagle* devoted a few lines to the Brooklyn cricket club when it played matches.

The Charleston *Daily Courier* covered water sports in the low country of South Carolina. That included rowing in Charleston Harbor. One story covered nine paragraphs and in a concluding sentence told readers of the sports benefits: "All who are interested in the promotion of innocent gymnastics, and in the physical health and welfare of our young men of sedentary pursuits and occupations should encourage this pastime." The *Courier* also devoted considerable space to hunting. A story about game bird hunting in October 1859 covered seven paragraphs. This highly detailed story was designed to attract tourists from the North to the Charleston area. It emphasized the warm fall and winter weather in the low country. "Come to the South, then, in winter ye who seek sport and healthful pastime," the *Courier* writer intoned.[73] The newspaper also published a weekly chess column on its front page. This included an engraved graphic of a chessboard with the pieces placed in certain positions to represent the problem under discussion for that day. The Wilmington *Herald* covered regattas.

In a fall 1859 race, the newspaper reported that a sailboat named *Anna* had won the race on a day of light wind.[74]

Other forms of entertainment news were popular in the Civil War press. *The New York Journal of Commerce* demonstrated a typical interest in the arts, especially literature, drama, and highbrow magazines. Their coverage included book reviews, dramatic notices, and updates on the latest in the periodical press. *The New York Times* provided information on Manhattan's plays and musical events. The *Times* also had notes about New York artists abroad. For example, it remarked on how pianist Nicholas Rubenstein was "playing in London with success."[75] *The New York Herald* had an "Amusements This Evening" list that included drama, music, and minstrel shows, publishing the program of music concerts in Central Park in the summertime. The Springfield *Republican* had a literature page on Fridays that included book reviews, poetry, short stories, and a notes column on various happenings in the arts.

Coverage of minorities mostly concerned slavery and the relationship with Native Americans, although some newspapers in larger Northern cities covered the Black community's reaction to major wartime events. This was especially the case with the Emancipation Proclamation and the passing of the Thirteenth Amendment. *The New York Tribune* sought foremost to refute the argument put forth by Southern journalists that slaves were content with their lives. The *Tribune*, in one case, provided a historical account of the insurrection led by Denmark Vesey in South Carolina in 1822. The *Tribune* wrote that slavery had "not improved in these forty years" since Vesey led his revolt.[76] On the other hand, the pro-Democrat Indianapolis (IN) *Daily Sentinel* expressed disdain for the idea of having Black children attend public schools. It commented: "The universal sentiment seemed to be that a little white child, born of honest and respectable parents, should not be set side by side with a nigger to learn her A, B, C's."[77]

As for coverage of Native Americans, most stories concerned the status of treaties or warfare in the West, especially in Minnesota. *The New York Tribune* reported on a neutrality stance taken by the chief of the Cherokee nation, noting that the chief had warned his people not to profit off the war. According to the *Tribune*, the chief had earnestly impressed upon his people the importance of non-interference, and trusted that God would keep the desolation of the war from their borders.[78] The *Daily State Register* reported on a meeting between the federal government and Native Americans in which the latter objected to having to move even further north. "It seems hard to persuade them to leave their present hunting grounds for strange lands, but after due deliberation it will be accomplished," the *Register* remarked.[79] The Des Moines newspaper did not specify which tribe was participating in the negotiations. Also in Iowa, the Dubuque *Herald* wrote about the U.S. Army fighting Native Americans in the West, including in Utah. The *Herald* noted that the Indians had cut telegraph lines.

Another important type of Civil War-era entertainment reporting was the travelogue. Horace Greeley himself took a journey west in summer 1859. He traveled by rail to Missouri and by stagecoach the rest of the way. As was the custom, the *Tribune* editor wrote letters for publication in the newspaper. At Yosemite, Greeley wrote that the balsam firs "were the most beautiful trees on earth."[80] In some cases, such as in Greeley's travels west, the amount of attention readers paid to individual editors became a central feature of the news itself.

Personal Journalism

While the best description of journalism from the Civil War era includes its combination of the interpretive and informative, it also had a personal component, with the voice and personality of the journalist adding an integral aspect to content and reader response. Certainly that was the case with the likes of Horace Greeley of *The New York Tribune*, Wilbur F. Storey of *The Chicago Times*, and Robert Barnwell Rhett of the Charleston *Mercury*. One of the most peculiar personalities of the war was Marcus "Brick" Pomeroy, editor of the La Crosse, Wisconsin, *Democrat*. Few editors in either section of the country unleashed a higher degree of vitriol than did Pomeroy.

For Pomeroy, the rhetorical war he conducted against the war was personal, in the sense that he constantly attacked Abraham Lincoln. He complained, for example, that the spending of the Lincoln administration in its first term exceeded that of "all the expenditure of government since its foundation." He also sought to rally Democratic journalists during the war.

> It is not child's play to edit a democratic newspaper in these times. None but brave men will hazard their lives at the hands of cowardly mobs—their property at the hands of insane rioters, or toil early and late to right the ship of state as democratic editors who have the pluck to speak plainly do every day in the week.[81]

Pomeroy claimed that "seventy five thousand tons of human blood" had spilled, and in another example of his bombastic style, he attacked Lincoln as an ineffective leader and lampooned the president for "for his imbecilic incompetency and for his success in ruining a great country." For all the bloodshed in the war, Pomeroy condemned Lincoln "for making a million of widows and five million of orphans." The La Crosse editor, who termed anyone who voted for the president a traitor, branded Lincoln the "widow maker of the 19ᵗʰ Century" in one column while hammering at the his tax policy in another. Yet his most vituperative comment suggested to his readers something far more sinister than simply Lincoln's personal and political faults. On August 2, 1864, Pomeroy wrote the following about Lincoln: "If he is elected to misgovern for another four years, we trust some bold hand will pierce his heart with dagger point for the public good."[82] Written during the Democratic convention of 1864, these words represented not only the ravings of an infuriated editor, but also the last gasp of life of the old Democratic Party. Free-speech arguments aside, inciting violence against the president instead of working to help the Democrats reclaim power was at the very least a poor business maneuver—costing readers and leading to a drop in Pomeroy's subscribers to a mere four hundred.[83]

The close of the war brought the eventual departure of personal journalism as well, as news slowly began to reassume a more formulaic quality. The transformation to content-driven information supported primarily by advertising and less according to editorial decisions took a decade or more to complete, but the first signs of the change came in early April 1865. *The New York Tribune* began putting all of its war news under the title "Virginia," as the Union Army had occupied Richmond and businesses on Main Street burned.

An enormous headline in Greeley's April 10 paper read: "Lee Surrenders! The Rebellion Ended!" All of the front-page reporting came from official dispatches from Secretary of War Edwin M. Stanton and Ulysses S. Grant, among others. Elsewhere in the *Tribune* was the sheet music and lyrics to the song "Victory at Last." The song ended: "Nail it to the mast, for there's victory at last, victory, victory at last."[84]

James Gordon Bennett's *Herald* met the close of the war with equal excitement, although he, too, was seeing his personal influence on coverage wane. His lead April 10, 1865, headline read simply, "The End" with ten more headlines following, including "Intense Enthusiasm." In Bennett's editorial that day, he wrote, "The grand climax has been reached." The *Herald* had a map that nearly took up the entire front page of central Virginia between Richmond and Lynchburg. Coverage in the *Herald* included how New Yorkers were reacting to the news. The *Herald* noted that students at New York University sang "America" and the doxology after morning prayers.[86]

Elsewhere, the end of the war signaled the close of not only of the nation's most terrible ordeal, but an era in journalism, with Henry Raymond's *New York Times*, April 10, reading, "Union. Victory! Peace!"[87] The Des Moines *Daily State*

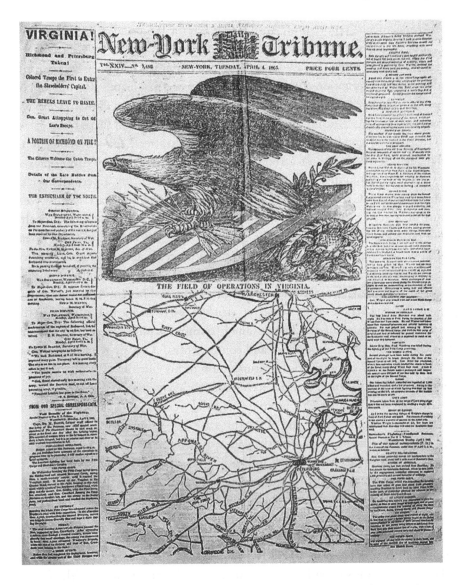

Image 6.1 *New-York Tribune*, April 4, 1865, front page. This spectacular issue features the headline "Richmond and Petersburg Taken!" The American eagle sits on a flag shield with arrows in its claws, while behind it are twigs of victory laurels, set on a cornucopia of the farm bounty of America. Below is as large a woodcut, being a map of "The Field of Operations in Virginia." The entire rear page filled with a topographical map of Richmond and the 30 miles surrounding the city.[85]

Register meanwhile reported on April 9 that "Grant Is Confident of Capturing" Lee, and two days later, it proclaimed "Surrender of Lee!"[88] In Chicago, the *Tribune* headline read, "The Old Flag Vindicated," with a lead story on Lee's surrender and the restoration of the Union. The Chicago newspaper also announced "The Draft Stopped and No More Recruiting."[89] Pomeroy's La Crosse *Democrat*, perhaps less enthusiastically, announced "The Great Rebellion Played Out."[90]

The tide of good feeling was short. Five days after Lee's surrender, John Wilkes Booth—who almost certainly had not heard of Pomeroy's 1864 plea—assassinated Lincoln at Ford's Theater in Washington during a performance of "Our American Cousin." Republican newspapers from the East to the West mourned. Greeley, who had at times a problematic relationship with Lincoln, wrote only kind words of him. The *Tribune* called the assassination a "Great Calamity" and reported that Booth was still at large. It also ran the Associated Press account of the assassination that included an almost minute-by-minute report of the physician at the scene. Greeley's editorial began: "The immediate presence of the horrible crime which has stricken the Republic to the heart, in the hour of its transcendent and long-awaited triumph, is unfavorable to a full and clear conception of its importance and consequences." Greeley went on to praise Lincoln for never stooping to the vituperation of his enemies. The editor added that Lincoln had fallen "a sacrifice to his country's salvation."[91]

In the West, under the headline "Terrible News," *The Chicago Tribune* informed readers that at the end of the third act, "a person entered the box occupied by the President, and shot Mr. Lincoln in the head." Two days later, the *Tribune* commented: "The nation mourns. Its agony is great. Its grief is dumb. Never before have the American people been so stricken. The ball that pierced the President has pierced the hearts of all of us."[92] Medill called the assassination the most horrid crime since the killing of Jesus.

Elsewhere in New York, the *Herald* used the same official dispatches as other papers, but Bennett also relied on his Washington correspondent, who reported, "The President was shot at Ford's Theatre. ... Result not yet known." The *Herald* announced a $10,000 reward for assistance in arresting the assassin and called the murder a "terrible calamity," noting that business in New York had nearly come to a halt.[93] *The New York Times* reporter wrote: "A stroke from Heaven laying the whole of the city in instant ruins could have startled us as did the word that broke from Ford's Theatre a half hour ago that the President had been shot." On Sunday, April 16, the *Times* reported that Booth was believed to be the assassin. Henry J. Raymond wrote, "The heart of the nation was stirred yesterday as it had never been before. The news of the assassination of Abraham Lincoln carried with it a sensation of horror and of agony which no other event in our history has ever excited."[94]

In the Midwest, the reaction was equally heartfelt, with the Des Moines *Daily State Register* publishing a dispatch of the "violent death of our beloved President" and calling Lincoln the "predestined savior of our country" It encouraged readers to "display a confidence in trust" in new president Andrew Johnson.[95] In Wisconsin, the lead headline of Pomeroy's La Crosse *Democrat* read "Assassination of Abraham Lincoln." Its lead story—ironically in view of a past statement from Pomeroy—demanded the blood of the man who shot the president. Like almost every other paper in the North, the *Democrat* had bold black lines in the alleys of its columns, an expression of sadness for the murdered president. On April 17, under the headline "General Sorrow," Pomeroy wrote, "The head of the nation has been foully murdered, and this at an hour when his goodness of heart and kindness of disposition gave promise of such hope for the nation."[96]

Pomeroy's political enemies believed he was somehow behind the plot to assassinate Lincoln. However, Pomeroy would defend his rhetorical excesses. His words were merely political, he held. Still, they could cite his editorial, which intimated the death of a president as a political solution, as a call to action. Pomeroy escaped punishment for his words, and after the war faced the challenge of reinventing himself. First, he moved to New York to edit a Democratic newspaper for Boss Tweed, and then he returned to Chicago to publisher a paper called *Pomeroy's Democrat*. Finally, he ended up in Denver running the *Great West* newspaper. Perhaps Pomeroy never stopped practicing personal journalism, but in many ways, the personal and political were in their nadir. A decade after the war, the number of newspapers claiming to be political had dropped from 80 to 67 percent. Thus, a major lesson of journalism in the Civil War era was limitation of the interpretive press.

Notes

1 Frankfort (KY) *Commonwealth*, October 24, 1859.
2 *Republican Banner and Nashville Whig*, October 24, 1859.
3 Nashville (TN) *Union and American*, October 21, 1859.
4 Charleston (SC) *Mercury*, October 19, 1859.
5 Chicago *Press and Tribune*, October 22, 1859.
6 Richmond (VA) *Whig*, October 18, 1859.
7 Wilmington (NC) *Daily Herald*, October 18, 1859.

8 Augusta (GA) *Chronicle & Sentinel*, October 22, 1859.

9 Wilmington (NC) *Daily Herald*, October 20, 1859.

10 New Orleans *Picayune*, October 25, 1859; Austin (TX) *Texas State Gazette*, November 5, 1859; Wilmington (NC) *Daily Herald*, October 26, 1859.

11 Baltimore *Sun*, October 19, 1859, December 2, 1859.

12 Reynolds and Reddin van Tuyll, *The Greenwood Library of American War Reporting*, 7.

13 Baltimore *Sun*, July 24, 1861.

14 Cleveland *Plain Dealer*, July 24, 30, 1861.

15 Baltimore *Sun*, July 24, 25, 1861.

16 Ibid, July 27, 1861, August 9, 1861.

17 New York *Tribune*, July 21, 22, 23, 1861.

18 New York *Herald*, July 22, 1861, August 3, 1861.

19 New York *Times*, July 23, 1861.

20 New York *Journal of Commerce*, July 23, 1861.

21 Dubuque (IA) *Herald*, July 23, 1861.

22 Drew Gilpin Faust, *This Republic of Suffering: Death and the American Civil War* (New York: Vintage Books, 2008), 104.

23 Wallace B. Eberhard, "Editors in Uniform: The Historiography of Civil War Soldier Newspapers," presented to the Symposium on the 19th Century Press, the Civil War and Free Expression, University of Tennessee at Chattanooga, November 10, 2006, 2.

24 Richmond (VA) *Examiner*, September 22, 23, 25, 1863.

25 New York *Tribune*, September 21, 22, 23, 1863.

26 New York *Herald*, September 21, 24, 1863.

27 New York *Times*, September 24, 1863.

28 Des Moines (IA) *Daily State Register*, September 23, 24, 25, 1863.

29 Baltimore *Sun*, June 18, 1863.

30 New York *Tribune*, August 6, 1861.

31 New York *Herald*, August 7, 1861.

32 New York *Journal of Commerce*, August 7, 1861.

33 Baltimore *Sun*, August 7, 1861.

34 New York *Herald*, August 8, 1861.

35 Richmond (VA) *Examiner*, January 1, 1863.

36 St. Louis (MO) *Republican*, September 25, 1862.

37 Dayton (OH) *Daily Empire*, January 2, 1863.

38 New York *Journal of Commerce*, June 22, 24, 1861.

39 Chicago *Tribune*, April 30, 1863.

40 Baltimore *Sun*, March 10, 1863.

41 Springfield (MA) *Republican*, July 17, 1862.

42 Baltimore *Sun*, August 9, 1861.

43 Chicago *Tribune*, April 30, 1863.

44 Springfield (MA) *Republican*, July 10, 14, 1862.
45 Wilmington (NC) *Daily Herald*, December 21, 1859.
46 Cleveland *Plain Dealer*, July 24, 1861.
47 Springfield (MA) *Republican*, July 12, 1862.
48 Baltimore *Sun*, March 25, 1863.
49 New York *Tribune*, September 5, 1863.
50 Des Moines (IA) *Daily State Register*, September 23, 1863.
51 Dubuque (IA) *Herald*, July 4, 1862.
52 Wilmington (NC) *Daily Herald*, July 13, 1859.
53 Baltimore *Sun*, August 19, 1861.
54 Springfield (MA) *Republican*, July 10, 17, 1862.
55 Baltimore *Sun*, August 13, 1864.
56 Wilmington (NC) *Daily Herald*, May 10, 1859.
57 New York *Tribune*, August 6, 1861.
58 Indianapolis (IN) *Daily Sentinel*, April 3, 1862.
59 Springfield (MA) *Republican*, July 8, 1862.
60 Wilmington (NC) *Daily Herald*, July 9, 1859.
61 Baltimore *Sun*, August 17, 1864.
62 Baltimore *American*, December 30, 1861.
63 Wilmington (NC) *Daily Herald*, December 21, 1859.
64 Waukesha (WI) *Freeman*, August 30, 1864.
65 Indianapolis (IN) *Daily Sentinel*, April 3, 1862.
66 Des Moines (IA) *Daily State Register*, July 14, 1863.
67 New York *Tribune*, May 20, 1861.
68 Ibid, September 5, 1863.
69 New York *Times*, June 9, 1863.
70 Baltimore *Sun*, August 19, 1861.
71 Baltimore *Sun*, August 27, 1864, September 2, 1864.
72 Cleveland *Plain Dealer*, October 24, 1861.
73 Charleston (SC) *Daily Courier*, August 6, 1859, October 18, 1859.
74 Wilmington (NC) *Daily Herald*, September 24, 1859.
75 New York *Times*, June 30, 1861.
76 New York *Tribune*, May 21, 1861.
77 Indianapolis (IN) *Daily Sentinel*, May 19, 1862.
78 New York *Times*, June 26, 1861.
79 Des Moines (IA) *Daily State Register*, March 7, 1863.
80 Greeley, *An Overland Journey from New York to San Francisco in the Summer of 1859*, Charles T. Duncan, ed. (New York: Alfred A. Knopf, 1859, 1964), 257.
81 La Crosse (WI) *Democrat*, July 29, 1864, August 1, 1864.
82 Ibid, August 2, 3, 5, 1864.

83 Frank L. Klement, "'Brick' Pomeroy: Copperhead and Curmudgeon," *Wisconsin Magazine of History*, 35, 2 (Winter 1951): 113.

84 New York *Tribune*, April 10, 1865.

85 New York *Tribune*, April 4, 1865, Library of Congress, accessed October 27, 2021, at <loc.gov/item/sn83030213/1865-04-04/ed-1>.

86 New York *Herald*, April 10, 11, 1865.

87 New York *Times*, April 10, 1865.

88 Des Moines (IA) *Daily State Register*, April 11, 1865.

89 Chicago *Tribune*, April 10, 14, 1865.

90 La Crosse (WI) *Democrat*, April 10, 1865.

91 New York *Tribune*, April 15, 17, 1865.

92 Chicago *Tribune*, April 15, 17, 1865.

93 New York *Herald*, April 15, 17, 1865.

94 New York *Times*, April 15, 16, 1865.

95 Des Moines (IA) *Daily State Register*, April 15, 16, 1865.

96 La Crosse (WI) *Democrat*, April 17, 1865.

7

Classifieds of the Era: The Case of Ads about Runaway Slaves

$50 Reward
"Broke Jail in Sampson County, on the 28th inst., my negro man Stephen. Said negro is about 5 feet 8 or 10 inches high, dark complected, spare built, and quite intelligent. He can write very well, and will undoubtedly attempt to pass as free. He has been confined in the Newbern Jail for the last six months. He represented himself as free … I will pay the above reward for his delivery to me, or his confinement in any Jail so that I can get him." E. F. Shaw, Clinton, North Carolina, published in *Fayetteville Carolinian*, January 5, 1850.

During the nineteenth century, U.S. newspapers routinely ran notices or advertisements about runaway slaves. While the majority of the advertising did occur in Southern newspapers, some appeared in Border State and Washington, D.C., newspapers. The following will examine how American newspapers constructed these notices—essentially classified advertisements (although that term was not used in journalism at the time). Some notices were from the slave owners (sometimes called the "subscriber" in the ad) asking for help in finding runaways. Others were from law enforcement agents asking owners to come collect their slaves from far-flung places. The ads were generally ten to twenty lines in length, with a concise headline such as "Runaway Negro in Jail," "Committed to Jail," "Negroes Lost or Stolen," or "Run Away." They generally appeared on the inside of these often-weekly newspapers, usually on the third or fourth page. Occasionally they were accompanied by visuals, called "ornaments." The ads varied in terms of their placement on the page—sometimes near the top, sometimes near the bottom, sometimes in the middle, but usually within a gray sea of text. They were nothing like modern advertising, but rather more closely resembled classified advertising.

Most were written objectively and in the third person. However, the slave owner attempting to locate his runaway slave or slaves, with a reward for the person returning the runaway, wrote some in the first person—as a narrative, usually.

News media in the United States in the first part of the nineteenth century (with the exception of abolitionist journals) were complicit in the perpetuation of slavery. Media continued slavery's legitimatization at a time when there was a major national debate about how the nation would proceed with this economic, social, political institution. It also shows the national divide, as these ads disappeared in Northern newspapers in the nineteenth century. Thus, newspapers, by publishing notices about runaway slaves, essentially acted as conservative agents for the constitutional maintenance of slavery. The sheer volume of runaway advertising shows us the nature and strength of the resistance to slavery, as well.

The following study features ads between 1800 and 1865, focusing on key phrases, such as skin color, clothing, personality traits, physical size—height and/or weight—scars from whippings, and the magnitude of reward, as well as points of view, attitudes toward the slaves, and number of lines of type. It shows that these ads helped legitimize slavery by normalizing activities associated with the retrieval of runaways. The study includes ads found in Gale's Nineteenth Century U.S. Newspapers archives, the Chronicling America website, the University of North Carolina at Greensboro's "North Carolina Runaway Slaves Advertisements" projects, Runaway Slave Ads from Baltimore County by Julie DeMatteis and Louis S. Diggs Sr., and the Texas Runaway Slave Project.

Slavery and Nineteenth-Century Journalism

American newspapers in the nineteenth century were full of information about slaves and slavery. As a topic, slavery was a mainstay in the journalistic agenda. Much of the information came in news stories about how state and national government were dealing with the issue. These stories often were about ordinances on either side of the issue that passed or failed in city council or state legislature votes. There also were editorials expressing opinions about slavery and abolition, such as one in the *Baltimore Clipper* in 1851 that criticized whites who had held that there was a higher law than the Constitution, and that slaves were thus justified in "forcible resistance"—that is, in committing violence against their masters.[1]

Another kind of story was about crimes that runaway slaves had committed. These were usually cautionary in nature, such as the story of how a slave (a nurse) kidnapped a white four-year-old in New Orleans who was playing outside her house in a city street. The slave carried the four-year-old into the woods near an Army camp, and a police officer happened to notice the pair. He took both to the camp and discovered that the slave was lying about the situation. The white girl was returned to her family, which filed a complaint, and the slave was "sent to prison to await an examination."[2] The messages to the public were: (1) be careful with your children, and (2) slaves will steal and lie.

Yet another kind of story was one that recounted a successful attempt to apprehend a runaway or runaways. For example, an 1858 story in the Evansville (IN) *Daily Journal* recounted how a bounty hunter and policeman in Vincennes ambushed three runaways from Kentucky who were headed toward Canada.[3]

A final kind of story—advertisements about runaway slaves—usually included a specific reward. These advertisements had their roots in eighteenth-century American newspapers, when slavery was legal even in most Northern states.

Image 7.1 "$150 Reward [cut of runaway slave]. Ranaway from the Subscriber, on the Night of the 2d Instant, a Negro Man, Who Calls Himself Henry May,... William Burke, Bardstown, Ky., September 3d, 1838." The Library of Congress includes notes about this broadside indicating it was created in Bardstown, 1838, and gifted to the archives from Arthur Douglas, Hulls, York, England. The original woodcut is in Wilberforce House, Hulls.[4]

These advertisements (really announcements, almost of a legal status, often under a heading of "General Notices") were concise—usually ten to twenty lines of copy. They included a brief description of the runaway and an announcement of a reward for returning the slave to the owner, jailer, or sheriff. Some were about runaways found, jailed, and waiting for their owners to claim them. A small work of art called an ornament, which usually depicted a Black man walking with a stick over his shoulder, sometimes accompanied the ads. Tied to the stick was a handkerchief stuffed with whatever possessions the man had. The ornament cost a printer approximately $1.50 from a type cast company.[5]

These advertisements dehumanized the slaves—conferring on them the same status as other items for sale on the pages of American newspapers, such as boots, Christmas presents, cutlery, dry goods, firearms, furniture, groceries, hardware, hats, homes, pianos, real estate, and stationery. They appeared on the same pages as did service ads for attorneys, dentists, doctors, and schools. Typically, owners, sheriffs, or jailers bought the classified advertisements. The sponsors of the ads generally gave rewards as an incentive for a member of the public to return the slave. If a runaway ended up with law enforcement, the advertisement asked the owner to prove possession of this runaway up for sale "to the highest bidder" in front of the courthouse.[6] In some cases, the ads stated that if the owner did not come forward, law enforcement would sell the runaway at auction. An 1850 fugitive slave advertisement from St. Louis, Missouri, states that the owner had three months from the date of publication to retrieve the slave. The worst punishment was being returned to the owner, who often administered medieval lashings from a leather strap—as much as one hundred in a day.[7] In some instances, owners may have preferred to let runaways go because they did not want to travel great distances for retrieval or to pay fees associated with regaining the slave from law enforcement—especially if the slave was in poor health.

By the nineteenth century, most of these ads were appearing solely in Southern newspapers as slavery was gradually abolished in Northern states. American journalism, perhaps unintentionally, essentially helped underpin slavery as the cotton producers in the South fed textile manufacturing in the North, with much of the venture capital coming from British financial houses. By charging owners, sheriffs, and jailers to publish advertisements informing the public about lost or found runaways, newspapers helped buoy the slave system. Runaway slave ads were part of the ecology of nineteenth-century American journalism. They were a source of revenue for editors/publishers (often the same person), and they evinced two contradictory facets of American life: (1) an openness and acceptance of a labor system that many of the founding fathers had known was immoral; and (2) a very public demonstration of the discontent that existed among the slaves themselves. Instead of hiding what could have been construed as a disgraceful and evil system (which was the growing sentiment in the North), American journalism broadcast the fact that thousands of slaves had fled their masters. This helped stoke the flames of abolitionists, whose leadership included editors William Lloyd Garrison and Frederick Douglass.

In the following study, the authors look at the uniformity and presence of these ads from 1800 to 1865 (the latter being the year the Civil War ended) and analyze how these classifieds became a staple of American journalism in this period. The study examines one hundred and twenty-five runaway slave advertisements. These ads included the first name of the slave, the gender (approximately eighty percent of the runaways were male), approximate age, some sort of physical description (often height and skin color, as well as blemishes, scars, and infirmities), and the reward for returning the slave to the owner.[8]

Again, most of the advertisements appeared in Southern or Border State newspapers. In the eighteenth century, they had been common in newspapers in the North, but they gradually lost their popularity there and decreased over time. This was largely due to Congress passing the Act Prohibiting the Importation of Slaves in 1807, which became law in 1808. The Constitution allowed it, and President Thomas Jefferson promoted it.

The status of runaway slaves in America had a complicated history leading up to the 1808 law. Before the Revolution, there was a sense in the South that slave runaways were not a serious problem since it was cheaper just to purchase another slave than it was to track one down. In addition, most runaways at that time preferred to seek refuge in swamps or other relatively remote places that whites preferred to avoid. Still, runaways were an issue, and South Carolina had a fugitive slave law in place as early as 1683. That law gave sheriffs the power to raise a group of men to track down runaways, and the taxpayers had to pay the bill. A little more than a century later, Georgia had a law that required Savannah to have a nightly crew of law enforcement officers scouring the port city for absconding slaves.[9] Even in the North, when those colonies still had slavery, there had long been a custom of returning a slave as long as the master could prove the slave belonged to him.

The Founding Fathers were no strangers to the fugitive issue. George Washington, Benjamin Franklin (when he was a printer, he allowed slaves-for-sale advertisements in his journals), and Thomas Jefferson saw some of their slaves flee. During the Revolution, as a wartime strategy, the British encouraged slaves to abscond from their masters. Indeed, the British told slaves they would win their freedom if they came and worked for the Redcoats. Of course, the war's result left slaves in limbo. The treaty made it a British responsibility to return slaves to their owners, but this was more theory than practice. George Washington gave up on getting back his slaves lost during the Revolution, as many of them had run away to what would later be called Canada, mainly the eastern provinces. Later, Andrew Jackson, hero of the War of 1812 and eventually the President of the United States, owned slaves and had runaways. In an advertisement that appeared in the *Tennessee Gazette,* Jackson wrote that he would provide a $50 reward and pay all expenses related to retrieval of a "Mulatto Man Slave" who was headed toward Ohio or to the western part of the Louisiana Territory. There would be a bonus for anyone returning the slave from beyond the borders of Tennessee.[10]

The U.S. Constitution made it mandatory for slaves who left their masters in a slave state and ended up in a free state to be returned to their masters. Furthermore, masters in the Southern states wanted to be sure that they could take their slaves into free states and not have them confiscated.[11]

> *Article IV, Section 2, Clause 3*: No person held to service or labour in one state, under the laws thereof, escaping into another, shall, in consequence of any law or regulation therein, be discharged from such service or labor, but shall be delivered up on claim of the party to whom such service or labour may be due.[12]

This clause was added to the Constitution in part to ensure that non-slavery states would not discredit or undermine laws in slave states. The hope was that this would prevent the establishment of safe havens. There was some backlash from a few Northern politicians who thought it was unfair for citizens of non-slave states—or those masters possessing only a small numbers of slaves—to have to pay for enforcement of escaped slaves from states retaining slavery or having a large number of slaves. The Southern delegates to the Constitutional Convention believed joining the Union would help with the retention of slaves, simply because as the Union of states strengthened over time, so would extradition laws.

The Northwest Ordinance of 1781, Fugitive Slave Act of 1793, and Missouri Compromise of 1850 bolstered the Fugitive Slave Clause. The Northwest Ordinance outlawed slavery north of the Ohio River in the then-territories that the United States possessed, but it also stated that runaway slaves "may be lawfully reclaimed, and conveyed to the person claiming his or her service."[13] The 1793 act put fugitive slaves at risk for recapture their entire lives while setting a $500 fine (a large sum then) for anyone who obstructed the attempt of an owner or his agent to regain an escaped slave. It required the governor of the state from which the runaway had fled to send an indictment to the governor of the state to which the slave fled.[14] The 1850 law required law enforcement to uphold it and essentially made it an act of treason to help an escaped slave. Indeed, Democratic newspapers in the North would rail at the "Black Republicans" for claiming the Fugitive Slave Act of 1850 was subversive and "abhorrent to the moral sense of the civilized world," especially when Republicans said that resistance to the law could include the use of violence in helping the slave escape.[15]

The legality of slave retrieval at the federal level made newspaper ads for runaways legal and socially acceptable. Throughout the period under study here, no institutional organization existed to consider ethical and professional standards for journalism; that would not come until the early twentieth century. So, publishers and editors were free to run the runaway slave ads without consideration of any professional standards. Hence, many American journalists had no moral qualms about running ads that helped masters, their agents, or law enforcement track down runaway slaves—ads that, at same time, helped editors pay their bills.

The journalists who printed these runaway ads seemed unconcerned about how their newspapers might look to the public, especially south of the Mason-Dixon Line. In the South, publishing runaway slave ads was ordinary business in journalism in both the eighteenth and nineteenth centuries. The practice was common and open, and the price of publishing such an advertisement was a pittance. Furthermore, the ads were striking in their casual depiction of the mutilation of the slaves at the hands of their masters, as well as the harsh conditions slaves faced in their labor environments. Mentions of scars on the face, shortened legs, limb wounds, and lost fingers were commonplace.[16] There was little attempt to hide the fact that the slaves had been whipped or beaten. Another frequent description was the "inclination to steal."[17]

The Eighteenth-Century Precedent

But what went before, in terms of advertising about slaves in the U.S. press before the nineteenth century? Patricia Bradley examined "Slave Advertising in the Colonial Newspaper" (Association for Education in Journalism and Mass Communication, 1987). She observed that the ads of the eighteenth-century press, both North and South, sometimes unintentionally humanized slaves by mentioning their relatives in the notices. Bradley emphasizes that Colonial press depictions had an inherent paradox, in that masters legally owned the slaves, yet lived with them on a day-to-day basis and knew that they were human—even if they did not treat them so. As Bradley put it, "slave advertising served as an ongoing reminder of the dilemma of slavery."[18]

Lathan Algerna Windley's *Runaway Slave Advertisements: A Documentary History from the 1730's to 1790* (Routledge, 2013) notes that an extraordinary amount of energy and money was spent on attempts to apprehend runaway slaves, not to mention the loss of labor and the need to compensate for that. Indeed, the "number of runaways was large enough to sap a part of the economic advantage of a slave labor force."[19] Andrew Delbanco's *The War Before the War: Fugitive Slaves and the Struggle for America's Soul from the Revolution to the Civil War* (Penguin, 2018) shows how runaway slaves were a central issue leading to the U.S. Civil War. Delbanco helps provide context for the ads, as he provides an analysis of the policies in U.S. history that governed fugitive slaves and the attempt to recover them. Gordon S. Barker's *Fugitive Slaves and the Unfinished American Revolution: Eight Cases, 1848-1856* (McFarland, 2013) uses case studies to show the inhumane nature of slavery and the legal quandaries runaway slaves faced in a key period leading up to the Civil War.

Runaway Ads

In analyzing one hundred and twenty-five runaway slave ads, the authors found certain themes and common traits. The title of the ads and their locations within the newspaper offer important windows into the views and attitudes of society. The most common titles (or headlines) read something along the lines of "Runaway" or regarded the reward amount (in dollars) for returning slaves. "Committed," "Slave in Custody," and 'Notice" were also popular headlines for advertising runaway slaves in the papers. The short and uninformative titles of runaway slaves were similar to those for runaway animals and criminals, thus further marginalizing slaves. The majority of the ads analyzed were mixed amongst home and product sales, wanted posters, and lottery postings. The location of the ads within the paper spoke to the lower status of slaves in the nation and suggested the lack of humility that slaves possessed. The runaways were nuisances who nevertheless deserved attention because they were property. However, the editors rarely splashed these advertisements on the front page or gave the notices more than fifteen lines. They usually appeared under small headlines of no more than 12 or 14 picas. The language tended to be succinct, no-nonsense. For example, an ad from a Democratic newspaper in Port Gibson, Mississippi, implored the owner of an escaped slave to "comply with the law and take him (the slave) out (of the jail)."[20] A local jailer had taken out the advertisement.

In one hundred eighteen of the ads, the slave's name was given, and in ninety-three, the slave's complexion was described. The vast majority of the advertisements cited physical characteristics of the slaves, including height and build. Distinguishing marks were often cited, especially permanent scars. The *Western Union* newspaper in Hannibal, Missouri, for example, described a runaway named Cornelius Hudson as: "five feet, four inches high, about 25 years old, is of a copper color, full faced, and has a heavy beard, and is altogether a very well made man." In addition, the runaway belonged to Richard Southgate of Cincinnati and likely would be found wearing "black casinett pants, calico shirt, and an old fur cap."[21] Others ads included descriptions of facial blemishes or wounds. An ad from a New Orleans newspaper described a female runaway named "Hannah, about forty years of age," as having only one eye.[22]

The advertisements also stated whether the runaways were male or female. A male runaway was usually called a "boy," not a man, which arguably lowered his status in the eyes of readers and differentiated him from their white male masters. Most of the men in the advertisements were between 20 and 30 years old. The other two age groups of significance were teens and thirties. One New Orleans runaway named Nancy was termed a "wench" and was said to have "very dark skin, a large breast, and a fearful look."[23] Height and build were commonly mentioned in the ads. Most of the runaways were between five feet and six feet tall. Weight was cited less commonly. However, body type was described as "clumsily built," "fat and lusty," "heavy made," "slender," "light built," or "well built."[24] Runaways were described as "light complexioned," "black complexioned," "freckled," "ginger-cake colored," "very black," "mulatto," "light mulatto," "dark copper complexioned," and "almost white."

The runaways were primarily seen as physical laborers such as field hands or in regards to women, seamstresses, or cooks. Some were described as being good readers or good writers—or even suspected of being literate. One runaway slave was described as being a good fiddler, and several were described as playing musical instruments, including the violin. Others were portrayed as being garrulous or quiet, or as of having "a stoppage in speech" (likely stuttering).[25] Some were described by their personalities ("a very likely girl").[26] One runaway was described as speaking both English and Dutch.

There often is reference in these ads to either family members or acquaintances—especially those living in free states, or former slaves who had achieved their freedom. These references bespoke the human dimension of the slaves and almost certainly had a strong effect on both free Blacks and abolitionists. Many advertisements expressed fear that the runaways would be heading toward freedom. There also was a veiled fear that sympathetic whites had helped the runaways or were harboring them. Another key trait is the legal status of the runaway. Advertising tended to cast doubt on runaways who claimed they were free. Here is an example from the Wilmington (NC) *Journal* from January 1851, about a runaway named George Aaron, in a notice written by a sheriff: "He [George] came as a seaman from Boston in September last. He pretends he is free, and was raised in Brooklyn, New York."[27] Note the word *pretends* in the sheriff's clause. In another ad that same day in the *Wilmington Journal*, there is mention of a runaway who has a "free wife."[28] However, there is no further information about the incongruity of how a runaway in southeastern North Carolina could have a free wife. In another case from North Carolina, a runaway was said to "write very well" and would "undoubtedly attempt to pass as free."[29] Literacy was a negative trait in the eyes of the masters.

While it is easy to see these advertisements as formulaic and relentlessly similar, each tells the story of an individual runaway—and in some cases multiple runaways. All that we know of these slaves is their first names (in most cases), ages, builds, distinguishing physical characteristics, and perhaps what clothes they were wearing when last seen by their owners. However, these were living and breathing human beings. The names alone hint at some social standing; after all, they did represent being three-fifths of human, according to the Constitution, for the apportionment of representatives in the U.S. House.

The ornaments, or stereotyped images, that accompanied some of the ads also hinted at a certain perspective and intention. These slaves were runaways seeking permanent freedom, which, of course, meant heading to the North, to Canada, or to a ship that could take them abroad, perhaps to a Caribbean nation or back to Africa. In some cases, their skills were noted—hinting at their aptitude and values as a worker. However, these skills did not serve their own interests— another way that the slave ideology ran antithetical to the free, independent, self-reliant, laissez-faire capitalism that became the centerpiece of the emerging Republican Party in the mid-1850s. The images also suggest that the Black male is on the run, with one foot off the ground and sometimes a stick in hand that is helping him move along. Perhaps the stick could be used as a weapon against would-be captors, or against wild animals, including snakes, as many runaways ran into swamps where whites were loath to go. The printing of these stereotypes was not highly detailed or clear, and this further made each runaway seem the same—desperate, mobile, merely a problem for the owner—not a person to be respected for his or her inherent worthiness.

Other characteristics of runaways mentioned in the ads might include scars, deformed limbs, or other physical conditions. For example, in an advertisement in the *Port Gibson* (Mississippi) *Correspondent* in August 1844, a runaway named Stephen (or William) was reported as being "badly whipped" and "his left leg appears to be shorter" than his right.[30] Another example is that of a Milledgeville, Georgia, runaway named Harper, who had a "scar in the upper corner of his forehead."[31] Yet another example is that of Solomon from Cabarrus County, North Carolina. The *Charlotte Western Democrat* described Solomon thusly: "The forefinger of his left hand has been cut off, and a sharp hard knot has grown on the end of it."[32]

Sometimes the runaways were associated with crimes. For example, a slave named Claibourn in Alabama was said to have stolen $150 before he fled from his master. Claibourn also had changed his name to John Scott, "a free man, and got a pass to that effect."[33] Deception was often highlighted in these notices. A woman in New Orleans named Mariah, a hairdresser, attempted to pass herself off as a boy. The advertisement stated, "she has frequently dressed up in boy's clothes, and has her hair cut short for this purpose."[34] Other runaways, the ads said, would forge documents or purchase papers that stated they were free. One owner who placed his ad in the *Maryland Gazette* in May 1860 stated that his runaway slave was "of a saucy disposition, but if resolutely spoken to is a great coward."[35] The owner emphasized the slave's negative characteristics, also saying that he had stolen certain equipment.

The sheer cruelty of the fugitive system could be seen in a runaway slave advertisement from a Raleigh, North Carolina, newspaper. The *North Carolina Confederate* described a fugitive named John who had been captured in Guilford County. John, weighing approximately 145 pounds, standing five feet and eight inches, and being 22 years old, had belonged to a man in Tarboro in eastern North Carolina, approximately one hundred fifty miles away, and he testified he had been hired to work in the western part of the Tar Heel State. He had been free for nearly a year and had been discovered "worn out and nearly naked."[36] When the ad was printed, John had already been in the Guilford County jail for a while. In other words, how long the slave had been on the run had no bearing on his status. He was still a slave, with no citizenship rights or freedom in the eyes of law enforcement and the editor.

Slave Ads as Newspaper Revenue

So, why did newspapers run these notices? First, editors were making money by selling these ads. That was a primary incentive. However, editors in the South and Border States also were part of a slave-owning society and saw no reason not to publicize information about fugitive slaves. They did not see what they were printing as a barometer of slave discontentment, although almost certainly free Blacks and abolitionists did see them that way. Effectively, these advertisements helped uphold the system of slavery in the United States. This endorsement of slavery contributed to the entire ecology of American journalism. It meant that appeals to decency and morality about slavery were trumped by the need to make money on classified advertisements of these sorts, as well as the desire to maintain the social order, especially south of the Mason-Dixon Line. Runaway slaves were seen as a threat to the domestic tranquility, especially in the South. American liberty was reserved only for white men, and, to a lesser degree, white women. African slaves were merely property for compartmentalization. The inherent contradiction that they were also human seemed lost to American journalism of the nineteenth century, although editors from the eighteenth century had passed along this phenomenon. This also suggests that the mainstream journalism of this time merely reflected the political, social, and moral norms of the nation. Yes, there were abolitionist newspapers that would never run such advertisements, but those represented a small minority of American journals. (As the Republican Party grew, Republican papers abstained from running runaway ads.)

The descriptors used within these ads affirmed negative views of and attitudes toward slaves. The position of the advertisements on back pages, the concise headlines (often announcing a reward), and the terms used to describe the slaves' physical characteristics all conspired to reinforce societal views of the time. Runaway slaves were important enough to be in the newspaper as an open source of information, and therefore to be before the public's eye, but they were rarely important enough to be put on the first or the second page (which in that century was often the critical page of the journal), or to be spotlighted with large, eye-catching headlines. Analyzing these advertisements provides insight to the culture and norms of the day, as well as the ecology of nineteenth-century American journalism, which as the century progressed became more sensational while opening eyes to the evil of slavery.

These advertisements essentially had a dual role: (1) upholding slavery as an ingrained economic system and (2) illustrating the casual and callous attitude toward these forced laborers by their owners and the society that surrounded them. Slavery was an essential part of what made America function and grow, and losing slaves because they were running away was destructive to the economic system, social order, and accompanying lifestyle. The ads showed how much time, money, and effort were put into retrieval of runaways. Yet at the same time, these notices added fuel to growing resentment in the North of the slave system.

Our research also points to several other avenues of investigation on press coverage of fugitive slaves. For example, in 1861, several newspapers in Chicago printed notices to runaway slaves advising them they should leave the city immediately "and make tracks for Canada."[37] There also was considerable coverage of fugitive slaves related to the Compromise of 1850 and the Dred Scott decision, as their plight became a public issue of prime importance, as well as resistance to the Fugitive Slave Act in the North. Republican editors would ask how runaway slaves could be arrested on free soil. Other stories concerned attempts to help runaway slaves gain their freedom over land and by sea, including a case in 1848 in which a captain of schooner named *The Pearl* attempted to take seventy-seven slaves out of Washington and ship them out into the Atlantic. However, the schooner was seized at the mouth of the Potomac and the slaves were returned in chains to Washington.[38] Other articles were crime stories about the collection of runaways by law enforcement.

Notes

1   "From the Baltimore Clipper. The 'Higher Law' Party," Washington (DC) *The Republic*, September 18, 1851.

2   "A Runaway Slave Steals a Little Girl and Carries Her into the Woods," Shreveport (LA) *Southwestern*, November 13, 1861.

3   "Arrest of Fugitive Slaves at Vincennes," Evansville (IN) *Daily Journal*, June 14, 1858.

4   "$150 Reward [cut of runaway slave]. Ranaway from the Subscriber, on the Night of the 2d Instant, a Negro Man, Who Calls Himself Henry May,... William Burke, Bardstown, Ky., September 3d, 1838," Library of Congress, accessed July 23, 2021, at <loc.gov/resource/rbpe.0220120b>.

5   Andrew Delbanco, *The War Before the War: Fugitive Slaves and the Struggle for America's Soul from the Revolution to the Civil War* (New York: Penguin Press, 2018), 23.

6   "Notice of a Runaway Slave," Hannibal (MO) *Western Union*, November 7, 1850.

7 John Hope Franklin and Loren Schweninger, *Runaway Slaves: Rebels on the Plantation* (New York: Oxford University Press, 1999), 239.

8 Delbanco, *The War Before the War*, 107.

9 Ibid, 46.

10 "Stop the Runaway," Nashville (TN) *Tennessee Gazette*, October 3, 1804.

11 Donald L. Robinson, *Slavery in the Structure of American Politics* (New York: Harcourt Brace Jovanovich Inc., 1971), 228.

12 U.S. Constitution, accessed May 30, 2019, at <archives.gov/founding-docs/constitution-transcript>.

13 Article the Sixth, Northwest Ordinance, 1787, accessed May 31, 2019, at <loc.gov/resource/bdsdcc.22501/?sp=2>.

14 Robinson, *Slavery in the Structure of American Politics*, 286.

15 "The Sole Issue," McArthur (OH) *Democrat*, July 28, 1859.

16 "$500 Reward," Charleston (SC) *Mercury*, October 6, 1857.

17 "Twenty Dollars Reward," Nashville (TN) *Whig*, May 26, 1813.

18 Patricia Bradley, "Slave Advertising in the Colonial Newspaper: Mirror to the Dilemma," conference paper, Association for Education in Journalism and Mass Communication, San Antonio Texas, August 1987, 5.

19 Lathan A. Windley, *A Profile of Runaway Slaves in Virginia and South Carolina from 1730 to 1787* (New York: Garland Publishing, 1995), 4.

20 "Committed on the 2nd Steven or William," Port Gibson (MS) *Correspondent*, August 17, 1844.

21 "Notice of a Runaway Slave," Hannibal (MO) *Western Union*, November 7, 1850.

22 "Horses and Negro Lost," New Orleans *Daily Picayune*, April 15, 1837.

23 "Fifteen Dollar Reward," New Orleans *L'Abeille*, January 28, 1828.

24 "Ran Away," Norfolk (VA) *Herald*, December 9, 1800.

25 "A Runaway in Jail," Richmond (VA) *Enquirer*, December 18, 1840.

26 "Louisiana Notice for Molly," New Orleans *Picayune*, September 22, 1859.

27 "Notice," Wilmington (NC) *Journal*, January 17, 1851.

28 "$50 Reward," Wilmington (NC) *Journal*, January 17, 1851.

29 "$50 Reward," Fayetteville (NC) *The Carolinian*, January 5, 1850.

30 "Committed," Port Gibson (MS) *Correspondent*, August 17, 1844.

31 "Brought to Jail," Milledgeville (GA) *Federal Union*, February 14, 1842.

32 "$100 Reward!" Charlotte (NC) *Western Democrat*, January 1, 1860.

33 "Fifty Dollars Reward," Huntsville (AL) *Weekly*, October 26, 1824.

34 "$500 Reward," New Orleans *Picayune*, March 25, 1837.

35 "Thirty Dollars Reward," Annapolis (MD) *Maryland Gazette*, May 1, 1800.

36 "Runaway Slave," Raleigh (NC) *North Carolina Confederate*, June 29, 1864.

37 "The Chicago Papers," Washington (DC) *Evening Star*, April 16, 1861.

38 "Wholesale Equipment and Speedy Apprehension," Tarboro (NC) *Press*, May 6, 1848.

8

Abolitionism and the Fight to End Slavery

"Give us Disunion with liberty and a good conscience, rather than Union with slavery and moral degradation. What! Shall we shake hands with those who buy, sell, torture, and horribly imbrute their fellow-creatures, and trade in human flesh! God forbid!" "Remarks of Mr. Garrison," *The Liberator*, March 12, 1858.

In the middle of the nineteenth century, a new form of American journalism arose, mostly in the North, although some of its earliest practitioners were in the Upper South. The publishers of this niche political journalism practiced an advocacy or interventionist approach at a time when partisanship in the press was still conventional in the United States. These intensely partisan journalists did a deep dive on a single issue, issuing a call to action on the subject of slavery.

While abolitionist editors were not numerous—and while their newspapers, with a single exception, lacked the circulation numbers of the big urban newspapers—they had a measurable impact on public opinion, even if the majority of readers in both North and South felt their views were too extreme.

Abolitionist journalism had begun in earnest in the early 1830s, but it was the murder of Elijah P. Lovejoy on November 7, 1837, in Alton, Illinois, that began to move public discourse toward the abolitionists' point of view. Lovejoy, who in addition to being an editor was a Presbyterian minister, had to defend his mainly religious newspaper, *The Alton Observer*, on three occasions, having to see his printing equipment thrown into the Mississippi River by pro-slavery vigilantes. Originally, he had run the newspaper in St. Louis, but his ideas about ending slavery upset many. He chose to move it to Alton, which he thought would be a better environment, as Illinois was a free state. Ultimately, however, an angry

SLAVE MARKET OF AMERICA.

THE WORD OF GOD.

THE DECLARATION OF AMERICAN INDEPENDENCE.

THE CONSTITUTION OF THE UNITED STATES.

CONSTITUTIONS OF THE STATES.

DISTRICT OF COLUMBIA.

"THE LAND OF THE FREE."   THE RESIDENCE OF 7000 SLAVES.   "THE HOME OF THE OPPRESSED."

RIGHT TO INTERFERE.

PUBLIC PRISONS IN THE DISTRICT.

FACTS.

FACTS.

PRIVATE PRISONS IN THE DISTRICT, LICENSED AS SOURCES OF PUBLIC REVENUE.

Published by the American Anti-Slavery Society, 143 Nassau-street, New-York, 1836.

Image 8.1 "Slave Market of America." William S. Dorr, American Anti-Slavery Society. New York: Published by the American Anti-Slavery Society, 144 Nassau Street, 1836. This broadside condemns the sale and keeping of slaves in the District of Columbia. The Library of Congress' caption indicates it was issued during the 1835-36 petition campaign waged by moderate abolitionists led by Theodore Dwight Weld and buttressed by Quaker organizations to have Congress abolish slavery in the capital. At the top are contrasting scenes of the Declaration of Independence captioned "The Land of the Free" juxtaposed with a scene of slaves being led past the capitol by an overseer entitled "The Home of the Oppressed." Between them is a plan of Washington with insets of a suppliant slave and a fleeing slave with the legend "$200 Reward" and implements of slavery. On the next line are views of the jail in Alexandria, the jail in Washington with the "sale of a free citizen to pay his jail fees," and an interior of the Washington jail with imprisoned slave mother Fanny Jackson and her children. On the bottom level is an illustration of slaves in chains emerging from the slave house of J. W. Neal & Co. (left), a view of the Alexandria waterfront with a ship in the process of having slaves loaded on it (center), and a view of the slave establishment of Franklin & Armfield in Alexandria.[1]

mob—plied by alcohol and seeking to destroy *The Observer*'s new printing equipment, which had been hidden in a grocery warehouse—attacked on November 7. Lovejoy and several friends (a pro-*Observer* "militia" of about thirty) battled back with guns.

The mob of between fifty and eighty was initially only armed with clubs, but they eventually acquired guns. There was an exchange of gunfire, and one participant, a carpenter named Lyman Bishop, was struck. A lull in the battle ensued after Bishop's wounding. However, Bishop died about a half hour after being shot, and that caused the mob to attempt to set the warehouse on fire and burn the editor and members of his friendly militia. The mob used a ladder to try to set the roof on fire. When Lovejoy, only thirty-five years old, attempted to push the ladder away from the building, five bullets struck and killed him. The national response was strong. Edward Beecher called Lovejoy a "martyr."[2] William Lloyd Garrison's pro-abolition newspaper, *The Liberator*, termed the murder of Lovejoy a "Horrid Tragedy" in its first headline related to the editor's death.[3] The *Liberator* story ran with thick black gutters on the second page of that November 24 edition. In another article in that day's edition, Garrison also called Lovejoy a "martyr."[4]

Lovejoy and Garrison were among a group of abolitionist editors who plied their trade in the decades before the Civil War and then throughout the conflict. When it ended, their reason for existing dried up—in 1865, Garrison, for example, closed operations. Other major abolitionist editors included Benjamin Lundy,

James G. Birney, Lewis Tappan, Gamaliel Bailey, and Frederick Douglass. The relationship between Douglass and Abraham Lincoln holds particular intrigue, as does the relationship between abolitionist journalists in the United States and the abolitionists of Great Britain, including those in the British press.

Leading Abolitionists: From Lundy to Douglass

While there had been several abolitionist newspapers before 1821 (including Elihu Embree's *Manumission Intelligencer* in Tennessee and William Swain's *Greensboro Patriot* in North Carolina), Lundy opened the abolitionist press era in earnest with his newspaper the *Genius of Universal Emancipation*. He was a New Jersey-born Quaker who had migrated to Ohio, where he started an organization called the Union Humane Society. He wanted free African Americans to have civil rights and equality, and he advocated an end to slavery.

Lundy started publishing the *Genius of Universal Emancipation* on January 1, 1821, in Mount Pleasant, Ohio. He had no printing background. He made harnesses, and he started his newspaper from scratch. It would last until 1839, and he would move it around—to Baltimore, Washington, D.C., and Philadelphia. His newspaper, which never attained a sizable circulation, would nevertheless provide the model for future abolitionist editors, including Garrison, Bailey, and Douglass. That model featured what became a staple of abolitionist editors—lecturing around the country spreading the anti-slavery word.

Garrison, in fact, began working as an editor for Lundy's newspaper in 1829. Lundy named Garrison co-editor, and the Massachusetts native immediately began to write more forcefully for the end of slavery. Garrison wanted immediate, not gradual, emancipation. He also tried something a bit different journalistically. He began a column titled the "Black List," which publicized barbaric, inhumane acts against slaves, including kidnapping, whippings, and even murder. However, the "Black List" column led to a libel suit that Garrison would lose. In Baltimore, he was convicted of libel after he tried to go after someone involved in the underground slave trade. A ship owner named Francis Todd sued Garrison for publishing a piece about Todd's ship the *Francis*, which transported slaves from Massachusetts to New Orleans. Garrison wrote that men like Todd were "enemies of the species" and that the ship owner should be placed in solitary confinement for life for his crimes.[5] The jury in Baltimore did not buy his truth-as-a-defense argument, and Garrison lost the case. He was ordered to pay a $100 fine, which he could not afford, so the journalist had spent nearly fifty days of a sixth-month sentence in jail when Arthur Tappan, another abolitionist, paid his fine. (As it turned out, Garrison did not have the facts about the shipment of slaves precisely right: There were 88 slaves, not 85, onboard the ship.[6]

Birney was perhaps the most intriguing of the abolitionist editors, in that he was not only a Southerner (born in Kentucky) but had also been a slave master in Alabama. In 1836, he started *The Philanthropist* in Cincinnati, Ohio, and began to advocate for abolition, although with a moderate tone. The newspaper would be associated with the Ohio Anti-Slavery Society. Despite its moderation, twice mobs destroyed Birney's printing operation, and on the second occasion, they threatened to tar and feather Birney. The same mobs nearly destroyed the entire Black community of Cincinnati. Birney opted to move his family to New York, where he became secretary of the American Anti-Slavery Society.

Lewis Tappan founded the *National Era* in Washington, D.C., in 1847. It was connected to the American and Foreign Anti-Slavery Society and was "an advocate of the Anti-Slavery cause."[7] Tappan hired Bailey to run the newspaper, which would become the most successful of the abolitionist papers, with a circulation of about 25,000 at its zenith. Tappan's enterprise showed that abolitionist journalism could capture a sizable audience. It helped that Tappan and Bailey wanted the newspaper to be a conventional journal that appealed not just to the one political cause but could also be embraced by anybody in the family. Bailey called it a "safe and instructive Family Newspaper."[8] The *National Era* ultimately helped promote through serialization *Uncle Tom's Cabin* by Harriett Beecher Stowe. The newspaper also was larger than most papers of the era, with text spread across seven instead of six columns of type.

Bailey, a native of New Jersey who grew up in Philadelphia (his father was a Methodist minister and silversmith), began his journalism career with the *Methodist Protestant* newspaper in Baltimore. He moved to Cincinnati in 1831 and started working for Birney's *Philanthropist* in 1836. Bailey became editor of the newspaper the following year. He was a moderate, and his editorials in *The Philanthropist* maintained such a tone. He assumed ownership of the newspaper in 1841 after the Garrisonians in the Ohio Anti-Slavery Society broke from the organization and formed the Western Anti-Slavery Society, which published a new journal, *The Anti-Slavery Bugle*. Lowering the cost for a year's subscription to a dollar, Bailey doubled *The Philanthropist*'s circulation from 3,000 to 6,000.[9]

In 1843, he began editing the *Cincinnati Morning Herald*, a daily. Bailey ran the *Herald* for three years and then moved to Washington, D.C., to edit Tappan's *The National Era*—which while quite moderate faced considerable agitation from pro-slavery mobs. Indeed, Bailey and his printers were held hostage by a mob for three days in 1848. *The National Era*'s circulation exceeded 15,000 and, in 1851-1852, serialized Harriett Beecher Stowe's *Uncle Tom's Cabin*. The popularity of Stowe's novel pushed *The National Era*'s circulation to nearly 20,000. Bailey would also co-found the Liberty Party and go on to move most of the members of that party into the Free Soil movement. He eventually would help build the Republican Party in response to Stephen A. Douglas' popular sovereignty policy for Kansas and Nebraska.

The son of a sailing master, Garrison was born in Newburyport, Massachusetts, in December 1805. His parents were from Nova Scotia, but his father had obtained an American visa and moved to Newburyport. The son began his journalism career as a teenager, learning how to set type. Garrison also wrote articles under the pseudonym Aristides. He started working for the *Newburyport Herald* in 1818. He would ply the trade in Newburyport, Boston, and Bennington. He met Lundy in 1828, when he agreed to become co-editor of the Baltimore-based *Genius of Universal Emancipation*. In that Maryland city, Garrison boarded with free Blacks.[10] After his term in jail for libeling the Newburyport shipping merchant Todd, Garrison returned to Boston to start his own newspaper, *The Liberator*. It is not clear if Garrison and Lundy had a falling out, but Lundy had decided to make *The Genius* a monthly rather than a weekly, and may no longer have had the financial resources to retain Garrison's contributions. It is possible that the two parted company because of Garrison's hardening view toward immediate emancipation without colonization.

The Liberator, born on January 1, 1831, represented a turning point in the history of abolitionist journalism. Garrison's newspaper would become the leader of the abolitionist movement and ultimately would introduce Douglass to the world. Douglass offered a real-life perspective on the ideas of the movement as a one-time slave— whereas most of the abolitionist editors were white and had no direct experience with slavery. Garrison laid his extreme stance on slavery in the first edition.

> I am aware, that many object to the severity of my language; but is there not cause for severity? I will be as harsh as truth, and as un-compromising as justice. On this subject, I do not wish to think, or speak, or write, with moderation. No! no! Tell a man whose house is on fire, to give a moderate alarm; tell him to moderately rescue his wife from the hands of the ravisher; tell the mother to gradually extricate her babe from the fire into which it has fallen;—but urge me not to use moderation in a cause like the present. I am in earnest—I will not equivocate—I will not excuse—I will not retreat a single inch—AND I WILL BE HEARD.[11]

Garrison knew his position was extreme, but he also advocated for nonviolent abolition. Southerners, however, wondered how slavery could end without violence, and Southern states enacted laws meant to silence Garrison and his ilk.

The Liberator reached a circulation of 2,000 in 1834, and the majority of its readers were African Americans. The newspaper was given away to legislators, governors, and federal officers in Washington, including members of Congress. It was also delivered to the White House, which was paid for by benefactors and receipts from Garrison's speaking tours that included abolitionists and even Douglass.

Image 8.2 "The Hurly-Burly Pot." New York: James Baillie, 1850. The artist attacks abolitionist, Free Soil, and other sectionalist interests of 1850 as dangers to the Union. He indicts abolitionist William Lloyd Garrison, Pennsylvania Free Soil advocate David Wilmot, editor Horace Greeley, and Southern states' rights spokesman Senator John C. Calhoun. The three wear fool's caps and gather, like the witches in Shakespeare's "Macbeth," round a large, boiling cauldron, adding to it sacks marked "Free Soil," "Abolition," and "Fourierism" (added by Greeley, a vocal exponent of the doctrines of utopian socialist Charles Fourier). Sacks of "Treason," "Anti-Rent," and "Blue Laws" already simmer in the pot. Wilmot says, "Bubble, bubble, toil and trouble! Boil, Free Soil; the Union spoil; come grief and moan; peace be none; til we divided be!" Garrison says, "Bubble, bubble, toil and trouble; abolition; our condition shall be altered by Niggars [sic] strong as goats; cut your master's throats; abolition boil! We divide the spoil." Greeley says: "Bubble, buble [sic], toil and trouble! Fourierism, war and schism. Till disunion come!" In the background stands the aging John Calhoun, who says, "For success to the whole mixture, we invoke our great patron Saint Benedict Arnold." The latter rises from the fire under the pot, commending them, "Well done, good and faithful servants!"[12]

The newspaper became the place to distribute pro-abolition news. It ran letters from abolitionists around the country and abroad, and it published news about abolitionist meetings and resolutions from various abolitionist associations. Establishment of the anti-gradualist *Liberator* in Boston led Garrison to create another organization devoted to abolition, the New-England Anti-Slavery Society. Later, this organization would re-name itself the American Anti-Slavery Society.

Frederick Douglass was born a slave with the name Frederick Augustus Washington Bailey in Talbot County, Maryland, in 1818. He was separated from his mother, Harriett Bailey, as a baby. Douglass grew up with his enslaved maternal grandmother, Betsy Bailey, and free grandfather, Isaac. He was taken from his grandparents when he was six years old. During that time, he witnessed the brutal lashing of his aunt Hester.[13] Two years later, he was moved to Baltimore, Maryland, where he worked as a servant for the Auld family.

His primary responsibility was serving as a companion to the Aulds' young son. Sophia Auld, the woman of the house, taught Douglass how to read and write (in part, because he was curious upon hearing Sophia reading aloud from the Bible). Master Hugh Auld, however, forbade the teaching of a slave, fearing Douglass would learn to crave liberty and be prone to escape. Auld told his wife that literacy obtained from the Bible would make slaves "disconsolate and unhappy."[14]

Accordingly, Sophia Auld ceased teaching him, but Douglass kept reading secretly. When he was older and working on the farm owned by William Freeland, he taught other slaves to read and write. Douglass later stated that this period of instruction was the genesis of his becoming an orator.[15] In Baltimore, Douglass came under the spell of Bethel AME Church's Charles Lawson, who led him into Christianity. Lawson continually advised Douglass that he would find his freedom from slavery through God and would become "a useful man."[16]

In 1834, Auld moved Douglass to the farm of Edward Covey in rural Maryland. There, he received severe lashings. Indeed, Auld believed Covey would break the teenager. Covey nearly did, but eventually Douglass fought back, and the Maryland farmer left the slave alone thereafter. Historian David W. Blight believes the time on the Covey farm was a transformative experience for Douglass. "Covey's savagery is forever cloaked in some of his [Douglass's] most beguiling and lyrical prose," Blight writes. "Douglass's great gift, and the reason we know of him today, is that he found ways to convert the scars Covey left on his body into words that might change the world."[17]

For the next few years, Douglass worked in Baltimore shipyards as a caulker. He fell in love with Anna Murray, a free Negro and daughter of slaves, and in 1838 escaped slavery by visiting Philadelphia first and then meeting Murray in New York where they wed. They moved to New Bedford, Massachusetts, where he changed his name to Frederick Douglass in an attempt to skirt bounty hunters and found work at a whale oil refinery.[18]

Early on in New Bedford, he subscribed to Garrison's *Liberator*. Garrison's influence was critical to Douglass, who had experienced firsthand the violence of slave masters. Douglass also came to realize from Garrison's example that public speaking was another way to fight against slavery. In 1841, he spoke at an anti-slavery conference about his time as a slave. His life was his text, and, while he was nervous speaking in front of a large gathering, his words had a strong effect on the audience. Garrison and Wendell Philips were among the notables in the crowd that evening. In fact, Douglass's first public speech was so compelling that it led to his appointment as an agent for the Massachusetts Anti-Slavery Society, for which he became a regular lecturer on the abolitionist circuit. Douglass quit his job in Bedford and moved his family to Lynn, Massachusetts, to became a full-time communicator for emancipation. From that day forward, he made his living through journalism and public speaking.

Douglass began his journalism career writing letters that Garrison published in *The Liberator*. In 1845, Douglass published his autobiography, *Narrative of the Life of Frederick Douglass, Written by Himself*, which he based on his stump speech. It sold more than 30,000 copies in the United States and Great Britain. Douglass also wrote a regular letter for the *National Anti-Slavery Standard* and for *The Ram's Horn*. His first *Standard* piece recalled the emancipation of slaves in the West Indies in the 1830s, from whom he thought the South's slaves might gain inspiration.

Douglass started *The North Star* newspaper in December 1847 after a speaking tour in Great Britain. The tour raised $2,175 for Douglass, and he decided to purchase a printing press and start his own newspaper.[19] During his stay in Britain, he had gone on the offensive against churches that took donations from Southern Christians who owned slaves, holding that slavery was incompatible with Christianity. The success of his publications aroused not only those who supported abolition but those who supported slavery. Douglass was injured at a mass meeting in Indiana, and bounty hunters attempted to capture him. On the lecture circuit, Garrison and Douglass frequently faced other forms of hostility, including hurled vegetables and other objects. Garrison suggested that Douglass take a tour of Great Britain to give things time to cool down. During his nineteen-month tour, Douglass he earned money speaking to abolitionist organizations in England, Ireland, and Scotland.

Douglass, who had moved to Rochester, New York, hired Martin Delany to be co-editor of *The North Star*. A second hire was William Cooper Nell, who served as publisher, and a third was Englishman John Dick, who would be the printer. Douglass housed *The North Star* at Rochester's Memorial AME Zion Church. The newspaper was a four-page weekly with an annual subscription rate of $2. The front page usually consisted of current events involving the abolitionist movement. The second page, as was common in the middle of the nineteenth century, featured Douglass's editorials. Douglass wrote that *The North Star* was "a journal devoted to the cause of liberty and progress"—meant to "impress my sable brothers in this country with the conviction that … progress is yet possible, and bright skies shall yet shine upon their pathway."[20]

A War and a Proviso

Division with Garrison came over how each man saw the U.S. Constitution. Garrison believed the document was flawed, but that since it allowed slavery, the political system would continue to perpetuate it. For a while, he urged New England to secede and form an anti-slavery country in the mold of Great Britain, which had abolished slavery in 1833. On the opposite side of the argument, Douglass thought it folly to call for secession. Douglass, like many Northerners, including Abraham Lincoln, came to the see the Constitution as an anti-slavery document. Their argument went like this: Freedom is the rule in the American political and economic system, slavery the exception. These anti-slavery constitutionalists rejected the argument, posed by Supreme Court Justice Roger B. Taney, that slaves were property. They argued that the nation's founders prized freedom above all, and in the end, the American system would strangle slavery. In fact, many politicians among the founding generation had worked against slavery from the day of the Constitution's ratification.

These abolitionists, including Lincoln, were optimistic that the anti-slavery nature of the Constitution would ultimately win the day. They pinned their hopes on slavery never being allowed in expanding federal territories—all of which was put in jeopardy in 1854 when Congress, led by Illinois Democratic Senator Stephen A. Douglas, embraced the idea of popular sovereignty and ended the ban on slavery above the 36-30 line. Prior to this, as part of the Missouri Compromise of 1820, this line had divided prospective slave and free states west of the Mississippi River, with the exception of Missouri. Douglass used his new newspaper to argue for an anti-slavery reading of the Constitution. His publication reached an average circulation of 3,000 and cost Douglass $80 a week, lasting until 1851 before *Frederick Douglass' Paper* replaced it.[21]

In the late 1840s, Garrison, Douglass, Bailey, and the other abolitionist editors grappled with the Mexican War. Douglass termed it "disgraceful, cruel, and iniquitous" and urged its speedy end.[22] He criticized the Democrats for starting the war and the Whigs for fueling it with arms and other materials. He called it a "slaveholding crusade."[23] Douglass railed against the Whigs for not asking about the ultimate purpose of James K. Polk's war.

Garrison called Polk's war "atrocious" and wrote in a letter to Richard Davis Webb in July 1847 that it was "carried on against the deep moral convictions of the sober portion of the people; its real object, the extension and preservation of slavery, no intelligent man honestly doubts." He acknowledged to Webb, however, that criticizing what was proving to be a successful and popular American war subjected abolitionist editors to "great odium," and "brings down upon our heads the heavy charge of 'treason' and 'traitors to the country.'" He continued, "our testimony is not in vain. It burns like fire upon the national conscience."[24]

Garrison reported that most citizens of Massachusetts opposed the war. His evidence was a report to the Massachusetts House of Representatives stating that volunteers to the state militia did so to serve their state, not out of patriotic fervor for the war. In February 1847, Garrison published resolutions of the Pennsylvania legislature that instructed the state's delegation to the Congress to vote against any laws that might make it legal to include slavery in any new territory. These resolutions were made in response to the war and potential "acquisition of new territory to the Union."[25] Garrison also published resolutions against the war made at Faneuil Hall in Boston. Those resolutions called the war an "unjustifiable invasion" and advised against "voluntary aid" of the war effort.[26] Garrison published a list of congressman who had voted against the military appropriations bill that would bankroll the war effort. *The Liberator* editor noted that all the "no" voters were Whigs.

An important policy issue during the war was the Wilmot Proviso, an amendment by Pennsylvania's David Wilmot to an appropriations bill that would require any new territory acquired by the United States to be perpetually free. Wilmot's amendment would have prohibited any land captured during the Mexican War becoming slave territory. Garrison accepted its defeat in the Senate as inevitable, since the South was "numerically superior" in representation in that legislative body. The editor called the amendment's failure a "temporary defeat of freedom," but held that an "everlasting victory over [America's] slaveholding foes" would occur in the future.[27]

Douglass welcomed Wilmot's amendment as indicating "a great principle in the national heart"—that is, the urge to be free.[28] He skewered the "servile dough-faces" in the North who quietly empowered Southern politicians by failing to support Wilmot. *The North Star* editor also observed that those legislators who supported Wilmot were too few in number, too young, and not in positions of leadership in their parties. "They are the weak against the wrong," he pointed out.[29]

Bailey's opposition to the war had begun with his stance against the annexation of Texas in 1845, which he thought damaged America's relationship with Mexico. Bailey called Northern congressmen who opposed the Wilmot Proviso traitors, but he also agreed that the numbers simply weren't there in the U.S. Senate, so the proviso would expire there. However, Bailey praised Wilmot for pushing for no slavery in the territories: "It ought to be the subject of rejoicing in all the land; for if slavery be an evil, what wise man, what good man, could wish to multiply such an evil?"[30] Bailey excoriated South Carolina Senator John C. Calhoun. The Washington editor suggested that Calhoun offered a "metaphysical distinction" in describing Polk's war as predicated on the annexation of Texas and caused by the U.S. Army's presence in Mexico. Bailey, whose newspaper also carried news stories about battles and military strategy, wrote that Congress was "sorely perplexed" at how the president was prosecuting the war. The journalist ended the piece with a flourish of sarcasm: "What a war! What a President! What a Congress!"[31]

Bailey wrote: "Santa Anna had not been elected dictator. A Mexican Army of 30,000 had not been assembled. A project of attacking General Scott had not been entertained … The conclusion of the whole matter is, that peace had not been conquered, and it is not known when it will be."[32] In July 1847, Garrison printed in the *Liberator* an open letter to President Polk from Francis Jackson, president of the Massachusetts Anti-Slavery Society. In it, Jackson encouraged the president to emancipate his slaves because, he wrote, "no greater sin can be committed against God" than owning slaves. Jackson called slavery "man-stealing" and accused Polk of "kidnapping human beings."[33]

Garrison clearly took an anti-war position. When General Winfield Scott neared Mexico City and appeared ready to capture the capital, the *Liberator* editor wrote that he had hoped the Mexicans would have "mustered enough strength" to counter Scott and give him "a good licking."[34] Garrison did not want Americans killed or wounded for such a cause.

The Senate ratified the Treaty of Guadalupe Hidalgo in March 1848. Mexico gave 525,000 square miles of its territory to the United States in exchange for $15 million. This encompassed what is now the entire southwestern part of the continental United States. The U.S. government pledged to take over $3.25 million in debts Mexico owed to American citizens. Garrison's take was that the treaty put "no restriction on the Slave Power," nor did it appear there was "any attempt" to include "the Wilmot Proviso with the territorial acquisition." He concluded: "Once more the Slave Power wields the resources and the power of the nation to accomplish its own diabolical purposes."[35] Bailey's newspaper reported who voted for the treaty and who voted against it.

Douglass likewise opposed the treaty, and he made his reasons known publicly in *The North Star*.

> In our judgment, those who have all along been loudly in favor of a vigorous prosecution of the war, and heralding its bloody triumphs with apparent rapture, and in glorifying the atrocious deeds of barbarous heroism on the part of wicked men engaged in it, have no sincere love of peace, and are not now rejoicing over peace, but plunder. ... They have succeeded in robbing Mexico of her territory, and are rejoicing over their success under the hypocritical pretence of a regard for peace.[36]

When Polk died in 1849, Garrison called him "an unrepentant man-stealer" whose administration "has been a curse to the country." He added: "Neither humanity, nor justice, nor liberty, has any excuse to deplore" Polk's death.[37] Bailey wrote that Polk had "sacrificed thousands of lives."[38] Moreover, the *National Era* editor quoted the *Jacksonville News*, which wrote that Mexico would "be settled by slaveholders."[39]

The *Dred Scott* Decision

Dred Scott, a slave who had been taken to free states and territories by his owners, attempted to sue for his freedom. It became clear that Chief Justice Roger B. Taney and the Supreme Court intended to settle the slavery issue once and for all, ruling that "a negro, whose ancestors were imported into [the US], and sold as slaves," whether enslaved or free, could not be an American citizen and therefore had no standing to sue in federal court.[40] Moreover, the Court ruled that the federal government had no power to regulate slavery in the federal territories acquired after the creation of the United States. Rather than settling the slavery issue, this decision inflamed sentiments on both sides, causing Southerners to toughen their stand on the absolute right of slavery everywhere, and causing outraged abolitionists to reject the ruling.

The events of the next four years would ignite these sentiments into war. In October 1859, John Brown and his followers captured Harpers Ferry, Virginia, intending to incite a slave insurrection. The raid triggered fear in the South, a fear that multiplied with the realization that Republican Party presidential candidate Abraham Lincoln could win the 1860 presidential election. In turn, South Carolina, Mississippi, Florida, Alabama, Georgia, Louisiana, and Texas all seceded from the Union before Lincoln assumed office on March 4, 1861, and as Lincoln said in his Second Inaugural Address, "And the war came."[41]

The Dred Scott decision had made those associated with abolitionist press apoplectic. In the 7-2 decision, Chief Justice Roger B. Taney wrote for the majority that Scott could not sue for his freedom because he was not a human being, but rather property. Furthermore, the federal government had no power to regulate slavery in the territories. The Taney court also struck down the federal Fugitive Slave Act, which had been part of the Compromise of 1850.

Douglass called *Dred Scott* a "devilish decision" that obviously came from "the Slaveholding wing of the Supreme Court" and struck down the notion that slavery was a local or regional custom. Now it had been nationalized, and Congress could no longer "prohibit slavery anywhere." Slaves were no different from "horse, sheep, and swine," in that they were mere material property. Douglass added that the "National Conscience will be put to sleep by such an open, glaring, and scandalous tissue of lies as that decision." He said the *Dred Scott* case was a wakeup call—"proof that God does not mean that we shall go to sleep, and forget that we are a slaveholding nation."[42]

Bailey, who had paid Scott's legal expenses, urged his readers to take action by using the ballot box to end slavery. Accordingly, the *National Era* editor predicted Republican victory in the election of 1860, saying it was time for the voters of the North to cease being "political slaves of the slaveholders."[43] Garrison called the court's decision "infamous and tyrannical." He praised the dissenting judges, John McLean of Ohio and Benjamin R. Curtis of Massachusetts, observing that they had protested against the "usurpations and encroachments of slavery."[44] Garrison then fired his rhetorical cannon: "Give us Disunion with liberty and a good conscience, rather than Union with slavery and moral degradation. What! Shall we shake hands with those who buy, sell, torture, and horribly imbrute their fellow-creatures, and trade in human flesh! God forbid!"[45]

Garrison and Douglass in Great Britain

There was another factor in the development of the abolitionist press in the North: namely, their relationship to abolitionists across the ocean in Great Britain. Indeed, the connection between abolitionist journalists of the United States and abolitionists in Great Britain is underplayed in the history of American slavery.

Garrison and Douglass looked to England for support and intellectual encouragement. Timing alone suggests a strong connection between groups on each side of the Atlantic. As Garrison, in 1831, was beginning his career as an abolitionist editor in Boston (and only a year after the publication of David Walker's *Appeal*), the British were moving to outlaw slavery. Indeed, Walker and other blacks in America saw the British—with their vast empire—as great allies against Southern slave owners. He wrote: "The English are the best friends the colored people have on this earth. They have done one hundred times more for the melioration of our condition, than all the other nations of the world put together."[46] Historian Enrico Dal Lago comments of the early 1830s: "The most progressive antislavery forces were creating a network of Atlantic abolitionism that spread throughout the English-speaking world to engage more effectively in the struggle to abolish slavery in the British Empire, a struggle that Garrison followed and supported."[47]

In 1823, the British Society for the Mitigation and Gradual Abolition of Slavery throughout the British Dominions was formed. Other like-minded societies followed, including the Edinburgh New Antislavery Association, Glasgow Emancipation Society, and Belfast Antislavery Society. Parliament and Prime Minister Earl Grey outlawed slavery with passage of the Slavery Abolition Act in 1833 just before William Wilberforce died, and a decade after the Anti-Slavery Society had been formed in London. The Abolition Act took effect in August 1834; Garrison had been in London the previous year, when much of the debate took place.

Adopting the British conception of abolition made the crusade in New England international in character. In other words, Garrison, and then Douglass, were essentially developing the concept of what today would be called human rights. That is, freedom was not merely local, regional, or national; rather, it was international—universal. Just as the two American journalists would travel to Great Britain to preach and listen, they would invite British abolitionists, in turn, to tour New England.

Pamphlets produced by British abolitionists flowed onto American shores. Likewise, British and American churches of the same denominations routinely communicated, with the former often urging their American counterparts to work toward slavery's end. One method suggested by those churches was an economic boycott of Southern products. Thus, a trans-Atlantic superhighway of abolitionism was born in the 1830s and would only gain speed with the invention in that decade of the telegraph (although transatlantic telegraph cable would not be laid until the Civil War). American abolitionist newspapers often re-ran speeches from Parliament that took on slavery and espoused pro-abolitionist points of view. These speeches were published in key British newspapers that made their way to Boston by ship.

These ideas did not just organically transmit themselves from England to New England. Communication and transportation played key roles. Americans often traveled to Britain by ship, and American newspapers often reprinted articles from British newspapers that arrived in America aboard British ships. Both Garrison and Douglass made several trips to Great Britain during their journalism careers. These were tours—that is, they traveled around to mass meetings on abolition, where resolutions were made on the immorality of slavery and the need to outlaw it. Both journalists often spoke elsewhere in the cities where these mass meetings took place.

The British press covered the trips of Garrison and Douglass in the 1830s and 1840s, and Douglass's trip in 1859—a pivotal time in the development of American abolitionism, as the nation moved toward civil war. Garrison went to England in 1833, again in 1840 to attend the World Antislavery Conference, and in 1846. Douglass journeyed to Ireland, Scotland, and England in 1845-47 and again in 1859. It was as if Garrison was the opening two acts, and Douglass the third, in an American-abolitionists-in-Britain play. Whereas Garrison went voluntarily, Douglass had to leave the United States or face violence from his enemies in the entire South and later in what became known as the Border States (Delaware, Kentucky, Maryland, and Missouri).

Garrison's readers—many of whom, including Walker, were African Americans—funded his trip in 1833. He would be representing the New England Anti-Slavery Society. The trip's purpose, according to *The Liberator*, was to procure funds that would help sponsor work for Boston's "colored youth" and to deliver to the British "the truth" about slavery in the United States.[48] When he returned from England, Garrison was inspired to form the American Antislavery Society. *The Liberator* would lead the cause and sound the refrain of immediate emancipation. Both Garrison and Douglass made money on their tours of Britain by speaking at pro-abolition rallies. They also wrote about their trips, and these letters made their way back to the British press. Garrison and Douglass further invited British abolitionists to speak in the United States. For Garrison, the connection to the wider world was critical. He wrote in his newspaper's motto: "Our country is the world—our countrymen are mankind."[49]

The New England journalist was in the relatively early phase of developing his newspaper when he made his first trip across the Atlantic. Garrison's 1833 trip to England was designed for him to raise money for black schools—one of the founding purposes of *The Liberator*. He arrived in Liverpool on May 22. In June, the *Times of London* ran a letter in which the American journalist challenged Elliott Cresson, an advocate of colonization of emancipated slaves to Liberia and a member of the American Colonization Society, to a debate. During it, Garrison focused on the racial dimensions of the difference between those in the American Colonization Society and those in the New England Anti-Slavery Society. The journalist asked Cresson: Did not the American Colonization Society "maintain that the whites and blacks can never amalgamate and live in harmony together?" Did not the society "contend that the coloured population of the United States must for ever remain a separate, degraded, and miserable population in their native country?"[50]

A month later, the *Bristol Mercury* reported that Garrison had challenged Cresson to a debate on the issue of colonization, which *The Liberator* editor opposed. Cresson was also touring Great Britain, hoping to raise funds for colonization of African Americans in Liberia. *The Mercury*, which based its report on an article in the *Sheffield Iris*, called Garrison an "Agent of the New England Anti-Slavery Society" and noted that Cresson had declined to face Garrison in a debate in London.[51] In response to Cresson's refusal to debate Garrison, *The Liberator* back in Boston commented: "Mr. Cresson probably thinks 'discretion is the better part of valor.'"[52] The *York Herald* also waded into the Cresson-Garrison row, covering a dialogue between Cresson and pro-Garrison speaker George Impey in Scarborough, Yorkshire. In that debate, Cresson, noting that Garrison had been charged with libel in Baltimore, said he therefore was of "very little credit" in his attacks on Cresson's call for gradual emancipation combined with colonization.

Also in July 1833, the *London Morning Advertiser* reported on Garrison's talk at Exeter Hall. The newspaper noted that Garrison had called the black man was his "brother" and was for "the total extinction of slavery." The purpose of Garrison's trip to England, the *Advertiser* wrote, was to provide a "message of mercy," because he sought immediate, not gradual, emancipation. Garrison also told the audience that he believed blacks and whites could live "in friendly intercourse in the United States."[53] In late July 1833, the *Chelmsford Chronicle* announced that Garrison would speak on "the present state of the anti-slavery question" at a "Public Meeting" at the Independent Chapel.[54]

Later, in the fall, the *Waterford Chronicle* in Ireland reported that Garrison wisely was absent from a meeting on abolition in New York. The purpose of the meeting was to resolve in favor of immediate emancipation of the slaves in the United States. The *Chronicle* article stated that Garrison's "only crime" was trying to emulate British abolitionists like Wilberforce and Clarkson. If Garrison had appeared, he would have been "tarred and feathered." The writer added: "Whatever opinion may be entertained as to the policy of the immediate abolition of slavery throughout America, a people who pride themselves on their free institutions might have at least heard with temper a proposal to relieve two millions of their fellow creatures from slavery."[55]

The *Reading Mercury* reported in November 1833 that Garrison had published in August a pamphlet entitled "An Appeal to the Friends of Negro Emancipation throughout Great Britain." (The same story would appear in the *Aris's Birmingham Gazette*, the *Bath Gazette*, and the *Manchester Times*. The Glasgow Emancipation Society would later reprint it.) In the pamphlet, Garrison appealed to the British sense of family and treating women well, detailing in contrast how slave masters broke up families, and how children were "ruthlessly torn from their [parents'] arms."[56] The *Mercury* story included Garrison's description of female slaves being placed onto scales and "sold like meat by the pound." The *Mercury* noted that, due to the successes of abolitionists in England, "it appears the spirit of abolition is traversing the whole length and breadth of the United States."[57]

An influential British abolitionist was George Thompson, a native of Liverpool whose father had worked on a slave-trading ship. He joined the Anti-Slavery Society of London in 1831. Garrison met Thompson in Scotland, and they became friends. In 1834, Garrison invited Thompson to speak in the United States, with the Edinburgh Emancipation Society providing financial support for the trip. On April 26, 1834, *The Liberator* reprinted a *Scotsman* story on Thompson's antislavery speech from the previous October. In the *Scotsman* piece, Thompson called out the hypocrisy of Americans who "boasted of their liberty and equality," yet held more than two million slaves who faced "iniquitous laws and the most malignant prejudices."[58] That same April day, back in England, the *Bristol Mercury* reported on a speech delivered by Thompson at the Methodist church in Bristol's Old Market. The *Mercury* reported that Thompson said it was "just, expedient, wise, and necessary to emancipate every slave on the face of the earth." Thompson asked, "What gave the white man claim to America?" and answered, "Fraud and force, gin and gunpowder, the almost annihilation of the Red Man, trampling on treaties, crime and depravity."[59]

Douglass' first trip to Great Britain came on the heels of publication of his book *Narrative of the Life of Frederick Douglass* in 1845. For years, he had lectured in the North. Douglass always feared speaking in cities that were near Southern states. Now, with the publication of his autobiography, which sold well, he was leery of even the big cities of the North. Thus, he traveled to Britain, his visit funded by friends who noted that the memoir of his early years had provoked the pro-slavery crowd, especially his former owner. The thinking was that Douglass would be much safer in Great Britain, where he could promote the book and boost sales. Still, on the passage from Boston to Liverpool, when Douglass lectured about slavery he agitated a group of passengers who had Southern connections. They loudly criticized him and threatened to throw him overboard, and the captain had to intervene. News of the incident reached Britain, and it created extensive commentary.[60] Douglass spoke in northern England, Scotland, and Ireland. His lectures were well attended, and the British press covered them with significant interest.

Writing to Garrison, Douglass observed with "wonder and amazement" that the British did not judge him by the color of his skin the way Americans did. He contrasted "American skin autocracy" with relative enlightenment on race by the British.[61] Douglass also expressed gratitude to the press of England for being fair in its coverage of him in a letter to Garrison.

> I can truly say, I have spent some of the happiest moments of my life since landing in this country. I seem to have undergone a transformation. I live a new life. The warm and generous co-operation extended to me by the friends of my despised race—the prompt and liberal manner with which the press has rendered me its aid—the glorious enthusiasm with which thousands have flocked to hear the cruel wrongs of my down-trodden and long enslaved fellow-countrymen portrayed—the deep sympathy for the slave, and the strong abhorrence of the slaveholder, everywhere evinced—the cordiality with which members and ministers of various religious bodies, and of various shades of religious opinion, have embraced me, and lent me their aid—the kind hospitality constantly proffered to me by persons of the highest rank in society—the spirit of freedom that seems to animate all with whom I come in contact.[62]

A typical story about Douglass in the British press would center on a lecture event. For example, the *Leeds Times* reported on a Douglass speech at Wakefield Corn Exchange, including the editor's description of the "horrors of American slavery." The Leeds newspaper commented that Douglass's "statements of the tyranny, oppression, and most abominable cruelty of the slave-holders, elicited from the audience the strongest manifestations of the abhorrence of the system."[63] The report also stated that resolutions were made condemning slavery and that the speech-making went on for hours.

In July 1846, the *Belfast Commercial Chronicle* reported on Douglass speaking at the Primitive Wesley Chapel in Donegal. He told his audience that his goal was to prove that slavery was a sin. The journalist, the paper reported, then enumerated how the laws of God were violated by the slave system. That is, without "the fetters, the thumbscrews, and the cowhide," slavery could not be kept in place. These brought the slave down to the level of animals. The church should excommunicate all slave masters and those who enabled them, Douglass said, asking how the church could accept man stealing.[64] The *Belfast News Letter* also covered the meeting, writing that Douglass attacked the Free Church of Scotland for being sympathetic to slave masters rather than the slaves. Douglass pointed out that the Free Church had taken a donation from a church in South Carolina that supported slavery. According to the *News Letter* article, Douglass told his listeners that the cry "send back the money" should be "raised throughout Ireland."[65]

The *Dundee Courier* reported on a meeting at which Douglass told the audience that slave masters in America refused to let the slaves read the Bible and "dreaded the spread of the Gospels" among them.[66] A number of publications reviewed Douglass's book. A review in London's *The Atlas* described Douglass's narrative as "thrilling and absorbing," as it showed how slavery "was fraught with moral death" for both slave and master and "debauches the public mind, destroys the public sensibility."[67]

One of the most reported aspects of Douglass's trip concerned his treatment by the Cunard Line, from whose agent he purchased a ticket in London for his return trip to Boston from Liverpool. When he got on the ship, he found someone in his berth. He was told to go to the agent in Liverpool to determine what had gone wrong. The agent there told him the London agent had sold him the wrong ticket. Douglass would only be allowed on the ship if he agreed to eat alone and not visit the bar. Douglass wanted the story of his mistreatment to be published everywhere. He wrote: "I have travelled in this country nineteen months and have always enjoyed equal rights and privileges with other passengers, and it was not until I turned my face toward America, that I met with anything like proscription on account of my colour." Eventually, the ship's captain agreed to let Douglass stay in his room. Still, the *Tyrone Constitution* of Omagh, Ireland, called it a "shameful" incident.[68]

By the time Douglass returned to the United States, he had garnered enough money to pay off his former master. British abolitionists, having heard his first-hand accounts of his early life as a slave and his criticisms of the politics and economics of slavery, had given him enough to pay for his freedom.[69] Douglass had contemplated starting his own newspaper, and although he would not chase that dream yet, he wrote for the *National Anti-Slavery Standard* and did a lecture tour with Garrison. Probably in part because of his treatment on that tour—crowds usually would not even let him speak—Douglass opted to proceed with his newspaper.

A group of abolitionists in North East England raised £450 to pay Douglass for the lectures he gave there during his nearly two years in Britain, according to the *Newcastle Guardian*. The money was sent by steamer to Boston. The newspaper also noted that Douglass had become editor of *The Ram's Horn*. On December 3, 1847, in Rochester, New York, he published its first edition. Within its pages, he would advocate for immediate and universal abolition, as well for other measures to enhance the lives of African Americans.[70]

Douglass returned to England in late 1859 for another speaking tour, as he wanted to get away from America after John Brown's unsuccessful raid on Harpers Ferry, Virginia. He again was greeted warmly. An audience in Leeds appreciated that he had to flee to England after Harpers Ferry because Southerners and their sympathizers believed Douglass was behind the attack. The *Leeds Times* paraphrased what Douglass said in his December 1859 speech to the Leeds Young Men's Anti-Slavery Society. Southern slaveholders, Douglass said, were in state of war against the black man, with "Slavery itself was an insurrection."[71] The *Sheffield Daily Telegraph* called Douglass "the best living refutation of the arrogant assumption of those who talked of the inferiority of the negro race."[72] Like many British newspapers, the *Peterhead Sentinel* printed Douglass's explanation of why he was touring England in 1859. This included his adamancy that he had nothing to do with John Brown's insurrection, although he sympathized with Brown and his followers and deemed them "martyrs to a righteous cause."[73] Another British newspaper, the *Sheffield Independent*, wrote that Douglass was not involved in Harpers Ferry attack and that he was happy "to be under the dominions of Queen Victoria rather than under the protection of the American President" (James Buchanan).[74] In Scotland, the *Alloa Advertiser* lamented that Douglass would not be speaking in that city. The newspaper praised the American journalist for his "noble eloquence" and "heart stirring appeals."[75]

In Falkirk, Douglass praised the citizenry for being so predisposed to anti-slavery views. He also told that audience that the American slavery system was far more brutal than, say, the Brazilian model, from which a slave could purchase his freedom. In America, he told the Falkirk audience, the master owns everything the slave possesses, and American slaves were "liable at any time to be sold or resold at the slave markets like cattle to the highest bidder."[76] The *Paisley Herald* reported that Douglass, speaking in Glasgow, said that voting for supporters of abolition was the way to end slavery in America. Echoing his anti-slavery view of America's founding document, Douglass said he denied the interpretation that the U.S. Constitution gave one man the right "to own property in men."[77]

Some of the articles on Douglass at this time were, while not negative, more neutral than they had been on his previous visit to Britain. *Bell's Weekly Messenger* reported that Douglass was presumed to be in Canada after he failed to show up for a speaking engagement in Boston. It also stated that it was believed that he was part of the Brown conspiracy. The *Lancaster Gazette* ran a *New York Herald* story that claimed Brown had implicated Douglass and "other abolitionists."[78] The *Western Daily Press* also stated that Brown had implicated Douglass.[79] The *London Daily News*, on the other hand, quoted Douglas from his own newspaper as having stated that there was no way he could have been part of a plan to attack Harpers Ferry, as he was elsewhere, planning a lecture tour in New York and then in England at the same time that Brown had attacked the federal arsenal. He also said he was not "ashamed of endeavouring to escape" from the kind of justice that would be delivered to a black man accused of a major crime in Virginia.[80] The *Times of London* and the *Teesdale Mercury* both reported that a letter from Douglass had been found in Brown's possession. No further commentary was given, but some readers might have seen that piece of information as damaging to the American journalist. The *Mercury* did note that Robert E. Lee had been dispatched to Harpers Ferry to make sure there were no further attacks, while the citizens of Virginia "were arming" in preparation for other possible uprisings.[81] The *Times of London* stated that Governor Henry A. Wise of Virginia had stated that he would have destroyed the ship that had taken Douglass to England.[82]

Douglass also noted that there had been a slight shift in British perspective on American slavery. While the British remained committed to abolition, he no longer could persuade audiences to embrace the need for British intervention in stopping slavery in the United States. Douglass noted that the British were holding to "non-intervention" as a policy toward American slavery, acknowledging as much in his talk in Leeds.

The *Leeds Mercury* reported the "vile system of blood" inherent in slavery "was an outrage upon all the great principles of justice, liberty, and humanity, principles which belonged alike to all men of whatever country, colour or clime." Douglass said eradicating slavery was not an American, English, or European question; rather, it was "a great human question."[83] The *Leeds Mercury* article added: "They in England had a right to the expression of an opinion on this subject, and he did not ask them with him to take up arms and go to the Southern states to rescue slaves by force, he did not ask for materials to buy implements of war. All he asked of British men and women was that they would lend him their moral influence and aid for the abolition of slavery."[84]

These reports represented a shift toward neutrality from views expressed during Douglass's previous visit to the British Isles. The *Scottish Banner* took aim at the *Times of London* as the main British party espousing non-interventionism. The newspaper applauded the large turnout for Douglass's talk in Glasgow.[85] The *Banner* also noted that some working-class Scotsmen had expressed their disdain for the British upper class who had expressed sympathy for slaves, but yet expressed no sympathy for the conditions that hard working laborers of Great Britain faced.

The *Anti-Slavery Advocate*, published in London, consistently alluded to Douglass's trip to Britain in terms of a larger discussion about whether or not the U.S. Constitution was pro-slavery. The *Advocate* pointed to Douglass arguing in Glasgow, and against Garrison, that the document was not pro-slavery. He said in Glasgow: "I ... deny that the Constitution guarantees the right to hold property in man, and believe that the way to abolish slavery in America is to vote such men into power as will use their powers for the abolition of slavery. This is the issue plainly stated, and you shall judge between us." As an example, Douglass noted that the three-fifths clause actually deprived slaveholding states of two-fifths of their representative population for the purpose of congressional representation.[86]

Abolitionist editors of the Civil War era were clearly a subset of American journalism. They could not make enough money from their journals to sustain their newspapers. Men like Garrison and Douglass toured the country lecturing about abolition. They also traveled to Great Britain to raise money, to inform the British public about the nature of American slavery, to stimulate interest in abolition, and, sometimes, to avoid violent anti-abolitionists back home—or, in Douglass's case, to avoid being captured and returned to his master. Generally, abolitionist editors were better received in Britain than stateside, but they built sizable readerships in American cities, especially among Black readers.

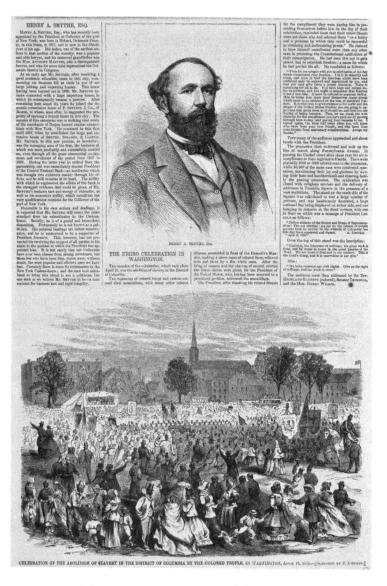

Image 8.3 "Celebration of the Abolition of Slavery in the District of Columbia by the Colored People, in Washington, April 19, 1866." Henry A. Smythe, Esq., sketched by Frederick Dielman, 1847-1935, artist. New York: Harper & Brothers, May 12, 1866. This page includes two illustrations showing African Americans celebrating the abolition of slavery in Washington, D.C., and portrait of Henry A. Smythe, newly appointed Collector of Customs of New York; also includes articles about the celebration and Smythe's appointment.[87]

The locations of abolitionist newspapers were critical to the success of abolitionist journalists. Garrison published in Boston, on the direct shipping line to England. Douglass went inland, but Rochester was on the last stop of the Underground Railroad before freedom in Canada—the great Northern beacon, part of the British Empire, and therefore under the aegis of Parliament's abolition act. Bailey's great contribution was building an abolitionist paper that reached a broad audience, proving that a decent number of Americans were receptive to advocacy journalism—a medium that focused on a single issue.

Bailey died before the Civil War commenced, but Garrison and Douglass continued to fight the good fight. Douglass effectively got out of journalism before the end of the war, and Garrison closed *The Liberator* late in 1865. Advocacy journalism would not die, however. Rather, it would soon focus largely on such subjects as women's suffrage and temperance.

Notes

1 "Slave Market of America," Library of Congress, accessed October 25, 2021, at <loc.gov/item/2008661294>.
2 Paul Simon, *Freedom's Champion: Elijah Lovejoy* (Carbondale, IL: Southern Illinois University Press, 1994), 126, 131, 147.
3 "Horrid Tragedy," Boston (MA) *The Liberator*, November 24, 1837, 2.
4 "The First Martyr—Another Mob at Alton," Boston (MA) *The Liberator*, November 24, 1837, 3.
5 Risley, *Abolition and the Press: The Moral Struggle against Slavery* (Evanston, IL: Northwestern University Press, 2008), 22.
6 Bernell E. Tripp, "The Antebellum Press," in William David Sloan, ed., *The Media in American: A History* (Northport, AL: Vision Press, 2008), 147.
7 "The Fourth Volume of the Era," Washington (DC) *The National Era*, January 3, 1850, 2.
8 Ibid.
9 Risley, *Abolition and the Press*, 94.
10 William E. Cain, *William Lloyd Garrison and the Fight against Slavery: Selections from The Liberator* (Boston, MA: Bedford/St. Martin's, 1995), 4.
11 "To the Public," Boston (MA) *The Liberator*, January 1, 1831.
12 "The Hurly-Burly Pot," Library of Congress, accessed October 25, 2021, at <loc.gov/item/2008661525>.
13 D. H. Dilbeck, *Frederick Douglass: America's Prophet* (Chapel Hill, NC: University of North Carolina Press, 2018), 15.
14 Ibid, 23.

15 David W. Blight, *Frederick Douglass: Prophet of Freedom* (New York: Simon & Schuster, 2018), 68.

16 Dilbeck, *Frederick Douglass*, 19, 30.

17 Blight, *Frederick Douglass*, 60.

18 Dilbeck, *Frederick Douglass*, 49, 50.

19 Brewington Perry, "Before the *North Star*: Frederick Douglass' Early Journalistic Career," *Phylon*, 35, 1 (1974): 96.

20 Frederick Douglass, *My Bondage and My Freedom*, ed. by William W. Andrews (Urbana, IL: University of Illinois Press, 1987), 247, 248.

21 Carter R. Bryan, "Negro Journalism in America before Emancipation," *Journalism Monographs*, Columbia, SC: Association for Education in Journalism, 12 (September 1, 1969): 22.

22 "The War with Mexico," Rochester (NY) *The North Star*, January 21, 1848, in Philip S. Foner, *The Life and Writings of Frederick Douglass: Early Years, 1817-1849* (New York: International Publishers, 1950), 292.

23 "The War with Mexico," Rochester (NY) *The North Star*, January 21, 1848, in Foner, *The Life and Writings of Frederick Douglass*, 293, 295.

24 Garrison to Richard Daniel Webb, "On the Mexican War," July 1, 1847, accessed September 28, 2017, at <teachingamericanhistory.org/library/document/letter-on-the-mexican-american-war>.

25 "Pennsylvania Resolutions," Boston (MA) *The Liberator*, February 5, 1847, 22.

26 "Anti-War Resolutions," Boston (MA) *The Liberator*, February 12, 1847, 25.

27 "Slavery Again Triumphant," Boston (MA) *The Liberator*, March 12, 1847, 42.

28 Quoted in Wu Jin-Ping, *Frederick Douglass and the Black Liberation Movement: The North Star of American Blacks* (New York, Garland Publishing, 2000), 49.

29 "The North and the Presidency," Rochester (NY) *The North Star*, March 17, 1848, in Foner, *The Life and Writings of Frederick Douglass*, 299.

30 "The Wilmot Proviso," Washington (DC) *The National Era*, February 25, 1847, 2.

31 "The Causes of the War," Washington (DC) *The National Era*, March 4, 1847, 2.

32 "From the Seat of War," Washington (DC) *The National Era*, July 15, 1847, 2.

33 "To James K. Polk, President of the United States," Boston (MA) *The Liberator*, July 2, 1847, 106.

34 "The New Conquest of Mexico," Boston (MA) *The Liberator*, September 17, 1847, 150.

35 "Ratification of the Treaty," Boston (MA) *The Liberator*, March 17, 1848, 42.

36 "Peace! Peace! Peace," Rochester (NY) *The North Star*, March 17, 1848, in Foner, *The Life and Writings of Frederick Douglass*, 300.

37 "Death of Polk," Boston (MA) *The Liberator*, June 22, 1849, 2.

38 "The Point Conceded—Important Correspondence," Washington (DC) *The National Era*, March 4, 1847, 2.

39 "The Object," Washington (DC) *The National Era*, January 27, 1848, 2.

40 US Supreme Court, *Dred Scott v. Sandford*, March 6, 1857, 60 U.S. (19 How.), 393, accessed March 22, 2022, at <supreme.justia.com/cases/federal/us/60/393>.

41 Abraham Lincoln, "Second Inaugural Address," March 4, 1865, accessed March 26, 2022, at <loc.gov/item/mal4361300>.

42 "The Dred Scott Decision," in Foner, *The Life and Writings of Frederick Douglass*, 410–12.

43 "The Supreme Court and Slavery—The Duty before Us," Washington (DC) *The National Era*, March 12, 1857, 2.

44 "The Decision of the Supreme Court," Boston (MA) *The Liberator*, March 13, 1857, 42.

45 "Remarks of Mr. Garrison," Boston (MA) *The Liberator*, March 12, 1858, 43.

46 James B. Stewart, "Boston, Abolition, and the Atlantic World, 1820-1861," in Donald M. Jacobs, *Courage and Conscience: Black & White Abolitionists in Boston* (Bloomington, IN: Indiana University Press, 1993), 110.

47 Enrico Dal Lago, *William Lloyd Garrison and Giuseppe Mazzini: Abolition, Democracy, and Radical Reform* (Baton Rouge, LA: Louisiana State University Press, 2013), 40.

48 "Garrison Appointed to Go to England," Boston (MA) *The Liberator*, March 9, 1833, 2.

49 "Our Country is the World—Our Countrymen Mankind," Boston (MA) *The Liberator*, January 1, 1831, 1.

50 "To Mr. Elliott Cresson, Agent of the American Colonization Society," *Times of London*, June 28, 1833, 3.

51 "American Colonization Society," Bristol (UK) *Mercury*, July 6, 1833, 2.

52 "Mr. Garrison," Boston (MA) *The Liberator*, August 3, 1833, 123.

53 "American Colonisation Society—Meeting at Exeter-Hall," London *Morning Advertiser*, July 15, 1833, 2.

54 "Public Meeting," Chelmsford (UK) *Chronicle*, July 26, 1833, 1.

55 "Slavery in the United States," Waterford (UK) *Chronicle*, November 9, 1833, 6.

56 Quoted in Rachel A. Jezierski, "The Glasgow Emancipation Society and the American Anti-Slavery Movement," dissertation, University of Glasgow, 2010, 17.

57 "Slavery in the United States of America," Reading (UK) *Mercury*, November 4, 1833, 6.

58 "Slavery in the United States: Mr. Thompson's Lecture," Boston (MA) *The Liberator*, April 26, 1834, 65.

59 "Mr. Thompson's Lecture on Slavery," Bristol (UK) *Mercury*, April 26, 1834, 2.

60 Timothy Sandefur, *Frederick Douglass: Self-Made Man* (Washington, DC: Cato Institute, 2018), 43.

61 Waldo E. Martin, *The Mind of Frederick Douglass* (Chapel Hill, NC: University of North Carolina Press, 1984), 115.

62 Douglass, letter to William Lloyd Garrison, from Belfast, Ireland, January 1, 1846.

63 "Frederick Douglass at Wakefield," Leeds (UK) *Times*, January 23, 1847, 5.
64 "Anti-Slavery Meeting," Belfast (Ireland) *Commercial Chronicle*, July 13, 1846, 1.
65 "American Slavery," Belfast (Ireland) *News Letter*, June 19, 1846, 1.
66 "Anti-Slavery Meeting," Dundee (Scotland) *Courier*, September 22, 1846, 2.
67 *Narrative of the Life of Frederick Douglass, an American Slave. Written by Himself.* Webb and Chapman. Dublin, 1845," London (UK) *The Atlas*, November 1845, 726.
68 "Departure of Frederick Douglass, Disgraceful Proceedings," Omagh (Ireland) *Tyrone Constitution*, April 16, 1847, 4.
69 Paul Kendrick and Stephen Kendrick, *Douglass and Lincoln: How a Revolutionary Black Leader and a Reluctant Liberator Struggled to End Slavery and Save the Union* (New York: Walker Publishing, 2008), 34.
70 Risley, *Abolition and the Press*, 115.
71 "Mr. Frederick Douglass on the Harper's Ferry Insurrection," Leeds (UK) *Times*, December 24, 1859, 3.
72 "Frederick Douglass," Sheffield (UK) *Daily Telegraph*, December 14, 1859, 2.
73 "The American Refugee," Peterhead (Scotland) *Sentinel and General Advertiser for Buchan District*, December 2, 1859, 3.
74 "Lecture by Fredk. Douglass," Sheffield (UK) *Independent*, December 17, 1859, 5.
75 "Frederick Douglass," Alloa (Scotland) *Advertiser*, January 28, 1860, 4.
76 "Frederick Douglass on American Slavery," Falkirk (Scotland) *Herald*, February 9, 1860, 3.
77 "Mr. Frederick Douglass' Lecture on the American Constitution," Renfrewshire (Scotland) *Paisley Herald and Renfrewshire Advertiser*, March 31, 1860, 2.
78 "The Harpers' Ferry Insurrection," Lancaster (UK) *Gazette*, November 5, 1859, 5.
79 "The Harper's Ferry Insurrection," Bristol (UK) *Western Daily Press*, November 26, 1859, 3.
80 "Frederick Douglass," London (UK) *Daily Times*, November 24, 1859, 5.
81 "The Negro Rebellion," Durham (UK) *Teesdale Mercury*, November 9, 1859, 3.
82 "Whatever May Be the Actual Burdens," *Times of London*, January 14, 1860, 8.
83 "Mr. Frederick Douglass on Non-Intervention, in Regard to American Slavery," Leeds (UK) *Mercury*, December 10, 1859, 7.
84 "Mr. Frederick Douglass on Non-Intervention, in Regard to American Slavery," Leeds (UK) *Mercury*, December 10, 1859, 7.
85 "Frederick Douglass," Glasgow (Scotland) *Scottish Banner*, February 4, 1860, 4.
86 Douglass, "The Constitution of the United States: Is It Pro-Slavery or Anti-slavery," speech to the Scottish Anti-Slavery Society, Glasgow, Scotland, March 26, 1860.
87 "Celebration of the Abolition of Slavery in the District of Columbia by the Colored People, in Washington, April 19, 1866," Library of Congress, accessed October 25, 2021, at <loc.gov/item/2015647679>.

9

Beyond the War: Everyday News in Wartime

"The woman had a child in her arms. The wretch who would sell such a woman liquor deserves hanging." La Crosse (WI) *Democrat*, August 12, 1861.

While battles dominated news coverage throughout the war, editors also published international and local news. Far from abandoning their obligation to inform readers of events in their towns and cities, the press developed a level of sophistication in local reporting—which had until the war remained an extraordinary style of coverage—as most of the public was uneasy about the sensationalized content of stories about fires, murders, and accidents.

Local news stories—and the sometimes sensationalized reporting of such information—had been in newspapers from the earliest days of reporting, flourishing in some periods and fading into the background in others. News featuring local crime, accidents, and the bizarre could even be found in the city streets of Rome millennia ago, with postings of events throughout the city and around the empire on a white tablet with copied-out newsletters.[1] Donald L. Shaw and John W. Slater noted that the earliest newssheets highlighted "the seamier side of life."[2] Such content, which Shaw and Slater called popular news, also was visible in American journalism before the nineteenth century. For example, in the seventeenth century, information about droughts, epidemics, and premature deaths were found in the almanacs of New England.[3] Later, in 1732, the first edition of the South-Carolina *Gazette* included a bizarre account of an entire family dying in a single afternoon.[4] Then, in

1816, *The New York Evening Post* in another example carried a story about a "surly old mastiff dog" that mauled a child in a "shocking manner."[5] Mitchell Stephens found local news content in other parts of the world—in the news books and news ballads of sixteenth-century England, for example, including a lurid account of an assault by Sir John Fites, an infamous hell raiser who was newsworthy for his otherwise aristocratic lineage.[6]

Press historians have underplayed the significance of local news, including the sensational content that often accompanied such stories, even though this style of content had long established itself as a standard part of American journalism. Although historians have recognized the local and sensational content prominent before the war in the Penny Press and after the war during the progressive era at the cusp of the twentieth century, everyday news and its sensational tone did not simply disappear between 1861 and 1865. In fact, to some extent, this type of news thrived, especially in the urban newspapers of the East Coast. Yes, war and political news had their stages in this journalistic drama, but local news did, too, and the volume of local news in both North and South played a significant role in the makeup of daily newspapers. The Baltimore *Sun* and the Richmond *Examiner*, notable examples, had columns devoted to events in their cities on a daily basis. For these papers, as well as other popular ones during the era, there seemed to be no end to the supply of crime, accidents, and the bizarre.

The war clearly affected the way journalists told local news stories, with a new kind of content that blended crime, accidents, and the grotesque with politics and race. In the South, for instance, there were more stories about runaway slaves and Black-on-white crime, especially after Union President Abraham Lincoln's Emancipation Proclamation took effect on January 1, 1863. Another type of story concerned the health of public figures. For example, in summer 1862 the Baltimore *Sun* published an article about the death of Stonewall Jackson nearly a year before he actually died.[7] Newspapers routinely wrote about the relative well-being of officers, especially those from a paper's city. Yet another trend was a spike in the number of stories about money issues, especially counterfeit currency. The war also brought stories about the misdeeds of soldiers. Yet the vast majority of stories when both sections of the country are combined show that crime and accidents remained the two main areas of local news—a kind of content that had originated in the century before the war, and, by the era of Joseph Pulitzer and William Randolph Hearst, had become a staple of American journalism. Writers produced a large percentage of that content using sensationalism, although they reported much of it matter-of-factly.

Image 9.1 "War News." George Stacy, publisher. New York: George Stacy, between 1861 and 1866. Photograph of a staged scene showing men gathered at a table socializing and discussing the latest news about the American Civil War. Crate in foreground shows the stereograph publisher name and studio address "Geo. Stacy 691 Broadway, New York."[8]

Crime Sells

Mitchell Stephens is among historians describing sensational local news as having roots in coverage that preceded the events of the nineteenth century. In some cases, the printed materials of the sixteenth, seventeenth, and eighteenth centuries employed a moralizing tone and included what he described as a "preachy voice," often employing "a moral façade" that allowed journalists to rationalize and partly disguise, even from authorities, what might be seen as their true vocation, "exploitation of the baser human instincts."[9] Reasons for moralizing about sensationalized content were not limited to simple concealment of base interests—they were also coldly economical.

Although this sensationalized content was unaccompanied by the bold headlines of the content common in the Penny Press of the 1830s and 1840s, sensationalized local content was "standard fare" in eighteenth-century American journals, according to David Copeland, among historians to delve into the genre.[10] A moral tone was often central to these local-news stories, which must have created a good deal of buzz in the small towns and cities of colonial and revolutionary America. In a study on journalism in the seventeenth and early eighteenth century, David Paul Nord found that local news served a religious and public purpose. Indeed, stories of "unusual private occurrences" in those centuries showed the hand of God in everything, as the Puritans of New England saw it.[11] For example, a stillborn baby from a follower of Anne Hutchison showed God's disfavor with the famous dissenter. Nord noted that such local news stories had a direct bearing on the concept of election. Clearly, the Hutchison follower was being judged and was not one of the elect.

In another study on the topic, Warren Francke suggested that the primary rationale for such local-news content in the 1800s was business. Nineteenth-century editors who published sensationalized local stories did so to sell newspapers, although they might not have admitted it. Francke noted that if crime news came in without lurid details, editors of the time would be sure to add them. Most criminal cases were not witnessed firsthand, but the editors could imagine the crime scene and would add "the rotting body," or "brains thrown throughout the room."[12] Shaw and Slater commented that society's elites saw sensationalized local news as "lighter topics." These were common subjects for the common person. "Serious people," the authors noted, "were expected to be repelled by these lighter topics, at least publicly."[13]

The sensational reporting of local crime news became a staple of nineteenth-century journalism. It could be seen, for example, in a story about a crooked mayor who embezzled money, or a well-known doctor who went insane and murdered his entire family.[14] Homicide in particular seemed to resonate with readers, one example being coverage of the April 10, 1836, murder of Ellen Jewett (also known as Helen Jewett), a prostitute in New York City whose death brought attention to a number of her customers who were among Manhattan's elite. Press coverage of the murder and trial was highly polarized, with reporters either sympathizing with Jewett and vilifying Richard P. Robinson, her alleged killer, or attacking Jewett as a seductress who, in keeping with nineteenth-century moral standards, deserved her fate. James Gordon Bennett's *New York Herald* provided the most complete coverage of the event. The newspaper was also among the few to question Robinson's guilt and attempt to describe Jewett's personal history and her character. However, at the same time, Bennett emphasized the sensational nature of the story and worked to exploit the sexual, violent details of Jewett's death for the newspaper's gain.[15]

As reporting of sensationalized local news evolved, its makeup of crime and accident news changed and made room for stories with unusual and grotesque content. Newspapers during the Civil War era were especially fascinated with entertainer General Tom Thumb and his marriage to Lavinia Warren. Almost every American newspaper featured the story. Thumb and Warren, both dwarves, wedded in New York, evoking odd emotion that editors exploited. Some newspapers even went so far as to comment on what their children would look like if the two decided to start a family. Other odd and sensational topics found in the era's newspapers included a two-headed baby, Siamese twins, beggar girls, student pranks, cheating husbands, a drunken woman, and the depraved saloonkeeper who plied her with liquor, and a fistfight between brothers that led to the death of one.

While it is important to note which content was preferred in sensationalized news accounts, it is also useful to understand the style of writing used to communicate these stories. Such items often were written in a poetic manner, in which the words almost bounced along as if written to a musical beat. The story of two drunken men beating each other bloody, for example, was turned into a poetic play on words of the two gentlemen dodging the fists of the other until one was finally caught across the cheek. In another sample, the Cleveland *Plain Dealer* described the characteristics of local beggar girls: "They are ragged and sorry-looking objects. ... Their fathers are invariably dead. ... For the most part, they are bad children with worse parents. They can counterfeit grief and poverty and wretchedness more naturally than the most skillful stage players can."[16]

The writers of sensationalized local news items added another rhetorical twist when they attached a moral to their stories—such as Wisconsin editor Marcus Pomeroy's description in the La Crosse *Democrat*. Of a "nearly dead drunk" woman who, while crossing the street, fell down in the mud. "She was picked up by several gentlemen and taken to a more comfortable place." Pomeroy wrote. "The woman had a child in her arms. The wretch who would sell such a woman liquor deserves hanging."[17] Waiting until the very last sentence, he revealed what most bothered him most about the story—the irresponsibleness of the barkeep and the mistreatment of the woman involved.

From the perspective of editors, these stories sold newspapers. From the perspective of readers, they provided an entertaining escape from the real world and war-stricken times. Instead of telling readers told how to think and behave politically, or informing them about what was going on in England, these stories told

American readers stories about the human condition. They were about the very world they lived in, the ordinary mishaps and difficulties endemic to the modern city. While some of the public would criticize and shun newspapers for their sensationalized and exaggerated content, as one scholar observed, the real reason for anger at the sensationalism of the mass media might be that most adults realize they are fascinated by sex and violence and they wish they were not.[18] It is much the same reason that the contemporary auto-racing fan attends the competitive race, hoping to see a wreck.

This is not to say that the sensationalized content of the era went unchallenged. Indeed, Henry Raymond's *New York Times*, one of the major newspapers to survive the era all the way through until today, was founded in 1851 primarily as a reaction to what Raymond perceived as the excesses of his contemporaries. Raymond, a protégé of Horace Greeley, had first written for Greeley's *The New-Yorker* at the age of 18, while still in college. In 1841, when Greeley founded the *Tribune*, he hired the aspiring editor as his chief assistant. "Abler and stronger men I may have met," Greeley wrote, but "a cleverer, readier, more generally efficient journalist, I never saw."[19] Although the two initially separated amicably, Raymond later suggested Greeley's taste for eccentric content (a sensationalism of a different sort) drove him from the *Tribune*.[20] And, while many of the issues Raymond and Greeley subsequently quarreled about had roots in petty personal rivalries, their editorial antagonisms grew to the point where the *Courier and Enquirer* (where Raymond began working as managing editor in 1843), and later the *Times*, nearly always opposed measures favored by the *Tribune*.[21] Also shunning the exploitative tendencies of Bennett's *Herald*, Raymond sought his own niche by publishing what he had described as content "without passion"—a publishing style that took decades to mature but in time proved successful.

On a professional level, then, it is understandable that Bennett would willingly cover crime and exploit the guilty pleasures of sex and violence. And, at the same time, it can be understood why members of New York society (in the name of upholding a moral order) organized to impose a boycott of the *Herald*. Compounding the social phenomenon, Lambert A. Wilmer in 1859 published an analysis of the issue titled *Our Press Gang, or, A Complete Exposition of the Corruptions and Crimes of American Newspapers*, alleging that sensationalized news content sometimes had negative consequences for a publisher and at the same time taught the nation's youth how to be criminals.[22]

Aside from Raymond's challenge to rival editors, American journalism had experienced major changes before the start of the Civil War. In the 1840s, the telegraph sped the delivery of information, helping make news more informative than ever before, and its political function became gradually less prominent. As part of the transformation, newspapers had begun to put more emphasis on local news at the expense of political and foreign news. Urban journals had learned to tap larger audiences by selling subscriptions for substantially less. These penny papers benefited from improvements in printing technology and management of human and non-human resources, including the development of a more profitable advertising model. They also had already developed a stable news commodity in the form of sensational reporting.

If sensationalism and many of the other major achievements of nineteenth-century journalism were not new, the Civil War was the first major event on domestic soil since the adoption of penny press innovations. The war was a national catastrophe of the first order, and it directly affected journalism. Many journalists, especially in the South, had to decide whether to fight or stay home; due to a shortage of laborers in the Confederate military, many of those editors and printers chose to fight. Thus, their newspapers had to shut down for the duration of the war, and many did not resume publication afterward. In the North, the press established a completely new reporting corps, one that covered the war instead of the crime beat or other local news. Additionally, editors devoted a considerable amount of space to long lists of dead, wounded, sick, and missing, as well as official orders and proclamations from the Union military and federal government.

In preceding decades, Bennett's *Herald* had made crime and other types of sensational news popular by targeting the rising immigrant class in New York with news of the streets. It worked fantastically, and the newspaper's circulation skyrocketed. These immigrant readers apparently could not get enough of crime, accidents, and the bizarre. An 1863 story in the *Herald* typified the approach, describing a particularly grizzly murder. "This morning," the story began, "the members of the family of William Steele found his chamber deluged with blood, and Mr. Steele lying dead on the floor, with his throat horribly cut. His wife was on the bed with her throat cut from ear to ear and an infant, six months old, had its head almost cut off. All were dead—the child still warm."[23]

Following Bennett's lead, the nation's urban newspapers were also filled with stories about assaults, suicides, homicides, explosions, robberies, burglaries, mob violence, bigamy, epidemics, obituaries, and oddities (or oddball, as historian W. Joseph Campbell calls them).[24] Newspapers in the urban North ran hundreds of sensational stories each month during the war. Even though much of Southern journalism seemed to disdain this type of reporting, almost every newspaper in the South carried some sensational stories.

Sensationalized Local News

Mass communication scholars have changed their definitions of what constitutes a sensationalized news story, with successive generations having either having either a more or less expansive concept of it than the previous one. One definition suggests that almost any article fits the mold of sensationalism as long it contains a certain rhetorical edginess and that sensationalized topics were recurrent by the middle of the nineteenth century. As scholar John D. Stevens has commented, some content is made sensational and some content is inherently sensational.[25] Because it is impossible precisely to determine how Civil War readers interpreted each local news article, the following analysis of news content focuses on categories that tended to be sensationalized or that treated topics that were inherently sensational.

For immediate purposes, sensationalized content was interpreted as local stories that fell into the categories of crime, accidents, health, weather, and a miscellaneous category arbitrarily called "others" (most of these would be seen as bizarre or odd in nature). These are categories made inductively through a content analysis of local news in January 1863 in seven Northern and seven Southern newspapers. The examination of local news content that follows focuses on categories where sensationalized writing would be found during the Civil War. This analysis is not rhetorical in nature. That is, it does not measure the degree of sensationalism, although it does look for "sensationalized" or raw language, with phrases such as "scalded to death," "horribly burned," and a "rapid decay of the bodies." An analysis of the degree of sensationalism would be useful, and is highly recommended by the authors for a further study of sensationalized local news at mid-century.

In the current analysis, two coders examined an entire month of two of the fourteen newspapers first to determine the five categories of sensationalized local news stories. They looked for stories with a twist—some odd fact or occurrence; and/or crude, raw, or graphic language. The coders kept in mind the notion that readers would have engaged the articles primarily for moral or entertainment purposes. For example, the tone of the following *New York Herald* story might not contain inherent sensationalism, but the topic was sensational, and the diction and inclusion of key facts added to this nature. Under the headline "Coroner's Inquest," the *Herald* story concerned the suicide of a domestic named Bertha Uhley who apparently took too much morphine and died. "Deceased, it appears, was formerly an inmate of a lunatic asylum, and had often threatened to destroy herself. She drank the poisonous draught before going to bed, and the following morning was found a corpse."[26]

Referring to Uhley as "deceased" and a "corpse" dehumanized her. The editor's word choice implied that the woman was somehow unfit to live among the active, bustling mass of New Yorkers. In essence, Uhley was twisted. Yet, stories like this were abundant, and the categories unfolded. Also, for the health category, a story on an abortion was counted as being sensationalized, especially since these articles dealt with criminal prosecutions of doctors performing abortions, and the tone of such stories showed a disdain for the physicians' actions.

Two categories dominated this Civil War-era journalism analysis: crime and accidents. Civil War newspapers, large and small, were full of such stories. A typical crime story from a Civil War newspaper was one in the Baltimore *Sun* under the headline "Serious Case of Assault." The article described a group of youths who attacked a Baltimore man at a saloon on Light Street. The story was written in a matter-of-fact tone. The boys broke the man's skull, and the paper called his condition "precarious."[27] Although the rhetoric is neither sensational nor bizarre, the story stands out among other briefs in two columns of "Local Matters." There is an implied morality of idle youth doing terrible things to an older citizen.

A typical accident story from this era was the explosion of a "kitchen range" in New York during winter 1863. This "range" was a type of washing device, and the water in it had become frozen. When a woman began using the range, the steam was unable to escape, and that resulted in an explosion. "The woman was struck, and badly injured," reported *The New York Herald*, which also noted that the story was being printed as a "caution to housekeepers."[28] The main "other" categories included politics, race, and the bizarre. While some of these types of news items might not be seen as being sensational today, in the middle of the nineteenth century readers were much more likely to see them as titillating, appalling, and meaningful.

The content analysis of stories from the era, surveying nearly 1,000 articles from the fourteen newspapers in January 1863, revealed that some sensationalized local news included simply crime stories only a few lines in length, while others ran for several columns and depicted the unusual and the weird. The analysis also discovered different styles of sensationalized local reporting between the North and South, with Northern newspapers including three times as many stories of this type as the Southern newspapers. This suggests that Northern newspapers more thoroughly developed local news content as a journalistic staple. However, when one considers that two of the Southern newspapers studied here were weeklies and re-adjusts the comparison to the number of lines expended per sensational story, a relatively unified approach to sensationalized local news reporting appears. Southern journals averaged about sixteen lines per story and Northern newspapers twenty lines. In other words, these items were short in length when compared to the much longer editorials, administrative orders, and battle stories that appeared in Civil War newspapers. Viewed in this way, it is clear that a similar amount of space was devoted to this type of news in both the North and South.

A representative number of newspapers from both sections of the country were chosen so that a broader understanding of how sensationalized local news worked in the press of the Civil War could be seen. It was decided that a period near the halfway point of the war would be representative, leading to a selection of January 1863 as the month for analysis. News of the month included the Emancipation Proclamation taking effect on January 1; the battle of Stones River, in Murfreesboro, Tennessee (a key conflict in the Western theater); and the demotion of Major General Ambrose E. Burnside. Additionally, it was a winter month with relatively few major battles, which contributed to a demand for at least some sensationalized local news even in newspapers a long way from the East Coast publishing epicenter. Finally, following the fall elections of 1862, the political hegemony that the Republicans had enjoyed in the North for two years was in jeopardy, and political tensions in the Union put greater stress on the military. Likewise, the grassroots peace movements in the North gave the South some sense of optimism that their independence might be recognized or that defeat might be avoided, even though the Confederacy had witnessed very little inspiring news from the Western theater.

The analysis focused on newspapers with a strong reputation in their communities and a degree of operational stability, seeking to develop a sample over a large area, North and South, as to not overemphasize the content of a particular region. Thus, only one New York newspaper is examined here. Yet another consideration was having a balance of Republican and Democratic newspapers. Approximately 80 percent of newspapers at the start of the war were political in nature, so having a representative sample from both parties was necessary to be historically accurate. Of course, there were no Republican newspapers in the South.

Another factor in the choices made was the availability of newspapers on microfilm through interlibrary loan. In frequency of publication, daily newspapers were preferred. However, two North Carolina weeklies (*Weekly Standard* of Raleigh and Greensborough *Patriot*) were chosen among the Southern newspapers because of their prominence in their state. The *Weekly Standard* was a key player in Tar Heel politics, and its editor, William W. Holden not only led the peace movement in that state but also ran for governor. The four-page *Patriot* would be the longest running of the wartime newspapers in Greensboro, a leading city in the Piedmont. The *Patriot* would last nearly another century after the war.

Northern newspapers chosen included the *Baltimore Sun, Chicago Tribune, Cleveland Plain Dealer, Des Moines* (Iowa) *Daily State Register, Louisville* (Ky.) *Journal, New York Herald,* and *Springfield* (Mass.) *Republican.* Southern newspapers chosen included the *Atlanta Intelligencer, Augusta* (Ga.) *Chronicle & Sentinel, Charleston* (S.C.) *Mercury, Greensborough* (N.C.) *Patriot, Lynchburg Virginian, Richmond Examiner,* and the *Weekly Standard* of Raleigh, North Carolina. Each edition of the fourteen papers chosen was examined for the month of January 1863. The unit of analysis was local informational stories, which included city news, news summaries, individual articles, letters, and, in a few cases, paid-for classified advertisements that had news information.

These newspapers were examined for news content that included crime, accidents, medical or health news, weather, and a miscellaneous category that included the bizarre. In addition to the news of unusual nature, newspapers ran offbeat stories of a political and racial nature. Thus, these three categories were lumped together for convenience under the term "other" because, while there were nowhere near as many of these types of stories as of, say, crime or accident articles, they still occurred regularly.

The page on which they appeared and their length determined the classification of each article. By far, most of the sensationalistic local content appeared on inside pages, and few of these stories were very long. Indeed, the Southern sensationalistic stories averaged approximately fifteen lines and Northern stories averaged twenty lines. Longer stories often were court news roundups or general news summaries. It was found that Northern newspapers as a whole had a greater volume of sensationalistic news than their Southern counterparts did. Seven Northern newspapers had 725 sensationalistic articles in January 1863 that covered 13,546 lines. By contrast, seven Southern newspapers had 237 articles in that month for 4,205 lines. The Baltimore *Sun,* for example, had 244 sensational articles in January 1863—nearly eight per day. (The *Sun* was among newspapers with local news on the front page, usually the last right column.) Two of the Southern newspapers were weeklies, although one of those had more sensational articles in January 1863 than several of the dailies did. Because it was a weekly, the editor likely hoarded news he had seen in the other dailies in his city, thus publishing a week's information in one edition.

The fact that the sheer volume of sensationalized local news was greater in the Union newspapers is explained in part by the fact that Northern journalists were less likely to have to fight in the war than were Southern journalists. Southern editors simply did not have the human resources to chase down local news. An editor in the South was often lucky if he had a single man or boy to help him with the printing, and many Southern editors simply closed their papers during the war. Northern editors fought in the war, too, and many Yankee papers closed, but not to the same degree as did Southern journals. Furthermore, Southern newspapers covered the war quite acutely. The war was a defensive one in the minds of Southern editors. The homeland had to be defended from the invading Union military. Thus, Southern newspapers tended to have a higher percentage of their news space devoted to the military action.

There also was a greater emphasis on crime reporting in the Northern newspapers. Approximately 51 percent of the sensational stories in the North were about crime, contrasted to 32 percent in the South. One factor behind the crime-reporting differential came at the level of editorial gatekeeping. Southern editors tended to look down on the sensationalistic news in the Northeast urban papers and chose to downplay reporting on criminal activity. Confederate journalists saw the over-reliance on sensationalism as a sign of moral failing and frequently ranted about it in editorials. Furthermore, they may have disagreed with James Gordon Bennett of *The New York Herald* and instead taken the viewpoint that covering criminals encouraged their behavior—or, at least, that such coverage did not discourage it.

Southern newspapers also focused more on crime and accidents, but the combined percentage was lower than that for both categories in the seven Northern papers (77 percent) combined. Indeed, Southern newspapers had nearly 20 percent less crime coverage than the Northern papers. On the other hand, health reporting consumed a larger percentage of the total among Southern newspapers, except in the Richmond *Examiner* (at 65 percent for crime) and Charleston *Mercury* (at 42 percent for accidents). Both of those papers had low health totals. But health stories accounted for 15 percent or more of the sensational totals in four Southern papers, with the *Weekly Standard* coming in at 42 percent. Indeed, health and accidents combined for more than 46 percent of Southern sensational stories. Northern papers had almost 38 percent combined for health and accidents.

Since accidents are unintended, editors could not account for their numbers in terms of moral failure. Likewise, health issues such as smallpox epidemics and death from tuberculosis or diphtheria were not so much about morality as concerning physiological problems or matters of public policy. It is worth noting that no Northern newspaper could come close to the 42 percent level of health stories that appeared in the *Weekly Standard* of Raleigh, North Carolina. The highest percentage of health stories in the Northern newspapers came from the *Daily State Register* of Des Moines at 16 percent. A higher emphasis on health issues, though, may also be attributed to the general lack of resources for Confederate local governments and a lower level of hygiene in the South. Several Southern editors complained about the lack of quality healthcare during the war. Health stories may have also been more prevalent in the South because of the greater presence of tropical diseases there—illnesses that were not limited to one or two seasons of the year.

Furthermore, newspapers that were more thoroughly political in their orientation stuck to interpretation as opposed to the investigative function required in the local reporting of crime, accidents, and health. Indeed, Southern newspapers relied on political spin and military news (either from reporters in the field or the telegraph) to fill their columns. The Confederacy was in a defensive position. If it could prevent the Union military from capturing Richmond and hold its own throughout the other theaters of war, then it would survive and gain international recognition—at least that was the theory in the South. On the other hand, Northern newspapers were more likely to have room for city or local news columns that had a high degree of sensationalistic stories. The economy was more robust in the North, and except for Antietam and Gettysburg, the Union was not under attack. Northern readers, therefore, were treated to a greater variety of news—and greater depth of sensationalism. Moreover, the desire to read sensationalism seems to have grown as the level of sensational reporting increased—at least that was the perception of Northern editors, and even the editors of the more sophisticated Richmond newspapers. Journalists believed that readers wanted these types of stories, and newspapers served them up readily.

One notable consistency was observed in the authors' analyses of these fourteen newspapers: In both Southern and Northern publications, crime and accident reporting accounted for most of the sensational news, with 76 percent of Northern stories consisting of crime and accidents, compared with 63 percent of the Southern stories. This shows that the national paradigm for sensational news was to emphasize these two types of stories. Even if the Southern papers had more health news, the overall approach of emphasizing crime and accident news was well established, and the notable attempts of Southern editors at making a moral point about the debauchery of the North apparently could not overturn human nature.

Another consistency was the average size of an article in all newspapers. Northern and Southern sensational stories for January 1863 totaled 936. The sum of lines for both sections was 17,070. Thus, the average sensational story that month was 18.2 lines in length (Northern stories were 20.7 and Southern 16.7). By nineteenth-century standards, these stories were concise, and they reflected a trend in news presentation during the war: the summary story. Because of the nature of warfare, with its emphasis on who won a battle and the casualty news, editors began to write in a more pithy manner, in large part due to the fact that they paid for the transmission of information over the telegraph lines by the word. Thus, the wordy stories of the pre-war era began to be replaced by a more concise form of journalistic writing, though reporters in the field still tended to be quite prolix, especially the star writers. In general, though, Civil War journalism began to feature a shorter form of writing, and the sensational news fit into that trend.

Local news stories were presented in remarkably similar ways, North and South, during the Civil War. Newspaper readers not only could expect uniform length in city-news articles, but they generally found these stories inside—usually on the second or third page, and with either very simple headlines ("Runaway," "Railroad Accident," or "Small Pox") or with no headlines at all. Likewise, there was no attempt to supplement these stories with complementary graphics (logos, etchings, or maps). They were generally concise and full of concrete information. For example, the Baltimore *Sun*'s "Local Matters" column in May 1863 carried a story about a two-horse team serving Union soldiers that panicked and caused serious damage to individuals and property.[29]

The Baltimore *Sun*, a penny paper, had the highest percentage of crime stories, at 71 percent. The Cleveland *Plain Dealer* and Louisville *Journal* also had more than 50 percent of their sensational stories come under the crime category. Only the Richmond *Examiner* exceeded the 50-percent mark for crime among Southern newspapers—approximately 65 percent of the newspaper's sensational stories were about crime. The next closest among Southern newspapers was the Augusta *Chronicle & Sentinel* at 38 percent. It is also worth noting that newspapers in the North and South had a similar percentage of stories about accidents— 25 percent for the North and 26 percent for the South, suggesting this type of story was a consistently important part of the news for readers throughout the country.

Beyond Crime and Accident News

Perhaps the most illustrative of the sensational categories has been described as the "other," including stories of the grotesque, ghoulish, or generally bizarre. "Other" stories perhaps provided the kind of guilty pleasure historian John D. Stevens referred to in his work on sensationalism in the nineteenth-century press. For example, the Raleigh (N.C.) *Weekly Standard* ran a story about a Black girl who had two heads, contrasting the story with an accompanying description of Siamese twins. "At this mysterious union, science recoils. She, however, is worthy of personal observation, and we anticipate if she is carried through the South, that the student of nature and the curious must make her that subject of close scrutiny, and return amazed at the works of nature."[30] The newspaper also noted that the two-headed girl was intelligent and had considerable musical talent.

Other freakish news came from agriculture. Under the headline "A Monster Pear," *The New York Herald* told of a piece of fruit that weighed thirty-one pounds and seven ounces.[31] The Baltimore *Sun*, meanwhile, had a story about the arrest of a woman dressed in a man's clothing and sporting a fake set of whiskers. The woman was dressed as a man as part of an elaborate marriage scheme with a man from Philadelphia who could not travel to Baltimore at the time.[32] A similar story appeared in the *Sun* a week later. This time the woman dressed as a man said she was leaving behind her mother and a young daughter to start a fresh life.[33]

The unusual was a staple of Civil War-era local news. *The Chicago Tribune* ran a story about a pickpocket who chose to steal a pocket book instead of a more valuable watch.[34] Northern newspapers also delighted in reporting about the marriage of General Tom Thumb and Lavinia Warren, both dwarves. The Cleveland *Plain Dealer* speculated that the couple's boss, the entertainer P. T. Barnum, had wanted to marry Warren first, and the paper believed that Barnum would therefore fire Warren for marrying his employee. "Barnum is a happy man no more," the Cleveland newspaper reported. "The jewel has been snatched from his grasp."[35] Another love story, printed in the Louisville *Journal*, involved the double-suicide overseas of an eighty-year-old man and a sixty-six-year-old woman. The couple had jumped in the Seine and drowned together. "They were locked in each other's arms and kept in position by a true-blue handkerchief," the *Journal* reported.[36] Another love story involved a high-society divorce in New York. *The New York Times* reported on a civil suit in which a man sued his aristocratic wife for being adulterous. One of her lovers just happened to be the man's brother.[37] The Baltimore *Sun* ran a story about a "stone" fight between two rival groups of boys in the city that resulted in the death of one of the youths. It turned out he had been shot by one of the boys on the other side—a boy who claimed he did not know the gun was loaded. There is no mention that the other boys were merely using rocks in the affray.[38]

The ghoulish was another type of bizarre story. *The New York Herald* frequently reported on the desecration of graves in the city's cemeteries. It also had an article about a haunted house. The *Herald* reported that the police were guarding a ghost. Yet another *Herald* story was about juveniles breaking into a church and destroying Bibles.[39] Another type of bizarre story involved class. The Atlanta *Intelligencer* ran a cautionary story about a New York woman who married her father's coachman. The article narrates how the coachman attempted several business ventures that failed. He began to abuse his wife physically, and she eventually entered an insane asylum. "The fashionable, accomplished, and elegant belle of Fifth Avenue—a few years ago—is now the associate of beggars and paupers," the Atlanta paper observed. Another type of bizarre story dealt with the existence of female soldiers. For example, the *Intelligencer* ran a reprint of a story from the Jackson *Mississippian* about a Confederate female soldier named Amy Clarke who had joined the Army with her husband. Both fought in the battle at Shiloh in Tennessee, where he was killed. The Union Army captured her after she was wounded twice, and granted her parole. She was permitted to return home once "she had donned female apparel." Both the Jackson and Atlanta editors ran the story to highlight the faithfulness of Southerners to the Confederate cause. Yet another type of bizarre story was the use of runaway slaves in the Union military. The *Intelligencer* ran such a story about Blacks in the Union Navy.[40]

That piece in the Southern paper was meant to outrage its reader; however, *The Chicago Tribune* played with their emotions, describing a fifteen-year-old boy found at a train station. "He is a bright boy, and should be taken care of," the *Tribune* noted. "He has no friends here." The boy was from Mississippi and had migrated up the Mississippi River and eventually landed in Springfield, Illinois, where he had worked in the fields during harvest.[41]

Confederate newspapers shared incidents of Yankee atrocities, such as the destruction of farms and churches and the plundering of houses.[42] The Augusta (Ga.) *Chronicle & Sentinel* reported on the Yankee shooting of a young woman who was out in the country riding on horseback in Fairfax County, Virginia. The bullet fractured her leg. The editor commented, "Not much humanity about acts of this kind."[43] Another article in the Augusta newspaper recounted the robbery of an orphan girl in Mississippi by William T. Sherman's troops.[44] On the other hand, Northern newspapers took aim at racism and slavery. The Iowa *Daily State Register* expressed outrage at the arrest of an African American boy, saying it was "lawless."[45] The same newspaper also made fun of Democrats who held an anti-Negro rally.[46]

The Augusta newspaper also ran a story about how a New Orleans bookseller was fined for exhibiting a painting of "Stonewall" Jackson in his shop window.[47] The artist who painted the Jackson portrait was also fined. Another humorous story, under the headline "The Merry Wives" in the Richmond *Examiner*, related to the arrest of seven women on whiskey smuggling charges. The *Examiner* noted, "The women were conveyed to the Provost Marshal, where the inner curtain of the skirts were raised, and lo and behold, were exposed about twenty gallons of the fluid concealed in beef bladders around their waist."[48] The Baltimore *Sun* sometimes used very subtle humor in its city items, such as when the editor wrote about a Black man who had violated city law "by allowing nauseous liquors to flow on his premises."[49]

Some of the bizarre stories were not intended to be funny, but must have provided some comic relief. One such story, appearing in the Charleston *Mercury*, concerned the son of Louisville *Courier* editor George D. Prentice. His son, Major Clarence Prentice, served in the Confederate Army, and the Charleston newspaper observed that during a truce the major contacted his journalist father and told him that he was doing well—that he was "fat, ragged, saucy, and rebellious."[50] A story in the Iowa *Daily State Register* reported on a train accident that resulted in the death of a bunch of hogs.[51] *The Chicago Times* ran a story about two farmers who had a dispute about manure that caused them to come to blows.[52] The Chicago newspaper also ran a story about how a woman who owned a boarding house had killed a dog. The Scottish Terrier was a nuisance, having "biting and snapping propensities." Apparently, the woman could tolerate the dog's actions no longer and "cut short the existence of this troublesome member of the canine species."[53]

Republican editors in the North enjoyed picking at their Democratic rivals. These so-called Copperhead editors were often the butt of Republican jokes. The pro-Lincoln Iowa *Daily State Register* hammered the pro-Democratic Muscatine *Courier* for reporting that a Muscatine-based cavalry regiment had made a pact that it should not fight the Southern army, but only Indians. The Des Moines editors called the policy "plain, palpable, damnable mutiny" and claimed that Iowa's integrity was on the line. "We hope for the honor of Iowa soldiers that the charge of the Copperhead organ is groundless," the *Register* editors commented. "There is a motive for such charges in such organs."[54]

On the other hand, the more conservative *New York Herald* liked to poke fun at rival Greeley at the *Tribune*. *Herald* editor Bennett reveled in Greeley's miscues. In an article titled "A Little Mistake," Bennett criticized Greeley for saying that one side or the other had to win each battle. "This sentence strikes the reader as both inelegant and sophistical. Are there no drawn battles?"[55] Some local news had national political overtones. For example, the Baltimore *Sun* ran a story headlined "The Wooden Horse" about a Baltimore group whose political aim was to oppose the federal government. Those members who took the loyalty oath were released, and those who did not were detained. The story was not particularly sensational in tone, but the unusual wording of the headline drew attention to the brief.[56]

These stories often had a moral twist. For example, the Louisville *Journal* reported on a man in a seedy coat who took a spot in a pew near the front of a fashionable New York church. An usher asked him to move to a less auspicious place. Later, the man, Nathaniel P. Banks, removed his coat, revealing he was a Major General in the Union Army. Suddenly, the congregants became courteous, but he refused their civilities. The *Journal* noted: "Gen. Banks quietly declined these flunkey attentions, and concluded his devotions in the free pew near the door, having egregiously mistaken Grace Church for a Christian institution, in the character of some of its frequenters."[57]

While health stories were generally less numerous than crime, accidents, and those articles in the "other" category, they provided important news to Civil War readers. The Greensborough (N.C.) *Patriot* ran a story about a smallpox epidemic that caused a cotton factory in Randolph County to suspend its operations until the situation improved.

> [The] spread of the deadly disease, we think is owing in a great measure to care-lessness on the part of army and hospital surgeons. They should be more careful than send suspected cases of smallpox through the country, which can only be characterized as committing wholesale murder.[58]

Newspapers not only gave information about epidemics or unusual deaths, they also provided calls to action. For example, the *Weekly Standard* encouraged smallpox prevention, informing readers that the state's surgeon general had free vaccinations. A follow-up article on vaccination emphasized that revaccination worked well after the age of thirty-five.[59] The Atlanta *Intelligencer* in one article suggested quarantining could slow the disease, and, in another, that burned leather could act as a "disinfectant against the disease." Weather stories were not that plentiful, especially in inland cities. However, newspapers tended to run stories about extreme weather events—snowstorms, tornados, floods, nor'easters, and hurricanes. Some stories were about extreme weather oddities, such as snow-fall in Jackson, Mississippi.[60] *The New York Herald* reported on ships colliding because of fog in New York Harbor.[61] The Baltimore *Sun* reported on constant rain in March 1863, saying that while temperatures were mild, the overall feel of the weather was "disagreeable." The twist was a little commentary on the city, as editors observed the "the streets were resuming their filthy appearance."[62]

Summarizing Local News during the Civil War

The sheer volume of local news reporting in Civil War newspapers indicates that this type of journalism was well entrenched when the war began. In the decades before the war, the leading penny press papers had made such reporting a staple in American journalism. What changed in the war was the nature of news items that made their way into the newspapers. For the high percentage of sensationalized local news stories, drama was still an essential trait. Yet there were new dramas, ones that came out of the drama of war itself. For example, stories about runaway slaves in Southern newspapers were plentiful. There were also even more stories about the grotesque as editors, it seemed, sometimes tried to provide escapism. To take the attention away from the state of the war as well as the wounded and dead, editors gave readers stories about unusual crimes and weird individuals.

Space was tight because war news took up so much room, and few newspapers had the revenue to hire reporters to cover local beats. This was the convention before the war, but it made even more sense during the war for these local news items to be short and to the point, for the major news of the day was the war itself, not everyday happenings in the cities. While there was a major difference in how Northern and Southern newspapers used sensationalism, it is also worth noting that there was a major difference between large cities and small cities. Newspapers in Baltimore and Chicago, for example, had high percentages of crime news—both exceeding 65 percent. Smaller cities like Des Moines, Iowa, and Springfield, Massachusetts, as well as Greensboro, North Carolina, and Augusta, Georgia, had less than fifty of its sensational total in crime reporting.

Clearly, though, Northern newspapers had a far more pronounced bias toward crime and accident reporting, in large part because these cities were more industrialized and growing. But what did having sensationalistic reporting in the newspapers of the Civil War mean for nineteenth-century journalism? It continued the trend away from the interpretive (political) function of the press toward the informative (news). A decade after the war, the number of newspapers saying they were politically orientated was down from 80 percent to 67 percent. In continuing to include sensational news content along with an increasing amount of military news, Civil War editors made American newspapers more informative.

Contents from the Local News section of the Charleston (SC) *Mercury* on January 10, 1863, typify the material published in newspapers of its size, and for respective audiences. While the news of the day was not nearly as extensive as was coverage of the war, it occasionally contained sensational items that paralleled national headlines, with the local news column containing the following content:

> The Confederate Court is still occupied with the consideration of cases under the Act of Sequestration. On Thursday, Judge Magrath delivered an opinion sustaining the constitutionality of that portion of the Sequestration Act which gives to the next of kin of an alien enemy the sequestered property of each alien enemy. ... The Legislature.—The Secretary of War has extended the leaves of absence and furloughs, heretofore granted the members of the *South Carolina Legislature* ... The Post Office known as "Allison Creek," York District, SC, has been discontinued. ... A Lot of Salt sold at auction in Richmond ... the owner of the salt lost $1,000. ... Found Dead.—On Friday of last week Mr. J. A. Johnson, an old and respectable citizen of Newberry, was found dead in his office. At an inquest returned a verdict that the deceased came to his death by a bullet from a gun in his hands ...[63]

The header of the newspaper featured the name Robert Barnwell Rhett, Jr., the fiery editor of the *Mercury*, as well as the price per paper (5 cents) and price per year ($10).

In general, sensationalized local news during the war reflected the chaotic, violent nature of American society at mid-century. In the urban newspapers in particular, it exposed a dangerous world of industrial accidents and venal crime, as well as bizarre happenings. Yet no similar outrage existed during the war, perhaps in part because the war itself was far more serious an issue than the condition of the cities. When the New York draft riots occurred in July 1863, for example, most New York newspapers did not over-sensationalize the horrible events in the city's streets. Even Democratic editors who exploited the barbarism during the draft riots for their own political reasons still wanted to see the safety and security of the city maintained. While sensationalized local news pervaded the columns of newspapers both North and South, the war had generally both softened and sobered editors as a whole. Still, they understood that their readers needed both local news and entertainment, and they frequently married the two.

Perhaps all the attention on crime, accidents, and the bizarre made local news in the Civil War frivolous in contrast to the solemnity of the war news. However, these story types gave newspapers a steady stream of material with which editors could fill their columns. Add a dash of sex, pranks, and the bizarre, and the entertaining quality of sensationalized local news may well have provided a bit of an escape from the realities of the nation's bloodiest war.

Notes

1 John D. Stevens, "Sensationalism in Perspective," *Journalism History*, 12, 3-4 (Autumn/Winter 1985): 78.

2 Donald L. Shaw and John W. Slater, "In the Eye of the Beholder? Sensationalism in American Press News," *Journalism History*, 12, 3-4 (Autumn/Winter 1985): 86.

3 David Paul Nord, "Teleology and News: The Religious Roots of American Journalism," *Journal of American History*, 77, 1 (June 1990): 14.

4 David Copeland, *Colonial American Newspapers: Character and Content* (Newark, DE: University of Delaware Press, 1997), 18, 19.

5 Carol Sue Humphrey, *The Early Republic: Primary Documents on Events from 1790 to 1820* (Westport, CT: Greenwood Press, 2004), 306, 307.

6 Mitchell Stephens, "Sensationalism and Moralizing in 16th and 17th-Century Newsbooks and News Ballads," *Journalism History*, 12, 3-4 (Autumn/Winter, 1985): 92.

7 Baltimore *Sun*, July 4, 1862.

8 "War News," Library of Congress, accessed October 22, 2021, at <loc.gov/resource/stereo.1s05160>.

9 Mitchell Stephens, *A History of News* (New York: Oxford University Press, 2007), 102; Stevens, "Sensationalism in Perspective," 94.

10 Copeland, *Colonial American Newspapers*, 69.

11 Nord, "Teleology and News," 10, 11.

12 Warren Francke, "Sensationalism and the Development of 19th Century Reporting: The Broom Sweeps Sensory Details," *Journalism History*, 12, 3-4 (Autumn/Winter, 1985): 80, 84.

13 Shaw and Slater, "In the Eye of the Beholder?" 87.

14 Borchard, Bates, and Mullen, "Violence as Art and News: Sensational Prints and Pictures in the Nineteenth Century Press," in *Murder, Mayhem, Mudslinging, Scandals, Stunts, Hoaxes, Hatred, and Disasters: Sensationalism in 19th Century Reporting*, eds. Sachsman and Bulla, (Piscataway, NJ: Transaction, 2013), 53-74.

15 Patricia Cline Cohen, *The Murder of Helen Jewett* (New York: Alfred Knopf, 1998), 37.

16 Cleveland *Plain Dealer*, January 24, 1854.
17 La Crosse (WI) *Democrat*, August 12, 1861.
18 Stevens, "Sensationalism in Perspective," 79.
19 Greeley, *Recollections of a Busy Life*, 138.
20 Parton, *Life of Horace Greeley*, 205.
21 Augustus Maverick, *Henry J. Raymond and the New York Press* (New York: Arno, 1870, 1970), 34, 88, 89; Willard G. Bleyer, *Main Currents in the History of American Journalism* (Boston: Houghton Mifflin, 1927), 240; Dorothy Dodd, *Henry J. Raymond and the New York* Times *during Reconstruction* (Chicago: University of Chicago Libraries, 1936), 4.
22 David R. Spencer, *The Yellow Journalism: The Press and America's Emergence as a World Power* (Evanston, IL: Northwestern University Press, 2007), 100.
23 New York *Herald*, June 9, 1863.
24 W. Joseph Campbell, *The Year That Defined American Journalism: 1897 and the Clash of Paradigms* (New York: Routledge, 2006), 79.
25 Stevens, "Sensationalism in Perspective," 78.
26 New York *Herald*, January 20, 1863.
27 Baltimore *Sun*, April 22, 1863.
28 New York *Herald*, January 1, 1863.
29 Baltimore *Sun*, May 9, 1863.
30 Raleigh (NC) *Weekly Standard*, January 21, 1863.
31 New York *Herald*, January 20, 1863.
32 Baltimore *Sun*, April 22, 1863.
33 Baltimore *Sun*, April 30, 1863.
34 Chicago *Tribune*, January 14, 1863.
35 Cleveland *Plain Dealer*, January 13, 1863.
36 Louisville (KY) *Journal*, January 9, 1863.
37 New York *Times*, March 15, 1865.
38 Baltimore *Sun*, May 28, 1863.
39 New York *Herald*, January 19, 20, 23, 1863.
40 Atlanta *Intelligencer*, January 6, 11, 13, 1863.
41 Chicago *Tribune*, January 16, 1863.
42 Chicago *Times*, quoted in the Atlanta *Intelligencer*, January 15, 1863.
43 Augusta (GA) *Chronicle & Sentinel*, January 3, 1863.
44 Ibid, January 4, 1863.
45 Des Moines (IA) *Daily State Register*, January 21, 1863.
46 Ibid, January 6, 1863.
47 Augusta (GA) *Chronicle & Sentinel*, January 20, 1863.
48 Richmond (VA) *Examiner*, January 5, 1863.
49 Baltimore *Sun*, January 2, 1863.
50 Charleston (SC) *Mercury*, January 5, 1863.

51 Des Moines (IA) *Daily State Register*, January 9, 1863.

52 Chicago *Times*, March 17, 1865.

53 Ibid, March 20, 1865.

54 Des Moines (IA) *Daily State Register*, January 30, 1863.

55 New York *Herald*, January 31, 1863.

56 Baltimore *Sun*, May 21, 1863.

57 Louisville (KY) *Journal*, January 16, 1863.

58 Greensborough (NC) *Patriot*, January 8, 1863.

59 Raleigh (NC) *Weekly Standard*, January 1, 28, 1863.

60 Augusta (GA) *Chronicle & Sentinel*, January 27, 1863.

61 New York *Herald*, January 16, 1863.

62 Baltimore *Sun*, March 9, 1865.

63 Charleston (SC) *Mercury*, January 10, 1863.

10

The Naval War Mediated in Newspapers and Magazines

"The naval action which took place on the 10th instant between the *Monitor* and *Merrimac* at Hampton Roads... has excited general admiration and received the applause of the whole country." Gideon Welles, Navy Department, March 15, 1862, letter to Lieutenant John L. Worden, US Navy, published in "Letter to Lieut. Worden," Washington (DC) *National Republican*, March 26, 1862.

Historians have generally neglected to study naval conflict during the U.S. Civil War. Most of what professional historians have written focuses on the ground war, especially that in the Eastern theatre between the Union Army of the Potomac and the Confederate Army of Northern Virginia. Yet the Union naval blockade of the South—the so-called Anaconda Plan—as well as the *Trent* Affair and the British sale of warships to the Confederacy, especially the CSS *Alabama*, were critical to the war's meandering plot and outcome.

Even less examined had been the coverage of the two navies by the press, yet various journals, including magazines, covered major aspects of the naval conflict. Their coverage included narratives about battles, description of ships and fleets, profiles of officers, analysis of naval strategy, news from the office of the Secretary of the Navy, and accounts of appropriations by Congress. In a few newspapers and in magazines like *Harper's Weekly* and *Frank Leslie's Illustrated Newspaper*, coverage included images and woodcuts that showed ironclads, submarines, officers, and sailors.

On the eve of the Civil War, the U.S. Navy had only 8,000 men serving and forty-two ships in commission. Another forty-eight ships were ready to sail after the commissioning of crews, with twenty more ships serving in revenue collection and surveying. Thirty steamers were purchased in the first month after Sumter to help with the planned blockade, and the total tonnage of the U.S. Navy fleet was 149,841.[1] Essentially, no Confederate Navy existed in April 1861, although some states had small fleets; rather, the Confederacy had a relatively modest merchant marine and a few shipyards. Indeed, the strategic planning of the Confederacy for the war put almost all of its focus on its army and the ground war. Meanwhile, on the U.S. side, the Naval Academy at Annapolis, Maryland, on the site of the old U.S. Army Fort Severn, was only sixteen years old. When the war started, the three upper classes of the academy were ordered to sea. The rest of the students were moved to Newport, Rhode Island. Many officers who were trained at Annapolis switched over to the new Confederate Navy. This included the first USNA superintendent Franklin Buchanan and Sidney Smith Lee, who was the second commandant of the midshipmen and the older brother of Robert E. Lee.

The U.S. Navy's strategy during the Civil War included:

1. Engaging in a blockade of the South and "closing of all the insurgent ports," with the goal of reducing exports of cotton, tobacco, and sugar cane;
2. supporting Union Army operations on major rivers, particularly the Mississippi, using shallow-draft boats;
3. seeking and destroying Confederate commerce raiders, the most famous of which was the CSS *Alabama*, with all of this occurring outside U.S. boundaries on the high seas;
4. and, using U.S. boats to weaken Confederate defenses over nearly three thousand miles of Southern coastline.[2]

The main areas of operations included the Atlantic and Gulf coasts, the Mississippi and Potomac rivers (the latter for the defense of the federal capital), and the high seas in pursuit of commerce raiders.

Fort Sumter and the Anaconda Plan in the Press

Coverage of the naval war essentially started with the bombardment of Fort Sumter on April 12, 1861. It was technically not a naval engagement, as South Carolina militia batteries on surrounding islands shelled Sumter. However, U.S. ships, including the *Star of the West*, provisioned and provided the fort with more men. Hired for troop transport and owned by Cornelius Vanderbilt, the ship had resupplied U.S. Major Robert Anderson and his men, and the cadets at The Citadel fired on it.

Image 10.1 "The Blockade of Charleston." *Harper's Weekly*, 5, 247 (September 21, 1861): 599. The summary from the Library of Congress for this image includes the note, "three sailing ships: 'Vandalia,' the prize 'Arthur Middleton,' and 'Roanoke.'"[3]

Few newspapers covered the naval conflict more intensely than the *New York Herald*. On the first day after the battle, under the headline "The War Begun," Bennett's newspaper initiated its war coverage with this declarative statement: "The war has at last begun." The story announced that South Carolina commander P. G. T. Beauregard's men had begun firing their cannons on Fort Sumter, but it also reported that the U.S. Army was returning fire. The exchange would last thirty-four hours before Sumter was surrendered.

The following day, the lead headline in the *Herald* was simply "The War."[4] The story included narrative of the bombardment of the fort and the surrender of Anderson, who took down the Stars and Stripes and replaced it with a white flag. The *Herald*'s front-page story included a sketch of Fort Sumter, which is situated in Charleston Harbor. The image was rare in newspapers of the war period, and that gave the *Herald* a major advantage over its competition. On April 15, the Baltimore *Daily Exchange* termed what had happened "Civil War" and wrote "Fort Sumter Surrenders Unconditionally."[5] The Baltimore newspaper stated that a naval fleet had attempted to re-provision the fort.

The *New York Daily Tribune*, the newspaper of Republican stalwart Horace Greeley, called Sumter the start of a revolution. Greeley commented that the attack on Anderson and his garrison in Charleston Harbor "inaugurated the second Revolutionary War which is to free forever from the hateful domination of the Slaveholding Aristocracy, who for a quarter of a century past have trampled on the principles of the Fathers of the Republic."[6] The *National Republican* of Washington, D.C., reported on appropriations to pay for shipbuilding, as well as officers and sailors' salaries.

Newspapers in smaller markets also covered Sumter. The *Toledo Transcript* in Iowa noted that Sumter was fortuitous to the South: "The Traitors in Luck!"[7] It also stated that the U.S. Navy had attempted to reinforce Major Anderson and that ships that had run aground were sailing again. The Iowa journal also commented that the war had started because Beauregard refused to let resupplies get to Anderson. Like most Northern newspapers, the *Marshall County Republican* in Plymouth, Indiana, ran telegraphic dispatches about Fort Sumter. On April 18, its lead headline read, "The War Begun! Fort Sumter attacked by the Rebels! Thrilling War News."[8] In a similarly excitable tone, the *Bedford Inquirer* in Ohio claimed: "The traitors have attacked United States forces at Fort Sumter!" Editor David Over used an allusion to assess the situation: "Regardless of the calamity of civil war which they were forcing on the nation, and in contempt of the opinion of the whole civilized world, they assume the aggressive, and force upon the Government a defensive war. They have passed the Rubicon."[9]

Southern newspapers had a different perspective on Sumter. The *Richmond Dispatch* used the headline "The Civil War" for its coverage on April 17, stating that Anderson had surrendered. The *Dispatch* also noted that President Abraham Lincoln had made a call for 75,000 troops in response to the Sumter crisis. The *Dispatch* editor urged North Carolina governor John W. Ellis not to respond to Lincoln's call for enlistments, as the Upper South was still in the Union at this point. The *Abbeville* (South Carolina) *Press* ran communication between Beauregard and CSA Secretary of War LeRoy Pope Walker in which the brigadier general outlined what had happened after Anderson refused to "evacuate Fort Sumter, and to agree meantime not to use his guns against us."[10]

The *Nashville Patriot* re-ran an article from the *Charleston Courier* under the headline "Hostilities Commenced! Bombardment of Fort Sumter." The *Courier* editor wrote after Anderson refused to evacuate: "The crisis had arrived, and we were fully prepared to meet it. The work that awaited the morrow was a momentous character, but we had counted the cost, and had resolved to do it or die in the attempt."[11] The *Alexandria Gazette and Virginia Advertiser* countered the *Washington Republican*'s claim that the number of applicants for the U.S. Navy after Sumter, including those from the South, was more than the resignations of Southerners in the Navy before Sumter. "We must be permitted to doubt the accuracy of the statement concerning 'a huge number from the South.'"[12]

Image 10.2 "The Expedition to Beaufort—Before the Attack." *Harper's Weekly*, 5 (November. 30, 1861), p. 757. According to the Library of Congress, this illustration shows three scenes of naval warfare off the coast of South Carolina during the Civil War. The caption from *Harper's Weekly* reads, "Army and navy reconnaissance, Tuesday morning, Nov. 5—Signaling the flag-ship Wabash—The Winfield Scott losing her masts in the gale of Nov. 1st & 2nd."[13]

The *Wilmington* (North Carolina) *Journal* reported on naval operations at Cape Hatteras. The flag officer of the Atlantic Blockading Squadron reported the capture of 615 men after the bombardment of Confederate States Navy batteries at Cape Hatteras by the U.S. Navy fleet. The *Journal* also included a report on the wounded. The *Western Sentinel* from Winston-Salem, North Carolina, reported on the U.S. Navy taking Virginians prisoner in Norfolk, and that a French marine in New Orleans had "offered his service to the Confederate Government."[14]

Union General-in-Chief Winfield Scott proposed to strangle the South with a naval blockade of Southern ports and an attempt to cut the Confederacy in two by gaining supremacy along the Mississippi River. The *Chicago Daily Tribune* criticized Scott's plan in June 1861, claiming it would not cause the Confederates to starve because the crops were "abundant" in their fields despite the war, and because foreign powers dependent on cotton would recognize the Confederacy and would then break through Scott's blockade.[15] The *Cincinnati Commercial* complained, "Scott's anaconda moves his giant coils but slowly"—a frequent criticism of the strategy, especially with so few Union victories early in the war, especially in the East.[16] In July 1861, *Tribune* editors noted that the strategic nature of the Anaconda Plan had slowed the U.S. Army to a crawl, and that General Irvin McDowell's seventy thousand men along the Potomac River "are burning with impatience for the order to advance on the rebels."[17] After McDowell's Union Army was defeated at Bull Run, the *New York Herald* wrote that the Anaconda Plan had led Lincoln and the Union "on the broad highway to destruction" and that "General Scott's grand and infallible plan for a short war has thus already been destroyed."[18]

The *Cedar Falls Gazette* in Iowa praised Scott's strategy, calling it "slow but sure."[19] On the other hand, the *Buchanan County Guardian*, also in Iowa, praised Congressman John Addison Gurley of Ohio for his attack on the Anaconda Plan, which the newspaper pronounced a "miserable failure."[20] The *Cleveland Morning Leader* indirectly criticized Scott's plan by eulogizing Frederick W. Lander, who had recently died from pneumonia. The *Morning Leader* editor wrote: "Inaction was death to him, and to sit down in the mud and wait for the development of the 'anaconda' plan chafed against his restless spirit."[21] Later, the *Chicago Tribune* would make fun of Major General George B. McClellan's "anaconda plan" of a grand strategy—that is, not taking the war to Robert E. Lee and the Army of Northern Virginia when he had overwhelming manpower and material advantages. At the same time, the *Tribune* praised new Secretary of War Edwin M. Stanton for emphasizing "the active use of carnal weapons as the most efficacious way of bringing traitors to repentance and converting rebels from the error of their ways."[22]

In the South, the *Shreveport Daily News* suggested it would take a "miracle" for Scott's plan to work, despite his huge advantage in men and the "converted movement of flotillas down the Ohio and Mississippi."[23] The *Texas Republican* described Scott as working "slowly" and with "thorough preparation." Another characteristic of the Scott plan, the Texas newspaper noted, was only attacking with "overwhelming numbers" on the Union side.[24]

The Politics of the Press and the *Trent* Affair

The *San Jacinto-Trent* Affair was perhaps the greatest naval story of the Civil War. Captain Charles Wilkes, commander of the USS *San Jacinto*, intercepted the RMS *Trent*, a mail steamer, on November 8, 1861, off the Bahamas and captured two Confederate diplomats, James Mason and John Slidell, who were headed for England on a mission to secure recognition of their new nation and establish business and military ties. Wilkes considered Mason and Slidell to be contraband, but there was no legal precedent for his boarding a neutral nation's ship and taking prisoners, even though many British newspapers were quite sympathetic to the South and wanted Lord Palmerston's government to recognize the Confederacy as an independent nation. In fact, Palmerston, the British prime minister, had warned U.S. Minister to England Charles Francis Adams that removing Confederate diplomats from British ships would breach international law.

Northern newspapers at first were quite excited by telegraphic reports of the *Trent's* capture. Many editors considered the capture of the two Confederate envoys to be a necessary extension of the blockade of Southern ports under Scott's Anaconda plan. The *New York Herald*, which had the most intense coverage of the *Trent* Affair, made the capture of Slidell and Wilkes the lead story of its November 18, 1861, edition. The newspaper examined the legality of Wilkes' action, as well as looking at comparable cases of boarding neutral ships and arresting passengers. On December 13, the *Herald* reprinted a *Times of London* story that stated the *San Jacinto* fired a live shell across the bow of the *Trent*—which the *Times* described as "contrary to all acknowledged law."[25] The *Herald* also reported that Winfield Scott, writing in a letter published widely, held the opinion that Wilkes should not have merely detained Mason and Slidell; rather, Wilkes should have escorted the *Trent* to the closest U.S. port and had the British ship "condemned by a prize court, in order to justify her seizure."[26]

The *New York Daily Tribune*, Greeley's newspaper (with its national readership), held that the detention of the *Trent* and removal of Mason and Slidell were both "fully justified here by all who have made international law a study. The case is strengthened by the recognition which England has so persistently given to the right of maritime search." The *Tribune*, which claimed Wilkes had acted on his own, defended the *San Jacinto* captain for "exercising his lawful privilege."[27] The *Tribune* observed that the captain of the *Trent*, Captain James Moir, was acting in violation of Queen Victoria's command that Britain remain neutral by harboring the Confederate commissioners.

As the British seemed to be preparing for war by sending ten thousand soldiers to Canada, the *Tribune* opined that the taking of the two Confederate envoys hardly was a strong enough cause for initiating war against the United States. The *Tribune* editor called the taking of Mason and Slidell "minute" in terms of real international incidents.[28] Later, the *Tribune* commented, "England has suffered infinitely greater outrages at our hands than the capture of Mason and Slidell, without declaring war against us, and that, too, at a time when the animosity existing between the two nations was far more rampant than at present."[29]

The *Tribune* ran a report from its Paris correspondent stating that Mason and Slidell were getting greater publicity from their capture by Wilkes than they ever would have from their own diplomatic effort. The reporter added, "their actual quality as United States prisoners forcibly taken on the high seas from under the British flag, is for the moment of more aid and service to the cause they were coming to advocate, than anything they could have said or done on European soil," which resulted in "rousing a hostile spirit" toward the Union government.[30]

The *Daily Green Mountain Freeman* in Vermont claimed that the *Trent* affair was being blown out of proportion and that the British were using the capture of Mason and Slidell as an excuse to go to war with the United States. Furthermore, the newspaper held that "the whole conduct of England looks thus far like an attempt to frighten us into an acquiescence with her demands."[31] On December 27, the *New York Sun* reported, "the evidence is accumulating that we are to surrender Slidell and Mason," as the seizure of the two diplomats was "without precedent in international customs."[32] In Pennsylvania, the *Columbia Democrat and Bloomsburg Advertiser* ran a letter to the editor by Massachusetts Democratic Congressman Caleb Cushing stating that Wilkes had acted justifiably, and that "it was an act, which it cannot be doubted, that Great Britain would have done under the same circumstances."[33] The *Cecil Whig* in Elkton, Maryland, stated that the press in Great Britain was "generally excited" and that Palmerston's government was demanding the release of the two envoys and an apology from the Lincoln government. The *Whig* also said that the *Times of London* and the *Observer* were demanding "ample reparation" for what the British perceived as an insult to the Union Jack.[34] The *Port Tobacco Times*, also in Maryland, reported that Secretary of State William H. Seward was willing to release Mason and Slidell if the British agreed that the international law governing the situation was "applicable to both nations."[35]

Wilkes was generally seen as a hero in Northern newspapers. The *New York Sun* printed a block-image drawing of Wilkes on its front page on November 29, 1861, under the headline, "Another Efficient Officer of Our Gallant Navy," describing him as "the officer who boldly arrests traitors, wherever found."[36] However, the Lincoln Administration would eventually decide infuriating Great Britain was not worth it, and the president was not willing to fight two wars at the same time. The *Chicago Daily Tribune* announced on December 28, 1861, that the "Government will disavow the act of Capt. Wilkes, and give up the captive rebels."[37] In the South, the *Richmond Dispatch* reported in late December 1861 that the United States would return Mason and Slidell to British authorities, adding that the *Trent* Affair would cause the Union a "shame yet unrecorded in the annals of the history of any nation." The *Dispatch* also commented that the United States "may only avert, but only for a while, war with England."[38]

In the British press, the *Times of London* covered the *Trent* Affair carefully. It ran without comment a speech by J. W. Edmonds in Boston on November 29, 1861, praising Wilkes for his "patriotic instincts" in arresting Mason and Slidell.[39] The *Times* ran a letter by J. Randolph Clay, a former American diplomat, who cautioned that the British in the eighteenth and earlier in the nineteenth century had acted "with the most unscrupulous severity towards neutrals, and, indeed, may be said not have paid any regard to their rights or to the declarations and protests of neutral powers."[40] In an editorial, the *Times* did criticize Lincoln and his administration for its handling of the *Trent* Affair and in particular for not censuring Wilkes: "It is hardly possible to imagine a Government sunk so far below its duties and responsibilities as to allow all this to go on." The *Times* added that Lincoln had "abandoned the vessel of the State to drift helpless before the gale of popular clamour."[41] By the end of December, the *Times* correspondent in Washington, D.C., was reporting that public opinion "has become calmer, and the idea prevails that there will be no war" between the United States and Great Britain.[42]

The Cork (UK) *Herald* was pessimistic about a diplomatic solution. "The *Herald* feels that peace is almost hopeless. The vote of thanks by Congress to Captain Wilkes amounts to a declaration of war, and such a vote can only be intended as a direct insult to England."[43] The *Salisbury and Winchester Journal* in England reported on December 28, 1861, that Lincoln's Cabinet had decided to cave to British pressure and would release the two Confederate envoys. That journal also reported that the Austrian government told Washington that the British were justified in asking reparations for the *Trent* Affair.[44] In London, the *Thame Gazette* reported that the Prussian government also "condemned the act of the commander of San Jacinto."[45] The *Maidstone Journal and Kentish Advertiser* reported, "Confederates in Kentucky are stated to be jubilant at the prospect of a [Union] war with England."[46]

Ultimately, Lincoln and Seward decided to give in to the British. The United States freed the Confederate prisoners and apologized to the British government. Behind the scenes, John Bright, a Quaker and Liberal Member of Parliament, had worked to cool British ire and sought a diplomatic solution to the *Trent* Affair. Bright gave a speech at Rochdale on December 4 that urged the British to not to run into war with the United States without dialogue. "Let us be calm," he said. "You recollect how we were dragged into the Russian war—how we 'drifted' into it." Bright went on to remind his audience that the Crimean War had cost hundreds of millions of pounds and "the lives of forty thousand Englishmen." Moreover, it hurt the economy and caused a general alarm in Europe that "nearly doubled the armies of Europe; that it placed the relations of Europe on a much less peaceful footing than before."[47]

By mid-December, Seward believed releasing Mason and Slidell allowed the United States to take the high moral ground by not breaking with international law and custom. Furthermore, it was time to work against any international recognition of the Confederacy by taking the *Trent* Affair off the pages of newspapers in both England and the United States. Seward prevailed upon Lincoln to rebuke Wilkes' action—which, while well received by most of the press in the North, had been undertaken independently of the administration. Most Republican newspapers proclaimed Wilkes a Union hero at a time in the war when positive Union military news was scarce.

Newspaper Coverage of the Naval Conflict

On March 9, 1862, a premier ironclad on each side of the war fought in the Battle of Hampton Roads, Virginia. The USS *Monitor*, an ironclad steamer, faced off against the CSS *Virginia*, an ironclad ram that had been the steam frigate USS *Merrimack* before the war. It was the first—and only—conflict between two ironclads. From its base in Norfolk, the *Virginia*, the much bigger of the two ironsides, was attempting to upset the U.S. Navy's blockade of the Virginia coast and its ports, including Norfolk. On the previous day, the *Virginia* had destroyed two U.S. ships (with one hundred casualties reported in one case) and was about to send a third, the steam frigate *Minnesota*, to the bottom, but darkness fell.

The next morning, the *Virginia* intended to pummel the listless *Minnesota* again, but by this time the *Monitor*, which had not been involved in the action the previous day, was at the *Minnesota*'s side to defend the U.S. ship. There ensued a four-hour battle between *Monitor*, with its two large guns, and *Virginia*, with its ten smaller ones, which would result in a stalemate, although the Confederate ship would leave the battle zone. The *Monitor* did not pursue the *Virginia* because its acting commander feared losing the only ironclad of the Union.

The *New York Herald* termed the ironclad battle a "Tremendous Naval Conflict."[49] The *Herald*, which ran woodcut drawings of both *Monitor* and

Image 10.3 "Submarine Infernal Machine Intended to Destroy the 'Minnesota.'" *Harper's Weekly*, 5, 253 (November 2, 1861), p. 701. The Library of Congress summary reads (only), "a submarine and a sailing ship."[48]

Virginia, stated that the Union ship "sustained herself" through the day's battle, "showing herself capable of great endurance."[50] The *Herald* added: "The magnificent war steamer *Monitor* has proved herself to be all that her friends and distinguished constructor had anticipated for her."[51] A few days later, the *Herald* ran a woodcut of the map of the battle, showing the relative position of the two ironclads. On March 11, the *Chicago Daily Tribune* called the *Monitor-Virginia* clash a "Great Naval Engagement," and ran a map of Hampton Roads on its front page. In England, the *Banbury Guardian* in Oxfordshire reported that the *Monitor-Virginia* engagement, an "absorbing subject," was the talk of the town.[52]

The *Chicago Daily Tribune* commented that the result left "little ground for rebel rejoicing," but added that the *Monitor*'s commander, Lieutenant John L. Worden, had sustained a wound in the battle, having been hit by shrapnel in the eyes as he manned the pilot house. He would be promoted to commander after the battle. The *Daily Tribune* reported a few days later that a bill "would be rushed through Congress" to appropriate funds for the building of more gunboats like the *Monitor*.[53] The bill appropriated $15 million for construction of these ironclads. The *New York Herald* reported that President Lincoln formally commended Worden for his "gallant conduct" in the Battle of Hampton Roads.[54]

In Washington, D.C., the *Evening Star* wrote that the *Monitor*'s "two big guns" were "too much for anything secesh [secession] can get up."[55]

In the Southern press, the *Richmond Enquirer* reported that the builder of the *Monitor*, John Ericsson, stated that both ships "were well fought" and that the *Virginia* had hit the *Monitor* twenty-two times, with the Confederate ship hit nearly a hundred times.[56] The Richmond (VA) *Whig* reported that the two ironclads made contact with one another several times during the engagement. The *Whig* stated that the *Virginia* retreated and that the *Monitor* was "uninjured" in the battle.[57] The Southern press invested great hope in the *Virginia*, but this would be its only battle. When the base at Norfolk was abandoned ahead of a looming attack by the Union a few months later, orders came to sink the ironclad.

The Union Navy would go on to build eighty-four ironclads, sixty-four of them in the mold of the *Monitor*. The press in the North got behind the legislation to build these ships, although the ironclads had questionable long-term value for several reasons: (1) they were slow; (2) they had uncomfortable living spaces for the sailors; and (3) they were only somewhat buoyant. The Confederacy would commission twenty-two ironclads during the war and had another twenty-eight under development when the war ended in April 1865.

Nonetheless, the March 9, 1862, battle between the *Monitor* and the *Virginia* produced excitement on both sides. Gideon Welles, the Union Secretary of the Navy, spoke for most when he wrote: "The performance, power, and capabilities of the *Monitor* must effect a radical change in Naval warfare."[58] The *Times of London* went a step further, remarking that the *Monitor* "can neither be destroyed nor captured," and added: "A boat once alongside of the *Monitor* is perfectly safe."[59] Thus, the ironclads could serve as ships that would protect larger vessels from enemy attack.

The other Confederate ship that would loom large in the war was the CSS *Alabama*, which was built near Liverpool by John Laird Sons, a shipbuilding firm. It was launched as ship number 0290, or the *Enrica*, in May 1862. The *New York Daily Tribune* noted, "in the Alabama everything was sacrificed for speed."[60] The 220-foot-long propeller-driven sloop of war had two 300-horsepower horizontal steam engines and travelled at 15 miles per hour. Confederate States Navy Commander James Bulloch had worked to get the ship constructed by Laird. Bulloch went through an intermediary in Liverpool with ties to the cotton industry. The *Alabama* was commissioned in a secretive fashion.

Once christened, it sailed to the Azores, where the Confederate Navy's Raphael Semmes took command. The *Alabama* prowled the Atlantic and Indian oceans, nearly approaching Australia, and preyed upon American merchant and naval ships, and usually leaving alone European shipping interests. The *San Francisco Daily Evening Bulletin* reported on the *Alabama* on November 28, 1862, stating that the Confederate ship had overtaken the brig *Baron de Casline* off Cardenas, Cuba, with Semmes demanding a $6,000 ransom. The captain of the *Baron de Casline* also had to take on forty-five passengers, Americans captured by the *Alabama* who had watched their ships burn.

A typical story on an *Alabama* attack appeared in the Wisconsin-based *Manitowoc Pilot* in February 1863. Based on a report by Captain Homer C. Blake that had been routed through the U.S. Consulate in Kingston, Jamaica, the *Pilot* (a Democratic newspaper) reported that the *Alabama* had sunk the USS *Hatteras* off the coast of Texas, near Galveston. Semmes had flown a British flag but then pulled it down and raised the Confederate banner. Soon after, Semmes began to pelt the *Hatteras* with his cannons. Despite the sinking, Blake praised his men: "Their enthusiasm and bravery were of the highest order."[61] The *Abbeville*, South Carolina, *Press* reported that the *Alabama* had sunk the *Hatteras* in just thirteen minutes of engagement, and that the Confederate ship then sailed to Jamaica. The *Press* report was based on a letter from Secretary of Navy Stephen R. Mallory to CSA President Jefferson Davis about the engagement.

In another typical story about the ship, the *Cleveland Morning Leader* reported in April 1863 that the *Alabama* had attacked two merchant vessels off the Turks: "One went to pieces. The cargo of the other would be saved."[62] In June 1863, the *Washington Evening Star* claimed that the *Alabama* was burning cargo from neutral ships—one of which, the *Nora*, was a British cargo vessel. The *Evening Star* editors believed the British government would "take instant action in the matter."[63] The USS *Vanderbilt* was sent to chase down the *Alabama*, and the *Cleveland Daily Herald* reported that the U.S. ship was in Mauritius and the Confederate ship was off India's east coast in the Bay of Bengal. The Cleveland newspaper added: "The captain of the Vanderbilt is believed to be well informed with regard to the rebel pirate's course."[64]

The *Chicago Daily Tribune* called the *Alabama* "the terror of the seas" in October 1862.[65] The *Tribune*, which kept close tabs on the Southern ship, reported on its sinking of the *Amanda* and *Winged Racer* in the Indian Ocean in fall 1863. On November 6, Semmes attacked the Boston-based *Amanda* (whose owners were from Maine)—which was carrying hemp and sugar—and set it afire. This occurred near the Strait of Sunda, between Java and Sumatra. Three days later, Semmes attacked the *Winged Racer*. The *Tribune* story, which the *Java Times* had originally reported, said both American ships were left "in almost destitute condition."[66] Once the attacks occurred, Semmes had the Confederate flag hoisted. In December 1862, the *Nashville Daily Union* (Nashville was occupied by the Union Army at the time) reported that the *Alabama* would fly the U.S. flag as it attacked Union ships, had a French pilot, and "received coals from an English brig."[67]

U.S. Secretary of the Navy Welles made it a special priority to gather a fleet of U.S. Navy ships that were equal to the *Alabama*. The New York *Tribune* on January 1, 1863, listed eighteen ships the Union government had refurbished that could vie with the Confederate raider, including its eventual nemesis, the *Kearsarge*. The *Tribune* stated: "And now, after twelve weeks work, the following fleet is on the ocean, every vessel belonging to it a match for the Alabama, save in speed, and several well able to overhaul her." Another of the eighteen was the *San Jacinto*, the ship used to intercept Mason and Slidell in 1861. The *Tribune* added that the fleet had been built for "fighting and chasing."[68] The *New South* newspaper in Port Royal, South Carolina, commented in September 1863 that the building of warships like the *Alabama* was alarming the *Times of London*, which feared that the British providing the Confederacy with arms might lead to war with the United States.[69]

Despite its menacing record described by most Northern newspapers, the *Alabama* was had its weaknesses. The *Delaware Gazette* in Ohio announced the sinking of the *Alabama* by the USS *Kearsarge* on June 19, 1864, off Cherbourg, France, stating: "This destroyer of our merchant ships has gone down in her first fight." The newspaper added, "This is the first regular sea fight between two naval vessels that has taken place in this war."[70] The *Chicago Daily Tribune* wrote that the *Alabama* was destroyed in "honorable combat with an equal adversary. Heretofore, with a single exception, she has been known only by her victories over the unarmed and defenseless."[71]

The *Alabama* and *Kearsarge* circled one another seven times, and their engagement lasted nearly two hours before the Confederate ship began to sink. The pro-Republican *Caledonian* in St. Johnsbury, Vermont, reported that the *Alabama* went down in half an hour, with "one officer and six men killed, and sixteen wounded."[72] The *Caledonian* also reported that the *Kearsarge* was probably "a formidable overmatch for the Alabama" because it had more power and twice as many men as did the Confederate ship.[73]

In Indiana, the *Plymouth Weekly Democrat* reported the capture of sixty-eight crewmembers; however, Semmes and a few of his men escaped to either French or British ships. The newspaper reported that the *Kearsarge* "sustained but little injury."[74] The *Burlington Weekly Hawkeye* in Iowa called the *Alabama* "the most stupendous and systematic fraud on record" because it had been built allegedly as a merchant ship and had been constructed by those British who were, in fact, enemies of the Union.[75]

The *Chicago Daily Tribune* also reported that most of the men working on the *Alabama* were British. A newspaper in California reported that Secretary of State William H. Seward said, "the British Government was responsible for the depredations of the *Alabama*."[76] After the war, Seward would seek reparations for the damages caused by the *Alabama*.

The *Soldiers' Journal* praised *Kearsarge* Captain John A. Winslow—"nobly has he done"—and noted that he was a native of Wilmington, North Carolina, had become a midshipmen at age fourteen, and had been in the Navy for thirty-seven years in 1864.[77] Winslow, like Wilkes before him, received plenty of plaudits in the press, although some editors wondered why he had not apprehended Semmes. The *Chicago Daily Tribune* said Winslow should be promoted from captain to commodore, and that "his last act will be remembered in naval history."[78] Later, though, the Chicago newspaper wrote that Winslow's allowing Semmes to escape on an English yacht was "inexplicable."[79]

In the Southern press, the Richmond (VA) *Whig* praised the volunteers who had signed up to be sailors on ships like the Alabama. The *Alexandria* (VA) *Gazette* reported that the USS *Vanderbilt* was "in pursuit of the Alabama" out of St. Helena in fall 1863.[80] The *Gazette* announced the *Alabama*'s sinking in July 1864, noting that Semmes had been wounded slightly and was headed to Paris to meet with a Confederate commissioner. The *Gazette* reported that the key blow was when the *Kearsarge* "sent a projectile right through the Alabama's boiler."[81] The Alexandria newspaper also reported that Semmes would soon be in command of a "new Alabama"—a corvette with "powerful artillery."[82]

In South Carolina, the *Lancaster Ledger* reported that the *Alabama*'s "carnage was awful" in its sinking by the *Kearsarge*.[83] Meanwhile, the *Camden Daily Journal* reported that a new *Alabama* would "be cutting the salt sea foam" soon and "sinking and burning" enemy ships.[84] A few weeks later, the Camden newspaper reported on the exploits of the *Tallahassee*, which had destroyed seven U.S. ships off the coast of Connecticut. The *Daily Journal* called that ship the "new apparition that has burst upon the Yankees."[85]

The Richmond *Daily Dispatch* praised "numerous acts of gallantry" by several onboard the *Alabama* during the final duel with the *Kearsarge*—including the captain's coxswain, who was wounded in the arm, and two sailors who picked up an 11-inch shell from the Yankee ship and threw it overboard.[86] Although not a Southern newspaper, the conservative Democratic *Dayton Daily Empire* pronounced the *Alabama* "so worn out that it was thought she would have to be

abandoned" when in the port at Cherbourg before the fight with the *Kearsarge*—as if the Dayton newspaper was excusing the defeat of the Confederate raider.[87]

Magazine Coverage of the Naval Conflict

Harper's Weekly, an illustrated magazine, also covered the naval war. *Harper's* ran stories on this subject, but its major contribution to journalism about the naval aspect was inclusion of woodcut drawings based on either artist sketches or photographs. The first example of such images in *Harper's* came on April 20, 1861, with a depiction on two inside pages of the "United States Fleet off Fort Pickens, Florida."[88] There also was an image of Fort Pickens on the bottom of the front page of that week's edition of the magazine. In September, *Harper's* would run a cover drawing of the CSS *Merrimac* (i.e., the *Virginia*). In that same edition, a spread showed "The Great Naval Expedition," including the USS *Oriental*, *Great Republic*, and *Wabash*.

In November 1861, *Harper's Weekly* ran a three-panel illustration of the U.S. Navy ships *Wabash* and *Winfield Scott* at the bottom of the page, and, at the top of the page, an illustration of about a dozen ships doing reconnaissance. In the illustrations, the *Wabash* is a signaling ship—a key in the communication chain for the U.S. fleet—and the *Winfield Scott*, listing along, has been decimated by a gale. The title of the page, "The Expedition to Beaufort," refers to the capture of the fort in that South Carolina port by the South Atlantic Blockading Squadron.[89] Commodore Samuel F. Dupont of Delaware led the expedition.

Harper's showed the blockade of Charleston in September 1862. The image featured the USS *Roanoke* with the Stars and Stripes displayed prominently, and the USS *Vandalia* sandwiching the blockade-runner the *Arthur Middleton*, flying a Confederate flag. On the same page is an image of the interior of a tent for U.S. military personnel at Cape Hatteras, North Carolina. Maintaining a Union military presence at Hatteras Inlet, the magazine editors noted, "is of vast importance to the cause of the Union" because the inlet opens up to the vast Pamlico, Albemarle, and Currituck sounds.[90] In November, *Harper's* ran a woodcut engraving of a submarine. The two-man Confederate vessel is beneath the USS *Minnesota*, and "the infernal machine" possesses primitive torpedoes—that is, tethered beer barrels armed with friction triggers that would ignite black gunpowder if a barrel made contact with an enemy ship's hull.[91]

In its March 1, 1862, edition, *Harper's Weekly* detailed several naval actions, including Western battles along the Mississippi and Ohio rivers, and their tributaries. The magazine ran an image of the capture of Fort Henry in Kentucky in this issue. Fort Henry was on the Tennessee River, and the battle included both Army and Navy forces. Indeed, U.S. Navy gunboats bombed the Confederate-held fort, helping then-Brigadier General Ulysses S. Grant notch a much-needed early victory in the war. This fleet was the Western Gunboat Flotilla led by Flag Officer Andrew Hull Foote.

Reporting on Fort Henry also included a profile of Captain William D. Foster, commander of the *Essex*. The story noted that while that Foster had been born in Louisiana and owned property in Virginia, he remained "faithful to the noble old Government" after Sumter.[92] *Harper's* also ran a series image of naval images from Georgia, including warships on the Savannah River outside Fort Pulaski. In the June 14, 1862, issue, the magazine showed an image of the Confederate ironclad *Manassas* and a raft that was afire. The Manassas pushed the raft into a Union sloop-of-war, the *Hartford*, commanded by David G. Farragut. This was tactic used to torch Union ships along the Mississippi, in this case at Fort Jackson and Fort St. Philip. Farragut's men put out the fire, and later engineers had to work feverishly to free the boat after it ran aground. In the *Harper's* piece, the reporter wrote that Navy engineers "worked like beavers ... and soon got the ship astern and afloat."[93]

Frank Leslie's Illustrated Newspaper also covered the naval war. One illustration, for example, depicted a battle on the Mississippi River between the Confederate ironclad *Arkansas* and the USS *Carondelet* near Vicksburg, Mississippi. The *Carondelet*, a gunboat, is flying the Stars and Stripes, which is prominent in the drawing. The text notes that the crew of the U.S. ship boarded the *Arkansas* to try to take prisoners, but the Confederate crew had "retired below, and the iron hatches were closed, so that it was utterly impossible to continue the action."[94]

Another *Frank Leslie's* drawing shows Farragut's fleet bombarding Port Hudson, Louisiana, in May 1863. Farragut was assisting Nathaniel Banks' siege of Vicksburg, and again the ships display the U.S. flag prominently in this wood-cut. Although the battle depicted in this drawing was a Union defeat, ultimately the Army and Navy would subdue both Vicksburg and Port Hudson—a key moment in the war since it came just after Gettysburg. The drawing was one of two involving this campaign featured in this edition of *Frank Leslie's*. The other drawing was of the Second Louisiana Colored Regiment attacking the Confederate works at Port Hudson. Again, the Stars and Stripes, in this case held by an African American soldier, is prominent in the drawing.[95]

The Civil War press paid a great deal of attention to the war at sea, and the two major magazines shared that focus with the world. *Harper's Weekly*, in particular, chronicled the modernization of the U.S. fleet. Advances in technology and a greater degree of industrialization were critical to the Union victory. In fact, Craig L. Symonds, a historian of the Civil War navies, believes that construction of the ironclads during the war "led to the emergence in the North of a truly modern industrial system. Because the various components of the monitors had to be manufactured at different sites and then brought together to be assembled," he holds, "the whole program provided an important boost to both metallurgy and fabrication, and allowed the U.S. Navy to create and maintain a stockpile of spare parts."[96] This industrialization included a major project undertaken during the war, the laying of the transatlantic telegraph cable.

Notes

1 "Our Navy for 1861," Columbus (OH) *Daily Statesman*, May 31, 1861, 1.

2 "Secretary Welles' Report," Potter (PA) *Journal*, December 11, 1861, 1.

3 "The Blockade of Charleston," Library of Congress, accessed October 14, 2021, at <loc.gov/item/00652823>.

4 "The War," New York *Herald*, April 14, 1861, 1.

5 "The Civil War: From Charleston," Baltimore *Daily Exchange*, April 15, 1861, 1.

6 "Lexington and Concord," New York *Daily Tribune*, April 19, 1861, 4.

7 "Latest News! War Begun!" Toledo (IA) *Transcript*, April 18, 1862, 2.

8 "The War Begun!" Plymouth (IN) *Marshall County Republican*, April 18, 1862, 2.

9 "War Begun!" Bedford (OH) *Inquirer*, April 19, 1861, 2.

10 "Official Report of the Bombardment of Fort Sumter," Abbeville (SC) *Press*, May 17, 1861, 1.

11 "Hostilities Commenced! Bombardment of Fort Sumter!!" Nashville (TN) *Patriot*, April 16, 1861, 2.

12 "It Is Asserted," Alexandria (VA) *Gazette and Virginia Advertiser*, April 30, 1861, 2.

13 "The Expedition to Beaufort—Before the Attack," Library of Congress, accessed October 14, 2021, at <loc.gov/item/99404907>.

14 "War Vessels Ashore!" and "From New Orleans," Winston-Salem (NC) *Western Sentinel*, April 26, 1861, 2.

15 "The Anaconda Plan," Chicago *Tribune*, June 28, 1861. 1.

16 "Gen. Scott's Policy," Cincinnati *Commercial*, reprinted in St. Paul (MN) *Weekly Pioneer and Democrat*, July 5, 1861, 1.

17 "The Torpid Anaconda," Chicago *Tribune*, July 15, 1861, 2.

18 "President Lincoln Puts His Foot Down for His Cabinet," New York *Herald*, July 26, 1861, 4.

19 "The War," Cedar Falls (IA) *Gazette*, February 21, 1862, 2.

20 "Words Fitly Spoken," Buchanan County (IA) *Guardian*, February 11, 1862, 1.

21 "Death of Gen. Lander," Cleveland *Morning Leader*, March 4, 1862, 2.

22 "The New Secretary," Chicago *Tribune*, February 4, 1862, 2.

23 "Gen. Scott's Plan," Shreveport (LA) *Daily News*, September 11, 1861, 1.

24 "The Position of Military Affairs in Virginia," Marshall (TX) *Texas Republican*, July 20, 1861, 1.

25 "The Mason-Slidell Affair," New York *Herald*, December 13, 1861, 3.

26 "The Latest Relative to the Slidell-Mason Affair," New York *Herald*, December 21, 1861, 1.

27 "The War for the Union: The Search of the British Steamer," New York *Tribune*, November 18, 1861, 4.

28 "The News from England," New York *Daily Tribune*, December 19, 1861, 4.

29 "Naval Precedents," New York *Daily Tribune*, December 27, 1861, 4.

30 "The Mason and Slidell Seizure in France," New York *Daily Tribune*, December 19, 1861, 7.

31 "The Griefs of England," Montpelier (VT) *Daily Green Mountain Freeman*, December 24, 1861, 2.

32 "The Fact of Surrender becoming Clear," New York *Sun*, December 27, 1861, 2.

33 "Slidell and Mason's Arrest," Bloomsburg (PA) *Columbia Democrat and Bloomsburg Advertiser*, December 21, 1861, 2.

34 "Warlike News from England," Elkton (MD) *Cecil Whig*, December 21, 1861, 2.

35 "The Trent Affair," Port Tobacco (MD) *Times and Charles County Advertiser*, December 26, 1861, 2.

36 "Our Gallant Navy, Captain Wilkes, of the Frigate San Jacinto," New York *Sun*, November 29, 1861, Library of Congress, accessed November 2, 2021, at <loc.gov/item/sn83030272/1861-11-29/ed-1>. "Another Efficient Officer of Our Gallant Navy," New York *Sun*, November 29, 1861, 1.

37 "The Trent Affair," Chicago *Tribune*, December 28, 1861, 1.

38 "Rebel Opinions on the Trent Imbroglio—Southern News," Richmond *Dispatch*, quoted in the Cincinnati *Daily Press*, December 28, 1861, 1.

39 "America," *Times of London*, December 10, 1861, 9.

40 "The Trent Affair," *Times of London*, December 11, 1861, 7.

41 "The Style of the American President," *Times of London*, December 17, 1861, 6.

42 "America: The Trent Affair," *Times of London*, December 30, 1861, 10.

43 "The President's Message," Cork (UK) *Herald*, December 17, 1864, 3.

44 "The Trent Affair," Salisbury and Winchester (UK) *Journal*, December 28, 1861, 2.

45 "Prussia and the Trent Affair," London *Thame Gazette*, December 31, 1861, 2.

46 "American: The Trent Affair," Maidstone (UK) *Journal and Kentish Advertiser*, December 31, 1861, 4.

47 John Bright, "On the 'Trent' Affair," speech given at Rochdale, England, December 4, 1861.

48 "Submarine Infernal Machine Intended to Destroy the 'Minnesota,'" Library of Congress, accessed October 14, 2021, at <loc.gov/item/00652824>.

49 "Important from Fortress Monroe: The Merrimac out of Norfolk," New York *Herald*, March 10, 1862, 1.

50 "The Great Naval Conflict," New York *Herald*, March 11, 1862, 10.

51 "An Account of the Engagement by an Eyewitness," New York *Herald*, March 11, 1862, 10.

52 "The Budget," Banbury (UK) *Guardian*, April 10, 1862, 2.

53 "A Bill," Chicago *Tribune*, March 13, 1862, 1.

54 "Congress," New York *Herald*, December 12, 1862, 4.

55 "Iron Clad War Ships," Washington (DC) *Evening Star*, March 11, 1862, 2.

56 "The Monitor," Richmond (VA) *Enquirer*, March 25, 1962, 1.

57 "The Late Battle in Hampton Roads," Richmond (VA) *Whig*, March 13, 1862, 3.

58 "Letter to Lieut. Worden," Washington (DC) *National Republican*, March 26, 1862, 2.

59 "How to Take the Monitor," *Times of London*, in the Surrey (UK) *Comet*, April 19, 1862, 2.

60 "Chasing the Alabama," New York *Daily Tribune*, January 1, 1863, 8.

61 "The Fight between the Steamers Hatteras and Alabama," Manitowoc (WI) *Pilot*, February 27, 1863, 1.

62 "From Boston," Cleveland *Morning Leader*, April 25, 1863, 1.

63 "The Pirate Alabama Burning British Cargoes," Washington (DC) *Evening Star*, June 3, 1863, 2.

64 "Telegraphic: This Day's Report," Cleveland *Daily Herald*, November 23, 1863, 3.

65 "The Rebel Privateer '290' or Alabama," Chicago *Tribune*, October 21, 1862, 3.

66 "The Privateer Alabama: Her Capture of the Amanda and Winged Racer," Chicago *Tribune*, February 2, 1864, 3.

67 "The Rebel Pirate Alabama Again," Nashville (TN) *Daily Union*, December 13, 1862, 2.

68 "Chasing the Alabama," New York *Daily Tribune*, January 1, 1863, 1.

69 "News from the North," Port Royal (SC) *The New South*, September 19, 1863, 1.

70 "Naval Victory," Delaware (OH) *Gazette*, July 8, 1864, 2.

71 "The Pirate Alabama: A Few Facts Relative to Her Origin, Career and End," Chicago *Tribune*, July 29, 1864, 3.

72 "The Alabama Again," St. Johnsbury (VT) *Caledonian*, July 8, 1864, 2.

73 "The Sinking of the Alabama," St. Johnsbury (VT) *Caledonian*, July 15, 1864, 2.

74 "The News," Plymouth (IN) *Daily Democrat*, July 7, 1864, 2.

75 "A Refuge of Lies," Burlington (IA) *Weekly Hawkeye*, July 16, 1864, 1.

76 "From the War," Weaverville (CA) *Weekly Trinity Journal*, January 23, 1864, 2.

77 "Capt. Winslow, of the Kearsarge," *Soldiers' Journal*, July 20, 1864, 7.

78 "Sketch of John A. Winslow, U.S.N.," Chicago *Tribune*, July 8, 1864, 1.

79 "Capt. Winslow," Chicago *Tribune*, July 12, 1864, 2.

80 "Later from Europe," Alexandria (VA) *Gazette*, October 8, 1863, 4.

81 "The Loss of the Alabama," Alexandria (VA) *Gazette*, July 6, 1864, 1.

82 "The New Alabama," Alexandria (VA) *Gazette*, July 15, 1864, 2.

83 "The Great Naval Duel between the Alabama and Kearsarge," Lancaster (SC) *Ledger*, July 26, 1864, 1.

84 "The Augusta Chronicle and Sentinel," Camden (SC) *Daily Journal*, July 19, 1864, 1.

85 "The Confederate Steamer Tallahassee," Camden (SC) *Daily Journal*, August 23, 1864, 1.

86 "Heroism of Some of the Confederate Crew," Richmond (VA) *Daily Dispatch*, July 11, 1864, 1.

87 "The Alabama Affair," Dayton (OH) *Daily Empire*, July 6, 1864, 3.

88 "United States Fleet off Fort Pickens, Florida," *Harper's Weekly*, April 20, 1861, 248, 249.

89 "The Expedition to Beaufort," *Harper's Weekly*, November 30, 1861, 757.

90 "Forts Hatteras and Clark," *Harper's Weekly*, September 21, 1861, 599.

91 "Submarine Infernal Machine Intended to Destroy the Minnesota," *Harper's Weekly*, November 2, 1861, 701.

92 "Captain Porter," *Harper's Weekly*, March 1, 1862, 140.

93 "The Hartford in the Mississippi," *Harper's Weekly*, June 14, 1862, 373.

94 "Desperate Combat between the Confederate Ram 'Arkansas' and the Federal Gunboat 'Carondelet,'" *Frank Leslie's Illustrated Newspaper*, July 15, 1862, in the Mississippi Archives of History, accessed: October 16, 2021, at <da.mdah.ms.gov/series/photos/detail/532834>.

95 "Bombardment of Port Hudson, La., by Admiral Farragut's Fleet," *Frank Leslie's Illustrated Newspaper*, May 27, 1863, 216, 217.

96 Craig L. Symonds, *The Civil War at Sea* (New York: Oxford University Press, 2012), 35, 36.

11

Press Suppression, North and South

"Every man felt, as he listened to this appeal of liberty and law, the day of lawless tyranny was drawing to a close." *New York World*, February 21, 1863.

No period in American journalism history has produced a greater degree of press suppression than the Civil War years. The press suppression of the era encompassed the closing of newspapers, seizure of property of the publisher, barring of publications from the mail, and arrests of editors or reporters. It was also a strategy for silencing journalists.

These forms of suppression amounted to prior restraint of publication—something that had been out of favor since publication of John Blackstone's *Commentaries* in the eighteenth century. Other forms of Civil War press constraints included banishment of reporters from army camps and censorship of the telegraph lines. These measures did not prevent a journalistic operation from printing, but they made it more difficult for correspondents to gather news. Two other types of constraints, both of which were informal, included intimidation via mobs and blocking potential advertisers. Often mob intimidation became mob violence. This, too, was a form of suppression if it resulted in closing of a newspaper.

Yet it is important to note that these constraints occurred in a piecemeal fashion. They were far from systematic or bureaucratized. The most intense suppression came from officers who for one reason or another believed the government ought to control the press. Furthermore, most suppression acts resulted only in temporary closing of newspapers, and such squelching of the press often backfired, prompting some editors to be even more vituperative. Still, there were newspapers that did close permanently. For example, in Indiana, after Brigadier General Milo S. Hascall attempted to rein in the dissident press in 1863, Democratic newspapers in four of the eleven cities where press suppression occurred soon ceased to exist.[1]

President Abraham Lincoln oversaw the greatest governmental censorship in American history, but he was not dogmatic about the issue. Indeed, Lincoln had mixed feelings about suppression and increased his tolerance of the press during the war. However, Secretary of War Edwin M. Stanton had no such qualms, and he often pushed Lincoln toward less lenience for wayward journalists. Author Shelby Foote has claimed that the Lincoln administration suppressed three hundred newspapers in the North.[2] While historians David Herbert Donald and James G. Randall do not necessarily dismiss such numbers, they maintain that press suppression was minimal, and that "the government as a general rule refrained from control of the news, both on the positive and negative sides." Donald and Randall concede, though, that the Lincoln administration "swerved from the course of democratic government and departed from the forms of civil liberty."[3]

Certainly most of the suppression happened in the North, but it also occurred in the South. In September 1863, Confederate troops transiting through Raleigh, North Carolina, attacked and caused the temporary closing of that city's *Standard* newspaper—an incident very similar to mob intimidation in the North, such as the attack by Union soldiers on the *Jeffersonian* in Richmond, Indiana, in March 1863. Yet Southerners generally were too busy fighting the war to worry about things like dissent in newspapers. Moreover, most Southern editors were on board first with secession and then war, but this does not mean there were not disagreements about policy or criticisms of political and military leaders.

Press constraints had been in place before the war, although the South had been relatively tolerant of abolitionist sentiment until the publication of David Walker's *Appeal* in 1829 and the slave revolt in Virginia led by Nat Turner in 1831. After these two events, the abolitionist campaign against slavery led to formal and informal press restrictions in the South. Countering the abolitionist rhetorical campaign were laws that would restrict freedom of expression. Most Southern states would have liked to hush the agitating radicalism of such journalists as William Lloyd Garrison, Frederick Douglass, or Gamaliel Bailey. These censorship laws made it illegal to publish anti-slavery sentiment in certain Southern states. Southern leaders on a local level also put in place policies that prohibited the circulation and possession of abolitionist literature in the mail. Penalties included imprisonment or fines, but some laws prescribed execution as the sentence for a second offense.[4] Furthermore, Southern states attempted to have violators of these laws extradited from Northern states. No such extradition occurred, but some Northern states genuinely considered such cooperation.

While attempts to silence abolitionists through legal means had mixed results, less-formal constraints had a more powerful effect on public opinion. No incident was stronger in this respect than the November 7, 1837, murder of Elijah P. Lovejoy in Alton, Illinois. Born in Maine, Lovejoy was the son of a Congregationalist minister. After attending Waterville College, Lovejoy taught for a year before heading west. He went to Illinois first but could not find adequate employment and ended up in St. Louis, where he opened a school and then bought half-interest in The St. Louis *Times*. (Ironically, under the Missouri Compromise of 1820, Maine was the free state and Missouri the slave state that were admitted to the Union under the tit-for-tat plan, and now, Lovejoy had moved from one to the other). A supporter of Kentucky Whig Henry Clay, Lovejoy was not initially an abolitionist. Indeed, the *Times* under his ownership ran advertisements for selling slaves.[5]

Lovejoy's attitude toward slavery changed after he heard Presbyterian minister David Nelson's sermons against it. Nelson charged that the selling of human beings was just as great a sin as murder or adultery. Nelson's words transformed Lovejoy, who took action by selling his share in the *Times*. Thereafter, he returned east to attend Princeton Theological Seminary and was ordained a Presbyterian minister. In 1832, he also became editor of a religious newspaper, the *Observer*, and over the next five years, in the pages of his pro-Presbyterian newspapers, he crusaded against slavery, Catholicism, and tobacco. Lovejoy described how slavery was dehumanizing, writing of the "lacerated bodies of helpless men, and women, and children."[6] He also took aim at non-slaveholding Missourians, saying that their apathy toward slaves was also criminal. Words like Lovejoy's were anathema in a slave state, and Lovejoy and his newspaper were not that popular with the public. In May 1836, his opponents chased him out of town after he criticized a judge who failed to charge anyone in the lynching of a free African American.

Lovejoy decided to move across the Mississippi River to Alton, Illinois. There, he began the Alton *Observer* and resumed his rhetorical war against slavery. In that town, mobs decided to take matters into their own hands. Hooligans destroyed the *Observer*'s printing press three times. When Lovejoy purchased a fourth press, a mob attacked the warehouse where it was being stored. The editor defended his press as the mob tried to set fire to the building, but two pro-slavery physicians shot the journalist five times, killing him as he and a supporter tried to push a ladder away from the warehouse.[7] The editor was buried two days later, on his thirty-fifth birthday. The *Missouri Republican* in St. Louis (a pro-Democratic newspaper) called the incident regrettable but put the blame on Lovejoy for trying to "establish an abolitionist press" in the part of the country that was pro-slavery.[8]

Historians have called Lovejoy the first casualty of the Civil War because his death showed the depth of resistance to abolition—that is, a willingness to act to slow or stop opponents of slavery. It also demonstrated that words mattered to Americans at mid-century, and that the super-charged language of the era could lead to violence. Moreover, mob action against Lovejoy established a primitive frontier paradigm for dealing with unpopular words.

Maryland, Missouri, Mahoney

During the war, Northern conservatives composed a leading minority. The group, mostly Democrats who initially opposed coercing the South to return to the Union, later opposed the degree of blood and treasure spilled in pursuit of the war's ultimate twin goals of reunion and abolition. Officials made Democratic journalists swear the loyalty oath after arresting them, jailing them and implored them to temper their criticism of the war and the Lincoln administration. Their offices were ransacked, their advertising dried up, and their publications were barred from the mail. They stood on the opposite side of the political divide from the abolitionists who faced intimidation before the war, but with the outbreak of hostilities, Democrats ironically resorted to using the same arguments for freedom of the press that the anti-slavery journalists had used for decades.

Press suppression at the beginning of the war was especially intense in Maryland, a slave state that stayed in the Union. Unlike antebellum suppression, the new attempts to squelch civil liberties came against those who opposed abolition. In April 1861, the Baltimore press was generally pro-South. Baltimore's editors tended to take the side of the tobacco farmers on the eastern shore of the state—men who owned slaves and espoused states' rights. Baltimore journalists thought the South had the right to secede. A coercive war was seen as incompatible with the principles that had led to the nation's creation almost a century earlier.

Baltimore was one of the nation's best newspaper cities at the time, rivaling New York, Boston, and Philadelphia. The Baltimore *Sun* was a penny paper of the first order under the direction of publisher Arunah S. Abell. Being in a slave state, the Rhode Island native could not promote abolitionism even if he abhorred slavery. Indeed, being anti-slavery was simply not a good business decision in Baltimore. To support the position of Horace Greeley, for example (expressed by the *Tribune* in the leading anti-slavery newspaper of the North), would have ruined the *Sun*'s advertising revenue. In Abell's view, Maryland's economic future rested with Southern cotton, rice, and sugar interests, not any items produced in the more industrial North.

The prosperous *Sun* shunned Abraham Lincoln just as the rest of Maryland did: He received only 2,294 of the 92,241 votes cast in the state in November 1860. In March 1861, when Lincoln traveled through Baltimore on his way to Washington for the inauguration, federal agents determined that the city was too dangerous and had him transited through downtown in the middle of the night. The *Sun* called the nighttime trip through Baltimore "stupendous folly," labeling it the "Underground Railroad Journey."[9] Those kinds of words did not endear the newspaper to the new administration.

Just a week after the attack on Fort Sumter, some 1,700 members of the Sixth Massachusetts Regiment entered the Maryland port city on their way to Washington. Baltimore law forbade locomotives downtown, so the city did not have a continuous railroad line from north to south. Thus, horse-drawn rail cars moved the troops from the President Street depot to Camden Station via Pratt Street. A mob of anti-Republicans met the soldiers' railroad cars at the city's inner harbor. The hooligans grabbed loose stones and hurled them at federal soldiers. Anchors were placed on the track in front of the soldiers' cars, and the volunteers continued their journey on foot. As the Massachusetts regiment marched through downtown, the mob pelted them with rocks. Two soldiers were injured.

To avoid the projectiles, the soldiers picked up the pace and then defended themselves by firing on the crowd on Pratt Street. Members of the mob searched for guns, bringing Baltimore to a full-fledged riot. Four soldiers and twelve civilians were killed, and thirty-six soldiers and an unknown number of civilians wounded.[10] The Baltimore *Republican* remarked that the riot would "remain forever a foul and damning blot upon the fanatical administration which has brought the curse of civil war upon our land."[11]

George W. Brown, Baltimore's mayor, called on the city's police and militia to restore order. He asked citizens with firearms to loan their weapons for the city's defense if Lincoln sent troops to restore order.[12] A mass meeting was held the day after the riot, and 10,000 Baltimoreans assembled. Brown had the Maryland flag unfurled to wild cheering. In the month after the event, skirmishes occasionally broke out in Baltimore between pro-Southern and pro-Northern groups. For example, on April 22, 1862, a mob attacked the Baltimore *Wecker*, a German-language newspaper with abolitionist sentiments. The editor asked Mayor Brown for protection, and he sent police to the newspaper's office. Despite the city's official attempt to show that Baltimore could be peaceful, Northern newspapers reacted with quick criticism. Union soldiers vowed revenge for the treatment of the Massachusetts troops.

The *Sun*, modeled on the penny papers of New York, ran extensive coverage of the riots. This was an unusual practice since local news usually was placed on an inside page. Riot stories covered more than half of the front page. The multi-decked headline on the main story included the words "Citizens of Baltimore Shot Down in Our Streets," showing the paper's bias against the Lincoln administration. In its editorial on the same day, it expressed "profound regret" at the "scenes of bloodshed" in the city. "There is no doubt," it read, "the people of Maryland have cherished an almost inalienable love of the Union, and men have hoped against hope, that the Union would survive even the terrible ordeal to which it has been exposed since the administration of Mr. Lincoln was inaugurated." It concluded that Maryland's citizens were "zealously devoted to the honor, the interests, and the welfare of our State."[13]

Two days later, the *Sun* called the Union troops "invaders," and Abell's newspaper proclaimed that the alternative to letting the South go in peace would be a "long, bloody, profitless war, with no adequate result possible to either" side.[14] Again, the paper warned that war would result in a collapse of commerce. The *Sun* indicated that Lincoln would be wise to concentrate on the affairs of the North.[15] Spending the federal government's treasure on war would be foolish, the editorial writer commented. Repeatedly, the Baltimore newspaper conflated war with desolation and peace with prosperity. If Lincoln would maintain the peace, "wisdom and civilization" would triumph.[16]

In May 1861, President Lincoln sent troops under Benjamin Butler to occupy the city. At that point, the *Sun* began to modulate its tone, and in September, the power of the military was used against the Maryland press. On September 10, Postmaster General Montgomery Blair prohibited mail circulation of three Baltimore newspapers—*The South*, the *Republican*, and *Daily Exchange*.[17] Then, on September 13, Secretary of War Simon Cameron had Allan Pinkerton and the provost marshal of Baltimore arrest Frank Key Howard, editor of the *Daily Exchange*, and Thomas W. Hall, editor of *The South*, as well as several correspondents for Hall's paper. Later, federal officers arrested William W. Glenn, one of the publishers of the *Daily Exchange*. The officers escorted Glenn to Fort McHenry, where they gave him over to the custody of General Dix. The *Sun* noted that the "arrest of Mr. Glenn was not unexpected, and he had made arrangements for such events."[18]

Cameron said the arrests were a military precaution, and Union soldiers discovered a list of Marylanders who swore that the federal government should recognize the Confederacy and that they would be willing to support the secession of Maryland if Virginia left the Union. As it turned out, the newspapers did not publish the list. Over time, Maryland's newspapers became far less openly pro-Southern, though they continued to carry clippings from newspapers in the South, especially the Richmond papers. While the federal government was reining in journalists in Maryland, it also took aim at gaining control over the telegraph, which was a critical medium for spreading news.

In August 1861, just over the Maryland border in Pennsylvania, a group of perhaps half a dozen men from out of town destroyed the pro-Democratic *Jeffersonian* newspaper in West Chester after editor John Hodgson continually criticized the Lincoln administration. Later, U.S. marshals seized Hodgson's printing equipment. Republican newspapers in the state held that silencing the *Jeffersonian* was overdue. However, Hodgson would not go quietly. The Pennsylvania journalist and Hodgson's father, William Hodgson, believed Philadelphia Republicans were behind the assault on their newspaper, and they sued the federal marshals for illegally confiscating more than $7,000 of their property. The case ended up in the state supreme court, and the Hodgsons won. The decision was an affirmation of press freedom. "Every man felt, as he listened to this appeal of liberty and law," *The New York World* remarked, that "the day of lawless tyranny was drawing to a close."[19]

Two years later, Union soldiers arrested Albert D. Boileau, editor of the Philadelphia *Evening Journal,* for his criticism of Lincoln. Later, the provost marshal took control of the *Evening Journal* building. Both orders came from Major General Robert C. Schenck, commander of the Middle Department. The military authorities ordered Boileau to sign a letter expressing his regret for being critical of the president and for praising C.S.A. President Jefferson Davis. The Democratic newspapers in New York thought Boileau to be a coward for recanting his views, but the Philadelphia journalist had little choice. After signing the letter, Boileau won his release. However, he decided to close the *Evening Journal.*

Like Maryland, Missouri experienced a high degree of press suppression and intimidation during the Civil War precisely because it had stayed in the Union as a slave state. With divided loyalties, Missouri had great political instability, and the civil liberties of its citizens were often in jeopardy—sixty-three newspapers in the state faced suppression between 1861 and 1864. It is probable that more journals faced censorship, but those papers no longer exist, and the military records that might shed light on their suppression were destroyed.

In the first year of the war, the Union side in the state took aim at the pro-Confederate journals. Once the Union military was able to gain the upper hand in Missouri in the summer of 1861, Brigadier General Nathaniel Lyon began systematically suppressing the pro-Southern press. For example, a mob destroyed the Booneville *Observer* newspaper on June 18, 1861.[20] One month later, a leading pro-Confederate paper in St. Louis, the Missouri *State Journal*, was seized after editors published words that gave, in the view of Union authorities there, aid and comfort to those in active rebellion against the U.S. government.[21] The suppression order used to enforce the seizure also said the newspaper had encouraged citizens to take up arms against the United States and had published unreliable news about Union troops. While the printing equipment was confiscated, Joseph W. Tucker, editor, fled before the Union soldiers came to his office. Indeed, Tucker joined the pro-Southern state militia and called the Union military "the enemy."[22] The journalist called Lincoln a monarch. Of course, pro-Union newspapers praised the decision to close the *State Journal*, while pro-Confederate journals condemned the action. One month after Lyon closed the St. Louis *State Journal*, he suppressed both the *Evening Missourian* and the *Bulletin*.

In April 1862, a military commission convicted Edmund J. Ellis, editor of the Boone County *Standard* in Columbia, of treason. The commission punished him by sending him to the front, where Confederate forces assumed control over him. Four months later, military officers suppressed the Sainte Genevieve *Plaindealer*. Military authorities also suspended the Platte City *Conservator* in May 1863 for writing critically of the Emancipation Proclamation, and they arrested the editor of the St. Joseph *Tribune* in October 1863 for unknown reasons. In 1864, a mob attacked the office of the *Union* newspaper in Louisiana, Missouri.[23]

St. Louis was the epicenter of journalism in the state, and the pro-Republican *Missouri Democrat* feuded with the pro-Democratic *Missouri Republican*. Started in 1808, the *Republican* was one of the first newspapers in the state, and it became a daily in 1836. Established in 1853, the *Democrat* supported Thomas Hart Benton's political aspirations. (Benton, a Democrat, served five terms in the U.S. Senate, having a background in journalism after editing the Missouri *Enquirer* when he came to the state in 1815). Indeed, with at least a bit of irony, the pro-Republican newspaper was called the *Democrat* and the pro-Democratic paper was called the *Republican*. Yet confusion was the rule in Missouri. The Blair family had been Democrats before the founding of the Republican Party. When

Francis Preston Blair, Jr., founded the paper, it was still in the Democratic camp. After the war, he would actually switch back to the Democrats and run for vice president. The *Republican* went so far back in Missouri history that its name mirrored the name of the party of Jefferson and Madison, which, of course, would later become the Democratic Party under Andrew Jackson.

Early in the war, pro-Confederate mobs threatened the *Democrat*, as the state was divided into pro-Union and pro-Confederate camps.[24] The *Democrat* would help lead the state into the Union column and would serve as the public opinion leader for a pro-abolition state government, as Missouri would be the first of the slave states that stayed in the Union to emancipate its slaves. The *Republican* was moderate, and its editors thought Missouri should stay in the Union. However, the newspaper also maintained that it would stand by its Southern neighbors.[25] Later, the *Republican* criticized Lincoln for allowing the Fort Sumter situation to move the two sides to war. For St. Louis' most popular Democratic newspaper, the idea of forcing the South back into the Union was anathema.

Major General John C. Frémont, who served as commander of the Department of the West in 1861, he had the support of the *Democrat*. Frémont declared martial law in August of that year and barred five New York newspapers from circulating in his department.[26] Frémont also emancipated the slaves of all Missourians who opposed the Union and confiscated the property of any secessionist—orders that President Lincoln would rescind for political reasons. Wanting to show that Missouri was a strong member of the Union, the *Democrat* supported the emancipation order. Ironically, Frémont arrested Blair Jr. co-editor of the *Democrat*, after he had heard that Blair, also a congressman from Missouri, had criticized the general in a letter to his brother Montgomery Blair, the postmaster general, as being incompetent as a military leader. Francis Blair was, in fact, a brigadier general in the Union Army serving under Frémont, so this was a matter of insubordination. Eventually, Frémont had Blair freed.

Secretary of War Cameron approved of military control of the telegraph in spring 1861, and by July 8 of that year Winfield Scott, Lincoln's leading general at the time, laid down the law to journalists. With Cameron's approval, Scott wrote: "Henceforth the telegraph will convey no dispatches concerning the operations of the Army."[27] Reporters, however, prevailed upon Scott to let them cover battles as they were occurring without giving away troop location, movement, or strength. (At the same time, the Confederate secretary of war had begun making similar recommendations for Southern journalists.) Scott did not keep his word. When the first battle of Bull Run transpired, the old general truncated the journalists' transmissions.[28] Many Republican newspapers cheered telegraphic censorship, especially those that did not have reporters at the front. Some Republican editors urged Draconian measures. However, the problem was that uncensored Southern newspapers penetrated the North. Furthermore, it would be difficult for the federal government to control all the newspapers scattered throughout the North, many of which printed letters home from soldiers—missives that might contain sensitive information or criticism of officers.[29]

The U.S. House of Representatives investigated telegraph censorship in late 1861 and early 1862. The House Judiciary Committee concluded that the Lincoln administration had the power to censor since Congress had given him that control of the telegraph and railroads.[30] E. S. Sanford of the American Telegraph Company monitored all messages sent along the telegraphic lines. Although the Judiciary Committee did not address the constitutionality of censorship, the panel did say that government censors should not stifle political or personal information. The legislative committee entreated the executive branch to censor only military information that might aid the enemy.

Postmaster General Blair and several generals promoted a form of prior restraint by limiting the circulation of certain newspapers. In 1862, the War Department assumed authority over U.S. Post Office, giving officers in the field the ability to determine what publications they could seize. Blair justified the measure as a matter of national security—that, in effect, the military was serving the public good. However, nothing in the Constitution gave the executive branch such extraordinary powers; authorities simply assumed these powers under the rebellion clause (Article I, Section 9), which provided for the suspension of habeas corpus in times of invasion or rebellion. The Lincoln administration believed the Civil War was such a time, and accordingly reduced civil liberties, including freedom of the press.

Among generals who limited newspaper circulation in the mail was General J. W. Davidson, who in 1862 barred the Montreal (Canada) *Commercial Advertiser* in Missouri. A year later, the provost marshal in St. Louis barred seven newspapers from circulation in that city, including *The Chicago Times*, Columbus (Ohio) *Crisis, New York World*, and *New York Journal of Commerce*—all pro-Democratic newspapers. A year later, Major General Ambrose Burnside banned *The New York World* in the Department of the Ohio. Burnside called the *World*'s words "pernicious and treasonable," saying that they created "distrust" in the administration's war policy.[31] Under pressure from the president, Burnside revoked the order a few days later when he lifted his suppression of *The Chicago Times*, one of the most anti-Lincoln papers in the North. A week later, Major General James G. Blunt barred *The Chicago Times*, the Columbus *Crisis*, the *New York World*, and two other newspapers from the mail in Kansas. General William Rosecrans barred *The Chicago Times* from the Army of the Cumberland in 1863, and in 1864, Kentucky banned the Illinois newspaper.

One of the most prominent cases of arrest and imprisonment of an editor was that of Dennis A. Mahony, editor of the Dubuque (Iowa) *Herald*. Mahony, a native of Ireland who became an active Democrat, supported the war at the outset and even wanted to raise an Irish regiment from the city, although Iowa's Republican governor refused Mahony's request. But the conservative Democrat was extremely critical of the president and his party. On orders from Secretary of War Edwin M. Stanton, U.S. Marshal Herbert M. Hoxie (a former editor of the Des Moines, Iowa, *Daily State Register*) arrested Mahony early in the morning of August 14, 1862. P. H. Conger, the deputy U.S. marshal, made the formal arrest. As authorities apprehended him, Mahony reportedly said, "Here I am, a martyr to Liberty!"[32] The federal agents did not say exactly what Mahony had done to merit arrest.

The *Herald* reported the next day that Mahony would not retract any of his published words because he had said nothing wrong.[33] Mahony did not write anything directly that encouraged citizens of Dubuque to resist enlisting.[34] In Democratic neighborhood meetings, Dubuque made resolutions that described "abolition treason" of two types: (1) suspension of the writ of habeas corpus and (2) wartime financial policy, including the personal income tax.[35] Mahony routinely encouraged Republicans to enlist if, as they alleged, the president's war policy so enthralled them. The editor did concede that if the president or Congress subverted the Constitution, "the people have the right to resist such subversion."[36]

Hoxie also arrested David Sheward, editor of the Fairfield *Union and Constitution*, then took both journalists to Washington, D.C., by train. The two men stayed in prison there until after the November elections. They were released only after they swore a loyalty oath. Democrats in Iowa actually nominated Mahony for the Third Congressional District race. The Iowa *Daily State Register* called the nomination "bold, to say the least," and it told the Democrats they should not run an incarcerated man.[37] Mahony lost without uttering a single speech. Meanwhile, Stilson Hutchins, Mahony's assistant at the Dubuque *Herald*, ran the newspaper while his boss was in jail.[38] Mahony returned to Dubuque to a "huge concourse of citizens," bonfires on the levee, a band, speeches by local dignitaries, and a parade through the streets to the editor's home.[39] Sheward came home to a more modest display of support. A procession of approximately fifty to seventy men led him through Fairfield.[40] The Davenport *Democrat* argued that the release of Mahony and Sheward after the election was proof that Republicans had conspired to rig the congressional contest, and that Democratic gains in the Midwest were in large part a consequence of their arrests. "Those who could not, or would not, see the object of these arrests before, see it now, and must confess the outrage as beyond parallel in the history of our free country," the *Democrat*'s editor wrote.[41] Mahony's arrest irritated Democrats in the Midwest, it had far less of an impact on the election than did Lincoln's announcement of the Emancipation Proclamation on September 22, 1862. Mahony eventually returned to the editor's post at the *Herald* and wrote a book called *The Prisoner of State* about the federal government's abridgement of his civil rights.

Content Constraints

While formal press constraints left editors in jail and newspaper offices closed, another form of injury was informal yet equally—if not more—effective. This was the use of boycotts to dry up revenue. In the winter of 1863, Republicans in the Muskingum River Valley of Ohio conspired to injure the economic well-being of three Democratic newspapers in that part of the state—the McConnelsville *Enquirer,* Zanesville *Citizens' Press,* and Marietta *Republican.* For example, operatives in the Republican Party circulated a document that stated that the *Enquirer* had discouraged enlistments. The document encouraged merchants to boycott advertising in the *Enquirer.* In addition, Cyrus McGlashan, the newspaper's editor, received a letter warning him that if he did not leave within fifteen days, he would be shot as a traitor. Later, someone in McConnelsville posted a bulletin promising a $250 reward for anyone who shot McGlashan.[42] Despite these obstacles, McGlashan kept the *Enquirer* afloat.

In March 1863, a mob ransacked the office of the Marietta *Republican.* In response, Democrats in Washington County held a mass meeting at which they fashioned resolutions in favor of a free press and the right to a free conscience, even in wartime. Two months later, the sheriff in Zanesville had to arrest *Citizens' Press* editor Samuel Chapman to protect him from a Republican mob. Later, Chapman received a letter from Burnside reminding him that General Order No. 38 prohibited the editor from discouraging patriotism.[43] That was enough for Chapman, who decided to suspend his journalistic endeavor. Also in March 1863, Company M of the Second Ohio Volunteer Calvary attacked the Columbus *Crisis,* a relatively new Democratic newspaper owned by Samuel Medary. The soldiers, carrying hatchets, clubs, axes, and pickets, were from Camp Chase, which was located on the west side of Columbus. With Medary in Cincinnati, the Ohio troops smashed windows and tossed furniture, books, paper, and maps into the street. *The Crisis*, only two years in operation, did not have a press, so it was not a total loss. Medary, a former governor of the Kansas Territory and member of the Ohio legislature, owned another Columbus newspaper, the *Daily Statesman*, which soldiers also trashed in a quest to find the type that *The Crisis* used. Columbus police stopped the mob before it could do significant damage to the *Daily Statesman*. Medary said he had "no quarrel with the military" and claimed two Republican newspapers, the Ohio *State Daily Journal* and the *Fact*, had provoked the mob.[44] Medary said both papers told falsehoods about *The Crisis*, and that *State Journal* personnel plied the soldiers with liquor and encouraged them to do harm to Medary's newspaper offices.[45] Medary also printed a letter from members of the regiment who did not take part in the attacks condemning the actions of their fellow soldiers. Those members of the Second Volunteers who were not involved wrote: "We are all entirely and utterly opposed to all such demonstrations."[46]

Similarly, the press in Wisconsin, far from the war front, experienced relatively more informal violence. Almost comically, Marcus "Brick" Pomeroy, editor of the La Crosse *Democrat*, had a turkey pushed into his face. In 1864, Pomeroy suggested that Lincoln should be assassinated if reelected. When he was fatally shot the following year, a mob threatened the editor. He also had to face questioning from the local sheriff, although he was not arrested. While the pro-Democratic Prairie du Chien *Courier* never actually faced informal press constraints, William D. Merrell's newspaper covered the murder of a Democratic politician by a mob of Union soldiers in New Lisbon, Wisconsin. Merrell said such mob violence would never happen in Prairie du Chien.[47]

After Congress passed the Habeas Corpus Act in March 1863, Milo S. Hascall, the commanding brigadier general in Indiana, decided to rein in the Democratic press of the Hoosier State. A resident of Goshen, where he was a Republican leader, Hascall knew the political structure of Indiana well. He would suppress ten newspapers in six weeks in the spring of 1863, all of them in the northern half of the state. Typical of those suppressions was the arrest of Plymouth *Weekly Democrat* editor Daniel E. VanValkenburgh on May 5. Citing Hascall's General Order No. 9, Union soldiers arrested VanValkenburg at 5 a.m. on that day for words to which the general objected—specifically, that the journalist had called him a donkey. The troops took the Democratic editor to the train station in Plymouth, and the editor ultimately stopped in Indianapolis at Hascall's office. After an interview, Hascall sent him to Cincinnati to meet with Burnside, the commander of the Department of the Ohio. In the Queen City,

VanValkenburgh took a loyalty oath and promised to cease his anti-Lincoln, anti-Hascall rhetoric. A week later, he resumed publication of his newspaper. At least for the next month, VanValkenburgh was more careful with what he wrote.

The VanValkenburgh episode was typical of Hascall's suppression efforts in Indiana. The general had editors arrested or threatened with arrest. The journalists did not stay in jail very long. Hascall's work generally had a temporary chilling effect, although it is worth noting that in four of the eleven cities in which suppression occurred Democratic newspapers did close in 1863.[48] In the eyes of even some of the state's Republicans, Hascall unnecessarily upset Hoosier Democrats, and Lincoln asked Stanton to relieve the general of his command in Indianapolis. Hascall took leave of his post on June 6, 1863. Thereafter, military interference in Indiana journalism decreased. Federal officials arrested several editors for draft evasion, and Joseph Bingham, editor of the pro-Democratic Indiana *State Sentinel* in Indianapolis, was arrested for conspiracy.[49] Officials later dropped those charges. For the most part, mob intimidation of the press would be the rule after Hascall resigned.

On the heels of Hascall's efforts in Indiana, Ambrose E. Burnside's suppression of *The Chicago Times* in June 1863 ranks as one of war's the most significant acts of censorship. Wilbur F. Storey was a brilliant journalist. He was Greeley's equal as an editor, but he stood on the opposite side of most issues published in the New York newspaper. Storey had risen to journalistic prominence as the editor of the Detroit *Free Press* before moving to the quickly developing city of Chicago in June 1861, just a month before the war's first major battle. He was an aggressive businessman, and the *Times*' advertising increased, as did its circulation. It became a first-rate rival of *The Chicago Tribune*, Lincoln's most loyal advocate in the press.

Initially, Storey was not anti-war, but he wanted no part of a war for emancipation. Once Lincoln announced the Emancipation Proclamation on September 22, 1862, Storey led the chorus of protest from what the Republican editors would call the Copperhead press. For Storey, a war of abolition was "an act of national suicide," a theft of property that interfered with local institutions, limited the power of the states, and would lead to freed slaves competing for jobs with whites in the North.[50] The latter was quite important, because Storey believed the freedmen would work for lower wages than white laborers. There was no question that Storey was a racist and that he did not ever foresee Blacks as being social equals to whites.

Image 11.1 "The Copperhead Plan for Subjugating the South." *Harper's Weekly*, 8, 408 (October 22, 1864), 688. This *Harper's Weekly* cartoon shows a delegation of Copperheads entreating a Southerner to return to the Union. The caption reads: "War and Argument—Cold Steel and Cool Reason—having failed to restore the Union, it is supposed that the South may be bored into coming back."[51]

Storey was a staunch defender of Democrat Clement L. Vallandigham, whom Burnside had arrested in May 1863. The *Times* editor led journalistic defense of the former Ohio congressman. While the Chicago editor provided cogent arguments for Vallandigham's release (including the point that civilian courts were open in Ohio), he also got very personal. This naturally angered Burnside, who was only a few months beyond the loss at Fredericksburg when he was the commander of the Army of the Potomac.

On June 1, 1863, Burnside issued General Order No. 84, the suppression order for Storey's newspaper. He called the paper both disloyal and incendiary, although the order offered no proof of either. Most Republican editors around the country despised Storey's rhetoric and cheered on Burnside's decision to close down the *Times*. Storey was warned not to publish his June 3 issue, but the wily editor applied for an injunction from the U.S. circuit court in Chicago. The judge issued a temporary injunction until a hearing could be held the next day on a permanent injunction. Just as 8,000 copies of the banned issue were about to hit the streets, two companies of the Sixty-Fifth Illinois Infantry overtook the *Times* building.

At the injunction hearing, the judge threw out the appeal because the Union captain had received no notification to appear in court. The judge, Thomas Drummond, though, did take a shot at the Lincoln administration, saying:

> I have always wished to treat the government as a government of law and a government of the Constitution, and not a government of mere physical force. I personally have contended ... for the right of free discussion, and the right of commenting, under the law and the Constitution, upon the acts of the officers of the government.[52]

Reaction to suppression of the *Times* was intense. Democrats gathered in front of *The Chicago Tribune* and threatened to do violence against the Republican newspaper. The presence of the local militia quelled that sentiment. The same day Drummond refused to hold the injunction hearing, the majority-Democratic state legislature condemned the closing of the *Times*. Legislators said Burnside's order was unconstitutional. A group of Republicans and businessmen signed a petition condemning the seizure and sent it to Lincoln. Lyman Trumbull, Illinois' Republican senator, and Isaac N. Arnold, an Illinois congressman, also urged Lincoln to revoke Burnside's order. The night after the order took effect, thousands gathered in downtown Chicago to protest the *Times'* suppression. Lincoln telegraphed an executive order to Burnside revoking General Order No. 84. Burnside, in turn, sent Storey a telegram saying the editor could resume publication of his newspaper.

However, this was not the end of the story. Lincoln had second thoughts about revoking Burnside's Order No. 84, in part because he disliked second-guessing his generals. The president had also heard from a number of Republican editors in Illinois who felt that Burnside had done the right thing in silencing Storey. (Lincoln had briefly been a reporter decades earlier and owned a German-language newspaper in Illinois.) Thus, the president sent his major general a second dispatch telling Burnside to hold off on the revocation order, if it were not too late. However, the rescinding telegram did arrive too tardily. Storey already had returned to business.

Later, Lincoln admitted that during the *Times* affair he was not sure how to balance freedom of the press with "what was due the Military service." The main reason he acted was public opinion, not because of loyalty to Burnside. The general later said Lincoln made a mistake in revoking General Order No. 84, but Burnside did not mention the rescinding order.[53]

All of this occurred at a time when tensions were running high in Chicago. In 1862, the city experienced a race riot when white teamsters attempted to keep Blacks from using the omnibus system. Meanwhile, the city council voted to segregate the common (public) schools. While the *Times* certainly continued with the anti- Black and anti-Lincoln rhetoric, Storey did one markedly smart thing as editor: he began to say that Major General Ulysses S. Grant was the only officer who could win the war. Accordingly, Grant refused to stop circulation of the well-reported *Times* in his camp, and when Grant did become head of all of the Union's armies, the Democratic newspaper was obliged to support him through Appomattox.[54]

Lincoln learned from the Hascall-Burnside suppression episodes that public opinion did matter. Later in 1863, he sent a letter to Major General John Schofield in Missouri telling the officer that prudence should guide any decision to suppress. In a letter on October 1, Lincoln counseled Schofield not to censor newspapers in Missouri. Moreover, Lincoln wrote, Schofield's officers and soldiers should not injure editors or printing offices. "You will only arrest individuals and suppress assemblies or newspapers when they may be working palpable injury to the military in your charge, and in no other case will you interfere with the expression of opinion in any form or allow it to be interfered with violently by others," Lincoln advised. "In this, you have discretion to exercise with great caution, calmness, and forbearance."

Lincoln essentially made an early case for the "clear and present danger" doctrine, while recognizing that unless the words clearly harmed the Army's war effort, they had to be protected from constraint. Two days after Hascall resigned as commander of the District of Indiana, a group of journalists met in New York to discuss censorship. At the Astor House Hotel in Manhattan, sixteen editors representing approximately two million readers met for what a New York newspaper termed "the most remarkable and important meetings which has occurred since the war" started.[55] Editors at Astor House made a stand for their profession via nonpartisan resolutions declaring freedom of the press to be a bedrock principle of a democratic society, including in times of war. The special circumstance of war that Lincoln and his generals had used to rationalize censorship did not impress them. Horace Greeley of the *Tribune*, Elon Comstock of the Albany *Atlas & Argus*, and James Brooks of the *Express*, made special note of the right of the press "to criticize freely and fearlessly" the administration, as well their civil and military insubordinates, "whether with the intent directly to secure greater energy, efficiency, and fidelity in the public service."[56] While the majority of the editors were Democrats, the presence of Greeley, a Republican, strengthened the impact of the resolutions.

Schulyer Colfax, editor of the St. Joseph County (IN) *Register* in South Bend, served in the House of Representatives during the war. Before becoming Speaker of the House, he served as the chair of the Committee on Post Offices and Post Roads. The Hoosier Republican introduced a bill targeting bulk mailing by private express companies that also would have made newspaper circulation more difficult by limiting relatively inexpensive transportation methods. Colfax maintained that if Congress failed to charge postage on express mailings, the Lincoln administration would urge legislators to enact a tax on newspaper circulation to help pay for the war—a sort of nineteenth-century stamp tax. As the editor of a small newspaper, Colfax was also worried that papers from larger cities might become more attractive to readers in South Bend if they sold for less than, say, his St. Joseph Valley *Register*.

Criticism of the bill from New York newspapers helped stymie it, as Colfax's proposal lost by fifteen votes in the full House. As it turned out, Congress did not consider a special tax on newspapers. However, Colfax was able to pass a different postal bill. The Indiana congressman wanted reform because the system of mailing printed items was too complex in his estimation. Indeed, there were more than three hundred different rates. He wished to reduce the types of charges to three. With the aid of Vermont Senator Jacob Collamer, Colfax moved his bill through the Senate and House. The law reduced the mailing rate for newspapers and magazines to thirty-eight cents. The publisher or the subscriber had to prepay this fee. During hearings on the bill, legislators considered petitions condemning constraints on the circulation of Democratic newspapers.[57] Montgomery Blair, the postmaster general, had claimed that public safety in wartime allowed him to stop the mailing of journals he deemed disloyal. Blair said he was not stopping dissident newspapers from publishing; rather, he was stopping their circulation. If they were criticizing Lincoln's war policy or somehow giving aid to the Rebels, then he had the power to stop their circulation. The House Judiciary Committee investigated and sided with Blair.

While arresting editors and closing newspapers were blunt instruments for contracting press freedom, reporters faced constraints as they gathered information, including exclusion from a commander's camp, having their press passes revoked, and incarceration without a writ of habeas corpus. In February 1862, Secretary of War Edwin M. Stanton had *New York Herald* reporter Malcolm Ives incarcerated for fourth months for being a spy. Apparently, Ives wanted special access to the War Department and told Stanton's people that he would withhold favorable treatment in the *Herald* if he did not receive such access.[58]

The Lincoln administration drafted certain guidelines for reporters. In 1861, Secretary of War Simon Cameron established General Order No. 67, which said a government censor had to read all journalistic dispatches. The Lincoln administration also designed a pass system to give reporters access to camps and battles. However, the system did not have the backing of Major General Henry W. Halleck, who served as field commander in Missouri, Ohio, Kentucky, and Kansas. Halleck issued Special Field Order No. 54, which removed "hangers-on" from Union camps. Correspondents who were caught evading the order were punished with construction labor. Journalists protested but Halleck ignored them. He did allow Associated Press reports from his camp, but he had to review them first.[59]

Major General William T. Sherman had reporter Thomas W. Knox of *The New York Herald* tried for being a spy. Knox, a former teacher, was not happy to begin with about Sherman's staff reading his mail. He wrote a story in winter of 1862 that said Sherman's obsession with the press had an effect on a battle in Mississippi, a Union loss. Knox even suggested that Sherman was insane. Sherman had Knox arrested even though he was not in the Army. Ultimately, Knox was found not guilty of being a spy. Indeed, Ulysses S. Grant had given him a press pass, and none of his information could be construed as aiding the Rebels. However, the court did convict Knox of not submitting his story to censors. No American reporter has faced a court martial since that time, so, in this sense, members of the press and the military created a wall separating each other that remains recognized today.[60]

Reporters also faced becoming prisoners of war—and this, too, served as a kind of constraint. This happened to Albert D. Richardson and Junius Browne of *The New York Tribune*. The Confederate Army captured them at Vicksburg in May 1863, after which they spent twenty months at the Salisbury Military Prison in North Carolina. Horace Greeley and Sydney Howard Gay of the *Tribune* attempted to gain their release. Also appealing for their freedom were President Lincoln, Secretary of War Stanton, Major General Benjamin F. Butler, *New York World* reporter Richard Colburn, and Cincinnati *Gazette* correspondent Whitelaw Reid.[61] The pair escaped in December 1864 and walked in frigid conditions across the Appalachian Mountains to Knoxville, Tennessee.

One reporter who figured out that a close relationship with a commander in the field might make his job easier was Sylvanus Cadwallader, who first worked for *The Chicago Times* and then *The New York Herald*. Cadwallader earned the respect of Ulysses S. Grant when he covered the Western theater for the *Times*. Grant liked the fact that the correspondent did not hide behind a pseudonym and admitted when he wrote something critical of Union military operations. Because of their close relationship, James Gordon Bennett hired Cadwallader away from Wilbur Storey to make sure the *Herald* had better access to Grant. Cadwallader had begun working for the general during the war and helped hide Grant's drinking problem. After the war, he worked in the *Herald*'s Washington bureau.

On the other hand, some reporters conflicted with temperamental generals. In June 1864, at Cold Harbor, Virginia, Major General George G. Meade arrested reporter Edward Crapsey of the Philadelphia *Inquirer*. In a published article, Crapsey criticized Meade for being too cautious. Meade asked Provost Marshal Marsena R. Patrick to remove the journalist from the field. Patrick then paraded Crapsey around camp, facing backward on a mule. On his back was a sign reading "Libeller of the Press."[62] Whitelaw Reid of the Cincinnati *Gazette* condemned the actions of Meade and Patrick. Meade eventually let Crapsey return to his camp to cover the Army. Correspondent Cadwallader would write that journalists protested Meade's actions as much as possible by simply ignoring him. Likewise, Major General Benjamin Butler would intimidate journalists by making them perform hard labor.[63]

Southern Suppression

Dissent was much rarer in the South than in the North. Before the war, the pro-Union editor of the Fort Worth (Texas) *Chief* decided to sell his newspaper rather than face hanging from a mob. Texas was a bitterly divided state, with Governor Sam Houston opposing secession, though the majority in the legislature favored it. In Tennessee, Parson William G. Brownlow, editor of the Knoxville *Whig*, opposed secession, and he claimed that Unionists in the deeply divided city only wanted to be left alone. J. A. Sperry, editor of the Knoxville *Register*, consistently called for the arrest of Brownlow and other anti-secessionists. The *Whig* editor countered by calling Sperry a "low-down, ill-bred, lying, debauched, drunken scoundrel"—a man of "groveling habits" who wrote "slanderous editorials."[64] Brownlow, whose paper would continue to carry an American flag even after Tennessee seceded, would pay a steep price for his opinions. He stopped publishing the *Whig* on October 26, 1861. In that last edition, he wrote that Confederate authorities would arrest him, and that he would face a charge of treason before a grand jury. Brownlow attacked Jefferson Davis for not upholding freedom of the press, as the Confederate constitution did. He refused to hold his tongue and print only the "articles as meet the approval of a pack of scoundrels in Knoxville."[65]

A few days later, the *Whig* editor fled Knoxville as the Confederate stranglehold on the city intensified. While he was gone, military authorities seized his newspaper. Brownlow just happened to leave three days before Unionists burned nine bridges in an attempt to help what they thought would be a federal invasion of the city from Kentucky.[66] Authorities arrested as many as 1,000 citizens of East Tennessee. Some were executed. Brownlow sent a letter to a Confederate official saying that he did not have prior knowledge of the bridge burnings, which he condemned. The editor said he would be willing to face a trial, but that he did not want to face a mob. Knoxville attorney John Baxter wrote a letter to Confederate Secretary of War Judah Benjamin seeking safe passage for Brownlow to the North. Benjamin agreed to the plan, guaranteeing the *Whig* editor safe passage to Kentucky.

In December, when Brownlow returned to Knoxville, Tennessee district attorney J. C. Ramsey had the journalist arrested for treason, despite the arrangements for Brownlow to be safely transported to the Union lines. At the same time, *The New York Times* printed a story about Brownlow leading a group of 3,000 Unionists into battle in northeast Tennessee.[67] This report was false. Benjamin decided it was best not to make Brownlow a martyr, and the war secretary had the editor released. Eventually, the Confederate government told Ramsey to ship Brownlow to Union authorities in Nashville.[68] Brownlow would return to Knoxville to edit his newspaper, but he would modulate his tone to a degree, relying more and more on criticism by other Southern newspapers rather than from his own pen, in part because his advertising was decreasing. Furthermore, once the war started, the Knoxville *Whig* was the only remaining pro-Union sheet in the South (not counting slave states that stayed in the Union), thus isolating Brownlow.

Midway through the war, approximately thirty Southern journals began to question its continuation. Influential Augusta *Chronicle & Sentinel* editor Nathan S. Morse led this group of editors, who were supporting a handful of Southern politicians who had come to see the war as futile. These politicians included C.S.A. Vice President Alexander Stephens and Georgia Governor Joseph E. Brown. Stephens and Brown had hatched a plan to nullify the power of the Richmond government, toward the end of opening peace negotiations with the Lincoln administration. Morse believed Georgia should act alone, if necessary against what he saw as illegal actions by Jefferson Davis and the C.S.A.

Congress in narrowing civil liberties in the South. In particular, Morse objected to conscription, which he believed changed the war's cause. He also abhorred the Confederate Congress passing a law that suspended the writ of habeas corpus. Morse felt what made the South different from the North was its love of the same liberties the founding generation so cherished. The Augusta editor encouraged Georgia legislators to assemble and call for the end of the Confederate Congress in Richmond.

Another prominent Southern peace editor was William W. Holden, editor of the *Standard* newspaper in Raleigh, North Carolina. Holden supported the war for two years. Before the war, like many Tar Heels, he had held Unionist sentiments. When South Carolina and the Lower South succeeded, Holden opposed it. However, that all changed after Fort Sumter and Lincoln's call for 75,000 volunteers for the Union Army. The North Carolinian believed by summer 1863 that a Southern triumph was unlikely. He felt that the majority of people in both the North and the South had grown tired of the war and desired an honorable peace.[69] If the South sued for peace early enough, he believed, it could remain an independent Southern nation with slavery still legal. The Raleigh editor counted on a grassroots peace movement that would change public opinion, forcing Davis to assemble a diplomatic mission to discuss peace with Lincoln.

While many Tar Heels agreed with Holden, most Confederate soldiers did not. Many regiments passed resolutions condemning the *Standard*. Indeed, North Carolina regiments met at Orange Court House, Virginia, on August 12, 1863, and inked a resolution in support of the Confederate government. On a September night in 1863, Georgia soldiers traveling through Raleigh came to the *Standard* office and at first called for suppression of the newspaper. Then, to go a step further, the Georgians ransacked the *Standard* office, except for the printing press. Editor Holden heard about the mob and went to see North Carolina governor Zebulon Vance at his mansion to seek a police detail to regain the peace. Vance, a long-time Holden ally, walked to the *Standard* office and told the soldiers to cease their illegal activities. The soldiers agreed to stop and left Raleigh.

The next morning, a pro-Union mob countered the soldiers' destructive actions by razing the pro-Confederate *State Journal*. It is worth mentioning that Confederate troops did not attack the Raleigh *Progress*, another pro-peace newspaper. Vance then telegraphed C.S.A. President Davis and asked for an end to the transiting of troops through Raleigh. Vance also requested permission for the recall of North Carolina soldiers to help restore order in the state. Two days later, an Alabama regiment threatened the *Standard*. Again, Vance was on the scene to restore order. Holden fled Raleigh before returning to restart his newspaper in October.[70]

Holden resumed publication in October 1863 and condemned the Raleigh *Register*, the *State Journal*, Charlotte *Bulletin*, and the Richmond *Enquirer* for inciting the soldiers against his newspaper. Holden wrote that these newspapers "had urged the government, the people, and the soldiers to suppress the paper by force," and he added that his readers would "bear witness that I have at all times opposed mob law. Nothing will justify a resort to it." Holden said if he had committed treason in advocating peace, then the governor should have arrested him and tried him in the civilian courts. "I was assailed in a cowardly manner, my property injured, and my Constitutional rights trampled down, *on account of my opinions*," Holden wrote. The state of the war effort for the Confederacy was so dire, he continued, that every battle was "an argument for peace, and every improvement by statesmen and people at home of the results of battle, is an argument for peace."[71] He urged Robert E. Lee, commander of the Army of Northern Virginia, to continue allowing soldiers to read the *Standard* in camp. Moreover, he refused to acquiesce in his conviction that the South should sue for peace—eventually splitting with Vance, as the Tar Heel governor found himself backed into a corner. Vance chose to stay on Davis' side and support the war. Accordingly, Holden ran against Vance in 1864, but lost. After the war, he would become the leader of the new Republican Party in the state, and although he became governor, he was later impeached.

The greatest constraint on Southern journalism during the war was the number of printers and editors who served in the Confederate military. If a journalist was a member of a regiment, he might post letters home for publication in the newspaper. This put that journalist in position of having to accept an order saying that he could not print something. In 1862, the C.S.A. Congress in Richmond passed a conscription bill that gave journalists an exemption to avoid service. This was because legislators considered the work that editors and printers did to be critical to the political cause.

Two years later, however, President Jefferson Davis proposed removing all exemptions from the conscription law, including the one for journalists. Davis held that the Confederate Army was so undermanned that it could no longer afford exemptions. He also began calling for the freeing of slaves in order that they might be mustered into service. Davis envisioned a Southern form of journalism consisting of just a handful of strong, widely circulated newspapers. He hoped depriving the other papers of their labor would cause them to close. Employees of the closed journals would then serve in the Confederate military. The press in the South saw Davis' concept as an infringement on freedom of the press, a liberty explicitly provided for by the C.S.A. constitution. Editors noted that Davis could arbitrarily choose which papers would survive and which he would close (ostensibly, so their personnel could fight the war)—a form of tyranny against which the Confederacy was supposed to be fighting. One government official who took the side of the journalists was Alexander Stephens, the C.S.A.'s vice president. Because of the strong opposition to Davis' proposal, he never tried to make it law, and there were no cases of overt press suppression by the Confederate government.[72]

Leroy Walker, the Confederate secretary of war, wrote in a letter in the Richmond *Enquirer* on July 1, 1861, about what topics Southern journalists could not discuss publicly. These included troop strength, size, and quality of arms, as well as location and movement of Confederate troops. The only major dissenter to Walker's call for self-restraint came from the Charleston *Mercury*. That newspaper held that Washington did not read the Southern newspapers to find out what was going on in the Confederate military. Otherwise, while the Southern press agreed to voluntarily censor itself. General Robert E. Lee had an agreement with the press to be discreet in what news they published.[73] Telegraph lines in the South also faced censorship. Another form of de facto censorship was closing sessions of the Confederate congress to the press and public.

Whatever degree of censorship occurred in the South, one factor that worked against it was the professionalism of the Press Association of the Confederate States. John S. Thrasher, general manager of the P.A., insisted that the military leave reporters alone to do their jobs. Thrasher also insisted that Confederate correspondents stick to the facts and not print rumors or falsehoods. Another constraint on Southern editors was losing a newspaper when the Union conquered a city. The Memphis *Appeal* was able to avoid such a fate by constantly moving its operations, but other Southern newspapers, such as The *Daily Times* in New Bern, North Carolina, were turned into pro-Union, pro-Republican journals. Freedom of the press was likely stronger in the South during the war. Certainly, no newspaper faced direct central government suppression. Furthermore, many Southern editors consistently disparaged Northern suppression. After the Baltimore suppression period in the fall of 1861, Richmond *Examiner* editor John M. Daniel condemned "the utter prostration of liberty" in Maryland.[74] Southerners generalized liberty and saw a linkage between the right to own slaves and freedom of the press.

Sensational and General Censorship

A notorious journalistic moment during the war that resulted in restrictions on two New York newspapers was the Gold Hoax in May 1864. The *World* and the *Journal of Commerce* had reported that Lincoln was calling for a draft of 400,000 more men into the Union army. The two newspapers' source for the information was the Associated Press. The news, coming during tightly fought battles in Virginia, caused prices on the New York Stock Exchange to plummet. At the same time, investors saw the price of gold increase and they began buying the metal. Yet readers were perplexed that only the *World* and *Journal of Commerce* published the report. The AP later issued a statement saying it had not sent such a dispatch. Soon thereafter, Secretary of State William H. Seward, a New Yorker, declared the report of the call for 400,000 more men a forgery. As it turned out, the foremen at both newspapers had received the news at 3:30 a.m. from a courier. They thought the dispatch looked legitimate and stopped the presses and found a place for the story in that day's paper. Other newspapers got the dispatch but were more skeptical. After checking with each other, these editors papers decided to hold the story.

The city editor of the Brooklyn *Eagle*, Joseph Howard, Jr., had perpetrated the fraud. After his arrest, Howard confessed to the ruse, having purposely sent the dispatch just as night editors had gone home early in the morning on the day of publication, knowing that foremen at the papers would be in control for a period with no ability to double-check facts. Guessing negative war news would cause gold prices to rise, he had invested heavily in the metal the previous day. When the news from the *World* and *Journal of Commerce* made its way around the city, Howard sold his investment. The *World* defended the story because it said there was "no time to be lost" over deliberating Lincoln's call for more men. The newspaper also claimed one of its paperboys had heard concerns about the dispatch, but that the boy had no authority "to tamper with the working of the press" and could not therefore delete the story. The *World* figured out the hoax by late in the morning of the eighteenth and proclaimed it so on the bulletin board outside the office. The *World* promised $500 to anyone who could help authorities find the forger of the bogus AP dispatch. The AP offered a $1,000 reward.

Lincoln, who had told General John Schofield to be cautious the year before, overreacted. Spurred on by Secretary of War Edwin M. Stanton, the president ordered Union Major General John A. Dix to send soldiers to seize the offices of both newspapers. The military also arrested the editors of both journals, which were generally critical of Lincoln, and charged them with treason. Those charges were dropped, but the editors could not re-enter their offices, which remained under armed guard. The editors of both papers published their side of the story and protested the fact that their buildings were still under lockdown. "We protest against the assumption of our complicity with this shameless forgery," they wrote. "We protest the suppression of our journals."[75]

Stanton wanted them tried by a military commission, but public reaction was against the president. He soon lifted the suppression order. New York governor Horatio Seymour said that suppression of the *World* and *Journal of Commerce* was part of a pattern of civil liberties abuse that included the exile of Clement L. Vallandigham and Ambrose Burnside's closing of *The Chicago Times*. Seymour asked the New York district attorney to charge Dix and the other officers who had carried out Lincoln's orders to suppress the newspapers. The judge in the case ruled against Lincoln, Dix, and the other Union Army officers, claiming that the Habeas Corpus Act of 1863 was invalid. However, no action was taken against the president and the military officers.[76] Meanwhile, Howard was jailed for three months. That summer, Lincoln did call for 500,000 more men to serve in the Union military.

Ironically, the pro-Democratic Brooklyn *Eagle* had no idea that Howard had perpetrated the fraud. Editor Isaac Van Anden refused to condemn the *World* and *Journal of Commerce*. He understood that both newspapers "were made the innocent victims of the heartless fraud." Their worst offense was just being careless. The *Eagle* supported *The New York Tribune* when the latter criticized Lincoln's decision to suppress the *World* and *Journal of Commerce*. When the *Eagle* discovered Howard's role in the hoax, it quickly distanced itself from his "transgression." Van Anden wrote that it was not possible for the Eagle to denounce the ruse sooner because he had no prior knowledge of Howard's deceit. It regretted the shame that Howard had brought upon his friends and "disgrace upon himself."[77]

So, why did the North have a higher degree of suppression than the South? In part, because the South had one basic political party, the Democrats. Yes, there were liberal, moderate, and conservative Democrats, but political dissent was far less conspicuous in the South. On the other hand, the North had two parties— the Republicans and the Democrats (who were divided between War and Peace factions). The North, therefore, was more politically heterogeneous. Thus, there was a greater degree of dissent, and, with far more publications operating, many more dissident voices in the press.

Historian John D. Stevens hypothesized that "the more heterogeneous a society, the more freedom of expression it will tolerate."[78] Under Stevens' construction, one would have expected more suppression in the less-populated, more-homogeneous South. Yet Stevens also leaves a caveat: If one is living in an urban society, one is more likely to be actively tolerant of a wide variety of views. Tolerance is harder earned in the city than in the countryside, where one is apt to live ten or fifteen miles from the nearest neighbor. Thus, Stevens, keeping in mind the North's population of 22 million and the South's 9 million (which included 3.5 million slaves), actually expected more tolerance of dissent in the South because it had far fewer big cities, and because its population was more diffused over its land mass.

Another reason for greater press suppression in the North is that it had a more vigorous press. The North had about seventeen hundred newspapers, of which three hundred were dailies. The South had about eight hundred newspapers, of which about seventy-five were dailies. Some 80 percent of able-bodied white men in the South fought for the Confederate military. Thus, a larger percentage of Southern editors, reporters, and printers served in the armed forces, and, because there were fewer newspapers and journalists, less opportunity for suppression existed. Furthermore, most of the suppression and intimidation in the North came from mobs, usually from soldiers or veterans outraged by published words of dissident. Since at least a million more men served in the Union military, there were far greater chances that they might act against a newspaper.

Yet another factor was the size of the non-fighting military government in the North. The Lincoln administration divided the North into military districts that acted as federal shadow governments. These were seen as particularly important in the slave states of Delaware, Maryland, Kentucky, and Missouri. In effect, these shadow governments had the time and resources to handle political problems that arose, including press dissent. The Confederacy did not have the human power for a similar sort of internal structure. The best and the brightest in the South were all fighting the war. Then there was the overwhelming advantage in the number of West Point men that the Union Army had. The U.S. Military Academy was the place where American men of the nineteenth century learned to be soldiers, and a logical place for the development of anti-journalism attitudes such as that displayed by William T. Sherman, who believed freedom of the press to be a relic of the past and irrelevant to the wartime situation. Yes, the South had the Citadel and the Virginia Military Institute, but the two did not have comparable resources as graduates at West Point.

Finally, a school of researchers has suggested that the South simply valued liberty more than the North did. Southerners had written the Bill of Rights. Yet those who espouse this view must clear the hurdle of slavery. It is more likely that both sides cherished freedom of the press, especially in peacetime. Because of its greater available resources to fight the war, the North had more men sitting on the sidelines second-guessing the president and Congress. For many of those in the military, especially those who had gone to West Point and knew the sacrifices made to quell the rebellion, the dissent of Democratic journalists was too much to bear. With Lincoln and Congress suspending the writ of habeas corpus, military and federal officers had the necessary legal backing to take action against wayward journalists. In the first two years of the war, officers acted, especially in Maryland and Missouri. This sent a signal, and then mob action became the dominant mode of constraining the press in the final years of the war. Mobs took out their frustrations on a few newspapers in the South, but Confederate soldiers were too busy fighting or too tired to enforce a political orthodoxy the way the North did.

Notes

1 Bulla, *Lincoln's Censor: Milo Hascall and Freedom of the Press in Civil War Indiana* (West Lafayette, IN: Purdue University Press, 2009), 8.

2 Shelby Foote, *The Civil War, A Narrative: Fredericksburg to Meridian*, Vol. 2 (New York: Vintage Books, 1986), 635.

3 Donald and James G. Randall, *The Civil War and Reconstruction*, 2nd Edition (Lexington, MA: D. C. Heath and Company, 1969), 308.

4 Bulla, *Lincoln's Censor*, 68.

5 Paul Simon, *Freedom's Champion: Elijah Lovejoy* (Carbondale, IL: Southern Illinois University Press, 1994), 14.

6 St. Louis (MO) *Observer*, July 31, 1864.

7 Simon, *Freedom's Champion*, 130, 131.

8 *Missouri Republican*, November 10, 1837.

9 Baltimore *Sun*, February 25, 1861.

10 Harold A. Williams, *The Baltimore Sun, 1837–1987* (Baltimore, MD: Johns Hopkins University Press, 1987), 47.

11 Baltimore *Republican*, April 20, 1861.

12 George W. Brown, Mayor of Baltimore, Maryland, Proclamation, Published in the Baltimore *Sun*, April 22, 1862.

13 Baltimore *Sun*, April 20, 1861.

14 Ibid, April 22, 1861.

15 New York *Tribune*, December 17, 1860.

16 Baltimore *Sun*, April 22, 1861.

17 Sidney T. Matthews, "Control of the Baltimore Press during the Civil War," *Maryland Historical Magazine*, 36, 2 (June 1941): 152.

18 Baltimore *Sun*, September 16, 1861; Matthews, "Control of the Baltimore Press during the Civil War," 154; Baltimore *Sun*, September 14, 1861.

19 New York *World*, February 21, 1863.

20 Harper, *Lincoln and the Press*, 148.

21 Colonel John McNeil, Third Regiment, U.S. Reserve Corps, Proclamation, St. Louis, Missouri, July 11, 1861.

22 Dennis F. Saak, "Newspaper Suppressions in Missouri during the Civil War," Master's Thesis, University of Missouri (1974): 15.

23 Harper, *Lincoln and the Press*, 148.

24 Lucy Lucile Tasher, "The *Missouri Democrat* and the Civil War," *Missouri Historical Review* 34, 1 (July 1937): 406.

25 Erika J. Pribanic-Smith, "The War within the State: The Role of Newspapers in Missouri's Secession Crisis," presented at the Symposium on the 19th Century Press, the Civil War, and Free Expression, University of Tennessee at Chattanooga, November 11, 2005, 3.

26 Harper, *Lincoln and the Press*, 142.

27 Robert N. Scott, *The War of the Rebellion: A Compilation of the Official Records of the Union and Confederate Armies*, 3, 1 (Washington, DC: Government Printing Office, 1880–1902), 324.

28 Jeffery A. Smith, *War and Press Freedom: The Problem of Prerogative Power* (New York: Oxford University Press, 1999), 100.

29 Starr, *Bohemian Brigade: Civil War Newsmen in Action* (Madison, WI: University of Wisconsin Press, 1987), 39.

30 *House Reports*, "An Act to Authorize the President of the United States in Certain Cases to take Possession of the Railroad and Telegraphic Lines, and for Other Purposes," Thirty-Seventh Congress, Second Session, 3, 64-1 (March 20, 1862).

31 General Orders, No. 84, Hdqrs. Department of the Ohio, Cincinnati, Ohio, June 1, 1863.

32 Des Moines (IA) *Daily State Register*, August 21, 1862.

33 Dubuque (IA) *Herald*, August 15, 1862.

34 Robert K. Tharp, "The Copperhead Days of Dennis Mahony," *Journalism Quarterly*, 43, (Winter 1966): 681.

35 F. T. Oldt, ed., *History of Dubuque County, Iowa* (Chicago, IL: Goodspeed, 1911), 355.

36 Dubuque (IA) *Herald*, May 7, 1862.

37 Des Moines (IA) *Daily State Register*, August 26, 1862.

38 Dubuque (IA) *Herald*, quoted in the Des Moines (IA) *Daily State Register*, August 21, 1862.

39 Martin E. McGrane, "Dubuque—Editorial Battleground 1860–1862," Master's Thesis, Iowa State University (1972), 90, 91.

40 Des Moines (IA) *Daily State Register*, November 19, 1862.

41 Davenport (IA) *Daily Democrat and News*, November 14, 1862.

42 Brett Barker, "Communities at War: Ohio Republicans' Attack on Democratic Newspapers," presented at the Symposium on the 19th Century Press, the Civil War, and Free Expression, University of Tennessee at Chattanooga, November 9, 2007, 4, 5.

43 Barker, "Communities at War," 8, 10.

44 Columbus (OH), *The Crisis*, March 18, 1863.

45 Harper, *Lincoln and the Press*, 338.

46 Columbus (OH), *The Crisis*, March 18, 1863.

47 Phillip J. Tichenor, "Copperheadism and Community Conflict in Two Rivertowns: Civil War Press Battles in Prairie du Chien and La Crosse, Wisconsin, 1861–65," presented at the Symposium on the 19th Century Press, the Civil War, and Free Expression, University of Tennessee at Chattanooga, November 2, 2002, 17, 19.

48 Bulla, *Lincoln's Censor*, 8.

49 Stephen E. Towne, "Works of Indiscretion: Violence against the Democratic Press in Indiana during the Civil War," *Journalism History*, 31, 3 (Fall 2005): 142.

50 Chicago *Times*, September 23, 1862.

51 "The Copperhead Plan for Subjugating the South," Library of Congress, accessed July 1, 2021, at <loc.gov/pictures/item/2003663130>.

52 *American Annual Cyclopedia and Register of Important Events*, 1864, Vol. 3, 424.

53 Craig D. Tenney, "Major General A. E. Burnside and the First Amendment: A Case Study of Civil War Freedom of Expression," Ph.D. dissertation (Bloomington, IN: Indiana University, 1977): 254, 255.

54 Donald B. Sanger, "*The Chicago Times* and the Civil War," *Mississippi Valley Historical Review*, 17, 4 (March 1931): 569.

55 New York *Journal of Commerce*, June 9, 1863.

56 New York *Tribune*, June 9, 1863.

57 Kielbowicz, *News in the Mail*, 91, 92.

58 Harris, *Blue & Gray in Black & White*, 141.

59 Smith, *War and Press Freedom*, 103, 104.

60 John F. Marszalek, *Sherman's Other Way: The General and the Civil War Press* (Kent, OH: Kent State University Press, 1999), 162.

61 Mary Cronin, "'The North Is to Use Like the Grave': New York *Tribune* Reporter Albert D. Richardson's Confederate Prison Letters," presented at the Symposium on the 19th Century Press, the Civil War, and Free Expression, University of Tennessee at Chattanooga, November 12, 2009, 1.

62 Perry, *A Bohemian Brigade*, 251, 282.

63 Smith, *War and Press Freedom*, 104.

64 Knoxville (TN) *Brownlow's Weekly Whig*, October 12, 1861.

65 Ibid, October 26, 1861.

66 Robert T. McKenzie, *Lincolnites and Rebels: A Divided Town in the American Civil War* (New York: Oxford University Press, 2006), 103.

67 Ibid, 107.

68 Reddin van Tuyll, "What Freedom of the Press Meant in the Confederacy," presented at the Symposium on the 19th Century Press, the Civil War, and Free Expression, University of Tennessee at Chattanooga, November 12, 2009, 6.

69 William C. Harris, *William Woods Holden: Firebrand of North Carolina Politics* (Baton Rouge, LA: Louisiana State University Press, 1987), 131.

70 Horace W. Raper, *William W. Holden, North Carolina's Political Enigma* (Chapel Hill, NC: University of North Carolina Press, 1985), 48, 50.

71 Raleigh (NC) *Weekly Standard*, October 7, 1863, emphasis included.

72 Reddin van Tuyll, "What Freedom of the Press Meant in the Confederacy," 4, 19.

73 J. Cutler Andrews, *The South Reports the War* (Princeton, NJ: Princeton University Press, 1970), 76, 77, 529.

74 Richmond (VA) *Examiner*, September 23, 1861.

75 New York *World*, May 23, 1864.

76 Smith, *War and Press Freedom*, 118.

77 Brooklyn (NY) *Daily Eagle*, May 19, 21, 1864.

78 John D. Stevens, "Freedom of Expression: New Dimensions," in *Mass Media and the National Experience*, Ronald T. Farrar and John D. Stevens, ed. (New York: Harper & Row, 1971), 17.

12

Three Newspapers that Supported the President

"How different our candidate! He never speaks that he does not bring forward something new." "The Galesburg Debate," Chicago *Press and Tribune*, October 9, 1859.

While the opposition Democratic press faced outright suppression, intimidation, and mob violence, the majority Republican press did not support President Abraham Lincoln uniformly, and some pro-Lincoln newspapers faced suppression. In 1863, the commander of the Union force in Missouri arrested the editor of the pro-Republican St. Louis *Democrat* because the latter published a letter from the president to the general that the military officer considered private.[1] Federals suppressed a pro-war Democratic newspaper in Albany, Indiana, for describing the assignments of various Hoosier regiments, and Lincoln sometimes faced criticism even from editors within his own party.[2] Indeed, during the war, newspapers that both supported the president and enjoyed support from the administration were generally the exception and not the norm.

Support for the president was qualified based on the degree of an editor's consonance with the policies of the Lincoln administration. For example, some Republican editors believed he moved too slowly on key policy issues, while others felt he was going too fast. The issue of abolition, for example, illustrated the various levels of support—or opposition—to the president's goals. Horace Greeley, often perplexed by the president's slow prosecution of the war and moderate position on abolition, used his *New York Tribune* to push and prod Lincoln on the issue. Meanwhile, Springfield, Massachusetts, *Republican* editor

Samuel Bowles—although he would have preferred seeing William H. Seward as president—accepted Lincoln as better than any of the other alternatives and held a generally moderate tone, even in his assessment of abolition as problematic North and South. Whereas Joseph Medill's *Chicago Tribune*, the president's home-state cheerleader, rarely found fault with its favorite son, and helped frame the Lincoln legend with praise for the liberation of millions in bondage.

Although most Republican editors did support the president, *The New York Tribune*, The Springfield *Republican*, and *The Chicago Tribune* in particular represented the relationship between Lincoln and his allies in the press. While *The New York Tribune* tended to push the president on policy issues and was the most willing to be critical, and *The Chicago Tribune* offered unconditional support, the *Republican* more consistently considered a broad political context, and hence proved to be the most moderate—albeit staunchly in the Republican ranks.

From Lincoln's Debates to Lincoln's War

The nation had a political press on the eve of the Civil War, but this type of journalism faced a crisis in part because of national political shifts. Democrats, who had dominated policy for most of the nineteenth century, had fragmented over slavery with the election of 1860, leaving Republicans, led by Lincoln, the beneficiaries of the disarray.

In order to understand better this changing of the guard, a model for the American political system provides a way of explaining what also happened in the newspaper industry at the start of the Civil War. The model was proposed by Samuel Lubell, a writer, reporter, and political analyst who made the case that partisan competition in the American political system consisted more often than not of two unequal parties, rather than of competitive factions. Lubell called the dominant group, which often stayed in power for decades, the "sun party" and termed the minority group the "moon party."[3] According to Lubell's analysis, the rise of Andrew Jackson and his brand of democracy marked an age in which the western frontier, together with the tensions between the agrarian South and commercial East, fought out the issues of slavery. Not until the Democrats splintered in 1860 did the Republicans begin their ascendancy as the latest sun party, making the Democrats the moon party and heirs to a new set of post-war issues.

However, without the benefit of hindsight, at the outbreak of war Lincoln had not held office for even a year, so it was not clear to editors, journalists, or even politicians of the time if the Republicans would maintain power for any length of time. (Certainly, winning the war was the major historical event that factored into the Republicans developing into the sun party.) However, as the nation headed in unknown directions—toward ruin, some feared—politics did not end, and newspapers continued to function to a considerable extent like agents of the parties. Republican wartime editors then had two major objectives: (1) winning the war and (2) expanding the power of the party. It was their job to support the president, mobilize the party's base, and marginalize Democratic opposition.

Antecedents to war coverage came in the major events leading up to Fort Sumter in April 1861. As Lincoln's rise to national prominence began with his failed U.S. Senate bid in 1858, differences separating Republicans and Democrats were on full display in his debates with Senator Stephen Douglas. Editor Joseph Medill's *Chicago Tribune* covered all seven of the debates and provided commentary. *The New York Tribune* also followed the debates closely, remarking that "perhaps no contest in this country ever excited so general or so profound an interest as that now waging in Illinois."[4]

Political debates were part of small-town culture in what would become the Midwest (at the time, still known as the "West"). They provided a source of entertainment for citizens, and the seven Lincoln-Douglas debates in August, September, and October 1858 represented one of the most highly anticipated and well-attended demonstrations of the type. Towns swelled with attendees, well beyond their usual populations. Hotels, churches, and homes served as the resting places for those who came from all over the state to witness the event.[5]

The first debate took place at Ottawa, Illinois, on August 21, 1858, with *The Chicago Tribune* reporting first on the arrival of the two candidates by train, and then on the debate itself. The format allowed Douglas to open for sixty minutes, followed by ninety minutes from Lincoln, then thirty minutes from Douglas. The news report, which fixed attendance at 12,000 in the pro-Republican city of 7,000 on a hot summer day, noted that the crowd filled Lafayette Square at 1 p.m. The debate started late because of the large crowd. The *Tribune* reported in a story headlined "The Dred Scott Champion Pulverized" that "The rush was literally tremendous. The speaking stand had been foolishly left unguarded, and was so crowded with people, before the officers of the day arrived, that half an hour was consumed in a battle to make room for the speakers and reporters." A complementary editorial led the attack against the Democratic senator, describing Douglas as "cunning, unfair, and cowardly" and accusing him of avoiding the issues of the campaign in order to put Lincoln on the defensive and force him to reply to "irrelevant matter."

One day later, the *Tribune* claimed that its Democratic rival, *The Chicago Times*, had mangled Lincoln's words.[6] The *Tribune* wrote that two Democratic lawyers dictated what Lincoln said and distorted both his meaning and style. What appalled the *Tribune* editors the most, though, was Douglas's attempt to paint Lincoln as a radical abolitionist based on alleged resolutions made by Republicans in Springfield in 1854. Lincoln replied that he was not in Springfield when the resolutions were drafted and that his hero was Henry Clay, the Kentucky Whig and slaveholder. Lincoln, who at the time used the word "nigger" twice, tried to paint himself as a moderate.[7]

Horace Greeley's *New York Tribune* declared that Lincoln had the advantage in the first debate. His editorial, complemented by a reporter's account, stated that Lincoln had better positions than Douglas and Lincoln stated them "with more propriety and cogency, and with an infinitely better temper."[8] The Springfield *Republican*'s account cast the talk on both sides as "mostly personal." While the newspaper praised Lincoln for being "entertaining" and felt he had "handsomely" defended himself, it also suggested he should have been more assertive in countering Douglas.[9]

Switching the speaking order, the second debate occurred at Freeport on August 27, and one of *The Chicago Tribune* headlines proclaimed: "Lincoln Tumbles Him [Douglas] all over Stephenson County." According to the *Tribune*, attendance was 15,000 in another Republican stronghold (this one in far Northern Illinois) on a chilly, damp day. The newspaper called Douglas a "desperate, dishonest" demagogue.[10] Lincoln, who came to the speaker's stand from the Brewster Hotel in a Conestoga wagon, responded to questions that Douglas had posed at the Ottawa debate. The Springfield lawyer noted that the pro-abolition resolutions passed in 1854 had not been at a state convention but rather at a county meeting.

Lincoln then asked four of his own questions. The most important dealt with popular sovereignty, and Douglas responded by saying that local governments in a territory could exclude slavery if agreed, even if citizens of the United States wanted slavery in that territory.[11] Douglas said that even if a new state included slavery in its constitution, local authorities could ignore such a law. Without local enforcement by the police, slavery would not survive, Douglas held. Lincoln pressed Douglas on this question at the urging of the *Tribune*'s Medill.[12] Douglas's answer certainly infuriated Southerners. Noting that one of Lincoln's advisers was Frederick Douglass, Douglas said, "Those of you who believe that the negro is your equal and ought to be on an equality with you socially, politically, and legally, have a right to entertain those opinions, and of course vote for Mr. Lincoln."[13]

After this debate, *The New York Tribune* accused Douglas of having his eyes more on the White House than on serving the citizens of Illinois. Greeley's newspaper also inveighed against the Democratic senator for overemphasizing westward expansion. For the *Tribune*, this was code for allowing slavery to expand beyond the restrictions of the Missouri Compromise.

The third debate, at Jonesboro in southern Illinois on September 15, drew approximately 1,500 people. In this more conservative part of the state, Douglas attempted to paint Lincoln as a radical on slavery. *The Chicago Tribune's* headline the next day said that Douglas was merely rehearsing the same old speech. On the other hand, the *Tribune* believed Lincoln had successfully put Douglas on the defensive on popular sovereignty, and that the former had shown how the Dred Scott decision by the U.S. Supreme Court made that policy moribund because the ruling made it impossible to bar slavery in the in the new territories.

Three days later, the fourth debate took place in Charleston, with 12,000 to 15,000 in attendance. The *Tribune* headline read: "Lincoln Tomahawks His Antagonist with the Toombs Bill."[14] This referred to Lincoln attacking Douglas for his role in a bill by Georgia Senator Robert Toombs that would have required a federal commission to register voters in Kansas before they voted on delegates to attend a state constitutional convention. More significantly, Lincoln said he did not believe in full equality for Blacks. In its analysis of the debate, the *Tribune* described Lincoln's performance as his best to date. The Springfield paper, meanwhile, claimed that Douglas had the upper hand, scoring well on popular sovereignty and Black inequality. In a hopeful note, the Massachusetts journal also believed the Republicans were gaining on the Democrats in Illinois.

The fifth debate, at Knox College in Galesburg on October 7, drew between 15,000 and 20,000, and Douglas reminded this pro-Republican crowd that Lincoln had spoken against equal rights for Blacks in Charleston. Lincoln countered by saying that slavery was both a moral and political failing. The *Tribune* continued to attack Douglas as being narrow-minded and offering nothing new to the debate. "How different our candidate! He never speaks that he does not bring forward something new," observed the *Tribune* editors of Lincoln.[15]

After the sixth debate, at Quincy with 12,000 attendees, the *Tribune* described Douglas's performance as "fainter and weaker."[16] Meanwhile, the Chicago paper described Lincoln "as fresh, vigorous, and elastic as when the contest began." The editors used a boxing analogy to claim that the verbal jabs that Lincoln was now landing on Douglas were doing more damage than before.

For the final debate, at Alton, the *Tribune* continued to harp on Douglas for voicing the same debate each time while Lincoln appropriately offered a comprehensive summary of the law and evidence "before the jury of the people."[17]

Image 12.1 "Our Political Snake-Charmer," *Vanity Fair*, February 11, 1860. This British political cartoon shows Stephen Douglas with snakes labeled with the political positions "Old Line" (Whig), "American," "So. American," "Anti-Lecompton," "Democrat," and "Republican." The caption includes dialogue from Douglas, who says, "You perceive, ladies and gentlemen, that the creatures are entirely under my control." John W. Forney, a Democrat who switched sides and became a Lincoln supporter, says, "Hope the Brutes won't bite!" Forney later published in Washington, D.C., the *Sunday Morning Chronicle*, which in 1862 changed to a daily and supported the Lincoln administration.[18]

After the debates, the next major event leading to the war was John Brown's raid on Harpers Ferry, Virginia, on October 16, 1859. *The New York Tribune* sympathized with Brown, although the newspaper insisted that change should come without violence.[20] The Southern journalistic response to the raid and its press backing in the North was caustic. For example, the Augusta *Constitutionalist* denounced Greeley's *Tribune* for justifying those who supported and planned Brown's attack, and the Savannah (Ga.) *News* railed against Northern newspapers

Image 12.2 "Honest Old Abe on the Stump. Springfield 1858. Honest Old Abe on the Stump, at the Ratification Meeting of Presidential Nominations. Springfield 1860." A caricature of Abraham Lincoln, likely produced after his 1860 nomination as Republican presidential candidate. The artist contrasts Lincoln's modest posture at the Illinois Republican state convention in Springfield in 1858 with his confident appearance at the 1860 Illinois Republican ratifying convention, also held in Springfield. The two Lincolns are shown joined at the back and seated on a stump. The 1858 Lincoln (facing left) addresses a small audience of men, including a young Black man, denying any presidential ambitions. His words appear in a balloon: "Nobody ever expected me to be President. In my poor, lean, lank face, nobody has ever seen that any Cabbages were sprouting out." In contrast, the 1860 Lincoln (facing right) says, "I come to see, and be seen." The illustration apparently criticizes Lincoln's reticence about his political views during the 1860 campaign, when from May to November he made no speeches except for a brief address at the meeting in Springfield, which likely explains the puzzled look of several of his listeners here. Although clearly by a trained and able artist, the lithograph is not readily attributable to any of the major known cartoonists of the time.[19]

that suggested the event showed the need for the South to protect itself from Black revolt.[21] The Augusta *Chronicle & Sentinel* called the raid "reckless, foolhardy, and insane," and editor William S. Smith hoped that a paper trail would connect Brown to abolitionists Gerrit Smith and Frederick Douglass, resulting in the hanging of both men.[22]

The Chicago Tribune pinned Harpers Ferry on the Democrats, claiming that their policies would mean another decade or two of such insurrections. According to Joseph Medill's newspaper, those policies—including popular sovereignty, the Fugitive Slave Law, and the Dred Scott decision—had alienated the Southern Democrats' closest friends in the North. While extremists like Brown were beginning to act, the *Tribune* noted that the slaves had improved their conditions to the point of "dangerous acquirements."[23] The *Tribune* wrote that freed slaves who had gone to Canada were likely returning to their former plantations to instruct those still in chains about the blessings of freedom.

Six months after Virginia executed John Brown, the Republicans chose Abraham Lincoln as their candidate for president at the Wigwam in Chicago. At about the same time, Lincoln penned an autobiography to help promote his campaign, which was submitted to John L. Scripps, an editor at *The Chicago Tribune*, who revised it, published it, and allowed Greeley's *New York Tribune* to reproduce it en masse.[24] While the Springfield *Republican* predicted William H. Seward would win the nomination, both *Tribunes*, which intensely covered the convention, went for Lincoln. *The New York Tribune* held that Lincoln possessed the "greatest running qualities" of those seeking the Republican nomination, and that the public perceived the Illinois attorney to be "of sterling stuff."[25]

The Chicago Tribune wrote that the "age of purity" had returned with Lincoln's nomination, adding that Honest Abe's presidency would "guaranty that the country, wearied and outraged by the malfeasance of those invested with the Federal power, desires a return to the sterling simplicity and Democratic simplicity which marked the Administrations of Jefferson, Madison, Adams, and Jackson." The Chicago newspaper praised Lincoln for the clarity of his record on slavery, calling the Springfield resident a conservative with an antislavery fiber and noting that New York, Indiana, Ohio, and Missouri had received Lincoln's nomination with enthusiasm, as he embodied "the genius of our free institutions."[26]

In November, on the day of the national election, the Springfield *Republican* claimed Lincoln had the necessary electoral votes to win, but that the heads of Wall Street had urged voters to go against Lincoln and were holding onto their investments. The next day, *The New York Tribune* was quick to point to the division of the Democratic Party as the major reason for the Republican victory. In

Greeley's editorial on Lincoln's victory, he reminded Democrats that it was their turn to play the role of the minority party. "It is decidedly pleasanter to be on the winning side, especially when—as now—it happens also to be the right side." Greeley also told his readers that if the Southern states needed to mediate on the subject of secession, "let them do so unmolested." He added that his *Tribune* had a "chronic, invincible disbelief in Disunion as a remedy for either Northern or Southern grievance."[27]

The Union Imperiled

The national fabric unraveled after the election, with South Carolina seceding on December 20, 1860. The Springfield *Republican* responded bluntly: "At last the agony and suspense are over," wondering how "the little grand empire" would handle its debts now that it was on its own.[28] *The Chicago Tribune* warned other states not to follow or recognize the newly independent Southern state, remarking "Wo [*sic*] onto him who makes himself a party to treason."[29] *The New York Tribune* defended Lincoln's election as stock prices fell on Wall Street and Southern banks suspended specie payments. Greeley lambasted Southern legislators for asking for their 1861 salary before the state seceded. The editor also wrote that Washington, D.C., should allow any state that wanted to leave the Union to go peacefully: "We loathe the idea of compelling them to stay." He further wrote that South Carolina's succession had "not appalled nor seriously disturbed the country." He then threw a verbal jab at the Palmetto State: "South Carolina must be certainly wanting in any serious intention of setting up in business on her own account, or else she is singularly destitute of men of ability."[30]

At the time that South Carolina left the Union, Congress was considering the Crittenden Compromise. A Senate group led by Kentucky Senator John J. Crittenden (a moderate Democrat) proposed amendments to the Constitution that it believed would help avert war. These included a guarantee that the government would not impede slavery in the states where it existed and re-establishment of the Missouri Compromise line (no slavery above 36 degrees and 30 minutes). Another amendment would guarantee slavery in the District of Columbia as long as it existed in either Virginia or Maryland. Among the resolutions was a statement to the effect that fugitive slave laws were valid and that the government should enforce them.

Both the Senate and the House of Representatives rejected the Crittenden Compromise. *The New York Tribune* called the proposal a "concession of the most radical and vital character." The *Tribune* editors noted that the New Mexico Territory was situated both below and above 36-30, but that slavery might flow through it once it became a state. Likewise, Utah, "where a condition of society exists that is capable of anything, Slavery may very possibly be introduced when she becomes a member of the Union." Greeley and his colleagues would have none of this, and urged rejection of the compromise. "We are half through this battle," they wrote. "Let us finish it like men, and be done with controversy forever."[31] Medill's *Chicago Tribune* called the 36-30 amendment "a quack remedy—no less than staving off an important settlement a few years longer, merely for lack of courage to meet it now." Republicans should not compromise, the newspaper insisted, and the party should stand behind the Constitution and the Union. The editors had no interested in tinkering with the Constitution, and believed that such a resolution in the North would mean the "secession blast will soon blow out."[32]

During his March 4, 1861, inaugural oath, Lincoln made the case for a permanent Union. "Perpetuity is implied, if not expressed, in the fundamental law of all national governments," he said. "I therefore consider that, in the view of the Constitution and the laws, the Union is unbroken."[33] *The New York Tribune* held that the North now had to intervene in the South. The editors dared the president to be decisive, demanding "energetic" and "effective" action in order to maintain the government.[34] According to the *Tribune*, if Washington was not willing to fight, then the Lincoln government had to accept the Confederacy as an accomplished fact.

After C.S.A. Brigadier General P. G. T. Beauregard and his troops captured Fort Sumter on April 13, 1861, *The New York Tribune* declared that the war had begun, although it maintained the war had begun earlier when the South had taken other forts in Charleston Harbor. The *Tribune* editors believed the Confederacy had the temporary upper hand militarily, but that in the end the Washington government would triumph. "There is no more thought of bribing or coaxing the traitors who have dared aim their cannon balls at the flag of the Union and those who gave their lives to defend it."[35]

The Springfield *Republican* wondered of the war: "What the end will be, no human eye can foresee, but all eyes can see that we are in the midst either of revolution or a gigantic rebellion." The *Republican*, with a headline that read, "Treason Wins the First Battle," also described a comprehensive military plan from the federal government to counter the Confederacy. The *Republican* called on readers to fight because a "peace that fosters corruption" was the worst curse a nation could face.[36]

Three months later, the first major battle occurred southwest of Washington at Manassas, Virginia. First Bull Run took place July 21, 1861, after the *Tribune* had forced Lincoln's hand with its "On to Richmond" editorial. The Union Army was not ready to fight and suffered a demoralizing setback, but Greeley's team of writers had made the case for military action by arguing that the Constitution had to bend in times of rebellion: "The Nation must live though a locality or interest should have to die."[37]

The Springfield *Republican* was sober in its assessment of First Bull Run, calling the loss the "saddest day this country ever saw." The *Republican* explained that the Rebels had routed a large number of Union troops and that a march to Richmond would not be as "easy and rapid as some have supposed." Still, the *Republican* editors did not fear Washington's capture because of the artillery that defended the capital city. Three days after the battle, the Springfield newspaper rationalized the defeat by saying that Union troops retreated because of the distractions from spectators who had come from Washington to watch the skirmish. In future battles, the paper urged, spectators should not be allowed anywhere near the field. A similar policy should apply to journalists, the paper held. The *Republican* commented: "If reporters must go, let them go in the ranks, with a gun in their hands."[38]

The North did not notch its first major victories of the war until February 1862, with twin triumphs at Fort Henry and Fort Donelson. The latter was a decisive win, with a 5-to-1 ratio in casualties in favor of the Union. Most of the 13,846 Confederate casualties were captured prisoners. The wins gave Republican newspapers a chance to give their readers encouraging news. According to *The New York Tribune*, "'The American Flag waves over Fort Donelson!' was the electric response that last evening repaid the days of intense anxiety with which the fate of the attack upon the Rebel stronghold was regarded by the community." As it had done with skirmishes since Bull Run, the *Tribune* ran a map of the battle area, beside headlines saying "Our Troops Won't Let Them Run Away," "Our Troops Making Good Progress," and "No Re-Enforcements Possible."[39]

A month later came the bloodiest battle of the war so far, at Pittsburg Landing, Tennessee. The Battle of Shiloh was a Union victory. However, the North suffered more losses—13,047 casualties, compared to 10,699 for the South, although the number of killed was almost equal. *The New York Tribune* called Shiloh a "great" victory and described the contest as "the hardest-fought battle that has ever taken place on this continent." The triumph in Tennessee did not have the dash of the Fort Henry and Fort Donelson victories, according to the *Tribune*, but the editors recognized the effectiveness of the operations had contributed to overall Union war aims.[40] The Springfield *Republican* believed the battle might result in the end of the Western campaign.

Changing Coverage and Course

The summer of 1862 saw the Union military in Virginia gradually lose ground to Robert E. Lee's army. Yet the most important event of the season in the North may well have been Greeley's publishing an August editorial titled "The Prayer of the Twenty Millions," which the editor had sent to the president the day before.[41] Greeley expressed his disapproval of the way the president was running the war. He was especially critical of the president's policy regarding slaves in Southern areas re-conquered by the Union military. The *Tribune* editor wrote that the Northern people wanted both the rebellion and slavery squashed, and that even if federal forces crushed the rebellion the next day, it would spring up again a year later without the extermination of slavery. In other words, Greeley encouraged Lincoln to make the war not only about reunion but also for abolition of slavery.

> I do not intrude to tell you—for you must know already—that a great proportion of those who triumphed you in election, and all who desire the unqualified suppression of the Rebellion now desolating our country, are sorely disappointed and deeply pained by the policy you seem to be pursuing with regard to the slaves of the Rebels. ... As one of the millions who would gladly have avoided this struggle at any sacrifice but that Principle and Honor, but who now feel that the triumph of the Union is dispensable not only to the existence of our country to the well being of mankind, I entreat you to render a hearty and unequivocal obedience to the law of the land.[42]

Lincoln responded publicly that he intended to save the Union—and that this was his top priority, above all else. In print, he downplayed the role of emancipation in his wartime decisions, leaving Greeley unimpressed (although the latter said privately that he would forgive the president if he ever freed the slaves).[43] However, Lincoln had indeed already drafted an emancipation order in July 1862 that allowed for arming of slaves to help the Union fight the war—a strategy to create confusion in the South while the white men were off fighting. Cabinet members William H. Seward and Gideon Welles had reviewed the edict and protested it, with Seward urging the president to wait for a Union victory. Almost a month before Antietam, Greeley published his open letter.

The second battle at Manassas, Virginia, occurred a week after publication of Greeley's letter, did not produce the victory that Lincoln needed. Again, the Confederates, whom many Northern editors believed would attack Washington if unchecked, proved the winners. Led by Robert E. Lee, Stonewall Jackson, and A. P. Hill, the Army of Northern Virginia attacked the Union left south of Bull Run, a small river on the Manassas-Sudley Road. *The New York Tribune* reported on the Rebels' August success and wrote that Union Major General John Pope, head of the Army of Virginia, should have been "on his guard" against a repeat of the battle the previous summer on the same field.[44] Pope fought alone, as Major General George McClellan and his troops remained stationed at Aquia, Virginia. Pope's army held its own against Lee until C.S.A. Major General James Longstreet used a flanking attack to defeat Pope's army.

The Springfield *Republican* initially credited the Union Army with victory, but backtracked a few days later. Once it was clear that Lee's army had won, the *Republican* speculated that Lee would either attack the Northern capital or invade Maryland. The Massachusetts paper predicted that the Union military leadership would focus on the defense of Washington. Editor Samuel Bowles felt the federal capital would stay safe, but added: "But we look for something better than the safety to Washington."[45]

It was a remarkable time for Lee and his top generals, as they had repelled McClellan's peninsular advance on Richmond and had driven the Union Army back to Washington. Pope would be demoted on September 12, replaced by McClellan. Historians David Herbert Donald and James G. Randall noted that the loss at Second Bull Run left Washington in disorder, as the government's control of the military had fallen into confusion, with Secretary of War Edwin M. Stanton and General Henry W. Halleck urging their plans on Lincoln and creating situations in which coordinated command was impossible.[46]

Lincoln still did not have the victory he believed he needed in order to announce his emancipation plan. However, such a triumph came just a few days later, in what would be the bloodiest single day of the war. On September 17, the North scored a tactical victory at Sharpsburg, Maryland, when Lee was forced to retreat to the Potomac. *The Chicago Tribune* relied heavily on the Associated Press for coverage of the battle, with an AP correspondent commenting: "Some of the most desperate fighting ever recorded in history took place on the field. In passing over the ground today, the evidence was manifest where the most deadly contests occurred—the dead lying thick and in rows where they had fallen on the enemy's centre."[47] The AP overestimated Confederate casualties at 18,000 to 20,000. In fact, the South had 13,724 casualties, compared to 12,410 for the Union.[48]

Initially, *The New York Tribune* reported that the battle at Antietam Creek "closed without definite result," but the next day the newspaper claimed the advantage had clearly swayed to the Union.[49] Greeley's editors, though, cautioned readers not to be surprised if the Antietam victory proved to be only a temporary setback for the Confederate Army. Nonetheless, the *Tribune* predicted Lee would retreat across the Potomac back into Virginia. The Springfield *Republican* interpreted Antietam as a decisive Northern win because the Rebels had invaded Maryland "with the expectation of staying there" and enlisting 50,000 Marylanders in their army. The Confederates had risked "their whole pile on the great game," Bowles wrote, "and they have failed."[50]

Although a narrow Northern victory, Antietam provided the president with the opportunity to announce the Emancipation Proclamation. On September 23, newspapers across the nation published this executive order, which would take effect on January 1, 1863. Greeley was ecstatic, writing that it was "one of the most stupendous facts in human history which marks not only an era in the progress of the nation, but an epoch in the history of the world." He wrote that he "trembled at the responsibility" and claimed that emancipation would occur not only for the Blacks slaves but also for Northern men and women who had been taught to revere the institution of slavery.[51] Most importantly, Greeley wrote, emancipation began the rebellion's end.

Bowles, in the *Republican*, was more sober in his assessment of the proclamation. He suggested it would not have much of an effect on Southern slavery and it would not alter the course of the war. He claimed that nine-tenths of the Republican Party approved of the plan. Bowles anticipated "no bad effects" on the slave states that stayed in the Union. The Massachusetts editor commented insightfully. "The whole scope of the proclamation makes it evident that the president is faithful to his declared policy of resorting to emancipation only as a means of subduing the rebellion and restoring the Union, and probably the only objection that will be made, North or South, will be that it is an error of judgment."[52] Yet there would be at best only a minimally propitious effect gained from the proclamation, in that those who wanted to see the war's main cause to be freedom now could no longer criticize the president.

The rest of the year would be disastrous for Lincoln. The Democrats would make decent gains in the House of Representatives and regain several state houses. Lincoln would sack George McClellan in November, an unpopular move with Union soldiers. Then, McClellan's successor, Ambrose E. Burnside, would try a more aggressive approach against Lee, one that led to disaster at Fredericksburg, Virginia, on December 13.

Lincoln removed McClellan from his command as the chief of the Army of the Potomac on November 5, 1863, as the North was voting in the off-year election. Greeley's *Tribune* described McClellan as having "a chronic incapacity for getting on," and added that Lincoln had no choice but move on.[53] Greeley also noted that it was not good for the Union that Southern soldiers called McClellan the greatest Northern general. Moreover, McClellan had too many friends, and his lieutenants were willing to appease the South. While McClellan had been unsuccessful in pursuing Lee, Burnside's aggressive approach proved an even greater failure. So hopeful was *The Chicago Tribune* that it ran a headline on the day of the battle, saying "Forward the Whole Line!" Joseph Medill's newspaper believed the Union soldiers' crossing the Rappahannock River was a positive sign that gave "promise of an energetic campaign in Virginia."[54]

However, Fredericksburg would be one of the two worst Union losses in the war. The Confederates held a defensive ground on a hill called Marye's Heights on the southern side of the Rappahannock River. As the Union soldiers crossed the river and attempted to climb the heights, Rebel sharpshooters mowed them down. Bowles' *Republican* called the Fredericksburg battle a "Step Backward" and wrote that the Union army would have to postpone its march on Richmond.[55] *The Chicago Tribune*, which ran a December 19 headline saying, "Fearful Carnage of our Forces," applauded Burnside's "moral courage" in retreating once he realized the dangers facing his men. The *Tribune* also reported that every man from instructional camps on the East Coast was en route to Washington, and that eventually the Union Army would complete "the pulverization of the Rebel army."[56] A congressional investigation of the disaster would follow, and Lincoln would demote Burnside in January.

In the spring 1863, Robert E. Lee would continue his dominance of the Union military, no matter who the leader of the Army of the Potomac happened to be. After Fredericksburg, he was successful again in early May 1863, this time at Chancellorsville, just southwest of the city where he had so humiliated Burnside in December. Major General Joseph Hooker was at the helm of the Army of the Potomac, but he, too, was no match for Lee. However, it proved to be a costly victory as Lieutenant General Thomas J. "Stonewall" Jackson, Lee's top subordinate, died when killed by friendly fire as he tried to keep the battle going into the night. Jackson, who earlier that day had executed a long march to the west and then the north to attack Hooker from behind, would actually die not from his wounds but from pneumonia.

The New York Tribune was critical of Major General Daniel E. Sickles' Eleventh Corps for losing their nerve and running. The defeat shocked Greeley because Sickles had planned well and had his troops in position to win. Greeley wrote that the country expected the war's decisive victory at Chancellorsville but did not get it. The *Tribune* editor even praised the Confederates: "The Rebels seem to have acted with signal energy and skill from the moment that they found Hooker in force on their right flank."[57]

The Chicago Tribune, which for days cheered Hooker on (on May 8, the editors wrote that they still "believed in Joe Hooker"), eventually called Chancellorsville a disaster for the Union but urged readers not to despair. Editor Joseph Medill and his colleagues wrote that the defeat would teach the North important lessons. "We notice that the sun still shines, as if nothing particular had happened," a *Tribune* editorial observed, "and nothing particular has happened, so far as the final issues of the war are concerned."[58] Medill noted that the North had plenty of men to carry on the war, but urged aggressiveness in recruiting Black soldiers.

Lincoln relieved Hooker of command of his army in late June 1863, just as the Army of the Potomac was about to encounter Lee for the second time in the North. The turning point of the war in the eastern theater would occur at Gettysburg, Pennsylvania, when Lee's winning streak finally ended. Major General George G. Meade would be the victor, losing 5,000 fewer men in a three-day battle that resulted in 51,000 total casualties.[59]

The New York Tribune claimed the Confederates had been defeated outright, and announced with a "joy and gratitude that have had no parallel since the war began" that the Army of the Potomac had won "a magnificent victory." According to Greeley's newspaper, which focused on Meade's achievement, no amount of praise for the general would have been gratuitous.[60] *The Chicago Tribune* called the news from Pennsylvania "cheerful" and reported that Lee's "scared army" was in "full retreat."[61]

Winning the War

Only a day after news of the triumph at Gettysburg came word that Ulysses S. Grant had finally notched a victory at Vicksburg, Mississippi. Grant suffered only 8,873 casualties, contrasted to 39,491 for the C.S.A.'s John C. Pemberton.[62] After Gettysburg and Vicksburg, the Springfield *Republican* gloated that the twin victories meant the end for the Peace Democrats. Editor Bowles, who often took a relatively moderate position on the issues of the day, presciently forecast the end of the peace movement from conservative Democrats.

Noting that nothing harmed peace advocates' cause more than a Union battle victory, Bowles wrote, "Copperheadism is the northern thermometer that indicates the state of the rebellion. When the Union armies win, copperheadism goes down; when the Rebels succeed, they go up again. The fall of Vicksburg now would take it down to zero, and the culmination of our victories in Pennsylvania in the capture or destruction of Lee's army will run it so low that not even a spirit thermometer can tell where it is." Bowles told Pennsylvania peace proponents that it was time for them to leave for Canada. Their movement had ended with Robert E. Lee's defeat at Gettysburg, and, the *Republican* editor added, "What is true of that state will be true everywhere if our successes continue. Copperhead politics will die out with the rebellion, and in fact a little in advance of it."[63]

The Chicago Tribune described the Vicksburg victory, after Meade's win in the East, as giving "fresh luster to the National birthday."[64] In New York, the draft riots that occurred the following week tempered the luster. Some of the rioters came to the *Tribune* office and challenged Greeley to show his face in public, denouncing him and the president for their abolitionist sentiment. They stormed the building and set it ablaze before police arrived.[65] Greeley's newspaper duly noted the racial component of the riots and observed that many Black families left the city with no intention of returning.

The remainder of 1863 saw another bloodbath, this time at Chickamauga Creek in Georgia (a Confederate victory, with 34,500 casualties). It also saw the Union triumph at Chattanooga and Lincoln's oratory at Gettysburg. Then William T. Sherman began to maneuver across the South, en route to Atlanta and ultimately his scorched-earth campaign. In March 1864, Lincoln named Ulysses S. Grant commander of all Union troops. In May and June of that year, Grant would witness several resounding defeats: the Wilderness, where he lost 17,666 men, contrasted to only 7,750 for Lee; Spotsylvania, where he lost 18,399, almost 9,000 more than Lee; and Cold Harbor, the greatest Union disaster of the war, with 14,931 Northern casualties and only 1,700 Confederate.[66]

Greeley's *New York Tribune* did not concede these reverses, and instead wrote that despair that was overtaking the citizenry of the Southern states. "The people [in the South] are called upon to pray now or never, and besiege the Almighty with entreaties for victory," he wrote. "The gravity of their position is reluctantly confessed, and it is clear to see that they look upon the defeat of Lee's army as fatal."[67] *The Chicago Tribune* admitted that Lee had been able to hold his entrenchments at Cold Harbor, and the Illinois newspaper praised Grant for his high regard for

290 | *Journalism in the Civil War Era*

the lives of his men. The Chicago paper still predicted that Grant would "do a prodigious amount of damage to the enemy."[68] The *Tribune*'s position was similar to that of *The New York Times*, which noted that Lee had held the "main line strongly and persistently" at Cold Harbor. The *Times* also held that the "contest for Richmond bids fair to be prolonged and desperate."[69]

Farther south, Sherman's troops fought those of John Bell Hood in Atlanta on July 22. *The New York Tribune* reported: "Gen. Sherman is firmly established in siege of Atlanta."[70] Greeley's paper reported Confederate losses to be three times greater than those of Sherman's troops did. Two days after the battle, *The Chicago Tribune* ran the following lead headline: "Glorious News from Georgia—Atlanta in Our Possession." The *Tribune*'s special correspondent also observed that Georgians were unable to provide adequate provisions for the Confederate Army in the state because the Rebel military had already used up the corn and wheat. The reporter wrote that citizens of the state might go without food because the Union Army was eating whatever was left over. "Such destitution and poverty," the correspondent observed, "so universally and abject in so rich and fruitful a country, is found only in the fields desolated by war."[71]

While the Confederates had won the battle of Ezra Church on July 26, by September 2 all of Atlanta had fallen to Sherman's forces. He would raze the city and march his soldiers to the sea. By December 21, the Union general possessed Savannah. The improving military news coincided with Lincoln's reelection in November 1864. *The Chicago Tribune* called the election one day after polling—rare at a time when election results from around the country would often take days and weeks to tally. The *Tribune* headlines read: "A Victory of Gigantic Proportions," "Re-Election of Abraham Lincoln," and "The Peace Sneaks Utterly Destroyed."[72]

The New York Tribune, which prided itself in accurately counting the vote, reported on November 9 that Lincoln had won New York, Pennsylvania, Delaware, New Jersey, Maryland, Ohio, Indiana, Michigan, Illinois, Wisconsin, Minnesota, Iowa, and Kansas. That gave Lincoln 190 electoral votes. Greeley was happy in particular with Republican successes in congressional elections. An addition of fifty Republican seats gave Lincoln's party more than a two-thirds majority in the House of Representatives—enough to ensure passage of the Thirteenth Amendment, which outlawed slavery forever. The Springfield *Republican* called Lincoln's victory "one of the glorious events of the world's life" and wrote that it gave new life to republican institutions. "The grand triumph is nearly completed."[73]

Lincoln's reelection, as well as Sherman's campaign in Georgia and the Carolinas, signaled the impending end of the Confederate military. With the major cities of Virginia re-conquered, Lee determined there had been enough carnage and surrendered on April 9, 1865. *The New York Tribune* reported that once the city discovered the news, "cheer upon cheer rang through the night."[74] Only a few days before Lee surrendered, *The Chicago Tribune* praised Grant's April 3 capture of Richmond and acknowledged that although the cost of the war was significant, "the cost was far greater to the enemy than to ourselves." When news of Lee's capitulation reached the city on Lake Michigan, the *Tribune* reported, "a universal uprising, out-pouring, procession-forming, speech-making, banner-displaying, bonfire-burning, rocket-blazing, day of glory as Chicago and its people have never before seen."[75]

However, the celebration lasted only a few days. On April 14 came news that an assassin had killed Lincoln at Ford's Theatre in Washington. *The Chicago Tribune* wrote that the news sent "profound grief throughout the nation." Medill observed: "Our President has fallen, in the prime of his energy and usefulness, another martyr to the Demon—Slavery."[76] *The New York Tribune* provided the following assessment of Lincoln's life: "He filled a larger space in the public eye than any American before him, partly because of the stupendous events in which he bore a conspicuous part."[77] In the Springfield *Republican*, Samuel Bowles printed a eulogy of Lincoln by Josiah G. Holland, who wrote: "I do not think it ever occurred to Mr. Lincoln that he was a ruler. More emphatically than any of his predecessors did he regard himself as a servant of the people—the instrument selected by the people for the execution of their will."[78]

Lincoln was gone, and the nation would struggle to find its balance after the war. Yet, as Lubell would predict, the Republicans enjoyed a long national dominance. Between Lincoln's death and Woodrow Wilson's election in 1912, the Republicans would see only one Democrat successfully challenge their monopoly—Grover Cleveland. Indeed, the Republican hegemony would continue until Franklin D. Roosevelt assumed office, as three consecutive presidents after Wilson came from Lincoln's party. During this run, the Republican newspapers of the North grew stronger, none more so than *The Chicago Tribune*. In the last quarter of the nineteenth century, the Republican press would continue to espouse the ideals Lincoln championed during a time when journalism would become a profession and an industry.

Notes

1 Harper, *Lincoln and the Press*, 144, 145.

2 Bulla, *Lincoln's Censor*, 112.

3 Samuel Lubell, *The Future of American Politics*, 2nd ed. (Garden City, NY: Doubleday & Company, 1956), 212.

4 New York *Tribune*, August 26, 1858.

5 White, *A. Lincoln: A Biography*, 264.

6 Chicago *Press and Tribune*, August 23, 24, 1858.

7 Holzer, ed., *The Lincoln-Douglas Debates* (New York: Harper Collins, 1993), 42.

8 New York *Tribune*, August 26, 1858.

9 Springfield (MA) *Republican*, August 27, 1858.

10 Chicago *Press and Tribune*, August 30, 1858.

11 Holzer, *The Lincoln-Douglas Debates*, 88, 89.

12 White, *A. Lincoln: A Biography*, 270.

13 Chicago *Press and Tribune*, August 30, 1858.

14 Ibid, September 22, 1858.

15 Ibid, October 9, 1858.

16 Ibid, October 9, 15, 1858.

17 Ibid, October 18, 1858.

18 "Our Political Snake-Charmer," Library of Congress, accessed November 10, 2021, at <loc.gov/item/2002707238>.

19 "Honest Old Abe on the Stump. Springfield 1858. Honest Old Abe on the Stump, at the Ratification Meeting of Presidential Nominations. Springfield 1860," Library of Congress, accessed November 11, 2021, at <loc.gov/item/2008661607>.

20 New York *Tribune*, October 19, 1859.

21 Louis T. Griffith and John E. Talmadge, *Georgia Journalism, 1763–1950* (Athens, GA: University of Georgia Press, 1951), 54.

22 Augusta (GA) *Chronicle & Sentinel*, October 22, 1859.

23 Chicago *Press and Tribune*, October 22, 1859.

24 Fred Kaplan, *Lincoln: The Biography of a Writer* (New York: Harper Collins, 2008), 315, 316.

25 New York *Tribune*, May 19, 1860.

26 Chicago *Press and Tribune*, May 19, 23, 1860.

27 New York *Tribune*, November 9, 1860.

28 Springfield (MA) *Republican*, December 21, 24, 1860.

29 Chicago *Press and Tribune*, December 21, 1860.

30 New York *Tribune*, December 24, 25, 1860.

31 Ibid, December 20, 1860.

32 Chicago *Press and Tribune*, December 19, 20, 1860.

33 Carl Sandburg, *Abraham Lincoln: The Prairie Years and the War Years* (New York: Sterling Publishing Company, 2007), 140.

34 New York *Tribune*, March 16, 1861.

35 Ibid, April 15, 1861.

36 Springfield (MA) *Republican*, April 15, 20, 1861.

37 New York *Tribune*, July 20, 1861.

38 Springfield (MA) *Republican*, July 22, 24, 1861.

39 New York *Tribune*, February 15, 17, 1862.

40 Ibid, April 9, 1862.

41 Williams, *Horace Greeley*, 233.

42 New York *Tribune*, August 20, 1862.

43 Williams, *Horace Greeley*, 233.

44 New York *Tribune*, August 29, 1862.

45 Springfield (MA) *Republican*, September 4, 1862.

46 Donald and Randall, *The Civil War and Reconstruction*, 219.

47 Associated Press, September 20, 1862, in "The Battle Field—The Retreat of the Rebel Army," New York *Herald*, September 22, 1862.

48 Gil Hinshaw, *From 10,500 Battles: A Handbook of Civil War Engagements* (Hobbs. NM: Superior Printing Company, 1996), 27.

49 New York *Tribune*, September 18, 19, 1862.

50 Springfield (MA) *Republican*, September 20, 1862.

51 New York *Tribune*, September 24, 1862.

52 Springfield (MA) *Republican*, September 24, 1862.

53 New York *Tribune*, November 10, 1862.

54 Chicago *Tribune*, December 13, 1862.

55 Springfield (MA) *Republican*, December 17, 1862.

56 Chicago *Tribune*, December 19, 1862.

57 New York *Tribune*, May 8, 1863.

58 Chicago *Tribune*, May 8, 1863.

59 Hinshaw, *From 10,500 Battles*, 36.

60 New York *Tribune*, July 6, 1863.

61 Chicago *Tribune*, July 6, 8, 1863.

62 Hinshaw, *From 10,500 Battles*, 36.

63 Springfield (MA) *Republican*, July 7, 1863.

64 Chicago *Tribune*, July 9, 1863.

65 Iver Bernstein, *The New York City Draft Riots: Their Significance for American Society and Politics in the Age of the Civil War* (New York: Oxford University Press, 1990), 19.

66 Hinshaw, *From 10,500 Battles*, 45, 46.

67 New York *Tribune*, June 6, 1864.

68 Chicago *Tribune*, June 18, 1864.

69 New York *Times*, June 6, 1864.
70 New York *Tribune*, July 26, 1864.
71 Chicago *Tribune*, July 24, 1864.
72 Ibid, November 9, 1864.
73 Springfield (MA) *Republican*, November 10, 1864.
74 New York *Tribune*, April 10, 1865.
75 Chicago *Tribune*, April 4, 11, 1865.
76 Ibid, April 15, 17, 1865.
77 New York *Tribune*, April 18, 19, 1865.
78 Springfield (MA) *Republican*, April 19, 1865.

13

The International Dimension of Civil War Journalism

"The sympathies of Mr. Gladstone are openly with the North, and if his conclusions tally not with those sympathies, we may perhaps afford to forgive him his temporary deductions in consideration of the principles permanently friendly to freedom and to a free Union which he resolutely utters." "Mr. Gladstone on Southern Nationality," *New York Times*, October 25, 1862.

British Chancellor of the Exchequer Sir William E. Gladstone made a speech in Newcastle-Upon-Tyne, England, on October 7, 1862, in which he stated that Jefferson Davis and the Confederate States of America had "made an army; they are making, it appears, a navy; and they have made what is more than either, they have made a nation." He also said: "We may anticipate with certainty the success of the South, so far as regards separation from the North." In fairness to Gladstone, he also said that England had no desire for the "disruption of the American Union" and that, thus far, a "strict neutrality" had been in the best interest of the British government. Nonetheless, the "made a nation" comment was a stunning pronouncement, and the *Newcastle Chronicle* reported that it brought "prolonged cheering."

Indeed, for the Union government in Washington, D.C., it was a galling line, coming from a major figure in Viscount Palmerston's London government. Benjamin Moran, who was the secretary of the U.S. legation in London, called Gladstone's words an "insulting attack" on the United States. For the Davis government in Richmond, Virginia, it was validation—while not, however, the same as official recognition. The timing of the speech was critical, as it came just two weeks after President Abraham Lincoln announced his Emancipation Proclamation and three weeks after the Union's narrow victory over the C.S.A.

at Antietam. From the Southern perspective, Gladstone appeared to be hinting that the Palmerston government was about to recognize the Confederacy, but that never happened.

Press Coverage of Gladstone's Confederacy Recognition Speech

In fall 1862, Gladstone toured the northern part of England. In Manchester, he talked about problems with the cotton trade due to the U.S. Civil War.[1] He then stayed in Carlisle awhile before heading north to Newcastle-Upon-Tyne, where he spoke at the Town Hall after inspecting Grey Street, the city's marvelous downtown avenue. His words would prove to be sensational, even if Gladstone had not intended for them to be.

The *Observer* on October 12 reported Gladstone stating of the American situation, "We may anticipate with certainty the success of the South, so far as regards separation from the North." The British official, whose father had owned slaves, also said: "Jefferson Davis and the other Confederate leaders have made an army; they are making, it appears, a navy; and they have made what is more than either—they have made a nation."[2] These words were the most significant spoken by a member of the British government during the U.S. Civil War. No matter Gladstone's intent, they suggested the British were about to recognize the Confederacy—and, perhaps more importantly, they suggested that the United States (the Union) had lost its bid to force the Southern states back into the federal compact of states.

However, Gladstone's Newcastle words did not represent the official policy of Lord Palmerston, the prime minister, and his cabinet. Palmerston and Foreign Minister John Russell were hoping to coax both sides in the conflict to mediation. The British leadership believed that if it could convince the governments of France and Russia to join the British in pressuring the North and South to the peace table, a negotiated solution to the conflict could be found. The British view was that there had been enough bloodshed after more than a year of warfare, and that England no longer could tolerate the U.S. Naval blockade that made it impossible to get cotton from the South to Lancashire textile mills. Palmerston wrote to Gladstone, stating that negotiations with both sides would pre-suppose separation, and if both sides declined such mediation, Great Britain would "acknowledge the independence of the South."[3]

Still, the fact that a single member of the British cabinet had publicly spoken them gave the words an air of gravity. Great Britain was neutral at the time. Gladstone assumed that General Robert E. Lee was still invading the Union, in Maryland, but that invasion had ended after the Confederate Army's tactical defeat at Antietam. Furthermore, Gladstone was friends with Charles Sumner, the pro-abolition senator from Massachusetts, and he found slavery and the racism behind it "detestable."[4] In addition, it is unlikely that there was much pro-slavery sentiment in the Northeast of England.[5] After all, abolitionist societies in that part of the country had been bringing the likes of William Lloyd Garrison and Frederick Douglass over to speak and raise funds for several decades.

If anything, Gladstone's views, though, echoed sentiments of many Northern Democrats, in that what he wished for most was "restoration" of the old American union.[6] Oddly, in his comments he wished both sides well—seeing in both "the elements of future power and good," as well elements of "danger and mischief."[7] Yet a month after his Newcastle speech, he wrote that he had never "expressed any sympathy with the Southern cause," nor had he praised Jefferson Davis.[8] Behind the scenes, Russell tried to soothe Charles Adams, the U.S. minister in London, telling the American that Gladstone had not really meant what he said.[9] Russell also mildly scolded Gladstone, writing to the Chancellor of the Exchequer: "You must allow me to say that I think you went beyond the latitude which all speakers must be allowed, when you said that Jeff. Davis had made a nation. Recognition would seem to follow and for that step I think the cabinet is not prepared."[10]

The British Press Response

Newspapers around Great Britain and the United States responded vigorously, and the timing could not have been more discomforting for President Abraham Lincoln and his government in Washington, D.C., as only sixteen days before Gladstone's Newcastle speech Lincoln had issued his Emancipation Proclamation. Response to the speech in Newcastle Town Hall was "prolonged cheering" from those assembled there, according to the account in *The Observer.*[11] However, reactions ran the gamut in newspapers around Great Britain and the United States. In England, *The Guardian* would comment that the cheers that followed Gladstone's "have made a nation" remarks unfairly drew attention to that portion of his speech. *The Guardian* held that while Gladstone said Davis had made an army and a nation, he was not saying the Confederacy deserved "recognition of independence from other states."[12] *The Guardian* also reported on the opinions of Members of Parliament for Birmingham, and it noted that MP William Scholefield also believed that Davis had made a nation, and that the Confederacy "ought to be recognized by the British Government."[13] While editors of *The Globe* of London could not state when the British government would recognize the South as an independent nation, "it cannot be deferred long," they wrote.[14] Instead of directly referring to his words in Newcastle, the Birmingham *Daily Post* called Gladstone the "most hopeful statesman of the age" and "one of the boldest men in England," adding, "His speeches are substantial; they wear well, and their splendour is equal to their utility without eclipsing it."[15]

According to *The Economist*, it was unlikely Gladstone merely spoke for himself at Newcastle, although he was known for his "impulsive temperament." He expressed the sentiment of the country, the editors held, and the South had "made the Confederacy a nation" with no chance for its re-annexation by the Union. *The Economist* conceded, however, that the British cabinet had "no immediate intention of acting on the thought."[16]

The *Newcastle Courant* reported on what other newspapers were saying about Gladstone's remarks. Citing the *Daily News*, it wrote that Gladstone had never tried to hide that he is "favourable to Southern independence." The *Morning Herald* stated that Gladstone's words "will be taken as the deliberate conviction of the cabinet of which he is a member."[17] The *Essex Standard* chastised Palmerston for not following Gladstone's Newcastle speech with a clear explanation of the British government's position on the American Civil War.[18] The *Saturday Review* called the manner in which Gladstone couched the American conflict an "extraordinary indiscretion" that caused Liverpool to "fall into a state of panic" and the price of cotton to plummet.[19] The *Durham County Advertiser* scolded Gladstone for being too liberal and for not coming to his view on Davis establishing an army and a nation sooner, stating "the confession comes with less grace than it would have done some time ago."[20]

Many of the English newspapers focused on Gladstone's comments about slavery. For example, the *South Bucks Free Press, Wycombe and Maidenhead Journal* reported Gladstone as saying the slaves "would be better off if the States were separated, as on the basis of the Union the law against the slaves were enforced by the whole power of the Federal United Government." The *Free Press* also reported Gladstone's claim that British neutrality "had been more against the South than the North."[21] The *Birmingham Daily Gazette* summarized the response of the British to the concept of a British-brokered mediation. The Birmingham newspaper ran excerpts from the *Times of London*, stating "the present is not the moment for strong measures" and that mediation in the fall of 1862 would be "manifestly an act of favourtism to the South." The *Star* questioned why peace would be invoked for the masters of the South—a "tyrant minority."[22]

In Scotland, the *Elgin Courier* wrote that Gladstone's words implied that "he spoke for the government," and it was "probable that all the members of the cabinet hold the same position."[23] *Courier* editors went on to speculate that Palmerston's government believed Confederate independence had probably been established, but that his cabinet was not quite ready to recognize the South officially. The *Aberdeen Press and Journal* said the public was "startled" by Gladstone's pronouncements in Newcastle, and that the public assumed "the Ministry had come to a decision to acknowledge the independence of the South." The Aberdeen newspaper concluded that Gladstone was just speaking "his mind on the American question."[24] The *Dunfermline Saturday Press* wondered why Gladstone had not "shown his heart stirred by the prospect of freedom to the slave, which the war in question presents."[25]

In Ireland, the *Wexford Constitution* reported that Gladstone "treated the South as a successful cause."[26] The *Belfast Weekly News* criticized Palmerston for not addressing Gladstone's Newcastle commentary, remarking that his "apathy" was "surprising and painful."[27] The *Banner of Ulster* said that Gladstone was correct to say the South had become an independent nation, because that "is the bare fact," and Davis had merely given the nation "name and form."[28] The *Dublin Evening Post* referenced Gladstone's comments on the Confederacy, stating that the minister had called the North a "virtual despotism" since the start of the war. The Irish newspaper reported that Gladstone was pessimistic about the future of the American experiment and, quoting his words spoken in York a few days after the Newcastle speech, that "'an influence unfavorable to freedom has been strengthened by the unhappy experience of what may be called American democracy.'"[29] The *Sligo Champion* observed that both major political parties in England were "fraternising with the South." The *Champion* editors added: "We are of the opinion that there will be NO OPEN interference on the part of England."[30] The *Belfast News-Letter* said all indications were that France was eager to begin mediation. The Belfast newspaper agreed with Gladstone—that the South had made itself an independent nation—and stated that Britain, France, and Russia "should recognize that fact."[31]

In January 1863, the *Bedfordshire Mercury* published a letter by J. Lothrop Motley, the U.S. minister to Vienna, to William H. Seward, the U.S. Secretary of State in Washington, D.C., about Gladstone's "unfortunate speech." In the letter, Motley told Seward that he did not believe Gladstone's words represented "the policy of the Government or the nation."[32]

The American Press Response

In the United States, Henry J. Raymond's *New York Times* stated that Davis had "unquestionably not" made a nation.

> That speech, while it treats the separation of the American States as an accomplished fact, breathes only regret over the fact which it assumes; and finds the only consolation which a statesman can discover in the calamity, to be the hope that the Confederacy may be less competent to perpetuate Slavery than the Union had proved to be. The sympathies of Mr. Gladstone are openly with the North, and if his conclusions tally not with those sympathies, we may perhaps afford to forgive him his temporary deductions in consideration of the principles permanently friendly to freedom and to a free Union.[33]

Note the negative praise of Gladstone for hoping that the Southern "nation" would be an incompetent perpetuator of slavery. The Evansville *Daily Journal* in Indiana remarked that Gladstone's Newcastle talk had attracted "great attention" and claimed that it had caused "a flatness in cotton" prices.[34]

The Boston *Daily Advertiser* reported that while the British government would "persist in the policy of perfect neutrality" regarding the American Civil War, some non-governmental organizations were endorsing Gladstone's comments, including the Liverpool Chamber of Commerce and the Liverpool Southern Association.[35] The *Bangor Whig & Courier* in Maine paraphrasing the *Times of London*, stated that sentiments toward recognition of the Confederacy had more attraction in the north of England than in the south. The Washington, D.C., *Daily National Intelligencer* referenced remarks by the *London Shipping News* that Gladstone was perhaps "premature in the announcement of his views" on the American situation.[36]

The Boston *Advertiser* also quoted the correspondent of the *Paris Patrie*, who stated that Gladstone's speech "has produced the greatest possible confusion in the political world." It noted other members of Palmerston's cabinet who considered the Chancellor of the Exchequer to have been indiscreet.[37] The *North American and United States Gazette*, published in Philadelphia, held that Gladstone was "stirring up the people of England against the United States," and referred to Gladstone's remarks as "impertinent."[38] The Philadelphia newspaper characterized the British government as having "two mouths" on every issue and speculated that Russell was the other mouth on the American issue. The Biddeford, Maine, *Union and Journal* felt that while Gladstone wanted recognition for the

Confederacy, the "sentiment of the English people had not yet arrived at this point." The Maine newspaper characterized Gladstone's pronouncement on slavery as "novel," as the British minister argued in Newcastle that the permanent separation of the two nations would benefit the slave, as a relatively weak Southern nation would be unable to sustain the institution without benefit of the strong Union (federal) law enforcement. Slavery, the *Union and Journal* wrote, was the "corner stone" of the Southern general government.[39]

The Boston *Investigator* wrote that Gladstone claimed that the American "national struggle would be dangerous to individual liberty."[40] The *Daily Citizen and News* in Lowell, Massachusetts, reported that Richard Cobden, a leading Liberal in Great Britain, believed "it would be a waste of time for foreigners to attempt to influence the combatants" in America, and that it would do "more harm than good."[41] The *Daily Cleveland Herald* reported that Cobden asked to predict how the war would end, said he "would not make the same guess that Earl Russell and Mr. Gladstone did." The *San Francisco Daily Evening Bulletin*'s London correspondent wrote that Gladstone's speech was seen as "a semi-official announcement of the fact that the Palmerston ministry is now at least tending towards a recognition of Southern Independence."[42]

Frank Leslie's Illustrated Newspaper, a visually oriented weekly magazine, noted that Gladstone's speech revived rumors in London of the British government recognizing the Confederacy, and characterized the Chancellor of the Exchequer as holding "a lurking hostility" toward the United States "which he shares with all Englishmen of the governing class." *Frank Leslie's* also stated that the pro-Southern press around the world saw this as a "semi-official expression" of the entire cabinet's point of view on the American matter.[43] The *Daily Ohio Statesman* quoted the *New York Daily News* as claiming Gladstone "has made a few proselytes" in England "to the Confederate cause."[44]

The conservative and generally anti-Lincoln *New York Herald* published an exchange of letters between Gladstone and a Professor Newman that had first been printed in the *London Star*. In the letter, Gladstone maintained that he had not praised Davis, nor "expressed any sympathy with the Southern cause." He also wrote that he was a great friend of the North Americans, and stated that he was not encouraging both sides to continue in their "hopeless and destructive enterprise."[45] The *Herald* printed Gladstone's talk at York—where, speaking again of the American crisis, he said, "freedom itself seems to be in danger." Gladstone added, "the longer this terrific struggle continues the more doubtful becomes the future of America." He called slavery "the saddest of social calamities."[46]

On the other hand, from the Southern perspective, the *Richmond Daily Dispatch* welcomed Gladstone's words, stating: "But it is now plain that the British Cabinet sees—as all the rest of the world sees—as the Yankees themselves see—that the attempt to subjugate the Confederate States is utterly hopeless."[47] The *Daily Dispatch* held that the British now saw the conquest of the South by the North to be "utterly impossible," and that the neutrality of Britain was not in its national interest before Gladstone's speech.[48] The *Memphis Daily Appeal* welcomed Gladstone's remarks, writing: "Mr. Gladstone concludes very reasonably that the rebels, who are a nation, will remain so, and that their nationality will not be absorbed back into the Union."[49]

The *Fayetteville Observer* in North Carolina observed that Gladstone's remarks in Newcastle "seem to indicate recognition" of the Confederacy.[50] However, the Fayetteville newspaper also reported the *Times of London* as holding that England "does not mean to interfere," although the British government "regrets the shedding of blood."[51] Also in the Tar Heel State, the *Raleigh Register* assumed that Gladstone had consulted his Cabinet colleagues, and that they concurred with his assessment of the American situation. The newspaper concluded, "early recognition is not improbable."[52] In South Carolina, the *Camden Confederate* reported the *Liverpool Journal* having stated that Gladstone's speech "has convinced nearly everybody that Lord Palmerston ... is about to recognize the Confederacy."[53]

Gladstone likely did not change the views of the Union government and their sympathizers when he had his secretary, Charles L. Ryan, respond to a letter from a constituent published in the *Times of London* and reprinted throughout both countries. The letter stated that his boss had long held the position "that the effort of the Northern States to subjugate the Southern ones is hopeless, by reason of the resistance of the latter."[54] This squared with Lord Palmerston's desire to seek mediation by couching the American conflict as "hopeless"—that is, the U.S. Civil War was a stalemate and the bloodshed unnecessary.

Mediation in the Press

It is worth remembering that Great Britain received news of the narrow Union victory at Antietam almost two weeks after the battle and did not get the news about Lincoln's Emancipation Proclamation until October 5, 1862. *The Spectator* excoriated Lincoln for failing to liberate the slaves in the Border States. The *Times of London* accused Lincoln of planting the seeds of a slave revolt in the South. With the announcement of the Proclamation, British politicians of a more liberal stripe saw Lincoln as unfit to lead a war in which abolition had to be the main reason for fighting because he did not free the slaves in the Border States. *The Economist* said Lincoln was being deceptive, in that it was unlikely he would have announced the order if the Union Army was about to conquer the South, and if the North should conquer the South, the men of the North would put the former Black slaves to good use as laborers on Yankee-owned farms.[55] The *Liverpool Evening Post* reported straightforwardly that sixteen state governors supported Lincoln's order.[56]

Just before Gladstone's speech in Newcastle, Lord Granville, the top-ranking Liberal in the House of Lords, told Foreign Minister Russell that Britain must stay out of the war. Granville reasoned that even a good-faith mediation effort would ultimately drag the British Army and Navy into the fray. Another major British political figure, Benjamin Disraeli, who led the opposition Tories, also believed that it was folly to declare war on the United States.

Image 13.1 "The Right Hon. W. E. Gladstone and the Right Hon. Benjamin Disraeli." *Harper's Weekly* (July 4, 1868), 429, 430. The *Harper's Weekly* caption describes these illustrations as character sketches of Gladstone and Disraeli seated and full length. The text in the accompanying article on the following page offers flattering descriptions of both men but praises Gladstone as morally superior: "Gladstone obliterates his own prejudices when justice demands and opportunity favors reform, while Disraeli stands ready to use any prejudice—even ones which he has never adopted as his own—for the advancement of his selfish designs."[57]

Disraeli observed in a November 1862 letter that neither the United States nor Palmerston's government would accept a peace negotiated by France, Russia, and Great Britain.[58] Furthermore, Palmerston had blocked a House of Commons resolution in favor of mediation in summer 1862. Russell, however, still believed in mediation, and that was perhaps what gave Gladstone the impetus to speak his mind in the Northeast. Moreover, the British cabinet was scheduled to meet on October 23, 1862, to discuss the American situation.

Both President Lincoln and U.S. Secretary of State William H. Seward, however, had a standing policy that mediation was a non-starter, and that if the British were to force it on the United States, the Union would declare war on Great Britain—with the understanding that Russia would enter into an alliance with the Lincoln government.[59] The October 23 cabinet meeting did not include Palmerston, so nothing was decided. Charles Francis Adams, Lincoln's envoy in London, would meet with Russell that day to discuss the matter. Adams told Russell that Gladstone's words would "have a bad effect on popular feeling in America" and was affecting public opinion against the North in Britain.[60] The American learned that the British position in fact had not changed: there would be no request for mediation. Russell also told Adams that Gladstone's Newcastle remarks had been misinterpreted.[61]

The bloodbath in Maryland reinforced Gladstone's belief that the U.S. Civil War had become a humanitarian crisis. No modern war had ever been this bloody, and Antietam remains the deadliest single-day battle in American history. Gladstone, who knew Palmerston's cabinet would be meeting on the subject of mediation in mid-October, did not interpret Antietam as a major defeat for the Confederates. He was probably right in this estimation, as it was at best a tactical victory for the Union, only because Lee took his troops back across the Potomac. In December and May, the Confederates would score significant victories over the Army of the Potomac in Virginia to the southwest of Washington. Gladstone also wanted to say something that would seem to be good news for the cotton-starved textile industry in Lancashire—although Newcastle-upon-Tyne, long a haven for abolitionist sentiment, hardly seemed the appropriate locale for his statement about the South being an independent nation

The Chancellor of the Exchequer also harbored hopes that the Democrats would make significant gains in the House of Representatives in the fall elections. The party did gain twenty-seven seats, but the Republicans maintained narrow control by forming a coalition with the Unionist Party. Speaker of the House Galusha A. Grow of Pennsylvania, however, was defeated in his quest for re-election and would be replaced by Indiana Republican Schuyler Colfax (even the seat representing Springfield, Illinois, went Democratic in 1862). With Russell cheering on the Democrats in the election, they did very well on the state level in fall 1862, winning back control of the legislatures in New York, Pennsylvania, Ohio, Indiana, and even Illinois.[62] Still, Lincoln and the Republicans had the upper hand in Congress, where the federal purse strings reside.

Behind the hullabaloo over Gladstone's Newcastle speech was the fact that the British had outlawed slavery three decades before. Ultimately, unless the South emancipated its slaves (there was some discussion of this by C.S.A. diplomats in Europe), the British people would be unhappy with recognition. In fact, the biggest error in Gladstone's thinking was that an independent Confederacy would be beneficial for the slave—who somehow would be treated better without the North coercing the South to accept emancipation. This is how he stated this case: "I can understand those who say—and it is my own opinion—that it is greatly for the interest of the negro race that they should have to do with their own masters alone, and not their own masters backed by the resources of the Federal power."[63]

In mid-October, Russell did write a memorandum endorsing Britain's intervention, toward the goal of helping to end the war.[64] Two days later, Sir George Cornewall Lewis, the Secretary of State for War, contradicted Gladstone's assertion that the Confederacy was a nation.[65] Lewis's word proved to be the final one by the Liberal Palmerston cabinet on this issue, and the leadership of the opposition Tories continued to hold that Britain should avoid entanglement in the American war.[66] The Tories did not want to irritate Lincoln and Seward and then see the United States declare war on Great Britain over its recognition of the Confederate States of America. That would put Canada in jeopardy.[67] At the same time, the Americans were beginning to get very irritated with Britain over its selling of war ships to the Confederacy. The New York Chamber of Commerce passed resolutions in October 1862 stating that the sinking of the American ship *Brilliant* by the British-constructed Confederate ship *Alabama* was a "crime against humanity."[68]

In November, France announced a mediation proposal, but neither Great Britain nor Russia went along with it.[69] Thus, the Confederacy received no recognition as a sovereign nation. Thirty-four years after the Newcastle speech Gladstone, described his comments about the Confederacy as an "unwarranted" indiscretion of "incredible grossness."[70] He added, in the third person, that he had made the statement "with no authority other than his own."[71] Three and a half decades earlier, the press of the North would not have objected to the characterization. The journals of the South only wished Gladstone and Russell had persuaded Palmerston to adopt mediation as national policy.

Notes

1 Roy Jenkins, *Gladstone: A Biography* (New York: Random House, 1995), 236.

2 "Mr. Gladstone at Newcastle," London *The Observer*, October 12, 1862.

3 Henry John Temple (Viscount Palmerston) letter to William E. Gladstone, September 24, 1862, quoted in John Morley, *The Life of William Ewart Gladstone* (New York: Macmillan, 1903), 70.

4 Morley, *The Life of William Ewart Gladstone*, 71.

5 Jenkins, *Gladstone: A Biography*, 238.

6 Morley, *The Life of William Ewart Gladstone*, 71.

7 Letter to the Duchess of Sutherland, November 1862, quoted in Morley, *The Life of William Ewart Gladstone*, 72.

8 Ibid.

9 Jenkins, *Gladstone: A Biography*, 237.

10 John Russell letter Gladstone, October 20, 1862, quoted in Morley, *The Life of William Ewart Gladstone*, 80.

11 "Mr. Gladstone at Newcastle," London *The Observer*, October 12, 1862.

12 "Summary of the News," Manchester (UK) *The Guardian*, December 6, 1862.

13 "The Late Meeting," Manchester (UK) *The Guardian*, December 20, 1862.

14 "Mr. Gladstone and America," London *The Globe*, quoted in the Bristol (UK) *Western Daily Press*, October 9, 1862.

15 "William Ewart Gladstone," Birmingham (UK) *Daily Post*, October 16, 1862.

16 "Recognition of Mediation," *The Economist*, quoted in the London *Morning Post*, October 20, 1862.

17 "Opinions of the London Press, Regarding Mr. Gladstone's Speech at Newcastle on America," Newcastle (UK) *Courant*, October 10, 1862.

18 "Mr. Gladstone on Jefferson Davis' Nation," Essex (UK) *Standard*, October 17, 1862.

19 Quoted in "Mr. Gladstone's Slip of the Tongue," Edinburgh (Scotland) *Evening Courant*, October 27, 1862.

20 "Mr. Gladstone at Newcastle," Durham County (UK) *Advertiser*, October 10, 1862.

21 "Mr. Gladstone at Newcastle," *South Bucks Free Press, Wycombe and Maidenhead Journal*, October 10, 1862.

22 "The American Civil War. Mediation. Opinions of the Press," Birmingham (UK) *Daily Gazette*, November 14, 1862.

23 "Mr. Gladstone and America," Moray (Scotland) *Elgin Courier*, October 17, 1862.

24 "Mr. Gladstone on America," Aberdeen (Scotland) *Press and Journal*, October 15, 1862.

25 "Mr. Gladstone at Newcastle," Dunfermline (Scotland) *Saturday Press*, October 11, 1862.

26 "Mr. Gladstone at Newcastle," Wexford (Ireland) *Constitution*, October 11, 1862.

27 "The Coming Session," Belfast (Ireland) *Daily News*, January 24, 1863.

28 "Mr. Gladstone on the Independence of the South," *Banner of Ulster* (Ireland), October 11, 1862.

29 "Mr. Gladstone in York," Dublin (Ireland) *Evening Post*, October 14, 1862.

30 "Mediation," Sligo (Ireland) *Champion*, October 11, 1862.

31 "Notwithstanding," Belfast (Ireland) *News-Letter*, November 13, 1862.

32 "Mr. Motley and Mr. Gladstone," Bedfordshire (UK) *Mercury*, January 5, 1863.

33 "Mr. Gladstone on Southern Nationality," New York *Times*, October 25, 1862.

34 "Later from Europe," Evansville (IN) *Daily Journal*, October 25, 1862.

35 "From Europe," Boston *Daily Advertiser*, October 25, 1862.

36 "Mr. Gladstone on American Affairs," Washington (DC) *Daily National Intelligencer*, October 27, 1862.

37 "Mr. Gladstone's Speech," Boston *Daily Advertiser*, November 4, 1862.

38 "Mr. Gladstone and England's Double Dealing," Philadelphia (PA) *North American and United States Gazette*, October 29, 1862.

39 "Mr. Gladstone's Speech," Biddeford (ME) *Union and Journal*, October 31, 1862.

40 "Mr. Gladstone Again," Boston *Investigator*, November 12, 1862.

41 "From England," Lowell (MA) *Daily Citizen and News*, November 13, 1862.

42 "Signs of Southern Recognition," San Francisco *Daily Evening Bulletin*, November 28, 1862.

43 "'Recognition in England,'" *Frank Leslie's Illustrated Newspaper*, November 8, 1862.

44 "Latest from Europe," Columbus (OH) *Daily Statesman*, November 9, 1862.

45 "Mr. Gladstone Defines His Position," New York *Herald*, December 20, 1862.

46 "Another Speech from Chancellor Gladstone," New York *Herald*, November 2, 1862.

47 "Mr. Gladstone's Speech," Richmond (VA) *Daily Dispatch*, November 3, 1862.

48 Ibid.

49 "The London Press on Mr. Gladstone's Speech," Memphis (TN) *Daily Appeal*, November 12, 1862.

50 "More Rumors of Recognition," Fayetteville (NC) *Observer*, November 3, 1862.

51 "The Intervention Question," Fayetteville (NC) *Observer*, November 17, 1862.

52 "The Probabilities of Recognition," Raleigh (NC) *Register*, November 5, 1862.

53 "The Very Latest from Europe," Camden (SC) *Confederate*, November 7, 1862.

54 "Mr. Gladstone on the American Struggle," *Times of London*, October 20, 1862.

55 "The Emancipation Proclamation," *The Economist*, quoted in the Lancaster (UK) *Gazette*, November 1, 1862.

56 "America," Liverpool (UK) *Daily Post*, October 9, 1862.

57 "The Right Hon. W. E. Gladstone and the Right Hon. Benjamin Disraeli," Library of Congress, accessed August 5, 2021, at <loc.gov/item/2003653728>.

58 Benjamin Disraeli letter to Lord Baron Lyndhurst, November 9, 1862.

59 Walter Stahr, *Seward: Lincoln's Indispensable Man* (New York: Simon & Schuster, 2012), 351.

60 "Mr. Gladstone's Speech," Edinburgh (Scotland) *The Scotsman*, December 23, 1862.

61 Amanda Foreman, *A World on Fire: An Epic History of Two Nations Divided* (London: Allen Lane, 2010), 323.

62 McPherson, *Antietam: The Battle That Changed the Course of the Civil War* (New York: Oxford University Press, 2002), 93.

63 "Mr. Gladstone at Newcastle," London *The Observer*, October 12, 1862.

64 Foreman, *A World on Fire*, 320.

65 Ibid.

66 Ibid, 321.

67 Stahr, *Seward: Lincoln's Indispensable Man*, 351.

68 "Complaint from Federal America against England," Leeds (UK) *Mercury*, October 30, 1862.

69 Stahr, *Seward: Lincoln's Indispensable Man*, 351.

70 Jenkins, *Gladstone: A Biography*, 239.

71 Morley, *The Life of William Ewart Gladstone*, 81.

14

Abraham Lincoln's Legacy Emergent

"Never before have the American people been so stricken. The ball that pierced the President has pierced the hearts of all of us." *Chicago Tribune*, April 15, 17, 1865.

As a tragic irony of history, the murder of Abraham Lincoln—the most widely covered story of the nineteenth century—secured his place as an enduring figure. Indeed, prior to the president's death, newspapers in the North and South, as well as in Europe, had cast aspersions on both his war policy and his character. With Lincoln's body at the White House on Easter Sunday 1865, *The New York Herald* suggested the press had played a role in the assassination—editorializing that it was "clear as day" that the "fiendish and malignant spirit developed and fostered by the rebel press North and South" had encouraged the event. "That press has, in the most devilish manner, urged men to the commission of this very deed."[1]

The president's body left Washington, D.C., the next week on a train draped in black. After traveling to Baltimore, Harrisburg, Philadelphia, and New York City, then to Albany, Utica, Syracuse, Buffalo, Cleveland, Columbus, Indianapolis, Chicago, and finally to Springfield, mourners laid Lincoln's body to rest at Oak Ridge Cemetery on May 4, 1865. In the time between his death and funeral newspapers, poured a torrent of eulogies on Lincoln—praising him in a manner that has remained unequalled in both quantity and quality. Newspaper readers, in the final weeks of April 1865, were spared the brutally partisan tone of the preceding years. Editors who had had savaged the president now blessed him with touching lines.

"Today every loyal heart must suffer the terrible shock, and swell with over-burdening grief at the calamity which has been permitted to befall us in the assassination of the Chief Magistrate," read *The New York World*—the same newspaper that had (wrongly) blasted him less than a year before for allegedly joking about the bloodshed at Antietam.[2] The war's end and Lincoln's refusal to seek retribution against his enemies moved the *World* to reassess its tone. Lincoln's death was a loss deeper than "if our first soldier had fallen by a hostile bullet."[3]

In the South, reactions were more complex, ranging from a horror deeper than that expressed in northern newspapers to rage comparable to that of secessionists before the war. The Richmond (VA) *Whig*, speaking for many war-weary Confederates, described the killing of Lincoln as "the heaviest blow" inflicted on the South, recognizing that the late president had intended to restore the Union on beneficent terms. However, deep-seated hatreds bubbled elsewhere, with the *Texas Republican* (Marshall) showing no interest in reconciliation, calling Booth an agent of God, and pronouncing his action a "thrill" for the ages.[4]

Many of the initial stories about the Lincoln assassination were based on official dispatches from Secretary of War Edwin Stanton. Because of the rapidly moving news cycle and the technological constraints of telegraphy, many initial "facts" about the assassination were incorrect.[5] An early account from *The New York Herald*, for example, reported that the Ford's Theatre shooting had occurred at 9:30 p.m. Friday; later reports confirmed the bullet was fired just after 10 p.m. Other reports suggested that John H. Surratt, Jr., had killed William H. Seward. In fact, Lewis Thornton Powell had attempted the assassination of the Secretary of State, and, while Seward was gravely injured, he would live to serve in President Johnson's cabinet.[6] Newspapers subsequently added details, with editors relying on War Department reports and correcting previous reportage as new information became available.

Southern newspapers generally received assassination-related news more slowly than did their Northern counterparts.[7] The Richmond (VA) *Whig* (no doubt because of its proximity to Washington) was the first Southern newspaper to announce the assassination in boldface type, in its April 17 edition. "The heaviest blow which has ever fallen upon the people of the south has descended! Abraham Lincoln, the President of the United States, has been assassinated," announced the *Whig* to readers, many of whom were still reeling from the surrender of native son Robert E. Lee. "The decease of the Chief Magistrate of a nation at any period is an event which profoundly affects the public mind," the *Whig* mourned, "but the time, manner and circumstances of President Lincoln's death render it the most momentous, most appalling, most deplorable calamity which has ever befallen the people of the United States."[8]

The New Orleans (LA) *Daily Picayune* described the assassination a "hellish deed." The New Orleans (LA) *Delta* did not publish news of the assassination until its April 20 edition, whereupon black borders framed the front-page text.[9] In addition to the Marshall, Texas, *Republican* called Booth an agent of God and his action a "thrill" for the ages.[10] The Galveston (TX) *News*, moreover, held that Lincoln had committed "innumerable crimes and sins," while the Chattanooga (TN) *Rebel* deemed the assassination divine retribution: "Abe has gone to answer before the bar of God for the innocent blood which he has permitted to be shed."[11]

Lincoln's Martyrdom in New York's *Times* and Chicago's *Tribune*

When, on the night of April 14, 1865, John Wilkes Booth fired a bullet into President Abraham Lincoln's head and killed him, many Americans began grieving with a sorrow as profound as that which had afflicted families who lost loved ones during the war.[12] *The New York Times*, which under the leadership of Henry J. Raymond had become the Republican newspaper of record, reported that the heart of the nation stirred like never before. "The news of the assassination of Abraham Lincoln carried with it a sensation of horror and of agony which no other event in our history has ever excited."[13] *The Chicago Tribune*—a newspaper that had effectively become Lincoln's hometown journal under the editorships of Joseph Medill and then Horace White—reinforced that sentiment. Some columns described the assassination as the worst crime since Jesus's crucifixion. "The nation mourns. Its agony is great," reported the *Tribune*. "Its grief is dumb. Never before have the American people been so stricken. The ball that pierced the President has pierced the hearts of all of us."[14]

In the following analysis, news items on the front pages of *The New York Times* and the *Chicago Tribune* were studied relative to other stories that did not contain assassination-related content in order to develop a perspective on the relative amount of assassination coverage. Stories that focused on Lincoln's death, his presidency, the assassination plot, the search for conspirators, details about John Wilkes Booth, and the fate of William H. Seward all formed the basis of analysis. Content not included in the analysis that was featured on the front page in varying degrees includes general news on local, state, national, and international levels, as well as advertisements for various products.

The proportion of Lincoln-related stories to non-Lincoln stories generally—as anticipated—peaked in the days following his assassination and for the most part waned in the later days of April. However, the tone of each day's news varied greatly. The hard news of his death would be replaced by themes of heroism, martyrdom, and a legacy that would long outlast Lincoln's tenure as president. An overview of the daily editions of these two papers from Saturday, April 15, to Saturday, April 29, shows the quantity and quality of articles about the president, and—more importantly—foretells how his legacy would emerge.

Henry Jarvis Raymond founded *The New York Times* on September 18, 1851, and thereafter formed an alliance with Senator William H. Seward, becoming New York Assembly speaker as a Whig, and later, as a leading supporter of the Republicans.[15] He acted as one of the chief spokespersons for the nation's business interests, using his political offices to protect them. He had written for *The New-Yorker* and *The New York Tribune*, newspapers published by Horace Greeley, who recognized a brilliance in Raymond from the outset of his career.[16]

The first issue of the *Times* sold for one cent, aiming for circulation levels as large as the *Tribune*'s. Unlike other penny press publications, the paper shunned sensationalism. "We do not mean to write as if we were in a passion," Raymond wrote, "unless that shall really be the case; and we shall make it a point to get into a passion as rarely as possible." In his first *Times* editorial, he wrote that "There are very few things in this world which it is worth while to get angry about," adding, "they are just the things that anger will not improve."[17]

Upon Lincoln's election to the presidency, Raymond called upon him to take precautionary measures. "The main the thing," Raymond wrote, was to have the new president say that the South misunderstood the Republican Party, and that a Republican administration alone "could correct the error" by taking a conciliatory tone. Lincoln's reply to Raymond expressed his common-sense approach to matters. His shrewd pragmatism was built on an uncommon trust in his countrymen to the south. "I have too much faith in the good sense & patriotism of the people of the South to apprehend any violent disruption on their part from the mere fear of future aggressions—while I have too much faith in their honor to expect them to submit to such aggression when actually committed."[18]

Lincoln was part of a new generation of politicians and editors to arise throughout the Midwest in the 1840s that included Illinois' Stephen A. Douglas—Lincoln's counterpart and rival and would remain so through their years competing for office—as well as Joseph Medill and Charles Henry Ray—editors of *The Chicago Tribune*. These mavericks challenged both the East's dominance over political affairs and the influence of New York's *Herald* and

Tribune over the perceptions of voters. While leading editors and politicians in the Northeast would vacillate through the 1850s in their support of western candidates (with *The New York Tribune*, for example, suggesting that a Douglas victory over Lincoln in the 1858 Senate campaign would benefit New York's Republicans), *The Chicago Tribune*, first published in 1847, relentlessly supported Lincoln before and during his presidency.[19]

Medill had met Lincoln in Decatur, Illinois, at an 1856 convention of editors who were opposed to the Kansas-Nebraska Act. Lincoln attended and gave a speech that impressed *Chicago Tribune* representatives in particular, and Medill subsequently was among the first to lend support to Lincoln's bid for the presidency in 1860. During the Civil War, Medill supported the administration, organizing the powerful and influential Union Defense Committee, which became a mainstay in Illinois and the Midwest. Medill took a keen interest in recruiting and enlisting volunteer regiments in Chicago, encouraging even the enlistment of *Tribune* employees. During the final two years of the war, Medill was for the first time editor-in-chief, and the *Tribune* supported the president administration on every occasion.[20]

As Lincoln's most consistent supporters throughout the Civil War, *The New York Times* and *The Chicago Tribune* served as organs representing the interests of the Republican Party, the Union, and more specifically, in developing Lincoln's legacy. While *The New York Times*—more than *The New York Herald* or even *The New York Tribune*—had steadfastly supported Lincoln and the Republicans in general, *The Chicago Tribune* had supported Lincoln throughout his entire political career—during his congressional term, his campaign for the Senate in 1858, and his presidency.[21]

The newspapers' front pages reveal that both the *Times* and *Tribune* covered post-assassination news almost continuously for a two-week period from Saturday, April 15, to Saturday, April 29. The first front page analyzed for both papers was April 15, the day after Lincoln was shot and while his fate was still unknown. Although the number of front-page stories varied in the days after the assassination, the share of front-page column space dedicated to the assassination in both cases averaged about 80 percent. Generally, the *Times* focused on information and factual descriptions, while the *Tribune* featured analyses that were more personal in nature, attributable to Lincoln's hometown connection with Chicago.

The first major and noticeable difference between the front pages of the newspapers can be seen in the *Times'* six news columns with little or no advertisements, whereas the *Tribune* always had nine columns with anywhere between one and four of them filled with ads. The *Tribune* typically had six columns of news, making the two papers comparable in the proportion of front-page space devoted to it. However, another difference between the two papers was the number of issues within the two-week period from April 15 to April 29: The *Times* published a Sunday issue, while the *Tribune* did not. At the outset of the assassination coverage, the first columns of both newspapers contained content almost entirely devoted to the deadly event. A week after the assassination—on Saturday, April 22—related coverage for the first time did not comprise the majority of content in the first column of page one. At that time assassination coverage started to shift from the first few columns of the issue to the middle and latter columns. However, overall coverage of the assassination on the front page remained high throughout this two-week period, not once dropping below 40 percent.

The Times

Overall, 65 percent of *The New York Times* Saturday, April 15, 1865, edition was devoted to the news from Ford's Theatre. Sunday, April 16, eight of the ten headlines in the first column were devoted to Lincoln's death. On Monday, April 17, details of the event began to be described in feature stories.[22] On Tuesday, April 18—the first day that the first two columns were completely absent of Lincoln stories—the *Times* resumed coverage in column three with a story noting sombrely that the mood across the city of New York was one of "great grief," with signs of it "apparent on every hand."[23] On April 19, the *Times* published accounts of the funeral ceremony held at the White House and printed the full sermon given by Reverend Phineas D. Gurley of the Presbyterian Church in Washington.[24]

Columns of the *Times* on Monday, April 24, were the only ones during the two-week period that contained no front-page stories about Lincoln's assassination, his funeral, or the pursuit of assassin Booth. On this day, all of the stories centered on details and updates related to the concluding Civil War. The first story, like many of the others, included an official dispatch from Secretary of War Edwin M. Stanton. However, the next day, April 25, 100 percent of the content of stories on the front page were about Lincoln's assassination and funeral. On April 26, every front-page headline and story were again about Lincoln. The first story that day—one of the longest on Lincoln during the period—spanned well into the fourth column and described the departure of the funeral train. This piece included one of the most chilling literary passages published in the *Times*, describing Lincoln's corpse as a "face dark to blackness, features sharp to a miracle, an expression almost horrible in its un-nature, a stiff, starched countenance resembling none they knew of and expressive of nothing familiar."[25]

The April 28 *Times* published reports of the death of John Wilkes Booth, with every story on the front page including details about his pursuit and death.[26] The first column began with nine headlines about the events of the previous night, and the first short story was a notice from Secretary of War Edwin M. Stanton. The second story contained details on Booth's capture. The first story in column three was a dispatch to the *Evening Post* of the pursuit and capture of Booth, followed by a similar story from the Associated Press with more details about Booth's apprehension.

By the end of April 1865, the phraseology of the *Times* reflected the national mood more appropriately than did past or continuing criticisms of the president. The *Times* wrote of "Washington, the Father; Lincoln, the Saviour of his country."[27] *The Chicago Tribune*, generally more expressive than the *Times*, sought revenge for the assassin's deeds. "None but a fiend incarnate could have been guilty of the great crime, and the sooner the assassin is swept from the face of the earth the more satisfactory will it be to the civilized world."[28]

An atypical—and often morbid—descriptiveness crept into the *Times* throughout the final week of April. "The gloom in the atmosphere accorded with the gloom in the hearts of our citizens," read an April 22 account of memorials. "It was a funeral day in every sense."[29] A front-page article on April 27 expressed "disgust" for Booth, a "dastardly wretch" who had committed a "diabolical deed."[30] An April 28 account of the assassin's death noted his final words, "Tell my mother that I died for my country."[31] In one of the final issues of the month, the *Times* on April 29 described the estimated 180 mourners per minute who came to pay their respect to the martyred president. "Their sad countenances attest stronger than words the heavy grief which affects all hearts."[32]

For the most part, the *Times* held to publisher and founder Henry Raymond's devotion to dispassionate news reportage, with two days during this period consisting of front-page news entirely focused on the assassination and only one day with none. The *Times* also suggested that Lincoln's legacy at home already had undergone a powerful transformation, with those who had doubted and blasted him at last appreciating his role in preserving the nation. "Abraham Lincoln came here untried, unpopular, and almost despised among Washington people," the *Times* reflected. "His body, as it goes forth from the gates of the city, is the recipient of an homage and devotion unexampled in the history of the nation."[33] At the same time, the president had shown a remarkable spirit of clemency that had vouchsafed for Americans "a victory greater than any they had on the field, namely, a victory over themselves," by which "they were truly able and worthy to hold the reins of self-government."[34]

The Tribune

The front pages of the *Tribune* during this period contained a range of 20 to 41 stories. Typically, the number that were assassination-related (in comparison to the total number of stories) did not correspond directly to the amount of coverage the assassination received, as assassination stories were generally longer than other stories. Some assassination-related stories, especially those detailing Lincoln's funeral cortege, took up significantly more than an entire column. Even toward the end of the two-week period, assassination-related stories typically consumed more column space than did other stories.

On Saturday, April 15, the Tribune first published news of Lincoln's assassination.[35] The front page consisted of nine columns, with five and a half dedicated to news and three and a half to ads. Less than two columns worth of news were assassination-related, and, other than a short announcement of the news at the top of column one, all assassination stories were in the final two news columns. The tone of the initial stories focused much more on the emotional impact of Lincoln's death than on the factual accounts surrounding it. "The Spectacle is sickening. The human heart revolting from it with disgust loses faith in humanity, and sinking back like a child into the arms of its parent, we cry unto the God of the bereaved," read the contents of a front-page column.[36] "Not even within our nation's history has excited so deep and heartfelt emotions of sorrow," read another. "None but a fiend incarnate could have been guilty of the great crime, and the sooner the assassin is swept from the face of the earth the more satisfactory will it be to the civilized world."[37]

In Chicago, news of the assassination had reached the *Tribune* as it was going to press, but the information available was published regardless as "too fearful, the blow has fallen too suddenly almost to comprehend."[38] In every daily issue of the *Tribune* during this period, at least half the content on each front page was devoted to coverage of Lincoln's death; in the days immediately following the assassination, nearly every bit of front-page space was devoted to such coverage. Every issue throughout the end of April had stories about Lincoln in the first column, and each front page contained a range of twenty to forty stories about him.

As details of the assassination plot reached news offices, stories turned to the perpetrator. The *Tribune* reported on April 18 that an ad in the *Selma Dispatch* (AL) might link the Confederacy directly to the plot, as it offered an award of $1 million to anyone who would take the lives of President Lincoln, Vice President Andrew Johnson, and Secretary William H. Seward.[39] Days later, the *Tribune* noted efforts in Chicago to collect funds for an entirely different cause. "A movement has been started here to raise $100,000 by one dollar subscriptions, to be presented to Mrs. Lincoln as a token of respect and veneration felt by the people for their departed President."[40] Lincoln's home-state editors at the *Tribune* reminded both readers and reporters of Illinois' special link with the slain president. "The press is now respectfully requested to be present and attend the funeral of the late Chief Magistrate of the nation in this city."[41] Indeed, editors throughout Illinois made extraordinary efforts to remember the president. Edward Lewis Baker, publisher of the *Illinois State Journal*, arranged to host reporters from around the country and internationally in the rooms of the U.S. District Court at Springfield. The *Tribune* posted bulletins emphasizing that rooms would be fitted in style for visiting members of the press. Editors and reporters from parts of the United States and Canada who visited Springfield during the funeral ceremonies were invited to report to the offices of the *State Journal* or *State Register* for accommodations.[42]

The April 22 front page contained the least amount of assassination coverage during the period. The majority of the content was descriptive pieces on Lincoln's funeral, which comprised about 75 percent of assassination-related coverage. It was also the first issue after the assassination in which ads occupied more than three columns. On Wednesday, April 26, the *Tribune* reported that E. L. Baker, editor of the *Illinois Daily State Journal*, had helped secure rooms for members of the press to use while covering Lincoln funeral ceremonies. The event required direct involvement from the press, as attendance and participation in the processional, according to the *Tribune*, had "surpassed anything known."[43]

The *Tribune*'s coverage of the assassination on its front page in the two weeks following the event generally focused on the life of Abraham Lincoln, and secondarily on the fates of Secretary of State William Seward and assassin John Wilkes Booth. The amount of space devoted to assassination content averaged about half (50 percent) of front-page columns during this two-week period, after an initial spike to as high as 90 percent during the first two days. Placement of the coverage shifted over the two-week period (from the first columns to columns on the right side of the page), but there was not one issue that did not at least mention the assassination in the first column. The front page of the April 28 *Tribune* was the first since Lincoln's assassination in which his death did not receive the majority of coverage. Due to Booth's capture and death, the assassin received the most coverage in this issue.

Initial accounts in both the *Times* and *Tribune* expressed shock and disbelief over the events, and included descriptions of the scene at Lincoln's deathbed. In the first few days after the assassination—April 15 to April 20—the first column in both newspapers was almost entirely assassination coverage. Starting on April 22, such coverage no longer dominated the first columns, but rather the middle and later ones. Reports in both the *Times* and *Tribune* in the days after Lincoln's death were generally solemn and reflective, with the majority focusing on events that preceded Lincoln's funeral and the effects of his death on the nation. There were anecdotes of grief or literary descriptions of mood. Newspapers resonated with the same sentiments of loss and grief expressed in the *Times* and *Tribune*, but these two newspapers served as prototypical sources for readers following events both at home and abroad. Editors formerly opposed to each other in their positions on the Lincoln administration put aside differences and united in agreement that the events of late April had changed their opinions about the president, as they had those of their readers.[44]

The President Abroad

Within a week after Lincoln's death, the *New York Times* had extended its attention overseas. "No single event of the present century in America can at all compare with it in effect on the popular mind, and we think that in England the shock will be nearly as deeply felt," noted an April 19 article. Another piece anticipated changed perceptions of Lincoln abroad. While some foreign newspapers—particularly in Great Britain—had savaged Lincoln, characterizing him as a buffoon or backwoods rube, it was clear that much of the criticism would now temper.

"His simplicity of character, his straightforward honesty, his kindliness, even his bluntness of manner," the *Times* noted, "seem to have won the popular heart, even among a foreign, and in matter of opinion, a hostile nation."[45] The *Times* also published a Lincoln tribute from Canada, reprinting a speech by T. D'Arcy McGee from *The Montreal Herald* in which the Canadian nationalist had praised Lincoln's "spirit of clemency and moderation." The late president's spirit of conciliation, McGee had said, was a virtue "uncommon, almost unexampled, in time of Civil War"—one whose "sweet savor must have ascended before him to the judgment seat to which he was suddenly summoned."[46]

By the end of April, reactions overseas to Lincoln's death were widely reaching American readers. In London, Americans learned, the *Morning Star* had expressed regret that the British had not appreciated Lincoln's role as a leader until his death, and had in fact ridiculed him.[47] The Parisian *Le Constitutionnel*, which had supported each side during the course of the Civil War, now wrote that the French people felt "sorrow and indignation" at Lincoln's assassination: "All differences of political opinion vanish before assassination, and all honorable people, however they may be divided upon the questions of the day, feel the same horror. The death of Mr. Lincoln is a cause of mourning for all civilization."[48] Elsewhere in France, the *Epoque* noted that Lincoln had tragically paid for victory "with his blood," but added that he would be "admired and recorded in history as the restorer of the Union, and will be likened to that great man [George Washington] by whom it was founded."[49]

The assassination was a turning point, as suspicion toward the United States began to take shape in Canada. According to the *Hamilton Spectator* editors, Canadians who were interested in the restoration of peace could not but "deeply sympathise with the Americans in the hour of their great calamity."[50] However, Canadians worried about the United States as a major military power without its victorious and moderate president. Canada would have to build its defenses to prevent the Americans from launching a war of aggression. While no attack was imminent, the newspaper noted, Canada must "be able to rely on its own strength" to deter an American power grab.[51]

From London came one of the most poignant verses about Lincoln. The *London Star* recognized the role of the press not only in covering Lincoln's presidency, but also in what would be his legacy. The press, it reflected—as had James Gordon Bennett's *New York Herald*—bore responsibility for honoring the president in ways it had failed to do before his calamitous death. "History will proclaim, to the eternal humiliation of our country, how an influential section of the British press out bade the journalists of the South in their slander and invective against the great man," the *Star* intoned. "[H]is every action was twisted and tortured into a wrong, his every noble aspiration spoken of as a desire for blood, his personal appearance caricatured, his lowly origin made the theme for scorn by men as base-born as he, but without the nobleness of soul which made Lincoln a prince among princes."[52]

As the country mourned in the days and weeks after his death, editors—and, later, historians—grappled with the larger question of Lincoln's legacy. He had brought the young nation to a new union not realized by its founders. Lincoln's Emancipation Proclamation had re-revolutionized American notions of equality, promising that the nation would more closely reflect Thomas Jefferson's declaration of the "self-evident" truth "that all men are created equal." As history would show, Lincoln not only cast a long shadow over America's subsequent struggle with equality during the next century, but over the struggles of other nations as well.

While in general the kinds of works published about Lincoln by historians over the years since his death have ranged from respectful to revisionist and critical, a surge of studies in "new history" have placed historical characters and events into an international perspective. Michael Knox Beran's *Forge of Empires* (2007) reinterprets Lincoln by juxtaposing his role with those of nationalist leaders in Germany and Russia. "Lincoln called his revolution a 'new birth of freedom.' Bismarck spoke of a revolution accomplished through an expenditure of 'blood and iron.' Alexander implemented what he described as a revolution 'from above,'" Beran wrote. "Their revolutions were made in the name of freedom, and were to varying extents consecrated to the freer movement of people, goods, and ideas."[53] Beran's angle is compelling in a contemporary sense—and worth considering in writing a biography of any nineteenth century figure—because it rightfully places Lincoln in a global context. While Lincoln's international appeal reached its height during the last third of the nineteenth century and the early decades of the next, he enjoyed further phases of visibility during the Cold War and in recent years.

Recent scholarship from Richard Carwardine and Jay Sexton in *The Global Lincoln* (2011) also makes the case that "admiration of Lincoln was not confined to the English-speaking world."[54] Lincoln's post-death popularity has been highest in countries that underwent development and economic growth, with his life serving as an example of how the interests of an individual, self-improving laborer could contribute directly to the development and modernization of a national economy. This view of Lincoln, the authors note, was championed in nations such as Argentina and Japan in the early twentieth century, where Lincoln's example served as reassurance that economic modernization would benefit both the individual and larger policy. Elsewhere, Lincoln as "The Great Emancipator" resonated as a model for abolishing slavery. In Russia, involuntary servitude was banned primarily because it was the most convenient way to keep an antiquated social and political system from collapsing, and in Spain the anti-slavery movement helped modernize national infrastructure.[55]

Even today, Lincoln remains the personification of "America" for people throughout the world. Indian society in particular, UCLA historian Vinay Lal writes, continues to look to Lincoln as the Great Emancipator, being inspired by the man who overcame obstacles to reach the pinnacle of success. His popularity in India is not necessarily attributable to widespread circulation of his story; rather, his commonality among people makes him appealing. Indians prevalently view Lincoln as a pragmatic and incorruptible leader, steadfast in his resolve—and a martyr, much like Gandhi, to the causes of liberty and human dignity.[56]

The years surrounding sesquicentennials of a number of events during Lincoln's administration afforded scholars opportunities to reexamine some of his most famous decisions. While books published by academic and commercial presses varied in their attention to the press as a primary source, most included newspapers stories to detail the president's activities. One such recent account, *Lincoln Mediated: The President and the Press through Nineteenth Century Media*, describes the president as the both the producer and product of various nineteenth-century media. Authors Gregory Borchard and David Bulla suggest that much of what can be known about Lincoln has remained the same since 1865, so an accurate understanding of Lincoln's legacy requires contemporary readers to see him from outside their current contexts—"stepping outside modern times to see history as it truly was."[57] Revisiting primary sources—including *The New York Times* and *Chicago Tribune*—is part of this process.

The Legacy Today

The years surrounding the sesquicentennial of Lincoln's presidency afforded scholars an opportunity to revisit some of his most famous decisions—the Emancipation Proclamation 0f 1862 among them. While books published by academic and commercial presses varied in their attention to the press as a primary source, most included newspapers stories to detail the president's activities.

Since the 1960s, many books and articles have emphasized Lincoln's role in changing the national understanding of race and civil rights. Among them, Brian R. Dirck's *Abraham Lincoln and White America* (2012) explores Lincoln's personal, professional, and political understanding of race. Dirck's analysis examines the extent to which race was present in politics and written material, and the extent to which Lincoln walked a fine line between anti-slavery and abolitionist endorsements. Such strategy was present even in the publications Lincoln chose to read. Dirck's discussion of Lincoln's relationship with race commences at the time when Lincoln was a young student and reader of *The Kentucky Preceptor*, a provocative book that was the subject of student debates. The *Preceptor* often posited questions of moral equity in regard to subjugation of minority populations such as Native Americans and African Americans. "He likely read a poem by Englishman William Cowper (in a literary compilation called *The English Reader*, which he saw while a boy in Indiana), criticizing the British Empire's complicity in the slave system."[58] Dirck also notes Lincoln's proclivity as a young lawyer to read *Commentaries on the Laws of England* by Sir William Blackstone. Although the text was essentially nonracial, Lincoln's reading of Blackstone may have reinforced his general detestation of slavery as a system; so too may have Blackstone's emphasis on the supremacy of "natural law" over any man-made law, "such as that which created slavery."[59]

Part of a remarkable multi-volume series published by Southern Illinois University Press, "The Concise Lincoln Library," Richard Striner's *Lincoln and Race* (2012) examines Lincoln's ideas on race throughout his political career. Striner references various primary sources describing the dissemination of white-supremacist propaganda before the 1864 election. Since 2011, a dozen "Concise Lincoln Library" books have been published, with more planned. The series represents one of the various angles scholars have taken to personify complex social and historical subjects through the personhood of Abraham Lincoln.[60]

Another increasingly common focus among historians and biographers has been to analyze Lincoln's political development relative to his legal career. Guy G. Fraker's *Lincoln's Ladder to the Presidency* (2012) does exactly this, examining Lincoln's career as an attorney and his progression into politics. Fraker provides significant detail on Lincoln's legal history, as well as his involvement with the press. He meticulously traces Lincoln's story as a lawyer. Melding that career with his political life, Lincoln made sure to align himself with the right individuals: those responsible for the printed word. Lincoln received unwavering political support from Simeon and Josiah Francis, founders and editors of the *Sangamo Journal* (later, the *Illinois State Journal*), the first newspaper in Springfield, Illinois.[61] Having allied himself with key figures in the legal and political community, Lincoln's ties to the press made him a semi-celebrity long before his presidency and martyrdom at the hands of John Wilkes Booth.[62]

Recent works have also tended to focus on the people, personalities, and characters who associated themselves with Lincoln—an increasingly common form of creating a biography—based on the traits he shared with his contemporaries. Robert S. Eckley's *Lincoln's Forgotten Friend, Leonard Swett* (2012) documents Leonard Swett's accomplishments as a writer, attorney, and politician, primarily during Lincoln's tenure in the White House. Eckley describes Swett's relationship with Lincoln as an emergent attorney, a writer, and a biographer. Swett was part of a group of aspiring memoir writers with close contacts to Lincoln who shared and debated their experiences with Lincoln from differing vantage points.[63] Indeed, just as Swett mentored Lincoln, Lincoln entrusted Swett with confidential and sensitive information, such as the initial draft of the Emancipation Proclamation in August 1862.[64]

Similar to Eckley's work on Swett, Russell Freedman's *Abraham Lincoln and Frederick Douglass: The Story Behind an American Friendship* (2012) is a dual biography of Abraham Lincoln and Frederick Douglass—noting in particular the times their lives intersected. Freedman notes Lincoln's and Douglass's shared interest in *The Columbian Orator*, a publication that contained "speeches and dialogues about freedom, democracy, and courage."[65] The author describes the impact such a publication may have had on those who came of age during an era of extreme prejudice. Lincoln discovered the publication, which Douglass first secretly read in Baltimore at age 12. Like Douglass, Lincoln found the book to be a wonderful self-help manual for rhetoric.[66]

While biographies of Mary Lincoln have been written, her role in Lincoln's life—indeed as a singularly important historical character—has also reemerged as a subject for inquiry in recent years. Frank J. Williams and Michael Burkhimer's *The Mary Lincoln Enigma: Historians on America's Most Controversial First Lady* (2012) provides thorough descriptions of her as a political figure and wife, featuring contributions from leading historians. Williams and Burkhimer provide evidence that the press vacillated in its coverage of Mrs. Lincoln's political activities, especially with regard to her impact on the president. The volume provides accounts of Mary and Abraham's interaction with the press and Mary's role as Lincoln's political partner and supporter.[67] Lincoln aficionado Harold Holzer—who has in his own right published perhaps more recent works than any other scholar of the Sixteenth President—contributes a chapter to the book, paying particular attention to Mary's image as depicted graphically. While she remained supportive of her husband, she never allowed any photographs—public or private—to be taken of the two together.

Two treatments of Lincoln's relationship with the military—Chester G. Hearn's *Lincoln and McClellan at War* (2012) and David Alan Johnson's *Decided on the Battle Field: Grant, Sherman, Lincoln and the Election of 1864* (2012)—explore another angle historians have used to understand the president. Hearn details the political battle between Lincoln and McClellan during the 1864 presidential election and Lincoln's experiences as Commander in Chief. Hearn's account centers on Lincoln's tactical strategies during the war and political maneuverings during the election, with secondary attention on press issues during the campaign. In this regard, Hearn provides an account of a war between press editors and politicians, as opposed to armies.

Secretary of War Edwin Stanton exemplified this in his efforts to obtain support from the widely circulated *New York Herald.*[68] Including materials from *The New York Times, New York World, Chicago Tribune, Cincinnati Daily Commercial, Richmond Press, Harper's Weekly,* and *Philadelphia Press,* David Johnson's *Decided on the Battle Field* (2012) covers nearly the entire span of the Civil War. The focus of Johnson's analysis is Lincoln's efforts to secure presidential tenure over George B. McClellan during the 1864 election. Johnson notes opposing sides *The New York World* and *The New York Times* took throughout the war.[69] But when General Sherman captured Atlanta, the Northern press in general lined up to support Lincoln for a second term, with *The New York Herald* emphasizing the victory as part of the "Great National Contest" that had ensured Lincoln's reelection.[70]

Truly a sesquicentennial book, David Von Drehle's *Rise to Greatness: Abraham Lincoln and America's Most Perilous Year* (2012) details the political and military struggles of the Lincoln administration during 1862, the most perilous and precarious year of the Civil War. A chapter is devoted to each month in successive order. Von Drehle's portrait of Lincoln is detailed indeed, and highlights his relations with various press editors, such as James Gordon Bennett of *The New York Herald,* Horace Greeley of *The New York Tribune,* and Henry Raymond of *The New York Times.*[71] Greeley, of the New York editors, was the most vocal in both praise and criticism of Lincoln. Von Drehle notes this in his description of Lincoln's timing of the Emancipation Proclamation. Responding to Greeley's call in August 1862 to make abolition a primary goal of the war, Lincoln waited until the tenuous victory at Antietam to announce his plans to free slaves in Rebel territories. An account of this exchange can also be found in Gregory Borchard's *Abraham Lincoln and Horace Greeley* (2011), another book in Southern Illinois University Press's "Concise Lincoln Library."[72]

Similar to 2012, 2013 marked another sesquicentennial in scholarship about Abraham Lincoln and the Civil War, with the 1863 Battle of Gettysburg and the Gettysburg Address in particular eliciting revisited attention. Two books provide a meta-historical understanding of the event, using contemporary sources to help understand Lincoln's link to Gettysburg. Martin P. Johnson's *Writing the Gettysburg Address* (2013) is a media-centric account that focuses on how Lincoln prepared the speech, as well as the process through which the press covered it. Johnson compares the editorial positions of *Harper's Weekly, The New York Tribune, The New York Times,* and the *Baltimore Daily Gazette,* among others. Contemporary reception of Lincoln's address—contrary to our modern appreciation for it—was not uniformly positive. In fact, a number of newspapers found the speech unremarkable. (The *Chicago Times*, for example, described it as "silly, flat, and dishwatery.") While the *Cincinnati Daily Gazette* described Lincoln's presence as less than graceful, it praised his "modest, unpretending style."[73] Likewise, the *Philadelphia Age*—the only opposition paper in the city admitted to the proceedings—described the speech as the best Lincoln had made, while the unfriendly *New York World* noted only that Lincoln's speech was brief but at the same time "calculated to arouse deep feeling."[74] Through these sources, Martin contextualizes Lincoln's journey in constructing a speech for the ages.

Jared Peatman's *The Long Shadow of Lincoln's Gettysburg Address* (2013) also highlights nineteenth-century media sources, attempting to uncover the purpose of Lincoln's message not only through his words, but also through those of other speakers at the event.[75] Peatman pays particular attention to the ways in which the Gettysburg Address has morphed in the understanding of subsequent generations. In the first two decades of the twentieth century, for example, the speech was popularly understood as an attempt to build reunification after an era of discord among sections.[76] During World War I and World War II, Peatman suggests, the speech at Gettysburg was oftentimes cited as a calling to build a nation with a greater purpose.[77] Peatman's analysis avoids a tendency of present-minded secondary literature to attribute to Lincoln civil rights developments that occurred only after the Civil War.

While much new scholarship has looked at Lincoln in a global context, a similar approach has examined him relative to specific geographical areas. Among authors publishing in 2013 and typifying this angle, Kenneth Winkle and Robert E. May, for example, reexamine Lincoln's ties throughout the United States and in specific international areas. Winkle's *Lincoln's Citadel: The Civil War in Washington, DC* (2013) looks at Lincoln in an immediate context, focusing on his doings in the nation's capital. Winkle describes Washington as a refuge for many during the war, providing food, shelter, and medical care for those who had escaped slavery. The story that emerges describes Lincoln's efforts to turn the city into a bastion for the Union, a symbol of the nation, and a beacon for freedom.[78] May's *Slavery, Race, and Conquest in the Tropics: Lincoln, Douglas, and the Future of Latin America* (2013) carries Lincoln's vision well beyond the confines of the capital, beginning with his opposition to the Mexican-American War as a member of Congress in 1847. First as a Whig and later as a Republican, Lincoln sought to prevent slavery from extending into the territories and into areas outside the U.S. border. As part of a life-long debate with rival Stephen A. Douglas, Lincoln internationalized the showdown over slavery, putting Cuba, Mexico, and Central America into a discussion about the practice of the institution in the

Western Hemisphere. At the same time, by the end of his first year as president, he had increasingly entertained the possibility of colonizing African Americans as a way to rid the United States of slavery.[79]

Chris DeRose's *Congressman Lincoln: The Making of America's Greatest President* (2013) revisits Lincoln's days as a member of the Thirtieth Congress. Lincoln had been elected to the U.S. House in 1846 as an Illinois Whig Representative with the support of the *Sangamon Journal*, which described him as "one of the strongest men of our state—possessing a well-disciplined, clear and comprehensive mind—a mind able to grasp any subject within the range of the statesman."[80] Lincoln fought for his beliefs even when they cost him. His opposition to the Mexican-American War more or less cost him another term as a legislator, as Democratic newspapers made a sport of questioning his patriotism, and the charges resonated with returning veterans in Lincoln's constituency. The Illinois *State Register* said Lincoln had deceived voters, who, it claimed, were caught by surprise at his opposition to the war.[81] Regardless, Lincoln used his first experiences in Washington, D.C., to build resilience that helped him through the nation's trials and eventually secured his spot in history as—in DeRose's estimation—our "greatest" president.

Lincoln Tomorrow

A famous portrait of President Abraham Lincoln, traditionally considered the last photo of him, encapsulates the evolving understanding of the ways in which media capture both a moment in time and our interpretation of events from current perspectives. On February 5, 1865, Lincoln visited Alexander Gardner's Washington studio for a portrait session. One of the reasons the photo holds such compelling symbolic value relates to Lincoln's own premonitions about his presidency. He had confided to a number of associates, including journalist Noah Brooks, the details of a haunting dream.

With Lincoln's reelection having occurred just months before this particular photography session, Gardner began the February 5, 1865, photo shoot with several multiple-lens pictures of the president. He moved his camera closer for the final studio portrait. For whatever reason—mechanical or accidental—the glass plate cracked. After making a single print of the image, the negative broke completely and Gardner threw it away.[82]

"It was just after my election in 1860," Lincoln told Brooks. "I was well tired out, and went home to rest, throwing myself down on a lounge in my chamber."

Opposite where I lay was a bureau, with a swinging-glass upon it … and, looking in that glass, I saw myself reflected, nearly at full length; but my face, I noticed, had two separate and distinct images, the tip of the nose of one being about three inches from the tip of the other. I was a little bothered, perhaps startled, and got up and looked in the glass, but the illusion vanished. On lying down again, I saw it a second time—plainer, if possible, than before; and then I noticed that one of the faces was a little paler, say five shades, than the other. I got up and the thing melted away, and I went off and, in the excitement of the hour, forgot all about it-nearly, but not quite, for the thing would once in a while come up, and give me a little pang, as though something uncomfortable had happened. When I went home I told my wife about it, and a few days after I tried the experiment again … sure enough, the thing came again; but I never succeeded in bringing the ghost back after that, though I once tried very industriously to show it to my wife, who was worried about it somewhat. She thought it was 'a sign' that I was to be elected to a second term of office, and that the paleness of one of the faces was an omen that I should not see life through the last term.[83]

Image 14.1 "Abraham Lincoln, Head-and-Shoulders Portrait, Traditionally Called 'Last Photograph of Lincoln from Life.'" Alexander Gardner, photographer, February 5, 1865.[84]

The stress from years of war is evident in Lincoln's features. He even appears ill, an observation confirmed by Harriet Beecher Stowe, who, having visited Lincoln at about this time, suggested he would feel relief at the pending conclusion of the war. "No, Mrs. Stowe," Lincoln replied. "I shall never live to see peace; this War is killing me." Stowe said Lincoln shared his sense that he would not live much longer and that, when the war was over, he would collapse.[85] Lincoln's friend Ward Hill Lamon, Marshal of the District of Columbia, also sensed the president's dread. Having discussed with Lincoln the latter's dream about the double image, Lamon said Lincoln believed the "ghostly" image foretold impending death.[86]

Before destroying the negative, Gardner produced only one print, which today resides in the National Portrait Gallery. In the surviving image, Lincoln smiles gently as one of his eyes fixes on the horizon beyond the studio; half of his face is unfocused. Historians and historiographers since have assigned various symbolic meanings to the crack in the image. According to one interpretation, the crack may foretell Lincoln's assassination (the bullet traced a similar line through his head). The crack also may represent a divided nation. When collector Frederick Hill Meserve acquired the cracked-glass portrait from Gardner's friend Truman H. Bartlett in 1913, he did so with the understanding that it was the last picture of Lincoln ever taken.[87] Previous histories had dated Gardner's traditionally known "last photograph" to April 10, 1865, but recent research supports the earlier February date. While modern historians have proved Meserve wrong, the myth behind this photo persists, sustained by the power of Gardner's candid image.

This chapter has tapped into a surge of attention to not only Lincoln himself, but also to Lincoln as a media figure and even a character in popular culture. What we know about Lincoln today has not changed over the course of time, but it is being taught in different ways. If generations of Americans are truly to know how to interpret Lincoln's prestige and memory correctly, they will need to view him from outside of their current contexts, stepping away from modern times and seeing history as it truly was. The proposition is not entirely abstract, as Lincoln's memory is preserved chiefly through texts that function both to teach us about the past and to enable us to live within it. These texts can serve as commemorative symbols and the means by which the past becomes part of our everyday life—learned and relearned in the mind of the living. Among these symbols, images from the era may have the most lasting communicative powers to understand the lives of Lincoln and his contemporaries.

The story that emerged from the shooting on Good Friday 1865 was transformative in its impact on newspaper readers, as the majority of their daily information came from print. The event also marked a rare convergence of history, technology, and journalistic innovation, as the Civil War had established patterns for reporting by large numbers of independent writers covering the same story. With the increasing sophistication of telegraphic transmissions, newspapers could update their editions with information from the best bulletins as they arrived, providing content for extra editions that were published in rapid succession for days and weeks after the event.[88]

Lincoln may forever be known as one of the most highly regarded presidents in U.S. history; however, unless Lincoln's stories are told differently, the true man will never be known. Another way in which this new dimension may be explored is in global perspective—how the people of other nations view and have viewed Lincoln. This narrative is a process that historians have just begun to explore.

Notes

1 New York *Herald*, April 16, 1865.
2 New York *World*, June 20, 1864.
3 Ibid, April 17, 1865.
4 Richmond (VA) *Whig*, April 19, 1865; Marshall (TX) *Texas Republican*, April 28, 1865, in Harper, *Lincoln and the Press*, 352–60.
5 Borchard and Bulla, *Lincoln Mediated*, 171, 172.
6 Donald and Holzer, *Lincoln in the* Times, 240–88; Michael W. Kauffman, *American Brutus: John Wilkes Booth and the Lincoln Conspiracies* (New York: Random House, 2004), 20–58.
7 Borchard and Bulla, *Lincoln Mediated*, 173.
8 "Abraham Lincoln Assassination," Richmond (VA) *Whig*, April 17, 1865.
9 New Orleans *Daily Picayune*, April 20, 1865; Cronin, "Fiend, Coward, Monster, or King: Southern Press Views of Abraham Lincoln," *American Journalism*, 26, 4 (Fall 2009): 52.
10 Marshall (TX) *Texas Republican*, April 28, 1865.
11 Galveston (TX) *News*, April 28, 1865; Chattanooga (TN) *Rebel*, April 20, 1865.
12 Borchard and Bulla, *Lincoln Mediated*, 170-79.
13 New York *Times*, April 15, 16, 1865.
14 Chicago *Tribune*, April 15, 17, 1865.
15 Maverick, *Henry J. Raymond and the New York Press*, 88, 89; Borchard, *The Firm of Greeley, Weed, and Seward*, 106-8.
16 Greeley, *Recollections of a Busy Life*, 138.
17 New York *Times*, September 18, 1851.

18 Raymond to Lincoln, November 14, 1860, *Lincoln Papers*, accessed July 1, 2021, at <loc.gov/item/mal0449700>.

19 Borchard and Bulla, *Lincoln Mediated*, 6, 7.

20 Chicago *Tribune*, March 22, 1899.

21 Borchard and Bulla, *Lincoln Mediated*, 175.

22 New York *Times*, April 17, 1865.

23 Ibid, April 18, 1865.

24 New York *Times*, April 19, 1865; "The New York *Times*: The Obsequies," in Holzer, *President Lincoln Assassinated!!: The Firsthand Story of the Murder, Manhunt, Trial and Mourning*, Google Books version (New York: Library of America, 2014), 360.

25 New York *Times*, April 26, 1865.

26 Ibid, April 28, 1865.

27 Ibid, April 25, 1865.

28 Chicago *Tribune*, April 17, 1865.

29 New York *Times*, April 22, 1865.

30 Ibid, April 27, 1865.

31 Ibid, April 28, 1865.

32 Ibid, April 29, 1865.

33 Ibid, April 22, 1865.

34 Ibid, April 20, 1865.

35 Chicago *Tribune*, April 15, 1865.

36 Ibid, April 15, 1865.

37 Ibid.

38 Ibid.

39 Ibid, April 18, 1865.

40 Ibid, April 22, 1865.

41 Ibid, April 24, 1865.

42 Ibid, April 26, 1865.

43 Ibid.

44 Holzer, *Lincoln and the Power of the Press: The War for Public Opinion* (New York: Simon and Schuster, 2014), 554.

45 Ibid, April 19, 1865.

46 Ibid, April 23, 1865.

47 London *Morning Star*, April 27, 1865; London *Daily News*, April 27, 1865; *The Assassination of Abraham Lincoln*, (Washington, DC: Government Printing Office, 1866), 1–717; Harper, *Lincoln and the Press*, 360–62.

48 *Constitutionnel*, April 29, 1865, in *The Assassination of Abraham Lincoln*, 113–15.

49 *Epoque*, April 28, 1865, in *The Assassination of Abraham Lincoln*, 113–15.

50 "Death of the President," Hamilton (ON) *Weekly Spectator*, April 26, 1865.

51 "Defence of Canada," Hamilton (ON) *Weekly Spectator*, April 12, 1865.

52 London *Star*, May 2, 1865.

53 Michael Knox Beran, *Forge of Empires* (New York: Free Press, 2007), 7.

54 Richard Carwardine, and Jay Sexton, *The Global Lincoln* (Oxford and New York: Oxford University Press, 2011), 5, 7.

55 Ibid, *The Global Lincoln*, 9, 10.

56 Vinay Lal, "Defining a Legacy: Lincoln in the National Imaginary of India," in *The Global Lincoln*, Richard Carwardine and Jay Sexton, eds. (Oxford and New York: Oxford University Press, 2011), 172, 174, 175.

57 Borchard and Bulla, *Lincoln Mediated*, 184.

58 Brian R. Dirck, *Abraham Lincoln and White America* (Lawrence, KS: University Press of Kansas, 2012), 19.

59 Ibid, *Abraham Lincoln and White America*, 50.

60 Richard Striner, *Lincoln and Race*, Carbondale, IL: Southern Illinois University Press, 2012.

61 Guy G. Fraker, *Lincoln's Ladder to the Presidency* (Carbondale, IL: Southern Illinois University Press, 2012), 17.

62 Ibid, *Lincoln's Ladder to the Presidency*, 257, 258.

63 Robert S. Eckley, *Lincoln's Forgotten Friend, Leonard Swett* (Carbondale, IL: Southern Illinois University Press, 2012), 3.

64 Eckley, *Lincoln's Forgotten Friend, Leonard Swett*, 110.

65 Russell Freedman, *Abraham Lincoln and Frederick Douglass: The Story Behind an American Friendship* (New York: Clarion Books, 2012), 9.

66 Ibid, *Abraham Lincoln and Frederick Douglas*, 38.

67 Frank J. Williams, and Michael Burkhimer, eds. *The Mary Lincoln Enigma: Historians on America's Most Controversial First Lady* (Carbondale, IL: Southern Illinois University Press, 2012).

68 Chester G. Hearn, *Lincoln and McClellan at War* (Baton Rouge: Louisiana State University Press, 2012), 71.

69 David Alan Johnson, *Decided on the Battle Field: Grant, Sherman, Lincoln and the Election of 1864* (Amherst, NY: Prometheus Books, 2012), 131.

70 Ibid, *Decided on the Battle Field*, 229.

71 David Von Drehle, *Rise to Greatness: Abraham Lincoln and America's Most Perilous Year* (New York: Henry Holt and Co., 2012), 95.

72 Borchard, *Abraham Lincoln and Horace Greeley* (Carbondale, IL: Southern Illinois University Press, 2011), 67-89.

73 Martin P. Johnson, *Writing the Gettysburg Address* (Lawrence, KS: University Press of Kansas, 2013), 188.

74 Johnson, *Writing the Gettysburg Address*, 190.

75 Jared Peatman, *The Long Shadow of Lincoln's Gettysburg Address* (Carbondale, IL: Southern Illinois University Press, 2013), 34.

76 Ibid, *The Long Shadow of Lincoln's Gettysburg Address*, 72.

77 Ibid, 129.

78 Kenneth J. Winkle, *Lincoln's Citadel: The Civil War in Washington, DC.* New York: W. W. Norton & Company, 2013).

79 Robert E. May, *Slavery, Race, and Conquest in the Tropics: Lincoln, Douglas, and the Future of Latin America* (Cambridge University Press, 2013), 250.

80 Chris DeRose, *Congressman Lincoln: The Making of America's Greatest President* (New York: Threshold Editions, 2013), 48.

81 DeRose, *Congressman Lincoln*, 130.

82 Hamilton and Ostendorf, *Lincoln in Photographs*, 231.

83 Noah Brooks, *Abraham Lincoln* (New York: Fred DeFau, 1894), 202.

84 "Abraham Lincoln, Head-and-Shoulders Portrait, Traditionally Called 'Last Photograph of Lincoln from Life," Library of Congress, accessed July 1, 2021, at <loc.gov/pictures/item/2009630692>.

85 DePew, *Reminiscences of Abraham Lincoln*, 251.

86 Ward Hill Lamon and Dorothy Lamon Teillard, *Recollections of Abraham Lincoln, 1847–1865* (Chicago: A. C. McClurg and Company, 1895), 113.

87 James G. Barber, ed., *Faces of Discord: The Civil War Era at the National Portrait Gallery* (Washington, DC: Smithsonian Institution, 2006), 257.

88 Borchard and Bulla, *Lincoln Mediated*, 171.

15

Reconstruction Journalism: Two Examples

"The white cliffs of England and the people of that realm are preparing to welcome General Grant with the honors due him as a soldier and statesman ... to receive him with the etiquette observed towards ex-sovereigns." "The Noble Steamship Indiana," Philadelphia (PA) *North American*, May 25, 1877.

The Georgia Republican newspaper first named *The Colored American* and later (1867) the *Daily Loyal Georgian* started as a daily but for financial reasons would become a weekly. It was associated with an African Methodist Episcopal Zion church in Augusta, the Republican Party, and the Georgia Equal Rights Association (later called the Georgia Education Association). At the center of development of *The Colored American* and the *Daily Loyal Georgian* were two men most associated with the newspaper, John Thomas Shuften and John Emory Bryant—the former an Augusta barber who would go on to a journalism and law career in Florida, and the latter a Freedmen's Bureau agent and leading Republican political operative. The Republican journal in Augusta did not last very long—only four years, eventually dying out as Reconstruction efforts struggled in the South. Similarly, Grant's rise and fall as president left him tired and anxious. Accordingly, he, his wife Julia, and a New York journalist decided to set sail for Europe in 1877 to see the world. He was met with enthusiasm, especially in the Midlands and Northeast of England, where he was seen as the great liberator of the slaves. The journalist—John Russell Young of *The New York Herald*— chronicled the tour and helped Grant regain some of the lost political traction from his scandal-plague two terms as president.

Journalism in the aftermath of the Civil War included an attempt to establish a pro-Republican newspaper for an African American audience in Augusta, Georgia. Press coverage of Ulysses S. Grant at the time—in particular, his voyage around the world after his presidency—also attempted to rehabilitate his image ahead of another potential run for the White House.

Building a Republican Paper in the Heart of Dixie

In the aftermath of the U.S. Civil War, a pro-Republican newspaper, *The Colored American*, arose in Augusta, Georgia—in the heart of the former Confederacy, yes, but in a city with a sizable African American population. African American editor John Thomas Shuften initially owned and operated the journal, serving a Black audience. It had the backing of both the African Methodist Episcopal Church in Augusta and the newly established Republican Party in Georgia. James D. Lynch, who was born in Baltimore, Maryland, had come to South Carolina and Georgia as an African Methodist Episcopal church missionary to build schools after the war, and he assisted Shuften, an Augusta native, with publication of *The Colored American*. Lynch, a moderate, later would publish the *Jackson Colored Citizen* in Mississippi and serve as that state's secretary of state. Lynch and the church helped pay for the type used for printing.[1] *The Colored American* also had a business manager in Thomas P. Beard, an Augusta grocer. The newspaper office was located in the back of the Globe Hotel on the corner of Ellis and Jackson streets.

Before *The Colored American*, there had been a single pro-Republican newspaper in the state: the *Savannah Republican*. *New York Tribune* correspondent John E. Hayes started that newspaper in 1864 when Major General William Tecumseh Sherman was ravaging east Georgia. The Union Army later seized it, and Hayes developed ties with the U.S. Department of War. Hayes emphasized economic recovery and called his political organization the Union Party—a mixture of northern Republicans who had moved to the South and Georgians who had been pro-Union Democrats, as well as a few former loyal Democrats who had supported the Confederacy but had become supportive of the Republicans. Hayes believed that acknowledging the death of slavery, affording Blacks civil rights, and educating former slaves would help Georgia become prosperous.[2]

Goal of the Newspaper: Racial Harmony

In the initial issue of *The Colored American*, Shuften spelled out its mission. He wrote that *The Colored American* was to be a publication that would diffuse religious, political, and general intelligence information.

> It will be devoted to the promotion of harmony and good will between the whites and Colored people of the south, and untiring in its advocacy of Industry and Education among all classes; but particularly the class most in need of our agency. Accepting, at all times, the decision of public sentiment and Legislative Assemblies, and bowing to the majesty of law, it will fearlessly remonstrate against legal and constitutional proscription by appeal to the public sense of justice.[3]

While Shuften hoped the newspaper would promote harmony between Blacks and whites, he did not want Blacks to cast aside their civil rights in service to racial accord. Shuften believed that post-war equality meant that Blacks could vote, serve on juries, and serve in public office. A subscription to the four-page, five-column newspaper cost $4 per year. A single issue was ten cents. Shuften had half a dozen agents in the community to solicit subscriptions. The newspaper was devoid of artwork for the most part.

On December 30, 1865, Shuften published a front-page story announcing that all of the states had ratified the Thirteenth Amendment in the former Confederacy with the exception of Mississippi. That same article stated that several Southern states were re-establishing their governments, which of course were loyal to the federal government and the Andrew Johnson administration. Another story in that edition of *The Colored American* found the *New York Evening Post* reacting to an article in the *New York Daily News* that predicted that white Southern laborers would find "pressure" from Black workers and that white workers in the North should watch what happened in the South to see what would transpire over time. The *Post* wrote that pro-Confederate whites in the North seemed to believe, on the one hand, that Blacks "will not work at all," but on the other hand that they "will work so much better than the white laborer, that the latter will be injured by the pressure of negro competition." The *Post* commentator called it a "curious" contradiction.[4]

Another story on the front page of the December 30 edition told the story of a woman who sold her land for approximately $1,000. A stranger called one evening and asked if he could spend the night in her home. She eventually agreed, and in the middle of the night, she thought she heard robbers trying to break into her house. She asked the boarder to help her scare them off. He told her to open the door and hide behind it, and that he would defend her. As the robbers came into the home, their faces greased in black, he shot two of them dead and wounded a third. When the grease was rubbed away from their faces, they turned out to be her son-in-law and a neighbor. The third was believed to be her son. Her boarder had saved "the old lady, her money, and perhaps her life."[5] A brief next to this story told readers that Robert E. Lee had visited Lexington, Virginia, to visit Stonewall Jackson's grave, and that a home in Lexington had been purchased for Lee.

On January 10, 1866, John Emory Bryant, who had been an agent in the Freedmen's Bureau until December 1865, attended the Freedmen's Conference at Springfield Baptist Church in Augusta, which would establish the Georgia Equal Rights Association, which took over *The Colored American*.[6] One of the conference's resolutions was "you are free, and free for ever. No mortal power can thrust you or your descendants back into slavery. You can never again be bought or sold."[7] The only white member of the association, Bryant—who had served in the Eighth Maine Volunteers in the Civil War, including a stint on the Sea Islands of South Carolina—was elected its president, and editor of the newspaper, as well, as he had been a journalist before the war. Shuften, relieved of his editor's duties, focused on his small business as a barber, which was more lucrative than his journalism post. He would eventually move to Jacksonville, Florida, and work for the *Florida Union*. He would earn a law degree from Howard University in 1876.

After the establishment of the Georgia Equal Rights Association, *The Colored American* changed names to *The Daily Loyal Georgian*, and Bryant, an attorney and a Methodist who supported temperance (his father was a Methodist minister), would run it. In all, the newspaper lasted four years, publishing on a weekly basis for two years and a daily basis for the other two years, and serving the Black community of Augusta. Its major themes were party politics, civil rights, agriculture, reconstruction, education (literacy), and religion. Eventually, Bryant changed the name of the Georgia Equal Rights Association to the Georgia Education Association and made the *Loyal Georgian* its official newspaper. He stated that the *Loyal Georgian* would fearlessly advocate the cause of equality. He added that he upheld the "doctrine of the supremacy of the National over State governments," and that he denounced "secession as not only unconstitutional, but inherently hostile to" a democratic-republican system of government.[8] Bryant planned to step back from the editor's role and have co-editors, one Black, and the other white. However, this plan never came to fruition.[9]

The *Loyal Georgian* cost $6 a year for a subscription. The Georgia Education Association also subsidized it, receiving contributions from Union League clubs around the state, as well from as Northern sympathizers. Bryant continued to emphasize political news (platforms and resolutions of the Georgia Republican Party) and economic developments (such as the price of farm commodities). A typical news story referenced Major General Edward Ord, who oversaw the Department of Arkansas, a military district. Ord had directed the Arkansas legislature to no longer pay for the printing of a former pro-Confederate newspaper. Ord also told the mayor of Jackson, Mississippi, to uphold the tax laws of his city, adding that if the mayor should need military aid, "he can obtain it by calling on the commanding officer at Jackson."[10] Another news story informed readers of the swift work done by 16,000 laborers on the Central Pacific Railroad. Bryant noted that a strike by Chinese workers only stopped work on the railway for one day, and that the Chinese did not receive any concessions from their strike. From Tennessee, Bryant heard that Major General Oliver Otis Howard, head of the Freemen's Bureau, pronounced the crops in that state "the best ever."[11]

In an example of an article that featuring political interpretation, Bryant reacted to a speech by Benjamin H. Hill on July 16, 1867. In it, given at Davis House in Atlanta, Hill—a Democrat who had opposed secession but also allied with Confederate States of America President Jefferson Davis—denounced the 1867 Reconstruction Acts of Congress, stating they were unconstitutional. Hill mainly criticized the fact that Unionists had forced Southerners to swear loyalty to the Constitution, and that Congress ran Southern states with military force. Hill said the Reconstruction Acts would "inaugurate a war of races," the Republicans were "buying up the Negro vote," and the effects of these acts would "exterminate the African race."[12] Bryant responded by writing: "It was shown that Mr. H. was only the mouthpiece of all of those who array themselves against the Republican Party." Bryant added that Hill's speech had "inconsistencies of logic and the fallacy of foundation."[13]

The editor called the *Loyal Georgian* a family newspaper that would include educational and religious items. One story, for example, combined the two subjects. It announced construction of a Baptist church in Athens, Georgia, and the intention of Black citizens of that city to build a school on a large plot of land they had purchased.[14] Most stories were from out of town, but occasionally Bryant spotlighted local news. An example was an announcement of a printers' picnic on the Fourth of July: "A class that labor as they do—night and day—should have a gathering at least once a year where they can enjoy themselves to their heart's content. From January to January they are the most assiduous in their attention to duty."[15]

Bryant also liked to run human-interest pieces. One of those was about orator and journalist Frederick Douglass, who had reunited with his brother Perry after more than four decades apart. When asked about the reunion, Douglass said, in part, "'how unutterably cursed is slavery, and how unspeakably joyful are the results of its overthrow.'"[16] As was common in nineteenth-century American journalism, Bryant also ran stories about oddities. For example, in July 1867 he published a piece about a 30-year-old man in Virginia who had died recently, who was still "a baby in size" and had always lived in his cradle. The article ended with this familial detail: "Father and mother were cousins."[17]

In 1867, Bryant made the journal a weekly, and another pro-Republican daily was started in Augusta. That newspaper, *The National Republican*, merged with the *Augusta Daily Press*. In the *Weekly Loyal Georgian*, meanwhile, Bryant constantly advocated for the establishment of pro-Republican Union League clubs in each county of Georgia. The Republicans, he reminded readers, have "protected you, and will continue to protect you."[18] Thus, his readers should go out and vote against the Democrats. Content was usually on politics and featured reports from Atlanta and Washington, news on educational and military issues, and market reports. Bryant also reprinted stories from other Republican newspapers, such as an article from *The New York Times* observing that the United States was not merely a two-race nation, with Asians also an essential group, particularly in the Western states. The *Times* railed against instances in the South in which Asians were paid far less than were their native counterpart. "'We want no modified Slavery introduced where we have just done away with its legalized form.'"[19]

The format of the *Weekly Loyal Georgian* was eight columns across each page. While there were usually had been advertisements on the right two columns of the front page of the *Daily Loyal Georgian*, the weekly confined ads to inside pages only. The military provided financial support, as Bryant ran military notices, which were much like classified advertising. Other ads were for schoolbooks, watches, paint, and hair products. These sometimes covered as many as three columns. Most of the ads were not local; rather, they were from New York, such as Harper & Brothers, Publishers, D. Appleton & Co. Publishers, or Wilson's School and Family Series, which the federal government subsidized. Bryant knew that educating the children of his subscribers was not only important for the future of his newspaper but also for the social and political advancement of Blacks in Augusta. Another ad was the Freedmen's Trust, a bank set up by the Freedmen's Bureau. A further source of income was printing contracts from the government, determined by U.S. House of Representatives Clerk Edward McPherson. Bryant won one of these contracts, thanks in large part to his ability to organize Blacks to support the Republican Party.

Subscribers paid $2 per year for the weekly. Bryant complained that he spent too much time raising funds to pay for the newspaper, and not enough on editorial content or to promote education, which he saw as his main calling. When the daily newspaper ended, he hoped to have "the pleasure of talking with [readers], each week, through the columns of the 'Weekly Loyal Georgian.'"[20] *The Colored American* and the *Loyal Georgian* were part of an effort in Georgia to build the Republican Party after the Civil War. This was standard procedure for political parties in the nineteenth century. Newspapers were seen as essential tools in developing a party in a city, town, or state. At its height, the Republican Party had six newspapers in Georgia during the early years of Reconstruction—and, briefly (1868-1872) Georgia was a Republican ("Radical") state. Although the six papers were six more than the state had had in 1860, the Georgia press still underrepresented Republicans. By contrast, there were fifty-three Democratic newspapers in the state in 1869. Despite their modest number, the Republican newspapers were deemed "radical" by the Democratic press for helping motivate Black citizens to cast votes in the 1868 election, when the party gained its short-lived control of state politics. Newspapers like the *Loyal Georgian* and *Savannah Republican* printed state and local tickets before the election to urge their readers to vote Republican.

The significance of *The Colored American/Loyal Georgian* is it tells how a particular communication medium operated in a specific historical circumstance. This was a time when the former Confederate states were undergoing a major transformation, as were the Black residents of Augusta, most of whom were former slaves—with a party that did not exist in the state in the 1860 election running government at all levels from 1868 until 1872.

Later, the *Loyal Georgian*, which had a woodcut of an American flag on its editorial page, laid out its guiding principles: "The equal political and legal rights of all citizens of the United States, except those who have been convicted of crime, or those who have voluntarily attempted to destroy the Government." Another major policy principle, per Bryant, was the "enactment of State laws for the inauguration and support of a system of common schools"[21]

While the purpose of the Augusta newspaper was to offer Black and Republican readers the news of the day, the journal also interpreted events and published party dogma. For example, in an article headlined "Colored Men, Remember," Bryant told his readers that the Democratic Party "fought to keep you in slavery, and that its leaders "have done all that they could to prevent you from voting."[22] Bryant consistently encouraged readers to form Union League clubs and instructed them how to set one up (with an organizational constitution). The newspaper was quite popular in Augusta's Black community, and ministers read it aloud in Black churches.[23] Shuften and Bryant both attempted to inform the Black community of local, state, and national political developments, and rallied the base at election time.

The editors had hoped to get Black-owned small businesses in Augusta to support their journal with advertising, but little ever came of that, which contributed to the newspaper's demise. This was at a time when the U.S. press still was largely partisan in nature, with many newspapers relying on the political parties for patronage. In the end, the Republicans were drummed out of Georgia, and this handful of Republican newspapers followed. Ultimately, then, the Republican newspapers' goals were informational, educational, and organizational. They wanted their readers to understand and navigate the new world of the post-war Georgia. Both Shuften and Bryant were well aware of the very concrete social, economic, and political obstacles their readers faced. They aimed to help them surveil this brave new world—and urged the Blacks of Augusta to embrace literacy and education as means to social equality. The price of editing a Republican newspaper with a Black audience was quite steep. Whites in Augusta shunned Bryant and his wife, and he was clubbed once.[24]

Ultimately, Bryant's newspaper failed because it lost its government printing contract in 1868 when Governor Rufus Bullock, also a Republican, asked McPherson to award the state government printing contracts to Samuel Bard, the moderately political editor of Atlanta's *Daily New Era*.[25] Without the printing contract, Bryant's *Weekly Loyal Georgian* eventually collapsed, publishing its last issue on February 15, 1868. Bryant would start another newspaper in Augusta in 1869 called the *Georgia Republican*. He would serve in the General Assembly as a Republican, and was the chair of the executive committee of the National Republican Club, which was based in Georgia. Bryant was able to launch the *Georgia Republican* because he had been made postmaster of Augusta. He called it a radical Republican newspaper that advocated for civil rights, internal improvements, and universal public education.[26]

Bryant moved the *Republican* to Savannah in 1872 and renamed it the *Journal*.[27] It was designated one of three official Republican Party newspapers in Georgia. He would close the *Journal* after the 1872 election in which incumbent Ulysses S. Grant easily defeated former *New York Tribune* editor Horace Greeley (who ran as a Democrat) for the presidency. Bryant started the Atlanta

Publishing Company in 1877 and restarted the *Georgia Republican* at that time. Later called the *Southern Advance and Georgia Republican*, it ceased in 1879—as usual with so many nineteenth-century newspapers, a victim of meager funding.[28] Bryant had been the rare white Republican journalist in the South who had championed the cause of civil rights for his Black readers. Shuften and Bryant's experiences in journalism after the Civil War show that the partisan press was not yet outdated in the United States. While major urban newspapers moved toward financial independence based on advertising, a majority of U.S. newspapers remained political in nature. In a democracy, politics is always changing, and those vicissitudes meant instability for party newspapers. *The Colored American* and *Loyal Georgian* were effective at motivating Black voters, but they existed in a state where the Republican hold on political power would soon slip away—ushering the end of Reconstruction and inaugurating the century-long nightmare of Jim Crow.

Grant's Redemption after Reconstruction

Ulysses S. Grant, the hero of the Union military in the American Civil War, served two terms as president, succeeding the nearly ousted Andrew Johnson. Grant had a number of achievements, including establishment of the Civil Service Commission and the Department of Justice, resolution of the CSS. *Alabama* claims with Great Britain, and prosecution of the Ku Klux Klan. However, he faced a major economic downturn in 1873, and his administration was replete with corruption. After the contentious and controversial election of 1876 that resulted in the election of Republican Rutherford B. Hayes, Grant, in May 1877, began a tour of Europe—landing in Great Britain before moving onto the continent. He eventually decided to go around the world, to the Middle East, India, China, and Japan—a trek that would last two and a half years.

The global journey was something of which he had long dreamed, and now that he was retired from politics and the military, he finally had the time—and enough money—to leave the shores of his native land. The Grants had saved $100,000 during his presidential years. Some of it was from his presidential salary and some of it came from investments in railroads, mining, and other ventures. His wife, Julia, also had cash from real estate holdings, and Grant intended to spend $25,000 of their savings on the world tour.[29] Joining him were his wife and his son Jesse. A fourth member of the party was journalist John Russell Young, a

Image 15.1 "Gen. Grant and Li Hung Chang, Viceroy of China, taken at Tientsin Jan. 1879," Shitai Liang, photographer. Photograph shows portrait of Grant and Li Hongzhang during meeting to discuss China's dispute with Japan over the Ryukyu Islands.[30]

long-time Grant supporter who would turn his *Herald* articles into a book entitled *Around the World with General Grant.*

The inclusion of Young afforded Americans the opportunity to follow the president's global tour in detail. The New York journalist also interviewed the ex-president about both the Civil War and his political career. Meanwhile, the U.S. Department of State sent a message to its consular offices around the world, urging consuls to give Grant whatever aid he needed, even though the tour's duration was "undetermined at the time of departure."[32]

Grant's time in Great Britain was covered with a medium-to-high level of intensity in both the U.S. and the British press. American newspapers examined included those available on the Library of Congress' Chronicling America website and on the Gale Nineteenth Century Newspaper database. British newspapers analyzed are from the British Newspaper Archive and Gale's *Times of London* database. Particular attention is paid to the coverage of *The New York Herald*, which was the only American newspaper that had a correspondent on the entire

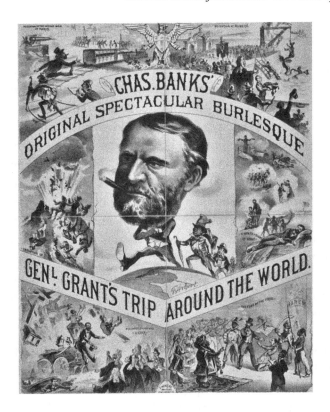

Image 15.2 "Chas. Banks' Original Spectacular Burlesque." F. Achert, lithographer. Cincinnati, OH: F. Achert, 1879.[31]

trip. *Herald* reports from Britain were obtained via telegraph and clipping by newspapers all over the country.

Newspapers in Great Britain tended to focus on Grant's exploits in the U.S. Civil War. This extended to calling him a liberator of the African American slaves and a friend of the common laborer—the latter designation based in part on his humble origins from a family of tanners in the American heartland. Young also tended to emphasize this frame to turn Americans' focus on Grant's military victories in the Civil War and the surrender of Robert E. Lee's Army of Northern Virginia at Appomattox, Virginia, in April 1865.

Young was very sympathetic to Grant. *The New York Herald* reporter seemed bent on restoring the ex-president's positive image after the many stains and scandals of his eight years in the nation's highest political office. In Great Britain, Grant was feted as a conquering hero, and was the guest of honor at one state dinner after another. He was accorded honors in every city he visited—including

Liverpool, Manchester, Birmingham, Newcastle-upon-Tyne, Sunderland, Edinburgh, Glasgow, Bristol, Brighton, Sheffield, Stratford-upon-Avon, Dublin, Belfast, Londonderry, and London. The British tour was interrupted in summer 1877 by a trip to the European continent that included Belgium, Germany, Alsace-Lorraine, and Switzerland. Later, after touring Africa, the Middle East, and Asia, Grant returned to Europe, and he made a trip to Ireland in January 1879.

The voyage from Philadelphia to Liverpool would take eleven days, but even before Grant arrived in England reports began to surface in the American press. The Philadelphia *North American* reported on May 25 that Grant's ship, the *U.S.S. Indiana*, was nearing "the white cliffs of England and the people of that realm are preparing to welcome General Grant with the honors due him as a soldier and statesman." The *North American* went on to report that the prime minister's cabinet planned "to receive him with the etiquette observed towards ex-sovereigns."[33] The newspaper also noted that Grant had stopped in Queenstown, Ireland, before heading for England. In Queenstown, the former president received an invitation to visit Liverpool from that city's mayor, the newspaper reported.

The New York Herald had the most intense coverage of Grant's tour. Young, the *Herald* correspondent, had been invited to cover Grant by the former president's inner circle. Young had covered early Civil War battles for the *Philadelphia Press*, having started at that newspaper when he was fifteen years old, and he was later managing editor of Horace Greeley's *New York Tribune*. The native of Ireland would go on to start the *Herald*'s London edition and would eventually become the Librarian of Congress. Young, who in 1877 had been with the *Herald* for five years, provided the narration of Grant's various public and social events as he wound through England and Scotland. Young had been chosen by Grant to accompany the former president's family on the tour because he had started the *New York Standard* in 1870. Grant supporters financed the *Standard*, which was created to challenge the *New York Sun*. However, the *Standard* failed, and two years later Young joined the *Herald*.[34] Others also contributed impressions of the tour, including actress Olive Logan, who was married to the U.S. Consul to Wales, Wirt Skiles.

The first stop in England was at Liverpool on May 28, 1877. There, Grant got a stirring reception, with every ship in the harbor hoisting the American flag. At the customs house, a crowd of ten thousand welcomed Grant to Merseyside. He had not expected such a public display and had no speech prepared to respond to the crowd. Next, he went to Manchester. It was there in the Midlands, and then in the Northeast of England, that the former president was received most enthusiastically—especially in Newcastle-Upon-Tyne, where eighty thousand greeted him.[35] The Newcastle throng was heavy with coal miners, metalworkers, tailors, carpenters, masons, sawyers, painters, and tanners—that is, the city's working class. In total, members of twenty-two trade societies attended the event.[36] This in large part was because Grant was seen as a great liberator, and Newcastle was the home to a large abolitionist contingent that had brought such luminaries as Frederick Douglass and William Lloyd Garrison to the area to lecture before the U.S. Civil War. Moreover, Grant's commoner roots heightened his attraction in a region of England known for its sizable working class. As noted previously, Grant's father had been a tanner, so the English labor class saw the former president as one of their own. And, of course, it would take a man of such background, in the view of these Englishmen, to be the great liberator—the man who would release Black slaves from the tyranny of their masters.

Young's coverage reads more like diary entries than a series of news articles. His pieces were written as letters, per nineteenth-century custom. Young, who was then thirty-six years old, described Grant's Newcastle reception as an "occasion of a most enthusiastic and remarkable demonstration." Grant told the throng that the two nations were really one people who "ought not only keep peace with each other but with all the world, and by their example stop the wars which are now devastating Europe." (The Russo-Turkish War started in April 1877.) Young observed that Grant was "loudly cheered" during his speech.[37] Grant also told the Newcastle crowd: 'I always was a man of peace, and I have advocated peace, although educated a soldier. I never willingly, although I have gone through two wars, of my own accord advocated war.'"[38]

After Grant's short oration, he rode in a steamer down the river Tyne, which borders Newcastle on its southern side. Along the way, citizens of Newcastle and Gateshead (on the other side of the Tyne) saluted Grant with gunfire, and "every available spot was crowded with people." The mayor of Gateshead and the town council also gave Grant a welcome. He said that his reception on the Tyne side had exceeded "anything he had expected," and that he was "glad the good feeling between England and America was warmer today than it had ever been."[39]

Young added that Grant stood on the bridge of the steamer and bowed to the crowd as they cheered from the banks of the Tyne. The *Herald* reporter estimated that 150,000 folks had come out to see the former American president and Civil War hero.[40] Young also wrote that there had been no assemblies of this size since the early 1830s—which the man saluted, then-Prime Minister Earl Grey, who was from Northeast England, had led.

Grant also was received enthusiastically in Liverpool. The U.S. consul there, the *Herald* reported, gave a speech expressing "the gratification of the American people at the reception of the ex-President in England."[41] The *San Francisco Evening Bulletin* noted that when Grant was in Manchester, the "factory girls turned out almost *en masse* in their morning attire and joined in the huzzahs."[42] The *Evening Bulletin* also stated that the mayor of Bedford called Grant the "'Hannibal of the American army.'"[43] Another *San Francisco Evening Bulletin* article mentioned that Grant had visited the Epsom Downs racecourse in Surrey, southwest of London, and attended The Oaks horse race.

Grant traveled to the Midlands and then on to London. Young describes the train's journey through the "Black Country," where coal was king. In Lancaster, the "elegant buildings formed a striking contrast to the black hills and valleys of the coal district."[44] Then, at Derby, Grant saw how the whole nature of the countryside had changed: "the General remarked that almost every foot of land was utilized or under cultivation." Young wrote that the factories of Nottingham were reminiscent of the Bethlehem factories in Pennsylvania. Young also wrote that Grant received a "warm reception" in Leicester en route to London.

The train then arrived at St. Pancras Station on Euston Road in central London, where, Young reported, "huge crowds thronged the entrance to the station and cheered loudly, though Grant gave no speech there."[45] Young also made comments about British supporters of the Union during the Civil War. These included Thomas Walker of the pro-Union London *Daily News*. "He it was," Young wrote of Walker, "who put that powerful journal on our side in 1861, and kept it there through the long period of disaster and discouragement which saw almost every other London paper steadily defending the cause of the Rebellion. This act Mr. Walker did against influences which would have overborne the judgment of most men—against even the remonstrances of the owners of the *Daily News*, who feared peril to their property from the policy it supported."[46]

One of Grant's get-togethers in London included members of the British press. This occurred on June 29, 1877, at the Grosvenor Hotel. Among the newspapers represented at that dinner were the *Daily News*, *The World*, *Fortnightly*, *The Observer*, *Pall Mall Gazette*, *Daily Telegraph*, *Mayfair*, and *The Times*. Young praised one *Times* correspondent for the "finish and accuracy of his work."[47] In addition, there from the United States press was George Washburne Smalley of *The New York Tribune*. Smalley, who had been a leading abolitionist, had earned a strong reputation as a reporter during the Civil War, particularly for his reporting on Antietam. He later covered the Austro-Prussian War in 1866 and became the *Tribune*'s European bureau chief, stationed in London.

Frank Leslie's Illustrated Newspaper noted that the University of Oxford issued Grant an honorary doctor of civil law degree: "The attentions showered so profusely upon ex-President Grant must ... be attributed to his being regarded as the greatest of living military commanders and as the representative of the country of which he had twice been elected president."[48]

Smalley in *The New York Tribune* remarked on Grant's visit with the Prince of Wales (Edward VII).

> It is something to have crushed a rebellion and to have been twice chosen President of the United States. But what true admirer of aristocracy can doubt that Gen. Grant felt that the climax of his career was reached when he found himself on that memorable evening on the right hand of the Heir Apparent to the Throne of England.[49]

The *Herald* tried going beyond Young's letters about Grant and his family touring around the countryside and London. For example, on June 16, 1877, the newspaper ran a woodcut-drawn map of London showing the route Grant took through London on the day he was made an honorary citizen of the British capital.

Grant would go on to the European continent during the summer before returning to London in August. In September 1877, Grant left London for the north. This led to a trip to Scotland, with Edinburgh as the first stop. There, Grant told Young in an interview that he planned to stay in Europe for a year, saying, "'I have a special reason for so doing. I am a private citizen now, and want nothing whatever to do with politics.'"[50] Grant also told Young that he had no fondness for handshaking, which he had to do as often in England as he had in the United States. "'I think handshaking a great nuisance, and should be abolished,'" he told the *Herald* reporter. Grant said he also did not believe in partisanship, but, rather, in the good sense of the American people, who he called "'sentimental, loyal, and brave,'" and who would only elect a high official on a "'common sense basis.'"[51]

Grant added that he fully supported the policies of President Rutherford B. Hayes. In response, *The Chicago Tribune* lambasted Grant as being too weak in defense of his own Reconstruction policy. "This is a frank admission that the policy of sustaining the carpet-baggers by bayonets was a failure, and it is confirmation of what was often suspected, viz.: That Grant, when President, rather yielded to the pressure of the bloody-shirt politicians than asserted his own conviction in pursuing the policy of armed intervention."[52]

In Edinburgh, Grant visited Sir Walter Scott's birthplace and the memorial to Robert Burns. His party also walked along the Cowgate, toured Edinburgh Castle and Holyrood Palace, visited a hostelry in White Horse Close where

Samuel Johnson had stayed, took a drive around Arthur's Seat, and paid a visit to the house where John Knox had lived. Grant referenced the Scots who had immigrated to the United States and became good citizens. He took in the town of Melrose and Abbotsford, the home of Sir Walter Scott, along the river Tweed.

Because the *Herald* had a correspondent within Grant's party, many newspapers quoted or clipped from the newspaper's reports. The pro-Republican *Chicago Tribune* was one such journal. For instance, its June 10, 1877, story, titled "Gen. Grant the Guest of Consul [Adam] Badeau [who would help edit Grant's memoirs] in London" relied entirely on a *Herald* story. The byline read, "Special Dispatch to the Tribune."[53] The Chicago *Inter Ocean* also published Young's *Herald* dispatches—including the one from Manchester stating that Grant appeared before "immense crowds," with the Stars and Stripes "being everywhere prominent."[54]

Not all of the U.S. press was kind to Grant. The tone of articles in many Southern and Northern Democratic newspapers contrasted sharply with that of *The New York Herald* and the Republican journals. For example, the *Indianapolis State Sentinel* called the fawning Europeans "snobs and fools" for their enthusiastic reception of the former president. The *Sentinel* editor also took aim at the "flunky journalism" of those Northern editors for believing Grant deserved the reception he was getting across the Atlantic. The writer continued: "The send off that Grant received at Philadelphia was in no sense a tribute of respect to him as a man, a soldier, or an ex-President." Rather, "the affair was deliberately gotten up by the Don Camerons of Pennsylvania as an insult to (President Rutherford B.) Hayes. It was intended to say, 'We prefer Grant the despot, the sot, the bribe taker, the associate of the thieves and debauchee of the Government, to a Presidential fraud who accepted power from crime-stained hands and had not the courage to stand by Grant's bayonet policy.'"[55]

The Macon *Georgia Weekly Telegraph and Journal & Messenger* reprinted an article from the *New York World* that stated that Grant had been "lionized, wined, and dined" in London. The article added, "another link has been forged in the chain which binds together the two great branches of the Anglo-Saxon race." However, the reporter also wrote that Grant's taciturn manner was seen as "absolutely appalling" and that he had nearly made a faux pas when he was about to light a cigar at Marlborough House in Westminster (a place for royal gatherings).[56] The Boston *Advertiser* clipped an analysis of Grant from *The Spectator*, the British magazine. While *The Spectator* was kind to Grant on military issues, it found him lacking in the political arena. "It is certain that General Grant will be remembered in history not as President, but as commander-in-chief, though it will be added that being the great commander he was, he rather detracted from, than added to, his fame by ruling the United States for eight years."[57]

On the other hand, the *Raleigh Register* was one Southern newspaper that was more enthusiastic about Grant's reception—commenting that Grant stood with Washington and Lincoln among the greatest American presidents, and that his reception in England validated that status. The *Register* added: "The unsurpassed reception which has greeted Gen. Grant in England, is most to gratifying to every American citizen," and "the continued ovation is a compliment to the United States."[58] Meanwhile, the *Galveston Daily News* reported on Grant in a more neutral tone. Of his visit to Sunderland (near Newcastle), the *Daily News* reported that nearly 10,000 members of "trade and friendly societies march in procession" on a day which "was observed as almost a general holiday." Grant, the article continued, observed the "laying of the corner-stone of the library and museum."[59]

Some tour-related stories were entertaining. One involved Grant sliding on the deck of the *Indiana*, falling down, and accidentally kicking "a newly married man in the ribs." In fact, Grant had tumbled on the deck twice. The correspondent added: "It was really laughable, though, to see the General in one of these escapades, on the floor, struggling and sprawling about, trying to regain his feet."[60] This took away from some of the pomp and fuss often reported when Grant was in London and other British cities.

Much of what was reported in American newspapers centered on whether Grant's tour would help or hinder any future political ambitions he should have. Before Grant began the tour, the nation had endured a presidential election fiasco that was not decided until two days before the inauguration. Republican Rutherford B. Hayes edged Democrat Samuel Tilden by a single electoral vote, 185-184, after Tilden received almost 51 percent of the popular vote. In essence, the Democrats conceded the disputed election, and in return, the Republicans agreed to end Reconstruction. The country was in such disrepair politically that many thought only a third term by Grant, starting in 1881, could turn things around. The *Delaware Gazette*, in an article titled "Third Term Hints," stated that former Pennsylvania Senator Simon Cameron, speaking in Philadelphia on the eve of Grant's trip to Europe, held that Grant "'may yet be asked to again take in his hands the helm of this government when the ship of State is going to destruction.'"[61] The New Orleans (LA) *Daily Democrat* commented that Grant's positive reception by European sovereigns would "give many people of the North a higher opinion of his greatness and reputation," and that Grant would not make any mistakes that "would hurt his cause." The *Democrat* editor believed Grant would return just in time to "secure the Republican nomination" for the 1880 election, but that, in the meantime, he was being kept "out of the way until the presidential race of 1880 was heating up.[62]

Other articles painted Grant and his family as being perhaps too common for the royalty of Europe. For example, in an article titled "Grant and Victoria," the *Watertown*, Wisconsin, *Republican* noted that Grant's party arrived early at Windsor Castle and had to wait for Queen Victoria, who was riding in a nearby park. The Watertown dispatch also stated that the dinner for Grant was held in the Oak Room, not in St. George's Hall, which was reserved for state occasions—emphasizing that Grant was no longer a government official, but rather merely a private citizen of the United States. In addition, the Oak Room was chosen because Victoria wanted to talk to each member of Grant's party, and so preferred the smaller, more intimate hall. That night the queen went off to bed at 10 p.m., but the guests were "entertained by the Queen's private band" afterward.[63]

Smaller American newspapers tended to run shorter articles that summarized news of Grant's voyage with less commentary. The *Princeton*, Minnesota, *Union* published a seventeen-line story on its second page on Grant's stop in Liverpool. The *Princeton Union* reported simply that crowds met Grant with "hearty cheers," and that Liverpool's mayor welcomed him.[64] An October 1877 story on Grant's tour in the *Yankton Daily Press and Dakotaian* of South Dakota was only twenty-two lines long. The Prescott, Arizona, *Weekly Arizona Miner* reported in a twenty-eight-line story that Grant enjoyed a "splendid and hearty reception" when feted at the Apsley House, with the Duke of Wellington as host.[65]

The *Daily Citizen and News* in Lowell, Massachusetts, similarly ran a twenty-eight-line story about Grant in London. In it, the newspaper noted that the Freedom of the City had been given to the likes of Napoleon III but never before to an American. The Lowell newspaper explained that the Freedom of the City was "a parchment in a gold box" that "warrants to the holder the right of franchise as a citizen of London, and many other privileges, the exercise of which are now mostly obsolete."[66] The *Rocky Mountain News* in Denver stated that Grant's visit was one of the two great stories in English newspapers at the time—the other being the Russo-Turkish War. The *Rocky Mountain News* article remarked that Grant's grand tour showed that "the government of the United States have [sic] achieved a great success, and have taken a position in the which places them even with their now dear brothers of the other branch of the Anglo-Saxon race, on the footing of the most favored nations."[67] The Daily *Arkansas Gazette* ran two stories on its front page on the day of Grant's departure for England from

Philadelphia. One was forty-six lines long and the other twenty-eight lines long. A typo called the ship Grant was on the *India*.

The *Times of London* covered Grant's tour with some interest but rarely placed those stories prominently. At Liverpool, the *Times* reported, Grant had remarked that his reception was "far beyond anything that I could have expected.'" Grant had added: "A solider must die, and when a President's term of office expires he is but a dead solider; but I have received an attention and a reception that would have done honour to any living person." Grant then, the *Times* added, discussed the relationship between the United States and Great Britain, commenting, "I feel that in this moment a good feeling and sentiment should exist between these two peoples above all other, and that they should be good friends. We are of one kindred, one blood, one language, and one civilization. In some particulars we believe that being younger we surpass you; but being older you have made improvements in the soil and the surface of the earth which we shall not take so long to do as it took you."[68] The *Times* also reported that Grant had received a telegram from Governor John F. Hartranft of Pennsylvania thanking Britain for "Grant's reception."[69] Hartranft hoped that his well wishes and thanks would be expressed to Queen Victoria.

The *Times* quoted Grant during his talk at the Town Hall in Manchester: "'The reception I have had since my arrival in England has been to me very expressive, and one for which I have to return thanks on behalf of my country, for I feel that it is my country that is being received through me.'"[70] While in Manchester, the *Times* reported, Grant and his family visited cotton mills. The newspaper stated that Thomas Cook, founder of the famous travel agency, presented the former president with a photograph of four letters by George Washington housed at the Leicester Museum. While the headline of the story was "General Grant," the London *Evening Mail* first referred to him in a June 1 story as "the ex-President of the United States."[71] The *Evening Mail* noted that Grant was taken to Sir Joseph Whitworth's artillery and machine works in Manchester. Whitworth was the inventor of a sniper rifle and a standardized size for screw threads.

At Manchester, Grant spoke to the mayor, the city council, and thousands of laborers. According to the *Leeds Mercury*, he cited his strong affiliation with Manchester, whose textile workers suffered mightily during the Civil War due to the Union blockade of the South, but who had supported the Union in its attempt to end slavery:

> I was very well aware, during the war, of the sentiments of the great mass of the people of Manchester toward the country to which I have the honor to belong,

and also of the sentiments with regard to the struggle in which it fell to my lot to take a humble part. It was a great trial for us. For your expressions of sympathy at that time there exists a feeling of friendship toward Manchester distinct and separate from that which my countrymen also feel, and I trust will always feel, toward every part of England.[72]

Speaking to those assembled, Manchester Mayor Abel Heywood recalled that he had welcomed a relief ship from the United States during the cotton crisis.[73]

When the former president reached London, the *Times* reported on Grant's reception at the Guildhall, where he was given the Freedom of the City, making him an honorary citizen. The Chamberlain of London, Benjamin Scott, noted that Grant was the first president to visit Great Britain, and said, "You must bear with use therefore, General, if we make much of an ex-President of the great Republic of the New World visiting the old home of his fathers.'"[74] After the Guildhall appearance, Grant visited the Crystal Palace. When he arrived, a band played "Hail, Columbia." There, the ex-president was presented with a portrait of himself. While in London, Grant also met with the Admiral of the British Fleet, Sir George Sartorius, who had fought at Trafalgar with Nelson.[75]

Three months later, the *Times* reported on Grant's reception in Glasgow, where he also received the Freedom of the City. Glasgow made Grant a burgess and guild brother of the city in part because of "his successful efforts in the noble work of emancipating his country from the horrors of slavery."[76] The City Hall, where the ceremony took place, "was filled with spectators." The Lord Provost of Glasgow stated that while Lincoln had struck down "'the upas tree of slavery,'" Grant had torn "it up by the roots, so that it should never live in his country to suck nutriment from its soil.'"[77] (The upas tree has a poisonous aroma.) It must be noted that the *Times* stories on the trip to Glasgow did not appear on the front page but rather on pages six and thirteen. The *Times* also praised Grant as "indispensable to the success of the Federal policy," as well as for his "dogged determination" during the Civil War—especially the capture of Vicksburg, Mississippi, in July 1863. The newspaper further applauded Grant's "prudent conduct of foreign affairs" and his skill in avoiding "collision with our own or with Continental Powers" while he was president—adding, "Here he will find that his eminent services to the cause of international peace are not forgotten," and that he was welcomed as "an illustrious statesman" and friend of England.[78] (The British had worried after the Civil War that the United States might attempt to conquer Canada over the *Alabama* issue.)

The *London World* told its readers that Grant was enjoying his trip to Great Britain. When asked if he overindulged with all the formal meals during his time in London, the former Union major general replied negatively, but added, "it is rather severe work." Grant went on to say that he found England "beautiful everywhere."[79] The *Sheffield Independent* called Grant "our distinguished American visitor" when he came to that city in September 1877.[80]

In Scotland, the *Dundee Courier and Argus* was more prone to see Grant as a politician, referring to him as "the distinguished ex-President."[81] The newspaper reported that Grant was shown the nearly completed Tay Bridge, which would carry a railroad track over the River Tay between Dundee and Wormit. The American flag flew from the lighthouse there. Grant also inspected the training ship *Mars*. A band on board played "Yankee Doodle Dandy." Grant watched the three hundred and fifty sailors training on the ship perform a fire drill, the *Courier and Argus* reported. The Dundee newspaper also noted that a "large number of people assembled" at Waverly Station in Edinburgh when the Grant party arrived in that city in late August 1877.[82] The *North British Daily Mail* in Lanarkshire reported that Grant received the Freedom of the City of Ayr. At that ceremony, Grant "received quite an ovation" and referenced his Scottish ancestry (his family also was English and Irish).[83] In Edinburgh, Grant once again was given freedom of the city, as more than two thousand attended a ceremony at the Free Assembly Hall.[84] Grant also visited Inverness and Granttown, ancestral home of the head of the Grant clan, the Earl of Seafield.[85]

Grant's party returned to Newcastle in September. This time he visited St. Nicholas Church, which was built in the eleventh century, and toured the medieval castle closer to the River Tyne. At the Merchants' Exchange, the *Newcastle Journal* reported, Grant met the president of the Chamber of Commerce. A proclamation from the chamber commented on the "brilliancy of [Grant's] achievements as a commander in the field," emphasizing his Civil War leadership over his presidential experience. The document also praised Grant's "higher work of making peace" during his presidency. Asked to speak after the proclamation, Grant said, "'We are two nations, having a common destiny; and that destiny has to be brilliant in proportion to the friendship and co-labour of the brethren on the two sides of the water.'"[86] Grant also said: "'During my eight years of Presidency, it was my study to heal up all the sores that were existing between us. That healing was accomplished in manner honorable to the nations.'"[87] The *Journal* also referred to Grant as a "peacemaker."[88] It had earlier reported that Grant was scheduled to visit Hadrian's Wall, but it does not appear that this happened. He did inspect the Tyne Swing Bridge, and rode on the steamer *Commodore* down the Tyne to Wallsend "amid the cheers of thousands."[89] These cheers were "uninterrupted" along the trip on the *Commodore* up and down the river, according to the *Journal*.[90] Grant claimed to have seen one hundred fifty thousand people along the Tyne that day.

On September 22, 1877, approximately eighty thousand laborers greeted Grant at the Newcastle town moor. This included workers from sixteen Northumberland mines. One sign among the masses read: "Welcome Back, General Grant, from Arms to Arts." Another read, "Let Us Have Peace."[91] Thomas Burt, a Member of Parliament representing Morpeth (and the first working-class MP in British history), spoke to the assembled and stated: "'Never was there a war in which English armies were not employed that went to directly to the popular feeling'" of the British people.[92] Burt went on to praise Grant for wiping "the stain of slavery" from the United States with "prompt zeal and unfailing fortitude."[93] The MP also praised the general for his courage. At another large gathering, Joseph Cowen, the MP from Newcastle (as well as the editor of the *Newcastle Chronicle* and an abolitionist), welcomed Grant, a representative of "'that great, free, and friendly nation, that Younger Britain on the other side of the broad Atlantic.'"[94] Cowen also praised Grant for his treatment of Robert E. Lee at the end of the Civil War and criticized William Gladstone for his 1862 speech in Newcastle in which he implied that the Confederacy had made itself into a nation. Cowen called this view a technical one that was in error.[95] A few weeks later, the *Morning Post* (UK) noted that Grant had visited several of "the more important manufactories," including the Cadbury confectionery in Birmingham, during his October visit to that city.[96]

The Grants would return to Great Britain in January 1879 after having toured Spain. Julia Grant would stop in London to visit her daughter, Nellie Satoris. The former president went on to Ireland, including Dublin and Belfast, as he wanted to visit the homeland of his great-grandfather John Simpson. In Ireland, Grant would meet with dissent when the Cork aldermen refused to hold an official reception for him in that city. Grant had to cancel his two-day trip to Cork and instead continued his stay in Dublin. Several Irish newspapers criticized Grant for not seeing a delegation that wanted Irish independence during his presidency, although Grant had welcomed a Fenian group when it arrived in New York.

The *Herald's* Mission: A Third Term for Grant

John Russell Young had reported in *The New York Herald* that an Irish nationalist in Cork said there was nothing in Grant's career that "called for sympathy from the Irish nation." One of the Cork aldermen echoed that Grant had "never given them [the Irish] the same recognition as the other inhabitants" of the United States.[97] Antipathy was also directed at Grant over his 1875 speech at Des Moines, Iowa, in which he called for the separation of church and state, and therefore refused to support public funding of Catholic schools. The New Orleans (LA) *Daily Democrat* reported that Irish Catholics saw Grant "as their great enemy," while Irish Protestants viewed the ex-president as a "hero and champion of Orangeism." The New Orleans newspaper reported that Grant had enjoyed a "grand triumphal reception at Belfast."[98] Grant was also given the Freedom of the City in Dublin. He told his audience there that he was proud to be a citizen of that city. He added: "I am by birth the citizen of a country where there are more Irishmen, native born or by descent, than in all Ireland."[99] He went on to say he had represented more Irishmen than Queen Victoria herself. Young reported that Grant's reception in Londonderry was "enthusiastic and cordial in the extreme."[100]

The *Times of London* reported that Grant had received a warm reception in Dublin, but that nationalists in Cork had responded otherwise. One Cork alderman was quoted as saying: "'I say it would be unbecoming for the Catholic constituency of Cork to entertain such a man [as Grant]. I do not see anything in the career of General Grant that calls for sympathy of the Irish nation.'" The *Times* wrote that another alderman "declared that the ex-President had gone out of his way to insult the Catholic religion."[101]

Led by *The New York Herald*, the American press covered Grant's tour with a great deal of interest. The *Herald* had been pro-Grant for many years and often supported the idea of a third term for the former president. The *Herald* tended to publish the stories on inside pages, but then again, most American newspapers at this time used the front page for commercial and miscellaneous items. The most important news was usually on the same page as a newspaper's editorials. The *Herald* articles usually spanned several columns; thus, the Grant tour was afforded thousands of words from Young almost daily.

For the most part, the American press saw Grant's generally positive reception as a validation that the United States was a worthy international player. On the other hand, the British press tended to see Grant's trek around Great Britain as an opportunity to pay homage to a notable warrior and to describe the

Anglo-American relationship—while always emphasizing that the British were the elder member of the duo. The British press quoted Grant liberally, especially when he made comments about the relationship between the United States and the United Kingdom. Newspapers in Britain usually placed the Grant stories well on the inside pages. Furthermore, the British press was more likely to paint Grant as liberator of the African American slaves. This was especially the case in the Northeast of England. The American press avoided this frame, and Southern newspapers chipped away at Grant's reputation as a military hero while emphasizing the debacle of his presidency.

The trip would not end in Britain, as Grant continued to the European continent, the Middle East, and Asia over the course of two and half years, bringing him back to the United States in time for the next election. However, he would lose to James A. Garfield on the thirty-sixth ballot of the 1880 Republican National Convention in Chicago, denying him a third term. Grant would go on to write his memoirs, edited by former London Consul Badeau, because he was in dire financial straits and dying from throat cancer. Mark Twain published the memoirs after Grant died in July 1885. They attracted a wide audience and earned acclaim as among the best autobiographical writing produced by a former president.

Notes

1 James C. Clark, "John Shuften Blazed a Pair of Trails," *Orlando* (FL) *Sentinel*, February 24, 1990, accessed June 3, 2021, at <orlandosentinel.com/news/os-xpm-1990-02-24-9002232594-story.html>.

2 Richard Abbott, "The Republican Party Press in Reconstruction Georgia," *The Journal of Southern History*, 61, 4 (November 1995): 726.

3 George W. Gore, "Negro Journalism: An Essay on the History and Present Conditions of the Negro Press," DePauw University, Greencastle, IN, 1922, 10.

4 "Hard to Please," Augusta (GA) *The Colored American*, December 30, 1865, 1.

5 "Terrible and Swift Justice," Augusta (GA) *The Colored American*, December 30, 1865, 1.

6 Abbott, "The Republican Party Press in Reconstruction Georgia," 727.

7 "Proceeding of the Freedman's Convention of Georgia, Assembled at Augusta, January 10th, 1866, Containing the Speeches of Gen'L Tillson, Capt. J. E. Bryant and Others," Office of the Loyal Georgian, Augusta, Georgia, 1866, 8.

8 "The Loyal Georgian is One of the Very Outspoken Republican Papers in the South," Augusta (GA) *Daily Loyal Georgian*, June 15, 1867, 4.

9 Ruth Currie-McDaniel, *Carpetbagger of Conscience: A Biography of John Emery Bryant* (New York: Fordham University Press, 1999), 72.

10 "News and Other Items," Augusta (GA) *Daily Loyal Georgian*, June 7, 1867, 1.

11 "Items," Augusta (GA) *Daily Loyal Georgian*, July 27, 1867, 1.

12 Benjamin H. Hill, ed., *Senator Benjamin H. Hill of Georgia: His Life, Speeches and Writings* (Atlanta, GA: H. C. Hudgins and Company, 1891), 298.

13 "Republican Meeting," Augusta (GA) *Daily Loyal Georgian*, July 25, 1867, 1.

14 "Communicated," Augusta (GA) *Daily Loyal Georgian*, July 10, 1867, 1.

15 "Printers' Pic-Nic," Augusta (GA) *Daily Loyal Georgian*, June 7, 1867, 1.

16 "Reunion," Augusta (GA) *Daily Loyal Georgian*, July 28, 1867, 1.

17 "Items," Augusta (GA) *Daily Loyal Georgian*, July 16, 1867, 1.

18 "Colored Men, Remember," Augusta (GA) *Weekly Loyal Georgian*, February 15, 1867, 2.

19 "'Red, Yellow, and Black,'" Augusta (GA) *Weekly Loyal Georgian*, August 10, 1867, 2.

20 "Valedictory," *Daily Loyal Georgian*, July 28, 1867, 2.

21 "The Principles We Advocate," Augusta (GA) *Weekly Loyal Georgian*, August 10, 1867, 2.

22 "Colored Men, Remember," Augusta (GA) *Weekly Loyal Georgian*, August 10, 1867, 2.

23 Abbott, "The Republican Party Press in Reconstruction Georgia," 727.

24 Ibid, 728.

25 Abbott, *The Republican Party and the South, 1855-1877: The First Southern Strategy* (Chapel Hill, NC: University of North Carolina Press, 1986): 134, 135; *The Weekly Loyal Georgian*, in Georgia Historic Newspapers, accessed June 6, 2021, at <gahistoricnewspapers.galileo.usg.edu/lccn/sn83027105>.

26 Abbott, "The Republican Party Press in Reconstruction Georgia," 750.

27 Ibid, 758.

28 Currie-McDaniel, *Carpetbagger of Conscience*, 150.

29 William B. Hesseltine, *Ulysses S. Grant: Politician* (New York: Dodd, Mead & Company, 1935), 26.

30 "Gen. Grant and Li Hung Chang, Viceroy of China, taken at Tientsin Jan. 1879," Library of Congress, accessed November 2, 2021, at <loc.gov/item/2016647812>.

31 "Chas. Banks' Original Spectacular Burlesque," Library of Congress, accessed November 2, 2021, at <loc.gov/resource/var.0282>.

32 John Russell Young, *Around the World with General Grant: A Narrative of the Visit of General U.S. Grant, Ex-President of the United States, to Various Countries in Europe, Asia, and Africa, in 1877, 1878, 1879*, Vol. 1 (New York: American News Company, 1869), 3.

33 "The Noble Steamship Indiana," Philadelphia (PA) *North American*, May 25, 1877, 1.

34 Ron Chernow, *Grant* (New York: Penguin Press, 2017), 863.

35 William S. McFeely, *Grant, A Biography* (New York: W.W. Norton & Company, 1981), 1.

36 "Grant in England," New York *Herald*, September 24, 1877, 4.

37 "General Grant at Newcastle," New York *Herald*, September 22, 1877, 4.

38 Newcastle (UK) *Daily Chronicle*, September 24, 1877.

39 "Grant in England: Remarkable Demonstration in His Honor at Newcastle," New York *Herald*, September 24, 1877, 3.

40 "General Grant at Newcastle," New York *Herald*, September 22, 1877, 4.

41 "Grant in England," New York *Herald*, September 24, 1877, 4.

42 "Grant in England," San Francisco *Evening Bulletin*, June 1, 1877, 3.

43 Ibid.

44 "General Grant," New York *Herald*, June 1, 1877, 4.

45 Ibid

46 Young, *Around the World with General Grant*, 36.

47 Ibid, 38.

48 "An Ex-President Abroad and at Home," *Frank Leslie's Illustrated Newspaper*, June 23, 1877, 2 (266).

49 "Gen. Grant in London," New York *Tribune*, July 5, 1877, 1.

50 "Grant in Scotland," New York *Herald*, September 25, 1877, 3.

51 Ibid.

52 "Grant on American Politics," Chicago *Tribune*, September 27, 1877, 4.

53 "Gen. Grant the Guest of Consul Badeau in London," Chicago *Tribune*, June 10, 1877, 8.

54 "At Manchester: Ex-President Was in That Great English Manufacturing Town Yesterday," Chicago *Inter Ocean*, May 31, 1877, 5.

55 "The Truth about Grant," *Indianapolis* (IN) *State Sentinel*, quoted in Bellevue (LA) *Bossier Banner*, June 21, 1877, 2.

56 "Grant in England," Macon (GA) *Georgia Weekly Telegraph and Journal & Messenger*, July 24, 1877, 5.

57 "General Grant in Europe," Boston *Daily Advertiser*, June 7, 1877, 2.

58 "The Latest News," Raleigh (NC) *Register*, July 10, 1877, 2.

59 "Grant in England," Galveston (TX) *Daily News*, September 25, 1877, 1.

60 "Gen. Grant: The Voyage," Chicago *Tribune*, June 11, 1877, 1.

61 "Third Term Hints: Grant Revived," Wilmington (DE) *Daily Gazette*, May 19, 1877, 1.

62 "Grant," New Orleans *Daily Democrat*, November 10, 1878, 4.

63 "Grant and Victoria," Watertown (WI) *Republican*, July 4, 1877, 1.

64 "Ex-President in England," Princeton (MN) *Union*, June 8, 1877, 2.

65 "Honors to Our Ex-President," Prescott (AZ) *Weekly Arizona Miner*, June 15, 1877, 1.

66 "Honors to General Grant," Lowell (MA) *Daily Citizen and News*, June 5, 1877, 3.

67 "Grant in England," Denver (CO) *Rocky Mountain News*, June 22, 1877, 2.

68 "Ex-President Grant," *Times of London*, June 29, 1877, 10.

69 Ibid.

70 "General Grant," *Times of London*, June 1, 1877, 11.

71 "General Grant," London *Evening Mail*, June 1, 1877, 8.

72 "Gen. Grant in Manchester," Leeds (UK) *Mercury*, May 31, 1877, 6.

73 Young, *Around the World with General Grant*, 15.

74 "General Grant at the Guildhall," *Times of London*, June 16, 1877, 13.

75 Young, *Around the World with General Grant*, 41.

76 "General Grant," *Times of London*, September 14, 1877, 6.

77 Young, *Around the World with General Grant*, 83.

78 "London, Wednesday, May 23, 1877," *Times of London*, May 23, 1877, 9.

79 "Gen. Grant Talks: His Opinion of England and Englishman," London *World*, reprinted in Milwaukee (WI) *Sentinel*, July 12, 1877, 7.

80 "General Grant: His Visit to Sheffield," Sheffield (UK) *Independent*, September 27, 1877, 2.

81 "General Grant in Dundee: Visit the Mars and the Tay Bridge," Dundee (UK) *Courier and Argus*, September 3, 1877, 3.

82 "General Grant in Edinburgh," Dundee (UK) *Courier and Argus*, September 3, 1877, 3.

83 "General Grant in Scotland, Presentation of the Freedom of Ayr," Lanarkshire (UK) *North British Daily Mail*, September 15, 1877, 3.

84 Young, *Around the World with General Grant*, 79.

85 Ibid, 82.

86 "General Grant in Newcastle," Newcastle (UK) *Daily Journal*, September 22, 1877, 3.

87 Young, *Around the World with General Grant*, 87.

88 "General Grant in Newcastle," Newcastle (UK) *Daily Journal*, September 22, 1877, 3.

89 Young, *Around the World with General Grant*, 87.

90 "Enthusiastic Welcome on the Tyne," Newcastle (UK) *Journal*, September 22, 1877, 3.

91 Young, *Around the World with General Grant*, 91.

92 Ibid, 92.

93 Ibid, 93.

94 Ibid, 101.

95 Ibid, 103.

96 "General Grant," London *Morning Post*, October 20, 1877, 5.

97 "Grant in Ireland: A Queer Discussion," New York *Herald*, January 6, 1879, 7.

98 "Grant's Visit to Ireland," New Orleans *Daily Democrat*, January 10, 1879, 6.

99 "Grant in Ireland," New York *Herald*, January 4, 1879, 6.

100 "Grant in Ireland," New York *Herald*, January 8, 1879, 7.

101 "General Grant in Ireland," *Times of London*, January 4, 1879, 6.

Conclusion: Renewing the History of Journalism in the Civil War Era

"There are few things in this world which it is worthwhile to get angry about; and they are just the things anger will not improve." Henry Raymond, "A Word about Ourselves," *New York Times*, September 18, 1851.

Historians reflecting on the sweeping changes brought by the Civil War have generally understood it relative to political and legal issues, casting it in constitutional terms as the Second American Revolution; they can write no less in describing both the changes the war brought to the press and how the press changed the war. While the First American Revolution set into motion a free press with the protection of the First Amendment, the Civil War made the press a permanent fixture of a democratized citizenry. For four fateful years, the content and the purpose of the press, in a number of quite literal ways, reflected institutional and cultural changes in American society. In studying the members of the Fourth Estate as commentators on these changes, an informed student of history could argue that the United States evolved developmentally during this period more than in any other era.

Issues explored by newspaper writers and readers between the Age of Jackson and Reconstruction defined the fabric of the United States. During its catastrophic yet transformative duration, the war definitively changed the professional and institutional purpose of the press and the nation as a whole. With the horrific events that had made a new kind of content necessary—one that explored the deepest and sometimes darkest issues of humanity, including freedom, liberty, life, and death—by the end of the war, the concurrent development of individual technological innovations transformed newspaper production and revamped the industry as a whole. These changes extended beyond American politics and law, affecting concepts of freedom among a global audience.

To recap, in basic, quantitative measures, the exponential increase in the number of newspapers in the United Sates illustrates the increasingly prominent role of the press in daily life. In the early 1830s, the United States had 1,200 newspapers, most of them weeklies.[1] During the 1840s, as the United States grew in both population and its number of political participants, a wide audience turned to the press as a source of not only political content, but also for news, information, and, in the penny press, sensational entertainment. In the 1850s, the influence of the press on politics grew, with larger numbers of newspapers becoming sufficiently independent to attack political abuses. While newspaper operations devoted resources to covering actual battles instead of circulation battles, efforts to expand the reach of the press into daily lives reemerged during Reconstruction. Between 1870 and 1890, the number of newspapers published and their aggregate circulation increased almost exactly threefold from the antebellum era—about five times as fast as the population was growing. During Reconstruction, the circulation of newspapers nationwide was more than four and a half billion copies, with about 60 percent publishing daily.[2]

The growth of the press in the mid-nineteenth century was so great that according to an 1880 census, newspapers were published in 2,073 of the 2,605 nation's counties.[3] The expansion of railroads and growth of cities increased the demand for newspapers, and by the turn of the century, the United States was home to approximately 25,000 of them, including 2,300 dailies. Spirited newspaper rivalries sprang up everywhere, especially among the most energetic metropolitan papers. Every town of 10,000 or more had its own journal, compiled to a large degree of stories from New York's *Herald, Tribune,* and *Sun,* which in previous decades had helped found penny press conventions.

At the same time, the way in which news was distributed and collected changed dramatically. Editors who had printed not more than two or three columns of telegraphic news a day before the war now printed two or three pages of it. Correspondence by mail still existed, but editors accepted it only with reluctance, when they could obtain no better sources. The war also marked a turning point in the habits of news consumers, as readers followed casualty lists with personal interest, wanting to know if their family members and friends would appear in them. Although consumers had long desired timely information, technology and the war itself allowed them to expect it, as publishers, in their efforts to meet the demand for daily updates, used their resources (especially the telegraph) at times with little regard for cost. Editors, in turn, collectively directed reporters from nearly every major newspaper in the country, sending as many as forty correspondents to report on battles. This increased reliance on timely, fact-based information changed the structure of the newspaper itself, with news replacing front-page editorials and commentary. By the war's end, editors realized that their audience, which had grown accustomed to highly professional reporting, no longer took much interest in the sensational or everyday content of the pre-war days.[4]

On another level, while historians have tended to interpret the Civil War in the ways it affected the Constitution, describing it as the Second American Revolution, they have also, from a technological perspective described it as the first Modern War. Again, a student of history could say the same of the changes brought to the press. Inasmuch as technology, including highly advanced weapons and machinery, played a major role in the outcome of the war, the war affected journalism similarly, as the media that emerged laid the foundation for modern news, using highly advanced technologies. Along with the human demands of readers, machinery became a determining factor in the availability of massive quantities of information in much shorter periods than before the war. Revolving cylinders had replaced the flatbed Hoe presses used during the penny press era, and the addition of the stereotype, allowing for simultaneous printing on both sides of the page, accelerated the process even more. By the 1870s, increased production capabilities allowed the printing of more than 10,000 eight-page newspapers in an hour. Combining the stereotype cylinders to a set of multiunit machines made possible the production of a half-million to a million individual copies of a single newspaper issue in a single day. The new contraptions of six or eight presses combined to make one large machine that printed, folded, cut, pasted, and counted as many as 96,000 newspapers in an hour.[5] In an additional measure to increase efficiency, printers fed paper from a giant roll instead of individual sheets. The development of a method for producing cheap paper from wood pulp allowed printers to saved costs and, in turn, produce even larger quantities of news.

Another profound technological transformation is still very much a part of contemporary information consumption—the use of visuals to accentuate news. In some cases, visuals were the news, with the photographic innovations engineered by Mathew Brady—who pioneered photojournalism with his first studio displays in 1862—helping transform newspaper content on a very human level. The proliferation of graphics, illustrations, and photographic reproductions brought immediacy to daily events that transcended the symbolic abstractions

364 | Journalism in the Civil War Era

of text alone. *Harper's Weekly*, a leading illustrated literary magazine, helped

364 | *Journalism in the Civil War Era*

of text alone. *Harper's Weekly*, a leading illustrated literary magazine, helped popularize that development, shocking readers with reproductions of images from Antietam and—later—of starving and dying Union prisoners held in Andersonville, Georgia. As major daily newspapers, including New York's *Herald* and *Tribune*, and, increasingly, the *Times*, followed suit, photos became a mainstay of news. The result was a press that depicted life and death well beyond the scope of penny press predecessors.

A Requiem for Personal Journalism

The development and popularization of the penny press in the 1830s and 1840s highlighted an aspect to journalism that was peculiar to the era: the association of particular newspapers with the personalities of those who published them. Although certain elements of individual personalities are still prominently featured in specific, contemporary news programs, the personal opinions of publishing giants (most notably, James Gordon Bennett of *The New York Herald* and Horace Greeley of *The New York Tribune*) figured heavily into the choices made by consumers of the day.

Newspaper content just before the war had been locally oriented and directed toward the individual. Afterward, it came to meet the demands of the emerging business ethos of the country. Changes in the economic basis of the newspaper contributed directly to the transition, as advertising became more general with the increase in circulation, appealing to a less-specific local audience. Revenues of newspapers consequently tended to depend more on the favor of the advertiser than upon subscribers, giving the former a powerful although indirect influence on editorial policies. While city news associations continued to collect local items of interest, national press associations, composed of newspapers across the country, collected and distributed news of national importance to cater to the new publishing model.

Before the war, leading editors had made sporadic attempts at cooperation in obtaining national news, with the 1848 formation of the New York Associated Press, composed of the *Journal of Commerce*, *Courier and Enquirer*, *Tribune*, *Herald*, *Sun*, and *Express*, marking the first successful collaboration. Out of this idea grew other local, then state, and finally national associations. The telegraph, on yet another revolutionary level, made possible the delivery of information on a global scale. With the establishment of the Trans-Atlantic Cable that in the 1860s connected the East Coast of the United States with Europe, information from thousands of miles away was available immediately for the first time in human history.[6]

As a result, the scope of news naturally broadened, and stylistically, it included innovations such as interviews that featured dialogue and direct quotation, resulting in reports on business, markets, and finance taking on a new professionalism. Another increasingly popular feature was series of letters from the editor or another member of the staff who travelled abroad and wrote about what he heard or saw. The growth of these features also meant an unprecedented growth of staffs—writers and manual laborers—that exceeded the size and professional organization of anything developed in preceding years. It also produced an added emphasis on the talents of individual writers over the style of a particular editor.

These developments gradually affected the salience of personal journalism, as Bennett, Greeley, and other leaders of the era were no longer able to point solely to their editorial philosophies as the primary quality of their newspapers. Even before the beginning of the war, this style of publishing—characterized by the association of content with the personal qualities of the newspaper's leading editor—was ending. But while talented editors before the war could take credit for the great expansion of the numbers and influence of American newspapers, the war led to heavy investments in the development of a wider range of information, making particular and general issues the work of many contributors instead of just one.

To some extent, perhaps ironically, a remarkable editor influenced the declining role of personal journalism. Henry Raymond, who once worked for Greeley as an editorial assistant at the *Tribune*, helped set modern trends with the formation of his *New York Times*, which he first published in 1851 with a philosophy that went against conventional wisdom but later came to represent the mainstay of news. "There are few things in this world which it is worthwhile to get angry about," he wrote, "and they are just the things anger will not improve."[7] Raymond, an active player in New York's Republican Party, had believed simultaneously that a newspaper might assume the role of a non-partisan publication that encouraged independent thought. It took time for Raymond's approach toward journalism to take hold, but the post-war press reveals strains of it. As the leading editors of the antebellum era began dying—in New York, Raymond passed away in 1869, and Bennett and Greeley in 1872—readers no longer considered the *Times* to be simply Raymond's paper, or the *Herald* as Bennett's, or the *Tribune* as Greeley's. Newspapers subsequently trended away from content that reflected individual personalities and instead focused on the interests of the groups of people that read it—away from the editorial that expressed the views of a well-known writer, to an editorial page that combined the labors of many anonymous contributors.

In the 1870s, shortly after Raymond's death, the *Times* and *Harper's Weekly* illustrated his vision for the press by featuring Thomas Nast's cartoons exposing the corrupt Tweed Ring in New York City—truly departing from the content and style of previous news operations. The combination of illustrations with serious investigative reporting was an approach that sought the attention of both a sophisticated and interested electorate and new audience members—including waves of non-English-reading immigrants.

Yet, in other respects, the content did not change—newspapers continued to hold party affiliations and were seldom free from a biased point of view. In New York, for example, while the *World* continued to print items that blamed the South for the war, the *Tribune* made efforts to bring reconciliation, and the *Times* maintained a neutral position, So, if readers wanted all of the perspectives on the issues of the day, they still had to read more than one newspaper. While formal hostilities between the North and South had brought to a close many of the bitter partisan attacks among editors that had marked previous decades, evolution of the ideal of objectivism took time. It advanced slowly during Reconstruction, a time in which the purpose of the press transformed from one of political agency to being a source of information.

Furthermore, cessation of hostilities at Appomattox did not mean the issues upon which opposing sides had warred simply went away. From a Northern perspective, editors sought to legitimize the battles in which thousands of Yankee soldiers had died—a war that also changed in purpose, beginning as an attempt to restore the Union and ending as a call for the elimination of slavery. From a Southern perspective, editors in major cities saw the efforts of the federal government, as exercised under the administration of former Union General and two-term president Ulysses S. Grant, as a continuation of impositions from Washington before the war. Their editorials marked both a departure from the secessionist furor leading to the war and a continuation of the idea of states' rights. By the time of the 1872 election, those in both the North and the South who saw the Grant administration as failing to address their interests picked an unlikely candidate to represent them.

Horace Greeley's failed campaign for the presidency in 1872 illustrates how much the public's perception of editors had changed, and, perhaps more than any other event personified the death of personal journalism. At the outset of Reconstruction, sectional and partisan loyalties still determined the political goals of the major parties. Republican newspapers in the North, including Greeley's *Tribune*, supported General Ulysses S. Grant; however, nearing the end of Grant's first term, Greeley came to resent what he considered the administration's zeal to punish the South. Greeley began encouraging dissident Republicans, including Senators Carl Schurz, Lyman Trumbull, and Charles Sumner, who opposed Grant's military-based Reconstruction efforts, and, in May 1872, they formed the Liberal Republican Party. The Liberal Republicans picked for their presidential nominee Greeley—a Whig leader, one of the founders of the Republican Party, and a lifelong antagonist of the Democrats who called for a restoration of the nation more closely resembling what he believed to be Lincoln's ideals. To Greeley's surprise, his campaign was endorsed by the weakened and desperate Democratic Party, which, seeing no chance for a Southern candidate in the election, also nominated him as its candidate for president—the only time in U.S. history when a major party endorsed the candidate of a third party.

Greeley was the candidate of two parties to which a year prior he had declared no interest or loyalty. His acceptance speech at the Liberal Republican convention reflected his belief in the possibility of benevolently rebuilding the nation. Resigning his *Tribune* editorship to deliver speeches across the country, Greeley stressed the need for national reconciliation. His campaign promoted Universal Amnesty, which made it possible for Southern Democrats to support him because he promised to restore rights to former Confederate officers. However, voters in the South were alienated by the call, as it also entailed the enforcement of rights for freed slaves. The dilemma at the heart of the 1872 election from the perspective of Southern editors was that neither the Republicans nor Greeley's parties—the Liberal Republicans and Democrats—promised to represent their constituents.

Among the leading newspapers of the South, The Atlanta *Constitution* typified the tensions of a readership still scarred by war but anticipating new opportunities. Other newspapers in the South, such as the Richmond *Dispatch* and the Charleston *Daily Courier*, reflected enduring regional interests, but the *Constitution* by the 1870s had established levels of readership that rivaled the major publications of the North.[8] Its nameplate in the early 1870s boasted that it had the highest circulation of a newspaper in the city, county, and state. Reflective of national trends, the newspaper's diverse content included local, national, and international news, along with advertising for commercial products of every kind. And although Confederates had formally abandoned their cause, arguments published in the *Constitution* bespoke continued resistance in the South to President Grant's Reconstruction programs. Among Republican efforts rejected by the *Constitution*, state governments throughout the South, editors suggested, ought not to recognize the Reconstruction Amendments—especially the Fifteenth Amendment, which granted the right to vote to former male slaves. The primary argument advanced by the *Constitution*, as well as other newspapers in the South, was that the new suffrage rights infringed on the rights of Southern citizen as a whole, and that the measure was unnecessary, as state constitutions throughout the South already provided male suffrage.[9]

Despite its resounding editorial resistance to Northern objectives, Georgia was the only state to award Greeley, once dubbed the "Ultimate Yankee" by *Harper's Weekly*, with electoral votes in the 1872 election. The editorial content of other newspapers in the South, especially the older Democratic or Whig news-papers founded before the war, featured similar reactions to the Reconstruction Amendments, with the firebrand Charleston *Daily Courier* describing the Fifteenth Amendment in particular as a measure that deprived states of "all juris-diction over suffrage within their limits."[10]

In addition to maintaining a slogan of "Universal Suffrage" as a cornerstone of his campaign, Greeley alienated Northern support with the second plank in his campaign that called for "Universal Amnesty." Greeley had shown that he was serious about his beliefs by helping to free Jefferson Davis from prison, but in doing so, he had angered readers in the North who could not forgive the rebellion.[11] The move had cost the *Tribune* thousands of lifelong readers, and, in Republican newspapers in the North, editors used the incident to Grant's advantage.

By the summer of 1872, the campaign for president had degenerated into a mudslinging melee, epitomized by the anti-Greeley cartoons of Thomas Nast in *Harper's Weekly* and the anti-Grant cartoons of Matt Morgan in *Frank Leslie's Illustrated Newspaper*. While Greeley's supporters branded Grant a dictator and a drunk, Grant's supporters depicted Greeley as a traitor and a fool. Anti-Grant editorials and illustrations focused on the corruption that newspapers began to expose, including the Crédit Mobilier scandal, a scheme devised to spend $72 million on railroad contracts worth only $53 million. The scandal delved deep into the Grant administration, touching Greeley's old friend Schuyler Colfax who, after his first term as vice president, was forced to resign the office.[12] Meanwhile, Greeley's critics, including Nast, had little trouble finding controversial editorials published in the *Tribune* over the previous forty years, pointing to many of them (typically out of context) as indicative of Greeley's radicalism. While Greeley had been no stranger to controversy, the incessant assaults on his character took such a mental and physical toll on him that toward the end of his campaign he complained, "I have been assailed so bitterly that I hardly knew whether I was running for the presidency or the penitentiary."[13]

In the weeks leading to the election, Greeley returned to his *Tribune* office, resigned to the fate of the campaign. Managing editor Whitelaw Reid, who worried about Greeley's deteriorating health and the negative effect it might have on the newspaper's circulation, forced him to relinquish the post. Compounding the travails of Greeley's personal life, in early October his wife Mary Young Cheney Greeley had fallen sick and died. Grant won the 1872 election in a landslide, and shortly after the election, exhausted, disheartened, and ill, Greeley was interned in an asylum in Pleasantville, New York. He died a broken man on November 29, 1872, at the age of 61. At his funeral on December 4, critics who had made sport of him and admirers alike, including President Grant, mourned the loss of a humanitarian spirit and the nation's best-known editor—remembering him, in the words of Henry Ward Beecher's eulogy, as "a man who died of a broken heart."[14]

A New History

The press of the Civil War era told the story of a tremendous struggle, one for freedom and for respect—that began to transcend the American experience continued through and after Reconstruction. The United States during the Civil War, as European society had done previously, began drifting away from old agrarian ways to the new and often bewildering values of an urban society.[15] Since there was a dramatic shift in the character of society, and because cities were filling up with new waves of European immigrants, there would be a need for more newspapers everywhere (many in foreign languages), and a need for existing papers to increase their number of pages and circulations. Editors could now obtain European news thanks to steamship service, and, in the 1860s, through the Trans-Atlantic Cable developed a foreign news service that reached unprecedented standards of reportage.

In the United States, changes happening in New York City encapsulated universal aspects of the war. By the 1860s, the city had a population of almost 1 million. Combining its population with that of Brooklyn, Queens, and other nearby communities, along with areas in New Jersey, Long Island, and Connecticut, the 1.6 million-people metropolis was a beacon for European refugees escaping economic and political hardships. And by mid-century, the United States in general had taken on a more cosmopolitan composition, with immigrants from Ireland,

France, Italy, and Germany fleeing famine and failed revolutions. From Germany alone, nearly a million refugees had settled in the United States, with approximately 120,000 immigrating to New York City, making up 15 percent of the city's population—the largest collection of Germans outside Berlin and Vienna.[16] If Manhattan's Germans had set up their own city at the time, it would have been the fourth-largest collection of urban dwellers in the United States—and third largest if joined by Brooklyn's Germans.[17]

Immigrants who had worked as journalists and editors in Europe found work at the newspapers that sprang up in their communities. A prototype of the refugees, Carl Schurz, an assistant editor of the Bonner (Bonn) *Zeitung*, had become involved in the nationalist movement. When the armies of Frederick Wilhelm IV crushed it, Schurz escaped to the United States. In the mid-1850s he embarked on an active political career, recruiting German farmers in Wisconsin, his new home, to join the Republican Party. In Illinois, the role of German voters became so influential that in 1859, Republican presidential candidate Abraham Lincoln became part owner of the Illinois *Staats-Anzeiger*, a German-American newspaper edited by Dr. Theodore Canisius in Springfield—using it for eighteen months to help secure the presidency.[18] In Schurz, the Republicans found a valuable ally who championed equal rights for all citizens whether native or foreign-born, homesteads in the West, and adequate compensation to all laborers. He also lobbied for the support of another Forty-eighter, Oswald Ottendorfer, editor of the *New-Yorker Staats-Zeitung*.[19] Although Ottendorfer, who had fought for German democrats in 1848, had been the voice for German-Americans affiliated with the Democratic Party, Schurz convinced him to switch alliances and support Lincoln in the 1860 election, subsequently securing for Schurz roles during and after the war as a brigadier general, statesman, and senator.

Ottendorfer's newspaper, meanwhile, grew to boast the largest circulation of any German paper in the world.[20] By 1861, the influence of refugees in Missouri even surpassed their successes in Germany. A militia of German immigrants formed in St. Louis, Missouri, and led by Franz Siegel, a veteran of the struggle against the Prussians, disarmed secessionist forces, seized the state's arsenal, and helped overthrow the pro-Confederacy governor of Missouri, saving the state for the Union.[21] During the war, Secretary of State William H. Seward acknowledged that both Austria and Prussia were more sympathetic to the Union than the maritime powers of Great Britain and France.[22] But the role of the European powers among contemporary histories deserves re-examination, especially given scholarship trends that have increasingly understood nineteenth-century events as inextricably linked to a global context.

Traditionally, the most widely noted international event of the war stemmed from an incident involving the British ship Trent, with European newspapers in November 1861 providing wide coverage of the affair. When Charles Wilkes, commander of the Union warship San Jacinto, forcefully removed Confederate envoys James Mason and John Slidell from the Trent, the English perceived that the United States had insulted their national pride and vehemently objected. The incident threatened to escalate the war beyond the scope of the continental United States. The British sent a note to their minister in Washington, D.C., demanding an apology and the release of the prisoner, and France, Prussia, and Austria sent notes supporting the British demand. While remarkable as a seemingly singular overseas event, twentieth-century accounts of the Trent affair generally cast it as an anomaly, with historians generally focusing on the domestic progress of the war.

A vein of new historical scholarship, also referred to as "the new history," casts not only the Trent affair but also the whole of Civil War history in a new light. Historians have generally neglected to note that Central Europe had a direct interest in the outcome of the war, with at least one event in Europe, the Polish Insurrection of 1863, reflecting the struggle as having a distracting impact on the diplomacy of the era's maritime powers.[23] Using a Trans-Atlantic—and indeed a global—frame to interpret such events allows press historians to look at the European press differently.

Although the current record begs for subsequent histories on the subject of European press coverage of the war, the work of Niels Eichhorn, a doctoral student at the University of Arkansas, provides a sample of work in progress. For example, Eichhorn's analysis of *Kladderadatsch*, a newspaper started in Berlin during the 1848 uprisings, notes how the newspaper cast slavery as the chief cause of the Civil War, a position not entirely common at the time on either side of the Atlantic.[24] David Kalisch, the newspaper's liberal Jewish editor, had built readership over a ten-year period from *Kladderdatsch*'s first run of a few thousand copies to more than 20,000 by the 1860s. As Eichhorn saw it, the Civil War, far from affecting Americans alone, quickly led to a cotton shortage in Europe, due in part to the Union blockade of the South's ports. With other cotton-growing regions, such as India and Egypt, being slow to satisfy the demand, Europeans attributed the root of their economic problems to the American slave system. Although Great Britain—despite the unemployment of their workers and a certain concern about a worker's revolt—liked the price increases and the chance to use up extensive stores of crops from previous years, in Germany the cotton shortage led to a 50 percent drop in the number of textiles produced.[25]

This global context for understanding the economics, politics, and culture of the nineteenth century has been observed increasingly in the twenty-first century, as historians have sought to reinterpret accounts provided by relatively singular treatments of events on American soil. Michael Knox Beran's *Forge of Empires* (2007), for example, offers a compelling reinterpretation of the Lincoln administration on an international level, juxtaposing his role with those of nationalist leaders in Germany and Russia. Beran's angle is compelling because it not only rightfully puts Lincoln in a global context, but because until recently (due to the election of another Illinois president), it has been paid scant attention.

The Civil War and Meta-Journalism

Of all of the names and events associated with the Civil War, Lincoln and Gettysburg generally rise to the top in both popular and historical memory. The fateful battle, Lincoln's timeless commemoration speech, and its role in both the war and subsequent history illustrate how a true understanding of the past transcends simplistic notions of "names and dates," making history very much alive in our understanding of both the present and the future. For contemporary historians, understanding of Lincoln, Gettysburg, the Civil War, and the press of the era has taken on another dimension, one that goes beyond names and dates and includes locations outside of the United States to interpret the course of the war.

But for the civilian population of Gettysburg, the toll had been immediately devastating. The proximity of the small town to Washington, D.C. allowed the government to act swiftly, and Gettysburg's 2,400 inhabitants endured the stench of more than 7,500 dead and rotting soldiers. Pennsylvania Governor Andrew Gregg Curtin, in an effort to give the soldiers a dignified burial, agreed to buy the land with the intent of building a National Cemetery funded by representative states. Months later, to commemorate the dedication of the cemetery, Abraham Lincoln delivered a speech that still resonates as one of his most famous acts as president. Yet, by all accounts, he did not know when he delivered it that it would become the most quoted piece of oratory in American history.

Lincoln delivered the Gettysburg Address four and one half months after Union armies had defeated the Confederacy in the battle near the commemoration site. In a little more than two minutes, the president espoused the principles of equality found in the Declaration of Independence, defining the struggle of the Civil War as "a new birth of freedom." Despite the speech's subsequently prominent place in history, to this day disputes exist over its exact wording, reception

Image C.1 "Lincoln's Gettysburg Address, Gettysburg." 1863, printed later. The Library of Congress's caption indicates this photo is a reprint of a small detail of a photo showing the crowd gathered for the dedication of the Soldiers' National Cemetery where Lincoln gave the Gettysburg Address. Lincoln faces the crowd, not wearing a hat, about an inch below the third flag from the left. Josephine Cobb first found Lincoln's face while working with a glass plate negative at the National Archives in 1952. Another photo of Lincoln at Gettysburg, part of the Mathew Brady Collection in the National Archives and Records Administration, was identified in 1952 as a shot taken by David Bachrach."[28]

among the audience, and depiction in the press. Five known manuscripts of the address differ in a number of details, and accounts of the audience's reception in newspapers the next day differ, with the press reaction generally split along partisan lines. The Democratic-leaning Chicago *Times*, for example, suggested that "the cheek of every American must tingle with shame as he reads the silly, flat and dishwatery utterances of the man who has to be pointed out to intelligent foreigners as the President of the United States."[26] In contrast, the Republican-oriented *New York Times* praised Lincoln for the solemn effort, noting (unlike many newspapers in the North) that enthusiastic applause on several occasions interrupted the speech.[27]

Image C.2 "Dedication Ceremonies at the Soldiers' National Cemetery, Gettysburg, Pennsylvania." Alexander Gardner, November 19, 1863. Historians have recently suggested that this previously obscure photo by Gardner is among the few photos of President Abraham Lincoln at the 1863 commemoration. In 2007, members of the Center for Civil War Photography determined Lincoln might be visible in the crowd (near the top center) when viewed through magnification.[29]

A discovery in 1952 by Josephine Cobb, photo chief in the National Archives and Records Administration, identified Lincoln in a David Bachrach photo of attendees at the Gettysburg Address from a previously unexamined plate in the Mathew Brady Collection.[30] Until recently, it was believed that the Bachrach photo was one of a kind, but with the approach of the two-hundredth anniversary of Lincoln's birth, clues of the imprint Brady left on history took more than a commemorative dimension with unexpected discoveries of historical artifacts.[31]

In 2007, John Richter of the Center for Civil War Photography identified two photographs by Alexander Gardner in the Library of Congress collection that may show President Lincoln in the procession at Gettysburg, and historians now suggest that one of the previously obscure photos includes an image of Lincoln visible through magnification. Richter determined that Lincoln might be visible in the crowd (near the top center).[32] Even more recently, upon closer examination of this photo in 2013, Christopher Oakley, a scholar of new media at the University of North Carolina-Asheville, determined that Lincoln's presence in the same photo was more likely in a different location than that previously identified—that the first "Lincoln" was actually someone else.[33]

Oakley, a former Disney animator, examined the same Gardner photo using sophisticated image detailing. He believes he has identified Lincoln, along with Secretary of State William Seward, about forty feet to the right of the location suggested by Richter. Moreover, Oakley believes that Gardner had assigned one of his associates to capture this photo, and that Gardner himself is visible in the immediate foreground (right). This would be the only instance in which Lincoln and Gardner appear together. In this respect, a portrait of Lincoln's life as depicted in pictures serves as an appropriate personification of his era; the complex events of the Civil War era and the artifacts from it have evolved on a meta-historical level.[34] Scholars estimate that approximately 130 unique photos of Lincoln exist, taken by thirty-six different photographers on sixty-six occasions.[35]

In the century and a half since the oration, the "new birth of freedom" described by Lincoln has taken new meanings for successive generations, with interpretations as varied as the times and circumstances to which they applied. This event, part of the organic nature of history, provides one sample of the way in which the media (in this case photography) is inextricably part of a timeless interpretation of events.

The Press and the Civil War in the Twenty-First Century

As the Civil War remains a permanent fixture in American memory, the authors trust that their readers—in considering the multi-faceted aspects of the era, in particular, the role of the press—will help keep alive the memory of these events and the people who helped to shape them. Interest in the Civil War among scholars, historians, and authors certainly has not abated since publication of the first edition of this book. In fact, over the past 12 years dozens of books on the subject have been issued.

The following list is a selection of publications issued between 2010 and 2021, representative of scholarship about the press and the Civil War after release of the first edition of *Journalism in the Civil War Era*. It focuses in particular on scholarship associated with Abraham Lincoln's ties to the press. While not exhaustive—it certainly does not include all publications on these subjects during those years—the list does include secondary sources that contributed to the second edition of this book.

2010

McNeely, Patricia G., Debra Reddin van Tuyll, and Henry L. Schulte. *Knights of the Quill: Confederate Correspondents and their Civil War Reporting*. Purdue University Press, 2010. *Knights of the Quill* features war correspondence in Southern newspapers during the Civil War. It shows that men and women who covered the battles and political developments for Southern newspapers were doctors, lawyers, teachers, editors, and businessmen, nearly all with college and professional degrees. Objectivity and accuracy became important news values, and *Knights of the Quill* shows that Southern war correspondence equaled in quality work produced by reporters for Northern newspapers.[36]

2011

Borchard, Gregory A. *Abraham Lincoln and Horace Greeley*. Carbondale, IL: Southern Illinois University Press, 2011. *Abraham Lincoln and Horace Greeley* explores the intricate relationship between two major figures of nineteenth-century America. Packed with insightful analysis and painstaking research, it draws upon the personal papers of both men. Gregory A. Borchard explores in depth the impact the two men had on their times and each other, and how—as Lincoln's and Greeley's paths often crossed, and sometimes diverged—they personified the complexities, virtues, contradictions, and faults of their era. The book also develops material later featured in *Lincoln Mediated: The President and the Press through Nineteenth Century Media* by Borchard and David W. Bulla (2015).[37]

Carwardine, Richard, and Jay Sexton, *The Global Lincoln*. Oxford and New York: Oxford University Press, 2011. *The Global Lincoln* makes the case that admiration of President Lincoln extends well beyond American borders. Lincoln's post-death popularity was highest in countries that were undergoing development and economic growth. He served as an example of how the interests of an individual, self-improving laborer could contribute directly to the development and modernization of a national economy. In the analysis of Carawardine and Sexton, global citizens began looking to Lincoln as a leader who related to individuals regardless of social standing. "This view of Lincoln was most frequently articulated in places undergoing rapid economic development—late nineteenth-century Argentina or Japan in the early twentieth century—where Lincoln served as hope or reassurance that the dislocating changes of economic modernization would benefit both the individual and the larger policy."[38]

Hogan, Jackie. *Lincoln, Inc.: Selling the Sixteenth President in Contemporary America*. Lanham, MD: Rowman and Littlefield, 2011. *Lincoln, Inc.* estimates there were 15,000 books on Lincoln in circulation by 2010, with more than 4,500 published between 2005 and 2010 alone. Treatments range from non-fiction to fiction and include biographies, military analyses, political analyses, sociology, psychology, and even imaginings of Lincoln as a superhero for modern popular culture. While many cite primary sources such as letters and articles from Lincoln and his contemporaries, others republish these documents in full. *Lincoln, Inc.*, specifically explores the image of Lincoln in contemporary society, providing a sociological study on how he and his story have been disseminated in culture, and how the story plays into ideas about nationalism and American identity.[39]

2012

Risley, Ford. *Civil War Journalism*. Santa Barbara, CA: Praeger, 2012. *Civil War Journalism* offers a unique synthesis of the journalism of both the North and the South during the war. Its cast of characters includes editors Horace Greeley and John M. Daniel, correspondents George Smalley and Peter W. Alexander, photographers Mathew Brady and Alexander Gardner, and illustrators Alfred Waud and Thomas Nast. The work provides an introductory overview of journalism in the North and South on the eve of the Civil War. Risley recognizes Abraham Lincoln as not only being concerned with press content, but as contributing to it as well. "More than any president before him," Risley writes, "Lincoln understood the role of the press, its tendencies, and its shortcomings."[40]

2013

Borchard, Gregory A., Lawrence J. Mullen, and Stephen Bates. "From Realism to Reality: The Advent of War Photography." *Journalism & Communication Monographs*, 15, 2 (June 2013): 66-107. The monograph "From Realism to Reality: The Advent of War Photography" focuses on a selection of images displayed to audiences during the American Civil War era, in two categories—illustrations and photographs. Illustrations include lithographs and handcrafted interpretations of events. Photographs include the mechanically based processes of the era that featured chemically captured images, or remnants of actual events. The chronological scope of this work is between the war's outbreak in 1861 and its close in 1865. Using theoretical approaches generally applied to the social sciences, the monograph interprets the content of images and places them in context with the origins of photography. It also compares both the common and dissimilar features of illustrated and photographic images from the era.[41]

Reddin van Tuyll, Debra. *The Confederate Press in the Crucible of the American Civil War*. New York: Peter Lang, 2013. Debra Reddin van Tuyll's *The Confederate Press in the Crucible of the American Civil War* focuses on the press as a social, political, and economic institution that both shaped and was shaped by the Confederacy's experience. It documents how the press changed, stayed the same, and evolved by examining its role in Confederate society relative to social and demographic characteristics of journalists and their audiences, legal regulation of the industry, and how the war influenced both the business side of journalism and editorial decisions. The story of the Confederate press provides a prime opportunity to study how a domestic war affects the American press.[42]

2014

Holzer, Harold. *Lincoln and the Power of the Press: The War for Public Opinion*. New York: Simon and Schuster, 2014. In *Lincoln and the Power of the Press*, Harold Holzer writes that Abraham Lincoln, along with a triumvirate of New York editors—Horace Greeley of the *Tribune*, James Gordon Bennett of the *Herald*, and Henry Raymond of the *Times*—contributed directly to a legacy that continues to shape our understanding of the American experience. Holzer's book shows how Lincoln interacted with these figures, among other newsmakers, and how the worlds of politics and the press intertwined to create a competition for ideals and policy that determined the course of the nation between the 1830s and the 1860s.[43]

2015

Borchard, Gregory A., and David W. Bulla, *Lincoln Mediated: The President and the Press through Nineteenth Century Media*. Piscataway, NJ: Transaction, 2015; Routledge 2020. *Lincoln Mediated* describes the ways in which Abraham Lincoln worked with the press throughout his political career. This connection on a national level began with his service in Congress in the late 1840s and developed into ties with newspapers in Illinois, New York, and Washington. Borchard and Bulla study how Lincoln used the press to deliver his written and spoken messages, how editors reacted to the president, and how Lincoln responded to their criticism. Reviewing his public persona through the lens of international media and visually based sources, the authors cite the papers of Lincoln, the letters of influential figures, and content from leading newspapers, as well as nineteenth-century illustrations and photographs.[44]

2016

Cronin, Mary M., ed. *An Indispensable Liberty: The Fight for Free Speech in Nineteenth-Century America.* Southern Illinois University Press, 2016. *An Indispensable Liberty* examines attempts to restrict freedom of speech and the press during and after the Civil War. The volume's contributors blend social, cultural, and intellectual history to untangle the complicated strands of nineteenth-century legal thought. By chronicling the development of modern-day notions of free speech, this timely collection offers both a valuable exploration of the First Amendment in nineteenth-century America and a useful perspective on the challenges we face today.[45]

2017

Sachsman, David B., and David W. Bulla, eds. *Sensationalism: Murder, Mayhem, Mudslinging, Scandals, and Disasters in 19ᵗʰ Century Reporting.* Piscataway, NJ: Transaction Publishers, 2017. Sachsman and Bulla compile a range of essays that explore sensationalism in nineteenth-century newspaper reporting. Featured chapters analyze the role of sensationalism—detailing the rise of the penny press in the 1830s and the careers of specific editors and reporters dedicated to this particular journalistic style. A section of the book focuses on subjects including yellow journalism, sensational pictures, and changes in reporting over a twenty-year span. Another section focuses on sensationalism, the American presidency, and the reasons why muckraking became a force during the Progressive Era. Other topics explored include the place of religion and death in nineteenth-century newspapers and the connection between sensationalism and hatred.[46]

Sachsman, David B., ed. *A Press Divided: Newspaper Coverage of the Civil War.* London and New York: Routledge, 2017. *A Press Divided* provides new insights into the sharp political divisions that existed among newspapers of the Civil War era. These divisions reflected and exacerbated the conflicts in political thought that caused the Civil War, as well as political and ideological battles within the Union and the Confederacy about how to pursue the war. In the North, dissenting voices alarmed the Lincoln administration to such a degree that draconian measures were taken to suppress dissenting newspapers and editors, while in the

South the Confederate government held to its belief in freedom of speech and was more tolerant of political attacks in the press.[47]

Sachsman, David B., ed. *After the War: The Press in a Changing America, 1865–1900.* New York: Taylor & Francis, 2017. *After the War* presents a panoramic view of social, political, and economic change in post-Civil War America by examining its journalism—from coverage of politics and Reconstruction to sensational reporting and images of the American people. Changes in America during this time were so dramatic that they transformed the social structure of the country and the nature of journalism. By the 1870s and 1880s, new kinds of daily newspapers had developed. New Journalism eventually gave rise to Yellow Journalism, resulting in big-city newspapers that were increasingly sensationalistic and entertaining, and designed to attract everyone.[48]

2018

Risley, Ford. *Dear* Courier: *The Civil War Correspondence of Editor Melvin Dwinell.* Knoxville, TN: University of Tennessee Press, 2018. *Dear* Courier appeals to those interested in the campaigns of Robert E. Lee's Army of Northern Virginia, as well as those seeking accessible primary documents from the Civil War. The *Courier* in the title of this book is the Rome, Georgia, newspaper that Vermont native Melvin Dwinell (1825-1887) purchased in 1853, after moving south to teach school two years earlier. This book consists of Dwinell's dispatches from the war zone to his paper back in Georgia throughout his service in the Army of Northern Virginia. Risley adds helpful chapter introductions, annotations, and an epilogue that together provide context to the dispatches.[49]

2019

Fuhlhage, Michael. *Yankee Reporters and Southern Secrets: Journalism, Open Source Intelligence, and the Coming of the Civil War.* New York: Peter Lang, 2019. *Yankee Reporters and Southern Secrets* details evidence of a secessionist conspiracy that appeared in American newspapers from the end of the 1860 presidential campaign to just before the first major battle of the American Civil War. This book tells the story of the Yankee reporters who went undercover in hostile places that became the Confederate States of America. By observing the secession movement and sending reports for publication in Northern newspapers, they armed the Union with intelligence about the enemy that civil and military leaders used to inform their decisions, in order to contain damage and counter the movement to break the Union apart and establish a separate slavery-based nation in the South.[50]

Guarneri, Carl J. *Lincoln's Informer: Charles A. Dana and the Inside Story of the Union War*. Lawrence, KS: University of Kansas Press, 2019. *Lincoln's Informer* profiles Charles A. Dana, who, as managing editor of Horace Greeley's *New York Tribune*, led the newspaper's efforts against proslavery forces in Congress and the Kansas territory. When his criticism of the Union's prosecution of the war became too much for Greeley, Dana was drafted by Secretary of War Edwin Stanton to be a special agent. Drawing on Dana's reports, letters, and telegrams, Guarneri reconstructs the Civil War through Dana's eyes.[51]

Lundberg, James M. *Horace Greeley: Print, Politics, and the Failure of American Nationhood*. Urbana, IL: University of Illinois Press, 2019. *Horace Greeley: Print, Politics, and the Failure of American Nationhood* examines one of the most significant and complex newspaper personalities in American history. Lundberg also provides a compelling analysis of nineteenth-century issues as reflected in the content of Greeley's *New York Tribune*. The author argues that after the Civil War, Greeley failed to read correctly the mood of the public that he had, in earnest, previously sought to engage—Americans North and South who had no reason to believe the American System he championed in previous decades could possibly heal rifts still raw during Reconstruction.[52]

Sachsman, David B., and Gregory A. Borchard. *The Antebellum Press: Setting the Stage for Civil War*. New York: Taylor & Francis, 2019. Editors David B. Sachsman and Gregory A. Borchard argue in *The Antebellum Press: Setting the Stage for Civil War* that journalism in the years leading up to America's deadliest conflict in some ways contributed to the war's outbreak. Major challenges faced by American newspapers prior to secession and war are explored—including economic development of the press, technology and its influence on the press, major editors and reporters (North and South) and the role of partisanship, and the central debate over slavery in the future of an expanding nation.[53]

Temple, Wayne C. *Lincoln's Confidant: The Life of Noah Brooks*. Baltimore: Johns Hopkins University Press, 2019. *Lincoln's Confidant* profiles Noah Brooks, an influential journalist best known as a biographer of Abraham Lincoln and as a longstanding political supporter and close friend to the president during the Civil War—a time unlike any other, in which Lincoln truly needed a confidant. In Temple's view, Brooks' claim to fame should not rest entirely on his friendship with Lincoln. Rather, through the nineteenth century and into the twentieth, "Brooks won 'world-wide fame' as a journalist and man of letters."

382 | *Journalism in the Civil War Era*

Temple's book not only provides new source material on Lincoln, but it spotlights a member of the nineteenth-century press who was remarkable in his own right.[54]

2020

Mitchell, Elizabeth. *Lincoln's Lie: A True Civil War Caper through Fake News, Wall Street, and the White House.* Berkeley, CA: Counterpoint, 2020. *Lincoln's Lie* provides a narrative linking Civil War-era newspaper offices and the White House. Mitchell profiles manipulators of news during the war and explains their motivations for engaging in deception through the press. Her account of Lincoln's troubled relationship with the press and its role in the Civil War speaks powerfully to our current political crises: fake news, profiteering, Constitutional conflict, and a president at war with the media.[55]

2021

Cronin, Mary, and Debra Reddin van Tuyll, eds. *The Western Press in the Crucible of the American Civil War.* New York: Peter Lang, 2021. Relatively little scholarly attention has been paid to the role of newspapers in the West during the Civil War. Cronin and Reddin van Tuyll's contribution to the body of literature reveals, however, that areas far removed from the Eastern theater were nevertheless not immune from battles, military recruitment, national anxieties, or partisan fights. Editors from the Great Plains to the Pacific Coast addressed secession, the war, and its immediate aftermath.[56]

2022

Through 2022, it can be said that these books collectively demonstrate that we, as readers and as participants in the American experiment of representative democracy, have both evolved in our social attitudes since 1865 and still think in ways that our ancestors would recognize. According to 2022 polling, for example, 31 percent of American voters believe a second civil war within the United States will occur before 2030. At the same time, national security experts have assessed the chances of a civil war in the next 10 to 15 years and have reached a consensus that such a war has a 35 percent chance of occurring.

- A corresponding poll conducted by Georgetown University in 2019 asked Americans about the nearness of a civil war on a scale of 0 to 100. Responses indicated a belief that we are nearly two-thirds of the way to conflict.[57]

- A likeminded survey published by the University of Virginia Center for Politics after the 2020 elections found that 41 percent of Biden voters and 52 percent of Trump voters at least "somewhat agree" that "the situation in America" makes them favor Blue or Red states "seceding from the union to form their own separate country."[58]

This political divide further corresponds to which states were free states and which were slave states before the Civil War. Yet, history has shown that the process of secession cannot result in the desired ends of those who advocate for it. The biggest reason to separate is the most glaring and the most frightful to contemplate: Citizens of the United States are losing faith in the validity of their institutions and the nation's founding myths.

"Americans hate each other," writes Stephen Marche in an ironically reassuring way. "But we aren't headed for civil war ... Talk of secession always gets U.S. history wrong." In place of solidarity, a vast and powerful anger is building— a rage that increasingly expresses itself in violence like the riots that erupted throughout 2020 and into 2021. And, while secession may be a painful option to confront, it is far less painful than the alternative suggested by those who favor disunion. Indeed, given the hurdles, it also may be far less possible. "A separate Texas wouldn't have the power of the current United States in global negotiations," Marche writes. "It would just be another midsize country with no history and no connections."[59]

At the same time, writes James McCarten of *The Canadian Press*, the slaying of a Las Vegas newspaper reporter in 2022 illustrates a reality that the United States has not confronted since the Civil War: Domestic journalism has become a practice that is clearly and increasingly dangerous. Jeff German, 69, a reporter for the *Las Vegas Review-Journal*, was stabbed to death in September, allegedly by an elected official after publication of an expose of the administrator's office. The U.S. Press Freedom Tracker, an online database managed by the Freedom of the Press Association, had concurrently cataloged twenty-eight assaults against members of the media, most of them the result of direct targeting. While thirty-nine journalists have historically been killed on U.S. soil—most of them during the Civil War—nine have died in the last 30 years, including four who were killed in a mass shooting at a Maryland newsroom in 2018. "I would like to have said, 'No, we didn't see this kind of thing coming in the United States,'" said Celeste González de Bustamante, a professor of journalism at the University of Texas at Austin. "But we've often said that what's happening in other parts of the world, where press freedoms are under significantly more pressure, is a harbinger of what could be coming in places like the United States."[60]

Much of what is known about the fateful years between 1861 and 1865 has not changed over the course of time; it is only being taught in different ways. If Americans truly are to interpret the Civil War correctly, they will need to view it from outside of their current contexts—stepping outside of contemporary moments to see history as it truly happened. This proposition is not entirely abstract, as the legacy of the Civil War is preserved through texts—namely the press and sources featured herein—that serve as commemorative symbols and means by which the past becomes part of our everyday life. Images of the era—including those provided in this book—may have among the most lasting communicative powers through which we can understand the lives of those who participated directly in the war.

Another such way in which this history may be explored is the global dimension—how the people of other nations have viewed the Civil War, as well as how they view it now. This narrative is a process that historians have begun to explore, and that this book makes part of its story as well. While the central issues of the war have changed according to those who both wrote about them and fought over them, we who read about them must think not only in the past tense, but also in the present and future. It is our hope that *Journalism in the Civil War Era* has helped you do so.

Notes

1 Simon Newton Dexter North, *History and Present Conditions of the Newspaper and Periodical Press of the United States* (Washington, DC: U.S. Government Printing Office, 1884), 47.

2 Charles Ramsdell Lingley, *Since the Civil War* (New York: The Century, 1920), 100.

3 North, *History and Present Condition of the Newspaper and Periodical Press of the United States*, 73.

4 Lingley, *Since the Civil War*, 100.

5 DePew, *One Hundred Years of American Commerce*, Vol. 1 (New York: D. O. Haynes, 1895), 171.

6 Blondheim, *News over the Wires: The Telegraph and the Flow of Public Information in America 1844–1897* (Cambridge, MA: Harvard University Press, 1994), 47–96.

7 "A Word about Ourselves," New York *Times*, September 18, 1851.

8 Borchard, "Taking No Rights For Granted: The Southern Press and the 15th Amendment," in Sachsman, S. Kittrell Rushing, and Roy Morris, eds. *Words at War* (West Lafayette, IN: Purdue University Press, 2008), 309–18.

9 Atlanta *Constitution*, March 12, 1869.

10 "The Fifteenth Amendment," Charleston (SC) *Daily Courier*, April 14, 1869.

11 Parton, *Life of Horace Greeley* (1872), 539–42.

12 James Ford Rhodes, *History of the United States from the Compromise of 1850 to the Final Restoration of Home Rule at the South in 1877*, Vol. 7 (London: MacMillan & Co., 1920), 13.

13 Alexander, *A Political History of the State of New York*, 301.

14 *A Memorial of Horace Greeley* (New York: *Tribune* Association, 1873), 76.

15 Michael F. Holt, *The Rise and Fall of the American Whig Party: Jacksonian Politics and the Onset of the Civil War* (New York, Oxford: Oxford University Press, 1999), 743.

16 Tyler Anbinder, *Nativism and Slavery* (New York and Oxford: Oxford University Press, 1992), 4.

17 Burrows and Wallace, *Gotham*, 745.

18 Donald, *Lincoln*, 211, 242.

19 "Oswald Ottendorfer Passes Away," New York *Times*, December 16, 1900.

20 Carl Schurz, *The Reminiscences of Carl Schurz*, Vol. 2 (New York: Doubleday, 1908), 67, 72.

21 Jonathan Sperber, *Rhineland Radicals: The Democratic Movement and the Revolution of 1848–1849* (Princeton, NJ: Princeton, 1992), 492, 493.

22 Lynn M. Case and Warren F Spencer, *The United States and France: Civil War Diplomacy* (Philadelphia: University of Pennsylvania Press, 1970), 68.

23 Dean B. Mahin, *One War at a Time: The International Dimension of the American Civil War* (Dulles, VA: Brassey's, 2000), 197–205.

24 Niels Eichhorn, "Kladderadatsch: A German Newspaper Perspective on the Civil War and Its International Context," paper presented at The Symposium on the 19th Century Press, the Civil War, and Free Expression, November 13–15, 2008, 4.

25 Ibid, 5, 6.

26 Chicago *Times*, November 22, 1863.

27 "The Heroes of July," New York *Times*, November 20, 1863.

28 "Lincoln's Gettysburg Address, Gettysburg," Library of Congress, accessed July 1, 2021, at <loc.gov/resource/ds.03106>.

29 "Dedication Ceremonies at the Soldiers' National Cemetery, Gettysburg, Pennsylvania," Library of Congress, accessed July 13, 2021, at <loc.gov/pictures/item/2018672029>.

30 "Dedication of Monument at Gettysburg cemetery," David Bachrach, photographer [attributed], November 19, 1863, Library of Congress, accessed July 1, 2021, at <loc.gov/pictures/item/2012647713>.

31 Borchard and Bulla, *Lincoln Mediated*, 47.

32 Allen, "Lincoln in the News," Library of Congress, accessed July 1, 2021, at <loc. gov/loc/lcib/0803/lincolnnews.html>.

33 Franz Lidz, "Will the Real Abraham Lincoln Please Stand Up?" *Smithsonian*, October 2013, accessed July 1, 2021, at <smithsonianmag.com/history/will-the-real-abraham-lincoln-please-stand-up-3431>; Jennifer Schuessler "Scholar Says He's Found New Photo of Lincoln at Gettysburg," New York *Times*, October 14, 2013, accessed July 1, 2021, at <artsbeat.blogs.nytimes.com/2013/09/24/scholar-says-hes-found-new-photo-of-lincoln-at-gettysburg>.

34 Borchard and Bulla, *Lincoln Mediated*, 34.

35 George Sullivan, *Picturing Lincoln: Famous Photographs that Popularized the President*. (New York: Clarion Books, 2000), 2.

36 Patricia G. McNeely, Reddin van Tuyll, and Henry L. Schulte, *Knights of the Quill: Confederate Correspondents and their Civil War Reporting* (Purdue University Press, 2010), 571-96.

37 Borchard, *Abraham Lincoln and Horace Greeley*, 67-89.

38 Carwardine and Sexton, *The Global Lincoln*, 5. 9.

39 Jackie Hogan, *Lincoln, Inc.: Selling the Sixteenth President in Contemporary America* (Lanham, MD: Rowman and Littlefield, 2011), 1-10, 29-49.

40 Risley, *Civil War Journalism* (Santa Barbara, CA: Praeger, 2012), 17.

41 Borchard, Mullen, and Bates, "From Realism to Reality," 66-107.

42 Reddin van Tuyll, *The Confederate Press in the Crucible of the American Civil War* (New York: Peter Lang, 2013), 75-324.

43 Holzer, *Lincoln and the Power of the Press*, 467, 556.

44 Borchard and Bulla, *Lincoln Mediated*, 29-186.

45 Cronin, ed., *An Indispensable Liberty: The Fight for Free Speech in Nineteenth-Century America* (Southern Illinois University Press, 2016), 41-60.

46 Sachsman, and David W. Bulla, eds., *Sensationalism: Murder, Mayhem, Mudslinging, Scandals, and Disasters in 19ᵗʰ Century Reporting* (Piscataway, NJ: Transaction Publishers, 2017), 53-74.

47 Sachsman, ed., *A Press Divided: Newspaper Coverage of the Civil War* (London and New York: Routledge, 2017), 3-18.

48 Sachsman, ed., *After the War: The Press in a Changing America, 1865–1900* (New York: Taylor & Francis, 2017), 3-20.

49 Risley, *Dear Courier: The Civil War Correspondence of Editor Melvin Dwinell* (Knoxville, TN: University of Tennessee Press, 2018), 54, 60, 294, 295.

50 Michael Fuhlhage, *Yankee Reporters and Southern Secrets: Journalism, Open Source Intelligence, and the Coming of the Civil War* (New York: Peter Lang, 2019), 3-18.

51 Carl J. Guarneri, *Lincoln's Informer: Charles A. Dana and the Inside Story of the Union War* (Lawrence, KS: University of Kansas Press, 2019), 8-348.

52 James M. Lundberg, *Horace Greeley: Print, Politics, and the Failure of American Nationhood* (Urbana, IL: University of Illinois Press, 2019), 113-45.

53 Sachsman, and Borchard, *The Antebellum Press: Setting the Stage for Civil War* (New York: Taylor & Francis, 2019), 1-13.

54 Wayne C. Temple, *Lincoln's Confidant: The Life of Noah Brooks* (Baltimore: John's Hopkins University Press, 2019), 8.

55 Elizabeth Mitchell, *Lincoln's Lie: A True Civil War Caper through Fake News, Wall Street, and the White House* (Berkeley, CA: Counterpoint, 2020), 3-247.

56 Cronin and Reddin van Tuyll, eds, *The Western Press in the Crucible of the American Civil War* (New York: Peter Lang, 2021), 1-20.

57 Stephen Marche, *The Next Civil War: Dispatches from the American Future* (New York: Avid Reader Press, 2022), 2.

58 Marche, "Secession Might Seem Like the Lesser of Two Evils: It's also the Less Likely," *Washington Post*, December 31, 2021, accessed February 18, 2022, at <washingtonpost.com/outlook/2021/12/31/secession-civil-war-stephen-marche>.

59 Ibid.

60 James McCarten, "Press Perils: Killing of Las Vegas Reporter Drives Home Dangers of Modern Journalism," *The Canadian Press*, September 13, 2022, accessed October 11, 2022, at <cfjctoday.com/2022/09/13/press-perils-killing-of-las-vegas-reporter-drives-home-dangers-of-modern-journalism>.

Appendix: Journalism and Abraham Lincoln

While posterity has celebrated Abraham Lincoln popularly as a one of the most extraordinary presidents in American history, certain misconceptions about his life have also made their way into American consciousness. According to folklore, for example, Lincoln could easily resemble a country bumpkin, one who failed at everything until he rose to his heroic place in history under difficult circumstances. The account, although an attractive myth, fails under scrutiny, as an accurate study of his life reveals Lincoln to be a successful lawyer and outspoken politician. Among other sources, *Chicken Soup for the Soul*, for example, has helped perpetuate the myth that Lincoln essentially failed at everything before becoming president, although researchers at Snopes.com, along with generations of historians, demonstrate the claims about Lincoln's failures are mostly false.[1]

Lincoln's biographers more generally agree that he had a conservative worldview—if not entirely conservative political beliefs—for most or all of his life. While the mention of only a few contemporary biographies here does not do justice to the depth and breadth of Lincoln scholarship, Ronald C. White's *A. Lincoln: A Biography* (2009), a widely-recognized recent account, describes an understanding increasingly accepted by historians of a transformation in Lincoln's outlook before, during, and after the Civil War. White notes that as a young man, Lincoln believed his generation's role was to "transmit" the values of the nation's founders, but over time, he came to believe that each generation must redefine America in relation to the current problems it faces.[2] By the middle of the Civil War, Lincoln declared, "The dogmas of the quiet past are inadequate for the stormy present," and at the same time, he began thinking in the future tense, saying, "we must think anew and act anew."[3]

Of the biographies by Lincoln's contemporaries, *Herndon's Lincoln*, first published in 1889 by the Springfield lawyer's partner William Herndon, has been a leading primary source for historians seeking to understand the personal characteristics of the president prior to his near deification for more than a century.[4] A more nuanced look at Lincoln was featured in the formal biography *Abraham Lincoln: A History* by the president's secretaries John Hay and John G. Nicolay, who in 1890 conveyed many essential details of the president's life that have subsequently become a matter of historical record. Lincoln's legacy before the end of the nineteenth century had already reached divine levels, the authors noted. Projecting the tone of subsequent secondary analyses on Lincoln's life, Hay and Nicolay described the Lincoln name as having become synonymous with the word liberty. "His work is finished," they wrote, "and sealed forever with the veneration given to the blood of martyrs."[5]

Since the nineteenth century, the path of Lincoln's legacy has taken various turns, with not every historian remembering him at the near-deified levels of today. Although he was able to finish only two of the volumes in his ambitious work, Albert J. Beveridge's biography *Abraham Lincoln, 1809–1858* (1928) remains a classic example, as well as one of the more controversial treatments of Lincoln's life. Beveridge, unlike many of those who preceded or followed him, expressed in his understanding of Lincoln's politics a sympathy for Southern independence by suggesting it was the radicals in the North, not secessionists, who had killed compromise. In Beveridge's account, Stephen A. Douglas, Lincoln's nemesis in other histories, emerged as a hero, with the Little Giant among those who tried desperately to save the Union. At the same time, Beveridge did see greatness in Lincoln, citing his Springfield speech in October 1854 that attacked the Kansas-Nebraska legislation. The speech, Beveridge wrote, displayed "exalted yet restrained eloquence" and the "generosity of spirit which is to be fully realized in the Second Inaugural."[6]

In a similarly revisionist approach to Lincoln's story, Randall's *Lincoln the President* (1945–1955) established the standard for interpreting previous scholarship, depicting Lincoln's greatest successes as fending off the designs of Radical Republicans who sought both to destroy the South and to punish it after the war. Randall's version of history pitted a conservative Lincoln against adversaries in

his own party who posed an even greater threat to his ability to lead than did anyone in the Democratic Party.[7] Among Lincoln's most difficult legal decisions—
perhaps still the most controversial exercise of his powers as president—was his
suspension of the writ of habeas corpus, which Randall noted, concerned even
Lincoln as a potentially dictatorial move and one that members of the press rightfully criticized.[8] While subsequent generations of students of history have come
to know Lincoln as the Great Emancipator, concerns about his management of
civil liberties, noted not only by Randall, are valid, as he remains the only president to have suspended the writ of habeas corpus and to have prosecuted and
censored opponents.

    In general, the tone of works published about Lincoln by historians since
the Civil War have ranged from respectful to revisionist and critical. A surge
of studies in "new history" has put historical characters and events into an
international perspective. Michael Knox Beran's *Forge of Empires* re-interprets
Lincoln by juxtaposing his role with those of nationalist leaders in Germany
and Russia. "Lincoln called his revolution a 'new birth of freedom.' Bismarck
spoke of a revolution accomplished through an expenditure of 'blood and iron.'
Alexander implemented what he described as a revolution 'from above,'" Beran
writes. "Their revolutions were made in the name of freedom, and were to varying
extents consecrated to the freer movement of people, goods, and ideas."[9]

    Other contemporary histories have departed from the classically oriented
studies about Lincoln and focused on his ties to political culture. Barry Schwartz's
Abraham Lincoln and the Forge of National Memory, for example, makes the president and the man the subject of a sociological study of the nation's collective
memory. He looks at the construction of Lincoln myths in the wake of his death
and traces them through the twentieth century. Some themes Schwartz explores
include the misconceptions of Lincoln as a defender of civil rights and as a self-
made man of humble beginnings.[10]

    Building on Schwartz's thesis, Jackie Hogan's *Lincoln, Inc.* explores specifi-
cally the image of Lincoln in contemporary society, offering a sociological study
of how Lincoln and his story have been disseminated in culture and play into
ideas about nationalism and American identity. Hogan develops a content analysis of Lincoln biographies published through 2010, identifies common themes
in twenty prominent ones, and categorizes themes by prominence over time.[11]

    Of contemporary biographies, Michael Burlingame's *Abraham Lincoln: A
Life*—a two-volume set of more than 2,000 pages that consumed more than
ten years of research and writing—has been credited by many historians as
being the most fully documented work on the man ever written. Burlingame

scoured thousands of nineteenth-century newspapers; read hundreds of oral histories, unpublished letters, and journals from Lincoln's contemporaries; and re-examined vast manuscript collections around the country that had long been neglected by even the most assiduous of his colleagues.[12] Among his analyses, Burlingame describes Lincoln's legacy in the immediate aftermath of his assassination as being the father of the United States. "The nation's enormous outpouring of grief testified to the profound love and respect that Lincoln inspired, an emotional bond like the one between a child and a nurturing, wise parent."[13]

Given that Lincoln used the press to his advantage and demonstrated understanding of how to address criticisms from it, scholars in a number of disciplines have examined Lincoln's place in press history. Among the more widely cited books about the role of the press in Lincoln's administration is Robert S. Harper's *Lincoln and the Press* (1951), which looked both at newspapers that supported the war and those that opposed it. As do a number of more recent publications, Ford Risley's *Civil War Journalism* (2012) recognizes Lincoln not only as being concerned with press content, but as contributing directly to it. "More than any president before him, Lincoln understood the role of the press, its tendencies, and its shortcomings."[14] This fact was known among Lincoln's associates, including William Herndon, who had written that his law partner cultivated relationships with journalists in his days as a country lawyer, as a contributor to Illinois newspapers. Lincoln had "never overlooked a newspaperman who had it in his power to say a good or bad thing of him," Herndon (1890) wrote.[15]

Among a number of First Amendment scholars studying the effect of Lincoln's wartime measures on the press, Mark Neely, in *The Fate of Liberty: Abraham Lincoln and Civil Liberties* (1991), explores masterfully controversy over Lincoln's relationship with the Constitution. Neely's sympathetic perspective depicts Lincoln's actions as well-intentioned attempts to address unprecedented wartime issues—including the threat to the nation's capital posed by secessionists in Maryland, the disintegration of public order in the border states, corruption among military contractors, the occupation of hostile Confederate territory, and the outcry against the first draft in U.S. history.[16] As a follow up to this Pulitzer Prize-winning book, Neely adds to his interpretation of Lincoln and the Constitution with *Lincoln and the Triumph of the Nation* (2011), an expanded look at the role of judicial decisions in the first half of the nineteenth century. His sources draw on the opinions of judges and those expressed in presidential state papers and political pamphlets.[17] Neely also includes the reflections of partisan editors and their newspapers in order to build an expansive interpretation of the role of the Constitution in the years before, during, and after the Civil War.

Departing from the classically oriented studies about Lincoln and his ties to political culture, Barry Schwartz's *Abraham Lincoln and the Forge of National Memory* (2000, 2003) makes the president and the man the subject of a sociological study in the nation's collective memory. Schwartz's book looks at the construction of Lincoln myths in the wake of his death, and traces those myths through the twentieth century. He explores misconceptions of Lincoln as a defender of civil rights and as a self-made man of humble beginnings.[18]

New sources and new approaches to understanding Lincoln's personality continue to emerge. Of contemporary biographies, Michael Burlingame's *Abraham Lincoln: A Life* (2008), a two-volume set of more than 2,000 pages that took more than ten years of research and writing, has been cited by historians as the most fully documented work on the man ever written. Burlingame scoured thousands of nineteenth century newspapers, read hundreds of oral histories, unpublished letters, and journals from Lincoln's contemporaries, and re-examined vast manuscript collections around the country long neglected by the most assiduous of his colleagues. Burlingame's use of an unprecedented number of sources—certainly not press-related alone—makes his work remarkable, providing a sense of the totality of material on Lincoln's life and, in doing so, a clearer understanding of how he influenced history.

From Herndon to Burlingame and into even more recent scholarship, Lincoln biographers continue to reinterpret his personal traits and the times in which he lived. For example, Fred Kaplan, an English professor and a biographer of authors, examines, in *Lincoln: The Biography of a Writer* (2008), Lincoln's literary skills. Kaplan deems Lincoln to be one of the great writers of his day, and second perhaps only to Thomas Jefferson as a writing president. Noting that Lincoln was an extraordinary president—inasmuch as we can be relatively certain that he wrote the material attributed to him, unlike a number of other presidents who had paid speechwriters—Kaplan cites an autobiography that Lincoln wrote for the 1860 campaign. Lincoln first submitted the piece to John L. Scripps, an editor at *The Chicago Tribune*, who revised it, published it, and republished it in *The New York Tribune*.[19]

The rise of the civil rights movement roughly 100 years after the Civil War helped—perhaps more than any event beyond Lincoln's presidency—to ensure his subsequent standing as a central figure in American history. With Martin Luther King Jr. quoting and in many ways elevating Lincoln's own words at the historic March on Washington, Lincoln's dream, first articulated at Gettysburg, became a more clearly identifiable reality. And, by the time of the election of the first African-American U.S. president two centuries after Lincoln's birth,

394 | *Journalism in the Civil War Era*

scholarship on Abraham Lincoln had become a field in its own right, as no other personality in American history has attracted so much print attention.[20]

This interest in part is reflected in biographical and fictional Hollywood productions ranging from Steven Spielberg's (2012) *Lincoln* to Timur Bekmambetov's literally sensational *Abraham Lincoln: Vampire Hunter* (2012).[21] Barry Schwartz's *Abraham Lincoln in the Post-Heroic Era: History and Memory in Late Twentieth-Century America* (2009) details this mainstreaming of Lincoln's legacy. Schwartz observes that modern technology, political changes, and a different-looking nation have actually contributed to the diminishment of Lincoln's stature in the twenty-first century. Contemporary Americans do not know much about Lincoln beyond that which is typically found in school history books, Schwartz writes. Much about Lincoln's personal life still lives in the shadows—representations that are "autocatalytic" or "path dependent," shaped not only by their original social contexts but also by contemporary conditions.[22]

Generally, historians have cast Lincoln in heroic light, but a few contemporary historians have ventured to view his record critically. One writer who has gone against conventional trends is Thomas J. DiLorenzo, a Loyola College economics professor who suggests that Lincoln does not merit undiluted praise. He argues that scholars have made more of Lincoln's moral disdain for slavery than can be verified, and ascribes Lincoln's opposition to the institution primarily to economic interests within the Whig mercantilist system. In another criticism, DiLorenzo suggests that a Lincoln "cult" has emerged among scholars. He describes both left- and right-wing ideologues who, over the past 150-plus years, have used Lincoln to justify and rationalize causes as opposite as North and South—from protection of First Amendment rights to legitimization of state-controlled media.[23]

Indeed, honest historians have recognized Lincoln as, at least, a shrewd politician and a masterful communicator. David Herbert Donald's Pulitzer Prize-winning *Lincoln* (1995) set a modern standard—it's considered a landmark in biographies of the president; among the first to recognize forces beyond his control, including his bouts with depression—and other recent accounts have reinterpreted the conditions surrounding Lincoln's life in much more modern, human, and fallible terms.[24] In this respect, Lincoln's life—indeed, all of the lives of those who experienced the Civil War directly—serve as personifications of the era, as the complex events of the and the journalism embedded in it have evolved on a meta-historical level.

Notes

1 Jack Canfield and Mark Victor Hansen, "Abraham Lincoln Didn't Quit," *Chicken Soup for the Soul* (Deerfield Beach, FL: Health Communications, 1993), 229, 230; "The Glurge of Springfield," accessed July 1, 2021, at <snopes.com/glurge/lincoln. asp>.

2 White, *A. Lincoln: A Biography*, 6.

3 Lincoln, *Annual Message to Congress* (Washington, DC), December 1, 1862.

4 William Henry Herndon and Jesse William Weik, *Herndon's Lincoln: The True Story of a Great Life* (Chicago: Belford-Clarke, 1890), xv.

5 Nicolay and Hay, *Abraham Lincoln: A History* (New York: Century, 1890), 580.

6 Albert J. Beveridge, *Abraham Lincoln, 1809–1858*. 2 vols. (New York: Houghton Mifflin, 1928), 2:127–8, 171, 185.

7 James G. Randall and Richard N. Current, *Lincoln the President*. 4 vols. (New York: Dodd, Mead, 1945–55), 1:138, 2:63, 204, 218, 221.

8 Randall and Current, *Lincoln the President*, 4:154, 266.

9 Beran, *Forge of Empires*, 7.

10 Schwartz, *Abraham Lincoln and the Forge of National Memory* (Chicago: University of Chicago Press, 2000, 2003), 293–312.

11 Hogan, *Lincoln, Inc.*, 33–6.

12 Lincoln, "Autobiography Written for John L. Scripps," June 1860, in Basler, *The Collected Works of Abraham Lincoln*, 4:60–7; Kaplan, *Lincoln: The Biography of a Writer*, 315–16.

13 Michael Burlingame, *Abraham Lincoln: A Life* (Baltimore, MD: Johns Hopkins University Press, 2008), 2:828.

14 Risley, *Civil War Journalism*, 17.

15 Herndon and Weik, *Herndon's Lincoln*, 2:45.

16 Mark E. Neely, *The Fate of Liberty: Abraham Lincoln and Civil Liberties* (Oxford: Oxford University Press, 1991), 12, 13.

17 Neely, *Lincoln and the Triumph of the Nation* (Chapel Hill: University of North Carolina Press, 2011).

18 Schwartz, *Abraham Lincoln and the Forge of National Memory*, 293-312.

19 Lincoln, "Autobiography Written for John L. Scripps," June 1860, in Basler, *The Collected Works of Abraham Lincoln*, 4:60-7; Kaplan, *Lincoln: The Biography of a Writer*, 315, 316.

20 Emery and Emery, *The Press and America: An Interpretive History of the Mass Media* (Boston: Allyn and Bacon, 1996), 105.

21 Timur Bekmambetov, *Abraham Lincoln: Vampire Hunter*, 20th Century Fox, 2012; Steven Spielberg, *Lincoln*, Dreamworks, 2012.

22 Schwartz, *Abraham Lincoln in the Post-Heroic Era: History and Memory in Late Twentieth-Century America* (Chicago: The University of Chicago, 2009), 219, 221, 222, 267, 268.

23 Thomas J. DiLorenzo, *The Real Lincoln: A New Look at Abraham Lincoln, His Agenda, and an Unnecessary War* (Roseville, CA: Forum, Prima Publishing, 2002), 54, 55, 67–76; DiLorenzo, *Lincoln Unmasked: What You're Not Supposed to Know about Dishonest Abe* (New York: Crown Publishing, 2006), 153, 154; DiLorenzo, "The Lincoln Cult," in Brian Lamb and Susan Swain, eds., *Abraham Lincoln: Great American Historians on Our Sixteenth President* (New York: Perseus, 2008), 255–65.

24 Bertram Wyatt-Brown, "A Volcano beneath a Mountain of Snow: John Brown and the Problem of Interpretation," in Paul Finkelman, ed. *His Soul Goes Marching On: Responses to John Brown and the Harpers Ferry Raid* (Charlottesville: University Press of Virginia, 1995), 1–28.

Selected Bibliography

Primary Sources

Newspapers by Location

<u>United States</u>

Alabama: Huntsville *Weekly.*

Arizona: Prescott *Weekly Arizona Miner.*

California: San Francisco *Daily Evening Bulletin*; San Francisco *Evening Bulletin*; Weaverville *Weekly Trinity Journal.*

Colorado: Denver *Rocky Mountain News.*

Connecticut: Hartford *Daily Courant.*

Delaware: Wilmington *Daily Gazette.*

Georgia: Atlanta *Constitution*; Atlanta *Intelligencer*; Augusta *Chronicle & Sentinel*; Augusta *Daily Loyal Georgian*; Augusta *The Colored American*; Augusta *Weekly Loyal Georgian*; Macon *Georgia Weekly Telegraph and Journal & Messenger*; Milledgeville *Federal Union*; Savannah *Republican.*

Illinois: Chicago *Inter Ocean*; Chicago *Press and Tribune*; Chicago *Times*; Chicago *Tribune.*

Indiana: Evansville *Daily Journal*; Fort Wayne *Dawson's Daily Times & Union*; Indianapolis *Daily Sentinel*; Indianapolis *State Journal*; Plymouth *Daily Democrat*; Plymouth *Marshall County Republican*; St. Joseph County *Register*; St. Joseph Valley *Register.*

Iowa: Buchanan County *Guardian*; Burlington *The Hawk-Eye*; Burlington *Weekly Hawkeye*; Cedar Falls *Gazette*; Davenport *Daily Democrat and News*; Davenport *Daily Gazette*; Des Moines *Daily State Register*; Dubuque *Daily Times*; Dubuque *National-Demokrat*; Fort Madison *Plain Dealer*; Muscatine *The Courier*; Toledo *Transcript*.

Kentucky: Frankfort *Commonwealth*; Louisville *Journal*.

Louisiana: Bellevue *Bossier Banner*; New Orleans *Daily Democrat*; New Orleans *Daily Picayune*; New Orleans *L'Abeille*; New Orleans *Picayune*; Shreveport *Daily News*; Shreveport *Southwestern*.

Maine: Biddeford *Union and Journal*.

Maryland: Annapolis *Maryland Gazette*; Baltimore *American*; Baltimore *Daily Exchange*; Baltimore *Republican*; Baltimore *Sun*; Elkton *Cecil Whig*; Port Tobacco *Times and Charles County Advertiser*.

Massachusetts: Boston *Daily Advertiser*; Boston *Investigator*; Boston *The Liberator*; Lowell *Daily Citizen and News*; Springfield *Republican*.

Minnesota: Princeton *Union*; St. Paul *Weekly Pioneer and Democrat*.

Mississippi: Port Gibson *Correspondent*.

Missouri: Hannibal *Western Union*; St. Louis *Missouri Republican*; St. Louis *Observer*; St. Louis *Republican*.

New York: Brooklyn *Daily Eagle*; *Frank Leslie's Illustrated Newspaper*; *Harper's Weekly*; New York *Daily Tribune*; New York *Evening Express*; New York *Herald*; New York *Journal of Commerce*; New York *Sun*; New York *Times*; New York *Tribune*; New York *World*; Rochester *The North Star*; *Vanity Fair*.

North Carolina: Charlotte *Western Democrat*; Fayetteville *Observer*; Fayetteville *The Carolinian*; Greensboro *Daily Southern Citizen*; Greensboro *The Times*; Greensboro *The Watchman and Harbinger*; Greensborough *Patriot*; Raleigh *Daily Progress*; Raleigh *North Carolina Confederate*; Raleigh *Register*; Raleigh *The Standard*; Raleigh *Weekly Standard*; Tarboro *Press*; Wilmington *Daily Herald*; Wilmington *Journal*; Winston-Salem *Western Sentinel*.

Ohio: Bedford *Inquirer*; Cincinnati *Daily Commercial*; Cincinnati *Daily Press*; Cincinnati *Enquirer*; Cleveland *Daily Herald*; Cleveland *Morning Leader*; Cleveland *Plain Dealer*; Columbus *Daily Statesman*; Columbus *The Crisis*; Dayton *Daily Empire*; Delaware *Gazette*; McArthur *Democrat*.

Pennsylvania: Bloomsburg *Columbia Democrat and Bloomsburg Advertiser*; Philadelphia *North American*; Philadelphia *North American and United States Gazette*; Philadelphia *Public Ledger and Daily Transcript*; Potter *Journal*.

South Carolina: Abbeville *Press*; Camden *Confederate*; Camden *Daily Journal*; Charleston *Daily Courier*; Charleston *Mercury*; Lancaster *Ledger*; Port Royal *The New South*.

Tennessee: Chattanooga *Rebel*; Knoxville *Brownlow's Weekly Whig*; Memphis *Daily Appeal*; Nashville *Daily Union*; Nashville *Patriot*; Nashville *Republican Banner and Nashville Whig*; Nashville *Tennessee Gazette*; Nashville *Union and American*; Nashville *Whig*.

Texas: Austin *Texas State Gazette*; Galveston *Daily News*; Galveston *News*; Marshall *Texas Republican*.

Vermont: Montpelier *Daily Green Mountain Freeman*; St. Johnsbury *Caledonian*.

Virginia: Alexandria *Gazette*; Alexandria *Gazette and Virginia Advertiser*; Alexandria *Soldiers' Journal*; Lynchburg *Virginian*; Norfolk *Herald*; Richmond *Daily Dispatch*; Richmond *Dispatch*; Richmond *Enquirer*; Richmond *Examiner*; Richmond *Whig*.

Washington, DC: *Daily National Intelligencer*; *Evening Star*; *National Republican*; *The National Era*; *The Republic*.

Wisconsin: La Crosse *Democrat*; Manitowoc *Pilot*; Milwaukee *Sentinel*; Watertown *Republican*; Waukesha *Freeman*.

International

Canada: Hamilton (Ontario) *Weekly Spectator*.

England: Banbury *Guardian*; Bedfordshire *Mercury*; Birmingham *Daily Gazette*; Birmingham *Daily Post*; Bristol *Mercury*; Bristol *Western Daily Press*; Chelmsford *Chronicle*; Cork *Herald*; Dundee *Courier and Argus*; Durham County *Advertiser*; Durham *Teesdale Mercury*; Essex *Standard*; *Illustrated London News*; Lanarkshire *North British Daily Mail*; Lancaster *Gazette*; Leeds *Mercury*; Leeds *Times*; Liverpool *Daily Post*; London *Daily News*; London *Daily Times*; London *Evening Mail*; London *Morning Advertiser*; London *Morning Post*; London *Morning Star*; London *Star*; London *Thame Gazette*; London *The Atlas*; London *The Observer*; Maidstone *Journal and Kentish Advertiser*; Manchester *The Guardian*; Newcastle *Courant*; Newcastle *Daily Chronicle*; Newcastle *Daily Journal*; Newcastle *Journal*; Reading *Mercury*; Salisbury and Winchester *Journal*; Sheffield *Daily Telegraph*; Sheffield *Independent*; *South Bucks Free Press, Wycombe and Maidenhead Journal*; Surrey *Comet*; *Times of London*; Waterford *Chronicle*.

Ireland: Belfast *Banner of Ulster*; Belfast *Commercial Chronicle*; Belfast *News-Letter*; Dublin *Evening Post*; Omagh *Tyrone Constitution*; Sligo *Champion*; Wexford *Constitution*.

Scotland: Aberdeen *Press and Journal*; Alloa *Advertiser*; Dundee *Courier*; Dunfermline *Saturday Press*; Edinburgh *Evening Courant*; Edinburgh *The Scotsman*; Falkirk *Herald*; Glasgow *Scottish Banner*; Moray *Elgin Courier*; Peterhead *Sentinel and General Advertiser for Buchan District*; Renfrewshire *Paisley Herald and Renfrewshire Advertiser*.

Collected Papers and Works

Basler, Roy P. ed. *The Collected Works of Abraham Lincoln*. Springfield, IL: Abraham Lincoln Association, 1974.

Colfax Collection. Northern Indiana Center for History. South Bend, Indiana.

Horace Greeley Papers, 1838–1872. Durham, NC: Duke University Library.

Lincoln, Abraham, John George Nicolay and John Hay. *Abraham Lincoln: Complete Works*. New York: Century, 1894.

Schuyler Colfax Papers, Indiana Historical Society, Indianapolis, IN, M55.

Thurlow Weed Papers, 1846–1858. Rochester, NY: New York Historical Society.

Images, Courtesy Library of Congress

"$150 Reward [cut of runaway slave]. Ranaway from the Subscriber, on the Night of the 2d Instant, a Negro Man, Who Calls Himself Henry May,... William Burke, Bardstown, Ky., September 3d, 1838." Accessed July 23, 2021, at <loc.gov/resource/rbpe.0220120b>.

"A Burial Party on the Battle-field of Cold Harbor, April 1, 1865." Accessed July 1, 2021, available at <loc.gov/pictures/item/2002713100>.

"Abraham Lincoln, Candidate for U.S. President, Three-quarter Length Portrait, before Delivering his Cooper Union Address in New York City." Accessed July 1, 2021, at <loc.gov/pictures/item/98504529>.

"Abraham Lincoln, Head-and-Shoulders Portrait, Traditionally Called 'Last Photograph of Lincoln from Life." Accessed July 1, 2021, at <loc.gov/pictures/item/2009630692>.

"Blockade of Charleston, The." Accessed October 14, 2021, at <loc.gov/item/00652823>.

"Campaign in Virginia—A Street in Harper's Ferry during the Passage of the Potomac by the National Troops from Maryland, October 24, 1862." Accessed July 1, 2021, at <loc.gov/item/2002714248>.

"Carte d'visite: Colfax, Schuyler, 1823-1885." Accessed July 1, 2021, at <loc.gov/item/mss4429700129>.

"Celebration of the Abolition of Slavery in the District of Columbia by the Colored People, in Washington, April 19, 1866." Accessed October 25, 2021, at <loc.gov/item/2015647679>.

"Chas. Banks' Original Spectacular Burlesque." Accessed November 2, 2021, at <loc.gov/resource/var.0282>.

"Copperhead Plan for Subjugating the South, The." Accessed July 1, 2021, at <loc.gov/pictures/item/2003663130>.

"Dedication Ceremonies at the Soldiers' National Cemetery, Gettysburg, Pennsylvania." Accessed July 13, 2021, at <loc.gov/pictures/item/2018672029>.

"Dedication of Monument at Gettysburg cemetery," David Bachrach, photographer [attributed], November 19, 1863. Accessed July 1, 2021, at <loc.gov/pictures/item/2012647713>.

"Expedition to Beaufort—Before the Attack, The." Accessed October 14, 2021, at <loc.gov/item/99404907>.

"Gen. Grant and Li Hung Chang, Viceroy of China, taken at Tientsin Jan. 1879." Accessed November 2, 2021, at <loc.gov/item/2016647812>.

"Gettysburg, Pa. Alfred R. Waud, Artist of *Harper's Weekly*, Sketching on Battlefield." Accessed July 1, 2021, available at <loc.gov/pictures/item/cwp2003000198/PP>.

"Hon. Abraham Lincoln, February 12, 1809." Accessed July 1, 2021, at <loc.gov/pictures/item/98518286>.

"Honest Old Abe on the Stump. Springfield 1858. Honest Old Abe on the Stump, at the Ratification Meeting of Presidential Nominations. Springfield 1860." Accessed November 11, 2021, at <loc.gov/item/2008661607>.

"[Horace] Greeley Statue, *Tribune* Office." Accessed July 1, 2021, at <loc.gov/item/2014699235>.

"How Illustrated Newspapers are Made." Accessed August 30, 2021, at <loc.gov/item/98510934>.

"Hurly-Burly Pot, The." Accessed October 25, 2021, at <loc.gov/item/2008661525>.

"'Impending Crisis'—Or Caught in the Act, The." Accessed February 28, 2022, <loc.gov/item/2003674580>.

Front Page, New York *Tribune*, April 4, 1865. Accessed October 27, 2021, at <loc.gov/item/sn83030213/1865-04-04/ed-1>.

"Our Political Snake-Charmer." Accessed November 10, 2021, at <loc.gov/item/2002707238>.

"Progress of the Century, The—The Lightning Steam Press, the Electric Telegraph, the Locomotive, [and] the Steamboat." Accessed July 1, 2021, at <loc.gov/resource/ppmsca.17563>.

"Reading the War News in Broadway, New York." Accessed July 13, 2021, at <loc.gov/resource/cph.3c12561>.

"Rebel Telegraph Operator near Egypt, on the Mississippi Central R.R." Accessed July 8, 2021, at <loc.gov/resource/cph.3a02101>.

"Right Hon. W. E. Gladstone and the Right Hon. Benjamin Disraeli, The." Accessed August 5, 2021, at <loc.gov/item/2003653728>.

"Slave Market of America." Accessed October 25, 2021, at <loc.gov/item/2008661294>.

"Statues and Sculpture. Robert E. Lee in Statuary Hall." Accessed October 27, 2021, at <loc.gov/item/2019681623>.

"Submarine Infernal Machine Intended to Destroy the 'Minnesota.'" Accessed October 14, 2021, at <loc.gov/item/00652824>.

"Virginia. Newspaper Vendor and Cart in Camp." Accessed November 4, 2021, at <loc.gov/resource/cwpb.01140>.

"War News." Accessed October 22, 2021, at <loc.gov/resource/stereo.1s05160>.

Books

Alexander, DeAlva Stanwood. *A Political History of the State of New York*. New York: Henry Holt and Co., 1906.

Bancroft, Frederic. *The Life of William H. Seward*. New York, London: Harper and Brothers, 2 Vols., 1900.

Beale, Howard K. ed., *The Diary of Gideon Welles*. Boston: Houghton, Mifflin, 1911.

Benton, Joel. *Greeley on Lincoln*. New York: The Baker and Taylor Company, 1893.

Bleyer, Willard G. *Main Currents in the History of American Journalism*. Boston: Houghton Mifflin, 1927.

Brooks, Noah. *Abraham Lincoln*. New York: Fred DeFau, 1894.

Coffin, Charles Carleton. *Abraham Lincoln*. New York: Harper and Brothers, 1893.

DePew, Chauncey. *One Hundred Years of American Commerce*. New York: D. O. Haynes, 2 Vols., 1895.

———. *Reminiscences of Abraham Lincoln*. New York: North American Review, 1888.

Douglass, Frederick. *My Bondage and My Freedom*. William W. Andrews, ed. Urbana, IL: University of Illinois Press, 1987.

Fehrenbacher, Don E. ed. *Lincoln: Speeches and Writings, 1859–1865*. New York: Library of America, 1989.

Gardner, Alexander. *Gardner's Photographic Sketch Book of the War*. Washington, DC: Philip and Solomons, 1865–66.

Greeley, Horace. *An Overland Journey from New York to San Francisco in the Summer of 1859.* Charles T. Duncan, ed. New York: Alfred A. Knopf, 1964.

———. *Greeley's Estimate of Lincoln.* Hancock, NY: *Herald* Printery. unpublished, 1868?

———. *Recollections of a Busy Life.* New York: Arno, 1868.

———. *The American Conflict.* New York, Chicago, Hartford: O. D. Case, 2 Vols., 1864, 1866.

Hale, Edward Everett. *James Russell Lowell and His Friends.* Boston and New York: Houghton, Mifflin and Company, 1899.

Herndon, William Henry, and Jesse William Weik. *Herndon's Lincoln: The True Story of a Great Life.* 3 vols. Chicago: Belford-Clarke, 1890.

Hill, Benjamin H., ed. *Senator Benjamin H. Hill of Georgia: His Life, Speeches and Writings.* Atlanta, GA: H. C. Hudgins and Company, 1891.

Hollister, Ovando James. *Life of Schuyler Colfax.* New York: Funk and Wagnalls, 1886.

Hudson, Frederic. *Journalism in the United States.* New York: Harper Brothers, 1873.

Lamon, Ward Hill, and Dorothy Lamon Teillard. *Recollections of Abraham Lincoln, 1847–1865.* Chicago: A. C. McClurg and Company, 1895.

Maverick, Augustus. *Henry J. Raymond and the New York Press.* New York: Arno, 1870, 1970.

Memorial of Horace Greeley, A. New York: *Tribune* Association, 1873.

Morley, John. *The Life of William Ewart Gladstone.* New York: Macmillan, 1903.

Nicolay, John G., and John Hay. *Abraham Lincoln: A History.* 10 vols. New York: Century, 1890.

North, Simon Newton Dexter. *History and Present Conditions of the Newspaper and Periodical Press of the United States.* Washington, DC: U.S. Government Printing Office, 1884.

Oldt, F. T. ed., *History of Dubuque County, Iowa.* Chicago, IL: Goodspeed, 1911.

Parton, James. *Life of Horace Greeley, Editor of the New York Tribune, From His Birth to the Present Time.* Boston: James Osgood and Company, 1872.

———. *Life of Horace Greeley.* New York: Mason Brothers, 1855.

Payne, George Henry. *History of Journalism in the United States.* Westport, CT: Greenwood Press Publishers, 1920.

Rhodes, James Ford. *History of the United States from the Compromise of 1850 to the Final Restoration of Home Rule at the South in 1877.* London: MacMillan & Co., 8 Vols., 1920.

Schurz, Carl. *The Reminiscences of Carl Schurz.* New York: Doubleday, 1908.

Scott, Robert N. *The War of the Rebellion: A Compilation of the Official Records of the Union and Confederate Armies.* Washington, DC: Government Printing Office, 1880–1902.

Strunsky, Rose. *Lincoln.* New York: MacMillan, 1914.

Taylor, Bayard. *Life and Letters of Bayard Taylor.* Boston: Houghton, Mifflin and Company, 2 Vols., 1884.

Weed, Thurlow. *Life of Thurlow Weed Including His Autobiography and a Memoir.* Boston and New York: Houghton Mifflin and Company, 2 Vols., 1883–84.

Young, John Russell. *Around the World with General Grant: A Narrative of the Visit of General U.S. Grant, Ex-President of the United States, to Various Countries in Europe, Asia, and Africa, in 1877, 1878, 1879.* New York: American News Company, 1869.

Zabriskie, Francis Nicoll. *Horace Greeley, The Editor.* New York: Funk and Wagnalls, 1890.

Online Documents

Abraham Lincoln Papers at the Library of Congress. Manuscript Division. Washington, DC: American Memory Project, 2000-2002. Accessed March 11, 2022. At <memory.loc.gov/ammem/alhtml/malhome.html>.

Article the Sixth, Northwest Ordinance, 1787. Accessed May 31, 2019, at <loc.gov/resource/bds-dcc.22501/?sp=2>.

Basler, Roy P. *The Collected Works of Abraham Lincoln.* 9 vols. New Brunswick, NJ: Rutgers University Press, 1953–55. Accessed July 1, 2021, at <quod.lib.umich.edu/l/lincoln>.

Douglass, Frederick, to William Lloyd Garrison. From Belfast, Ireland. January 1, 1846. Accessed March 23, 2022, at <digitalcommonwealth.org/search/commonwealth:dv142z173>.

———. "The Constitution of the United States: Is It Pro-Slavery or Anti-slavery." Speech to the Scottish Anti-Slavery Society, Glasgow, Scotland, March 26, 1860. Accessed March 23, 2022, at <laphamsquarterly.org/democracy/constitutional-intent>.

Dred Scott v. Sandford. 60 U.S. 393, 1856. Accessed March 22, 2022, at <supreme.justia.com/cases/federal/us/60/393>.

Garrison, William Lloyd, to Richard Daniel Webb. "On the Mexican War." July 1, 1847. Accessed March 23, 2022, at <teachingamericanhistory.org/library/document/letter-on-the-mexican-american-war>.

Harper's Weekly. New York: Harper's Magazine Co.. Accessed July 1, 2021, at <app.harpweek.com>; <elections.harpweek.com>.

Lincoln, Abraham. "Second Inaugural Address." March 4, 1865. Library of Congress. Accessed March 26, 2022, at <loc.gov/item/mal4361300>.

Lincoln's Gettysburg Address, Library of Congress. Accessed July 1, 2021, at <loc.gov/resource/ds.03106>.

Seth Kaller, Inc., *Historic Documents & Legacy Collections.* White Plains (NY). Accessed March 2, 2022, at <sethkaller.com>.

The Valley of the Shadow. Accessed July 1, 2021, at <valley.lib.virginia.edu>.

The Weekly Loyal Georgian. Georgia Historic Newspapers. Accessed June 6, 2021, at <gahistoric-newspapers.galileo.usg.edu/lccn/sn83027105>.

U.S. Constitution. Accessed May 30, 2019, at <archives.gov/founding-docs/constitution-transcript>.

Additional Documents and Texts

American Annual Cyclopedia and Register of Important Events. Vol. 3. New York: D. Appleton, 1864.

Assassination of Abraham Lincoln, The. Washington, DC: Government Printing Office, 1866.

Benton, Joel. "Greeley's Estimate of Lincoln," *The Century, a Popular Quarterly,* 42, 3 (July 1891): 371–83.

Bright, John. "On the 'Trent' Affair." Speech given at Rochdale, England, December 4, 1861.

Brown, George W. Mayor of Baltimore, Maryland, Proclamation, Published in the Baltimore *Sun,* April 22, 1862.

General Orders, No. 84, Hdqrs. Department of the Ohio, Cincinnati, Ohio, June 1, 1863.

House Reports. "An Act to Authorize the President of the United States in Certain Cases to take Possession of the Railroad and Telegraphic Lines, and for Other Purposes." Thirty-Seventh Congress, Second Session. March 20, 1862.

Lincoln, Abraham. *Annual Message to Congress.* Washington, DC, December 1, 1862.

McNeil, Col. John. Third Regiment, U.S. Reserve Corps, *Proclamation*, St. Louis, Missouri, July 11, 1861.

"Proceeding of the Freedman's Convention of Georgia, Assembled at Augusta, January 10th, 1866, Containing the Speeches of Gen'L Tillson, Capt. J. E. Bryant and Others," Office of the Loyal Georgian, Augusta, Georgia, 1866.

U.S. Census, 1850, 1860, 1870.

Secondary Sources

Books and Book Chapters

Abbott, Richard. *The Republican Party and the South, 1855-1877: The First Southern Strategy.* Chapel Hill, NC: University of North Carolina Press, 1986.

Anbinder, Tyler. *Nativism and Slavery.* New York and Oxford: Oxford University Press, 1992.

Andrews, J. Cutler. *The South Reports the War.* Princeton, NJ: Princeton University Press, 1970.

Barber, James G., ed. *Faces of Discord: The Civil War Era at the National Portrait Gallery.* Washington, DC: Smithsonian Institution, 2006.

Beran, Michael Knox. *Forge of Empires.* New York: Free Press, 2007.

Bernstein, Iver. *The New York City Draft Riots: Their Significance for American Society and Politics in the Age of the Civil War.* New York: Oxford University Press, 1990.

Beveridge, Albert J. *Abraham Lincoln, 1809–1858.* 2 vols. New York: Houghton Mifflin, 1928.

Blight, David W. *Frederick Douglass: Prophet of Freedom.* New York: Simon & Schuster, 2018.

Blondheim, *News over the Wires: The Telegraph and the Flow of Public Information in America 1844–1897.* Cambridge, MA: Harvard University Press, 1994.

Borchard, Gregory A. *Abraham Lincoln and Horace Greeley.* Carbondale, IL: Southern Illinois Press, 2011.

Borchard, Gregory A., and David W. Bulla. *Lincoln Mediated: The President and the Press through Nineteenth Century Media.* Piscataway, NJ: Transaction, 2015; New York: Routledge, 2020.

Borchard, Gregory A., Stephen Bates, and Lawrence J. Mullen. "Violence as Art and News: Sensational Prints and Pictures in the Nineteenth Century Press." In Sachsman, David B., and David W. Bulla. eds. *Murder, Mayhem, Mudslinging, Scandals, Stunts, Hoaxes, Hatred, and Disasters: Sensationalism in 19th Century Reporting*, 53–74. Piscataway, NJ: Transaction, 2013.

Borchard, Gregory A. "Taking No Rights For Granted: The Southern Press and the 15th Amendment," 309–18. In Sachsman, David B., S. Kittrell Rushing, and Roy Morris, Jr., eds. *Words at War.* West Lafayette, IN: Purdue University Press, 2008.

Bulla, David W. "The Popular Press, 1833–1865." In Sloan, William David, ed. *The Age of Mass Communication*, 148–51. Northport, AL: Vision Press, 2008.

——— . *Lincoln's Censor: Milo Hascall and Freedom of the Press in Civil War Indiana.* West Lafayette, IN: Purdue University Press, 2009.

Burlingame, Michael. *Abraham Lincoln: A Life.* 2 vols. Baltimore: Johns Hopkins Press, 2008.

Burrows, Edwin G., and Mike Wallace. *Gotham: A History of New York City to 1898.* New York: Oxford University Press, 1999.

Cain, William E. *William Lloyd Garrison and the Fight against Slavery: Selections from The Liberator.* Boston, MA: Bedford/St. Martin's, 1995.

Campbell, W. Joseph. *The Year That Defined American Journalism: 1897 and the Clash of Paradigms.* New York: Routledge, 2006.

Carey, James. *Communication as Culture.* New York and London: Routledge, 1989.

Carwardine, Richard, and Jay Sexton. *The Global Lincoln.* Oxford and New York: Oxford University Press, 2011.

Case, Lynn M., and Warren F. Spencer. *The United States and France: Civil War Diplomacy.* Philadelphia: University of Pennsylvania Press, 1970.

Chernow, Ron. *Grant.* New York: Penguin Press, 2017.

Cohen, Patricia Cline. *The Murder of Helen Jewett.* New York: Alfred Knopf, 1998.

Copeland, David. *Colonial American Newspapers: Character and Content.* Newark, DE: University of Delaware Press, 1997.

Cronin, Mary, and Debra Van Tuyll, eds, *The Western Press in the Crucible of the American Civil War.* New York: Peter Lang, 2021.

Cronin, Mary, ed. *An Indispensable Liberty: The Fight for Free Speech in Nineteenth-Century America.* Southern Illinois University Press, 2016.

Currie-McDaniel, Ruth. *Carpetbagger of Conscience: A Biography of John Emery Bryant.* New York: Fordham University Press, 1999.

Dal Lago, Enrico. *William Lloyd Garrison and Giuseppe Mazzini: Abolition, Democracy, and Radical Reform.* Baton Rouge, LA: Louisiana State University Press, 2013.

Delbanco, Andrew. *The War Before the War: Fugitive Slaves and the Struggle for America's Soul from the Revolution to the Civil War.* New York: Penguin Press, 2018.

DeRose, Chris. *Congressman Lincoln: The Making of America's Greatest President.* New York: Threshold Editions, 2013.

Dicken-Garcia, Hazel, and Giovanna Dell'Orto. *Hated Ideas and the American Civil War.* Spokane, WA: Marquette Books, 2008.

Dicken-Garcia, Hazel. *Journalistic Standards in Nineteenth-Century America.* Madison, WI: University of Wisconsin Press, 1989.

Dilbeck, D. H. *Frederick Douglass: America's Prophet.* Chapel Hill, NC: University of North Carolina Press, 2018.

DiLorenzo, Thomas J. "The Lincoln Cult." In Lamb, Brian, and Susan Swain, eds. *Abraham Lincoln: Great American Historians on Our Sixteenth President,* 255–66. New York: Perseus, 2008.

——— . *Lincoln Unmasked: What You're Not Supposed to Know about Dishonest Abe.* New York: Crown Publishing, 2006.

——— . *The Real Lincoln: A New Look at Abraham Lincoln, His Agenda, and an Unnecessary War.* Roseville, CA: Forum, Prima Publishing, 2002.

Dirck, Brian R. *Abraham Lincoln and White America*. Lawrence, KS: University Press of Kansas, 2012.

Dodd, Dorothy. *Henry J. Raymond and the New York Times during Reconstruction*. Chicago: University of Chicago Libraries, 1936.

Donald, David Herbert, and Harold Holzer. *Lincoln in the* Times: *The Life of Abraham Lincoln as Originally Reported in The New York Times*. New York: St. Martin's, 2005.

Donald, David Herbert, and James G. Randall. *The Civil War and Reconstruction*. Lexington, MA: D. C. Heath and Company, 1969.

Donald, David Herbert. *Lincoln*. London: Jonathan Cape, 1995.

Eckley, Robert S. *Lincoln's Forgotten Friend, Leonard Swett*. Carbondale, IL: Southern Illinois University Press, 2012.

Emery, Michael C., and Edwin Emery. *The Press and America: An Interpretive History of the Mass Media*. Boston: Allyn and Bacon, 1996.

Emery, Michael C., Edwin Emery, and Nancy Roberts. *The Press and America, An Interpretive History of the Mass Media*, 9th ed. Boston: Allyn and Bacon, 2000.

Esslinger, Dean R. *Immigrants and the City: Ethnicity and Mobility in a Nineteenth-Century Midwestern Community*. Port Washington, NY: Kennikat Press, 1975.

Faust, Drew Gilpin. *This Republic of Suffering: Death and the American Civil War*. New York: Vintage Books, 2008.

Finkelman, Paul, ed. *His Soul Goes Marching On: Responses to John Brown and the Harpers Ferry Raid*. Charlottesville: University Press of Virginia, 1995.

Foner, Philip S. *The Life and Writings of Frederick Douglass: Early Years, 1817-1849*. New York: International Publishers, 1950.

Foote, Shelby. *The Civil War, A Narrative: Fredericksburg to Meridian*. Vol. 2, New York: Vintage Books, 1986.

Foreman, Amanda. *A World on Fire: An Epic History of Two Nations Divided*. London: Allen Lane, 2010.

Fraker, Guy G. *Lincoln's Ladder to the Presidency*. Carbondale, IL: Southern Illinois University Press, 2012.

Franklin, John Hope, and Loren Schweninger. *Runaway Slaves: Rebels on the Plantation*. New York: Oxford University Press, 1999.

Freedman, Russell. *Abraham Lincoln and Frederick Douglass: The Story Behind an American Friendship*. New York: Clarion Books, 2012.

Fuhlhage, Michael. *Yankee Reporters and Southern Secrets: Journalism, Open Source Intelligence, and the Coming of the Civil War*. New York: Peter Lang, 2019.

Gallagher, Gary. *The Battle of Chancellorsville*. Washington, DC: Eastern National, 1995.

Gore, George W. "Negro Journalism: An Essay on the History and Present Conditions of the Negro Press." Greencastle, IN: DePauw University, 1922.

Griffith, Louis T., and John E. Talmadge. *Georgia Journalism, 1763–1950*. Athens, GA: University of Georgia Press, 1951.

Guarneri, Carl J. *Lincoln's Informer: Charles A. Dana and the Inside Story of the Union War*. Lawrence, KS: University of Kansas Press, 2019.

Hale, William Harlan. *Horace Greeley: Voice of the People*. New York: Harper and Brothers, 1950.

Hamilton, Charles, and Lloyd Ostendorf, *Lincoln in Photographs: An Album of Every Known Pose.* Norman, OK: University of Oklahoma Press, 1963.

Harper, Robert S. *Lincoln and the Press.* New York: McGraw-Hill, 1951.

Harris, Brayton. *Blue & Gray in Black & White: Newspapers in the Civil War* Washington, DC: Brassey's, 1999.

Harris, William C. *William Woods Holden: Firebrand of North Carolina Politics.* Baton Rouge, LA: Louisiana State University Press, 1987.

Hearn, Chester G. *Lincoln and McClellan at War.* Baton Rouge: Louisiana State University Press, 2012.

Hesseltine, William B. *Ulysses S. Grant: Politician.* New York: Dodd, Mead & Co., 1935.

Hinshaw, Gil. *From 10,500 Battles: A Handbook of Civil War Engagements.* Hobbs, NM: Superior Printing Co., 1996.

Hirshson, Stanley P. *The White Tecumseh: A Biography of General William T. Sherman.* New York: John Wiley, 1997.

Hogan, Jackie. *Lincoln, Inc.: Selling the Sixteenth President in Contemporary America.* Lanham, MD: Rowman and Littlefield, 2011.

Holt, Michael F. *The Rise and Fall of the American Whig Party: Jacksonian Politics and the Onset of the Civil War.* New York, Oxford: Oxford University Press, 1999.

Holzer, Harold. *The Lincoln-Douglas Debates.* New York: Harper Collins, 1993.

———. *Lincoln and the Power of the Press: The War for Public Opinion.* New York: Simon and Schuster, 2014.

Horner, Harlan Hoyt. *Lincoln and Greeley.* Urbana, IL: University of Illinois Press, 1953.

Howe, Daniel Walker. *What Hath God Wrought: The Transformation of America, 1815–1848.* New York: Oxford University Press, 2007.

Humphrey, Carol Sue. *The Early Republic: Primary Documents on Events from 1790 to 1820.* Westport, CT: Greenwood Press, 2004.

Huntzicker, William E. "Picturing the News: Frank Leslie and the Origins of American Pictorial Journalism." In Sachsman, David B., S. Kittrell Rushing, and Debra Reddin van Tuyll, eds. *The Civil War and the Press*, 309–24. New Brunswick, NJ: Transaction Publishers, 2000.

———. *The Popular Press, 1833–1865.* Westport, CT: Greenwood Press, 1999.

Isley, Jeter Allen. *Horace Greeley and the Republican Party.* Princeton, NJ: Princeton University Press, 1947.

Jacobs, Donald M. *Courage and Conscience: Black & White Abolitionists in Boston.* Bloomington, IN: Indiana University Press, 1993.

Jenkins, Roy. *Gladstone: A Biography.* New York: Random House, 1995.

Jin-Ping, Wu. *Frederick Douglass and the Black Liberation Movement: The North Star of American Blacks.* New York, Garland Publishing, 2000.

Johnson, David Alan. *Decided on the Battle Field: Grant, Sherman, Lincoln and the Election of 1864.* Amherst, NY: Prometheus Books, 2012.

Johnson, Martin P. *Writing the Gettysburg Address.* Lawrence, KS: University Press of Kansas, 2013.

Kaplan, Fred. *Lincoln: The Biography of a Writer.* New York: HarperCollins, 2008.

Kauffman, Michael W. *American Brutus: John Wilkes Booth and the Lincoln Conspiracies.* New York: Random House, 2004.

Kendrick, Paul, and Stephen Kendrick. *Douglass and Lincoln: How a Revolutionary Black Leader and a Reluctant Liberator Struggled to End Slavery and Save the Union.* New York: Walker Publishing, 2008.

Kielbowicz, Richard B. *News in the Mail: The Press, Post Office, and Public Information, 1700–1860s.* Westport, CT: Greenwood Press, 1989.

Lal, Vinay. "Defining a Legacy: Lincoln in the National Imaginary of India." In Carwardine, Richard, and Jay Sexton, eds. *The Global Lincoln*, 172–88. Oxford and New York: Oxford University Press, 2011.

Lamb, Brian, and Susan Swain, eds. *Abraham Lincoln: Great American Historians on Our Sixteenth President.* New York: Perseus, 2008.

Lingley, Charles Ramsdell. *Since the Civil War.* New York: The Century, 1920.

Lubell, Samuel. *The Future of American Politics*, 2nd ed. Garden City, NY: Doubleday & Co., 1956.

Lundberg, James M. *Horace Greeley: Print, Politics, and the Failure of American Nationhood.* Urbana, IL: University of Illinois Press, 2019.

Mahin, Dean B. *One War at a Time: The International Dimension of the American Civil War.* Dulles, VA: Brassey's, 2000.

Maihafer, Harry J. *War of Words: Abraham Lincoln and the Civil War Press.* Washington, DC: Brassey's, 2001.

Marche, Stephen. *The Next Civil War: Dispatches from the American Future.* New York: Avid Reader Press, 2022.

Marszalek, John F. *Sherman's Other Way: The General and the Civil War Press.* Kent, OH: Kent State University Press, 1999.

Martin, Waldo E. *The Mind of Frederick Douglass.* Chapel Hill, NC: University of North Carolina Press, 1984.

May, Robert E. *Slavery, Race, and Conquest in the Tropics: Lincoln, Douglas, and the Future of Latin America.* Cambridge University Press, 2013.

McFeely, William S. *Grant, A Biography.* New York: W.W. Norton & Co., 1981.

McKenzie, Robert T. *Lincolnites and Rebels: A Divided Town in the American Civil War.* New York: Oxford University Press, 2006.

McKivigan, John R. *Forgotten Firebrand: James Redpath and the Making of Nineteenth-Century America.* Ithaca and London: Cornell University Press, 2008.

McNeely, Patricia, Debra Reddin van Tuyll, and Henry L. Schulte. *Knights of the Quill: Confederate Correspondents and their Civil War Reporting.* Purdue University Press, 2010.

McPherson, James M. *Antietam: The Battle That Changed the Course of the Civil War.* New York: Oxford University Press, 2002.

———. *Ordeal by Fire: The Civil War and Reconstruction.* Boston, MA: McGrawHill, 2001.

———. *The Battle Cry of Freedom.* New York: Oxford University Press, 1988.

———. *Tried by War: Abraham Lincoln as Commander in Chief.* New York: Penguin, 2008.

Meredith, Roy. *Mr. Lincoln's Camera Man, Mathew B. Brady.* Mineola, NY: Dover, 1974.

Mitchell, Elizabeth. *Lincoln's Lie: A True Civil War Caper through Fake News, Wall Street, and the White House.* Berkeley, CA: Counterpoint, 2020.

Monaghan, Jay. *The Man Who Elected Lincoln.* Westport, CT: Greenwood Press, 1956.

Neely, Mark E. *Lincoln and the Triumph of the Nation*. Chapel Hill: University of North Carolina Press, 2011.

———. *The Fate of Liberty: Abraham Lincoln and Civil Liberties*. Oxford: Oxford University Press, 1991.

Nevins, Allan. *The War for the Union, Volume II: War Becomes Revolution*. New York: Charles Scribner's Sons, 1960.

Peatman, Jared. *The Long Shadow of Lincoln's Gettysburg Address*. Carbondale, IL: Southern Illinois University Press, 2013.

Perry, James M. A *Bohemian Brigade: The Civil War Correspondents*. New York: John Wiley and Sons, 2000.

Randall, James G., and Richard N. Current. *Lincoln the President*. 4 vols. New York: Dodd, Mead, 1945–55.

Raper, Horace W. *William W. Holden, North Carolina's Political Enigma*. Chapel Hill, NC: University of North Carolina Press, 1985.

Ratner, Lorman A., and Dwight L. Teeter. *Fanatics and Fire-Eaters: Newspapers and the Coming of the Civil War*. Champaign, IL: University of Illinois Press, 2003.

Redin van Tuyll, Debra. *The Confederate Press in the Crucible of the American Civil War*. New York: Peter Lang, 2013.

Reynolds, Amy, and Debra Reddin van Tuyll. *The Greenwood Library of American War Reporting: The Civil War, North & South*. Westport, CT: Greenwood Press, 2005.

Reynolds, Donald E. *Editors Make War*. Nashville, TN: Vanderbilt University Press, 1970.

Risley, Ford. *Abolition and the Press: The Moral Struggle against Slavery*. Evanston, IL: Northwestern University Press, 2008.

———. *Civil War Journalism*. Santa Barbara, CA: Praeger, 2012.

———. *Dear Courier: The Civil War Correspondence of Editor Melvin Dwinell*. Knoxville, TN: Uni-versity of Tennessee Press, 2018.

Robinson, Donald L. *Slavery in the Structure of American Politics*. New York: Harcourt Brace Jovanovich Inc., 1971.

Rosenblum, Naomi. *World History of Photography*. New York: Abbeville Press, 1997.

Sachsman, David B., and David W. Bulla, eds. *Sensationalism: Murder, Mayhem, Mudslinging, Scandals, and Disasters in 19th Century Reporting*. Piscataway, NJ: Transaction Publishers, 2017.

Sachsman, David B., and Gregory A. Borchard, eds. *The Antebellum Press: Setting the Stage for Civil War*. New York: Taylor & Francis, 2019.

Sachsman, David B., ed. *A Press Divided: Newspaper Coverage of the Civil War*. London and New York: Routledge, 2017.

———. *After the War: The Press in a Changing America, 1865–1900*. New York: Taylor & Francis, 2017.

Sachsman, David B., S. Kittrell Rushing, and Debra Reddin van Tuyll, eds., *The Civil War and the Press*. New Brunswick, NJ: Transaction Publishers, 2000.

Sandburg, Carl. *Abraham Lincoln: The Prairie Years and the War Years*. New York: Sterling Publishing Co., 2007.

Sandefur, Timothy. *Frederick Douglass: Self-Made Man*. Washington, DC: Cato Institute, 2018.

Schwartz, Barry. *Abraham Lincoln and the Forge of National Memory*. Chicago: University of Chicago Press, 2000, 2003.

———. *Abraham Lincoln in the Post-Heroic Era: History and Memory in Late Twentieth-Century America*. Chicago: The University of Chicago, 2009.

Simon, Paul. *Freedom's Champion: Elijah Lovejoy*. Carbondale, IL: Southern Illinois University Press, 1994.

Sloan, William David. *The Media in American: A History*. Northport, AL: Vision Press, 2008.

———. *Perspectives on Mass Communication History*. Hillsdale, NJ: Lawrence Earlbaum, 1991.

Smith, Jeffery A. *War and Press Freedom: The Problem of Prerogative Power*. New York: Oxford University Press, 1999.

Smith, Willard H. *Schuyler Colfax: The Changing Fortunes of a Political Idol*. Indianapolis, IN: Indiana Historical Society, 1952.

Spencer, David R. *The Yellow Journalism: The Press and America's Emergence as a World Power*. Evanston, IL: Northwestern University Press, 2007.

Sperber, Jonathan. *Rhineland Radicals: The Democratic Movement and the Revolution of 1848–1849*. Princeton, NJ: Princeton, 1992.

Stahr, Walter. *Seward: Lincoln's Indispensable Man*. New York: Simon & Schuster, 2012.

Starr, Louis M. *Bohemian Brigade*. New York: Alfred A. Knopf, 1954.

———. *Bohemian Brigade: Civil War Newsmen in Action*. Madison, WI: University of Wisconsin Press, 1987.

Startt, James D., and William David Sloan. *Historical Methods*. Northport, AL: Vision Press, 2003.

Stephens, Mitchell. *A History of News*. New York: Oxford University Press, 2007.

Stevens, John D. "Freedom of Expression: New Dimensions." In Farrar, Ronald T., and John D. Stevens, eds. *Mass Media and the National Experience*, 14–37. New York: Harper & Row, 1971.

Stewart, James B. "Boston, Abolition, and the Atlantic World, 1820-1861," 101–26. In Donald M. Jacobs, *Courage and Conscience: Black & White Abolitionists in Boston*. Bloomington, IN: Indiana University Press, 1993.

Stoddard, Henry Luther. *Horace Greeley, Printer, Editor, Crusader*. New York: G. P. Putnam's Sons, 1946.

Striner, Richard. *Lincoln and Race*. Carbondale, IL: Southern Illinois University Press, 2012.

Sullivan, George. *Picturing Lincoln: Famous Photographs that Popularized the President*. New York: Clarion Books, 2000.

Symonds, Craig L. *The Civil War at Sea*. New York: Oxford University Press, 2012.

Tatham, David. *Winslow Homer and the Pictorial Press*. Syracuse, NY: Syracuse University Press, 2003.

Temple, Wayne. *Lincoln's Confidant: The Life of Noah Brooks*. Baltimore: John's Hopkins University Press, 2019.

Tripp, Bernell E. "The Antebellum Press," 141–58. In William David Sloan, ed., *The Media in American: A History*. Northport, AL: Vision Press, 2008.

Van Deusen, Glyndon G. *Horace Greeley, Nineteenth-Century Crusader*. New York: Hill and Wang, 1953, 1964.

———. *Thurlow Weed: Wizard of the Lobby*. Boston: Little, Brown and Co., 1947.

———. *William Henry Seward*. New York: Oxford University Press, 1967.

Von Drehle, David. *Rise to Greatness: Abraham Lincoln and America's Most Perilous Year*. New York: Henry Holt and Co., 2012.

White Jr., Ronald C. *A. Lincoln: A Biography*. New York: Random House, 2009.

Williams, Frank J., and Michael Burkhimer, eds. *The Mary Lincoln Enigma: Historians on America's Most Controversial First Lady*. Carbondale, IL: Southern Illinois University Press, 2012.

Williams, Harold A. *The Baltimore Sun, 1837–1987*. Baltimore, MD: Johns Hopkins University Press, 1987.

Williams, Robert C. *Horace Greeley: Champion of American Freedom*. New York and London: New York University Press, 2006.

Windley, Lathan A. *A Profile of Runaway Slaves in Virginia and South Carolina from 1730 to 1787*. New York: Garland Publishing, 1995.

Winkle, Kenneth J. *Lincoln's Citadel: The Civil War in Washington, DC*. New York: W. W. Norton & Co., 2013.

Wyatt-Brown, Bertram. "A Volcano beneath a Mountain of Snow: John Brown and the Problem of Interpretation," 10–38. In Finkelman, Paul, ed. *His Soul Goes Marching On: Responses to John Brown and the Harpers Ferry Raid*. Charlottesville: University Press of Virginia, 1995.

Monographs and Journal Articles

Abbott, Richard. "The Republican Party Press in Reconstruction Georgia," *The Journal of Southern History*, 61, 4 (November 1995): 725–60.

Blondheim, Menaham. "The Click: Telegraphic Technology, Journalism, and the Transformations of the New York Associated Press," *American Journalism*, 17, 4 (Fall 2000): 27–52.

Borchard, Gregory A. "From Pink Lemonade to Salt River: Horace Greeley's Utopia and the Death of the Whig Party," *Journalism History*, 32, 1 (Spring 2006): 22–33.

———. "*The New York Tribune* and the 1844 Election: Horace Greeley, Gangs, and the Wise Men of Gotham," *Journalism History*, 33, 1 (Spring 2007): 51–59.

———. "*The New York Tribune* at Harper's Ferry: Horace Greeley on Trial," *American Journalism*, 20, 1 (Winter 2003): 13–31.

Borchard, Gregory A., Lawrence J. Mullen, and Stephen Bates, "From Realism to Reality: The Advent of War Photography." *Journalism & Communication Monographs*, 15, 2 (June 2013): 66–107.

Bryan, Carter R. "Negro Journalism in America before Emancipation." *Journalism Monographs*. Columbia, SC: Association for Education in Journalism, 12 (September 1, 1969): 1–33.

Cronin, Mary. "Fiend, Coward, Monster, or King: Southern Press Views of Abraham Lincoln." *American Journalism*. 26, 4 (Fall 2009): 3, 5–61.

Francke, Warren. "Sensationalism and the Development of 19th-Century Reporting: The Broom Sweeps Sensory Details," *Journalism History*, 12, 3–4 (Winter-Autumn, 1985): 80–85.

Klement, Frank L. "'Brick' Pomeroy: Copperhead and Curmudgeon," *Wisconsin Magazine of History*, 35, 2 (Winter 1951): 106–13, 156, 157.

Matthews, Sidney T. "Control of the Baltimore Press during the Civil War," *Maryland Historical Magazine*, 36, 2 (June 1941): 150–70.

Nord, David Paul. "Teleology and News: The Religious Roots of American Journalism." *Journal of American History*, 77, 1 (June 1990): 9–38.

Perry, Brewington. "Before the *North Star*: Frederick Douglass' Early Journalistic Career." *Phylon*, 35, 1 (1974): 96–107.

Risley, Ford. "The Confederate Press Association: Cooperative News Reporting of the War," *Civil War History*, 47, 3 (2001): 222–39.

Russo, David J. "The Origins of Local News in the U.S. Country Press, 1840s–1870s," *Journalism Monographs*, 65 (February 1980): 1–43.

Sanger, Donald B. "*The Chicago Times* and the Civil War," *Mississippi Valley Historical Review*, 17, 4 (March 1931): 557–80.

Shaw, Donald L. "At the Crossroads: Change and Continuity in the American Press News 1820–1860," *Journalism History*, 8, 2 (Summer 1981): 38–50.

Shaw, Donald L., and John W. Slater. "In the Eye of the Beholder? Sensationalism in American Press News," *Journalism History*, 12, 3–4 (Autumn/Winter 1985): 86–91.

Smith, Willard H. "Schuyler Colfax, Whig Editor, 1845–1855," *Indiana Magazine of History*, 34, 3 (September 1938): 262–82.

Stephens, Mitchell. "Sensationalism and Moralizing in 16th- and 17th-Century Newsbooks and News Ballads," *Journalism History*, 12, 3–4 (Winter-Autumn, 1985): 92–5.

Stevens, John D. "Sensationalism in Perspective," *Journalism History*, 12, 3–4 (Winter-Autumn, 1985): 78, 79.

Tasher, Lucy Lucile. "The *Missouri Democrat* and the Civil War," *Missouri Historical Review*, 34, 1 (July 1937): 402–19.

Tharp, Robert K. "The Copperhead Days of Dennis Mahony," *Journalism Quarterly*, 43, (Winter 1966): 680–86.

Towne, Stephen E. "Works of Indiscretion: Violence against the Democratic Press in Indiana during the Civil War," *Journalism History*, 31, 3 (Fall 2005): 138–49.

Theses and Dissertations

Borchard, Gregory A. *The Firm of Greeley, Weed, and Seward: New York Partisanship and the Press, 1840–1860*. Ph.D. Dissertation. Gainesville: University of Florida, 2003.

Jezierski, Rachel A. "The Glasgow Emancipation Society and the American Anti-Slavery Movement." Dissertation. University of Glasgow, 2010.

McGrane, Martin E. "Dubuque—Editorial Battleground 1860–1862." Master's Thesis, Iowa State University, 1972.

Saak, Dennis F. "Newspaper Suppressions in Missouri during the Civil War." Master's Thesis, University of Missouri, 1974.

Tenney, Craig D. "Major General A. E. Burnside and the First Amendment: A Case Study of Civil War Freedom of Expression." Ph.D. Dissertation, Bloomington, IN: Indiana University, 1977.

Conference Papers

Barker, Brett. "Communities at War: Ohio Republicans' Attack on Democratic Newspapers." Presented at the Symposium on the 19th Century Press, the Civil War, and Free Expression, University of Tennessee at Chattanooga, November 9, 2007.

Bradley, Patricia. "Slave Advertising in the Colonial Newspaper: Mirror to the Dilemma," conference paper, Association for Education in Journalism and Mass Communication, San Antonio Texas, August 1987.

Cronin, Mary. "'The North Is to Use Like the Grave': *New York Tribune* Reporter Albert D. Richardson's Confederate Prison Letters." Presented at the Symposium on the 19th Century Press, the Civil War, and Free Expression, University of Tennessee at Chattanooga, November 12, 2009.

Eberhard, Wallace B. "Editors in Uniform: The Historiography of Civil War Soldier Newspapers." Presented to the Symposium on the 19th Century Press, the Civil War and Free Expression, University of Tennessee at Chattanooga, November 10, 2006.

Eichhorn, Niels. "Kladderadatsch: A German Newspaper Perspective on the Civil War and Its International Context. A paper presented at the Symposium on the 19th Century Press, the Civil War, and Free Expression, November 13–15, 2008.

Pribanic-Smith, Erika J. "The War within the State: The Role of Newspapers in Missouri's Secession Crisis." Presented at the Symposium on the 19th Century Press, the Civil War, and Free Expression, University of Tennessee at Chattanooga, November 11, 2005.

Reddin van Tuyll, Debra. "What Freedom of the Press Meant in the Confederacy." Presented at the Symposium on the 19th Century Press, the Civil War, and Free Expression, University of Tennessee at Chattanooga, November 12, 2009.

Tichenor, Phillip J. "Copperheadism and Community Conflict in Two Rivertowns: Civil War Press Battles in Prairie du Chien and La Crosse, Wisconsin, 1861–65." Presented at the Symposium on the 19th Century Press, the Civil War, and Free Expression, University of Tennessee at Chattanooga, November 2, 2002.

Online Materials

Allen, Erin. "Lincoln in the News." Library of Congress, July 1, 2021, at <loc.gov/loc/lcib/0803/lincolnnews.html>.

Clark, James C. "John Shuften Blazed a Pair of Trails." *Orlando* (FL) *Sentinel*, February 24, 1990. Accessed June 3, 2021, at <orlandosentinel.com/news/os-xpm-1990-02-24-9002232594-story.html>.

"Glurge of Springfield. The." Accessed July 1, 2021, at <snopes.com/glurge/lincoln.asp>.

Holzer, Harold, ed. *President Lincoln Assassinated!!: The Firsthand Story of the Murder, Manhunt, Trial and Mourning*. [Google Books version]. New York: Library of America, 2014.

Howe, Daniel Walker. "What Hath God Wrought." *American Heritage*, 59, 4 (Winter 2010). Accessed July 1, 2021, at <americanheritage.com/what-hath-god-wrought>.

Lance, Rachel. "As U.S. COVID-19 Deaths Top the Civil War's Toll, We're Repeating Disease History." *Time*, August 14, 2021.

Lidz, Franz. "Will the Real Abraham Lincoln Please Stand Up?" *Smithsonian*, October 2013. Accessed July 1, 2021, at <smithsonianmag.com/history/will-the-real-abraham-lincoln-please-stand-up-3431>.

Marche, Stephen. "Secession Might Seem Like the Lesser of Two Evils: It's also the Less Likely." *Washington Post*, December 31, 2021. Accessed February 18, 2022, at <washingtonpost.com/outlook/2021/12/31/secession-civil-war-stephen-marche>.

McCarten, James. "Press Perils: Killing of Las Vegas Reporter Drives Home Dangers of Modern Journalism." *The Canadian Press*, September 13, 2022. Accessed October 11, 2022, at <cfjcto-day.com/2022/09/13/press-perils-killing-of-las-vegas-reporter-drives-home-dangers-of-modern-journalism>.

Ross, Janell. "Richmond's Robert E. Lee Statue Is Gone, Now It's Up to the City to Shape What That Means." *Time*, September 9, 2021.

Schuessler, Jennifer. "Scholar Says He's Found New Photo of Lincoln at Gettysburg." *New York Times*, October 14, 2013. Accessed July 1, 2021, at <artsbeat.blogs.nytimes.com/2013/09/24/scholar-says-hes-found-new-photo-of-lincoln-at-gettysburg>.

Additional Sources

Bekmambetov, Timur. 2012. *Abraham Lincoln: Vampire Hunter*, 20th Century Fox.

Canfield, Jack, and Mark Victor Hansen. "Abraham Lincoln Didn't Quit." In *Chicken Soup for the Soul*. Deerfield Beach, FL: Health Communications, 1993.

Spielberg, Steven. 2012. *Lincoln*, Dreamworks.

Index

T

U

V

About the Authors

David W. Bulla is a professor of communication at Augusta University. His books include *Lincoln's Censor, Why Slavery Endures,* and *Gandhi, Advocacy Journalism, and the Media.* He is assistant editor of *The Southeastern Review of Journalism History.* Dr. Bulla earned a Ph.D. in mass communication from the University of Florida and his master's degree in journalism from Indiana University. He is former sports editor and high school student newspaper adviser.

Gregory A. Borchard is a professor of mass communication and journalism at the University of Nevada, Las Vegas. His books include *A Narrative History of the American Press* and *Abraham Lincoln and Horace Greeley.* He co-authored with Dr. Bulla *Lincoln Mediated: The President and the Press Through Nineteenth-Century Media.* He edited the second edition of *The Encyclopedia of Journalism* for SAGE Publishing, the journal *Journalism History* for the History Division of the Association for Education in Journalism and Mass Communication, and the book *The Antebellum Press: Setting the Stage for Civil War.* Dr. Borchard earned a Ph.D. in mass communication from the University of Florida.

Mediating American History

SERIES EDITOR: KIMBERLY WILMONT VOSS

Realizing the important role that the media have played in American history, this series provides a venue for a diverse range of works that deal with the mass media and its relationship to society. This new series is aimed at both scholars and students. New book proposals are welcomed.

For additional information about this series or for the submission of manuscripts, please contact:

editorial@peterlang.com

To order other books in this series, please contact our Customer Service Department:

peterlang@presswarehouse.com (within the U.S.)
orders@peterlang.com (outside the U.S.)

Or browse by series:

WWW.PETERLANG.COM